E <del>Making</del> <del>Marsden-Wray</del>'s Indian
Converts

Experience Mayhew's *Indian Converts*

A Cultural Edition

JANE WORMSLEY.

Edited and with an introduction by
Laura Arnold Leibman

Experience Mayhew's
Indian Converts

JANE WORMSLEY.

Experience Mayhew's
Indian Converts
A Cultural Edition

Edited and with an introduction by
Laura Arnold Leibman

UNIVERSITY OF MASSACHUSETTS PRESS
Amherst

A VOLUME IN THE SERIES

Native Americans of the Northeast: Culture, History, and the Contemporary

LC 2008014530
ISBN 978-1-55849-661-3 *(paper)*; 660-6 *(library cloth)*

Designed by Sally Nichols
Set in Monotype Bell by BookComp, Inc.
Printed and bound by The Maple-Vail Book Manufacturing Group

Library of Congress Cataloging-in-Publication Data

Mayhew, Experience, 1673–1758.
Experience Mayhew's Indian converts : a cultural edition / edited and with an
introduction by Laura Arnold Leibman.
    p. cm. — (Native Americans of the Northeast: culture, history, and the
contemporary)
    New scholarly edition of Indian converts by Experience Mayhew published in
1727.
    Includes bibliographical references and index.
    ISBN 978-1-55849-661-3 (pbk. : alk. paper) — ISBN 978-1-55849-660-6 (library
cloth : alk. paper)
    1. Indians of North America—Biography.   2. Indians of North America—
Massachusetts—Martha's Vineyard.   3. Martha's Vineyard (Mass.)—History.
4. Wampanoag Indians—Missions.   5. Mayhew family.   I. Leibman, Laura
Arnold.   II. Mayhew, Experience, 1673–1758 Indian converts.   III. Title.
    E78.M4M64 2008
    970.004'97—dc22   2008014530

British Library Cataloguing in Publication data are available.

Frontispiece. Jane Wormsley [Wamsley], a Wampanoag Baptist Preacher at Gay Head
(1860). From Porte Crayon, illustrator, "Summer in New England," *Harper's New
Monthly Magazine,* September 1860.

Contents

/

Illustrations

Acknowledgments

No work of scholarship is possible without the hard work of other scholars. This edition was feasible only because of the prior perseverance of David Silverman, Jerome Segel, Andrew Pierce, Charles Edward Banks, and of course Experience Mayhew. I am also profoundly indebted to Michael Colacurio: almost every useful idea I have about the Puritans can be traced back to Michael's tutelage, though any mistakes are my own. In addition I thank Peter Steinberger, Eric Sundquist, Gary Nash, Lisa Gordis, Kathryn Lofton, Tobias Vanderhoop, Gordon Sayre, Chris Moses, Kent Coupe, Joanna Burgess, Alice Beckett, Andrew Nusbaum, and Sabrina Gogol. The staffs at the Newberry Library, Massachusetts Historical Society, Martha's Vineyard Historical Society, Library of Congress, Massachusetts Archives, Aquinnah Cultural Center, Plimouth Plantation, New England Historic Genealogical Society, American Antiquarian Society, Haffenreffer Museum of Anthropology, Harvard University, and the John Carter Brown University Library generously answered my questions and allowed me to examine their collections. Funding from the National Endowment for the Humanities, a Ruby Grant, and Reed College provided means to travel to these collections. Special thanks go to Sara Berkelhamer and Bob and Trudy Josephson for hosting me in Boston and Cape Cod. My deepest gratitude belongs to my husband, Eric Leibman, כי איש חיל אתה: רב אדם יקרא איש חסדו ואיש אמונים מי ימצא?.

Abbreviations

DCCR   Dukes County Court Records, Office of the Clerk of
        Courts, Dukes County Courthouse, Edgartown, Mass.

DCRD   Dukes County Deeds, Dukes County Registry of
        Deeds, Dukes County Courthouse, Edgartown, Mass.

DCRP   Dukes County Registry of Probate, Dukes County
        Courthouse, Edgartown, Mass.

DRMV   Edward Charles Banks, "Documents Relating to
        Martha's Vineyard." Manuscript. Massachusetts
        Historical Society.

EEBO   Early English Books Online. http://eebo.chadwyck.com.

HMV   Edward Charles Banks, *The History of Martha's Vineyard:
        Dukes County, Massachusetts* (Boston: G. H. Dean, 1911–25).

IC   Experience Mayhew, *Indian converts; Or, some account of
        the lives and dying speeches of a Considerable number of the
        Christianized Indians of Martha's Vineyard in New-England*
        (London: S. Gerrish, 1727). Page numbers followed by an
        asterisk indicate the primary biography of the individual
        mentioned.

MA Arc. Massachusetts Archives Series, Massachusetts State
        Archives, Boston.

MHS   Massachusetts Historical Society, *Collections*.

MVHS   Martha's Vineyard Historical Society, Edgartown, Mass.

Native Writings Ives Goddard and Kathleen J. Bragdon, eds., *Native
        Writings in Massachusett* (Philadelphia: American
        Philosophical Society, 1988).

NCRD   Nantucket County Registry of Deeds.

OED   *Oxford English Dictionary,* 2d ed. (Oxford University
                Press, 2005). Online at http://dictionary.oed.com.

SJC   Supreme Judicial Court Records, Massachusetts State
                Archives, Boston.

WGH   Jerome D. Segel and R. Andrew Pierce, *The Wampanoag
                Genealogical History of Martha's Vineyard, Massachusetts,*
                vol. 1. (Baltimore: Genealogical Publishing, 2003).

Experience Mayhew Timeline

1673	February 5, Experience is born in Chilmark to John and Elizabeth Mayhew.
1688	John Mayhew dies, is buried in West Tisbury Cemetery. Leaves property at Quansoo and Quenames to Experience Mayhew, his eldest son.
1693–94	Experience begins to preach to the Wampanoags.
1695	November 12, Experience marries Thankful Hinckley (1671–1706), daughter of Gov. Thomas and Mary (Smith) Hinckley of Barnstable; builds the Mayhew-Whiting home at Quenames around this time.
1696	Daughter Reliance born.
1700	Son Samuel born.
?	Daughter Mary born, year unknown.
1706	September 27, wife Thankful Mayhew dies. Her gravestone is in the West Tisbury Cemetery.
1707	Makes Algonquian translation of Cotton Mather's *The Day Which the Lord Hath Made*. Boston: B. Green.
1709	Publishes *The Massachuset Psalter; or, Psalms of David with the Gospel according to John, in columns of Indian and English. Being an introduction for training up the aboriginal natives, in reading and understanding the Holy Scriptures.*
1711	Marries second wife Remember Bourne (1683–1721), daughter of Shearjashub and Bathsheba (Skiffe) Bourne of Sandwich.
1712	October 8, son Nathan born.
1713	October and November, travels to Pequot and Mohegan Indians in Connecticut to missionize; submits journals of trip to Society for the Propagation of the Gospel.
1714	Makes Algonquian translation of Cotton Mather's *Family-religion, excited and assisted*. Boston: B. Green.
	May 6, daughter Abigail born.

September and October, second missionary trip to Pequot and Mohegan Indians in Connecticut.

November 4, submits journals of trip to Society for the Propagation of the Gospel.

1716   April 4, daughter Eunice born (later, wife of Moses Blecher of Braintree).

1718   May 14, son Zachariah baptized (the last of the "missionary Mayhews").

November 23, Experience preaches in Boston "A discourse shewing that God dealeth with men as with reasonable creatures."

1720   Publishes *A discourse shewing that God dealeth with men as with reasonable creatures.*

Retranslates Eliot's *The Indian Primer as The first book. By which children may know truely to read the Indian language. And Milk for babes.* Boston: B. Green.

October 8, son Jonathan born (celebrated Arminian clergyman; President John Adams called him "the transcendent genius" of his day).

1721   March 2, wife Remember Mayhew dies, is buried in Abel's Hill Cemetery.

Selections of *A discourse shewing that God dealeth with men as with reasonable creatures* reprinted with Cotton Mather's *India christiana.* Boston: B. Green.

1722   Letter to Honorable Paul Dudley regarding Indian languages and recent illness on the island (manuscript, printed in *New-England Historical and Genealogical Register* 39 [1885]: 12–17).

1723   July 3, Harvard College confers upon Experience an honorary degree of Master of Arts. Mayhew originally excused himself from the honor but was overruled by the college.[1]

1724   December 3, preaches in Boston "All mankind, by nature, equally under sin."

1725   Publishes *All mankind, by nature, equally under sin.*

1727   Publishes *Indian Converts, or, Some account of the lives and dying speeches of a considerable number of the Christianized Indians of Martha's Vineyard, in New-England* (to which is added, some

---

1 Prince, *Chronological History*, 107.

account of those English ministers who have successively presided over the Indian work in that and the adjacent islands by Mr. Prince).

1728/29   February 15, daughter Reliance marries Eliashib Adams. Experience sells land to Eliashiab to build house down the road from the Mayhew-Whiting home.[2]

1729/30   January 8, daughter Reliance (Mayhew) Adams dies in childbirth: "She was a pious prudent woman of blameless conversation."

1731   Son Nathan graduates from Harvard College.

1733   October 14, son Nathan dies.

Daughter Abigail marries Jonathan Allen.

1738   November 21, son Zachariah marries Elizabeth Allen (1720–1790).

1741   Publishes *A right to the Lord's Supper considered in a letter to a serious enquirer after truth. By a lover of the same.*

May 18, grandson Nathan born to Zachariah and Elizabeth Mayhew.

1742?   Granddaughter Reliance McGee born to Mary (Mayhew) McGee and John McGee.

1744   Publishes *Grace Defended, In a modest plea for an important truth.*

Son Jonathan graduates from Harvard College.

1746   July 25, son Samuel dies.

July 7, grandson William born to Zachariah and Elizabeth Mayhew.

1747   Mayhew's retranslation of *The Indian Primer* reprinted.

Publishes *A letter to a gentleman on that question, whether saving grace be different in species from common grace, or in degree only?* Boston: S. Kneeland and T. Green.

June 17, ordination of Rev. Jonathan Mayhew to the pastoral care of the West-Church in Boston. Ordination Sermon, "The alienation of affections from ministers consider'd, and improv'd." Preached by Ebenezer Gay, A.M. Pastor of the First Church in Hingham.

A Prefatory Address to the Church of Christ, and Inhabitants of Edgartown, by the Rev. Mr. Mayhew of Christian-Town is published with Thomas Balch, *Preaching the Gospel, tho'*

---

2 Scott, *The Early Colonial Houses of Martha's Vineyard,* 2:229.

foolishness to men, yet a saving ordinance of God. A sermon preach'd at Edgartown on Martha's-Vineyard, July 29th. 1747. When the Reverend Mr. John Newman was ordained Pastor of the church in the said town, in the room of the late Reverend and excellent Mr. Samuel Wiswall, deceas'd. Boston: S. Kneeland and T. Green.

1748   March, daughter Abigail marries second husband, Mr. Wilson.

1749   January 30, granddaughter Elizabeth born to Zachariah and Elizabeth Mayhew.

1752   Writes "Of Human Liberty" (manuscript, MHS).

1753   March 27, will written.

1754   Granddaughter Reliance McGee dies, is buried in West Tisbury Cemetery.

1755   January 7, grandson Jonathan born to Zachariah and Elizabeth Mayhew.

1756   September 2, son Jonathan marries Boston beauty Elizabeth Clarke (1733–1777), daughter of Dr. John and Elizabeth (Breame) Clarke.

1755   Records "Disbursements Given to the Indian Poor at Martha's Vineyard" (MHS manuscript).

1757   August 28, grandson Zachariah born to Zachariah and Elizabeth Mayhew.

1758   November 29, Experience dies, is buried in Abel's Hill Cemetery.

1759   January 2, estate probated.

Granddaughter Elizabeth born to Jonathan and Elizabeth Mayhew.

1763   Son Jonathan Mayhew publishes attack on the Society for the Propagation of the Gospel.

1829–30   *Indian Converts* republished posthumously in sections: *Indian narratives; Containing an account of the first native preacher on Martha's Vineyard* (Boston: J. Loring);

Narratives of the lives of pious Indian children, who lived on Martha's Vineyard more than one hundred years since (Boston: J. Loring);

Narratives of the lives of pious Indian men who lived on Martha's Vineyard more than one hundred years since (Boston: J. Loring);

Narratives of the lives of pious Indian women who lived on Martha's Vineyard more than one hundred years since (Boston: J. Loring).

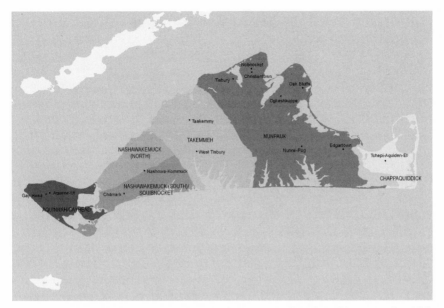

[Figure 1.] Map of Martha's Vineyard with Towns and Sachemships. Map by Alok Amatya and Taylor Smith (Reed College). Based on *WGH*, frontispiece.

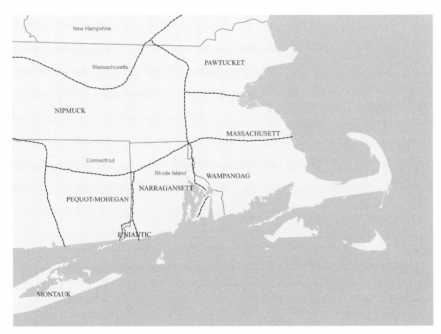

[Figure 2.] Map of Colonial New England with Algonquian Confederacies. Map by Alok Amatya and Taylor Smith (Reed College). Based on Salwen 161; Simmons, *Spirit of the New England Tribes*, 2.

Experience Mayhew's
Indian Converts

Introduction

A little over a hundred years after the first English interactions with the Wampanoags at Plymouth Plantation, Puritan missionary Experience Mayhew published the life stories of four generations of Wampanoag men, women, and children who had lived on the island of Martha's Vineyard. The history was unprecedented in scope and content. Although written in English for a primarily British audience, Mayhew's *Indian Converts* (1727) drew upon the Wampanoag sermons, oral history, and dying speeches that he and his family had been collecting and translating for over eighty years (1642–1727). A fluent speaker of *Wôpanâak*,[1] Mayhew dedicated his own life to ministering to the Wampanoag community on the island, like the previous three generations of Mayhews before him. By publishing *Indian Converts*, he hoped not only to raise interest and money for missionary activities but also to save souls: perhaps by reading about the lives of Christianized Wampanoags, his white readers would repent and rededicate themselves to the spiritual path of Calvinism. Whatever Mayhew's original intent, today his history provides the most extensive information we have about any Algonquian community during the early English colonial period.

Mayhew's text includes detailed biographies of twenty-two Wampanoag ministers, twenty "good men," thirty women, and twenty-two pious children. In addition, *Indian Converts* contains three appendixes with brief biographies of a further eight ministers, seventeen good men, and nine women. These 128 total biographies cover four generations of converts who lived on the island between the early 1600s and the 1720s, when Mayhew was writing. Although he recorded the life stories only of people who had already died and had lived exemplary lives, he frequently mentioned not only prominent Wampanoag Christians who were still living but also not-so-exemplary Wampanoags who served as foils to his heroes and heroines. We have no comparable series of biographies for any colonial community in

---

1 *Wôpanâak* is an Algonquian language that is closely related to *Massachusett*, the language used in Natick and several other New England praying towns.

New England, let alone any other Native American community. Moreover, Mayhew's personal knowledge of both the people and the language they spoke makes his history stand out from other tracts published by the Society for the Propagation of the Gospel. [2]

For readers of Mayhew's own day, *Indian Converts* provided more than just interesting historical information: its publication was an important typological event. On October 9, 1727, a small advertisement appeared for Mayhew's tome in the *Boston News-Letter* noting that the book was "Just arrived from *London*, and neatly bound." Colonists such as Rev. Jonathan Edwards scanned early periodicals for natural and human incidents—including book publications—that could be "signs of the potential fulfillment of biblical prophecies and the expansion of the kingdom of God."[3] Although some advertisements in the *News-Letter* were about runaway slaves, misbehaving wives, or land for sale, others—such as the advertisement for Mayhew's work—were more clearly framed as omens and lessons.[4] In the 1720s and 1730s, New England Protestants increasingly saw themselves as part of an international war against Catholicism in which Protestant missionary success would be an important harbinger of the second coming of Christ and the millennium. For ministers Benjamin Colman, Cotton Mather, Benjamin Wadsworth, Joseph Sewall, and other backers of Mayhew's book, *Indian Converts* was an essential confirmation that Protestants—not Catholics—were winning the theological war for America, and clear evidence that New England was doing important missionary work. [5]

Written on the cusp of the first Great Awakening, *Indian Converts* helps to illuminate the theological upheavals that rocked New England in both English and Native communities. I see the book's distinctiveness and significance in the context of two theological shifts: (1) the changing landscape of New England Puritanism leading up to the first Great Awakening, and (2) the changing landscape of Wampanoag cultural and religious life.

---

2 Established in 1649 and also known as the Corporation for the Promoting and Propagating of the Gospel in New England, this society mainly supported missionaries who espoused a Calvinist and Congregational creed. Missionary John Eliot published eleven pamphlets between 1643 and the 1670s which, in 2003, Michael Clark collected and reprinted as *The Eliot Tracts*. Eliot, however, was not nearly so fluent as Mayhew in Algonquian languages, nor was he raised near any Native communities.

3 Kidd, *Protestant Interest*, 57.

4 The advertisement following that for *Indian Converts*, for example, is an account of a Mr. Ashton, who was captured by and then "delivered" from Pirates and subsequently "liv'd alone on a desolate Island for about Sixteen Months." Mr. Ashton's account is accompanied by a sermon in which Rev. John Barnard explicates the significance of the captivity in light of the war between good and evil raging in the colonies. *Boston News-Letter*, September 4, and October 9, 1727.

5 Kidd, *Protestant Interest*, 43–44, 105, 138.

Martha's Vineyard: The Changing Landscape of New England Puritanism

As David Harlan notes, most historians have tended to characterize the First Great Awakening as "a conflict between extreme opposites: between formalism and enthusiasm, reason and piety, Arminianism and Calvinism, Old Light and New Light." For both Harlan and eighteenth-century New Englanders, however, such distinctions were rarely so clear-cut. As Samuel Mather, the minister of the Boston Second Church put it, most New England ministers were neither Old nor New Lights but "Regular Lights" who "understood the power and danger of revivalism."[6] As both a theologian and a chronicler of Native American lives, Experience stands out as a Regular Light: his work is marked by both innovation and orthodoxy. As such, *Indian Converts* helps us explore the middle ground of eighteenth-century millennialism.

Like most Regular Lights, Mayhew did understand both the power and the danger of revivalism. Although he rejected the dangerous fervor of enthusiastic preachers such as George Whitefield,[7] he understood that one of the great powers of the revival was its ability to combat the ultimate New England locus of fear: Catholicism. Thomas Kidd has recently argued that we should think of the 1720s and 1730s in New England not only as an period of eschatological revival but also as an era in which Protestants ignored sectarianism to draw together in a war against Catholicism.[8] *Indian Converts* was certainly intended as part of this anti-Catholic warfare, but Mayhew's tome also reveals the uneasiness of Protestant alliances.[9] As a narrator, he carefully navigates the treacherous water between coalition and heresy.

As a Regular Light, Experience Mayhew often appears as an odd mix of orthodoxy and innovation. One the one hand, he is a conservative force: in *Indian Converts* he writes as a Calvinist in an era of increasing theological

---

6 Harlan, *The Clergy and the Great Awakening*, 11, 4. The First Great Awakening is usually defined either narrowly as occurring between 1739 and 1745 or more broadly as occurring from 1720 to 1760. In general, "New Lights" were those who supported the Great Awakening, "stressed the emotions," and were "both pietistic and perfectionistic." "Old Lights," in contrast, "viewed revivalism as an unnecessary and disruptive element within church life" and "emphasized rationalism, which was born out of the Enlightenment and signified common sense, and self-control." Those on each side saw themselves as the true inheritors of Puritan Congregationalism. See Queen et al., *Encyclopedia of American Religious History*, 2:504. "Regular Lights" tended to pick and choose aspects of both camps and thereby founded a middle ground between the two poles.

7 See Akers, *Called unto Liberty*, 35.

8 Kidd, *Protestant Interest*, 12–13.

9 Although many missionaries "bent" the rules of Calvinism slightly to meet their audiences' state of preparedness, Mayhew loses no time pointing out the "heretical" nature of the Baptists on the island. Apparently for Mayhew there is bending and then there is broken.

leniency. Moreover, his choice of genre is an old-fashioned one, Indian biography having been more popular before King Philip's War (1675–76) than after it.[10] Indeed, as Mayhew himself acknowledges, his very mission appeared to many to be a figment of past dreams: in a lecture of December 3, 1724, in Boston, Mayhew laments that although missions in New England were once carried out with "Life and Vigour," now the work "goes on *heavily*," and "some will speak as if there was scarce *any good* to be hoped for concerning" Native American converts.[11]

On the other hand, Mayhew's text is highly innovative in the way it treats the genre of Indian biography, and it predicts a change of interest in women, children, and missionary activities in the eighteenth century. Mayhew significantly alters the form of the story of the deathbed saint: he provides more agency to Wampanoag converts and incorporates the oral tradition structurally and thematically into his accounts. In addition, the treatment of women and children in his text predicts major shifts in New England society. Long considered the most deviant members of Puritan society, women and children began to find their place among the ranks of Puritan exemplars during the eighteenth century. Mayhew's odd mix of orthodoxy and innovation reflects both the changing role of the Mayhew clan in island social and religious life and the life of a Regular Light. My analysis of the relationship between *Indian Converts* and New England Puritanism addresses Mayhew's combination of orthodoxy and innovation in the context of, first, the Mayhew clan and island life, and second, New England literary history.

The Mayhew Clan and Island Life

Experience Mayhew lived and wrote during an era in which the Calvinist hegemony of his ancestors was increasingly diluted. English settlement on Martha's Vineyard began as a Calvinist theocracy—a theocracy with Mayhews at the helm. By Experience Mayhew's day, his family had lost clear control of both the political and religious life on the island: whereas previous Mayhews had virtually monopolized colonial power there, Experience lived in an era of compromise.

As biographer Charles Akers notes, the early Mayhew family embodied a version of the Puritan dream that was more often desired than achieved: they

---

10 Sympathetic descriptions of deathbed scenes of Native American converts were popular before King Philip's War, but by the 1720s, when *Indian Converts* was written, Native Americans were more likely to be cast as villains and to have their role as "emblems of suffering souls" filled by white women. See Bross, *Dry Bones and Indian Sermons*, 147, 195–96.

11 E. Mayhew, *All mankind, by nature, equally under sin*, 25. Stout, "Word and Order," 26, 31–34.

controlled both church and state for colonists on the island. In 1641, Thomas Mayhew, the great-grandfather of Experience Mayhew, had acquired the title to Martha's Vineyard, an island off the southern coast of Cape Cod. Although Thomas Mayhew did not know much about the island before he bought it, history would confirm the value of the property; its exquisite coastline is complemented by a hundred square miles of farmland, ponds, and striking hills. In December 1642, Mayhew selected his homesite and granted rights to five of his former neighbors to settle on the island.[12] In the years that followed, Mayhew and his descendents established themselves as "Lords of the Manor" of the town of Tisbury and successfully missionized and converted many of the Wampanoags who lived there. While some of Thomas's descendants inherited his spiritual mission, others inherited the right to the island's political jurisdiction, for even though it was annexed by Massachusetts in 1691 when Experience was eighteen, the family continued to dominate island political life for many years.[13] Experience, like his father John before him, took the reigns of the family's spiritual kingdom. Although the Methodists did not settle the island until the 1780s, both Baptists and Presbyterians threatened its Calvinist hegemony during Experience's lifetime.[14]

The changes in the theological climate on the island and in New England more generally are reflected in the differences between *Indian Converts* and earlier missionary tracts by members of the Mayhew family.[15] Although many of Experience Mayhew's ancestors had published missionary tracts, *Indian Converts* stands out among the rest for its length, breadth, and point of view. As Laura Stevens has noted, words tended to outweigh deeds in the English colonial missions. The Mayhews were an exception to this rule: they spent more time missionizing than writing. The most prolific of the earlier Mayhews had been Experience Mayhew's grandfather Thomas Mayhew Jr. (1620/21–1657),[16] who began the missionary enterprise on the island and coauthored *Tears of repentance* (1653) with New England's most

---

12 Akers, *Called unto Liberty*, 5–6; *HMV*, 1:80–84.

13 Akers, *Called unto Liberty*, 6. The Mayhew hegemony clearly annoyed at least some of the colonists on the island and did not go undisputed. Simon Athearn, for example, repeatedly tried to undermine their rule and appealed to the courts that the Mayhews ran the island improperly: *Faith and Boundaries*, 83.

14 *HMV*, 2 (Annals of Oaks Bluffs): 45. The Wampanoag Baptist Church at Gay Head (Aquinnah) discussed later. Rev. William Homes, the minister of the meetinghouse in Chilmark, where Experience Mayhew lived, was a Presbyterian. *HMV*, 2 (Annals of Chilmark): 48–49.

15 Although here I compare *Indian Converts* only with writings by other Mayhew family members, later I compare it with works by non-Mayhew missionaries.

16 Prior to 1752, Puritans used two years to date events occurring between January 1 and March 24. The split date indicates those of the Old Style (Julian) calendar and the New Style (Gregorian) calendar.

famous missionary, John Eliot. Thomas Junior also had letters about his mission published in works by Edward Winslow (*The Glorious progress of the Gospel amongst the Indians in New England* [1649]) and Henry Whitfeld (*The light appearing more and more towards the perfect day* [1651]). These tracts were designed to raise both pity for American Indian converts and funds to continue the missionary activities that could alleviate Indians' spiritual suffering. Like Mayhew's *Indian Converts,* they were published under the auspices of the Society for the Propagation of the Gospel in New England.[17]

The early works by Mayhew family members can be distinguished from *Indian Converts* in both genre and length. *Indian Converts* is primarily a biographical history. In contrast, even when tracts such as *Tears of repentance* included conversion narratives, they relied heavily upon letters and the pity they induced.[18] As Laura Stevens so astutely argues, "Letters define and describe ties between individual or groups"; by using the letter genre, Thomas Mayhew Jr. and others tried to bridge the "physical or social distance by describing relationships in spiritually intimate terms, relying on the affective ties developed from a shared concern for Indian souls." For Stevens, such letters contrast sharply with narratives like Experience Mayhew's: whereas the narratives "present their accounts of missionary work to passive readers, letters reach out to those readers, asking them to become active contributors to the work."[19] Even though *Indian Converts* contains dedications, a preface "to the reader," and an introduction, the front matter does not directly address the reader and refrains from making a multitude of emotional pleas. Whereas John Eliot speaks in a personal tone to readers in 1653, in 1727 Experience Mayhew remains remote and logical.[20] For Stevens, Mayhew's social distance from his readers is reflected in his distance from the Wampanoags as well: the conversions are rendered "transparent to the reader's gaze." Experience Mayhew's distance, however, reflects the change in attitude toward emotion between his generation and that of his grandfather: whereas earlier missionaries such as Thomas Mayhew Jr. relied on pity, not empathy, to engage their

---

17 Stevens, *Poor Indians,* 3, 7–9, 13–14, 24–25.

18 For example, Eliot and Mayhew's *Tears of repentance* prefaces its "Relation of the Proceedings of the Lords Work" and its conversion narratives with letters to Cromwell by William Steel and John Eliot, a letter to the "much Honored Corporation" by Thomas Mayhew Jr., and letters to the "Christian Reader" by John Eliot and Richard Mather. These letters take up slightly less than half of the work.

19 Stevens, *Poor Indians,* 62–64.

20 Eliot begins, "Christian Reader, I Know thy Soul longeth to hear tidings of Gods grace"; in contrast, Experience Mayhew announces, "There are more especially *two Things* requisite, to render any *History* acceptable and entertaining to judicious Readers." Eliot and Mayhew, *Tears of repentance,* B; *IC* ix. Page numbers for *Indian Converts* in notes refer to the original.

readers,[21] Experience Mayhew relies on reason, not emotion, to be persuasive. Experience came of age not only amid the witchcraft fervor that swept New England but also during the enthusiastic revivals of the eighteenth century. When the First Great Awakening hit New England, Experience sided decidedly against "enthusiastic" religion.[22] The epistolary pleas for "pity" that his grandfather had found so useful two generations earlier had a completely different resonance when *Indian Converts* was composed, particularly for a Regular Light such as Experience Mayhew.

Indian Converts also stands in marked contrast to the narrative written by Experience's uncle, Matthew Mayhew: although both *Indian Converts* (1727) and Matthew Mayhew's *Brief narrative* (1694) are well-reasoned narratives,

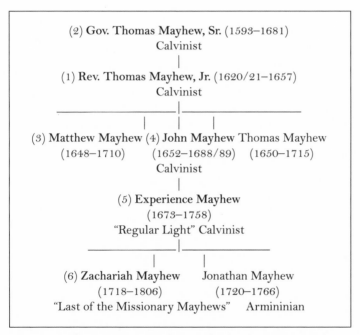

(2) **Gov. Thomas Mayhew, Sr.** (1593–1681)
Calvinist
|
(1) **Rev. Thomas Mayhew, Jr.** (1620/21–1657)
Calvinist

(3) **Matthew Mayhew** (4) **John Mayhew** Thomas Mayhew
(1648–1710)   (1652–1688/89)   (1650–1715)
Calvinist
|
(5) **Experience Mayhew**
(1673–1758)
"Regular Light" Calvinist

(6) **Zachariah Mayhew**   Jonathan Mayhew
(1718–1806)   (1720–1766)
"Last of the Missionary Mayhews"   Armininian

[Figure 3.] The Missionary Mayhews and Other Prominent Mayhews. Based on John D. Hannah, *Charts of Reformation and Enlightenment Church History* (2004); *HMV*, 3:301–12.

---

21 Stevens, *Poor Indians*, 190, 7–9.

22 When Experience Mayhew read Rev. George Whitefield's emotional autobiography, he concluded that Whitefield was not only a "*Miserable Enthusiast*" but also "under the Power of *Satanical Delusions*" (Akers, *Called unto Liberty*, 35). Mayhew's decreased emphasis on emotion should be compared with a similar moderation on the part of the eighteenth-century missionaries Jonathan Edwards and Samuel Hopkins, who "replaced the excessive emotion linked to revivals with the more moderate force of compassion, and emotion that prevented undue emphasis on the self" (Stevens, *Poor Indians*, 159).

Matthew's tract is more a natural history than a religious one. Matthew was the third missionary on the island: after Thomas Junior's early death at sea at the age of thirty-seven, Thomas Senior took over the mission until his grandsons were of age. Initially, Matthew Mayhew (1648–1710), the oldest grandson, succeeded his father and grandfather as head missionary of the island. He studied at Cambridge, mastered the *Wôpanâak* dialect, and wrote a tract explaining the third generation of the Vineyard mission: *A brief narrative of the success which the Gospel Hath Had, among the Indians, of Martha's-Vineyard* (1694).[23] His *Brief narrative* reads like many other natural histories from the colonial era: he discusses the language, political system, and religion of the Wampanoags and includes several letters by missionaries from other parts of New England. By emphasizing the monarchical and hierarchical nature of their society, Matthew Mayhew both implies and asserts that the Wampanoags will easily become both political and spiritual subjects of the Crown of England. Although the letters that accompany his natural history fluctuate between unemotional community reports by Samuel Trent and Rowland Cotton and the more direct emotional plea of Rev. James Noyce of Stonington, pity is clearly on the wane. The tract's overall interest in politics and society, rather than pity, may reflect in part the growing concern in New England about the role of emotional pleas. The shift in focus also reflects Matthew Mayhew's own predilection. As Charles Banks notes, ministry was not Matthew's true calling; thus, from the age of twenty-one until his death, John Mayhew (1652–1688)—Experience's father—took Matthew's place and became the minister to both the white population of Tisbury and the Wampanoags. Matthew went on to manage the family's estate.[24]

Between Matthew Mayhew's *Brief narrative* (1694) and Experience Mayhew's *Indian Converts* (1727), Experience published his own *Brief account of the state of the Indians on Martha's Vineyard* (1720). Although markedly different from either *Indian Converts* or Matthew Mayhew's tract, this account is a superb resource for understanding Wampanoag life on the island and, as such, is included as the Appendix in this edition. In style and content,

---

23 Experience Mayhew explains that Matthew Mayhew's "Narrative was Printed at *Boston* in the Year 1694 and Reprinted at *London* in the next Year, under the Title of, *The Conquests and Triumphs of Grace*, &c. The same, for Substance, being again Printed some Years after, in Dr. C. *Mather's* History of *New-England*." E. Mayhew, *Brief account*, 2.

24 Interestingly enough, Matthew Mayhew's education at Harvard was subsidized by the Society for the Propagation of the Gospel, which paid his expenses along with those of several "Indian youths." The commissioners expected Matthew to continue his father's and grandfather's work and explicitly recommended that he "learne the Indian Language" as well as his other subjects. *HMV*, 2 (Annals of Edgartown): 80–81; *IC* 302–6.

A Brief account lies midway between Matthew's report and *Indian Converts*: Experience fills in for his readers the missionary activities he performed between 1694 and 1720. Like *A Brief narrative* (1694), *A Brief account* (1720) summarizes general trends more than it details lives of individuals. Like *Indian Converts*, however, *A Brief account* provides clear evidence of the importance of the Mayhew mission for both the political and the religious future of New England: not only are the "*Indians* in *Dukes* County . . . wholly under the *English*" government, but many "may be justly looked upon as Exemplary Christians" and thereby help dispel English prejudices.[25] Experience also pays careful attention to the English dress, houses, and occupations of the Wampanoags—all important signs of how missions helped assimilate Wampanoags into colonial society.

A Brief account frames Mayhew's religious mission as both important and precarious. The tract congratulates readers on the support they have given to his missions in the past and makes a well-reasoned plea for more funds: when books and ministers are available, the Wampanoag community has taken great strides forward, and the "Influence of His [God's] Spirit" has been felt on the island. Like the mission itself, however, the spiritual future of the Wampanoag community is greatly dependent upon white readers' charity: perhaps the greatest plea Mayhew makes is for more Algonquian ("Eliot") Bibles, which had become incredibly scarce by 1720. From the missionary perspective, John Eliot's translation of the Bible was an essential means of making Algonquians into Christians. First published in 1663, the Eliot Bible (*Mamusse wunneetupanatamwe*) was reprinted in 1681 (New Testament only) and 1685. Although Wampanoags on the island made wide use of other Algonquian publications, the scarcity of Bibles should have struck horror into the hearts of any devout New Englander.[26] Mayhew and the Wampanoag converts must have been exceedingly disappointed when Mayhew's plea went unattended, and no further editions of the Eliot Bible were printed.

The precarious success recorded in *A Brief account* would have been interpreted typologically by most of Mayhew's readers. That is, readers would have been conscious not only of the biblical foreshadowing of Mayhew's work but also the way such foreshadowing predicted the second coming of Christ. In this reading, the success—or lack of success—of missionaries takes on cosmic significance. Mayhew constantly places his observations

---

25 E. Mayhew, *Brief account*, 6, 11.

26 Puritans laid great importance on individuals being able to read the Bible for themselves. See the section on literacy toward the end of this introduction.

about the Wampanoags within the language of the Bible, and his readers would have understood that such parallels predicted the imminent millennium. Like *Indian Converts*, Mayhew's 1720 tract should be read within the context of increasing pan-Protestantism and the theological war against Catholicism or, as it was sometimes thought of, the war of Gog and Magog.[27] If the Catholic missionary activity was a sore spot for millennial-minded New Englanders, "[Experience] Mayhew's successes on Martha's Vineyard proved of singular value in deflecting the sense that New Englanders were doing almost nothing with regard to missions, a particularly embarrassing deficiency given ongoing Jesuit missions and the recent sensations created by Danish missionaries."[28] When readers supported the Mayhew mission, they did more than ensure that New England's Native communities were assimilated into the physical and spiritual body of the colony; they helped guarantee that the colony would defeat its political and spiritual foes.

Like *A Brief account, Indian Converts* reflects not only a changing interest in the role of emotion in missionary reports but also the theological and political changes on the island. Experience Mayhew's missionary experience differed substantially from his father's: he lacked the authority his father had held with whites in the town of Tisbury, and the Calvinism he preached had began to lose its sway. Born on January 27, 1672/73 on Martha's Vineyard, Mayhew was a devoted and precocious Calvinist who was known for his modesty. He spent his early years training for the ministry he was soon to inherit, and he learned *Wôpanâak* from his infancy onward. When John died in 1688, Experience Mayhew was not quite sixteen years of age.[29] He immediately took over the running of the Mayhew household, but for five years the town of Tisbury was without a minister for either whites or Wampanoags. Finally, in 1694, the town invited Experience Mayhew to "teach" to them on Sundays. Experience was neither educated nor ordained as a minister; hence, he fulfilled the position of teacher rather than preacher. From 1694 onward he ministered to the Wampanoags, but until 1701 the whites of the town went without spiritual guidance or a leader for their services.

---

27 The prophecy of the war of Gog and Magog (Ezekiel 38–39) was the type that predicted not only the release of Satan in the book of Revelation (20.7–10) but also the antitype of the war between Protestants and Catholics ("Satan") in America. The reiteration of the antitype in New England predicted the imminent arrival of Christ. Mayhew's seemingly obsessive need to align his observations with quotations from the Bible exemplifies his desire to emphasize the importance of his mission for bringing about the millennium. For other uses of the Gog/Magog motif by New Englanders, see Kidd, *Protestant Interest*, 106.

28 Kidd, *Protestant Interest*, 44.

29 *IC*, 306–7.

These were dire years to be without leadership: on the mainland, Calvinism was increasingly under attack from heresies, perceived leniencies, and "satanic" visitations. If the threats against orthodoxy by "heretics" such as Quakers, Anabaptists, Presbyterians, and adherents of the Half-Way Covenant had decreased after the 1660s, such threats were "massively revived" in the 1680s and 1690s.[30] On the mainland, witchcraft hysteria gripped several towns and loomed large in the imagination of others. Moreover, "liberals" such as Rev. Solomon Stoddard continued to erode the Calvinist creed by abolishing the requirement of a public profession of faith altogether and thereby completely opening up communion. As George Willis Cooke points out, open communion "almost inevitably led to Arminianism because it implied . . . that man is able of his own free will to accept the terms of salvation which Calvinism had confined to the operation of the sovereignty of God alone."[31] Ironically Mayhew, who never advocated open communion, would later be accused of Arminianism himself, a charge which, I argue below, should be viewed with some suspicion.

In addition to the general upheaval Mayhew faced when taking on the Wampanoag mission, there were personal challenges that his father had not had to confront. John Mayhew had had sole control of the ministry of Tisbury and nearby Chilmark; Experience Mayhew, in contrast, not only did not control the pastorate but also did not always have the support of his clerical colleagues as to theology and behavior. Yet although Experience had not attended Harvard, he earned the trust and support of staunch Calvinists on the mainland such as Cotton Mather and was awarded an honorary degree from Harvard when he was twenty-five.[32] Mayhew's circle of friends—which included his nephew Thomas Prince, Judge Samuel Sewall, and the Mathers[33]—reads like a who's who of New England Calvinism. Indeed, many aspects of *Indian Converts* must have pleased the hard-line Calvinists who "attested" to Mayhew's tome: first, Experience insisted upon the correlation between salvation and the direct experience of grace; thus he directly challenged liberals who had opened church membership to those

---

30 The "Half-Way Covenant" extended church membership to the children and grandchildren of church members, even if they had had no describable religious experience. Many felt that this leniency paved the way for later Arminian heresies, and others believed that it was directly connected to the rise of witchcraft. Indeed, in Hartford, Connecticut, the introduction of the Half-Way Covenant and other Presbyterian schemes immediately followed witchcraft indictments. Demos, *Entertaining Satan*, 349–50, 380.

31 Cooke, *Unitarianism in America*, 28–29.

32 *IC*, 306.

33 Akers, *Called unto Liberty*, 11.

who had never had any describable religious experience. If Wampanoag converts didn't require leniencies, why should whites? Second, throughout *Indian Converts*, Experience directly connected grace and communion. Although years before, Stoddard and others had extended the Lord's Supper to people who appeared pious—even if they couldn't attest to an experience of grace—Mayhew's converts were exceedingly cautious about taking communion. Although Experience at times appeared frustrated that people who have clearly experienced grace couldn't recognize it, he never suggested that communion should be given indiscriminately.

Not all of Experience's colleagues were upstanding Calvinists. Given his somewhat unstylish Calvinist predilections, Mayhew must have been pleased when the town of Tisbury insisted in 1700 that they wanted "an orthidox [*sic*] Learned and pious person" to fill their long-vacant position of minister. He was soon to be disappointed. Although Rev. Josiah Torrey arrived in 1701 with the blessing of Calvinist divine Increase Mather, by the time of his death in 1723 Torrey was showing signs of recalcitrance: he "drunk too freely and too frequently of spirits [alcohol]."[34] Intemperance was a "sin" and hence an unfavorable sign regarding the salvation of Experience's colleague. Indeed, *Indian Converts*, published shortly after Torrey's death, often rails against the abuse of alcohol.[35] Torrey's successor, Nathaniel Hancock, similarly ended his pastorate under controversy and had his communion privileges and church membership suspended. The situation was different but equally troubling in nearby Chilmark: also left without a minister at John Mayhew's death, Chilmark was able to find a new pastor sooner than Tisbury, but even so, by 1714 that congregation was under the sway of Rev. William Homes, a Scotch Presbyterian. Putting aside the heated theological disputes between Calvinists and Presbyterians, some of the most biting personal criticisms we have of Experience Mayhew come from William Homes's diary. Although one hopes that Homes was kinder to Experience in person and in public, it seems unlikely that the two were close friends.[36]

---

34 *HMV*, 2 (Annals of West Tisbury): 79–82.

35 Mancall, *Deadly Medicine*, 16–20, 88–89.

36 Although Homes baptized Experience Mayhew's child, in private he was explicit about Mayhew's limitations as a preacher. He remarked in his diary of March 1718/19 that Experience's "sermon was well compressed but he [Mayhew] was at some loss in reading of it." That same June, Homes noted about one of Mayhew's sermons that "the matter of the discourse was not despisable [*sic*] but his delivery was flat and dull." See Homes, "Diary of Rev. William Homes of Chilmark, Martha's Vineyard, 1689–1746," 155–66; *HMV*, 2 (Annals of Chilmark): 47–52; *HMV*, 2 (Annals of West Tisbury): 76–82.

A major theological tension haunts *Indian Converts*, however, for despite his closeness to Mather at the time the book was written, in the 1740s, less than two decades later, Mayhew was accused of betraying Calvinism. In fact, Mayhew's final sermon, *Grace defended* (1744), has often been lauded as an early example of American Arminianism—a "heresy" that both fed the major controversies of the First Great Awakening and became the well-spring of what would become Unitarianism.[37] This charge is worth addressing, as there has been a tendency to read Mayhew's "Arminian beliefs" backward into his earlier works, including *Indian Converts*.

Arminianism was almost always an ambiguous charge. As in the case of Stoddard, most reactions against Calvinism in New England "took this designation . . . and to the Calvinists it was a word of disapproval and contempt." If by 1744 the Calvinists were particularly cantankerous, they had good reason. The First Great Awakening had posed a considerable threat to the Calvinist theology: on the one hand, the theatrics of non-Calvinist revivalists attracted great numbers of followers and made the "good old customs" of staid New England Congregationalism seem decidedly less appealing; on the other hand, a growing strain of liberalism within New England Congregationalism itself made some Calvinists retreat to a stricter Calvinism that they felt reflected the true purity of the early New England church.[38] It was a purity that Experience Mayhew and others doubted ever existed; indeed, as Mayhew points out in *Grace defended*, "There have been a great many eminent Divines" who "far from being *Arminians*" asserted many of the same "heresies" that were currently being denounced. His primary example is Dr. William Twisse (1578?–1646), whose 1653 work *The riches of Gods love unto the vessells of mercy* was an important—and effective—early refutation of Arminianism in England. Twisse's defense, as Mayhew notes, largely corresponds to what Mayhew himself argues in *Grace defended.*[39]

What did Mayhew's critics mean, then, when they called Mayhew's work Arminian? Although Arminianism could be applied to vice and social depravity, in the context of Mayhew's sermon the charge of Arminianism connoted a rejection of the Calvinist doctrines of "election, of God's absolute sovereignty, and of innate human sinfulness. Arminians liked to stress

---

37 As late as 1726, Cotton Mather had declared that he "knew of no Congregational pastor guilty of Arminianism and rejoiced that the contentions of English Nonconformists about justification 'have not yet straggled over the Atlantic to disturb this happy people.'" Quoted in Christie, "The Beginnings of Arminianism in New England," 154–55, 165.

38 Cooke, *Unitarianism in America*, 37, 46.

39 E. Mayhew, *Grace defended*, 42–45.

the importance of an individual's own effort in his or her salvation and individual moral responsibility."[40] Thus the grace that Mayhew "defends" in his 1744 sermon is at the crux of the Calvinist-Arminian conflict: was God's grace "irresistible," as Calvinists claimed, or was man "sufficiently free to resist divine grace," as the Arminians believed? Later generations would see this conflict as emblematic of the God-centered worldview of the Calvinists and the man-centered worldview of the proto-Unitarian Arminians. More recently, scholars have interpreted the divide between Calvinists and Arminians as conflict over whether the individual is the "key ingredient for salvation."[41] As a Regular Light, Experience Mayhew defends Calvinism for his readers and tries to find a middle way that will "quiet the tumultuating Thoughts" of both Arminians and Calvinists."[42]

Although Mayhew claims in *Grace defended* that he did not intend "at all" to overthrow Calvinism in favor of Arminianism, later readers believed that Mayhew "positively rejected the doctrine of election, and he defended the principle of human freedom."[43] Indeed, Professor Edward Wigglesworth of Harvard University criticized Mayhew's late work in 1741 as "a Medley of Arminianism and Pelagianism."[44] More significantly, Joseph Hawley, who became an Arminian after reading *Grace defended*, felt so moved by his new belief that he successfully spearheaded a campaign to remove Calvinist minister Jonathan Edwards from the pastorate of Northampton.[45] To be fair, the aging Mayhew may have honestly thought he was defending Calvinism in a language that Arminians—such as his own son Jonathan—would understand. In the prickly climate of the First Great Awakening, however, his work fed the very fires it may have been intended to extinguish.

The controversy over Mayhew's Arminianism at the end of his life is important for understanding *Indian Converts* because of the previously mentioned tendency to read Mayhew's "Arminianism" backward into his earlier works. Charles Akers, who wrote a biography of Experience's famous son Jonathan Mayhew, argues that Jonathan's Arminianism had its roots in his family's missionary activities: Experience Mayhew, Akers asserts, "found

---

40 Van der Wall, "Arminianism." http://www.oxfordreference.com/views/ENTRY.html?subview= Main&entry=t173.e031.

41 Corrigan, *Hidden Balance*, 3.

42 Quoted in Harlan, *The Clergy and the Great Awakening*, 82.

43 E. Mayhew, *Grace defended*, iii; Cooke, *Unitarianism in America*, 49–50.

44 Quoted in Akers, *Called unto Liberty*, 65. "Pelagianism is the heresy that man can take the initial steps towards salvation by his own efforts, apart from Divine grace": *Concise Oxford Dictionary of the Christian Church*, ed. E. A. Livingstone (Oxford University Press, 2000), *sv* "Pelagianism."

45 Akers, *Called unto Liberty*, 119.

it impossible to teach the complexities of Calvinism to the primitive [*sic*] Indians." For Akers, this early "simplification of doctrine in the interest of missions was not regarded as heresy" but was rather considered a necessity licensed by Cotton Mather and other strict Calvinists. Indeed, *Indian Converts* bears the seal of approval of Calvinist divines such as Cotton Mather, Benjamin Colman, Joseph Sewall, and Joshua Gee. Although Akers believes that Experience Mayhew found it difficult to keep his simplified missionary Calvinism separate from his "English" theology, that reading does not account for the unhappiness that the father felt over his "son's theological defection" and his plea to Jonathan as late as 1741 to "know the GOD of thy Fathers."[46] As I have already argued, Mayhew appears to have been a conservative force on Martha's Vineyard. In an era when the islanders increasingly decorated their tombs with more optimistic cherubs and willows, Mayhew and his immediate family clung to the fierce death's head of earlier generations (see, e.g., figure 4).[47] In death as in life, Experience Mayhew rests in the Calvinist camp.

In sum, Experience Mayhew wrote *Indian Converts* almost exactly midway through his missionary career, and the book reflects not only its author's Regular Light Calvinism but also his struggles and faith amid personal and theological hardships. His missionary career spanned sixty-four years, during which he preached, farmed, wrote, and educated his children. Both of his wives died young, and for over twenty years he was the primary caretaker—aided by his oldest daughters—for his two sets of young children. He wrote *Indian Converts* in the years immediately following his second wife's death in childbirth. The work's elegiac tone attests to Mayhew's belief in Calvinism to assuage not only the Wampanoags in a time of crisis but also the losses that he himself had suffered. Shortly after his second

---

46 *IC*, iii. Akers, *Called unto Liberty*, 63–66, 252 n 11.

47 Three motifs dominate early New England gravestones: "The earliest of the three is a winged death's head, with blank eyes and a grinning visage. . . . Sometime during the eighteenth century —the time varies according to location—the grim death's head designs are replaced, more or less quickly, by winged cherubs. This design also goes through a gradual simplification of form with time. By the late 1700's or early 1800's, again depending on where you are observing, the cherubs are replaced by stones decorated with a willow tree overhanging a pedestaled urn." The decline of the death's-head coincides with the decline of orthodox Calvinism: death's-head designs tend to stress decay and life's brevity; the more optimistic cherub stresses resurrection and heavenly reward. See Deetz and Dethlefsen, "Death's Head, Cherub, Urn and Willow," 29–30. Martha's Vineyard is not an exception to this trend: the cherub makes its appearance on the Vineyard first in West Tisbury in 1709 and by 1760 "the Cherub style begins to submerge the Death's Head in popularity," according to Richardson, "Death's Heads, Cherubs, Urn and Willow," 188. Interestingly, the early popularity of the cherub varies from cemetery to cemetery on the island. For example, from 1754 to 1758, when Reliance McGee's stone was made, cherubs were more popular in Chilmark than in West Tisbury. Iacocci, "Martha's Vineyard Gravestones from 1688 to 1804," 152–55.

[Figure 4.] "A Hopeful Child" (1754), detail of gravestone of Reliance McGee, Experience Mayhew's granddaughter, in West Tisbury Cemetery, Martha's Vineyard. Photo L. Leibman, 2007.

wife's death, Mayhew wrote to his friend and colleague Cotton Mather that if it weren't for the encouragement in seeing "here and there a truly pious person among the Indians" and "knowing that hundreds of them had gone to heaven," he would have "given out" long before.[48] For Mayhew the salvation achieved by Wampanoags gave meaning to his toil.

48 Akers, *Called unto Liberty*, 14–15, 10. Mayhew's missionary career spanned the years 1694–1758. He was married to Thankful Hinckley from 1695 to 1706 and Remember Bourne from 1711 to 1721/22. He had eight children who survived infancy, the youngest of whom (Jonathan) did not turn eighteen until 1738. *HMV* 3:305.

Indian Converts *and New England Literary History*

Mayhew's combination of orthodoxy and innovation can be felt in the structure and style of *Indian Converts*. By the 1720s both biographical history and the sympathetic figure of the "Praying Indian" were losing sway; Mayhew reclaims these forms in order to challenge the importance not only of Native Americans but also of women and children more generally, for New England and the millennium.

Kristina Bross has argued that the "possibilities of the Praying Indian figure for negotiating the Indians' role in Puritan New England" had largely ended with King Philip's War (1675–76). *Indian Converts*, however, is an exception to this trend. It reclaims the efficacy of the dying Indian saint to represent suffering and spiritual redemption; it also contradicts a general trend in American literature following King Philip's War in which Native Americans were cast as villains and in which white women took the place of Christianized Indians as "emblems of suffering souls rescued by God through the heroic efforts of Englishmen."[49] For Mayhew, suffering Wampanoags are figures with whom he and his readers can and should identify.

Indian Converts is similarly intriguing for its innovative use of the somewhat dated genre of biographical history. Just seven years after it was published, Rev. Thomas Prince rejected the utility of biographical history in favor of the "regular History" (annals) that had become more fashionable in England.[50] But Mayhew retains allegiance to the earlier, less stylish form of Puritan historiography, reinventing the genre to take into account changes in New England. Although roughly based on Cotton Mather's *Magnalia Christi Americana* (1702), Mayhew's *Indian Converts* radically reenvisions Mather's form to account for the growing interest in women and children during the eighteenth century. His text also differs from Mather's in that he cites Wampanoags, rather than white settlers, as the primary examples of saints' lives. This use of Wampanoags as *exempla fidei* has precedents in some of the earlier tracts by the Society for the Propagation of the Gospel; however, Experience Mayhew's biographies differ from these earlier conversion stories in that they relate the entire lives of a community of successful lifelong converts, rather than quoting the statements of a few key men at the moment of conversion. Furthermore, Mayhew's biographical

---

49 Bross, *Dry Bones and Indian Sermons*, 147. As Bross notes (195), King Philip's War is often seen as marking both a physical change in missionary activities and the way that those activities were represented.

50 Tichi, "Spiritual Biography," 65.

history is more indebted to the Wampanoag oral genre of the *memorate* than were the earlier tracts. His innovative use of the genre reflects not only his greater experience with the Wampanoags living on the island but also such changes in the theological climate as the eighteenth-century concern with the right to communion. In all these ways, Mayhew uses and adapts the traditional genre of New England biography.

Indian Converts reflects the influence of a seminal history of Mayhew's generation: Cotton Mather's *Magnalia Christi Americana* provides one of the clearest models for both the scope and structure of Mayhew's work. The *Magnalia*, like earlier Puritan histories by William Bradford, Nathaniel Morton, and Edward Johnson, relies upon biography as the basis for history. As Cecelia Tichi has argued, Mather's use of biographical history represented the Puritan settlers as a "Mosaic Tribe" analogous to the Children of Israel, the original "tribe of Moses." Biographical histories contributed to the social cohesion of Puritan life by presenting the disparate settlers as "organically unified and spiritually journeying in an atmosphere of frequent indifference and hostility."[51] Indeed, Mayhew's *Indian Converts* can be read as a mini *Magnalia Christi Americana*, but by focusing on the Wampanoags instead of the settlers, Mayhew not only weaves the converts into the fabric of the existing "Mosaic Tribe" of New England but also redefines the negative community against which the Mosaic Tribe is defined. As noted earlier, during the 1720s New England Protestants increasingly saw themselves as part of a shared Protestant war against Catholicism. They believed that the conversions of "pagans" and Jews by Protestants would help ensure Protestant England's spiritual and physical victory against the "popish" French and Spanish and speed the arrival of the millennium.[52]

Whereas earlier histories often posited New England Algonquians monolithically as the source of "the atmosphere of frequent indifference and hostility" against which the Mosaic Tribe struggled, in Mayhew's history the Wampanoag converts are part of the unified spiritual journey against paganism. The Indian militia on the island, led by converts such as Japheth Hannit of Chilmark, confirmed Mayhew's view that Wampanoag converts were part of the spiritual and physical battle against paganism and, later, Catholicism.[53] Wampanoag converts from Martha's Vineyard fought on the side of the

---

51 Ibid., 65–66, 69.

52 See Kidd, *Protestant Interest*, 14, 44–45, 138.

53 *HMV*, 1:296–97; *IC*, 46. Interestingly enough, the very day that the advertisement for *Indian Converts* appeared in the *Boston News-Letter*, an obituary on the same page connected the salvation of "Praying Indian" John Thomas of Natick with his willingness to fight on behalf of the English in the war against the Pequots.

English in both King Philip's War and the French and Indian Wars.[54] From a New England Calvinist point of view, these wars were effectively battles against two heresies: Catholicism (the French) and paganism (the Indians). A nice example of the blurring of the physical and theological war appears in the letters of some of the descendants of the converted sachem Mittark who were taken captive during the French and Indian Wars.[55] The captivity genre is itself modeled upon the Hebrew jeremiad and is designed to promote tribal unity through the exclusion of foreign elements and repentance. These letters use the language of captivity genre to align themselves with the British army and Protestantism and to define themselves in opposition to the Iroquois and the French priests.[56] Thus by the middle of the eighteenth century, it would seem that petitioners thought that invoking the language of the Mosaic Tribe, and Wampanoags' inclusion within it, was an efficacious and legitimate strategy. In *Indian Converts* and elsewhere, sympathetic writers sought to include Wampanoags within New England Protestantism.

Mayhew's *Indian Converts* also differs from Mather's *Magnalia* by positing a more positive role for women and children in Puritan society. Structurally, *Indian Converts* closely resembles books 2 and 3 of the first volume of the *Magnalia* in which Mather provided biographies of the governors and "divines" (ministers). Like those biographies, Mayhew's are designed to serve as *exempla fidei*: examples of people whose spiritual growth paralleled the "miraculous pattern of Christ's life [as it] unfolded in organic stages of spiritual growth."[57] The parallels between the saints' lives and Christ's life predicted the return of Christ himself. However, Mayhew's work expands upon Mather's model by adding chapters on pious women and children.

During the eighteenth century, women played an increasingly prominent role in New England religious life, yet for Mather, biblical matriarchs, not contemporary women, were the appropriate models for female Puritans.[58]

---

54 *HMV*, 1:296–320.

55 *IC*, 21–23; MA Arc. 33.73–74, 33.161, 97.283, 98.481, 133.98; *WGH*, 425–26.

56 See in particular "Joseph Metark, Indian ... petitioned for an allowance for military services under Capt. Thaxter and Capt. Dunlop, etc." (April 1761), MA Arc. 33.161–62A. This document is written in a very elegant script but signed in a different and less confident, albeit still impressive, hand, suggesting that Joseph had an official scribe write the letter and then signed it himself. It is hard to know for certain whether the invocation of religious captivity was Joseph's or the scribe's idea.

57 Bercovitch, *Puritan Origins of the American Self*, 9.

58 Mather's *Ornaments for the Daughters of Zion* remains a remarkably punitive work and is largely distrustful of women. *Ornaments* contains no biographies of actual women but rather relies upon the biblical poem "A Woman of Valor" (Proverbs 31) as the model of ideal womanhood. Mather alludes to Native American women only as negative examples of pride: white women who paint their faces with makeup are "sisters" to the sinful "*Squaws* in the Thickets of *America*." See Mather, *Ornaments for the Daughters of Zion*, 1, 19.

In contrast, Mayhew's willingness to see exemplary lives among contemporary Wampanoag women more accurately predicted the changing landscape for white women in the colony. Long considered the most deviant members of Puritan society, women and children began to find their place among the ranks of Puritan exemplars.[59] During the seventeenth century, both men and women had been more likely to think of women "as utterly depraved, as 'rebellious wretches against God,' bonded to Satan and bound for hell." Children were similarly seen as prerational and utterly sinful. As Kevin Hayes notes, however, by the middle of the eighteenth century, writers and theologians increasingly recognized that women were "rational Creatures" with souls and, like men, "deserved equal chances to improve them."[60] Narratives detailing the salvation of women and children (girls as well as boys) helped give women this equal chance. Mayhew's work, then, helped lay the groundwork for works by Jonathan Edwards (*Narrative of Surprising Conversions*) and Eleazer Wheelock (*Plain and faithful narrative*) which openly detailed the lives of women and children as a way to minister to their souls. *Indian Converts* is an early example of the use of women and children as positive exempla parallel to the men in their communities.

Yet although Mayhew's text accurately reflects the changing perception of women and children in white New England culture, it obscures and often inverts the changes in the status of Wampanoag women and children on the island itself: during the eighteenth century, Wampanoag women and children were often disenfranchised and dislocated from the community because of increasing debt and indenturement to white masters. Historian David Silverman's superb analysis of the wealth of other primary documents from colonial Martha's Vineyard has helped provide a corrective to Mayhew's view.[61]

Mayhew's text also differs from earlier New England literature in the extent to which he envisions Native Americans as part of the Mosaic Tribe. His use of Wampanoags as *exempla fidei* has precedents in some of the earlier tracts by the Society for the Propagation of the Gospel, including, in addition to the early writings by members of the Mayhew family, works by John Eliot and other missionaries. Although a number of such works were pub-

---

59 In ibid., 48, Mather estimated that between two-thirds and three-quarters of the members of a nearby church were women; according to Mather—and church records—this trend prevailed throughout New England. Porterfield, "Women's Attraction to Puritanism," 196–97.

60 Reis, *Damned Women*, 1; Hayes, *Colonial Woman's Bookshelf*, 1.

61 Silverman, *Faith and Boundaries*, 68, 197–215, 242. On this inversion, see below.

lished in Algonquian, stories about saintly Algonquians mainly appeared in English.[62] So did stories about the "success of the gospel," directed chiefly at white readers who might either be encouraged to help fund further missionary activities or be inspired to further piety themselves. The works in English fall into roughly four genres: dialogues, letters, historical and ethnographic narratives, and conversion narratives. In all four, Wampanoags serve as *exempla fidei*, though most particularly in the conversion narratives included in works such as Eliot and Mayhew's *Tears of repentance* (1653). Experience Mayhew's biographies differ from these earlier conversion stories in relating entire lives, not merely the moments of conversion. Moreover, Experience Mayhew often tells the story of Wampanoag families that had been Christians for as many as three or four generations. Hence, the biographies in *Indian Converts* more closely resemble the experiences of their white readers than do any of the earlier life stories found in the Eliot Tracts.[63] By focusing on a range of converts, *Indian Converts* is also more insistent in seeing the Wampanoags as part of New England's Mosaic Tribe.

Even as Mayhew includes the Wampanoags in New England's Mosaic Tribe, he incorporates elements of Wampanoag oral tradition into the traditional New England genre. His biographical history is indebted to the Wampanoag oral genre of the *memorate*: a concrete account of a personal encounter with the supernatural.[64] The *memorate* shares some important features with the standard Puritan conversion narrative: both can be either told in first person or retold by someone who was not involved in the incident. Just as conversion narratives were often told to gain church membership, *memorates* by *pniesok* (warrior-counselors) and *pawwaws* (shamans) were told as part of the rite of passage to become a spiritual leader, advisor, or practitioner. Unlike conversion narratives or experiences, *memorates* often came in the form of a dream or vision that might be deliberately induced through a "difficult ordeal" or "loss of sleep, fasting, and drinking

---

62 Works printed in Algonquian and used on the Vineyard included Bibles, primers, catechism, sermons, and translations of famous and essential theological works such as Richard Baxter's *Call to the unconverted* and Lewis Bayly's *Practice of pietie*. These works were aimed at an Algonquian audience and were used in the field by Protestant missionaries. (See the section below on literacy.)

63 The title "Eliot Tracts" refers to a series of tracts that were written by or feature missionary John Eliot and that were published by the England Company. As Hilary Wyss points out, "These writings establish patterns of conversion and set up the expectations and cultural assumptions of the missionaries under whose guidance conversions were to take place." Wyss, "Things That Do Accompany Salvation," 19.

64 William Simmons proposes that Wampanoag oral tradition can be divided into four genres: *memorate*, legend, myth, and folktale. Simmons, *Spirit of the New England Tribes*, 6.

mixtures that may have been hallucinogenic."[65] Also unlike Puritan conversion experiences, which involved an encounter with Jesus or God, a variety of spirits appeared to Algonquians in their dreams and visions. The figure associated with attaining the position of *pawwaw* or *pniese* was Hobbamock, "whose name was related to words for death, the deceased, and the cold northeast wind." Hobbamock was associated with night, black, and liminal spaces like "hideous woods and swamps." He could appear "in the shapes of Englishmen, Indians, animals, inanimate objects, and mythical creatures."[66] The conversion narratives told by Wampanoags in *Indian Converts* often reference the motifs, characters, events, and elements of the *memorate* tradition. In this sense, *Indian Converts* serves as a generic hybrid of Puritan and Wampanoag stories of the supernatural.

The hybrid nature of *Indian Converts* and the impact on his work of Mayhew's evangelical service to the Wampanoags can perhaps be best seen in the contrast between Mayhew's biographies of the Wampanoags and Rev. Thomas Prince's biographies of the Mayhew family. Mayhew's willingness to use Wampanoag oral tradition and to see Wampanoags as active and efficacious members of the Mosaic Tribe of New England differs sharply from the point of view offered by Prince, whose biographies of the Mayhew family are appendixed to *Indian Converts* in a section titled "Some Account of those English Ministers who have successively presided over the Work of Gospelizing the Indians on Martha's Vineyard, and the adjacent Islands." Thomas Prince (1687–1758) was the minister of Old South Church in Boston for forty years (1718–58), including the era when *Indian Converts* was published. Today his fame rests largely on his book collection, upon which his *Chronological history of New-England in the form of annals* is based.[67]

---

65 The word *pawwaw* (also *powwow* or *powah*) refers both to a religious ceremony and to the shaman who led such ceremonies. To distinguish between the two in this book, I use the spelling *pawwaw* to refer to the shaman and "powwow" to refer to the ceremony. These shamans provoked great fear in the Puritan colonists, who often associated their powers with witchcraft. *Pniese* (pl. *pniesok*) were warrior-counselors who gained their authority by virtue of having receiving a vision or dream of Hobbamock. Ibid., 6, 37–41. Anne Marie Plane has called attention the Wampanoag tradition of dream visions and dream interpretation embedded in Mayhew's text. As Plane observes, both Puritans and Wampanoags had a rich tradition of dream visions and dream interpretation, and both colonists and Wampanoags believed that dreams were a possible source of divine revelation and had a potential predictive significance. Plane, "Falling 'Into a Dreame,'" 86–87. Puritans were not as likely to try to induce their visions, however, or include them in the rites of passage leading to church membership.

66 Simmons, *Spirit of the New England Tribes*, 39.

67 Prince was also the nephew of Experience Mayhew's first wife, Thankful Hinckley (1671–1706). Prince was the son of Samuel Prince and Mercy [Mary] Hinckley, Thankful's sister. See *HMV*, 3:305; and "Barnstable, Mass., Vital Records vol. 1." The roughly 2,000 books that survive from his collection are housed at the Boston Public Library in the Thomas Prince Collection. Experience Mayhew bought a subscription for six copies of his history: Prince, *Chronological history of New-England*, 13.

Although Prince's history would effectively shift the genre of New England history back from biographical history to annals, "Some Account of those English Ministers" is faithful to the older biographical style of writing. In it, Prince gives the history of the Mayhews through portraits of the patriarchs rather than a year-by-year account. While Prince has been lauded for having "qualified himself for the service of history by [doing] so much conscious and specific preparation" like "no American writer before [him]," his research consisted primarily of book learning.[68] In contrast, Mayhew's biographies were based not only on personal experience but also on the oral histories he and his family had collected. Thus, the style and emphasis of Prince's account differs sharply from Mayhew's: although Prince repeats information already given in *Indian Converts*, he places the agency for Wampanoag conversion squarely in the hands of the Mayhews. Moreover, Prince is critical of rather than sympathetic to the Wampanoags, whereas Mayhew's work repeatedly emphasizes the achievement of Wampanoags through God's help and their own spiritual strivings. Mayhew's authorial self recedes into the background. The uniqueness of his account is vividly felt in the difference between his tone and Prince's.

In addition to reflecting his service to the Wampanoags, Mayhew's use of genre reflects a changing theological climate. On the one hand, *Indian Converts* attests to the ongoing importance of conversion narratives in New England life; on the other, the work also reflects the change in New England (auto)biography during the eighteenth century, particularly regarding concerns about the right to communion. Conversion narratives, as an important subcategory of spiritual (auto)biography, were almost always included in the life stories of New England saints, such as Thomas Shepard's *Autobiography*.[69] Conversion narratives were usually delivered publicly before the congregation (or, for women, sometimes privately before a minister) in order to gain church membership. Although the term "conversion narrative" might seem to imply the transformation from a nonbeliever to a believer, such narratives most often explain how the unsaved believer received God's grace and entered into his covenant. Listening to or reading the conversion narratives of other people allowed community members to recognize whether they themselves were saved. Perhaps even more crucially, these narratives allowed listeners and readers to take the first step toward salvation: "They learned how to see themselves as sinners worthy

---

68 Tichi, "Spiritual Biography," 65; Hill, *History of the Old South Church* 2:42.
69 See McGiffert, *God's Plot.*

of damnation."[70] The fear this knowledge of damnation engendered was assuaged by the "bright hope of grace" and the knowledge that even more sinful people had been saved before. Mayhew's life stories often depict how the converts have gone through this dual process of despair and hope. It is important that the converts, like the reader, are not perfect but still savable amid their flaws. Moreover, because these narratives were recited publicly, in New England they tend "more toward formalistic recitation and mechanical patterns than do contemporary counterparts."[71] This adherence to pattern was perceived not as a deficit but rather as making the narrative more convincing as testimony. Likewise, the conformity of Mayhew's stories would have attested to the strength of the conversions.

Jan Romein has suggested that biography is often "stimulated in periods of crises," since biographies provide guidance to individuals suffering a loss of confidence in other authorities and traditions.[72] Mayhew's biographies minister to the specific theological tensions of his day, particularly the crisis surrounding communion that came to a head during the First Great Awakening. Although the right to take communion would probably not strike many today as a source of dislocation and disruption, it reflected the ongoing crises of salvation in seventeenth- and eighteenth-century New England, perhaps most vividly portrayed by the concern the witchcraft trials raised about what kinds of evidence could be trusted regarding the salvation and damnation of others.[73] By the eighteenth century, although communion was usually still limited to the "elect," not all churches required conversion narratives for church membership. Removing the requirement undoubtedly increased church membership, but it did not solve the problem of how to identify who was a "saint" and who was not; it merely transferred the arena of identification to communion.

Mayhew's biographies reflect this eighteenth-century concern with the right to communion. As early as 1657–62, when the Half-Way Covenant extended church membership to descendants of church members, it denied them an automatic right to communion. For Arminians of Mayhew's day, the concern about communion was a nonissue, as they tended to view it as

---

70 Hall, *Worlds of Wonder*, 123.

71 Shea, *Spiritual Autobiography in Early America*, 90.

72 Murdock paraphrases Romein in "Clio in the Wilderness," 223.

73 The witchcraft trials raised questions about "spectral evidence"—that is, the assumption that "devils representing specific individuals must operate by consent of those individuals." As Cotton Mather and others pointed out, there was a basic problem when visible evidence relied on "the Devil's Authority." Godbear, *The Devil's Dominion*, 216, 220.

"a means of conversion rather than an emblem of holiness." Calvinist ministers such as Experience Mayhew, however, felt that one should be "visibly qualified" to partake of the Lord's Supper. Within the Calvinist camp there was great contention over what exactly was required to indicate inward grace: was a profession of belief enough, or was "a visibility of the circumcision of heart, or saving conversion . . . necessary"?[74] Perhaps even more pressing, how would one know one's heart *had* been "circumcised"? Although Mayhew claims that it "is *not probable*, that it should be very *difficult* for a serious Enquirer to know whether he has a *Right* to the *Lord's Supper*," practice showed otherwise.[75] Indeed, one of Mayhew's most common laments in *Indian Converts* is that righteous Wampanoags who clearly displayed the presence of God's grace often did not take communion for fear of overstepping their bounds.

Indian Converts responds to the question of "how do I know" by detailing the clear signs of "visible" saintliness; in this sense, it serves as a sort of practical guide and companion to Mayhew's sermon *A right to the Lord's Supper considered in a letter to a serious enquirer after truth* (1741). In that sermon, Mayhew insists that those who are qualified to take the Lord's Supper must not neglect to do so.[76] *Indian Converts* provides readers with real-life test cases for who should be taking communion and when. The debate surrounding communion raged throughout the eighteenth century. The topic of open and closed communion was treated by Solomon Stoddard (1709), Jonathan Edwards (1749, 1752), and William Stoddard (1751). Indeed, the controversy over the Lord's Supper during the First Great Awakening caused Solomon Stoddard's tract to be reprinted in 1751, and communion would continue to be the source of great debate in the 1770s through the 1790s, particularly for the Baptists. Mayhew's interest in restricting yet encouraging communion is yet another example of his Regular Light middle way. Moreover, his use of biography to illuminate the question predicts the importance of communion during the First Great Awakening and the changing nature of conversion narratives.

In spite of Mayhew's attempts to appeal to Protestants in England and America, *Indian Converts* was not a best seller in his own day. Few of his contemporaries refer to it; it was not used as a model for documenting other Native communities (though this may have been at least in part

---

74 Jonathan Edwards, quoted in Harlan, *Clergy and the Great Awakening*, 90–93.
75 Mayhew, *A right to the Lord's Supper*, 4.
76 Ibid., 3.

because other missionaries lacked the talent, resources, and personal history that made Mayhew's text possible); and it was not reprinted until the Second Great Awakening (1820s–1840), when its four chapters were published individually in 1829 and 1830. In part, this division points to the extent of the religious revolution in New England: the chapters on women and children were considered so interesting as to be printed separately for popular inspiration. Moreover, as Nathaniel Hawthorne lamented, women (and children) had become the primary consumers of literature, and their interests and taste often determined a book's popularity. Selections from *Indian Converts* were included in nineteenth-century children's books (such as chapter 11 of Benjamin Bussey's 1833 *Indian traits*), but general audiences appeared more interested in tales of Indian captivity, warfare, and "savagery" than in Indian conversion. Nevertheless, Mayhew's traditional plain-style Calvinism made his work important for nineteenth-century Calvinists who during the Second Great Awakening waged a new and intensive battle against Unitarianism, Methodism, and other more "liberal" forms of Christianity.

For nearly 150 years following the Second Great Awakening, Mayhew's text again languished in obscurity. With the rise of social history and Native American studies in the 1970s, however, it was once again brought to light. In addition to being cited in passing in larger studies on New England Algonquians in the colonial era, *Indian Converts* began to be used as a primary source for evaluating social and religious change among Algonquians in the seventeenth and eighteenth centuries. One of the earliest significant pieces of scholarship to focus on Mayhew's text was historian James P. Rhonda's "Generations of Faith" (1981), in which he argued that on Martha's Vineyard, converting to Christianity was not antithetical to maintaining a strong Wampanoag identity.[77] With Rhonda's article, scholarship began to focus on the ways Mayhew provided a corrective to the dominant stories told by historians about Algonquian life in colonial New England. In the 1990s, work on his text flourished. It has been used primarily by historian David Silverman to assess Indian-colonial relations and changes in Wampanoag life during the seventeenth and eighteenth centuries. Historian Ann Marie Plane has also relied on *Indian Converts* for an understanding of Algonquian marriage and gender relations. In the 1990s, it helped educational theorists and literary scholars to understand Native American literacy patterns and Native American narratives. The twenty-

---

77 Rhonda, "Generations of Faith," 369–94.

first century also saw the use of Mayhew's text for the first extensive published genealogy of Vineyard Wampanoags by Jerome Segel and Andrew Pierce.[78]

I take into account the place of Mayhew's converts in the larger history of Wampanoag life on the island. Today, many Wampanoags on the Vineyard and on the mainland practice some form of Christianity, often a Christianity blended with Native religious traditions. Although Mayhew's Calvinist congregations have not survived the test of time, the Wampanoag Baptist Church at Gay Head is alive and kicking. The varieties of Wampanoag religious experience that frame Mayhew's narrative include that of the Baptists, and I provide some ways of understanding how the lives of non-Puritan Wampanoags differed from those detailed in Mayhew's work. I also examine the economic, political, and cultural upheavals the Wampanoags faced in the seventeenth and eighteenth centuries which helped make Calvinism more appealing and fulfilling as a religion.

Noëpe: Alternative Paths to Modernity

Although white settlers called the island "Martha's Vineyard," the Wampanoags referred to their home as *Noëpe*, meaning literally middle (*noë*) of the waters (*pe*). As historian Edward Banks rightly points out, the name is not as generic as it sounds: there is another Algonquian word for island (*aquiden*), and *noëpe* probably refers to the fact that this island was the meeting place of currents coming from the northeast and southwest.[79] During the seventeenth and eighteenth centuries it became the meeting place of two other currents: classical Wampanoag society and early modern English culture. In order to understand the appeal of Calvinism to the Wampanoags on *Noëpe*, as well as the rejection of it by many Wampanoags, one must first understand the impact of the intersection of these two currents.

Although the island's offshore location saved it from the earliest Puritan migrations, which touched the mainland, it was not saved from the diseases that the settlers brought. Native Americans' lack of immunity to European disease wrecked havoc on the Wampanoags and other Indians. Early epidemics in 1616–19 and 1633 diminished New England's Native population by as much as 90 percent. An epidemic in 1643 further ravaged the tribes.

---

78 Silverman, *Faith and Boundaries;* Plane, *Colonial Intimacies;* Monaghan, "She Loved to Read Good Books," 492–521; Wyss, "Things That Do Accompany Salvation," 39–61; and *WGH.*
79 *HMV,* 1:32–34.

Historian David Silverman estimates that the outbreaks of 1643 and 1645 took half of the Wampanoag population on Martha's Vineyard.[80] By the time Thomas Mayhew settled on the island in 1642 and began his missionary activities, the Wampanoag community was already in crisis; although the physical presence of the settlers did not immediately disrupt island life, the diseases they brought most certainly did. The tragedy caused by death and disease continued as later epidemics swept the island.

The physical and psychological crises of the plague years were matched by the economic, social, and ecological upheaval that settlement would make during the seventeenth and eighteenth centuries. These upheavals impacted the religion as well as other aspects of life on the island. While some Wampanoags adapted their traditional religious practice to meet the challenges of these upheaveals, others sought out emergent religions—including Calvinism and the Baptist creed—to address the changes they saw around them. From an emic (insider) perspective such as that of Experience Mayhew or the Wampanoag converts, the appeal of Calvinism is simple: it is the Truth, and it emerges on Martha's Vineyard by the grace of God. From an etic (outsider) position, the appeal of Calvinism for the Wampanoags is less clear. Two primary arguments have been offered to explain the appeal of the Christian missions for New England Algonquians: (1) Christianity provided Algonquians with a new god (manitou) who appeared to be more efficacious than the manitous that they had previously worshiped, and (2) Christianity often came in a form compatible with precontact religious traditions. In contrast to these previous scholars, I argue that Calvinism is better understood as a religion that allowed Wampanoags to make sense of the newly "modern" world that emerged on the island between 1640 and 1720. Calvinism succeeded, then, for the ways it differed from traditional Wampanoag religion. In the words of Jill McMillan, Calvinism allowed Wampanoags to achieve "plausibility alignment": that is, it allowed the Wampanoag community to maintain "a correspondence between its worldview and information impinging on the group from the social context in which it resides."[81] Although the term is usually applied to the adaptation of traditional religions, plausibility alignment also helps explain the appeal of emergent religions: just as existing religions "are forced to re-evaluate continuously and adaptively" in order to remain credible, so too the success of an emergent religion can

---

80 Bradgon, *Native People of Southern New England*, 26; Silverman, *Faith and Boundaries*, 22, 74.
81 Piff and Warburg, "Seeking for Truth," 86; McMillan, "Institutional Plausibility Alignment," 326–44.

be measured by the extent to which it is both "believable" and useful in the face of cultural change. In this model, the ability of a religion to offer useful changes is equally important to its ability to connect to prior traditions.

Thus my approach differs from that of previous scholars who explained the success of the missions in New England primarily by showing how Christianity adhered to the preexisting Algonquian religious system. I argue instead that Christianity appealed to Wampanoags also in the ways it *differed* from precontact traditions. Scholars such as George Hamell, for example, argue that in the sixteenth and seventeenth centuries, Algonquians probably initially perceived Christianity "as another kind of medicine society, offering its members assurance of physical, spiritual, and social well-being"; at least initially, conversion to Christianity "was itself a kind of cargo cult phenomenon" whereby traditional mythical reality was "syncretized with a seemingly more efficacious strategy for assuring well-being."[82]

David Silverman makes a similar argument in *Faith and Boundaries:* Christianity's appeal to the Wampanoags, "was primarily ideological in character. Indians joined the meeting in anticipation of worldly results, particularly good health, but that hope was ultimately grounded in their conviction that a spirit of unrivaled power favored Christians for their adherence to him.... In a world wracked by epidemic disease, their choice rested on the belief that Christianity was the best way to regain some control over their lives."[83] For Silverman, the missions were successful primarily not because of offering a specific form of Christianity but because of directing "Wampanoag prayers toward a new, unprecedentedly powerful spirit, and reforming Wampanoag behavior to conform with His laws, thereby easing His wrath."[84] That is, Calvinism was successful because Wampanoags viewed it as analogous to but more efficacious than traditional Wampanoag religion. Although Silverman's argument is undoubtedly correct, his emphasis on continuity does not help us understand why certain forms of Christianity were more popular with Wampanoags than others during certain eras in island history. Was the Calvinist God sometimes deemed more "powerful"

---

82 Hamell, "Mythical Realities and European Contact," 80. Scholars of New England are not alone in making this argument. Studies of missions in the Spanish colonies or New France often argue that Catholic missions were more successful than Puritan missions because Catholics deliberately incorporated Native practice into Catholicism. For a superb comparison of the incorporation of Native religious practice and sacred space in the Spanish colonies versus the shunning of precontact traditions in New England, see Muldoon, *The Spiritual Conversion of the Americas,* 4–5, 17–35, 78–98.

83 Silverman does note, however, that Mayhew saw that doctrine as the Baptists' "strongest draw" (*Faith and Boundaries,* 38–39, 163).

84 David Silverman to author, May 5, 2006.

than the Baptist one, or were they the same God? What specifically made one form of Christianity appear more efficacious than another?

Other arguments about the appeal of Christian missions similarly fail to explain the appeal of Calvinism. William Simmons attempts to address the popularity of liberal Christianity for Algonquians during the 1740s, but his argument does not explain the appeal of Calvinism before this era.[85] In "The Great Awakening and Indian Conversion," he makes an argument similar to Hamell's about why Narragansetts converted to New Light Congregational-ism in the 1740s, contending that ministers such as Joseph Parks appealed to the Narragansetts because the "musical intonations, bodily movements, and appearance of trance which characterized many New Light preachers" was "strikingly similar to that described by William Wood, Roger Williams, and others from seventeenth century shamanistic performances."[86] If the main appeal of Parks and other New Lights, however, was that their preaching matched traditional Algonquian practice, why didn't the Narragansetts just have a revival of traditionalism? Moreover, as Silverman notes, during the eighteenth century, New England Algonquians were increasingly dislocated from traditional religion by indenturement with white families.[87] Why is it that the generation with the *least* access to traditional religion sought a form of Christianity most akin to Native practice? Simmons suggests three other reasons for the popularity of the New Lights: (1) the movement was new to all who participated; (2) the movement promised a new interracial society; and (3) "some kind of ideological breakthrough was imminent."[88] None of these explanations, however, nor the idea that New Light preaching was like traditional Narragansett religion, helps us understand why earlier forms of Calvinism, which weren't enthusiastic, were popular in an earlier era. Why was it that a highly segregated, nonenthusiastic, imported European religion prospered on the Vineyard during the seventeenth and the early eighteenth century and then had lost sway by the nineteenth century?[89]

---

85 Indeed, he argues that "a significant number of New England Indian groups rejected the domi-nant colonial religion" before 1740: Simmons, "Great Awakening," 26. More recently, Harold Van Lonkhuyzen has written that we need to rethink the idea that missions floundered after King Philip's War: Van Lonkhuyzen, "A Reappraisal of the Praying Indians," 396–428.

86 Simmons, "Great Awakening," 32–33.

87 Silverman, *Faith and Boundaries*, 208–15. Ruth Wallis Herndon and Ella Wilcox Sekatau make a similar claim about the dislocation of Narragansett children during the eighteenth century though they argue that, "Indian children . . . were not completely cut off from Indian ceremony and celebra-tion." Herndon and Sekatau, "Colonizing the Children," 152.

88 Simmons, "Great Awakening," 32–33.

89 I have not addressed Simmons's observation that an "ideological breakthrough was immi-nent" because of rampant "drunkenness, quarrelling, and indebtedness" ("Great Awakening," 33). Although I agree that these aspects would help us understand the appeal of religion in general, they don't explain the appeal of any particular kind of religion.

In contrast to previous scholars, I argue that the appeal of Calvinism for Vineyard Wampanoags must be understood in terms of the specific nature of Calvinism itself and the ways that it addressed the crisis facing the Wampanoags. As their social life changed during the eighteenth century, Calvinism became a less appealing "solution," and the Baptist church increased in prominence. Calvinism was born out of the crisis of modernization in early modern religion, the invention of by John Calvin (1509–64) as a way of coping with the rise of the "pragmatic, scientific spirit that slowly undermined the old conservative, mythical ethos."[90] It allowed practitioners to make sense of the radical changes in society while insisting upon the efficacy of "traditional" Christianity. From the 1640s to the 1720s, Wampanoags on the Vineyard underwent economic, political, and theological changes similar to the crises that Europeans had encountered a hundred years earlier, and Calvinism ranked high as a form of religion that could plausibly explain their changing world. During the eighteenth century many white New Englanders, however, found that traditional Calvinism no longer plausibly explained the world they faced: as Enlightenment philosophy shook New England's foundations, many New Englanders "adapted" Calvinism to make it more plausible. The Old Lights, New Lights, and Regular Lights disagreed as to how Calvinism should be adapted, but they all considered themselves to be the true inheritors of the Puritan tradition.[91] On the mainland and on the Vineyard, new "liberal" forms of Christianity gained acceptance in white communities during the second half of the eighteenth century. By 1811 most of the Wampanoags at Aquinnah (Gay Head) had also switched their allegiance, from the Calvinist Congregationalism to the Baptist church. While there were certainly political reasons for making this change, the preference for alternate denominations was echoed throughout New England Algonquian communities.[92] Thus it bears asking what changes occurring in Wampanoag society during the eighteenth century might have made

---

90 Armstrong, *Battle For God*, 62.

91 Queen, *Encyclopedia of American Religious History*, 2:504.

92 As William McLoughlin notes, it is difficult to lump all Baptists together during this era. The Baptist Church in Newport, R.I., heavily influenced the Baptists on Martha's Vineyard. While the Newport congregation was originally Calvinistic, by the 1730s the Second Baptist Church in Newport had incorporated leniencies that later historians would consider "Arminian," even if at the time the leniencies were largely considered consistent with "liberal" forms of Calvinism. For example, the Newport Baptist Church under the helm of William Peckcom held the doctrine of "Free Grace" as early as 1729. Without church records from Gay Head, it is very difficult to know if, when, and how their particular congregation might have become more lenient. McLoughlin, *Soul Liberty*, 13, 124; *HMV*, 2 (Gay Head):22; Backus, *A history of New-England*, 3:167–68. McLoughlin, *New England Dissent 1630–1833*, 304–5. Silverman, *Faith and Boundaries*, 238–39; Simmons, "Great Awakening," 25–36; Apess, *On Our Own Ground*, xxxiii, lviii–lx, 18–19, 34, 125–27, 135–36, 268.

Calvinist Congregationalism lose sway and the Baptist church seem more credible. Were the Wampanoags' reasons for turning to alternate forms of Christianity the same as those of white New Englanders?

Although the changes undergone on the island in some ways follow the general pattern of modernization in white New England, it is worth attending to the differences both in Wampanoag modernization and in the subsequent appeal to the community of various forms of Christianity. Between 1640 and 1730, Wampanoag society underwent a series of radical transformations: changes in the economy, changes in island political structure, changes in the status of women and children, and the rise of literacy. While these changes all appear to follow the general pattern that scholars of religion and social scientists refer to as "modernization," I seek to address the ways that in Wampanoag society they deviated from the general pattern of modernization. Thus I argue that Wampanoags on Martha's Vineyard paved an alternative path to modernity that has had far-reaching consequences for life on the island and for our understanding of New England Christianity. This alternative path helps explain the appeal of Calvinism, the mode it took on the island, and the ultimate favoring of other sources of spirituality by Vineyard Wampanoags.

In order for the concept of modernization to be useful to an understanding of the appeal of Calvinism on Martha's Vineyard, one must abandon the notion that modernization occurs in the same way in all societies. In the 1950s and 1960s, theories of modernization "were often based on the assumption of convergence. It was believed that modernization would wipe out cultural, institutional, structural, and mental differences and, if unimpeded, would lead to a uniform modern world." Any minor differences that remained between cultures would be due to the "persistence of premodern factors" which in the long run, theorists believed, would "fade away."[93] Such a theory of modernization clearly makes problems for an understanding of Wampanoag religion and society on Martha's Vineyard. First, it is highly Eurocentric: it assumes that after European contact, Wampanoag society developed in a predetermined evolutionary pattern that was only marginally, and briefly, impeded by Wampanoag culture itself. As Richard White and others have noted, however, contact between Algonquians and Europeans has more often taken the form of a "middle ground" in which "diverse peoples adjust their differences through what amounts to a process of creative, and often expedient, misunderstandings."[94] Because of their greater

93 Eisenstadt and Schluchter, "Introduction: Paths to Early Modernities," 2.
94 White, *The Middle Ground*, x.

numbers and autonomy, the Wampanoags on Martha's Vineyard played a larger role in the creation of this middle ground than Algonquians may have done elsewhere in New England.

It is also important to think about modernization as developing through several stages, rather than in a vague unspecified manner. As Richard Brown notes, in "one sense 'modern' is a purely relative term that simply means 'right now,' the present." Indeed, to sociologists such as Charles Lamert, "modernity" often sounds more like a state of being than a specific set of technological innovations: "Modernity," Lamert claims, "is a state of social affairs in which the spheres of social meaning are rent asunder." Even when historians use the term to talk about the "dramatic technological advances in communications, transportation, and production as well as . . . the creation of the nation-state," they often use the term to characterize not a specific moment but a *series* of technological and cultural shifts that began in the Renaissance and ended in the twentieth century.[95] In my discussion, modernization refers only to the early part of this transformation: the changes that occurred in four stages between 1536 (when John Calvin's *Institutes of the Christian Religion* was published) and 1760. These stages are (1) early "precontact" Calvinism (1536–1642): the introduction and popularizing of Calvinism in Europe as a means of coping with threats to "the old conservative, mythical ethos"; (2) the early Puritan importation of Calvinism onto Martha's Vineyard and its emergence as a Wampanoag form of religion that could plausibly grapple with the colonial world (1642–1730); (3) the Calvinist revival of the First Great Awakening (1730–60) caused by the influx of the Enlightenment into New England; and (4) the gradual erosion of Wampanoag Congregationalism in favor of the Wampanoag Baptist Church (1760–1820).[96] It is worth remembering that this trajectory attends only to the initial popularity of Wampanoag Congregationalism and its later demise. In all these stages, there was little consensus among the Wampanoags on Martha's Vineyard: different religious sects competed for the spiritual sovereignty of the island. The Wampanoag road to modernity was not a single footpath but a series of interconnected trails. Thus before turning to the specific appeal of Calvinism and its relationship to modernity, I want to examine the differences among Wampanoag religious traditions.

---

95 Brown, *Modernization*, 3; Lamert, "Foreword—1905," xi.
96 Armstrong, *Battle for God*, 62; McLoughlin, *Revivals, Awakenings, and Reform*, 28, 47.

Varieties of Wampanoag Religious Experience

Mayhew's portrait of the Wampanoag community on Martha's Vineyard documents a crucial turning point in Wampanoag history. Mayhew's biographies cover the period from 1642, when Indians dominated the island, until the late 1720s, when whites were in the majority. *Indian Converts* singles out the response of a significant segment of the Wampanoag community to this incursion. Perhaps even more significant, Mayhew reveals the role Wampanoags themselves played in creating the religious middle ground on the island. For example, he identifies the growing independence of the Native church and the role traditional leaders had in developing its distinctive practice. Although ravaged by disease, the island Wampanoags were relatively sheltered by the sea from the greatest excesses of the Puritan invasion of New England. The island sachems (leaders) maintained greater and longer control of their lands than did sachems of most places on the mainland, and converts were not expected to conform as strictly to white cultural practices as were Algonquian converts in mainland towns such as Natick. Even so, by the end of the period documented by Mayhew, the Vineyard Wampanoag community was experiencing major shifts: an erosion of the office of the sachem, increased debt, loss of land, and a rise in indentured servitude often accompanied by physical dislocation from the island hub. The converts in Mayhew's history tried to avoid the negative consequences of these trends by creating a new social hierarchy through the church, by raising their economic status through education and the church economy, and by redefining and extending their community to the larger world of Algonquian converts across New England.[97]

Not all Wampanoags on the island found Calvinism a useful or acceptable solution to the crisis caused by modernization and disease; indeed, the heroes of Mayhew's story represent only a fraction of the Wampanoags who lived on the Vineyard during those years. In Mayhew's day the Wampanoag converts to Puritanism would most likely have been called "Saints." This title did not mean that they were martyrs or holy people who had received honors from the church; rather, it indicated that they were Calvinists who had publicly declared their allegiance to the Puritan Congregational church and lifestyle. In addition to the Saints, there were at least three other spiritual communities of Wampanoags who organized their lives around religious beliefs and practices: the Traditionalists, the Baptists, and a com-

---

97 Silverman, *Faith and Boundaries*, 11–12, 276.

munity the Saints would have likely referred to as the "Goats." In Experience Mayhew's story, these three other communities serve as antagonists who seek to the lead the Saints away from the good life through various ploys. This antagonism, however, was not one-sided: the Saints were also clearly a threat to some, if not all, of the other communities. The variety of Wampanoag religious experience is also important as it helps outline the ways in which the Saints were part of a larger cultural change: indeed, the Saints' view of the good life represents only one possible solution to the problem of disease and colonization. It is therefore worth taking a closer look at all four Wampanoag communities on the island.

Saints

As Wampanoags, the Saints were connected through lineage and language to the network of Algonquian Indian confederacies that spread across New England. Yet they were also a people apart. During the seventeenth and eighteenth centuries in New England, religious identity was inextricably tied to social and political identities. The Wampanoags of Martha's Vineyard were no exception. The Wampanoag Saints lived at a crossroads between the other Algonquian communities on the island and the Christian settlers. James Rhonda suggests that the Wampanoag Saints of Martha's Vineyard lived in eight "praying towns" spread across the island.[98] More recently, however, David Silverman has argued that most Christian Wampanoags did not segregate themselves from nonbelievers but rather lived in long-standing communities to which they added new churches.[99] Living amid their unsaved brethren, they also formed a cohesive entity among themselves which was connected by both bodily and spiritual marriages to other converts. Like Algonquians in praying towns elsewhere in New England, Saints on the Vineyard reorganized Wampanoag life around the body of Christ. Just as earlier generations of Wampanoags had cemented relationships with nearby tribes and bands through matrimony, the Saints tightly wove their churches together through intertown marriages. The towns were similarly bound together through their spiritual marriage to Christ, as symbolized in the Eucharist.

---

98 Rhonda, "Generations of Faith," 376. "Praying towns" were an important innovation of New England's Puritan missionaries: whereas previous Algonquian communities generally organized themselves around tribal leaders (sachems) and kinship, the praying towns reorganized Wampanoag life around the body of Christ.
99 Silverman to author, May 5, 2006.

Traditionalists

The Traditionalists differed from the Saints in that they continued to practice the Wampanoag polytheist religion that had dominated island life before the arrival of the English. The Traditionalists attempted to heal the community by restoring balance to a world disrupted by social change. Although no religion is stagnant, Wampanoag polytheism differed from Puritanism in four key ways. First, rather than serving one tripartite God, the Traditionalists worshipped thirty-six manitous.

Second, Wampanoag traditionalism was primarily relational, whereas Puritanism was congregational. That is, the Traditionalists believed themselves bound to the sacred, the earth, and the natural world by ties of kinship, and they believed that "harmony with the nature beings and natural forms was the controlling ethic, [and] reciprocity the recognized mode of interaction."[100] In contrast, Puritans believed they were bound to a community of saved people through their kinship to Christ. Indeed, the underlying principle of congregationalism "is that each local congregation has as its head Jesus alone and that the relations of the various congregations are those of fellow members in one common family of God." Although God's design was present in nature, the natural world was a "shadow" or "image" of God, not God himself.[101] The relationship with nature prescribed in the Christian Bible was paternalistic not reciprocal.

The third way Wampanoag traditionalism potentially differed from the Puritanism of the Saints was in the relationship of their religious practice to the sachem, or tribal leader. In traditional villages, religious leaders such as *pawwaws* (shamans) and *pniesok* (warrior-counselors) played an important role in tribal politics and helped cement the power of the sachems. From the missionary's point of view, the church hierarchy was intended to replace such traditional leadership positions; however, sachems maintained their rule well after the establishment of these churches. Even more significantly, many sachems continued to connect their position to religion by converting to Christianity and taking their place within the church hierarchy.[102]

The fourth and final difference between traditional Wampanoag religion and Calvinism was that traditionally, religious credentials came through divine revelation, not book learning. *Pawwaws* and *pniesok* gained their power through experiences with otherworldly (sacred) beings and helped the tribes

---

100 Albanese, *Nature Religion in America*, 20–21, 23.
101 *Columbia Encyclopedia*, 6th ed.; J. Edwards, *Images or Shadows of Divine Things*, 44.
102 Silverman to author, May 5, 2006.

communicate with these beings. Visions and dreams allowed *pniesok* and *pawwaws* to provide advice to the sachems and to heal the tribe. Although Calvinists also believed in the predictive power of dreams, they regarded direct revelation as a potentially dangerous heresy, often linked to charges of antinomianism (the belief that Christians are not bound by established moral laws but should rely on faith and grace for salvation). As Mayhew's biographies reveal, the Traditionalists quite rightly saw the Saints as a substantial threat to their power structure on the island and to the harmony the Traditionalists maintained with the manitous and the natural world. Most of our information about the Traditionalists comes from two sources: missionaries' documents that record conflicts with settlers and Saints, and wills and deeds that record land transfers and transactions made by sachems.

Baptists

In addition to the Saints and Traditionalists, Martha's Vineyard was home to a community of Wampanoag Baptists, known more formally as the Gay Head Community Baptist Church in Aquinnah. The Baptists served as a midpoint between the Saints and the Traditionalists: they blended the strengths of innovation with their earlier autonomy. The beginning of the Wampanoag Baptist church on the island is a source of contention. Settlers such as Mayhew traced the Baptist heresies to renegade schoolmaster Peter Folger (1617–1690); however, Wampanoag oral tradition names Mittark, an important sachem, as the originator of the island sect.[103] Whatever its origins, the Baptist community differed from that of the Saints in four ways: it was more autonomous; it was limited to Gay Head; it more openly blended Traditionalism and Christianity; and it practiced the Baptist creed.

The first and most important difference was that the Wampanoags led the Baptist congregation themselves. Being self-led was a crucial selling point for Natives in the area: they had repeatedly emphasized their preference for Native preachers. As David Silverman notes, it is probably not a coincidence that "the Baptists' popularity spiked soon after the New England Company pressured the Aquinnah and Nashakemuck Congregationalists to replace their deceased pastor, Japheth Hannit, with Experience Mayhew."[104] Second, whereas the Saints' congregations and praying towns were under the jurisdiction of white missionaries who lived on the island, the Baptists

103 Author's conversations at Wampanoag Educational Center, Gay Head, Mass., June 2003.

104 The issue at stake was probably the loss of control rather than Mayhew himself, as Mayhew "had been and would continue to be a cherished advocate of theirs as a missionary, political advisor, and interpreter" (Silverman, *Faith and Boundaries*, 163).

were more cut off from white interference by virtue of their location in Gay Head, at the southeast end of the island. In addition, the community had only tangential ties to white Baptists on the mainland, though in the late eighteenth and the nineteenth century they did maintain ties to the Wampanoag Baptists at Mashpee.[105] Third, the autonomy and physical isolation of the community allowed this congregation to blend Traditional and Christian practice more openly than others did.[106] Although Experience Mayhew does not complain about this aspect of the Baptist church, oral tradition emphasizes its connections with traditional views; the Saints certainly also augmented Puritanism with Traditional practice (either intentionally or unintentionally) but were under more pressure to conform to dominant practice. Finally, the congregation at Gay Head adhered to aspects of the Baptist creed which the Puritans deemed heretical. These included a vigorous stand against infant baptism and a belief in the separation of church and state.

As Anabaptists,[107] the Gay Head community believed that "there should be a separation between the State and the Church; that no Christian should bear arms, take an oath, or hold public office; and that there should be complete religious liberty"—convictions that can be traced to the teachings of the "heretic" Roger Williams, who had been banished from Massachusetts Bay Colony in 1636.[108] The separation of church and state seriously challenged the Puritan theocratic model, in that religious conversion was no longer inherently tied to changes in political structure. To Calvinists like Mayhew, these were literally "damnable errors": that is, mistakes that jeopardized the authority and holiness of the community.[109] With this is mind,

---

105 Banks notes that the Wampanoag Baptists received money from the Massachusetts Baptist Missionary Society starting in 1855: *HMV*, 1:257.

106 John Cotton Jr.'s journal of his time as a missionary on Martha's Vineyard reveals that Calvinist Wampanoags also tested "Christianity's limits" and "refused to overlook Christianity's inconsistencies and ambiguities." Qtd. in Silverman, *Faith and Boundaries*, 56–57.

107 Later called Antipedobaptists, meaning literally "against infant baptism." Samuel Sewall reports that the congregation was largely what were later called Seventh-Day Baptists: in other words, those Baptists who opposed both infant baptism and Sunday worship; see Silverman, *Faith and Boundaries*, 58, 178, 182.

108 Schaff, *America*, 161–62.

109 One example of the use of the rhetoric "damnable errors" is in the abjuration made by the Walloon Baptists taken before minister Dr. De Laune in 1575, in London. It begins, "Whereas we being seduced by the devil, the spirit of error, and by false teachers, have fallen into the most damnable errors; that Christ took not flesh of the substance of the virgin Mary, that the infants of the faithful ought not to be baptized, that a christian may not be a magistrate, or bear the sword and office of authority, and that it is not lawful for a christian man to take an oath. Now by the grace of God, and the assistance of good and learned ministers of Christ's church, we understand the same to be most damnable and detestable heresies; and . . . henceforth utterly ⌈abandon and forsake⌉ all and every Anabaptistical error." Qtd. in Ivimey, *History of the English Baptists*, chap. 3 (cites Crosby, 1:61).

it becomes clearer why schoolmaster Peter Folger, when he began to preach these Anabaptist heresies, was run off the island in 1662.[110]

Although the Baptists on the island remained a minority during the seventeenth and early eighteenth centuries (roughly 20 percent of worshipers), they included some important members of the Wampanoag community and today remain a strong force in Vineyard Christianity; the Gay Head Community Baptist Church is the oldest Native Protestant church in continuous existence in the country. Many of its records have been lost in fires, but others are available in snatches in archives and early histories. According to one church elder, some of the main families still have some original church records under lock and key.[111] Although important players in Wampanoag Christianity, the Baptists play a small role in Mayhew's narrative. This erasure may reflect Mayhew's own anxieties: Mayhew's text is designed to note the "glorious progress of the gospel," and the Saints were less clearly the victors in the war against the Baptists.

Goats

The fourth and final Wampanoag community on the island during this era was a group I have labeled the Goats. In some sense they formed not a religious movement but rather a wandering away from religion altogether in search of more immediate solutions. The term "goat" is one that the Saints themselves might have used, as it refers to biblical parable in which Christ the shepherd will separate the saints from the sinners as "a shepherd separates the sheep from the goats."[112] One did not need to be a Wampanoag to be a Goat: indeed, the figure of the goat was popular in Puritan literature. In Michael Wigglesworth's best-selling poem about Judgment Day, while the sheep are gathered at Christ's right hand, "At Christ's left hand the Goats do stand, / all whining hypocrites."[113] To be a goat is to be a sinner: that is, to go against the laws or teaching of a particular religion, particularly if the sinner is conscious of the transgression. Goats, then, are identified by their unwillingness to follow the strictures of the other communities. All three religious communities on the Vineyard, as well as the colonial authorities, created common ground for what was generally seen as "sinful" behavior. Drink, for example, was an evil about which all three

---

110 Silverman, *Faith and Boundaries*, 55.

111 Author's conversations at Wampanoag Educational Center.

112 Matthew 25:32.

113 Wigglesworth, *"The day of doom: or, a poetical description of the Great and Last Judgment."* (Cambridge: Samuel Green, 1666. [Early American Imprints, 1st series, no. 112]), stanzas 25, 27.

[Figure 5.] "Divine examples of God's severe judgements upon Sabbath-breakers" (1671). From Solberg, *Redeem the Time*, 81. Courtesy, Houghton Library, Harvard University. Hollis No. 005233047.

religious groups agreed; sachems as well as ministers legislated against drunkenness. Other "sins" were community-specific: rules about sex outside of marriage, for example, differed between Saints and Traditionalists, as did keeping the Sabbath (see figure 5). Goats failed to adhere to either general *or* community-specific social laws.

For the Saint, the threat of the Goat was different from that posed by the other Wampanoag communities. In fact, the Goat represented two kinds of threats. First, the Goats not only transgressed laws but also potentially called into question the laws themselves, as well as the ability to lead the good life. Second, unlike Baptists or Traditionalists, Goats could not be expelled or exiled so easily from the community of Saints or even from the church. Mostly, the threat of the goat in *Indian Converts* is the threat of the "inner goat"—the sinner that every Saint could have been and sometimes was. According to St. Augustine, sin is a wandering from or a loss of self, and hence the life in the postlapsarian world is characterized by return— "an arduous journey back to God."[114] The Goats, however, by rejecting the strictures of the island's three religious communities, also rejected the basic premise that the goal of life is to "return" to the fold. Indeed, goats—unlike sheep—are characterized by their lack of need for community and their inherent love of wandering. Not all who wander, they seem to say, are necessarily lost.

Although the Goats had a less obvious and organized communal structure (certainly many of them lived among the Saints and Traditionalists), I have chosen to regard them as their own religious community, since they were often posited as such by the other communities. Increasingly, there were Wampanoags who lived outside of the religious communities and who wandered at will. The best records of the Goats occur in court records from Edgartown, where transgressions of noncommunity members were often recorded—stories such as that of "Elis" (Alice) Daggett, a half Wampanoag, half white woman who had three illegitimate children by three different men and who was punished by the courts for each transgression. There was also Elizabeth Uhquat, however, who had an illegitimate child but then settled into a happy Christian marriage.[115] Mayhew tells us the stories only of those who prevail over their inner goat, not those who lose or who never even wage the battle at all.

As one reads Mayhew's biographies of the Wampanoag Saints, it is important to remember that the heroes of his story are only a fraction of the Wampanoags who lived on the Vineyard. Their story is not the only one that could be told about this era, nor is their point of view the only one that existed. One person's antagonist is another man's hero. What does make Mayhew's account unique is the detail he provides about this community. Nowhere else is there a record of so many lives of many different people or so many segments of a Native population during this era.

Calvinism as a Solace for Modernity

Given the variety of spiritual options available to Wampanoags on Martha's Vineyard, why was Experience Mayhew's mission successful? Although

---

114 Qtd. in Dollimore, *Sexual Dissidence*, 136.
115 *IC*, 194–96, 257–60.

Mayhew himself attributed his success to the grace of God, I argue that Calvinism was successful at least in part because it helped Vineyard Wampanoags face the changing world of *Noëpe*. Calvinism emerged in early modern Europe as an attempt to heal the rifts caused by the social, psychological, economic, and philosophical innovations of modernization. As Karen Armstrong notes, Calvinism is essentially a conservative religion: it looks back in order to press forward. If Calvin felt that the "old medieval forms of faith no longer brought comfort . . . in these altered circumstances," the solution was to return to the "*ad fonts*, the wellsprings of the Christian tradition."[116] In this sense, Calvinism was doing nothing unusual: scholars of religion often argue that religions adapt to meet cultural and economic changes. These adaptations allow for "plausibility alignment"—that is, "the process by which a religious community . . . maintains a correspondence between its worldview and information impinging on the group from the social context in which it resides."[117] To the extent Calvin's religion was successful in Europe, it was so at least in part because he showed that Christianity made sense in spite of the changes in economics, politics, education, and logic unfolding in early modern Europe.

The success of Calvinism among some Europeans, however, only partially explains its success among Vineyard Wampanoags. Although it may at first appear highly implausible as a form of religion that could interest Native converts, the common ground between Wampanoag and European paths to modernization helps explain some of Calvinism's early appeal on the Vineyard. To the twenty-first-century American, Calvinism may appear to be highly implausible or at least potentially unappealing: the cycle of anxiety and assurance that accompanied the Puritan fear of damnation has been well documented by Elizabeth Reis and others.[118] The margins of Eliot Bibles, annotated by Wampanoags from Martha's Vineyard, Nantucket, and elsewhere, reveal the turmoil converts ingested: marginalia from Nantucket lament, "we are / pitiful, because of / our sin." Other marginalia from the same Bible, while still heart wrenching, begin to help twenty-first-century readers see the appeal of Calvinism for Wampanoags. In the margins of St.

---

116 Armstrong, *Battle for God*, 64.

117 Piff and Warburg, "Seeking for Truth," 86; McMillan, "Institutional Plausibility Alignment," 326–44.

118 Reis, *Damned Women*, 13–14, 17–21, 53–54. John Winthrop records in his journal the archetypal story of Anne Hett, a Puritan woman who "having been in much trouble of mind about her spiritual estate, at length grew into utter desperation . . . [and] took her little infant and threw it into a well, and then came into the house and said, now she was sure she should be damned." Qtd. in Ulrich, "John Winthrop's City of Women," par. 26.

Paul's epistle to the Romans, the scribe echoes Paul by asking, "Oh I am a pitiful man. / Who will save me from death's body?"[119] This cry not only formulates a pressing question for an epidemic-laden community but also necessarily invokes Paul's answer: "The law of the Spirit of life in Christ Jesus hath made me free from the law of sin and death."[120] Indeed, in many ways, Calvinism appears to be preadapted for the changes undergone by Native Americans during the colonial era: it attends to the very economic, political, and social changes that Wampanoags shared with early modern Europeans.

The differences between the Wampanoag and European uses of Calvinism reveal how Vineyard Wampanoags adapted European Calvinism to their own emergent crisis and thereby paved an alternative path to modernity. For them, Calvinism was not a return to the *ad fonts* (the wellsprings of the Christian tradition); rather it was an emergent form of religion. That is to say, for Vineyard Wampanoags—unlike early modern Europeans or missionaries—Calvinism was not fundamentalism strictly defined. Although like missionaries, Wampanoag converts practiced "scripturalism . . . , selective modernization, and the centering of the mythic past in the present," the Wampanoag converts in Mayhew's book did not "begin as traditionalists who perceive some challenge or threat to their core identity, both social and personal."[121] Instead, Calvinism was itself part of the challenge Wampanoag Traditionalists faced on the island. Although some early converts such as Wuttunnohkomkooh, the mother of Japheth Hannit, claimed a modicum of tradition by insisting that Christianity had been revealed to Wampanoags before the arrival of the English, this sort of plea is rarely made by the post-contact generations in Mayhew's work, and even in Wuttunnohkomkooh's case it does not posit a long-standing basis for the religion.[122]

Moreover, although the changes on the island mirrored those that had occurred in Europe, they differed in substantial ways. Most significantly, changes in Europe had happened more gradually; the changes on the island happened rapidly and dramatically. Second, change on the island was due to external intervention, not internal impetus. Third, the Wampanoags most often became the providers of goods and labor for others rather than benefiting economically from the changes themselves. Both the parallels and the differences between the transformation of Wampanoag and European

---

119 *Native Writings*, 1:409, 387. The originals are in *Wôpanâak*, translated by Goddard and Bragdon.

120 Romans 8:1.

121 Antoun, *Understanding Fundamentalism*, 2; Appleby, *Fundamentalisms Observed*, ix.

122 *IC*, 44–45, 135–37*.

Renaissance societies can help explain the appeal, and at times failures, of Calvinism on the island. For Wampanoags on the Vineyard, four key interconnected features mark the utility and failure of Calvinism and the Wampanoag path(s) to modernity: (1) the shift from a society based on agricultural surplus to one based on technologies that allowed people "to reproduce their resources indefinitely" and the influence of this change on the landscape; [123] (2) the change in political structures; (3) the changing role of women and children; and (4) literacy.

Economic Changes

The most famous arguments about the relationship between Calvinism and modernization is Max Weber's *The Protestant Ethic and the "Spirit" of Capitalism* (1905). For Weber there was a deep connection between the "practical ethics of seventeenth-century Protestantism and the emerging spirit of modern capitalism." His thesis has been attacked numerous times for the causal relationship he posits between Protestantism and the emergence of capitalism.[124] In contrast to Weber, I do not argue here that Calvinism caused capitalism but instead that Calvinism succeeded on Martha's Vineyard because it helped Wampanoags make sense of economic changes. During the seventeenth and eighteenth centuries, Vineyard Wampanoags moved first from a subsistence economy to one of agricultural surplus and then to early capitalism (see figure 6). Calvinism helped make sense of this transition through its asceticism of everyday life. The Wampanoag experience of this transformation differed substantially from that of the average white New Englander: not only was the change more rapid, but also possessions were never fully secularized. Furthermore, capitalism ultimately jeopardized the spiritual community rather than enhancing it. Thus, while in some ways the economic changes on the Vineyard paralleled the changes in eighteenth-century New England more generally, they also suggest an alternative path to modernity.

At the time of the first English settlement on Martha's Vineyard (1642), Wampanoags lived there in a subsistence economy. Thus after the impact of disease, perhaps the most radical effect of colonization for the Vineyard Wampanoags was the shift in the economic base of the community. During the Late Woodland period, Wampanoags like other Algonquians relied

---

123 Armstrong, *Battle For God*, xv.
124 Nielsen, "*The Protestant Ethic and the 'Spirit' of Capitalism* as Grand Narrative," 54, 64; MacKinnon, "The Longevity of the Thesis," 211.

[Figure 6.] John White, "The Tovvne of Secota" (1585–1593). From Thomas Hariot, *A brief and true report.* Courtesy, Dover Publications.

upon hunting and fishing as well as agriculture. Because of the richness of the Vineyard's tidal flats, marshes, and freshwater wetlands, island Wampanoags were more reliant on shellfish and other subsistence foods than the more agriculture-based New England Algonquian communities. If we take Nantucket as exemplary of Late Woodland life on the islands off Cape Cod, it would seem that island Wampanoags probably relied more heavily on intertidal plants than on maize cultivation, although archeological sites with evidence of maize production have been found on the island, and Wampanoag cornfields were used by colonists for feeding livestock in the early settlement period.[125]

Surplus from agriculture and hunting was traded throughout New England, though the ritual significance of trading and wampum should not be underestimated. Goods were more valued for the reciprocal relationships they helped establish than for their intrinsic worth. Thus hospitality and gift giving reinforced the status of the giver, not the receiver. Sachems and other Wampanoags of high status displayed their power by wearing wampum (shell currency) and other valuable items, which showed their "lack of immediate need for . . . money" (see figure 7). Goods could similarly establish harmony and reciprocity with manitous. The accumulation of goods for their own sake associated with early forms of capitalism was not a value shared by Late Woodland Wampanoags.[126]

With the arrival of English settlers, the Wampanoag community was forced to move away from a subsistence economy to one of agricultural surplus. Rather than being self-sufficient producers of food, Wampanoags increasingly were asked to see themselves as producing goods for other people to consume. One of the first changes made to their economy and ecology after the settlers arrived was the rise of animal husbandry. As David Silverman points out, the natural geography of the island was not compatible with English-style agriculture: "Imported grains depleted the glacial till soil and could be sustained only through extensive fertilization. . . . Yet the area's salt grass was excellent pasturage, especially when supplemented with English rye grass, blue grass, and white clover." Wampanoag culture also favored animal husbandry: even though Wampanoags considered farming "women's work," the raising of *Netasûog* (tame beasts) seems to have been

125 Bragdon, *Native People of Southern New England*, 37, 61–63, 82; Silverman, "We Chuse to Be Bounded," par. 22.

126 Hamell "Mythical Realities," 67–68; Bragdon, *Native People of Southern New England*, 97, 171; Arnold, "Now . . . Didn't Our People Laugh?" 16–17: Marten, "Wampanoags in the Seventeen Century," 19.

[Figure 7.] Paul Revere, "Philip. *KING* of Mount Hope." Courtesy, American Antiquarian Society and Lepore, *The Name of War*, 198. Notice the wampum belt that King Philip (Metacomet) is wearing.

gender-neutral. As Mayhew remarks, animal husbandry was not purely for subsistence: the Wampanoag "Samuel Coomes added beef and pork to the 'presents' wealthy natives conspicuously gifted to their less-fortunate neighbors." This example shows Wampanoags using surplus herd animals in a way compatible with their traditional reciprocal economy, rather than selling them for profit. Animal husbandry was part of a larger framework of jobs that were based on a surplus or early capitalist economy. Other lucrative activities for Wampanoags included whaling and fishing jobs, wage work, indentured service, and leasing out Indian pastures.[127]

Calvinism helped Vineyard Wampanoags make sense of both their surplus economy and the accumulation and devaluing of material possessions. As Donald Nielson notes, Protestantism in general and Calvinism in particular emphasized "an asceticism of everyday life that encourages work and wealth but refuses any enjoyment of one's possessions."[128] Indeed, throughout *Indian Converts*, Mayhew gives examples of Wampanoags who achieved "true happiness" by practicing the Puritan virtue of "weaned affections." The doctrine of weaned affections argued that individuals must learn to wean themselves away from earthly loves and instead focus on God. Earthly loves included not only material goods but also persons, such as one's husband, children, and grandchildren. Puritans feared that if one appreciated the sensual beauty and relations of this world, one might forget the everlasting beauty of the world of the spirit.[129] This view helped Wampanoags make sense of the economic changes that devalued and secularized material goods. Janawannit, whose story appears in Mayhew's first chapter, is only one of the many Wampanoags who found solace in this doctrine.

The economic changes undergone by Vineyard Wampanoags were parallel to but not the same as the changes made in Europe and white New England. First, they were much faster. In moving from a subsistence economy to one of agricultural surplus and finally to capitalism, the Wampanoags on Martha's Vineyard rapidly underwent economic and environmental changes that had taken Europeans two millennia. European and Middle Eastern economies had shifted from subsistence to agricultural surplus economies during what has been referred to the "Axial Age" (700–200 BCE). Changes in agriculture allowed these societies to produce surplus, which in turn led to the development of the arts, democratic city-states, and eventually empires. Dur-

---

127 Silverman, "We Chuse to be Bounded," pars. 20, 7–8, 26, 28; *IC*, 93, 141, 143.

128 Nielson, "*The Protestant Ethic and the 'Spirit' of Capitalism* as Grand Narrative," 64. Also see Chalcraft and Harrington, *Protestant Ethic Debate*, 128, 131.

129 See Tolles, "Of the Best Sort but Plain," 485.

ing a similar period of transition in the sixteenth and seventeenth centuries, European societies became capable of reproducing their resources almost indefinitely.[130] The colonization of the Americas was essential for providing the goods and labor needed for this transformation. The transformation from hunter-gatherers and subsistence farmers to capitalism occurred over a 2,400-year period. The economic, social, and ecological changes on Martha's Vineyard happened far more rapidly and were due to outside intervention.

The second difference between changes in the European economy and changes in the Wampanoag economy on the Vineyard is that material objects were never fully secularized. As David Silverman notes in "'We Chuse to be Bounded': Native American Animal Husbandry in Colonial New England," praying Indians on the Vineyard tended to place livestock within the traditional cosmos: rather than seeing all animals as consumable objects, they distinguished between *netasûog* (domestic animals) and wild beasts: "The tameness of domestic animals contrasted with the *manit*, or abstract power and uniqueness, that infused forest creatures. . . . [B]ehind every animal species was a giant double, or a boss spirit, that emanated manit to its smaller selves and directed their actions." Thus, Silverman argues, while "humans might lord over netasûog, . . . to hunt wild animals successfully men had to petition the boss spirits ritually to give their fleshly selves as gifts."[131] Gift giving remained an important way of creating physical and spiritual harmony between Wampanoags on the Vineyard. In 1749, Naomai Omausah narrated a will in which she not only left property to her kin but also indicated how the material goods served as symbols of preexisting relationships. The most expensive of her possessions, "six pewter dishes, and also seventeen pewter spoons," Naomai left to Wampanoag Congregational minister Zachariah Hossueit.[132] Pewter was not only the most costly item in her will but also the one most connected to the church, as the communion service used silver and pewter vessels. Naomai similarly paid careful attention to the relationships embedded in items deeded to her family members: her kinsman Henry Amos was to receive some red cloth "because of how kind he has been to me."[133] Her kinswoman Ezther Henry

---

130 Armstrong, *Battle For God*, xiv–v.

131 Silverman, "We Chuse to be Bounded," par. 7.

132 Naomai was probably the widow of Nehemiah Ommaush, a preacher at Tucker's Island. *WGH*, 281, 428. For more information on Zachariah Hossueit, see Silverman, *Faith and Boundaries*, 157–66.

133 Red was a color often worn by government officials and hence was given as a sign of respect to Algonquian leaders such as the Wampanoag sachem Massasoit. The most common articles mentioned in colonial records are coats, usually red ones, and stockings, shoes, and shirts. See Welters, "From Moccasins to Frock Coat and Back Again," 16.

is to be given "one dress of mine of blue (?) calico" because "I bought it from her late mother."[134] Many colonial wills mention items, but Naomai made sure as well that people would understand the relationship her gifts reflected. The repeated examples of hospitality in *Indian Converts* should be read within this context. For Wampanoag converts, hospitality invoked not only the Puritan asceticism that devalued possessions but also the Wampanoag understanding that goods could establish harmony and reciprocity between people and manitous and between individual people.[135] Even as the Wampanoag economy became more capitalistic, material goods retained some of their earlier associations.

The third difference between the Wampanoag experience of economic changes and the experience of white New Englanders was that by the middle of the eighteenth century, capitalism was jeopardizing the Calvinist community, not strengthening it. As white settlement of the island expanded, Wampanoags increasingly were unable to make ends meet by hunting or subsistence agriculture. Early venues into sheep herding were plagued by attacks from settlers' dogs, and settlers' livestock often broke through fences and decimated the Wampanoags' crops. During the eighteenth century, Wampanoags increasingly found themselves forced either to work as servants and laborers or to indenture their children in order to have food to eat. As David Silverman points out, indenturement not only decreased knowledge of Native languages but caused literacy rates either to stagnate or to decline.[136] Thus, although John Eliot and other missionaries had hoped that if Algonquians lived and worked like whites, they would be better able to become part of the visible church, this transformation actually weakened their access to the Bible. Whereas one purpose of the Mayhew mission was to spread knowledge of the Gospel and place the ability to read it in the hands of individual Wampanoags, the rise of capitalism inhibited this purpose.

Changes in Political Structure

A second connection Weber notes between Calvinism and the emerging spirit of modernism is "the Puritan demand for obedience to God alone, which encouraged democracy and an antiauthoritarian resistance to established powers."[137] During the seventeenth and eighteenth centuries Vine-

---

134 *Native Writings*, 1:55.

135 Hamell, "Mythical Realities," 67–68.

136 Silverman, *Faith and Boundaries*, 215.

137 Nielsen, "*The Protestant Ethic and the "Spirit" of Capitalism* as Grand Narrative," 64; Weber, *The Protestant Ethic*, 172.

yard Wampanoags moved from a relational political system, with sachems at the head, to a colonial theocracy led primarily by non-Wampanoags. In many ways this transformation inverts Weber's general pattern of modernization: Wampanoag society became less democratic as colonial government was more authoritarian. Whereas Weber envisioned Calvinism as modeling an antiauthoritarian stance, on the Vineyard it was more common that it modeled complete subservience to the white theocratic state. Thus in politics as well as economics, the Wampanoags traveled a path to modernity alternative to that of white New Englanders.

Before Thomas Mayhew Sr. arrived on Martha's Vineyard, the island was governed by sachems. *Noëpe* was divided into six sachemships (see map, page xvii): (1) Aquinnah/Gay Head, (2) Nashawakemuck (north), (3) Nashawakemuck (south)/Squibnocket, (4) Takemmeh, (5) Nunpauk, and (6) Chappaquiddick. Within these areas there were often "petty" sachems who were subservient to the more powerful sachem of the larger area. For example, the petty sachems of Sachakantacket and Nobnocket were under the influence of the Great Sachem of Nunpauk. Each of these six territories was governed by a hereditary leader who was part of an extended royal family. Only offspring of parents who were both members of a royal family could rule the territory. These royal families did, however, often intermarry with members of royal families from the other Algonquian confederacies throughout New England. Usually eldest sons or other male relatives inherited their father's sachemships, though on occasion, daughters such as Elizabeth Washaman inherited the position under the title of *squa-sachem*.[138] Marriage patterns of Indian converts with "royal blood" described in Mayhew's *Indian Converts* attests to the ongoing significance Wampanoags paid to hereditary status.

Although colonists sometimes translated *sachem* as "king" and *squa-sachem* as "queen," Wampanoag leaders differed substantially from European monarchs. Royal families did have a higher status than ordinary community members or resident nonmembers (such as slaves), but sachems ruled by consent and with the help of an advisory council of *ahtaskoaog,* or "principal men." Nominally, a sachem had the right to "marry, judge, make agreements, and the right to sell and assign land." In addition, the sachem and his council were responsible for "managing his territory's economic resources, hosting prominent visitors, maintaining relations with

---

138 *WGH,* 77; Plane, *Colonial Intimacies,* 16; Silverman, *Faith and Boundaries,* 124.

other communities, caring for the destitute, arbitrating disputes, punishing criminals, and organizing defense."[139]

In spite of their "hierarchical" status, however, sachems "had very little coercive power and maintained their influence largely through persuasion and generosity. Thus, though sachems and their councilors had "a distinct social status and lived quite ostentatiously on the tribute collected from followers," they, too, were required to give presents to members of their community. Gifts were mutual and a means of confirming and maintaining balance. Although bands "deferred to a certain amount of coercive power . . . they could transfer their allegiance if they found a leader did not measure up to their expectations." Traditionally, a sachem's right to redistribute land only lasted as long as his rule: with each new sachem, the land was to revert to the original owners. The difference between this concept of ownership and that of the colonists was the source of many conflicts between Wampanoags and whites, and between sachems and their kinsmen. A number of the court cases about Wampanoags "trespassing" on white lands appear to have been due to a conflict in opinion about whether lands had reverted to their original Wampanoag owners. Communities also contested the rights of individuals to sell communal lands, often by insisting that the person the English had recognized as the sachem had not in fact inherited this position.[140]

Though the sachemship persisted longer on the Vineyard than many other places in New England, the arrival of the English severely challenged the political structure of the sachemship throughout the region. Whereas the Wampanoags viewed island lands as owned by the sachemships, according to English colonial law they were part of the extended territories of William Alexander, Earl of Stirling, the secretary of state for Scotland under Charles I. In October 1641, Lord Stirling sold to Thomas Mayhew of Watertown and his son Nantucket, Muskeget, Tuckenuck, "Martin's" (Martha's) Vineyard, and the Elizabeth Islands; the deeds allowed the Mayhew family to "plant and inhabit" these islands. Although Mayhew decided that he would also endeavor to "obtain the Indian rights" to the land, he was not required by law to do so.[141] Mayhew continued to collect deeds from

---

139 Marten, "Wampanoags in the Seventeenth Century," 19; Bragdon, *Native People of Southern New England*, 142; *WGH*, 77; Silverman, *Faith and Boundaries*, 123.

140 Salisbury, *Manitou and Providence*, 42–43; Salwen, "Indians of Southern New England and Long Island," 167; March, *Uncommon Civility*, 47; Silverman, *Faith and Boundaries*, 124–25.

141 Silverman notes that the sachemship persisted longer among the Mohegans and Narragansetts than among Vineyard Wampanoags (message to author, May 5, 2006); *HMV*, 1:80, 81–84.

local sachems over the next twenty years, as he came to better understand the ownership of separate parcels of "his" land. Mayhew redistributed parts of "his" land to his Watertown neighbors, including John Daggett, who would become one of the first settlers and whose son would later marry the daughter of a sachem.[142] The result of this redistribution was that settlers increasingly saw the lands of *Noëpe* as owned by separate white colonists rather than by group of Wampanoags or sachems.

Thomas Mayhew Sr.'s reorganization of land reflects a larger change in political structure during the early colonial era. Mayhew served as the "governor" of the island, and his son Thomas Junior founded the island's church. After his son's early death, Thomas Senior was both the legislative and the spiritual leader for the island. This combination was not unique; rather, it reflected the New England ideal, for although Congregationalism encouraged a certain amount of popular participation the right to vote was determined by gender, wealth, and (at least initially) church membership. Ideally, governors were chosen by the governed and governed through their consent; since those who "chose" and "consented" were church members, not surprisingly the ideal governor was often himself a church father, as in the case of John Winthrop.[143] Although neither government nor church offices were hereditary, many of Thomas Mayhew's descendants continued to be either the chief missionary on the island (such as Experience Mayhew and his father John Mayhew) or the chief magistrate and "Lord of the Manor of Tisbury" (such as Major Matthew Mayhew).

In 1692 the island was annexed by the colony of Massachusetts, which wrested control of the government and courts from Mayhew hands.[144] The new government was more closely tied to the rest of Massachusetts and ruled less frequently in favor of the Wampanoags. The shift away from Mayhew control and their perceived indulgence of Wampanoags was long in the making: indeed, letters by non-Mayhew colonists provide good examples of the antiauthoritarian impulse that Weber admires.[145] For Wampanoags, however, antiauthoritarianism against island officials was more likely to get them in trouble with the courts than to curry favor.

---

142 John Daggett's marriage is one of the few cases of a legally recognized Indian-white marriage during this era in Massachusetts. Plane, *Colonial Intimacies*, 132–33.

143 Cooper, *Tenacious of their Liberties*, 5.

144 *HMV*, 1:174–89.

145 For example, Simon Athearn's 1675 letter to Gov. Sir Edmond Andros is as much a complaint about the Mayhew family's leniency with regard to the Wampanoags as it is about a desire to recoup losses.

From the colonists' point of view, the church, the local government, and the court system replaced or trumped many of the rights of the sachems. Sachems' right to sell and assign land was curtailed by the court system, which insisted upon signed documents rather than Wampanoag tradition. Heirs of sachems like Mittark tried to manipulate the court system by producing documents insisting that their families were "owners of this, this our Land forever"; the Mittark family attempt, however, was ultimately dismissed by the courts. Courts also overtook the sachems' rights to arbitrate disputes and punish criminals. Even their right to govern marriages was jeopardized by the differing definitions of marriage put forth by the Wampanoags, the church, and the courts.[146] Whereas the Wampanoags saw themselves as in charge of organizing defense, the colonial government formed its own militia, including Indian regiments, so that many of the Wampanoags fought on behalf of the English in both King Philip's War and the French and Indian Wars. Sachems' personal regiments were more likely to be seen as enemies of the state than as part of it. Time after time, the colonial government enforced its right to supersede the sachems' prerogatives.

The colonial government not only superseded the office of the sachem but altered the terms of governance. The relationship between the governing bodies and the poor stand as a clear example of this change. As sachems went into debt and were forced to sell their lands, their ability to manage their territory's economic resources and care for the destitute was also diminished; hence missionaries often assumed the role of caretakers of the poor. The differences between Algonquian and English views on exchange and reciprocity, however, undoubtedly affected each group's understanding of "charity" and relief. English exchanges tended to be unequal and based on perceived social status: those of higher status were expected to "govern and care for their inferiors," and in return, lower classes were expected to provide labor, obedience, and respect. Indeed, the poor were often separated into the "worthy poor" and "unworthy poor": those in poverty through no fault of their own, and those who had contributed to their own downfall.[147] In a theocracy like colonial New England, sinful behavior clearly contributed to one's downfall, while saintly behavior proved one's worthiness. Notably, many of the "worthy poor" in Mayhew's "Record of Disbursements Given to the Indian Poor at Martha's Vineyard" (1755) came from long-standing Christian families. How the receiving families interpreted this "charity," however, is another

146 Silverman, *Faith and Boundaries*, 141–43; Plane, *Colonial Intimacies*, 58, 70, 75–76, 78, 168.
147 Amussen, *An Ordered Society*, 134; Lee, "Public Poor Relief," 572.

question altogether. As Katherine Hermes notes, New England Algonquians' notion of reciprocity affected their understanding of justice in the colonial courts: "Algonquians involved in disputes with Europeans . . . expected that, if they had to pay a fine or damages, the European litigant would have to pay as well. The idea was that the sides exchanged something, so that in the end both parties had a material and a psychological gift."[148] Conflicting understandings of the meaning and role of reciprocity continued to confuse white and Wampanoag relationships throughout the colonial era.

One important result of the changes in political structure in the seventeenth and eighteenth centuries was the disenfranchisement of Wampanoags. Not only were the rights of the sachem and his council curtailed, but also the rights of consent of ordinary Wampanoags were virtually eliminated. The Puritan church, however, represented one important way that Wampanoags could reenter the colonial hierarchy: church membership was often accompanied by literacy, which in turn allowed Wampanoags to take part more effectively in the court system. Moreover, the church was tied to status, local governance, and the distribution of resources. As Mayhew's biographies attest, a high proportion of the early Native ministers and church deacons were sachems, royal family members, or councilors. Church membership also allowed access to other positions of authority in the colonial government. For example, convert Japheth Hannit "join'd as a Member in full Communion to the Church" and was subsequently "for a considerable time imployed in Offices civil and military, being first made a *Captain* over a Company of his own *Nation*, and also a[n Indian] *Magistrate* among them." Later, Hannit became a minister.[149]

Church membership could not overcome all barriers, however: for example, when an election was held on the Vineyard in 1692 regarding the proposed annexation of the island by Massachusetts, voting was restricted to owners of "a freehold of 40s per ann(um) or other property to the value of £40 sterling." This requirement reduced the voters to a small proportion of the population of two towns, Edgartown and Tisbury, where the island's wealth was concentrated.[150] It is unlikely that any Wampanoags voted in

---

148 Hermes, "Justice Will Be Done Us," 127.

149 *IC*, 46. To be an Indian magistrate entailed the power to enforce white colonial legislation upon Native communities. Native magistrates, like their white counterparts, adjudicated suits for sums under 20 shillings, punished drunkenness, swearing, lying, theft, contempt toward ministers, and church absence. Kawashima, *Puritan Justice and the Indian*, 29. In this sense, magistrates retained at least in part the power and prerogative of the sachems and *ahtaskoaog* (principal men, nobles) to govern and make decisions for the Wampanoag community.

150 *HMV*, 1:182.

this election, although its outcome would have a large impact upon their lives. In spite of these limitations, the church allowed Wampanoags to reenvision their political identities as members of the body of Christ rather than members of sachemships.

Although Calvinism wedded Wampanoags to the body politic, it also tried to help converts make sense of the subordination of Wampanoags within the political system. Weber hypothesized that the Puritan demand for obedience to God alone would encourage "democracy and an antiauthoritarian resistance to established powers," but his model was more applicable to white males than to women, children, or "Puritans of color."[151] Despite Edmund Morgan's contention that a Puritan wife in New England "occupied a relatively enviable position . . . for her husband's authority was strictly limited," Calvinism encouraged women, children, and servants to see themselves as completely subordinate to the patriarchs of the family. For Puritans, the relationship between husbands and wives mirrored the relationship between God and man: just as mankind was naturally subordinate and obedient to God, so too should a wife naturally obey and subordinate herself to her husband. The nuclear monogamous family functioned as the building block for society; indeed, as Plane argues, the "English marital/family/household unit mirrored the larger society in miniature." Compared with English women, "native women consistently played an unusually active and autonomous role in the household"; yet, Wampanoag converts seem to have internalized their spiritual dependency. In their marginalia in Eliot Bibles, converts repeatedly wrote of being "pitiful," and one remarked, "I am not able to defend myself /from the happenings in the world."[152] Calvinism not only made sense of such realizations but made them into a virtue: realizing one's dependence upon God was the first step toward salvation—or at least the *possibility* of salvation. Dependency was reframed as power.

Although Calvinism helped Wampanoags make sense of their decreased autonomy, the subordination of their political sovereignty to a larger imperial government structure in many ways inverted the normal pattern of political change in eighteenth-century Massachusetts. Even as suffrage was being extended to more whites, Wampanoag participation in politics became more limited. Although suffrage in early Massachusetts had been limited to adult male church members ("freemen"), the Township Act of 1647 made it legal for all non-freemen who were adult men to vote in town

---

151 Nielsen, *"The Protestant Ethic and the 'Spirit' of Capitalism* as Grand Narrative," 64.
152 Morgan, *The Puritan Family,* 45; Plane, *Colonial Intimacies,* 34, 178, 179; *Native Writings,* 429, 431.

meetings.[153] Even after 1647, however, property qualifications hindered nonwhites from voting. The property qualifications for voting were the possession of an estate worth at least £20, but as Richard Beeman notes, "Individual localities were free to enforce the qualification as stringently or leniently as they might choose. In most towns the combination of widespread property ownership and lax enforcement contributed to a broadly inclusive electorate, comprised of at least 75 percent of the towns' free adult males."[154] Massachusetts did not legally bar Wampanoags and other Algonquians per se from voting, but the high rates of debt and indenturement in the eighteenth century made suffrage unlikely at best.[155] Algonquians who were paupers or former paupers with no taxable property were only questionably citizens. Leavitt Thaxter, a nineteenth-century educator and "guardian" of the Vineyard Wampanoags, argued that the Indians had the legal status of children.[156] In sum, during the seventeenth and eighteenth centuries, Wampanoags entered into a more "modern" political system, albeit one that ironically limited rather than expanded their ability to participate in America's fledgling democracy.

Women and Children

For Weber, one important component of Puritan asceticism which foreshadowed the emerging spirit of capitalism and modernism more generally was the view of women and the family. As Donald Nielsen observes, Puritanism appropriated the monastic demand for total chastity and replaced it with "chastity with one exception, the spouse. Even this exception is coupled with the idea that sexuality is a duty, limited to the divine purpose of procreation, and should involve no creaturely enjoyment."[157] As noted earlier, during the eighteenth century white women and children began to find their place among the ranks of Puritan exemplars, yet on the island, Wampanoag women and children experienced a decrease in actual status.

---

153 Breen, "Who Governs," 461. As Katherine Brown notes, colonial Massachusetts was divided into two political classes: freemen (who were members of the Puritan church) and non-freemen. Not all men who went to the Puritan church were freemen: freemen were only those adult males who had recited their conversion narrative before the church. They constituted only about one-fifth of the adult male population. Brown, "Freemanship in Puritan Massachusetts," 865.

154 Beeman, *Varieties of Political Experience*, 75. On the complexities of determining how many people were actually allowed to vote, see Breen, "Who Governs," 460–74.

155 In 1800, forty "men of colour" voted in Boston. James Truslow Adams, "Disfranchisement of Negroes in New England," *American Historical Review* 30, no. 3 (1925): 544–45.

156 Cited in Ann Marie Plane and Gregory Button, "The Massachusetts Indian Enfranchisement Act: Ethnic Contest in Historical Context, 1849–1869," *Ethnohistory* 40, no. 4 (1993): 591.

157 Nielsen, *"The Protestant Ethic and the 'Spirit' of Capitalism* as Grand Narrative," 64.

Prior to contact and during the seventeenth century, women had held a fairly high status in Wampanoag society on the Vineyard. Whereas white women could not hold office or vote in colonial government, some Wampanoag women held the office of the sachem on the Vineyard. Seventeenth- and eighteenth-century documents regarding conflicts between colonists and island *squa-sachems* show that these women had broad bases of power and were supported by their communities. Wampanoag women also had status as members of extended royal families, a higher status that translated into material possessions and influence.[158] While postcontact sachems often recouped their power by becoming leading members of the church, this new hierarchy assigned women a less public social role. As *Indian Converts* and numerous other Puritan documents attest, Puritans valued women who were subordinate, subservient, unworldly, and self-denigrating—a view of the pious Puritan goodwife that was often in sharp conflict with the assertive, proud, and influential role that royal Wampanoag women took for granted.[159] But as women off the island were being given increasingly public roles and greater textual attention during the eighteenth century, Wampanoag women's roles on the island became increasingly domestic and private, and their leadership was temporarily curtailed.

The Calvinist church both contributed to the loss of status of women and helped make sense of it for practitioners. Through admission to the church, women were able to gain some status and influence, and this may help explain the appeal of Calvinism for female converts. As Mayhew notes in *Indian Converts*, "The number of *Women* truly fearing God, has by some been thought to exceed that of Men" on the island.[160] One benefit of conversion was education: early island schools, whether run by whites or not, were church-sponsored and open to girls as well as boys. In addition to being taught the catechism and the Bible, pupils learned to read and write, ideally in both *Wôpanâak* and English; as adults, Native women often taught their children to read and write at home. The Baptist church allowed an even greater role for women: by the 1860s Wampanoag women were being hired both as preachers and as schoolteachers.[161] This increased status may help account for the rise of the Baptist church on the island.

---

158 Marten, "Wampanoags in the Seventeenth Century," 19.

159 Arnold, "Now . . . Didn't Our People Laugh?" 1–28.

160 *IC*, 135.

161 See the example of Jane Warmsey and the Gay Head (Aquinnah) school in Strother, "Summer in New England," 442–61.

The experience of Wampanoag children paralleled that of Wampanoag women. Whereas the shift toward modernity is usually associated with an increase in the status of children, Wampanoag children on the Vineyard suffered a decrease in status during the eighteenth century. One of the early points of dispute between Wampanoags and white settlers had been the status and treatment of children, and during the eighteenth century, Native children were increasingly devalued, restrained, and indentured as potential sources of revenue for their families. The removal of children from the community during periods of indenturement decreased their ties to the community and their support systems and led to an internalization of their new racialized status.

Mayhew and other Puritan writers had commented (sometimes disparagingly) on the loving and often indulgent relationship between Wampanoag parents and their children.[162] In contrast, Puritan theology considered children sinful from birth and in dire need of restriction and instruction.[163] Puritan attempts to "tame" children led to a number of legal cases on the island as a result of the mistreatment of Wampanoag children by whites during the early contact period. By the middle to late eighteenth century, however, the economic instability of Wampanoag life on the Vineyard, combined with the increase in the number of children who were indentured, seems to have decreased Wampanoags' leniency: corporal punishment of Wampanoag children increased, and children's involvement in traditional religious life decreased.

The rise in acceptability of corporal punishment is one indicator of the lowered status of Wampanoag children. Puritans felt that "breaking the will" of children was often the kindest form of love; thus corporal punishment was common in both white homes and white schools. During the eighteenth century, more Wampanoag children lived with whites or white families—they went to work as "sailors, soldiers, farm hands, and domestic servants, often for ten years or more at a time"—and hence were also exposed to this system.[164] Wampanoag children were in a triple bind: they were beaten because they were children, because they were servants, and, as one boy put it, "I believe he [my master] Beats me for the most

---

162 Silverman, *Faith and Boundaries*, 209–10; Williams, *A Key into the Language of America*, 115–16; Gookin, *Historical Collections of the Indians in New England*, 149.

163 Minister Thomas Hooker argued that even children of ten or twelve years "lived the life of a beast" and were not yet rational enough to understand "the mysteries of life and salvation": qtd. in Brekus, "Children of Wrath," 302, 313

164 Silverman, *Faith and Boundaries*, 209–10; Brekus, "Children of Wrath," 307; Silverman, *Conditions for Coexistence*, 322.

of the Time because I am an Indian."[165] Over the course of the eighteenth century, Wampanoag families were increasingly unable (or unwilling) to defend their children from such attacks.

Emphasizing this point are two responses by Algonquian families to the treatment of their children, one from 1675 and one from 1767. In the first case, from 1675, we see white settlers defending the right to beat Wampanoag children and a Wampanoag family defending their child's right not to be beaten. Simon Athearn—an important and contentious member of the early white settlement on the Vineyard[166]—and his wife had repeatedly attempted to "break the will" of a Wampanoag boy and to assert their right to govern his behavior on the Sabbath. In his letter to the governor, Sir Edmond Andros, Athearn justified his right to reprimand the boy on the basis of the material goods he provided to the child and his family. Unfortunately for Athearn, both the boy and his family disagreed; the boy ran away repeatedly, and once after a beating one of his family members uttered "violant words to the great afrightning of my wife, & Caryed away my boy," or so Athearn complains. Thomas Mayhew Sr. also disagreed with Athearn's conduct: "Its a known thing," Athearn continues, that "it hath beene Mr Mayhews Judgment that no master should strik his servant and that if the servant is not willing to abid the master should let him go." In the Wampanoag servant's lack of subservience he sees dire political consequences: New England was at that moment engaged in King Philip's War, and hence Athearn pleads that in these "perilous times" Andros should "graunt us your Law to be our rule and square to walke, by that we may be delivered from all rible rable." For Athearn, Calvinism and the taming of the "rible rable" are synonymous: good ministers and schoolteachers are the first important step for keeping the island in line.[167] By ending with a plea for a stronger church to control "Indians" and children, Athearn's complaint highlights the way in which Calvinism gave white men license to be antiauthoritarian, even as they insisted upon the acquiescence of children and Wampanoags. During the seventeenth century, however, Wampanoags on the Vineyard still felt free to challenge these assumptions.

In contrast, the second case indicates that from the middle to late eighteenth century, Native parents were less likely to support and defend their children. A good example is a letter of January 15, 1767, written from a

---

165 Blodget, *Samson Occom*, 421 (qtd. in Silverman, *Faith and Boundaries*, 210).

166 Silverman (*Faith and Boundaries*, 83) notes that Athearn was a "perennial thorn in [Thomas] Mayhew's side."

167 "Simon Athearn to Gov. Sir Edmond Andros, Knt. &c, 1675," New York Colonial MSS in New York State Library, vol. 24, 159, transcribed by Charles E. Banks in DRMV, 105–7.

community near the Vineyard by Mary Occom, the wife of minister Samson Occom, to Rev. Eleazer Wheelock about her son, who was attending Wheelock's school. Mary comments that she writes "with Joy to hear that my Son has behaved himself the least so well as to give Reason to think that there is some hope of his Reforming" and to thank the minister "for taking so hard a task upon yourself as to take such vile Creature as he was into your Care." As if to emphasize the divide between herself and her son, Mrs. Occom signs the letter with the stock closing "Your Most Obedient and Very Humble Servant."[168] Mary's letter echoes rhetoric used by students at the school itself: those who misbehaved—including a Wampanoag boy—often wrote letters apologizing to Wheelock in which they described themselves as vile and degenerate, subservient to the minister and, by association, God. These letters help reveal changes both in the Algonquian attitude toward their children and in the attitude of the children themselves.

Changes in the perception of children's rights by children and their families alike may have been the result both of the internalization of white views and of economic necessity. On one level, writers such as Mary Occom constitute an intrinsically biased sample, since the writers were themselves literate and hence were successful survivors of white-style schooling. Similarly, as indentured children grew up, returned to the island, and had children of their own, they were more likely to have internalized and naturalized the treatment and punishment they had received. Whereas Simon Athearn's servant had kindred who might use "violant words to the great afrightning of [the master's] wife" and carry away the wounded boy, parents who had themselves been beaten as children, without any recourse, might (ironically) be less inclined to help their children. The economic dependency that characterized Wampanoag life on the Vineyard in the second half of the eighteenth century may have made parents less likely to sympathize with children or less likely to interfere. Women who, like Mary Occom, were often forced to beg whites such as Wheelock for money to buy food and basic necessities may have been less likely to be sympathetic when their children disobeyed the white patrons.

One possible reason for indentured children's decreased sense of self-entitlement is that they were denied access to the traditional community

---

168 Newberry Library Manuscript, Box Ayer MS 655 15 Jan. 1767. The boy may have been Aaron Occom; McCallum notes that Aaron "was thrice entered at Moor's Charity School: April 28, 1760, Dec. 3, 1765, Nov. 9, 1967. He was a poor student. At the age of eighteen he married an Indian named Ann Robin, and died February 1771. Occom was much disappointed with him." A letter from Aaron to Joseph Johnson appears in McCallum, *The Letters of Eleazar Wheelock's Indians*, 233.

and framework that might have allowed them to challenge the white value system they encountered. Indentured children often not only lost the ability to speak the *Wôpanâak* language and the opportunity to learn folkways but also—given their physical absence—were excluded from certain Wampanoag religious educational experiences that would have allowed them to take part in traditional Wampanoag social structures.[169] As indentured children increasingly internalized the racial and class assignment given to them in their masters' houses, their physical removal from the island took away their ability to access alternative values. Calvinism may have helped Wampanoag women and children make sense of their lower status, but it did not encourage them to rebel against it. The alternative path to modernity taken by Wampanoag women and children is an important reminder of the limitations of Weber's theory of the connection between Calvinism and antiauthoritarianism.

Literacy

As modernization created a crisis in authority for Wampanoags by challenging long-standing social and political structures, Calvinism provided a solution to these crises by replacing previous authorities with one authority—God. Within the Calvinist system a spiritual monarch supplanted worldly monarchs. Writing and reading were the crucial means by which to understand the will of this spiritual monarch; thus, Calvinism partially solved the crisis of authority through its insistence that "a particular script-language offered privileged access to ontological truth."[170] Missionary schools gave Wampanoags access to this sacred language and, almost as important, trained them in how to think about this language and the divine through the practice of logic. For Puritans, this educational process promised to transform children who would otherwise lead the life of "beasts" into mature souls wedded to the godhead. The transformation was not always a pleasant process. As José Rabasa argues, for the colonized, education itself is often a kind of violence, a process that "seeks to implant an institution of knowledge and European subjectivity."[171] Although the Calvinist mission on the Vineyard helped make Wampanoags literate and helped them understand the importance of literacy, their experience of literacy often differed dramatically from that of their white counterparts, in both the violence it entailed and the dislocation it created

---

169 Silverman, *Faith and Boundaries*, 209–22.
170 Anderson, *Imagined Communities*, 36.
171 Rabasa, "Writing and Evangelization in Sixteenth-Century Mexico," 69 (qtd. in Collins and Blot, *Literacy and Literacies*, 121).

from Wampanoag society. Whereas in Europe literacy often helped cement communities, for Wampanoags it just as often divided them.

Europeans had taken thousands of years to achieve print literacy; Vineyard Wampanoags moved from an oral to print culture over the course of a couple of decades. New England print culture was the result of centuries of technological innovations tied to the Protestant Reformation. In Europe the rise of literacy was a slow process that began around 800 BCE when the Greek alphabet began to be written in something resembling its modern form. The transformation of European civilization from an oral to a written culture was slow but revolutionary and was paralleled by the rise of an interest in analytical logic and the emergence of city-states.[172] The invention of the printing press by Johann Gutenberg in the 1450s further transformed Europe by making the duplication of written works cheaper and faster. Previously the domain of a cadre of specially trained monks, slowly the ability to read and write spread throughout the population. Rise of the printing press is intrinsically tied to the Protestant Reformation, as presses allowed for the distribution of the works of Martin Luther, John Calvin, and the Protestant English reformers who in 1560 produced the English translation called the Geneva Bible, which became so central to Puritan life. Puritans valued literacy and often memorized the entire Bible as well as large portions of other written works.

In part because of the Puritan emphasis on Bible reading, literacy was particularly high in colonial New England. Kenneth Lockridge's study of wills indicates that the proportion of New England males able to sign their wills was 60 percent, 85 percent, and 90 percent in the 1660s, 1760s, and 1790s respectively. Women's ability to sign their wills was lower but still remarkably high: 31 percent before 1670, 46 percent by the 1790s. Jennifer Monaghan and other scholars argue persuasively that New England women's ability to read (though not necessarily to write) was even higher.[173] Widespread literacy was significant for all aspects of society: the courts, for example, were much more likely to give weight to written evidence than to oral testimony. Colonial New England was indeed a culture of the book.

New England's print culture impacted Wampanoag culture rapidly after English settlement. A little over ten years after the Mayhews began to settle on Martha's Vineyard, John Eliot and several Algonquian translators

---

172 Vernant, *The Origins of Greek Thought*, is the classic text on the connection between literacy, logic, and the rise of the *polis*. Also see Havelock, *The Muse Learns to Write*.

173 Lockeridge, *Literacy in Colonial New England*, 13, 38–39; Monaghan, "Literacy Instruction and Gender in Colonial New England," 18, 19.

printed the Old Testament in *Massachusett* (1655). This work was quickly followed by others in Algonquian: a covenanting confession (1660), the Old and New Testament that were known as the Eliot Bible (1663), Richard Baxter's *Call to the unconverted* (1664), Lewis Bayley's *Practice of pietie* (1665), a primer (1669), a logic primer (1672), another New Testament (1681), Thomas Shepherd's *Sincere convert* (1689), John Cotton's *Spiritual milk* (1691), Increase Mather's *Greatest sinners* (1698), the Boston Synod's *Confession of faith* (1699), the Psalms (1709), and several sermons by Cotton Mather (1700, 1707, 1714).[174] These works were used widely by missionaries and were so beloved among converts that by 1720, when Experience Mayhew wrote his *Brief account*, there were no Eliot Bibles left.[175] Indeed, as early as the winter of 1652, Thomas Mayhew Jr. established a day school on the island in which he taught thirty students, both children and adults who sought to become literate, and the program was quickly expanded to include one other English teacher (Peter Folger) and eight Wampanoag schoolmasters. The early curriculum focused on the catechism, reading, and writing, mostly in *Wôpanâak*.[176] Eliot's publications were a help both to the school and to the readers it had created.

The most important book for the Wampanoag and white religious communities on Martha's Vineyard remained the Bible. Puritans laid great importance on individuals' ability to read scripture for themselves: literacy "destroyed the exclusive spiritual authority and efficacy of the priest. . . . Although the Puritan pastor retained the role of counselor, the printed manual took over some of the functions of the spiritual director of Roman Catholic monastic devotion." The Bible favored by the Puritans was the Geneva Bible, though over the course of the seventeenth century, the 1611 "Authorized Version" (King James Bible) increased in popularity in New England. Originally printed in 1560, the Geneva Bible was an important resource for the layperson: it was the first to divide scripture into numbered verses, and it offered extensive marginal notes that helped explain its contents. Importantly, it was also the first English Bible to be directly translated in its entirety from Hebrew and Greek, rather than via Latin. John Eliot's "Indian Bible," *Mamusse wunneetupanatamwe* (1663), and Experience Mayhew's Algonquian translation called *The Massachuset psalter* (1709) are indebted to this Bible and reflect its goal of reaching out to the common

---

174 *Early American Imprints, Series I, Evans* (1639–1800).
175 E. Mayhew, *Brief account*, 10.
176 Silverman, *Faith and Boundaries*, 51.

person. These translations played a key role in island religious culture and in allowing individuals to read the Bible for themselves, as well into the early eighteenth century, *Wôpanâak* was the dominant language for Algonquians even in religious communities on the island.[177]

The Eliot Bible was essential in building and maintaining religious life on the island, but it also reflects the variety of religious experience there. In *Indian Converts*, Mayhew remarks with favor which men and women on Martha's Vineyard were known for reading the Bible to their families. In the margins and blank spaces of the surviving Eliot Bibles, Wampanoags and other New England Algonquians wrote down commentaries, concerns, odd notes, and highlights of family histories. This practice was not unheard of in colonial New England: indeed, one great innovation of the Geneva Bible was that it provided a model for marginalia. The marginalia in Algonquian Bibles range from the mundane to the spiritually poignant: for some, the Bible represented a place to practice writing the alphabet or one's name; for others, it provided a space to reflect upon the relationship between the text and the precarious state of one's soul. In one Eliot Bible from Chappaquiddick (now in a private collection) the margins became a space to mark the dates of the death of family members.[178] In some of the most interesting cases, however, marginalia can help us trace the life history of an individual Bible as it moved through the hands of generations of worshipers, as in the case of one Eliot Bible originally used in Gay Head on Martha's Vineyard and now owned by the Library Company of Philadelphia.

The Gay Head Bible is particularly rich in the range and number of annotations.[179] During the first decades of the eighteenth century it passed through the hands of Simon, Joseph (1712, 1729), and Moses Papenau; and in 1738 Zachary Hossueit, the minister at Gay Head, annotated it. The Papenaus were members of Hossueit's congregation: the minister married Simon Papenau and Marcy Akoochik on November 13, 1750.[180] Hossueit

---

177 Hambrick-Stowe, *Practice of Piety*, 49; Silverman, *Faith and Boundaries*, 217–21. English would become the dominant language only as more children and adults became indentured servants in white households and as Wampanoag women married outsiders with greater frequency in the later part of the eighteenth and early part of the nineteenth century.

178 *Native Writings*, 1:459, trans. of B47.

179 The following books include marginalia: Genesis, Exodus, Leviticus, Numbers, Deuteronomy, Joshua, Judges, 1 Samuel, 2 Samuel, 1 Kings, 2 Kings, 1 Chronicles, 2 Chronicles, Ezekiel, Daniel, Amos, Nahum, Zephaniah, Malachi, Mark, Luke, John, Acts, Romans, Colossians, 1 Thessalonians, James, 1 Peter, Revelation, and metrical Psalms. Additional blank pages also contain marginalia. See *Native Writings* 1:416–45.

180 Marriage registry for the Gay Head Congregational Church, Huntington Library; *Native Writings* 1:12–14.

was a leading figure on Martha's Vineyard and an accomplished bilingual: as historian David Silverman remarks, "For almost a half a century Hossueit was the Indians' unrivaled master of the written word, translating the passages of God's book into plain speech for the people and interpreting the natives language for colonial authority."[181] This is only one of several surviving Algonquian texts from Martha's Vineyard that bear Hossueit's mark.[182]

Other Algonquian publications helped connect Wampanoag converts to their new spiritual authority (God) and weave them into the Mosaic Tribe of the island. Like the Eliot Bible, Mayhew's *The Massachuset psalter* (1709) played a crucial place in Wampanoag devotional practice for men, women, and children alike. The Psalms educated and entertained, and they were used socially at church and at home, as well as for private meditation and study. When sung, Psalms became, in minister John Cotton's phrase, a "converting ordinance": that is, a religious act through which God's grace might work in the worshiper's heart.[183] Devotional manuals such as Bayley's *Practice of pietie* (1665) and Baxter's *Call to the unconverted* (1664) helped the convert pray properly, prepare for death, and ultimately envision him- or herself as part of the larger community of Christ. *The Practice of pietie* was the most popular devotional manual in seventeenth-century New England. Like the Bible and sermons, New England devotional manuals were a form of social literature, often being read within prayer groups, including all female prayer groups.[184] Algonquian translations of popular New England sermons such as Cotton Mather's *Family-religion* (1714) not only provided important guidelines for normative Puritan practice but also modeled the ideal sermon structure for Algonquian ministers. Primers such as *The Indian primer* (1669), *The Logick primer* (1672), and *The Indian grammar* (1666) were part of John Eliot's educational program to teach Algonquian converts not only how to read and write but how to think; indeed, the books were designed to "teach them some of the Liberal Arts and Sciences, and

---

181 Silverman, *Faith and Boundaries*, 157.

182 Others include an Eliot Bible whose location is currently unknown. See B25 in *Native Writings*, 1:415; J. H. Trumbull's copy of *Manitowompae Pomantamoonk* [Bayley, *The Practice of pietie*, 1685]; a marriage registry for the Gay Head Congregational Church; and a letter from Hossueit to Solomon Briant [Priant], the Indian preacher at Mashpee. The John Carter Brown library in Providence, Rhode Island, houses the Zachariah Howwoswee Papers, which include examples of Hossueit's English writings. For an excellent biography of Hossueit and analysis of his role on Martha's Vineyard, see Silverman, *Faith and Boundaries*, chap. 5.

183 Hambrick-Stowe, *Practice of Piety*, 113, quoting Mather's *Singing of Psalmes*, 5–6, 48. Other "converting ordinances" included communion, hearing (or preaching) a sermon, and private devotional exercises such as Bible study, meditation, and prayer.

184 Hayes, *Colonial Woman's Bookshelf*, 43, 30.

the way how to analyze, and lay out into particulars bothe the Works and Word of God; and how to communicate knowledge to others methodically and skillfully, especially the method of Divinity."[185] Mayhew and other New England missionaries were indebted both to Eliot's translations and to the educational program he set forth.

Literacy entails not only learning to read and write but also learning to value the printed word itself. Thus the invasion of print into island life had radical implications not only for Wampanoag education but also for the Wampanoags' historiography and notions of truth. In *The Muse Learns to Write*, Eric Havelock suggests that cultures that use orality as the primary means of transferring and preserving information and history tend to have very different notions of what constitutes truth and valid historiography than "literate" cultures do. Havelock, like Walter Ong and others, suggests that oral-based cultures tend to valorize concrete thought, concrete language, active verbs, repetition, and experiential language. In contrast, communities that use primarily written speech can rely upon phonetic transcription rather than mnemonic devices and immediacy for relaying and preserving messages. Thus, literate cultures tend to privilege a more abstract discourse characterized by linear thought, passive verbs, detachment from the subject, "objectivity," and an emphasis on syllogistic logic and "rational" thought patterns.[186] As an oral-based community, the seventeenth-century Vineyard Wampanoags had stressed both orality and experiential knowledge in their language and culture.

One of the first places that the print revolution was felt was in the sphere of education. Traditional Wampanoag views on education contrasted sharply with Puritan practice and created conflicts between generations. Puritan education valued literacy, abstract thinking, and by-rote memorization; Wampanoag education focused on verbal performance, contextual and relational thought, and participation. As both colonial records and current storytelling attest, Wampanoags valued and continue to value the oral tradition as a means to impart knowledge about the Wampanoag worldview, cosmology, and cultural traditions. During the eighteenth century, as Wampanoag and other Algonquian children were dislocated from their homes, tribal languages, and families by either indenturement or schooling, the

---

185 Eliot, *Brief narrative*, 5, quoted in Wilberforce Eames, introduction to *The Logic Primer* by John Eliot, 9.

186 These generalizations about literate and oral cultures are summaries of information presented in conversations with Paula Gunn Allen and the written work of Havelock (*Muse Learns to Write*), and Ong (*Orality and Literacy*). As with any generalizations, there will be exceptions.

familiar letter became a means of confirming kinship.[187] These attempts did not always bridge the gap between generations. Good examples lie in the letters of other Algonquians who experienced dislocation during the eighteenth century.[188] Hezekiah Calvin, a Delaware Indian who went to Moor's Charity School, 1757–65, wrote to Narragansett John Secuter, asking for his daughter Mary's hand in marriage. The letter is full of the decorum and pomp we expect from an eighteenth-century writer eager to impress his readers with his social refinement and upward mobility. Calvin proclaims, "It may be no small thing that I have to acquant [*sic*] you [John] with, the design that lay, between your Daughter Moley and me, Pardon me if I blush to Name it, that is *Matrimony* but I shall not attempt it without yr Consent & approbation." Calvin's social claims fell on deaf ears, however, as not only did he not receive Mr. Secutor's consent, but the letter was bandied about by the Sachem Ninegrett and his family—presumably as a source of amusement—for a full four weeks before John even received it.[189] Although Calvinist educators hoped that reading and writing would tie Algonquian children to God's community, it seems sometimes to have done so at the cost of creating divisions between Algonquians.

The Calvinist education offered in missionary schools on the island helped prepare Wampanoag children for the abstract, logical view of the world valued by print-centered colonists. The goal of this education was to detach the child from the irrational fleshly life of a "beast" and instead develop the rational "Spirit" that would connect the child to Christ.[190] Logic and abstract thought, it was believed, could transform "children of wrath" into "children of grace."[191] By training children how to think as well as

---

187 The familiar letter—that is, "a mode of letter writing devoted to the expression of affection and duty among kin, family and friends"—was one of the genres taught to New England Algonquians. For many white letter writers of the "middling sort," familiar letters provided a way to "pursue their claims to social refinement and upward mobility." Dierks, "The Familiar Letter and Social Refinement in America," 31.

188 Surviving familiar letters by Wampanoags are rare; hence examples from other Native New Englanders are useful. At least one "Cape Cod Indian" (presumably a Wampanoag) named Nathan Clap attended Wheelock's school. Although we lack the response to Clap's letter, he too humbles himself before Wheelock and asks for the hand in marriage of a girl (Wheelock's maid). McCallum, *Letters of Eleazar Wheelock's Indians*, 68–69.

189 Ibid., 47, 53–54. The handwriting of John Secutor's response to Hezekiah Calvin is that of Edward Deake, the schoolmaster at Charlestown, R.I. The handwriting suggests, importantly, that John either did not write or felt he did not write well enough to address Wheelock, Hezekiah's teacher—which may help explain why the cultural codes of Calvin's highly literate and decorous style were unsuccessful. Moor's Charity School was an early Indian boarding school run by Eleazar Wheelock.

190 Anne Bradstreet's poem "The Flesh and Spirit" is a useful example of the Puritan perception of the conflict between the Flesh who "had her eye / On worldly wealth and vanity" and the Spirit who "did read / Her thoughts unto a higher sphere." *Works of Anne Bradstreet*, 215.

191 Brekus, "Children of Wrath," 301.

how to read, missionary schools offered cultural as well as physical literacy. During the period in which Mayhew wrote, the dominant pedagogy in white schools for both English and Algonquian children emphasized logic, catechism, and abstract thinking as a way to tame the "beast" found within all children. Because Puritanism valued abstract thinking, schoolbooks such as the *New-England primer* (see figure 8) emphasized by-rote memorization: children were instructed to learn the lessons "by heart," and even very young children were expected to be able to recite from memory the prayers and catechisms the primer contained. Learning to overcome natural depravity was the first step for every child, whose entire life was expected to be a preparation for salvation. Even so, this preparation was not always viewed as possible for children: according to first-generation minister Thomas Hooker, even children of ten or twelve years "lived the life of a beast" and were not yet rational enough to understand "the mysteries of life and salvation." With time, however, logic offered a solution to the "chaos" of the "irrational" child.[192]

The difference in the role of memorization in missionary education and Algonquian education reveals the extent to which Calvinism insisted upon conformity for Algonquians, rather than allowing for the antiauthoritarianism that Weber sees as the link between Calvinism and modernization. The text, as the word of God, became the ultimate authority. Thus, though memorization was crucial in both Puritan and Wampanoag education, the nature of what was to be memorized was different, as was the method. Whereas memorization in oral cultures relies on performance and participation, Puritan memorization was by rote. Just as young Puritans memorized the catechism, older Puritan children might commit to memory all 224 stanzas of Michael Wigglesworth's best-selling poem "The day of doom," and by the time they reached adulthood many knew the entire Bible as well. The Puritan capacity for memorization was so highly developed that it was common for congregants to remember an entire Sunday sermon and later transcribe it at home for future reference.

Though phenomenal, however, the Puritan recitation of memorized materials differed greatly from the transference of knowledge in such cultures as that of the Vineyard Wampanoags which emphasizes the value of the oral tradition. Whereas Puritans were expected to commit texts to memory word for word without changes or personal touches, oral storytelling is

---

192 Hayes, *Colonial Woman's Bookshelf,* 28–29; Cooke et al., *Encyclopedia of the North American Colonies,* 420; Brekus, "Children of Wrath," 302, 313 (quoting Thomas Hooker, *The Unbelievers Preparing for Christ,* 1638).

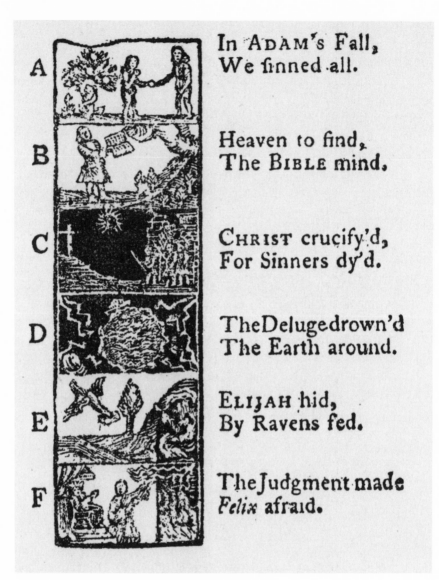

A — In ADAM's Fall, We finned all.

B — Heaven to find, The BIBLE mind.

C — CHRIST crucify'd, For Sinners dy'd.

D — The Deluge drown'd The Earth around.

E — ELIJAH hid, By Ravens fed.

F — The Judgment made Felix afraid.

[Figure 8.] Page from the *New-England primer* (1762).

fluid and adapts the stories according to context, circumstance, and audience. It is in this sense that unlike Puritan recitation, Wampanoag transmission of knowledge was "performative." As *pniese* initiation rituals and powwows show, the participation of the actors shaped the information received and transmitted. Likewise, Wampanoag students were expected to be active shapers of the education they received. Although Mayhew seems to have been aware of at least some Algonquian educational practices, his own primer is indebted to Puritan pedagogical values.

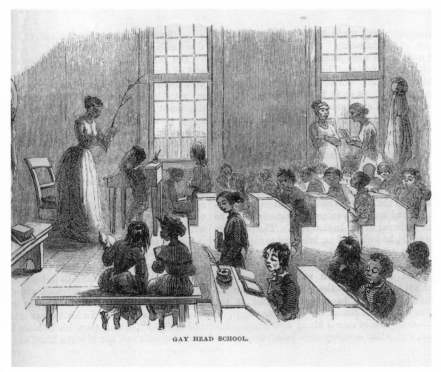

GAY HEAD SCHOOL.

[Figure 9.] Wampanoag School at Gay Head (1860). From Porte Crayon, illustrator, "Summer in New England," *Harper's New Monthly Magazine*, September 1860.

The God-centered education provided at the Vineyard's missionary schools and in white homes was intended to replace the traditional Wampanoag education that had helped connect the children to their community. As more children left home to serve in white households, access to a Wampanoag community-building education decreased. In contrast to Puritan practice, which placed education in the hands of paid professionals, chiefly men, many different members of society, both men and women, contributed to Wampanoag education.[193] Indeed, women educated the young in aspects of Wampanoag culture which Puritans would have considered more properly the domain of men. Women, for example, might teach their children how to build wigwams, tend fields, and prepare medicines, in addition to how to make traditional foods such corn stews and roasted fish and shellfish.[194] These technical skills were accompanied by stories from the oral

---

193 Puritans did often supplement or supplant grammar school education with "Dame Schools," which women ran from their homes and usually charged a small fee. Axtell, *School upon a Hill*, 175.

194 Silverman, *Faith and Boundaries*, 214, 242–43.

tradition and insights into the relationship between humans and the natural world.[195] Scholars have suggested that an emphasis on contextual rather than abstract wisdom is typical of cultures that value orality. Notably in the second half of the eighteenth century, when Wampanoag children were indentured out to white families, they not only lost their ability to speak the *Wôpanâak* language but also the opportunity to learn folkways, and Wampanoags began to rely more upon store-bought English foods and products. Certain traditions continued to be passed along orally, however, and during the cultural revival of the early twentieth century, Gay Head legends were once again being performed at pageants and powwows.[196]

When Wampanoag children were indentured out, they were similarly excluded from certain religious educational experiences that would have tied them to their communities. Non-Christianized Wampanoag children gained religious knowledge both from firsthand experience and from performances by spiritual leaders like the *pawwaws* (shamans) and *pniesok* (councilmen) at sacred and ritual settings, such as the powwows. These powwows conveyed knowledge that *pawwaws* and *pniesok* had obtained through dreams and visions. To become a *pniese*, a young man had to undergo an initiation that included loss of sleep, fasting, and hallucinogenic beverages. According to colonist Edward Winslow, this initiation culminated when "by reason of faintness [the initiates] can scarce stand on their legs, and then must go forth into the cold. . . . [T]hey beat their shins with sticks, and cause them to run through bushes, stumps, and brambles, to make them hardy and acceptable to the devil, that in time he may appear to them."[197]

This emphasis on revealed religion and participatory education contrasted sharply with the Puritan insistence upon exegetical authority and rote learning. The "devil" that the Wampanoags hoped to see was the manitou Hobbamock, who often appeared at night in the form of Englishmen, Native Americans, animals, or objects. He was associated both with death and with the color black (a fact that undoubtedly lent Wampanoags an interesting impression of the Puritan ministers' predilection for black frock coats).[198] Throughout *Indian Converts*, Mayhew relates the importance that

195 Examples of this trend include the teachings of Gladys Tantaquidgeon and cookbooks produced by Native New Englanders. See Fawcett, "The Role of Gladys Tantaquidgeon," 135–45; Sekatau, *Narragansett Indian Recipes;* Attaquin et al., *Wampanoag Cookery;* and Earl Mills Sr. and Betty Breen, *Cape Cod Wampanoag Cookbook.*

196 Silverman, *Faith and Boundaries,* 214; Simmons, *Spirit of the New England Tribes,* 28.

197 Winslow, *Good Newes from New England,* 346; cited in Simmons, *Spirit of the New England Tribes,* 40.

198 Simmons, *Spirit of the New England Tribes,* 39.

dreams and visions continued to play in Christianized Wampanoag culture and knowledge of the divine.[199]

Although literacy disrupted Wampanoag traditions, it became necessary for success within both the Algonquian church and colonial society. Indeed, one side benefit of conversion was the access to education and the economic and social advantages it potentially entailed. On the island, as elsewhere, colonists closely associated literacy with culture, intelligence, and rights. Education opened job opportunities for Wampanoag converts, both within the church (missionizing, teaching) and in the general community (writing letters, petitions, legal documents; record-keeping, and the like). From the early period, education was open to both Wampanoag women and men on the island. While there is little evidence that initially women were hired outside the home for jobs involving reading and writing, Experience May-hew remarks that women who had learned to read and write often taught these skills to their children, which increased the children's likelihood of earning a good living and of marrying into a literate household. In the nineteenth century, as more careers became open to women, Native women became teachers and even Baptist ministers.

During the eighteenth century, the pressure to become literate grew as New England's reliance on print increased; yet, opportunities for education decreased for Vineyard Wampanoags. For white New Englanders, the new forms of print complemented their Protestant identity and sense of spiritual community. As Thomas Kidd notes, late seventeenth-century New England "saw an enormous rise in the amount of print in circulation," which helped created a pan-Protestant identity that transcended sectarianism. The first single-issue newspaper appeared in Boston in 1690; in 1704 the *Boston News-Letter* became the first full-fledged newspaper for the colony. For Benedict Anderson, newspapers were crucial for representing the modern self and its relationship to the "imagined community" of the nation-state; like novels, they helped people who might never meet or interact see themselves as part of the same society. Algonquian-language newspapers, however, were not printed at the time in New England, and hence Algonquian converts were left out of this crucial connecting thread between themselves and other members of New England's Mosaic Tribe.

---

199 See, for example, his biographies of Elizabeth (*IC*, 241) and Abigail Manhut (*IC*, 219–22*). At a time in New England when "spectral evidence" had become suspect, Mayhew's unhesitating presentation of testimony for visitations by the dead and the devil in *Indian Converts* is interesting. Spectral evidence, obtained when a spirit visited a person in a vision or dream, was central to the cases made against witches in New England villages such as Salem at the end of the seventeenth century, but by 1727 it had been cast in doubt.

Moreover during the first two-thirds of the eighteenth century, as "more and more Natives served indentures, Indian literacy rates stagnated or declined"; only late in the eighteenth century did literacy rates begin to rise again, as servants began to be educated by white women in the home.[200]

Wampanoags and other Algonquians, however, *were* trained to write in the quintessential eighteenth-century genre of the familiar letter. Wampanoags who were sent to schools such as Moor's Charity School rather than being indentured were often forced to learn rudimentary chores rather devote themselves primarily to schoolwork. These schools did, however, train the students to write familiar letters.[201] For many white letter writers of the "middling sort," familiar letters provided a way to "pursue their claims to social refinement and upward mobility."[202] As seen in the example of Mary Occom's letter to Eleazer Wheelock, however, the power and subjectivity offered to Algonquians by literacy and letter writing was more often a power of subordination. Rather than increasing the status of the letter writer, eighteenth-century Algonquian letters often reflect the missionary's insistence on the lower status of Native Americans.

José Rabasa argues that literacy for the colonized was often as much a form of disempowerment as a form of empowerment. On the one hand, the skills of reading and writing provided Wampanoag converts with important opportunities within colonial society: the ability to read the Bible was crucial for those who wanted to attain positions of power within the fledgling Wampanoag church, and the education offered by missionary schools provided Wampanoag children with a way of understanding the very real changes they saw around them and an alternative authority for the language and leaders that they had lost. As James Collins and Richard Blot put it, "Literacy is both a weapon and shield."[203] On the other hand, literacy often helped dislocate Wampanoag children from the social fabric of traditional Wampanoag life.

Calvinism may have appealed to Wampanoags on Martha's Vineyard because it offered solace to the crises raised by colonization and modernization, including not only the rise of literacy but also significant economic,

---

200 Kidd, *Protestant Interest*, 53–57; Anderson, *Imagined Communities*, 25–36; Silverman, *Faith and Boundaries*, 215–17.

201 For example, see the letter from Daniel Simon to Eleazar Wheelock, September 1771, in McCallum, *Letters of Eleazar Wheelock's Indians*, 220–21.

202 Dierks, "The Familiar Letter and Social Refinement in America," 31.

203 Rabasa, "Writing and Evangelization in Sixteenth-Century Mexico," 69; Collins and Blot, *Literacy and Literacies*, 121, 122.

political, and social changes. Although Calvinism may at first appear highly implausible as a religion that could appeal to converts, the common ground between Wampanoag and European paths to modernization help explain some of Calvinism's early appeal on the Vineyard. The differences between the Wampanoag and European uses of Calvinism, however, reveal how Vineyard Wampanoags adapted European Calvinism to their own emergent crisis and thereby paved an alternative path to modernity.

Between 1760 and 1820, Calvinist Congregationalism gradually lost sway with Wampanoags on the Vineyard, and the Baptist church gained supremacy. During these years Wampanoags were increasingly riddled by debt and often had to indenture themselves or their children. Speakers of *Wôpanâak* decreased, and Wampanoags increasingly intermarried with African Americans. As Barry O'Connell, William Simmons, David Silverman, and others have noted, denominations such as the Baptists and Methodists offered more opportunities for Christians of color. It is also possible that the Baptist insistence upon the separation between church and state was appealing in an era of increasing Wampanoag disenfranchisement. Moreover, the Baptist church allowed Wampanoag women, such as Jane Wamsley, to serve as preachers. As women increasingly lost their traditional status, the freedom offered by the Baptist church may have been more appealing.[204]

Mayhew himself, however, saw that the main appeal of the Baptists was their doctrine itself; his portrait of Stephen Tackamasun, a convert who became a Baptist pastor, is that of a gentle man who wished people would be less "censorious." Even if the Baptists and the Congregationalists claimed to worship the same God, their representation of the character of this God—and his expectations for his worshipers—differed greatly. Although they did not favor infant baptism, Baptists at Gay Head emphasized a God more lenient and more welcoming than the Congregationalist deity. Mayhew complains in *Indian Converts* that sometimes the Wampanoags turned to the Baptists when they were rebuked by the Calvinists for "vile Immoralities" and that Baptists like Tackamasun were less inclined to "judge and censure others."[205] Mayhew's comments suggest that the Baptists may have had greater success leading the "Goats" and those suffering from the "inner goat" back into the Christian fold. As the Wampanoags became increasingly dislocated from their homes, language, and tradition, the more nurturing,

---

204 Silverman, *Faith and Boundaries*, 215–227, 230, 260, 163; Strother, "Summer in New England," 451.
205 *IC*, 43.

parentlike deity offered by the Baptists may have had greater appeal. The more Wampanoags served as actual servants, the less the "master" God of Calvinism seemed to appeal to them.

At this time, little has been published about the Baptist church on the Vineyard; most of what we know about it comes through ministers of other congregations. A full accounting of this rich community remains to be done. For Mayhew, however, the rise of the Baptist church on the Vineyard was an unforeseen future. Like many other important American writers of the First Great Awakening, he predicts a glorious and apocalyptic end to New England Calvinism—one in which the Wampanoag Saints of *Indian Converts* would play an important and efficacious role. In spite of the abundant deaths *Indian Converts* records, the story it tells is an optimistic one in which the millennium rapidly approaches.

Indian Converts

or, some ACCOUNT of the
LIVES and Dying SPEECHES of a
considerable Number of Christianized *INDIANS*
of *Martha's Vineyard,* in *New-England.*

VIZ.
I. Of Godly Ministers.
II. Of other Good Men.
III. Of Religious Women.
IV. Of Pious young Persons.

By *Experience Mayhew,* M. A. Preacher of the
Gospel to the *Indians* of that Island.

To which is added,

Some Account of those *ENGLISH* MINISTERS who have successively
presided over the *Indian* Work in that and the adjacent Islands. By
Mr. *Prince.*

Acts x.34, 35. *I perceive that GOD is no Respecter of Persons: but in every
Nation he that feareth him, and worketh Righteousness, is accepted with him.*

Acts xv.8, 9. *Giving them the Holy Ghost, even as he did unto us: and put no
Difference between us and them, purifying their Hearts by Faith.*

Mat. xxviii.19, 20. *Go ye therefore, and teach all Nations,* & c.

LONDON: Printed for *Samuel Gerrish,* Bookseller in *Boston* in *New-England;*
and sold by *J. Osborn* and *T. Longman* in *Pater-noster-Row,* M.DCC.XXVII

Page numbers of the original edition are given in square brackets throughout the text. The
running heads indicate the range of pages covered in each spread.

[3] To the
HONOROURABLE
William Thompson, Esq;
GOVERNOUR,
AND
To the rest of the *Honourable Company* for the Propagation of
the Gospel in *New-England*, and Parts adjacent in *America*.

Honourable Sirs,

VERY admirable and surprizing was the Favour of Heaven unto the
Aboriginal Natives of this Land, when it pleased the BLESSED GOD to
send them the glorious Gospel, after they had from Time immemorial
[4] *sat in Darkness, and in the Region of the Shadow of Death*.[1]
     It was still a further Manifestation of Divine Favour, and Beneficence
to them, when our GLORIOUS LORD stirred up the Hearts of many
well disposed People in *England*, to make liberal Contributions for the
Encouragement of those Servants of his, who, for the Glory of his great
Name, and out of Compassion to the Souls of the miserable *Heathen*,
were, without any Prospect of worldly Advantage, endeavouring their
Conversion.
     And it was yet an additional Mercy to the disconsolate *Indians*, in
these Ends of the Earth, and to such also as were engaged in the Work
of Gospelizing them, when the Society in *England* for the Propagation of
the Gospel here, were by *Royal Charter* erected into a *Corporation*, for the
more effectual carrying on that great and good Work.
     It is from your *honourable Company* so established, and acting on such
a Foundation, that such as are here employed for the Good of the *Indians*
[5] have, under GOD, their Encouragement to that Work and Service,
and Direction in it.
     And among the many Instances wherein the Wisdom and Care of
the *honourable Company* have been manifested, none has been more com-
prehensive than their directing and instructing a number of honourable
and reverend Persons here, to inspect and manage the Affair; and who
do accordingly heartily desire, and faithfully endeavour to promote the
Interest of Religion among those Natives of the Land.
     The Work of Gospelizing the *Heathen* being thus primarily under *your
Honours* Direction and Management, it is very fit and convenient, that
such as are here employed in that Service, should from time to time give
an Account of their Management to *your Honours*; as also the Successes

---

1 Psalm 107:10.

they meet with in the Work wherein they are engaged, and so of the good Effects of what has been expended for the great Ends already mentioned, and of the Care and Pains that have been taken, both by the *honourable Com[6]pany*, and their *honourable Commissioners* residing here.

From these Considerations I have thought it my Duty to dedicate this historical Essay unto *your Honours*, tho otherwise it might have been too great a Boldness: besides, I cannot doubt but such a Discovery of the Efficacy of Divine Grace in the Conversion and Salvation of Sinners, as is here exhibited in the Lives and dying Speeches of a considerable number of our christianized *Indians*, whose spiritual Good *your Honours* have been long labouring to promote, will be very acceptable unto you.

That my Induction of Examples of true Piety are only taken from *one small Island*, is not because there have not been many such pious Converts in other Places, but because I have not been so well acquainted with the State of the *Indians* in them, as I have been there, where my great Grandfather, Grandfather, and my self have successively laboured for these *fourscore Years*. Nor have I thought it convenient for me to enter into other Mens Lines, but rather leave it to them to [7] give an Account themselves of what was observable in the Places wherein they have respectively laboured.

Entreating therefore *your Honours* Acceptance of this Essay of mine to do my Duty, written at the Motion of some of your *honourable Commissioners* here, and praying, that He who is the Lord of all would please to direct you in all that Work and Service, wherein He is pleased to employ you, particularly in that of propagating the glorious Gospel among the *Aboriginal Natives* of these Parts of *America*; and giving you most hearty Thanks for all you have hitherto done for their Good, as well as for your Favours to me, I subscribe my self,

Honourable sirs,
Your most humble, and
most obedient Servant in
the Work of the Gospel,

Experience Mayhew

[ix] The AUTHOR's
PREFACE
TO THE
READER.

THERE are more especially *two Things* requisite, to render any *History* acceptable and entertaining to judicious Readers; namely, *first,* That the Matters of Fact related, be worthy to be observed and recorded. *The other* is, that the Things reported be well attested and worthy of Credit.

The *former* of these will, I hope, be granted, with respect to my present Essay: However, I am content to submit this to the Judgment of such as are impartial.

The *Truth* of the History which I here offer to the World, is *that,* the clearing up whereof is mainly intended in this Epistle.

For this end, the first Thing I shall assert, is *my own Fidelity and Concern for Truth* in this Performance. I know well that no Lye of mine can be necessary for the honour of GOD, or the Manifestation of the Glory of his Grace. And I can truly say, that I have not in this History imposed on others any thing which I do not my self believe. Indeed there are some things in it, which I lay no great stress upon, and therefore have but cautiously mention'd, and would have my Readers regard accordingly; yet I would not have related them, if I had not thought them probably true.

My Concern for Truth has been accompanied with proportionable Endeavours to avoid every thing contrary to it; and in giving these Examples of Piety, my first Care has [x] been, not to mention any of whom there was not Reason to hope, that they were indeed *Godly Persons,* as well as by many so esteemed.

The greatest number of those whose Characters I have given, being Persons with whom I was *my self acquainted,* I have had the less Occasion for the Testimony of others concerning them: Yet even with respect to these, I have made use of the best Information I could get, not relying wholly on my own Opinion.

Respecting the *Morals* of the Persons whose Lives I have written, I have made diligent Enquiry of such as I thought best able to inform me; and this not only of such as I conceived would be ready to give as favourable an Account as they could of them, but even of such also as I had reason to think would be very ready to mention such Miscarriages as they might have seen in them, or otherwise known them to have been guilty of. Nor have I confined my Enquiries about them to those of their own Nation only; but have also obtain'd the best Information I could of their *English* Neighbours, who were best acquainted with them: and on the Testimony of such as these, I have in this Case laid more stress than on that of the *Indians*: Nor can I think that I have represented any, as if they lived better Lives than they really did.

I know some of the Persons whose Characters I have given, have sometimes lived viciously; and this has been accordingly observed and confessed in the Accounts given of them. It will therefore be a vain thing for any to tell me what is already acknowledged; yet possibly some that are prejudiced against the *Indians*, will not cease to impute to them, the Sins committed by them before they were converted, not duly considering how great a Change there was wrought in them before they died, or how fitly that may be said with respect to them, I *Cor.* vi. II. *Such were some of you, but ye are washed,* &c.

Tho I could have mentioned many of our *Indians*, who have discovered very probable Signs of true Repentance in the Time of their last and long Sicknesses, many of them dying of Chronical² Diseases; yet considering the Doubtfulness of a Death-bed Repentance, I have not put any into my Catalogue of Penitents, in whom a remarkable Change did not appear while they were well and in Health: whatever Pains others, in the time of their Sickness, have taken to prepare for Death, and whatever [xi] Profession of Faith and Repentance they have made, or whatever Hopes in the Mercy of GOD thro' CHRIST they have declared; tho I could give several Instances of this kind, that would not be despised, if the Persons instanced in were of our own Nation.

With respect to the *Piety* of the Persons to whom this Account relates, with whom *I was not my self acquainted,* I have been obliged to rely much on the Testimonies of such of the *Indians* themselves, as had opportunity to observe their Deportment, and were in my Judgment worthy of Credit. But then I have not put any into my List, who were nor *generally* esteemed Godly Persons by such as knew them, how good an Opinion soever *some* might have of them.

Tho as to their Piety in *general,* I have had the Testimonys of *many* Witnesses, yet I confess that as to many of their *particular* Actions and Expressions, I have had no more but *single* Testimonies: But then I have diligently considered the *Quality* of such Witnesses, and what other Circumstances there were to strengthen the Testimonies given, and have not reported to others what I do not my self think I have good ground to give credit to.

As I have, when I thought it necessary, strictly charged such as I have received Relations from, to keep close to the Truth therein; so I should not do them justice, if I did not affirm, that I generally observed

---

2 Chronic (*OED*).

in them such an Appearance of *Caution and Impartiality*, as constrained
me to think them faithful Witnesses in the things related by them. Yea, I
observed in some of them Marks of true Piety in themselves, while they
were giving me an Account of the Piety of others; they sometimes opening their Mouths in the Praises of GOD for his distinguishing Goodness towards the Persons of whom they were speaking, at the same time
acknowledging and lamenting their own Sinfulness, in coming so far
short of what they saw in them; being much affected, and shedding many
Tears, while they were thus discoursing.

As for those mentioned in this Essay, who died *before my Time*, I have
in part taken my Information from Accounts formerly written by my
Father, Grandfather,[3] or others, being either printed or left in Manuscript; and partly from the oral Relations of Persons worthy of Credit,
whether *English* or *Indians*.

[xii] I confess I was not with some of the *Children* mentioned in this
History, when they discovered such Signs of true Grace, as they appear
to have done by the Accounts given of them, but have received what
I have related concerning them, from such Witnesses as I have above
described; and I think the Relation thereof so credible, that I doubt not
the Truth of them: particularly the Account given of *Joseph Peag*, Chap.
IV. *Examp.* 20. (which is very remarkable) is well attested; and some of
those from whom I have received that Relation, affirm to me, that some
remarkable Expressions uttered by that Child, were not related to me by
them, because they could not so distinctly remember what they were, as
they thought necessary in order to their giving an Account of them.

I asked a discreet *Indian Minister*, why I had not been sooner informed
of the eminent Piety of some *Children*, who died before I knew any thing
of the Grace of GOD manifested in them? He answered,

> That the *Indians* were a poor despised People, and were ready
> (as he supposed) to think it would look like Pride in them,
> if they should be forward to relate what GOD did for the
> Souls of their Children; and he thought this had made some
> of them backward to declare the Effects of GOD's Grace in
> and upon them.

But tho some of the Relatives of these pious *Children*, did not, *while
they lived*, declare to me what GOD had done for their Souls, yet others
of them did; and some with much Affection mentioned the Goodness
of GOD in this regard to their *Children*, soon *after they died*; repeating

---

3 His father is John Mayhew. His grandfather is Thomas Mayhew Jr., author of *The Glorious
progress of the Gospel amongst the Indians in New England* (1649) and *Tears of repentance* (1653),
both coauthored with John Eliot.

again, at my Desire, the same things to me, when I set about writing these Examples of early Piety. Others having preserved in *Writing* some Memorial of their pious Children, written immediately after their Death, put the same into my Hands while I was about this Work.

Thus have I told my Readers, how I came by the *Knowledge* of the Things related in this Historical Essay; and I hope what is now said, will, in some measure, satisfy unprejudiced Persons, that the Things reported are *worthy of Credit*.

I intended to have placed before these Examples of Piety some more *general Observations*, which I have made concerning the Efficacy of GOD's Grace on the Hearts of [xiii] our *Indians*; by which it appeareth, that they have such Knowledge, Convictions, Faith, Repentance, and other Graces of the HOLY SPIRIT, as do accompany Salvation, and which may be found among other sincere Professors of Religion: but since this will be manifest in the particular Examples of Piety hereafter mentioned, and lest this Book should grow larger than I would have it, I have determined to leave out what I intended should have been the first Chapter in it.

And now, wishing and praying that the following Relations may prove edifying to the Reader, and be a means to encourage further Essays, to save the miserable *Indians*, whether among us or in other Places, I shall here say nothing further.

Experience Mayhew

[xiv] AN
ATTESTATION
BY
The United Ministers of *Boston*

SO rich, so vast, so inexpressibly glorious are the Benefits *arising to Mankind from the true* Religion *of CHRIST, where it is well understood and embraced, that the want of Zeal for the* Propagation *of it, in very many of them that profess it, is a Thing most unnacountable and inexcusable. It is what more particularly calls for our Lamentation, that the Churches of the* Reformation *have done so little for the Propagation of a* Faith, *which emancipates Mankind from the worst of Slaveries and Miseries, and has a fair and sure Tendency to make us happy in both Worlds. While the Missionaries of* Antichrist *are more than can be numbred, and the Bigots are at prodigious Pains to* propagate *the* Romish Idolatries.

However, something has been done *for the* best of Purposes, *among those who are under peculiar Obligations to approve themselves the* best of Christians; *wherein the Men of GOD now at Work for him among the* Malabarians,[4] *as far as we understand, have done* excellent Things. *Indeed the* Romanists[5] *have their singular Advantages in the* Circumstances of their Clergy, *to* go to and fro in the Earth, and walk up and down in it,[6] *every where seeking whom they may seduce, and bring under their strong Delusions. But something has been done by the* Protestants, *to make the joyful Sound of the* Silver Trumpets[7] *heard in a GOSPEL* preach'd unto every Creature. *And, in the Prosecution of this noble* [xv] *Intention,* America *has been a Field of some Actions, not altogether unworthy to have some Notice taken of them.*

We can by no means imagine, that the Apostles, *or* Apostolical Men,[8] *carried the Gospel into the* American *World, or beyond the Bounds of the* Roman Empire, *which was then called,* All the World. *The Extent of Christianity celebrated by several of the Ancients, is most certainly to be taken with proper Limitations. What the* Spaniards *have done since the famous* Columbus *or* Colonus[9] *opened a Passage for their Colonies hither, has afforded but a very sad Story, which a* Bishop of their own[10] *has given us with a Pen dipt in*

---

4 Indians.

5 Catholics.

6 Job 1:7. Satan claims this is what he does.

7 Numbers 10.

8 An uninterrupted succession of spiritual authority that descended from the Apostles down to the Bishops (*OED*).

9 The Latin version of Columbus's name used by Pedro Mártir de Anglería.

10 Most likely Bartolomé de las Casas, the Bishop of Chiapas, author of *Devastation of the Indies* (1542).

Blood. Their boasted Conversions of the Pagans, *wherein one poor Friar has brag'd of his having baptized some* hundreds of thousands, *what will they be found when they are enquired into?*

It may after all be truly affirm'd, that the first Planters *of* New-England *are the* first Preachers *of what may be justly esteemed the* Gospel *to the* Americans, *that we certainly know of; and* that good Work *which was done in gospelizing the uncultivated Souls which were found in this hideous and howling* Wilderness, *most certainly deserves to be had in Remembrance. And tho there were some who did in the Time of it reproach the* first Planters *of this Country as most negligent of this good Work, a pious, candid, and learned Person, of the* Scots Nation, *whose Name is* Millar,[11] *in his late* History of the Propagation of Christianity, *has done the Justice to represent the good Work done here, as worthy, not only of a perpetual* Commemoration, *but also of an universal* Imitation.

Most certainly, to humanize *the Miserable, which our first* English *Planters found surviving the wasting Plagues which had so swept away the* Indians, *as to make room for a better People;[12] to cicurate[13] and civilize them was a Task of no little Difficulty. But then, to raise them up into the Knowledge and Practice of the* Christian Religion, *and bring them unto an Acquaintance of the Mystery of CHRIST, yea, to bring them into Experience of living to GOD, and by the* Faith of the SON of GOD, *how much more difficult is the Enterprize? But* it has been done.

[xvi] *Twice seven Years had not passed away, after the Beginning of the* Massachusets Colony, *before the renown'd* ELIOT, *a good Man, full of the Holy SPIRIT and mov'd by him, set on the good Work, and* the Hand of the Lord was with him;[14] *and, with a victorious Labour, he became a Master of the* Indian Language, *and then in that Language preached to many Villages of the Salvages; until, by the Blessing of GOD on his laborious Diligence,* many believed, and were turned unto the Lord.[15] *In the Harvest of GOD he soon had several Companions, and Successors, who did* worthily *in* Israel, *and have their Names in the* Book of Life.[16]

---

11 Robert Millar (1672–1752), author of *History of the propagation of Christianity and overthrow of paganism* (1723).

12 For a similar argument, see John Winthrop's "Reasons to Be considered for … the intended Plantation in New England" (1629).

13 To tame or domesticate (*OED*).

14 Ezra 7 and 8.

15 Acts 11:21.

16 Today this term is most often used by Jews, who believe that on Rosh Hashana (the New Year) the destiny of each person is inscribed by God in the "Book of Life." For the Puritans, however, "the Book of Life" was a metaphoric way of referring to those who have *eternal* life: that is, those who are saved. Exodus 32:32; Psalm 69:28; Malachi 3:16; Revelation 3:5, 13:8, 20:15.

The Indians *being so successfully instructed in the* Word of Truth, and Gospel of Salvation,[17] *soon had* Schools *erected among them; and learning to read and write, this indefatigable Servant of GOD first of all translated the whole BIBLE into their Language; and added a Version of the* Psalms *in* Indian Metre, *whereof they became skilful and graceful* Singers.[18] *It has had several* Editions *in this Country, and is the only BIBLE that ever was printed in* this Hemisphere *of the Universe.*

This great Light was quickly satellited with other Books of Piety *in their Language, which their Necessity and Edification called for: The Consequence has been, that in the several Villages of the* Indians *there have been formed* Assemblies,[19] *which meet every* Lord's Day *for the Worship of GOD our SAVIOUR, and Holy Sabbatizing, and occasional Days of* Supplication *and* Thanksgiving. *Besides these, and from among them, there were* gathered Churches *of* Indians, *who after strict* Examinations *of their higher Attainments in* experimental *PIETY, made before* English Synods, *enter'd into a solemn* Covenant *for the worshipping of the glorious ONE in THREE, into whose Name they were* baptized, *into the* Church State *of the Gospel, and Observation of all the Evangelical Institutions.*[20] *An* Eminent Person *present at the Examinations, then published to the World a large Testimony concerning it, and made this* Remark *on it,*

> There is so much of GOD's Work *in this Matter, that I cannot but count it a* great Evil, *yea a great Injury to GOD and his Goodness, for any to make light of it.*

[xvii] *This* good Work *has gone on, and there are* Churches of Indians *walking in the* Faith and Order of the Gospel, *besides many worshipping* Assemblies *preparing for the more advanced Church State, under the teaching of some* English *and more* Indian *Ministers. And tho we are glad when we are told of what our* Dutch *Brethren have done in the* East Indies,[21] *where the* Schoolmasters *have taught some hundreds of thousands to recite the* Lord's-Prayer, *the* Creed, *the* Ten Commandments, *a* Morning Prayer, *an* Evening Prayer, *a* Blessing before eating and after; *yet we in the* West Indies[22] *have pressed after a more* vital *Work in our* Proselytes; *and as little have we proposed the Religion of a* Party, *but have kept close unto the* golden Maxims

---

17 Ephesians 1:13.

18 John Eliot's *Mamusse wunneetupanatamwe* (1663).

19 Commonly called "praying towns" by the English.

20 For examples of some of the Algonquian conversion narratives proclaimed at these examinations, see Eliot and Mayhew, *A further account of the progress of the Gospel* (1653).

21 Present-day Indonesia.

22 The parts of America first discovered by Columbus and other early navigators (OED).

of the Everlasting Gospel,[23] *which all good Men approve as the Things that are* Excellent, *even* pure Religion and undefiled. *And tho this* good Work *has had many* Adversaries, *(for, as* Austin[24] *long ago told the Christians,* they should find the Devil was not yet become a Christian) *yet having* obtained Help from God, it continues to this Day.

But it must be confessed and bewailed, that, if our memorable ELIOT, *when he lay in his dying Languishments about Six and thirty Years ago,*[25] *saw Cause to mourn in* that Complaint,

There is a Cloud, a dark Cloud, upon the Work of the Gospel among the poor *Indians,* the LORD revive and prosper that Work, and grant it may live when I am dead:

There has been since his Death, a growing Occasion for such a Complaint. We cannot get the Indians *to improve so far in* English *Ingenuity, and Industry, and Husbandry,*[26] *as we could wish for. Some of the* English, *notwithstanding the tender Provision which the* Government *has made for their Protection, find Ways to incommode their Interests. Their* Numbers *are sensibly decreased by a strange Blast from Heaven consuming them. As the* older *and* wiser *People among them are by Mortality carried off, the Generation coming on feel a Decay, and a Remove of what would be their Glory. But what has the worst Aspect of all upon them is, the* Love of intoxicating Liquors, *which marvellously captivates them, and bewitches them; and which, not withstanding all the* Bars laid by our Laws *in the Way of both Sellers and Buyers,*[27] *finds the Way to come at them at such a Rate, as greatly to hinder the Interest* [xviii] *of* Religion among them. They that serve the Work *of* GOD *among the* Indians *with their most vigorous Essays, and have it most at Heart, upon Trial feel it,*

---

23 In Revelation 14:6–7, an angel flies "in the midst of heaven, having the everlasting gospel to preach unto them that dwell on the earth, and to every nation, and kindred, and tongue, and people, Saying with a loud voice, Fear God, and give glory to him; for the hour of his judgment is come: and worship him that made heaven, and earth, and the sea, and the fountains of waters" (King James version).

24 St. Augustine. Although today St. Augustine is often seen as a Catholic writer, Protestants such as Alexander Cooke argued that Augustine's belief was more in line with Luther and the Reformation: Cooke, *Saint Austins religion* (1624).

25 Eliot died in 1690.

26 One of the hallmarks of Eliot's mission was his insistence that in order to become good Christians, Indian converts needed to anglicize their lifestyle and to shed existing belief systems. Praying towns often mandated European attire or grooming, as well as the building of fences and the keeping of livestock (animal husbandry).

27 Puritans widely consumed alcohol but were fearful of its abuse. Wampanoag leaders were also concerned about the effect of alcohol in their communities: in 1676 the sachems on the island applied to the court to make it unlawful for "any person whatsoever to give sell or any way directly or indirectly furnish, any indian or indians, with any Beer, be it sip or greater quantitie; upon the penalty of paying 12sh per quart" (DCCR I.14, June 27, 1676). Selling rum to Wampanoags was also illegal. This legislation was widely violated by Wampanoags and colonists alike, either because the alcohol trade was so profitable, or because the demand was so great, or both.

that the Methods *of curing what is amiss, are much more easy in* Speculation *than they are in* Execution.

However, even at this Day there is what is not altogether to be despised. What remains, and is even ready to die, is far from *despicable. 'Tis worth not only all the* Care *of the* Commissioners *intrusted here for the Inspection and Management of it, but also of all the* Cost *which from the annual Remittances of the* Honourable Governor and Company, *who have commission'd them, is laid out upon it.*

That they who may ignorantly and imperiously say, Nothing has been done, *may be confuted, and that they who are desirous to see something that has been done, may be entertained and gratified; here is now exhibited a* Collection of Examples, *wherein the glorious Grace of our great REDEEMER has appeared to, and the* Indians *of* New-England.

It must not be imagined, that these are all *that could have been collected, for all these are fetch'd only from* one Island; *and, no doubt, other* Indian *Ministers could make a considerable Addition to those Relations: but certainly such a Specimen of what has been done will be highly acceptable to those good Men, to whom such* good News from a far Country will be as cool Waters to a thirsty Soul.[28] *And our* GOD *will be glorified in what his Grace has done for the poor Children of Men, and the veriest Ruins of Mankind in these Parts of the World.*

The Author *of this History,* Mr. EXPERIENCE MAYHEW, *is a Person of incontestable Veracity: He was born and bred in the midst of the* Indians, *and has been all along intimately acquainted with Occurrences among them, and is a Descendant from* Ancestors *that for several Generations have laudably done their Part in gospelizing of them.[29] He is a judicious, faithful, constant* Preacher *of the Gospel to them; and on the* Week-Days, *as well as on the* Lord's Days,[30] *he is an unwearied* Worker with GOD, *and for him among them. Among all the* Instruments *of the good Work which brings the* Indians *into the Kingdom of* GOD, *he shines as one of the* first Magnitude. *Several Things written* [xix] *by him, have by the Press been heretofore conveyed into the World, and found a favourable Reception.[31] And in* these Narratives, *we again say,* his Truth may be relied upon, his Fidelity is irreproachable.

---

28 Proverbs 25:25.

29 Experience Mayhew was a fourth-generation missionary on the island. Those that preceded him were Thomas Mayhew Sr., Thomas Mayhew Jr., and John Mayhew.

30 Sabbaths, i.e., Sundays.

31 His previous publications include an Algonquian translation of Cotton Mather's *The day which the Lord hath Made: A discourse concerning the institution and observation of the Lords-Day* (1707); *The Massachuset psalter* (1709); an Algonquian translation of Cotton Mather's *Family-religion* (1714); *A discourse shewing that God dealeth with men as with reasonable creatures* (1720); a retranslation of *The indian primer* (1720); and *All mankind, by nature, equally under sin* (1725).

We commend this History *to the due Consideration of all that wish well to the Cause of PIETY; and we bespeak the* Prayers *of such for the preserving and prospering of* good Woork *which it refers to.*

Boston, New-England,   Cotton Mather.
June 14, 1726.   Benjamin Colman.
                             Peter Thacher.
                             Joseph Sewall.
                             Thomas Prince.
                             John Webb.
                             William Cooper.
                             Thomas Foxcroft.
                             Samuel Checkley.
                             William Waldron.
                             Joshua Gee.

⌈xx⌉ THE
INTRODUCTION.

THE *Design* of the ensuing Historical Essay, is to make it evident that the Preaching of the Gospel to the *Aboriginal Natives* of this Land, has not not been in vain; but that there has been some desirable Fruit and Effect thereof.

Some may perhaps think, that a Performance of this nature is now become wholly unnecessary, since so many Accounts have been already published to the World, of the Conversion of these *Indians* from Heathenism to Christianity, and of Churches planted in divers Places among them.

But this notwithstanding, it appears to me on divers Accounts necessary at this time, that it be made yet more plainly to appear, that *the Grace of GOD, which bringeth Salvation* to Sinners, hath effectually appeared to some of these, *teaching them to deny all Ungodliness and worldly Lusts, and to live soberly, righteously, and godly in the World.*[32]

The *Things* that have inclined me to think thus, are such as *these*:

First. There be some of our *English*, who will hardly be persuaded that there is any thing of sincere Religion or Godliness among this poor People, or at least they think there is but very little of it to be found among them: And this their Opinion is apt to dishearten them from doing any thing for the promoting of their Spiritual Good, and sometimes causeth them to discourage others that do, or perhaps otherwise would take pains to further their eternal Happiness.

One Cause of their having so very low an Esteem of these *Indians*, I take to be the *Viciousness* of the Lives of many of that People; and that even of some that have made a good Profession among them. For this being seen ⌈xxi⌉ and observed by the *English*, as it cannot but be, some of them have been ready to think hardly of the *Indians* in *general*, on the account of those, whose vicious Conversations they have thus beheld, and been offended at.

Another Reason I take to be in the *English* themselves, *viz.* Their too great want of that *Charity* which would incline them to think as well as might be of these their poor Neighbours, and not to judge and condemn *all*, for the Miscarriages of *some* among them.

This I also fear does in part proceed from too much *Pride* in many of our *English* People. It is certain, that the *English*, in this Land, have many singular Advantages above their *Indian* Neighbours: And it must be acknowledged, that some of them have made a Proficiency in Religion,

---

32 Titus 2:12.

in some measure answerable to those their Privileges. Now I fear that this may have occasioned some of us to think too highly of *our own Nation*; and at the same time to think and speak too meanly of the *Indians*, whom GOD hath not done so much for. We have doubtless too much of that spiritual *Pride* among us, which many of the *Jews* had of old among them; which caused them to say to others, *Stand by thy self, come not near me; for I am holier that thou.*[33] Perhaps it may be from such Pride, that some of us are ready to look on the *Indians* as the proud *Pharisees*[34] did on the *Publicans*[35] in our Saviour's time: but *let us not be high-minded, but fear*[36] lest we be rejected when some of them are accepted, as in the Example of the *Pharisee* and *Publican*, Luke ch. xviii. *What have we that we have not received?*[37]

It must indeed be granted, that the *Indians* are generally a very sinful People: *Iniquity does abound* among them, *and the Love of many waxeth cold.*[38]

It is, therefore, *no part* of my Design to set them forth as a People generally eminent for Piety and Religion; but to shew that how vicious soever many of them be, yet there are others of whom better things may be hoped, and *things that do accompany Salvation.* And what if many of these miserable *Indians* believe not, their Unbelief cannot make the Faith of others to be of none Effect; nor will it hurt any, if they may upon good ground be prevailed on to entertain for the future, a better Esteem of this People than they have hitherto done.

[*xxii*] *Again*, There be many godly People, both Ministers and others, who do earnestly long to hear of the saving Conversion of the *Indians* in this Land. I find such, when I go among them, very inquisitive about the *Indians*. They ask me how the Work of the Gospel prospers among them: they inquire of me whether the *Indians* attend the Worship of GOD with Seriousness and Reverence? And they do most strictly enquire whether there be any number of them, of whom it may be hoped,

---

33 Isaiah 65:5.

34 A Jewish sect from the late Second Temple period that was characterized by strict observance of the oral law and written Torah, but perceived by Christ and his followers as having "pretensions to superior sanctity" (*OED*). Here Mayhew "poisons the well" against his opponents since Puritans would have disliked being associated with Pharisees, who, Puritans felt, mistreated Jesus and were guilty of following a covenant of "works" over one of faith.

35 Jewish tax gatherers in Roman-occupied Israel who abetted the Roman state. In Matthew 9:11, the Pharisees question Jesus for eating and drinking with publicans and sinners, to which Jesus responds that the sick (sinful), not the healthy, are those in need of a physician.

36 Romans 11:20.

37 In this parable, a Pharisee and a publican go to the temple to pray. Whereas the Pharisee reminds God that he fasts and tithes, and thanks God that he is not as sinful as other men, the publican smites his breast and asks for God's mercy on him as a sinner. Christ makes it clear that the humbled and abased publican will be forgiven before the (self-) righteous Pharisee is.

38 Matthew 24:12.

that they have experienced a Work of Regeneration or saving Conversion to GOD. Now I confess, that to give *Satisfaction* to such Inquiries, is a considerable part of my *Design* in this Essay: For I think it highly reasonable and necessary, that the People of GOD should be duly informed what Entertainment Religion meets with among the People I am speaking of, and that in order to their knowing their Duty with respect to them; and I wish I could give them a more satisfactory Account than I am able to do. However, I shall endeavour that the Account given may be a *true one.*

I shall *further* add, that since there has been a great deal of Pains taken, and Cost expended, by many *Gentlemen* and Well-disposed *Christians*, both in *England* and *this Country*, in order to the Conversion and eternal Salvation of these poor *Americans*; it is but just and reasonable, that such as these should from time to time be truly informed what *Effects* such Contributions and Collections have had, as have been made and distributed with such a pious Intention. To *neglect* to do this, would be such Injustice and Ingratitude as I would not be guilty of: Nor am I altogether without hopes, that the things now to be related concerning some of these our *Indian* Brethren, may prove a Means to quicken and *encourage* such as are concerned for their Welfare, to go on vigorously in the good Work wherein they are engaged, and to study diligently what is further to be done in order to the successful Management and carrying of it on; and to neglect nothing that may be necessary to the End thus proposed by them.

And I *may not here omit*, that it tends greatly to the Glory of GOD's *Grace*, that the saving *Effects* of it among any People of his, be taken notice of and owned by his Servants, who are obliged to give Glory and Honour to him. For as the Glory of GOD's *Grace* is won[xxiii]derfully *displayed* in the Conversion of Sinners to himself; so it is exceedingly to the praise of his Glory, so manifested in any Nation, or among any People, when the same is *acknowledged* and celebrated. The *Apostles* were therefore wont to publish to the Glory of GOD, and the Comfort of his People, the good *Effects* of their Ministry; as does abundantly appear in the *Acts of the Apostles*, and in their *Epistles*. If then GOD hath a *People* in these Ends of the Earth, *whom he hath saved and called with an Holy Calling*, we should endeavour to give him the Honour due on that account: and may he accordingly have Praise from what is here to be reported.

Thus much briefly concerning the *Design* of this Work, and the *Reasons* moving me to it. If I make good what I have undertaken, I shall have this further Satisfaction in it, that I shall thereby more fully illustrate and confirm what I have more *summarily* asserted concerning the Piety of some of our *Indians,* in *that brief Account* which was published concerning them in the Year 1720.[39]

I must, before I enter upon the Work designed, inform my Readers, that the *Indians,* of whom I am to speak therein, must be considered as a People in a great measure destitute of those Advantages of *Literature,* which the *English* and many other Nations enjoy. They have at present *no Scholars* among them; several that have been liberally educated, having by immature Deaths been removed out of the World before they had opportunity of being considerably serviceable in it: And tho considerable numbers of the *Indians* have learned to *read* and *write,* yet they have mostly done this but after the rate that poor Men among the *English* are wont to do: Nor have our *Indians* the same Advantage of *Books* as our *English,* few of them being able to read and understand *English Books* in any measure well. Moreover, there be but *few Books* comparatively yet published in the *Indian Tongue.* For *these Reasons,* nothing may at present be expected of them, that will look polite or accurate: nor can there be much published from any Writings of their own, which would be to my present purpose, and entertaining to *English* Readers. Yet, for the Satisfaction of such as may be thereby gratified, I shall, as occasion offers, translate and insert some *such Passages* written by them in their own Language, as I think will be subservient to the End herein aimed at. And however *inac[xxiv]curate* such Writings may be, yet I shall chuse to keep as much as may be the *very Words* of the *Indians* themselves, that the *Simplicity* of their Intentions may, by their own simple Expressions, the better appear; since it is not the *Learning* of any, but the *Piety* of some, that is here designed to be discovered.

Let me here *only add,* that there having been almost a total *Neglect* of preserving in Writing such *Sayings* of pious *Indians,* as would have been proper Materials for such a Work as this, (which I acknowledge to have been a Fault) the Work must, on that account, be much more imperfect than otherwise it might have been; for many things must for this Reason be only generally signified, whhich otherwise might have been particularly precisely expressed.

These things being said by way of *Introduction* to my following Essay, I shall, without any further Delay, apply my self to the Work intended.

---

39 Published with *A discourse shewing that God dealeth with men as with reasonable creatures* (1720). See Appendix.

[1] CHAP. I.

Containing an Account of several Indian *MINISTERS,*
both Pastors, Ruling Elders, *and* Deacons, *who have*
been justly esteem'd godly Persons.

GENERALLY where the Word of GOD has been preached by
godly Ministers, there have been Some godly People. Being therefore
now to shew, that there have been several pious People among our
Christian Indians; and that by instancing in particular Persons that
have been so, it will be very proper that I begin this Introduction of
Instances with mentioning sundry *Ministers* among them, that have
been exemplary for Piety; and that I bring *Ruling Elders* and *Deacons*[40]
into the same Catalogue, will appear the more natural, when I have
said that those in the *Indian* Churches, who have born this Denomination, have generally been *Preachers* of the Word of *God,* tho they
have been only chosen and set apart to the Offices by which they are
denominated.

I shall then, without any further Delay, proceed to the *Examples*
intended, and they are such as follow.

EXAMPLE I.
HIACOOMES *the first* Christian Indian,
and Minister *on the Island of* Martha's Vineyard.

THis *Hiacoomes*[41] was an *Indian* of *Great Harbour,* now *Egdartown,*[42]
where a few *English* Families first settled in the Year 1642.

---

40 Ruling elders assisted the minister and teacher. Their duties included admitting and excom-
municating church members, making sure all church members displayed saving grace, preventing
and healing corruptions in the church membership, preparing church assemblies, admonishing
church members, and visiting the sick. See Goodwin, "The Government and Discipline of the
Churches of Christ," 16, 19, 22. Next came the deacons, laymen who assisted the minister. An
important social role of the deacon was to be part of the seating committee that mapped out the
social hierarchy of the congregation: the closer the person sat to the minister, the higher his social
(and presumably spiritual) status. See Richard Archer, *Fissures in the Rock: New England in the*
Seventeenth Century (Hanover, N.H.: University Press of New England, 2001), 60. When Mayhew
notes that someone was a selectmen, town clerk, magistrate, or deacon, he is helping his reader-
ship mentally place the individual within the community's spiritual seating plan.

41 Hiacoomes was the father of Samuel Coomes (convicted of fornication with colonist Abigail
Norton), Joell Iacoomes (an early student at of Harvard), John Hiacoomes (a preacher), and
possibly Philip Coumes. *WGH,* 133.

42 A town on the southeastern side of Martha's Vineyard.

His Descent was but mean, his Speech but slow, and his Countenance not very promising. He was therefore by the *Indian Sachims*,[43] and others of their principal [2] Men, looked on as but a mean Person, scarce worthy of their Notice or Regard: However, living near the *English*, some of them visited him in his Wigwam,[44] and were courteously entertained by him; these endeavour'd to discourse a little with him about the way of the *English*, and the Man seem'd to hearken to them, and in a little Time began to pay them Visits again, going frequently to some of their Houses: And it was thought that he was trying to learn something of them that might be for his Advantage. About the same time he went also to the *English* Meeting, and observed what was done there.

This was soon observed by the Reverend Mr. *Thomas Mayhew*,[45] who was then Minister to the few *English* Inhabitants in that new Plantation, and was at the same time contriving what might be done in order to the Salvation of the miserable *Indians* round about him, whom he, with Compassion, *saw perishing for lack of Vision.*[46]

But now, observing in this *Hiacoomes* a Disposition to hear and receive Instruction; observing also, that his Countenance was grave and sober, he resolved to essay in the first Place what he could do with him, and immediately took an Opportunity to discourse him; and finding Encouragement to go on in his Endeavours to instruct and enlighten him, he invited him to come to his House every *Lord's-day* Evening, that so he might then more especially have a good Opportunity to treat with him about the things *of GOD*, and open the Mysteries of his Kingdom to him.

Hiacoomes accepting this kind Invitation, Mr. *Mayhew* used his utmost Endeavours to enlighten him. And *Hiacoomes* seem'd as eagerly to suck in the Instructions given him as if his Heart had been before prepared by GOD, and made good Ground, in order to a due Reception of his Word sown in it: *And thus as a new-born Babe, desiring the sincere Milk of the Word,*

---

43 Traditional rulers. Although sachems ruled by consent, the position was usually inherited on the island. People of "mean" descent who married into royal families would produce offspring who could not inherit the sachemship. See Plane, "Customary Laws of Marriage," 192. Even so, Mayhew is probably exaggerating the social hierarchies on the island to increase the miracle of Hiacoomes' rise to grace and power.

44 Traditional Wampanoag house. Wampanoags in colonial New England tended to build two types of wigwams: a smaller "round house" or *puttuckakuan*, and a larger, arborlike "long house," the *neesquttow* or "house with two fires." Thomas Mayhew Jr. describes the island wigwams as "made with small poles like an arbor covered with mats, and their fire is in the midst, over which they leave a place for the smoak to go out at." See "The Wetu or Native House"; and Scott, "The Early Colonial Houses of Martha's Vineyard," 1:50–52.

45 Thomas Mayhew the younger (1621–1657), grandfather of Experience Mayhew.

46 Proverbs 29:18.

that he might grow thereby,[47] he encreased daily in Knowledge; and so far as could appear, grew in Grace also.

But *Hiacoomes's* thus conversing with, and hearkening to the *English,* was soon noised about among the *Indians;* and the News of it coming to the *Sachims,* and *Pawwaws*[48] of the Island, they were, as obscure a Person as *Hiacoomes* was, much alarmed at it: and some of them endeavoured with all their Might, to discourage him from holding [3] Communication with the *English,* and from receiving any Instructions from them. But all that these could say or do to this end, was to no Purpose; for it seems that *God,* by whom *not many wise Men after the Flesh, nor many mighty, nor many noble are called,*[49] had by his special Grace especially called him *out of Darkness into his marvellous Light:*[50] and having now had a Taste of that Knowledge of *God* and *Christ,* which is Life eternal, he was resolved that nothing should hinder him from labouring after still higher Attainments in it.

About this Time therefore *Hiacoomes* going with some *English* Men to a small Island near by, called *Chapaquiddick,*[51] they there met a surly *Sagamore,*[52] whose Name was *Pahkehpunnsssoo,*[53] and the said *Sagamore* reviling him for his Communion with the *English* in things both *civil* and *religious,* and railing at him for being obedient to them, *Hiacoomes* replied, that he was gladly obedient to them; neither was it for the *Indian's* Hurt that he was so. Upon his Saying of which, the *Sachim* gave him a grievous Blow in the Face,[54] and would have struck him again if the *English* present would have suffered it; but the poor Man thus wrong'd, made this Improvement of the Injury done him, *I had,* said he, *one hand*

---

47 1 Peter 2:2. Puritan ministers often presented themselves as the "breasts" of God who deliver God's milk (word). Breasts are common on Puritan gravestones, including that of the Mayhew family.

48 Traditional Wampanoag religious leaders.

49 1 Corinthians 1:26.

50 1 Peter 2.9. The full verse reads, "But ye [are] a chosen generation, a royal priesthood, an holy nation, a peculiar people; that ye should shew forth the praises of him who hath called you out of darkness into his marvellous light."

51 Off the southeast end of the Vineyard.

52 Sachem, or traditional Wampanoag ruler.

53 Also known as Pakepanessit (ca. 1595–?); he had four wives and many children. *WGH,* 107.

54 As Kathleen Bradgon notes, the relative status of individuals in Wampanoag culture determined the form that interactions took, and the people's deference to communication etiquette, and status, helped acknowledge and reinforce an individual's power. Lower-ranking individuals would often display their deference to and esteem for the sachems with the phrase *"Cowaunckamish* 'my service to you'" and by stroking the sachems' shoulders and torso. Bragdon, "Emphaticall Speech and the Great Action," 103–5, 108.

for Injuries, and another Hand for God; whilst I received Wrong with the one, I laid the faster hold on God with the other.[55]

There was this Year 1643 a very strange Disease among the *Indians,*[56] they ran up and down as if delirious till they could run no longer; they would make their Faces as black as a Coal, and snatch up any Weapon, as tho they would do Mischief with it, and speak great swelling Words, but yet they did no Harm.

Many of these *Indians* were by the *English* seen in this Condition. Now this, and all other Calamities which the *Indians* were under, they generally then attributed to the Departure of some of them from their own heathenish Ways and Customs; but *Hiacoomes* being built on that Foundation that standeth sure, and being one of [t]hose whom *God* had *set apart for himself,*[57] *and knew [t]o be his,* none of these things moved him; but the [t]hings[58] which he had heard and learned he held fast: And that he might be in a Way to learn more than he had done, he now earnestly desired to learn to read; [4] and having a Primmer[59] given him, he carried it about with him, till, by the Help of such as were willing to instruct him, he attained the End for which he desired it.

A while after, in the Year 1644, *Hiacoomes* going to an *Indian's* House where there were several *Indians* met together, they laughed and scoffed at him, saying, *Here comes the* English *Man.* At this his old Enemy *Pahkehpunnassoo*[60] then asleep in the House, awaked, and, joining with the other *Indians,* said to him,

> I wonder that you that are a young Man, and have a Wife and two Children, should love the *English* and their Ways, and forsake the *Pawwaws;* what would you do if any of you were sick? whither would you go for Help? If I were in your Case, there should nothing draw me from our *Gods* and *Pawwaws.*

To this *Hiacoomes* at present answered nothing, perhaps foreseeing that, if he should answer, it would only put the Man into a Rage, as formerly:

---

55 This passage echoes theologians such as the Catholic Thomas à Kempis (ca. 1380–1471), who argued in *The Imitation of Christ* (131–32) that one should use Christ as a model for bearing injury with patience.

56 David Silverman estimates that the outbreaks of 1643 and 1645 eliminated half the Wampanoag population on Martha's Vineyard. Thomas Mayhew's success in helping provide cures during the epidemic enhanced his prestige and brought converts to Christianity. Silverman, *Faith and Boundaries,* 22–24, 74.

57 Psalm 4:3.

58 There is a printing error in the original, and the first letter of three lines is missing.

59 Probably an ABC or hornbook, or Coote's *English Schoole-maister.* See Cremin, *American Education,* 129. John Eliot's *Indian primer* was first published in 1669; the first solely Puritan educational manual in English was Benjamin Harris's *Protestant tutor* (1679). Ford, *The New England Primer: A History,* 34–35.

60 Sachem of Chappaquiddick.

However, he soon after told a Friend of his, *that he then thought in his Heart, that the God of Heaven did hear and know all the evil Words that* Pahkehpunnassoo *said*: And he was further confirmed in this, when a little after the said *Pahkehpunnassoo* was by the just hand of God terribly smitten with Thunder and fell down in Appearance dead, with one Leg in the Fire, then in the house where he was, the same being grievously burn'd before any of the People present were (it being in the Night and dark) aware of it, and could *pluck the Brand out of the Fire.* [61]

But for this Time *Pahkehpunnassoo* was spar'd, tho a young Man that was helping him to cover the Chimney of the House, at which the Rain then beat in, was killed outright at the same time. I shall have done with this *Pahkehpunnassoo*, when I have said, that as obstinate an *Infidel* as he was, yet so victorious is the Grace of *God*, that he afterwards renounced his *Heathenism*, and become a Worshipper of the only true *God*, in and thro' his Son *Jesus Christ*; so that it is to be hoped, that he was at last a *Brand pluck'd out of the Fire*, in a better Sense than that before mentioned.

In this and the following Year 1645, Mr. *Mayhew* went on with his Design of instructing his *Hiacoomes*, and several others of the *Indians*, as he had Opportunity; and now *Hiacoomes* begins to be so far from *needing to be taught the first Principles of the Oracles of God*, [62] that [5] he becomes a Teacher of others; communicating to as many as he could the Knowledge he himself had attained: And some there were that now began to hearken to him, yet seemed not to be duly affected with the Truths taught by him, and many utterly rejected them; but God now sending a general *Sickness* among them, it was observed by the *Indians* themselves, that such as had but given a Hearing to the things by *Hiacoomes* preached among them, and shewed any regard to them, were far more gently visited with it than others were; but *Hiacoomes* and his Family in a manner not at all. At this many of the *Indians* were much affected, for they evidently saw that he, who, for the sake of the Truth, exposed himself to the Rage of his Enemies, and such as adhered to him, fared better than those that opposed both him and *that*.

And being thus affected, many of the People desired to be instructed by him; and some Persons of Quality, such as before despised him, sent for

---

61 Zechariah 3:2. This passage refers to the cleansing of Joshua the High Priest, who was rescued from Satan not on his own merit but by God's intervention.

62 Hebrews 5:12. This verse is the text for Jonathan Edwards's sermon "The Importance and Advantage of a Thorough Knowledge of Divine Truth" (November 1739), which contains a good example of using milk as a metaphor for God's wisdom. In it Edwards argues that Christians must eventually mature into teachers (like Hiacoomes) who are "enabled to digest strong meat; i.e., to understand those things in divinity which are more abstruse and difficult to be understood" (2).

him (as *Cornelius* for *Peter⁶³*) to come and instruct them, and those about them: so in particular did one *Miohqsoo⁶⁴* afterwards to be mentioned.

And now the *Indians* began not only to give some Credit to the Truth by *Hiacoomes* brought to them, but were also awakened by what they heard and believed, so as humbly to confess their Sins, and be concerned how they should obtain the Pardon of them, and also to renounce their own *Gods* and *Pawwaws*, and promise to serve the true *God* only: and *Hiacoomes* could now tell Mr. *Mayhew*, that this was the first Time that ever he saw the *Indians* sensible of their Sins.

Hitherto the *Indians* had not any publick Preaching to them; but now (in the Year 1646) *Tawanquatuck*,⁶⁵ one of the chief *Sachims* of the Island, invited both Mr. *Mayhew* and *Hiacoomes* to preach to himself and such of his People as would hear them, and *Hiacoomes* was from this time forward heard as a publick Preacher by a considerable number of the *Indians*, and *God* gave him not only Light, but Courage also for this Work; and the *Indians* then said of him, that tho formerly he had been, a harmless Man among them, yet he had not been at all accounted of, and therefore they wonder'd that he that had nothing to say in all their Meetings formerly, was now become the Teacher of them all.

[6] The *Pawwaws*, and those that adhered to them, observing those things, and seeing two Meetings of the *praying Indians* set up, in Opposition to that Way which *themselves* and their *Fathers* had long walked in, were very much disturbed and enraged: and now they thought to terrify *Hiacoomes*, and the rest of the *praying Indians*, by threatening to destroy them by *Witchcraft.⁶⁶*

To this End several *Indians* went to a Meeting of the praying *Indians*, and there told many Stories of the great Hurt which the *Pawwaws* had in this way done to many, a thing of which these *Indians* could not be ignorant, and which seemed above any thing else to discourage them from embracing the true Religion now preached to them Then this Question was asked by one that was on *Pawwaws* side, Who is there that does

---

63 Acts 10, in which a Jewish Christian shared the Gospel with Gentiles who accepted the "good news" and were baptized. Cornelius (a Roman centurion) had a vision that Peter (a Jew) should talk with him; he sent for Peter, who shared the news of Jesus Christ. The presentation of Hiacoomes as a Jew who spread the word to the Indian "Gentiles" could be compared to Samson Occom's use of Jews and Gentiles in *A sermon preached at the execution of Moses Paul.* (New Haven: T. & S. Green, 1772).

64 Miohqusoo, Myxeo. *IC*, 5, 38, 76–80*, 153, 282.

65 Sachem of the east side of the island (? –ca. 1670). See *IC*, 80–82*. He is the Grandfather of the Squa-Sachem Nataquanam (Elizabeth Washaman). *WGH*, 132, 124–25. Petty sachems ruled under "chief sachems" in many New England confederacies.

66 Puritans often characterized Algonquian religious practices as witchcraft, designating them as heretical and in league with Satan. The term was particularly damaging, considering the execution of many white witches in Experience Mayhew's lifetime.

not fear the *Pawwaws?* To which another of answered, There is no Man that is not afraid of them; which said, he looked upon *Hiacoomes*, who protested most against them, and told him the *Pawwaws* could kill him: but he answered, that they could not; for, said he, *I believe in God, and put my Trust in him*,[67] *and therefore all the* Pawwaws *can do me no Hurt.* The *Indians* then wondering to hear *Hiacoomes* speak thus so openly, divers of them said one to another, that tho they were before afraid of the *Pawwaws*, yet now because they heard *Hiacoomes's* Words, they did not fear them, but believed in *God* too.

A while after this, on a Lord's-Day after Meeting[68] was done, where *Hiacoomes* had been preaching, there came in a *Pawwaw* very angry, and said, *I know all the Meeting* Indians *are Liars, you say you don't care for the* Pawwaws. Then calling two or three of them by Name, he railed at them, and told them they were deceived; for the *Pawwaws* could kill all the meeting *Indians* if they set about it. But *Hiaccomes* then told him, that he would be in the midst of all the *Pawwaws* on the Island that they could procure, and they should do the utmost they could against him; and when they should do their worst by their Witchcraft to kill him, he would without Fear set himself against them, by remembering *Jehovah*: He told them also he did put all the *Pawwaws* under his Heel, pointing to it. By which Answer he put the *Pawwaws* to Silence, so that they had nothing to say, but that none but *Hiacoomes* was able to do so. Such [7] was the Faith of this good Man! nor were these *Pawwaws* ever able to do the *Christian Indians* any Hurt, tho others were frequently hurt and killed by them. And with respect to *Hiacoomes* in particular, I cannot forbear here adding, that a converted *Sachim*, who was before a *Pawwaw*, did in his publick Protestation afterwards declare as followeth, *viz.*

> That having often employed his God, which appeared unto him in the Form of a Snake,[69] to kill, wound, or lame such as he intended Mischief to, he employed the said Snake to kill, and that failing, to wound or lame *Hiacoomes*, the first *Indian* Convert on the Island: all which prov'd ineffectual. And that, having seriously considered the said *Hiacoomes's* Assertion, that none of the *Pawwaws* could hurt him, since his God whom he now served was the great God to whom

---

67 An inversion of Psalm 78.22.

68 Church services were sometimes referred to as "meetings" and were held in "meeting-houses." This terminology helped Puritans distinguish their religious practices from those of the Anglicans and Catholics. "Meeting Indians" were those who had become Christian.

69 Colonist Edward Winslow was told by informants that Hobbamock, a principal manitou, usually appeared in the form of a snake. Receiving a vision or dream of Hobbamock was a distinguishing feature of being a *powwow* or *pniese*. See Winslow, *Good Newes from New England*, 343; and Simmons, *Spirit of the New England Tribes*, 41–42.

theirs were subservient, he resolved to worship the true God. *And he further added,* That from the time of his doing so, for seven Years, the said Snake gave him great Disturbance; but that he never after his praying to God in Christ, employed that said Snake in any thing; about which time the said Snake ceased to appear to him.

The Piety of our *Hiacoomes* did further appear in that which here followeth. None of the praying *Indians* or their Children, having died until the Year 1650, as if *God* would on purpose in this way distinguish them from the rest of their Neighbours, it now pleased him to begin with *Hiacoomes,* as being the best able to make a good Use of such a Providence, and carry well under it; *God* now by Death took a young Child from him, and he had Grace to shew an excellent Example under this Tryal, and so did his Wife also, who by the way was a very pious Woman. At the Funeral there were no black Faces or Goods buried, or howling over the dead, as the manner of the *Indians* in those Times was; but instead thereof a patient Resignation of the Child to him that gave it. At the Funeral Mr. *Mayhew* made a Speech concerning the Resurrection of the *Godly,* and their Children, to *Life eternal* at the *last Day:* which great Truth these good People believing, *mourned not as those that had no Hope were wont to do.*[70]

What I have hitherto related concerning this *Hiacoomes* being mostly extracted from some of Mr. *Mayhew's* Letters concerning the *Indians* Affairs, I shall add this Tes[8]timony concerning him, in one of them dated 1650: he says,

> I must needs give him this Testimony after some Years Experience of him, that he is a Man of a sober Spirit, and good Conversation; and as he hath, as I hope, received the *Lord Jesus* in Truth, so I look upon him to be faithful, diligent, and constant in the Work of the *Lord,* for the Good of his own Soul and his Neighbours with him.

To this Testimony of Mr. *Mayhew,* let me add one of the Reverend Mr. *Henry Whitfield's,* who was once Pastor to a Church of Christ in *New-*

---

70 Puritan funerary rites reflect the delicate Puritan balance between belief in salvation and fear of damnation: the burials helped console the mourners that the deceased was in the hands of God but also reminded the living of their own need to repent. Mayhew, like other Puritans, felt that the "excessive" grief of Algonquian mourning rituals expressed a doubt either of God's saving grace, God's goodness, or the salvation of the deceased. See Stannard, *Puritan Way of Death,* 100. On Algonquian mortuary rites and the significance of adaptation in burial practice, see Bragdon, *Native People of Southern New England,* 232–41. Bragdon provides passages from colonists Thomas Morton and Edward Winslow that describe traditional southeastern Algonquian funerals.

England.[71] This Mr. *Whitfield* in his Voyage to *Boston,* and so to *England,* was, by reason of contrary Winds, stopp'd at *Martha's Vineyard* about ten Days; in which Time he conversed frequently with *Hiacoomes,* and in a[72] Book which he published after his Return to *England,* he says,

> I had Speech with some of the *Indians,* (Mr. *Mayhew* being my Interpreter, above the rest I desired to speak with the *Indian* that now preacheth to them twice every Lord's-Day, his Name is *Hiacoomes*; he seem'd to be a Man of prompt Understanding, of a sober and moderate Spirit, and a Man well reported of for his Conversation both by *English,* and *Indians.* I thought him to be about thirty Years of Age; with this Man I had often Speech, and I asked him many Questions about the Christian Religion, and about his own Estate before God: as 1. Whether he had found Sorrow for Sin as Sin? 2. Whether he had found Sorrow for his Sins as they had pierced Christ? 3. Whether he had found the Spirit of God as an inward Comforter to him? Unto all which he gave me very satisfactory and Christian Answers.

As *Hiacoomes* was a good *Christian,* so he was doubtless a good *Minister,* and herein his being a *godly Man* was yet more evident. If any Man might say, *I believed, therefore have I spoken*[73] with respect to his entring on the Ministry, it seems our *Hiacoomes* might truly do so. As soon as he came to understand and believe the great Truths of the Christian Religion, he began to publish and declare them to his Countrymen; nor could he be hinder'd from doing so by all that the *Pawwaws,* and their [9] wretched Instruments could do or say, to discourage him from it: And as he daily increased in Knowledge under the Instructions of Mr. *Mayhew,* to whom he continually resorted for that end, so he went on to *Prophesy,* i.e. to preach to his Neighbours, *according to the Measure of the Gift of Christ,*[74] *which he had received*; and it pleased the *Lord* abundantly to succeed his Endeavours for the good of these miserable Creatures, to whom he sent him.

For three Years after his Conversion, this good Man only instructed his Neighbours in private, as he had opportunity: but after they were prepared and disposed to give him publick Audience, *viz.* in the Year

---

71 Henry Whitfield (1597–1657) was a founder and the first minister of the church in Guilford, Connecticut. His home (1639) still stands today and is the oldest stone house in Connecticut. He returned to England in 1650. He is the author of *Strength out of weaknesse; Or, A glorious manifestation of the further progresse of the gospel among the Indians in New-England* (1652), as well as *The light appearing more and more toward the perfect day; Or, a farther discovery of the present state of the Indians in New-England* (1651), from which this quotation is taken.

72 *Light appearing more and more, &c.* [Mayhew's note.]

73 2 Corinthians 4:13.

74 Ephesians 4:7. The last part of this citation is from the notes in the Geneva Bible.

1646, with what Zeal and Boldness did he preach to them? He then not only declared and opened the great Mysteries of Religion to them, as that of the *Trinity*, the *Covenant of Works* by *God* made with Man, Man's *Fall* and *Apostacy* by *Adam's* first Transgression, and the wretched Condition which Mankind was thereby brought into, and the way of *Redemption* which God has in and by his Son *Jesus Christ* provided for them, &c. I say, he not only instructed them in these things, but boldly charged them with the Sins and Abominations in which they daily lived; especially with their worshipping of false Gods, and adhering to *Paw-waws* or *Wizards*, and giving that Honour to Creatures that was due to *Jehovah* only.

Thus as *Hiacoomes* had *God's* Word, so he spake it faithfully, and *God* did abundantly own this his Servant in the Work to which he had called him: For when he reckoned up the Sins of the People to them, instead of being provoked at him for it, they would many of them, with Tears, confess their Guilt, and promise to turn to the true *God*, and serve him only, and seek for the Pardon of them thro' the Blood of his Son, the only Saviour of Sinners.

This good *Man* was a humble *one*, and in this, as well as in other things, his Piety did much appear. Tho *God* blessed his Ministry, giving him much Success in it, yet did he not at all appear to be exalted or lifted up therewith; nor did he thereupon think himself sufficient for the Work of his Ministry, but thought he still needed the continual Help and Instructions of Mr. *Mayhew*, by whom *God* had called him out of Darkness into his marvellous Light. To him, therefore he frequently still re[10]sorted, that he might be yet more taught and illuminated by him; and in particular, on the Day before the Sabbath he constantly did so, and that in order to his being the better prepared for the Duties and Service of that Holy Day.

This Course *Hiaccomes* held, till, to his great Grief, he lost Mr. *Mayhew* in the Year 1657;[75] which was indeed a very heavy Stroke on these poor *Indians*, and exceedingly lamented by them. However, this good Man went on still in the faithful Discharge of his Duty; and *God* so succeeded the Labours of this, and some other Servants of his, that most of the *Indians* here, were in a few Years brought to an acknowledgment of

---

75 Thomas Mayhew Jr. was lost at sea during a voyage to England intended to promote missionary work on the island. His own activities there must have been appreciated by at least some of the Wampanoags, as from 1657 to 1901 they honored the place he left the island by placing stones on a pile. In 1901 the Daughters of the American Revolution (DAR) established a monument in this location in honor of Mayhew. See *HMV,* 1:227–30; and Mather, *Magnalia Christi Americana,* 430.

the great Truths of Religion; and it is to be hoped, that many of them were effectually called.

However, there was no *Indian* Church here completely formed and organized till the Year 1670, when the Reverend Mr. *John Eliot,* and Mr. *John Cotton,*[76] came and ordained our *Hiacoomes,* and another *Indian* named *Tackanash,*[77] Pastor and Teacher[78] of an *Indian* Church on this Island.

After he was ordained, he went on steadily and faithfully in the Work to which he was called, till he arrived to so great an Age, that he was not able to attend the publick Ministry any longer. He survived his Collegue before-mentioned, made a grave Speech at his Funeral, and laid Hands on,[79] and gave the *Charge* to Mr. *Japhet*[80] at his *Ordination*; who succeeded the said *Tackanash* in his Office in the Year 1683.

My[81] Father, who then preached to the *Indians* on this Island, and assisted them in the Management of their Ecclesiastical Affairs, being present at the Funeral of the said *Tackanash,* took in Writing the Heads of the said Speech made by *Hiacoomes,* with what else he thought observable in the said *Tackanash's* Funeral Obsequies; which having now by me, among his reserved Papers, I shall here insert the said Speech, not knowing but that the same may be acceptable to some of my Readers.

It was this which followeth:

> [11] Here, *said he,* is my deceased Brother. *Paul* said, this Body is sown in Corruption, but it shall be raised in Strength.[82] Now it is a pitiful mean Body, but then it shall be a glorious Body: yea, however this Body shall be consumed, and be as if it had never been, as it were turned into nothing; yet the Power of God shall bring it forth again, and raise it up an excellent and glorious Body. Yea, this Body is now a precious Body for Example sake; tho this Body is but one, yet there are many people round about come together to see

---

76 John Cotton Jr. (1639/40–1699), who knew the Wampanoag language and preached on Martha's Vineyard, 1664–66. John Eliot (1604–1690) was perhaps the most important missionary in New England and the author of numerous tracts and books about and for New England's Algonquian converts.

77 See *IC,* 14–17*.

78 The office of teacher complemented that of minister: teachers were to "attend to doctrine," administer the seals of covenant, and censure congregants. See Cremin, *American Education,* 138. Some of New England's most famous ministers held the office of teacher, including John Cotton Sr.

79 To perform the rite of imposition of hands in confirmation or ordination (*OED*).

80 Japhet(h) Hannit; see *IC,* 44–54*.

81 *Mr.* John Mayhew, a *Son of Mr.* Thomas Mayhew *before-mentioned.* [Mayhew's note.]

82 1 Corinthians 15:42

it sown. But if a Man should go about to put one Grain of Wheat into the Ground, there would not be so many People present at the doing of it, as there are at the interring of this one Body. And as you see there are many People present at the Burial of this Body, so there shall be many People at the Resurrection also. But it shall not be then as you see it is now; now every one is diversly apparelled, some after one manner, and some after another, but all after a pitiful mean sort; but the Righteous at the Resurrection shall have all one uniform Glory.[83]

Thus much I Say as to that; but I shall now speak a short Word to the Relations of the Person deceased, especially to his Wife and Children. If you be desirous to see your Father, seek your Father;[84] for your Father went before you in every good Work, therefore seek your Father in every good Work, and you shall find your Father again; for God's Mercies are exceeding great.

Having finished his Speech, *saith the Writer thereof,* they proceed to their Work, *(viz.* of filling up the Grave) and this good Man standing by, I heard him say, *This is the last Work Man can do for him, the next Work God himself will do.* Which Words he often repeated; and further adds, that when this good Father spoke of the *Resurrection,* he uttered himself with such Fervency and Confidence, as would have become one who had himself actually seen the Dead raised.

Hiacoomes was of a great Age when this Speech was made by him; yet he lived several Years after it, if I mistake not, till the Year 1690; but was not able, for some Years before he died, to preach publickly. I saw him frequently when I was a Youth, and still remember him, the Gravity of his Countenance, Speech and Deportment: He seemed always to speak with much [12] Thought and Deliberation, and I think very rarely smiled. I was present when he laid hands on Mr. *Japhet,* prayed, and gave the Charge to him: which Service he performed with great Solemnity; and, as I have heard my Father say, with very pertinent and suitable Expressions. He was, by both the *English* and the *Indians,* looked upon as a Man of a very blameless Conversation. In his last Sickness, he breathed forth many pious Expressions, and gave good Exhortations to all about him, and so went into Eternal Rest.

---

83 Hiacoomes's assertion that all will be dressed the same at the Resurrection reveals his power as a minister and orator; his audience would undoubtedly have appreciated this message, given the importance of dress for establishing social status on the island and the role that white clothing played in creating new hierarchies.

84 A pun: "father" refers both to Tackanash and to God.

EXAMPLE II.

MOMONEQUEM, *the first* Indian *Preacher at* Nashauohkamuk, *now called* Chilmark.[85]

THIS *Momonequem* was the Son of one of the principal *Indians* of *Gay-head*, named *Annomantooque*. It seems this Father married a Woman of good Qualities, at a Place called *Nunpaug* now in *Edgartown*, and by her had this Son. At this Place our *Momonequem* dwelt, when Mr. *Mayhew* and *Hiacoomes* began to preach the Gospel there; and it was by the Ministry *Hiacoomes*, that he was converted in the Year 1649. For *Hiacoomes* now preaching a Sermon, wherein he reckoned up many of the great Sins of which the *Indians* were guilty, and as many good Duties which ought to be performed by them, there were no less than twenty two of his Hearers who at this time professed their Resolutions against the *Sins* mentioned, and that they would walk with *God* in Newness of Life.

Of this number *Mononequem* was one, and one who above all the rest seemed to be exceedingly affected; for to the great Admiration of all the *Indians* then present, with much Sorrow of Heart, and Indignation against Sin, he did now enumerate about twenty of his own Sins, manifesting his Repentaace [sic] of them, and professing his Resolution to follow the only living and true *God* against all Opposition.

He told those to whom he said these things, that he was brought into this Condition by *Hiacoomes's* Counsel from the Word of *God*; which at first he said he liked not, and afterwards laid by him as a thing to be considered of, not knowing well what to do: at last looking [13] over things again, I am come, said he, to this Resolution, which you have now heard; and Mr. *Mayhew*, out of some of whose Writings this Account of his Conversion is extracted, has added this Testimony of him:

> I confess, *saith he*, this Action of his makes me think he spake from more than a natural Principle, considering that the Man hath been since an earnest Seeker of more Light, both publickly and privately; for that he also refused the Help of a *Pawwaw* who lived within two Bow-shot of his Door, when his Wife was three Days in Travail, and waited patiently on *God* till they obtained a merciful Deliverance by Prayer.

Momonequem being himself thus effectually turned from Darkness to Light, and from the Power of *Satan* unto *God*, and being looked upon as a Man of much Wisdom and Prudence, the praying *Indians* soon began

---

85 *Nashauhkamuk* means "the halfway house." *HMV*, 2 (Annals of Chilmark): 3. The town is in the southwestern part of the Island.

to resort to him when they wanted Counsel and Encouragement in any of their Difficulties; and such as inclined to become *Christians* did so too: nor was he an unfit Person to be applied to in such Cases.

About this time, a famous *Pawwaw*, called *Tequanomin*,[86] entertaining Thoughts of turning from *the Devil* to the only true *God*, and *Jesus Christ* the only Saviour of sinful Men, providentially meeting with *Momonequem* in the Woods, opened his Case to him, and took his advice upon it; and the effect was, that that *Pawwaw* became, as there was reason to believe, a sincere Convert and good Christian.

After this, the next News I hear of *Momonequem* is, that he was become a Minister at *Nashouohkamuk* before-mentioned, a Place about five or six Miles from that where before he lived; and that he preached every *Sabbath-Day* twice to his Countrymen there. And to the end he might be the better provided for the Entertainment of his Hearers, he still waited on Mr. *Mayhew* on the last Day of the Week, in order to his assisting him in his Preparation for the Work of the approaching Day.

Thus was *Momonequem* imployed in the Year *1651*, as Mr. *Mayhew* has written; and in a Letter of that holy Man of *God*, the Reverend Mr. *John Wilson*, *Pastor* of the first *Church* in *Boston*,[87] dated *October 27*. 1651. I find the following Testimony concerning him:

> There was here, a few Weeks since, the Prime *Indian* of *Martha's Vineyard*, with Mr. *Mayhew (Momonequem)* a grave and [14] solemn Man, with whom I had serious *Discourse*, Mr. *Mayhew* being present as Interpreter between us. He is a great Proficient both in Knowledge and Utterance, and Love and Practice of the things of Christ and Religion, much honoured, reverenced, and attended by the rest of the *Indians* there, who are solemnly in Covenant together, I know not how many; between 30 and 40 at least. [He might have said near 200 of them.]

This and much more Mr. *Wilson* in that Letter speaks in his Commendation; and by all that I can learn, he was indeed a very excellent Man.

This good Man was taken out of this evil World so long ago, that there are not many now living on this Island, that remember him. But in what Year he dy'd I cannot find. However he has not been so long dead, but that there are some that do remember, that he was esteem'd a Man

---

86 In spite of the conversion of Tequanomin (ca. 1590–?), his descendants did not fare well under the new colonial administration and were charged with stealing, stabbing, supplying rum, and the like. *WGH*, 204, 255, 310, 372.

87 Rev. John Cotton served as "teacher" at the First Church of Boston under the leadership of Rev. John Wilson (c. 1588–1667). Wilson was coauthor of the tract *The Day-breaking, if not the sun-rising of the Gospell with the Indians in New-England* (1647).

very blameless in his Conversation, and one of whose sincere Piety none had any Reason to doubt.

EXAMPLE III.
JOHN TACKANASH, *who was ordained Teacher of the* Indian *Church at* Martha's Vineyard, *whereof* HIACOOMES *was Pastor.*

THis *John Tackanash*[88] was ordained as a Collegue with *Hiacoomes* above mentioned in the Year 1670, as has been declared. He was reckoned to exceed the said *Hiacoomes*, both in his natural and acquired Abilities; and, being accounted a Person of a very exemplary Conversation, was joined in Office with him, *viz.* as a Teacher of the same Church whereof *Hiacoomes* was Pastor.

These for some Years went on Hand in Hand, as Fellow-Labourers in the same Church: But whereas the Members of the Church whereof these were Officers, lived partly at *Chappaquiddick*, and partly on the *main* Island *of Martha's Vineyard*, at some Miles distance, and it was found on that Account difficult for the Church with its Officers to meet at one Place, it was at length agreed that the said Church with its Officers should divide into two: and it accordingly did so; *Hiacoomes* and *Joshua Mamachegin*,[89] one of the Ruling Elders, taking Charge of that Part which was at the said *Chappaquiddick*, (where they now dwell) and *John Tackanash* and *John Nohnoso*[90] [15] taking Charge of that on the main Island of the *Vineyard* where they lived. And thus they remained two distinct Churches, and carried on as such, until *Hiacoomes* being superannuated, was not able with Advantage to the Interest of Religion to carry on the Work of his Ministry any longer; and then both the *Indians* and the *English* being well satisfied in the Qualifications of the said *Tackanash* for his Office, and there not being a suitable Person found to take the pastoral Charge of the said Church at *Chappaquiddick*, these two Churches did, by Consent, become one again, under the pastoral Care of the said *Tackanash*; *Hiacoomes* still assisting him as Occasion call'd for, in such things as he still remained capable of.

That our *John Tackanash* was at the time of his Ordination esteemed a Person of good Abilities, and a very exemplary Conversation, has been already briefly hinted; but by that Time to which I am now arrived

---

88　John Tackanash was the brother of James Sepinnu (IC, 73), an Indian schoolmaster/teacher, and Hephzibah Paul, whose name appears on Mayhew's 1755 list of disbursements to the poor. His wife is Alanchchannum. *IC*, 173–75*; *WGH*, 128.

89　*IC*, 35*.

90　*IC*, 15, 17–18*, 29, 34, 164, 222.

in my Account of him, he was very much improved both in his Gifts and Graces. His natural Parts were esteemed very excellent, both by the *Indians* and *English*, that were in any measure capable to judge of them: And he diligently endeavoured to improve his Understanding, and increase his Knowledge. To this end he not only followed his Study and Reading closely, allowing himself, as I am credibly informed, but little Time for such Diversions as many Ministers, and other Persons use, but also frequently apply'd himself to such *English* Persons as took care of the *Indians* here for their Instruction in those things wherein he apprehended himself to need them.

By the Means now mentioned he so increased in Knowledge, as to be esteemed inferior to none of his own Nation that have succeeded him; and for a Preacher, no *Indian* in these Parts has been thought to come up to him.

Nor was the said *Tackanash* only esteemed a Person of good Knowledge, for he was, so far as I can learn, in his Conversation without Spot and blameless, being even wholly free from any Imputation of immoderate Drinking, which is the national Sin of our *Indians*. And he was look'd upon by all that knew him to be a very serious and godly Man, very devout and zealous in Prayer, Preaching, and administering the Sacraments of Baptism and the Lord's Supper. When there was no *English* Pastor upon the Island, some of our godly *English* People [16] very chearfully received the Lord's Supper[91] administered by him; and I suppose none would have scrupled[92] it, had they understood the *Indian* Language.

The last Time he administered the holy Ordinance, I was present, and saw with what Gravity and Seriousness he performed the Duty; which, tho then a Youth, I could not but take special notice of, as did many other *English* Persons then present. He was then indeed so weak and low of Body, as not to be able himself to Preach, but desired my Father to preach for him; which he did, and immediately repeated to the *English* then present the Heads of his Discourse. After this our *Tackanash* was never able to exercise his Ministry in publick any more.

He during the Time of his Ministry upheld and maintained a good Discipline in the Church, censuring and debarring from Ordinances[93] such as walked disorderly, till such time as by due Manifestations of Repentance, they qualified themselves for them.

---

91 The Lord's Supper, or communion, symbolized the consuming of Christ's body and blood; hence, in taking communion, church members symbolically joined themselves to the body of Christ, a common metaphor for the church.

92 Hesitated out of moral or ethical considerations.

93 Such as communion. In general only church members received communion in Puritan congregations.

He had in the Beginning of his last Sickness, as my Father has observed in the Account he gives of his Funeral, a very sore Conflict with Satan, the grand Adversary of Mankind; but, having obtained the Victory over this Enemy, his Mind was afterwards calm and serene to the End of his Life.

His Mind being thus quieted, he professed a stedfast Hope in the Mercy of *God*, thro' his only Saviour *Jesus Christ*, gave good Instructions and Exhortations to his own Family, and such as came to visit him; nominated three Persons to the Church, one of whom he desired might succeed him in the Office whom he was now about to lay down; and one of them accordingly did so.

He was highly esteemed in his Life, not only by those of his own Nation, but by such of our *English* as were acquainted with him. He was interr'd *Jan. 23d*, 1683-4. There were a great number of People at his Funeral, many of whom seem'd much to lament his Death: and there were two grave and serious Speeches then made, one by *Hiacoomes*, which my Reader already has in his Life; the other by good *Japhet*, which I shall give some of the Heads of when I come to speak of him, because the same will help to illustrate his Character.

He lived at the East End of *Martha's Vineyard* at a Place called *Nunpaug*,[94] and dy'd *Jan. 22d*, 1683-4.

[17] EXAMPLE IV.
JOHN NAHNOSOO, *Ruling Elder of the Church*,
whereof JOHN TACKANASH *above-mentioned was Pastor.*

JOhn Nahnosoo[95] lived on the East End of *Martha's Vineyard*, at a Place called *Sanchecantacket.*[96] I think he was one of those who soon imbraced the Christian Religion, when first published among the *Indians*; and he was, so far as I can learn, esteemed by all that knew him, to be one that *walked worthy of the Vocation wherewith he was called*,[97] as many of the first called among the *Indians* did. Upon strict Inquiry I cannot find that he

---

94 Edgartown.

95 Father of Joseph Nahnosoo (ca. 1665–1685; *IC*, 222–23*). John Nahnosoo's wife, Hannah (*IC*, 164–66*), was the daughter of the sachem of Holmes Hole (Vineyard Haven). One of her brothers, Ponit Cheeschamuck, inherited this position; another brother, Caleb Cheesechaumuck, was an early graduate of Harvard; her sister, Ammapoo (*IC*, 148–51*), was married to Wunnannauhkomun (IC, 18–20), another Indian minister. This family is a good example of how sachems and royal families preserved their social status and power on the island by becoming ruling members of the Indian churches.

96 Part of the Nunpauk sachemship near Edgartown.

97 Ephesians 4:1.

ever did by any Miscarriage bring any Blemish either on himself, or the holy Religion which he professed.

Being of such a good Conversation, and being generally esteemed a very pious and zealous Man, and a Person of good Knowledge in the Things of *God* and his *Law*, he was approved as Preacher of Righteousness in the Place where he lived, and was chosen, together with *Joshua Momatchegin*[98], a *Ruling-Elder* of the Church where of *Hiacoomes* and *John Tackamash* were ordained *Pastors* and *Teachers*: but when that Church was afterwards divided into two, as is abovementioned, this *Nahnosoo*, together with the said *Tackanash*, took the Oversight of that Part thereof which was on the East End of the *Vineyard*, some of the Members whereof lived in other Towns and Villages on the said Island.

He was esteemed by some of good Judgment to be a notable Preacher, a very zealous Reprover of Sin, and much set for the promoting of all Things that are holy, just, and good. He carefully inspected the Conversation of the Members of the Church, and faithfully admonish'd and reproved such as fell into Faults among them; and this both publickly and privately. Ruling Elders are by our *Indians* very frequently called *Aiuskomuaeninuog, i.e. Reprovers,* or *Men of Reproofs,* because they judge that their Office mainly consists in reproving of Sinners and censuring Offenders: Therefore in this Part of Church-Government they generally lead, as do the Pastors when any Members are to be admitted, &c. Now in the Ex[18]ecution of this *Office* I have heard that our *Nahnosoo* was very exemplary, and would not let Offenders go unrebuked, nor yet uncensured when the Case called for it; and so would not willingly let the holy Ordinances of *God* be prophaned by unqualified Persons partaking of them.

1 do not remember that ever I saw this excellent Man, he dying while I was but young, some time before his Pastor the said *Tackanash* dy'd, about the Year 1678; but he was so universally esteemed a good Man, that I could not forbear giving some brief Account of him.

I'm informed by Persons whom I esteem as worthy of Credit, who were well acquainted with him, that as he all along behaved himself as became a good Christian, and Minister of Jesus Christ, so in his last Sickness in particular he did so, then giving good Counsel to such as were about him, and professing to rely on the Mercy of *God* in *Christ* for the eternal Welfare of his own Soul: but what more particularly he then said, I cannot now inform my Reader. This good Man left behind him a good Wife and a good Son, whom I may afterward mention.[99]

---

98 *IC*, 34–35*.

99 Hannah and Joseph Nahnosoo, *IC*, 164–66*, 222–23*.

EXAMPLE V.
WUNNANAUHKOMUN, *an* Indian *Minister, who formerly preached at the Place now called* Christian-Town,[100] *and died there in or about the Year* 1676.

THis *Wunnanauhkomun*[101] was generally esteemed a very good Man, both by his *English* and *Indian* Neighbours. I'm informed that he constantly read the Scriptures in his Family, and usually sang Part of a Psalm[102] before Morning and Evening Prayer; and did very frequently and diligently instruct his Children and Houshold in the Things of *God,* and his Kingdom; that he used also frequently to catechize the Children of the Town,[103] yea and some that were grown up likewise. Such as knew him do affirm, that he would neither drink to Excess himself, nor keep Company with such as did. He used to labour diligently with his Hands for the supporting his Family, having little for them but what he got by his own Labour and Diligence; yet he used to spend some Time daily in the middle of the Day in Reading and Meditation, besides the last Day of the Week, which he intirely devoted to his Preparation for the *Sabbath.* He was highly esteem'd [19] and honoured by many of the poor People, to whom he dispensed the Word of *God,* who therefore frequently visited him, and performed many good Offices for him in the Time of his last and very long Sickness; and he at the same time shewed his Care and Concern for their Good, by frequently instructing, counselling, and exhorting them, and would then sometimes tell them, that tho he was about to die and leave them, yet, if they would love and serve the Lord their God, he hoped he should see them again with Comfort in *God's* eternal Kingdom.

Just before he dy'd, he called his Wife[104] and three Daughters to him, and told them, that, being speedily to take his Leave of them, he would

---

100 Josias, the sachem Takemmy, granted the lands for Christiantown to the praying Indians in his sachemship. The area was later known as West Tisbury.

101 Husband of Ammapoo (*IC,* 148–51*) and hence the brother-in-law of John and Hannah Nahnosoo; grandfather of Oggin Sissetom (*IC,* 184), Abel Sesetom, and Caleb Seaton (*IC,* 272); and great-grandfather of Deborah Sissetom (*IC,* 272–75*).

102 Psalms educated and entertained New Englanders and provided what minister John Cotton called a "converting ordinance"; that is, a religious act through which God's grace might work in the worshiper's heart. See Hambrick-Stowe, *Practice of Piety,* 113. Wampanoags on the island read psalms from John Eliot's *Mamusse wunneetupanatamwe* (1663) and Experience Mayhew's *Massachuset psalter* (1709).

103 The catechism was part of the child's (and converts') daily life in Puritan New England. Even children of only four or five years were expected to repeat it precisely at home and, after the age of seven or eight, in front of the entire congregation. See Ford, *The New-England Primer: A Reprint,* 81–83; and Axtell, *School upon a Hill,* 37–38.

104 Ammapoo, alias Abigail. The names of the daughters are unknown, though one was the mother of Oggin Sissetom, Abel Sesetom, and Caleb Seaton. *WGH,* 137, 158, 279, 335.

have them declare to him what Petitions they desired he should put up to God for them before he dy'd.[105]

His Wife then answered, that she desir'd that God would please to continue her Life until her Children were all grown up, and that he would give her Opportunity to instruct them in the Ways of *God* before she was removed from them. She told him also, that she earnestly desired, that *God* would extend his saving Mercies and Blessings to her self and all her Children, and that he would not take them out of this World before he had fitted and prepared them for a better. The Daughters then declaring their Acquiescence in what their Mother had said, the dying Man signify'd that he approved of the Petitions which they desired him to put up to *God* for them, and then immediately pray'd as they desired.

In this Prayer of his he earnestly intreated the Lord, that the Everlasting Covenant of his Grace might be established with his Wife and Children, and with his Childrens Children to many Generations; and that the Blessings of that Covenant might from Time to Time descend on them: and he now pleaded with *God* the great and precious Promises, which in his Word he has made to his People and their Seed.

Having finished this Prayer, he expressed his Hopes, that *God* would perform for his Wife and Children the Things that he had been seeking him for. He also then expressed a particular Concern for a little Grandson of his,[106] the Son of his eldest Daughter, who was married, and become the Mother of one Child before he dy'd: concerning this Child he said, if *God* had spared his Life, he intended diligently to instruct him in the [20] Ways of *God*, that so he might have been qualified to do Service for him; but since *God* had otherwise determined, he willingly submitted to his good Will and Pleasure.

This being said, he called them all to him, and took his Leave of them with Words of Comfort and Counsel; at the same time laying his hands on each of his Children, and blessing them.

Having done this, he immediately began another Prayer, wherein he expressed to *God* his Willingness to leave this World[107] and go to

---

105 It was not inappropriate for Wunnanauhkomun to assume that his family needed his petitions. As David Stannard notes, "Even the most apparently obvious candidate for Sainthood did not dare take his election for granted; there was no way of knowing in this world with certainty whether one was saved or not. In other words, the best sign of assurance was to be unsure." Stannard, *Puritan Way of Death*, 75.

106 Oggin Sissetom, alias Haukkings (*IC*, 184, 255), husband of Hannah Sissetom (*IC*, 184–87).

107 One of the most important theological doctrines for Puritans was the "doctrine of weaned affections." This concept argued that the individual must learn to wean him- or herself away from earthly loves (husband, children, grandchildren, material possessions), and to focus instead on God. Puritans feared that one who appreciated the sensual beauty and relations of this world might forget the everlasting beauty of the world of the spirit. See Tolles, "Of the Best Sort but Plain," 485.

him, which he declared his Hopes that he should, whenever his frail Life ended. And thus resigning up his Spirit to *God* that gave it, he immediately dy'd when his Prayer ended, without speaking one Word. I shall have Occasion afterwards to mention his Wife and his Offspring, for whom he pray'd, as has been now declared.

EXAMPLE VI.
JANAWANNIT, *who was formerly Minster at* Nashouohkmuk, *and died there about the Year* 1686.

JAnawannit[108] was an *Indian* of good Quality, being a younger Brother of one of their *Sachims* or Noblemen, *viz. Pamehannit,* Father of the memorable *Japheth,* to be hereafter mentioned. He was one of the first that embraced the *Christian Religion* in that Part of the Island, now called *Chilmark.* He learned to read and write, tho he had been for a considerable time a Man grown before he had an Opportunity for it. He was a Man of a very blameless Conversation, and was generally (and I believe on good Grounds) look'd upon as truly pious: And it was rather his Piety and Zeal that encouraged his being imployed in the Work of the Ministry, than any Excellency that appeared in his natural Endowments. I am informed by a credible Person, that lived a considerable time in his House, that he was a very diligent Reader of the holy Scriptures, and very constant and serious in his Performance of other religious Duties. He used to read a Chapter and *sing a Psalm* in his Family every Morning and Evening, and did also give frequent Exhortations to all that were about him. He was a most zealous Reprover of the Sins or Miscarriages, which he either [21] saw or heard of among any of his Neighbours, and that privately as well as in his publick Ministry. I once, when I was a Youth, heard him preach and pray, and still remember with what Zeal and Affection he expressed himself. Some that were well acquainted with him have observed, that when he reproved any Person for Sin, he would still condemn the very first Motions of the Heart towards it, as well as the Perpetration of the outward Acts. As he was himself no Drinker of strong Drink, so he was a very zealous Reprover of all such as followed after it.

I doubt not but that as a Minister he endeavoured to approve himself unto God and every Man's Conscience. But so sensible was he of his own Insufficiency for the great Work of the Ministry to which he was called, that he would not ordinarily preach a Sermon till he had sought and

---

108 Janawannit was the father of Hester Eanittus Wannit (China). *WGH,* 211.

obtained some Assistance in his Preparation for it, from the *English* Minister that assisted and directed the *Indians* here in their religious Affairs. I remember, that for this Purpose he generally waited on my Father once a Week. Those who were with this good Man in his last Sickness, can't now remember any of the good Sentences then uttered by him; but they remember plainly in general, that he talked like a good and holy Man, and that he had a firm Assurance of his own Salvation.

EXAMPLE VII.

MITTARK, *the first* Christian Indian, *and Minister at the* Gayhead, *on the West End of* Martha's Vineyard.

THe Substance of what I have to report concerning this *Mittark*,[109] whom I here mention and instance as a godly Man, and Minister of *Jesus Christ*, I find ready prepared to my Hand, being penned by my Father, who was well acquainted with him, and had a very high Esteem of him: which Account, tho for the Substance of it formerly published in Dr. *Mather's* History of *New-England*,[110] yet because proper to be put among the Examples which I'm now writing, shall be here inserted; and it is that which followeth, *viz.*

> *Mittark, Sachim* of the *Gayhead*, deceased *January* 20*th*, 1683. He and his People were all in Heathen[22]ism till about the Year 1663, at which time it pleas'd him who *worketh all Things after the Counsel of his own Will*,[111] *to call him out of Darkness into his marvellous Light*:[112] and his People being on that account disaffected to him, he left them, and removed to the East End of the Island, where after he had continued about three Years, he returned home again, and set up a Meeting at the said *Gayhead*, he himself dispensing the Word of *God* unto as many as would come to hear him; by which means it pleased *God* to bring over all that People to a Profession of Christianity.

---

109 Mittark's family is another good example of the way sachems maintained power bases after colonization by adapting to the new church hierarchies. Many members of Mittark's family became important in the early church on the island, including his son Joseph Mittark, who was both a sachem and a magistrate, and his brother Abel Waumompuhque Sr., who was a magistrate, preacher, and ruling elder. See *WGH*, 103; and *IC*, 98–99. Mittark's great-grandsons Phillip Metack and Joseph Matark fought in the French and Indian Wars and were taken captive. Descriptions of their captivities and petitions for pay can be found in MA Arc., 33.161, 33.73–74, 97.283, 98.481, and 133.98. See *WGH*, 426.

110 Mather, *Magnalia Christi Americana*, 436–37.

111 Ephesians 1:11.

112 1 Peter 2:9.

The Day before his Death I being with him, enquired of him concerning his Hope; and after he had treated some time of the Mutability of an earthly Life, he said, *I have Hope in God, that when my Soul departeth out of this Body, God will send his Messengers to conduct it to himself, to be with* Jesus Christ: And then with great Earnestness he pronounced these Words, *Where that everlasting Glory is. As for my Reasons,* said he, *I my self have had many Tens[113] of Enemies, against whom I have not sought any Revenge, nor return'd Evil in Thought, Word, or Deed, and also expect the same from God; but,* said he, *I proceed no further, for God is very merciful.*

Then asking of him of his Willingness to die, he reply'd, *It is now seven Nights since I was taken sick, and I have not yet asked God to give me longer Life in this World. In this World,* said he, *are some Benefits to be enjoy'd, also many Troubles to be endured; but, with respect to the Hope I have in God, I'm willing to die. Here I'm in Pain, there I shall be freed from all Pain, and enjoy that Rest that never endeth.*

Then pointing to his Daughters, he said. *There be three of my Daughters,* (relating how they were disposed of) *and you my Daughters,* said he, *if you lose your Father, mourn not for your Father, but mourn for your selves and for your Sins; for tho you are unwilling to spare me, and I might be helpful to you if I should live longer in the World, yet to die is better for me.*

[23] Thus far my Father's Account[114] of *Mittark:* I shall only add this further concerning him, that having made strict Enquiry about him, I can't find but that he was esteemed by all that knew him, as a Person of unblemished Morals, nor have I heard of any that have questioned his being truly pious.

EXAMPLE VIII.
PAUL, *otherwise called* MASHQUATTUHKOOIT,
who was a Deacon *of an* Indian *Church on* Martha's Vineyard,
and a Preacher of the Word of God at Sanchekantacket,[115]
and died in or about the Year 1688.

THe Person I speak of was commonly called *Holmes-hole-Paul,* because he generally lived near the Harbour called *Holmes-Hole.*[116]

---

113 *This is according to the* Indian *idiom; they say* Tens, *as we say* Scores. [Mayhew's note.]

114 Cotton Mather notes, "This I find written on the out-side of a book, in the library of Mr. John Mayhew": *Magnalia Christi Americana,* 436.

115 Part of the Nunpauk sachemship near Edgartown.

116 Vineyard Haven.

He was a Person of very good natural Parts; but was his younger Days too much inclined to strong Drink, and would sometimes drink to Excess: But God having effectually called him by his Grace, and enabled him in a publick and solemn manner to give up himself to him, gave him Strength against that Lust.

And thus becoming a new Creature, he liv'd a new Life, and was look'd on by those that knew him as an exemplary Christian. Some of his Neighbours of good Credit, both *English* and *Indians*, have informed me, that he appeared to them to be a *prudent, honest*, and *temperate* Man. They say he was diligent in his Business, provided well for his own Family, and was a good Neighbour to them that liv'd by him.

I am well assured, that he worshipped God constantly in his Family, praying both Morning and Evening in it; and that he used to read the Scriptures, and sing Psalms in his House: And likewise diligently instructed his Children[117] and Household, by catechising of them, &c.

Being so understanding and religious a Man, he was chosen to the Office of a *Deacon* by the Church, whereof Mr. *Japheth* was the *Pastor*, and did prudently and faithfully discharge that Trust; and was also called to preach the Word of God at the said *Sanchekantacket*.

He was reckoned a good Preacher by such as were best able to judge of his Abilities; nor did he only preach to the People under his Care and Charge, but did also [24] use to *catechise* publickly, not the Children only, but such as were grown up also.

He was sick a considerable while before he died, and in the Time of his Illness gave many good Instructions and Exhortations both to his own Family and Visiters; and called often on the Lord for his Mercy, both for himself and them.

About a Week before he dy'd, he fell into so deep a Sleep that none could wake him, for the greatest part of the Day; but at length awaking, he spake many good and comfortable Words to his good Wife, who carefully look'd after him. He exhorted her to *follow hard after God*,[118] live always to him, and continually put her Trust in him; telling her, that if she so did, God would take care of her, and the Children he left with her.

He then also professed a comfortable Hope of Eternal Life thro' Jesus Christ his only Saviour.

---

117 "And thou shalt rehearse them [God's commandments] continually unto to thy children, and shalt talke of them when thou tariest in thine house, and as thou walkest by the way, and when thou lyest down and when thou risest up." Deuteronomy 6:7 (Geneva Bible, 1560).

118 Psalm 63:8.

Having spoken to this Purpose, he took his leave of his Friends, telling them that his Distemper[119] lay so much in his Head, that he should
be no more capable of discoursing with them: and as he said, so it proved,
for soon after this he grew delirious, and so remained till he dy'd. But tho
his Reason thus fail'd him, yet we hope his Saviour did not forsake him.

EXAMPLE IX.
WILLIAM LAY[120] *alias* PANUNNUT at *Nashouohkamuk*,
i.e. Chilmark in or about the Year 1690.

HE in whom I here instance as a pious and godly Man, was Son of a
noted *Indian* called *Panunnut*, who formerly lived on the East End of
Martha's Vineyard. This *William* lived while he was a Youth with the worshipful *Thomas Mayhew* Esq;[121] who was Father to the Minister of the
same Name, by whose Ministry the *Indians* here were first gospelized;
and the Consequence of his living with so good a Man, and one who so
earnestly desired and endeavoured the Good of the *Indians*, was, that he
was well instructed in the Principles of Religion, and had without doubt
many good Counsels and Exhortations given to him.

When he became a Man, he married, and lived many Years on the
East End of the Island, where his Fa[25]ther lived, and was soon taken
notice of as a Person of such Sobriety and Discretion, that he was there
called to be a *Magistrate*[122] among his own Countrymen, and that with
the Consent and Approbation of the *English* Authority on the Island:
Nor was he then looked on as a Man merely *civil*, but was known to be

---

119 During this era, "distemper" was synonymous with illness or disease in general (*OED*).

120 A civil ruler and chief at a meeting of magistrates at Noëpe. *WGH*, 275.

121 Experience Mayhew's great-grandfather.

122 To be a magistrate entailed the power to enforce white colonial legislation upon Native
communities. Native magistrates, like their white counterparts, adjudicated suits for sums
under 20 shillings, punished drunkenness, swearing, lying, theft, contempt toward ministers,
and church absence. See Kawashima, *Puritan Justice and the Indian*, 29. In this sense, magistrates
usurped at least in part the power and prerogative of the sachems and *ahtaskoaog* (principal men,
nobles) to govern and make decisions for the Wampanoag community. Some of the early Indian
magistrates came from noble families and hence may have seen the new position as a way of
continuing their family's traditional role in island life. Indeed, at least six of the nine Indian
magistrates Mayhew mentions were members of a sachem's family or served as a sachem's
counselor, and at least sixteen of thirty church officials claimed royal or "elite" descent. See
Silverman, "The Church in New England Indian Community Life," 268. Others, however, came
from less notable families. It is interesting that some of the Indian officials on the island were
chosen by the community rather than solely by the white colonists; in this sense, the new ruling class continued the tradition of authority through consent, not force. See the example of
Tawanquantuck in *IC*, 82.

a Worshipper of God in his House; and being a better Singer than most of the *Indians* then were, used to set the Tune of the Psalm in the *Indian* Assembly to which he belonged.

Being so well disposed a Person, when there was an *Indian* Church gathered upon the Island, he soon offered himself to the Communion of that Society of Christians; and being admitted a Member of the same, did, so far as I can, on the strictest Enquiry, understand, live according to the Rules of that Religion which he professed, giving no Offence to any of God's People to the Day of his Death. I can't remember that ever he appeared guilty of any considerable Miscarriage; and the *English* that knew him as well as the *Indians*, will, I suppose, generally give him a very good Character.

After he had lived some time on the East End of the Island, and been a useful Man there, his Wife dying, and he marrying another[123] towards the West End thereof, removed thither, and was still imployed in the Office of a *Magistrate*, as he had formerly been; and was moreover frequently called to preach the Word of God to the People of his own Nation, and did, to very good Acceptation, perform that Duty, when he was by Providence called thereto: but the most remarkable Services of his Life were those which as a *Magistrate* were performed by him.

Mr. *Japheth*, to be hereafter mentioned, was the chief *Indian Magistrate* on the Island, until he was called to the pastoral Office on the Death of *John Tackanash*, of whom I have already spoken; but *Japheth* then laying down the Office of a Civil Ruler, this *William Lay* was chosen in his stead, and no *Indian* on this Island ever discharged that Trust with more Fidelity, and to better Advantage than he did. He was certainly in that Office a great Opposer of Sin, and did very much endeavour to be a *Terror to Evil Doers*,[124] and an *Encourager of them that did well.*

He used to open his Courts with solemn Prayer to God, for his Direction in the Affairs to be managed in [26] them; and did, with an agreeable Seriousness and Gravity, attend the Business to be heard and tried in them.

When Persons were conven'd before him for Miscarriages, of which they appeared to be evidently guilty, his Way was first to apply himself to them as a Minister of Religion, or of the Word of God, of which he was a Preacher, and endeavour to convince their Consciences of the Sins of which they were guilty, and bring them to a humble Sense and Confession of their Faults. If he succeeded in this Attempt, he dealt the more tenderly and gently with the Persons offending, according as the Nature

---

123 Rebecca Lay (? –ca. 1708), *IC*, 218.
124 Proverbs 21:15.

of the Thing would allow, which they were dealt withal for; but if they appeared stubborn and obstinate, he would very severely chastise them for their Offences, making them know what *Stripes for the Backs of Fools*[125] do intend.

My Father once telling him, that he feared he was rather too severe in the Punishments he inflicted on his Countrymen, he readily reply'd, that when an *English* Man was whip'd, the Shame of it was commonly at least one half of the Punishment; but the Case being not so with the *Indians, they ought to have the more in Smart, for that they had no more Shame in them.*

Having mentioned his Lenity towards such as could be humbled by his Reproofs, I shall give one Instance thereof which fell under my own Observation.

An *Indian* Servant that run away from his *English* Master,[126] had an *Indian* Officer sent after him to take him up, and bring him before some Authority, to answer for his Fault; but when the Officer found him, he refused to go with him: the Officer being therefore obliged to call in some Persons to his Assistance, they were necessitated to take him by Force, bind him Hand and Foot, and carry him against his Will some Miles to the Place intended, *viz.* the House of the *Indian Magistrate* of whom I am speaking; and the Master of the said Servant happening to be there present at the Time, desired the said Magistrate to deal with his Servant for the Miscarriages of which he had been guilty.

The Magistrate according to his Desire, took the stubborn Servant to task for his Naughtiness and Rebellion; and having some time expostulated with him for his Wickedness, and laboured to convince his Conscience of his great Sin against God in what he had done, the Servant, instead of justifying himself, burst into Tears, pray[27]ed his *Master* and the *Magistrate* to forgive him, and made Promises that he would endeavour to carry himself better for the future; and having so humbled himself was forgiven by both: and being further exhorted to his Duty, was sent about his Business, without having any Punishment at that time inflicted on him.

---

125 Proverbs 19:29.

126 The binding out of Wampanoag children became increasingly common during Experience Mayhew's lifetime. This case might be usefully compared to the Indian servant of Simon Athearn who ran away because of beatings; see Simon Athearn to Gov. Sir Edmond Andros, Knt. &c, [1675]. 24.159 N.Y. Colonial MSS. in New York State Library. In general, one divergence between Wampanoag and Puritan views on child rearing involved the use of corporal punishment: Puritans often disparaged the compassion and indulgence Algonquians showed their children—see Silverman, *Faith and Boundaries*, 68; Williams, *A Key into the Language*, 115–16; Gookin, *Historical collections*, 149—since they felt that "breaking the will" of children was often the kindest form of love. William Lay's rhetoric suggests that he has incorporated this Puritan value.

As the Man I am speaking of ruled well among those over whom he was a *Magistrate,* so he *ruled well in his own House also:*[127] He kept his Children in Subjection with all Gravity, while they dwelt at home with him. He prayed constantly every Evening and Morning in his House, and seldom fail'd of reading a Chapter, and singing a Psalm before he went to Prayer; and all that belonged to the House were obliged to attend soberly on those Exercises.

Tho he was but poor himself, yet it was observed of him, that he had a Heart to contribute freely out of the little which he had, to the Necessities of such as were in more need than himself was.

He always appeared to have a very cordial Affection for the *English,* highly priz'd their Labours among the People of his own Nation, and was ready to take Advice of them on all Occasions, and earnestly desired a Succession of *English* Labourers in the *Indian* Harvest.[128] When my Father dy'd, he earnestly desired me, who was then but a Youth, to study the *Indian* Tongue, and become a Preacher to them, as my Father and Grandfather had been before me: and truly his Importunity was none of the least of the Motives which influenced me to engage in that Work.

About half a Year before he dy'd, hearing that he was dangerously sick, I went to visit him, for which he was very thankful to me; and tho he was then in so weak and low a Condition, that he could say but little, yet what he said was very savoury, and such as did become a godly Person so nigh to Death as he then appeared to be.

I then took my Leave of him, expecting to hear of his Death by the next Intelligence, but was herein mistaken; for Mr. *Japheth* being a little after this sent for to pray with him, God very wonderfully recover'd him: of which Answer of Prayer there has been an Account given in Dr. *Mather's* History of *New-England, Book 6. p. 63.*[129]

[28] But this Recovery of his being perhaps principally to shew how prevalent with God the Prayers of his People are, he in a little time after fell sick again and died.

In the Time of his last Sickness he behaved himself as he had in the Time of his Health done, *viz.* as a truly godly Man ought to do. He desired his Relations and Visiters not to be much troubled at his Death; for that he had Hopes when he dy'd, thro' the infinite Mercy of God, to enter into Everlasting Rest. He told them, they should labour truly to repent of their Sins, and to be sincere and diligent Seekers of God, and should not be discouraged from so doing by any Difficulties which they

---

127 1 Timothy 3:4.
128 Presumably this is the metaphoric harvest of souls, the "laborers" being ministers.
129 *Magnalia Christi Americana.*

might meet withal; and that then he and they might again meet, and see one another with great Joy and Comfort.

As he used to pray with his Family[130] when he was in Health, so he continued to do so in the Time of his Sickness, even to the last Evening that he liv'd. When he was so ill that he was not able to sit up, he would still call them together, and put up a Prayer to God for them; but in the last Prayer which he made in the Evening before he dy'd, his Strength and Voice so fail'd, that none but God could hear and understand him.

This godly Man was the Son of a very pious Mother, who was living after he himself was above 60 Years old, tho he was the youngest of four or five Children which she had brought forth: and being also the last surviving of them, he took a tender Care of her till she dy'd, but a few Years before him.

EXAMPLE X.
ASSAQUANHUT, *alias* JOHN SHOHKOW, a *Ruling Elder,*
who died at Christian-Town *in the Year* 1690.

I Know nothing of the Father of this *Assaquanhut*,[131] saving that he was a praying *Indian* of *Taacame (alias Tisbury)* called *Nashohkow.* He had in all five or fix Sons, whereof this *Assaquanhut* was, if I mistake not, the eldest save one; and of these there were several that were esteem'd godly Men by those that were acquainted with them.

Two others of them may be hereafter mentioned.[132]

[29] But at present I shall speak of *Assaquanhut;* and he was look'd on as so pious and discreet a Man, that on the Death of *Nohnosoo,* the first *Ruling Elder* of the Church whereof *John Tackanash* was Pastor, of whom I have before spoken, he was chosen to supply his Place in that Office, and solemnly set apart to that Work, not long after the said *Nohnosoo's* Death, about the Year 1680.

He was a Person of a very blameless Conversation. My Father who was well acquainted with the *Indians,* and their Affairs, about the Time that this Man flourished, had a very good Esteem of him. I cannot learn

130 Mayhew's biographies reflect an emphasis on the importance of family prayer as displayed in Cotton Mather's *Family-religion,* a sermon that Mayhew translated into *Wôpanâak,* delivered on the island, and eventually printed (1714). It provided directions on how to pray as well as hymns matched to "extraordinary occasions."

131 Assaqunhut married Esther (Asquannit) Ahunnet and was the father of Joel Aquanuat (*IC,* 202).

132 Four are mentioned: Micah Shohkan (*IC,* 30–31*), Stephen Shohkau (*IC,* 54–56*), Pattompan (*IC,* 131), and Daniel Shohkau (*IC,* 131).

that he ever brought any Discredit on the Religion which he professed, by any Miscarriage whatsover. He not only abstained from the excessive Use of strong Drink himself, but was, as I am credibly informed, a sharp Reprover of them that followed after it.

The most credible and discreet among our *Indians* yet living, testify concerning him, that he did very faithfully and prudently discharge the Duties of that Office to which he was separated: and so far as I can learn, such of the *English* as knew him, do give him a good Character.

I am informed by a credible Person, who lived many Years in his House, that he was very constant and serious in his Attendance on the Duties which ought to be performed by every godly Housholder, such as praying with his Family, reading the Scriptures, singing of Psalms, and giving good Instructions and pious Exhortations to such as were about him.

He who thus informs me was a Son[133] which his Wife had by another Husband before he married her; who further affirms, that he carried himself like a kind Father to him all the while he lived with him, took care that he might learn to read, and frequently gave good Counsel to him; and that when he lay sick, and nigh to Death, he called him to him, and when he had renewed the Counsels formerly given him, he desired him to take a Father's Care of the little Son which, being now dying, he should leave behind him; desired him in particular to take care that his Son might not fail of being taught to read; also that he would give good Counsel to him when he should see him to need it: all which I think the Man has well and faithfully performed.

[30] Nor was this the only Person that this good Man gave good Connsels and Exhortations to, in the Time of his last Sickness, for he did the same to all in his Family, and such others as came to visit him. He charged all his Friends and Neighbours *to follow hard after God,*[134] told them, that they should not be weary or faint in their Minds, but go on sincerely and diligently to seek the Lord, and then they might expect to receive all needful Good from him.

As to himself he declared, that tho his Sins had been many and great, yet he had Hopes that thro' the Mercy of God, and Merits of his Son Jesus Christ, he should obtain Life eternal: and, being encouraged and influenc'd by such Hopes, he declared his Willingness to die, and go to his God, and continued calling upon him as long as his Ability for it lasted.

---

133 Probably Amos Ianoxso. Amos's mother was Esther Ahunnet, and his father was Henry Ohhunnut (*IC*, 126–28). He was the grandson of Mittark's brother, Ompohhunnut. Amos was involved in numerous court battles and was listed as a debtor. *WGH*, 149.

134 Psalm 63:8.

Mark the perfect Man, and behold the upright, for the End of that Man is Peace.[135]

EXAMPLE XI.
MICAH SHOHKAN, *who died at* Christian-Town *in the Year* 1690.

THis *Micah* was a Brother of that *Assaquanhut* last above-mentioned, and died near about the same time as he did. He was a Lover of strong Drink in the former Part of his Life, and was once charged with the Sin of Fornication, which as he deny'd, so it could never be prov'd against him. After he made a publick Profession of Religion, he appeared to walk more circumspectly than he had formerly done; yet still for some time shewed too much Inclination to drink of those Liquors in which many of our *Indians* have been drowned: However, he did not appear to be any of those who are *holden in the Cords of their own Sins;*[136] for after some Struggles, he appeared victorious over the *Sin which had most easily beset him,*[137] and carried himself so much like a true Christian, that he grew much in the Esteem of the *Indian* Church whereof he was a Member; and so far as I can learn, the *English* that were acquainted with him had also a good Opinion of him.

Being thus look'd on as washed and cleansed from the Sins whereof he had formerly been guilty, the *In[31]dian* Church did, on the Death of *Paul* before mentioned, separate him to the Office of a *Deacon* in his stead, and thought him well qualified for that Office.

He also frequently preached to the *Indians* on the Island, but especially those in that Town in which he lived and died: and his Labours in this way were very acceptable to his Countrymen.

I am credibly informed, that he was constant and serious in the Performance of the Duties of that Family Religion,[138] wherein all Masters of Families should with their Houses serve the Lord. He not only prayed, but read the Scriptures also in his House. Nor did he neglect frequently to instruct and exhort his Children, and others about him. When he was taken sick of the Fever whereof he dy'd, he gave many good Instructions and Exhortations to his Family and Visiters, and called very earnestly on God to extend his Favour to himself and them.

---

135 Psalm 37:37.

136 Proverbs 5:22.

137 Hebrews 12:1.

138 Since the family was seen as a microcosm of Puritan society, it was important that the father as patriarch should help his wife, children, and servants increase their piety. See Mather, *Family-religion urged.*

After he had been sick some Days, he grew better, and appeared likely to recover; but being suddenly informed of the Death of a Neighbour of his, an *Indian* Magistrate, for whom he had a great Respect, he appeared to be much affected with the News, and said, that if it were so then, he did not desire to live any longer, but was willing to die also, and did so accordingly: for his Fever presently returning, he in a few Days left the World with comfortable Hopes of entering into Life, thro' Jesus Christ his only Saviour.

EXAMPLE XII.
DAVID, *otherwise called* WUTTINOMANOMIN,[139]
an Indian *of the* Gayhead,[140] *and a* Deacon *of the Church whereof* Mr. Japheth *was the Pastor; who died in the Year* 1698.

I Remember that when I was young, this *David* was commonly called the honest Man, as tho he were eminently such; and such I think he was esteemed by all that had any knowledge of him: nor was a mere moral Honesty the best Part of his Character; for Piety toward God, as well as Honesty towards Men, was very conspicuous in him.

[32] Having two such excellent Qualifications, and having a considerable Measure of Wisdom, Prudence, and Courage also, he was sometimes called to the Office of a *Magistrate* among his Countrymen, and behaved himself in that Post as a *just Man, ruling in the Fear of the Lord.*[141]

Having tasted that the Lord is gracious, in that he had in loving Kindness drawn him to himself, he offered himself to the Communion of the Church whereof Mr. *Japheth* was then *Pastor*; but the Day proposed for his Admission being come, and he being grieved and affronted by some ungodly Persons, who would have discouraged him from proceeding in his pious Intentions, he turn'd his back on them, and fled from them, as if they had designed the greatest Mischief against him.

Thus saving himself from that untoward Generation, and not being ashamed of Christ before Men, he professed a good Profession before many Witnesses,[142] and the Church very gladly received him: nor did

---

139 The second husband of Abigail Ahhunnut (*IC*, 162–64*), possibly the progenitor of the David line on the island. *WGH*, 157.

140 A largely Wampanoag town at the southwest end of the island whose name has reverted to Aquinnah. The Wampanoag Cultural Center and Gay Head Baptist Church are still located in Aquinnah today.

141 2 Samuel 23:3.

142 In order to become a church member one had to make a public declaration of a conversion experience. This was true for white Puritans as well as Native Americans, though sometimes women could give their professions directly to the minister rather than in public for reasons of modesty. Church membership allowed congregants to receive communion and, potentially, vote.

he ever after this, as I have heard of, either say or do any thing that was a just Ground of Offence, either to his Brethren, or any other Person whatsoever.

As he would not be *drunk with Wine*, or any other strong Drink, so he seem'd to be *fill'd with the Spirit*.[143] He appeared to be a very devout and serious Christian, seemed evidently to have the Spirit of Prayer, and was, as I am informed, very constant in his Performance of that Duty, calling on God in his own House every Morning and Evening; and sometimes he prayed in publick also, as particularly on Days of fasting, which among our *Indians* are chiefly spent in Prayer, there being but one Sermon preached on them.

And whereas our Saviour tells us, that *of the abundance of the Heart of Man his Mouth speaketh*,[144] it was a considerable Part of this Man's Character, that his Discourses were very heavenly, his *Speech being with Grace, seasoned with Salt*;[145] and therefore *good for the use of edifying, and such as might administer Grace unto the Hearers*.[146]

In his own Family, as at other Times, so more especially just before Morning and Evening Prayer, he used to give serious Instructions and Exhortations to all that were about him. And when he went to visit any of his Neighbours, as he often did, I am credibly informed, that he [33] would not ordinarily take his leave of them, till he had let fall some serious Expressions of a religious Importance among them. And as his Discourses were serious and heavenly, so his Countenance had that Gravity in it, as did become a Soul mightily enriched with the Graces of God's Spirit, and a Man that was much *in the Mount with him*.[147] I think I never saw any Person whose Countenance appeared more serious.

Being thus *filled with the Spirit of God*,[148] he was well qualified for the *Office* of a *Deacon* to which he was called, and did accordingly very well and faithfully discharge the Truth reposed in him, until by Death he was advanced to a higher Station.

He lay a sick considerable Time before he died, and his Discourses were in that Time such as they used to be when he was in Health, *viz.* very serious, profitable, and comfortable. He then exhorted all that came about him, to the great and important Duties of Religion, and spake very comfortably with respect to his own Interest in the Blessedness of the

---

143 Ephesians 5:18.

144 Matthew 12:34.

145 Colossians 4:6.

146 Ephesians 4:29.

147 In Exodus, the "mount" is Sinai, and "him" is God. To be "in the Mount with him" is to be present at the moment of revelation.

148 Ephesians 5:18.

other World; but what in particular his Expressions then were, there be none now that can remember.

Some of the Persons that tended him in his Sickness, and were with him when he dy'd, have with great Assurance affirm'd, that tho his Brethren on Earth did some of them too much neglect to visit him, yet that then, while one was praying with him, there appeared in the Room where he lay far brighter Attendants, in human Shape,[149] than any which this lower World could have afforded, even such as those Spirits may be thought to be, who are *sent forth to minister for them that shall be Heirs of Salvation:*[150] but whether this Account be true or false I cannot determine, there being but one Witness now living, by whom the Affirmative is asserted; yet I doubt not but that the Man, to whom the Story relateth, *died in the Lord, and was carried by the Angels into* Abraham's *Bosom.*[151]

[34] EXAMPLE XIII
JOSHUA MOMATCHEGIN, *who died at* Chappaquiddick,
in or about the Year 1703.

WHen this *Joshua*[152] was converted to Christianity I never had any Account; but so good and prudent a Man he was esteemed to be, when the first *Indian* Church was gathered on *Martha's Vineyard,* in the Year 1670, that he was then chosen *a Ruling Elder* of that Church, and was by Mr. *Eliot* and Mr. *Cotton*[153] set apart to that *Office;* one *John Nohnosoo*[154] before mentioned, being then chosen and ordained to the same *Office* also. But that Church some time after dividing into *two,* good *Hiacoomes*[155]

---

149 The Wampanoags may have interpreted these forms differently: John Eliot and Thomas Mayhew Jr. were told that when Wampanoags died, they were "translated" into the form of Hobbamock. Indeed, the word "Hobbamock" is related to the word for death and was sometimes used in the place of dead man's name. See Eliot and Mayhew, *Tears of Repentance,* B3; Simmons, *Spirit of the New England Tribes,* 39.

150 Hebrews 1:14.

151 Luke 16:22.

152 He was the son of Momatchegin, an Indian schoolmaster and teacher: *WGH,* 379. In 1661, Momatchegin received roughly £3.75 for his work that year (there were eight Indian schoolmasters who received a total of £30). In contrast, the white schoolmaster received £20, and Matthew Mayhew received £5 for his clothing alone. This salary, however, was substantial compared with the £2 Mayhew distributed to "well deserving Indians": *HMV,* 1.237–38. Thus, Joshua was raised in relative spiritual and material prosperity.

153 John Eliot, the minister at Natick, and John Cotton Jr., the uncle of Cotton Mather. Cotton came to Martha's Vineyard in 1664 to preach to the Wampanoag population and became relatively fluent in the local language. He left in 1667 to run a congregation in Plymouth, where he continued to work with local Wampanoag communities. Plane, *Colonial Intimacies,* 56.

154 *IC,* 17–18*.

155 *IC,* 1–12*.

and this *Joshua* took the Charge of one of them, *viz.* that, the Members whereof lived on the Island of *Chappaquiddick*, where there were then a considerable number of very godly People.

But not many Years after this, many of the best of those People dying, and the aged and venerable *Thomas Mayhew* Esq;[156] who lived at *Edgartown* near them, and took much pains for their Good, being also by Death removed from that Work and Labour, which he performed for the People; good *Hiacoomes* also growing so old, that the Work and Service of his Life very much failed; and to add one thing more, the Life and Power of Religion being under great Decays among the *English* living near the same Place, it was so among the *Indians* also, insomuch that in a short time there were very few godly Persons left on that little *Island*; and those that still remained there with their aged Pastor, again join'd with the other Church on the main *Island* of the *Vineyard*, which some Years before they were a Part of: and now the *Indians* at the said *Chappaquiddick* were in a miserable State, the *Candlestick* which had been there, being *removed out of its Place.*[157]

The Place being thus *unchurched*, was filled with *Drunkards* instead of the *good People*, who had before inhabited it; and these were continually supply'd with the hot Liquors, by which they were debauched, from the *very Place* from whence the People of that Island had formerly received the good Instructions and Exhortations, which had been a Medium of their Happiness.

[35] In those dark and declining Times, the *Joshua*, of whom I speak, still lived, and that not only a natural Life, but that also which the Just are said to live.

And being such a righteous Man, he was *a Preacher of Righteousness*[158] among a poor sinful People, that needed *such a Preacher*, especially after *John Coomes*[159] the Son of *Hiacoomes* before mentioned, who was formerly a Preacher in that Place, removed to the Main, and left it.

I was acquainted with the Man of whom I now write, having divers times discoursed with him, and also heard him preach and pray very zealously; and I cannot but think by what I observed in him, that he was a truly godly Man, nor have any that knew him, so far as I can understand, different Apprehensions concerning him. All are agreed, that, in

---

156 Experience Mayhew's great-grandfather.

157 Revelation 2:5.

158 In 2 Peter 2:5, Noah is the "preacher of righteousness" who was spared when the rest of the world was drowned. Mayhew uses the flood motif in the rest of this paragraph; on Chappaquiddick it is liquor, not water, that drowns the sinners and destroys them.

159 John Hiacoomes preached at Assawamsot and later "removed" to Plymouth Colony. He was a preacher by the year 1687. *WGH*, 330.

the bad Times in which he lived, he had *no Fellowship with the Works of Darkness*[160] daily performed among his Neighbours, but did constantly and faithfully reprove them; and tho there was such a Flood of strong Drink, as drowned most of the People in the Place where he lived, yet he kept wholly free from any Excess in the Use of those Liquors by which his Neighbours were destroyed.

I cannot obtain so particular Account as I desire, how this good Man carried himself in his last Sickness, and at his Death: however, some that were with him do inform me, that he was not at all terrified at the Approach of the *King of Terrors*[161] to him, but was able to say he was willing to die, and go to his heavenly Father.

EXAMPLE XIV.
THOMAS SOCKAKONNIT, *an* Indian *of* Nunpang *in* Edgartown, *who died about the Year* 1703, *being an aged Man.*

THis *Thomas*[162] was, as I'm informed, among some of the first that were converted to Christianity, on the preaching of the Gospel to the *Indians* on this Island; and when an *Indian* Church was here first gathered by Mr. *Eliot*[163] and others, he was thought to be so good a Man, as to be qualified to be one of the first Members of it, and was accordingly one of those who did here first enter into Covenant to serve the Lord in a particular Church State.

[36] His Conversation, after he had thus solemnly entered into Covenant with God, continued to be such as it had been for many Years before, *viz.* very regular and blameless; for so far as I can learn, he never did by any Miscarriage dishonour God, or give offence to any of his People, from the time of his first imbracing and professing of Christianity, to the day of his Death.

He did indeed sometimes use strong Drink for his Comfort and Refreshment, but I never heard that he did once abuse himself with it in all his Life.

As he stood in Aw that he sinned not, so he carefully performed the positive Duties which he owed either to God or Man. Thus he constantly attended the publick Worship and Ordinances of God in his House, not

---

160 Ephesians 5:11.

161 I.e., death. Job 18:14.

162 Father of Jacob Sockakonnit, a justice of the peace (*IC*, 116–20*). His granddaughter married David Paul (*IC*, 113–16*) Thomas himself was an Indian surveyor. *WGH*, 132, 185, 333.

163 Missionary John Eliot of Natick, cotranslator of the Eliot Bible.

neglecting them as the manner of some is. He was likewise careful to uphold and maintain the Worship of God in his Family, praying constantly every Evening and Morning in it; and did often instruct and exhort his Household, and used also to exhort, admonish, and reprove his Brethren and Neighbours, when the Case called for it.

He was remarkable for his Care and Diligence in providing for those of his own House, kept at home, and minded his Business, taking Counsel of the *Ants*[164] in providing Meat in the *Summer*, to live upon in the *Winter*; nor was he backward to distribute to others out of the Effects of his Labour and Industry, when necessary Occasions called for it.

Being chosen to the Office of a *Deacon*, about the Year 1698, he continued in the faithful Discharge of Duties of that Trust till the end of his Life, about five Years.

Tho this good Man was no *Minster*, or preaching Officer, yet such was his Zeal for the Interest of Religion, that when it happened that there was no Minister to preach in the Place where he lived, he still used his Endeavours to persuade the People to meet together for the Worship of God, and to spend that time in praying, reading, and singing of Psalms, &c. And he himself did on such Occasions frequently pray in the Congregation, and used also with great Seriousness to give good Exhortations to the People, not in such a manner as shewed any Affectation of becoming a Preacher, but in such a way as discovered a Desire to promote the spiritual Good of his Brethren and Neighbours.

[37] With such a Gift and Spirit of Prayer did it please the Holy Ghost to indue him, that he was on that Account frequently desired to pray in publick, by such as preach'd in the Village in which he liv'd, as on Days of Fasting and Prayer, and sometimes on the Lord's-Day also. And I have my self on such Occasions sometimes heard this good Man pray very pertinently and very affectionately.

While he was in Health, he did sometimes express a Desire that he might not be long sick before he dy'd: and as he wished so it happened to him; for he was ill but three or four Days before his Death, and all that time he was able to sit up, except about half an Hour at last.

From the Beginning of his Sickness he declared his Apprehensions, that the time of his Departure out of this World was at hand, but did not appear to be at all amazed at what was coming on him. He now gave much good Counsel to his Children, and all others that were about him; especially he exhorted them to be earnest Seekers of God, as he told them he himself was and had long been.

---

164 Proverbs 6:6–8.

He did not profess to have a full Assurance of Life eternal,[165] but did frequently speak of Jesus Christ as an all-sufficient Saviour, and said, that he believed, that such as were true Disciples and Servants of his should certainly be saved; and that however it far'd with him as to the eternal Estate of his Soul, he was resolved to continue seeking the Lord as long as his Life lasted.

EXAMPLE XV.
JONATHAN AMOS, *who was a Deacon of the* Indian *Church, whereof Mr.* Japheth *was the Pastor, and a Preacher of the Word of* God *to the* Indians.

THis *Jonathan Amos*,[166] whom I here instance in, as a *pious* and *godly* Man, was the Son of a good Man called *Amos*,[167] who formerly lived on *Chappaquiddick*; the said *Amos* being one of the first Christian *Indians* on that Place, and a Member of the Church whereof *Hiacoomes*[168] was *Pastor*.

This his Son *Jonathan* was taught to read while he was a Youth, and was also taught his Catechism, and [38] otherwise religiously educated: but of his Carriage[169] in his younger Days I have heard nothing remarkable.

When he became a Man, he married a Daughter of a Man very much noted for Piety, whose Name was *Michqsoo*,[170] of whom I shall afterward give some Account. The Woman whom *Jonathan* thus took to Wife,[171] was also well instructed in her young Days, and prov'd a very pious Person, and so *a good and meet Help for him*.[172]

After he was married, he with his Wife lived many Years on the Main, (in the Town of *Dartmouth*,[173] if I mistake not) but being grieved to see Religion at so low an Ebb as it then was among the *Indians* in those

---

165 Puritans would have interpreted Thomas's lack of assurance as a good sign. As Calvinists, New England Puritans believed that God chooses certain individuals for salvation and that men cannot will themselves to be saved or be positive that they are saved. Even the most pious were expected to express uncertainty about their state. Indeed, many of the autobiographies of prominent Puritan ministers reflect this anxiety and self-loathing.

166 Jonathan Amos (ca. 1640–1706) was noted as attending services as early as 1666. *WGH*, 290.

167 *IC*, 131*.

168 *IC*, 1–12*.

169 Demeanor; deportment, behavior (referring to manners): archaic (*OED*).

170 Miohqusoo, *IC*, 5, 76–80*, 152, 282.

171 Rachel Amos, *IC*, 152–54*.

172 "Helpmeet," a Puritan term for wife, is based on Genesis 2:18–20.

173 A town in southeastern Massachusetts, an area originally ruled by the Wampanoag. Dartmouth Indian College was founded after Mayhew's book was published.

Parts, and apprehending that the Affairs of *God's* House were somewhat better ordered at *Martha's Vineyard*, where they were not wholly Strangers, having used to make Visits thither once in a Year or two at least; they resolved to remove to that Place, and actually did so, bringing all their Children, which were eight Daughters,[174] along with them.

Being settled in that Place of their Desires, they improved the Advantages which they came thither in pursuit of, join'd themselves to the Church of Christ there, whereof Mr. *Japheth* was the faithful Pastor, and did there enjoy Christ in all his Ordinances, *sitting under his Shadow with great Delight, and his Fruit was sweet unto their Taste.*[175]

Having these Advantages, they did diligently improve them. The publick Worship of God they constantly attended, and appeared very serious and devout in it; and their Conversations appeared to be in all respects well ordered.

But I shall henceforward confine my Discourse in *this Place* to the Man only, purposing to mention the Woman in another.[176] As then he behaved himself well in the *House of God*, so did he no less in *his own*, walking therein as far as could be perceived *with a perfect Heart.*[177] He very constantly and earnestly prayed to God in his Family both Morning and Evening, and at Meals, and did also frequently read the Scriptures to them, and sing Psalms with them, especially on the *Sabbath*, of which he was a strict Observer.[178] He used his Endeavours to bring up his Children in the Knowledge and Fear of God; to this end he used to make useful Observations on the Scriptures when he read them in his Family, and to ex[39]hort them to the Duties mentioned in them, and did often at other times instruct and admonish them: and how far God blessed the upright Endeavours of this his servant, may afterwards be observed.

This our *Jonathan* being so *serious* and *godly* a Man, and one that ruled well in his own House, the Church to which he belonged did, on the Death of the excellent Deacon *David*[179] before mentioned, chuse him into that

---

174 These included Bethiah Tuphaus (*IC*, 95, 228, 230, 242), Martha Christian, Abigail Amos (*IC*, 154–56*), Hannah Charles (*IC*, 156–57*), Abiah Paaonit (*IC*, 158–61*), Mary Coshomon (*IC*, 179–83*), Sarah Wompanummoo (*IC*, 187), and an unknown daughter. *WGH*, 290.

175 Song of Solomon 2:3.

176 *IC*, 152–54*.

177 Psalm 101:2.

178 In his first sermon at Nonantum, Eliot preached about the importance of keeping the Ten Commandments, including number four regarding the Sabbath, and Sabbath observance quickly became a concern for the Algonquian community at Natick. Praying towns throughout New England regulated the Sabbath and fined profaners. See Solberg, *Redeem the Time*, 183–85.

179 Wuttinomanomin, *IC*, 31–33*.

Office in his Room, nor could they have made choice of a fitter Person than he was: this Trust he therefore discharged both with Prudence and Fidelity, omitting nothing which was in his power to do for the Relief of the *Poor of the Flock*,[180] that were commited more especially to his Care. And one way in which he expressed his Care and Concern for these was, that he used when he stood up to receive the Contributions of the Church, to make a grave and serious Speech, tending to excite to a chearful and liberal Contribution for the Relief of *God's Poor*,[181] as he called them; and would at the same time express his most earnest Desires that God would graciously reward all those that opened their *Hearts* and *Hands* to them.

By thus using the Office of a Deacon well, he purchased to himself a good Degree not of Honour only, but a higher Advancement also in the Church which he so well and faithfully serv'd: For the Church observing how pious and prudent a Man he was, soon thought him fit to be imployed in that more honourable Work of the *Gospel Ministry*, and did accordingly call him to *it*; and I wish they had a greater number of so good Men as this was, for Preachers among them. At first he preached only transiently on necessary Occasions; but he was at length called to preach more constantly at the little Island of *Chappaquiddick*, the Place of his Nativity, and did very faithfully and zealously discharge that Duty.

He was very observable for that Gift and Spirit of Prayer, with which it pleased the *Holy Spirit* of *God* to endue him. I think I have scarcely ever heard any Man in Prayer plead with God with greater Importunity than he used to do; and these his *fervent Prayers availed much.* He had some remarkable Returns of them.

[40] I shall here mention one Instance, wherein it seem'd to me, that God had a respect to the Prayer of this Servant of his.

There was many Years since an extreme Drought in the Country, and on this Island in particular, insomuch that the Corn and Grass withered and dry'd up for want of Rain, the Cattle suffered for want of Grass, and Men were like to want their necessary Food.

In this Extremity there were Days of Fasting and Prayer observed in many of our Congregations, both *English* and *Indian*,[182] to seek for Relief

---

180 Zechariah 11:7.

181 Puritans, like many Christians, felt that the poor had a special relationship with God. Experience Mayhew and other members of his family regularly distributed money to the poor. Notably, many of the "worthy poor" in Mayhew's "Record of Disbursements Given to the Indian Poor at Martha's Vineyard" (1755) came from long-standing Christian families. *Papers of Experience Mayhew.*

182 Fasting was an important form of petition in both European Christianity and Algonquian tradition. Kathleen Bragdon notes that in Native New England, "rituals of many sorts were performed . . . according to season and need. These included calendrical rituals, life-cycle rituals, and critical rites (enacted during plagues, droughts, war, and famine." Feasting too was an important component of Algonquian ritual, as being fed "enhanced a sense of membership within the social group." See Bragdon, *Native People of Southern New England,* 217.

in this Case that did distress us; but *God* did not presently send us the Mercy for which we called upon him.

In this Day of Trouble the *Indian* Church, to which this good *Jonathan* belonged, appointed a Fast also, to *ask of the Lord Rain*[183] in a time wherein it was so much wanted; and there having in the former part of that Day, been a Sermon preached on *Jer.* xiv. 22. *Are there any of the Vanities of the* Gentiles *that can cause Rain?* &c. the Afternoon was spent wholly in Prayer, the *Indian* Minister and some principal Brethren of the Church in their several Turns, (as the Custom is in our *Indian* Churches) calling upon God for the Mercies needed, and the rest joyning with them.

Of those who thus prayed on that Occasion the pious *Jonathan* of whom I am speaking, was the last, excepting the Pastor only; in which Prayer of his I could not but observe a more than ordinary Pathos or Fervency. It was remarkably filled with most humble Acknowledgments of Sin and Unworthiness; and the Mercy of *God*, and the Merits of his Son were most earnestly pleaded, as the only Ground and Foundation on which we might build our Hopes of obtaining an Answer of Peace to our Requests. And in particular I remember there were in that Prayer such Expressions as these,

> O Lord we beseech thee, that thou wouldest not delay over-long to give us a gracious Answer to our Requests: We *Indians* are poor miserable Creatures, and our Faith is exceeding weak; if therefore thou shouldest long delay to answer us, we should be apt to be stumbled and discouraged: we therefore entreat thee to answer us speedily.

This Prayer was scarcely finished before there appeared a Cloud rising, which in a short time came up, and brought a plentiful Shower with it, with which the Face of the [41] Earth was very much refreshed; and People could not get home from Meeting before they received this Mercy.

I would not be misunderstood; I doubt not but many others besides the Person I speak of, received a gracious Answer to their Prayers in that Shower: I only say, that there seem'd therein to be a very remarkable Answer given to that Prayer in particular, a part whereof has been now related.

I was well acquainted with the Person of whom I now write, and cannot but look upon him as a truly godly Man, and I think he was thought so to be by all that knew him. He seemed to love the Lord and hate Evil, in his Discourses, Countenance and Behaviour. He appeared grave and serious, and in the general Course of his Life, he appeared to be *without Spot and blameless.*[184]

---

183 Zechariah 10:1.

184 2 Peter 3:14.

But as good a Man as this *Jonathan* was, that he might not be too much exalted, but might know what was in his Heart, and that others might not think too highly of him, it pleased God to permit him to fall very shamefully.[185]

When he was in the greatest Esteem among God's People, there began to be some Reflections cast on him, as if he appeared too much to thirst after those Liquors which the Generality of his Countrymen have an insatiable Appetite after; but while his Christian Friends and Brethren could scarcely believe such a Report of him, they were on a sudden convinced, that he had been deeply guilty of the Sin of *Drunkenness*: nor was there any need to produce any Witnesses to prove this Crime against him, tho perhaps he might have concealed his Fault if he had attempted it. But the Thoughts of his Sin herein so deeply wounded him, that he voluntarily took the Shame of it on him, and deeply humbled himself before the whole Church and Congregation on the account of it; nor did he ever, that I could hear of, return again to this Folly, but carried himself so circumspectly as wholly to recover that Esteem which the People of God had before had for him.

This good Man lay long sick before he dy'd; during all which time he did behave himself as became a true Servant of God, and an Heir of his Kingdom. His Discourses when I visited him were always serious and heavenly, and I was informed they were so at other times [42] also. He confessed himself to be a Sinner, and utterly unworthy of God's Mercy; and yet declared, that he had hopes of attaining eternal Mercy thro' Jesus Christ our only Saviour. He expressed himself willing to die whenever it should please God to call him out of this World, and said he had rather die before his Children, than undergo the Grief of parting with them while he lived. He told them,

> that tho he was going from them, yet the same God was the Preserver of both him and them; and if they did sincerely seek, and serve his and *their God*, they should come together again, and live in the same Place for ever.

He exhorted them to believe in Jesus Christ, and lay hold of the Mercy of God in and thro' him. He also told them,

> that God was exceeding merciful, and would extend his Favour to all such as would come to him for it; and that he

---

185 Honor was a doubled-edged sword, since if others thought too highly of a person, they might doom that individual to the sin of pride. Recounting Jonathan Amos's fall does not lessen the exempla Mayhew offers: salvation was *always* a struggle, even for the greatest of men; it involved a cosmic battle between the Spirit and the Flesh. For earlier Christian writers such as St. Augustine, attention to one's sins only reinforced the greatness of God when individuals were ultimately saved.

was the only Refuge which they could betake themselves to,
and be safe.

The last Words which he was heard to say were, *I trust in my Lord,
that he will give to me a better Life than this present Life is.* After this, being
unable to speak, he was observed divers times to lift up his Eyes and
Hands towards Heaven.

He dy'd in the Year 1706.

EXAMPLE XVI.
STEPHEN TACKAMASUN, *an* Indian *Minister,*
who died in Chilmark, *in the Year* 1708.

THis *Stephen*[186] was Son to an *Indian* of the main Land, called
Wuttattakkomasun.[187]

I am informed that he lived regularly while he was a young Man; but
however he carried himself then, he appeared afterwards to live soberly,
righteously, and godly in the World.

About so long ago as the Year 1690 he join'd himself as a Member
in full Communion to the Church of Christ. Nor did he ever after this,
that I can hear of, by any Immoralities in his Life, give Offence to God's
People.

He did indeed some Years after he had been a Member of the Church
to which he first join'd, become an *Antipedobaptist,*[188] and was re-baptized,
in which I doubt [43] not but that he was in an Error:[189] however, he
appeared to me to be so serious a Man, that I cannot but judge, that he

---

186 It is intriguing that Mayhew includes Stephen Tackamasun in his book, since many Puritans considered Baptists to be heretics. Even so, Mayhew's report underestimates the incred-
ible importance of Tackamasun for both island Christianity and the Wampanoag community:
he was the first minister of what would become the Gay Head Community Baptist Church in
Aquinnah, the oldest Native American Protestant church in continual existence in what was
then English North America.

187 *IC,* 31–33.

188 Meaning literally "against infant Baptism." Members of this sect of Baptists were also
called "Anabaptists." New England Baptists began as a splinter group of Roger Williams's Congregational church, but their theology and practice differed from Puritanism. Anabaptists, such
as those on the Vineyard, believed in the complete separation of church and state and complete
religious liberty, convictions that had gotten Roger Williams banished from Massachusetts Bay
Colony in 1636 (see Schaff, *America,* 161–62). To the Puritan, these were literally "damnable
errors" that jeopardized the authority and holiness of the community. Since Puritans throughout Massachusetts publicly beat, fined, and imprisoned Baptists, it becomes clearer why, when
schoolmaster Peter Folger began to preach these Anapaptist heresies, he was run off the island
in 1662. Silverman, *Faith and Boundaries,* 55, 110–11.

189 If Mayhew had not believed the Baptists to be in error and proclaimed their errors loudly,
he could potentially have lost his funding from the Society for the Propagation of the Gospel.

acted according to the Dictates of his Conscience in what he did, and not out of any such base and sordid Ends,[190] as those may be justly thought to do who go over to People of other Persuasions, when they are brought under Church-dealing for their vile Immoralities, which several of this good Man's Profession have, to my knowledge, here done.

He was chosen by the Church to which he belonged, to be their Pastor; and if the rest of the Officers of that Church had been qualified as he was, the other Churches here might have very comfortably held Communion with them in special Ordinances.

He was not apt to judge and censure others who were of a different Persuasion from him, but carried himself very Christian-like towards them, willingly holding Communion[191] with them in those things wherein he and they were agreed.

I had frequently Conversation with him while he was in Health, and did also sometimes visit him in the time of that long Sickness whereof he dy'd; and never from first to last saw any thing by him, that made me any ways suspect the Integrity of his Heart, but did ever think him to be a godly and discreet Man.

The last time I went to see him, he professed his good Opinion of those People and Churches from whom he differed in his Apprehensions about the Subjects and Mode of Baptism, and blamed some of his Brethren for being too uncharitable and censorious towards them; and he on other Subjects discoursed like a good Christian. He expressed much Grief at the sinful Miscarriages of some of those in the same Church with him, whose Conversation was blame worthy.

As he lived the Life of a righteous Man, so he dy'd the Death of such a one, and his last End was like his.[192] He before he dy'd gave many good Instructions and Exhortations to his Relations and Visiters, endeavouring to quicken and excite them to the great Duties of Religion in the Word of God required of them, and charged them continually to put their Trust in God, for all the Mercies which they did or might stand in need of.

---

190 New England Puritans often feared that deviation from Calvinist theology would be accompanied by a general breakdown in social mores, including sexual mores, for example, associating Anne Hutchinson's theological heresies with her "monstrous birth": Winthrop thought that the physically deformed child reflected the deformed spiritual life of the mother and foretold the deformation of civil society if the liberal Hutchinson were allowed to continue preaching. See Schutte, "Such Monstrous Births," 85–106.

191 In the previous paragraph Mayhew uses "Communion" to mean the sacrament that commemorates the Last Supper, but here he means a shared religious fellowship and identity. Mayhew's use of capitals emphasizes the relationship he sees between Communion (sacrament) and communion (shared religious fellowship and identity).

192 Numbers 23:10.

He confessed himself unworthy of God's Mercy, and yet declared his Hopes of obtaining it, thro' the Merits [44] of his only Saviour Jesus Christ. He seemed not to be at all terrified at the Approaches of Death towards him, of which he was very sensible, but appeared to enjoy that Peace in his Soul which passeth Understanding. He spake much of the Vanity of this World, and all things in it, and spake of Heaven as a Place infinitely more desirable than this. He called God his heavenly Father, and as such a Father called frequently on him in the last Hours of his Life, and professed a steadfast Hope that he should go to him, and be for ever happy in the Enjoyment of him.

He was observed to look up as stedfastly thro' the Chimney of his Wiggwam towards Heaven, when he was dying, as tho he had, like another *Stephen*,[193] seen the heavens open'd, and had such a View of the Glory of them as he had; but I rather think, that the Sight which he by Faith had of *him that is invisible*,[194] might cause him thus to look towards the Place whither he was going.

EXAMPLE XVII.

Mr. JAPHETH HANNIT, *the third Pastor of the* Indian *Church on* Martha's Vineyard, *who died* July 29, 1712.

JApheth Hannit[195] was born in or about the Year 1638, in the Place now called *Chilmark*, on *Martha's Vineyard*. His Father was an *Indian* of prime Quality there, named *Pamchannit*; which Name being contracted into *Hannit* only, by leaving out the two first Syllables of it, became afterward the Sirname of his Son *Japheth*, and others of his Offspring: a thing very common among our *Indians*.

This *Pamchannit* and his Wife having buried their first five Children successively, every one of them within ten Days of their Birth, notwith-standing all their Use of the *Pawwaws* and Medicines[196] to preserve them,

---

193 Acts 7:55.

194 Hebrews 11:27.

195 Japheth was the progenitor of an important Christian family on the Vineyard: the father of Bethia Escohana (*IC*, 102–3), Jerusha Jobe (wife of Job Somannan: *IC*, 51–52, 105, 110–13*), Jedidah Hannit (*IC*, 232–34*), Jeremiah Hannit (*IC*, 223–24*), Joshua Hannit (*IC*, 224), and Hannah Tobe (wife of Elias Wauwompuque: *IC*, 70). He was also the grandfather of Japheth Skuhwhannan (*IC*, 102–6*) and Mehitable Keape, who kept school at Christiantown and whose house was used for church meetings. *WGH*, 126–27, 244, 338–39. His wife is Sarah Hannit (*IC* 166–170).

196 Traditional medicine and Christianity were not mutually exclusive: Indian convert Hannah Nohnosoo, daughter of the sachem of Holmes Hole, continued this practice of Native healing. See *IC*, 165.

had a sixth (a Son) born to them, the same whom I am here speaking of, a few Years before the *English* first settled on the said *Vineyard.*

The Mother[197] being then greatly distressed with fear that she should lose this Child as she had done the former, and utterly despairing of any Help from such Means had been formerly try'd without any Success, as soon [45] as she was able, which was within ten Days after his Birth, she with a sorrowful Heart took him up and went out into the Field, that she might there weep out her Sorrow. But while she was there musing on the Insufficiency of human Help, she found it powerfully suggested to her Mind, that there is one *Almighty God*[198] who is to be prayed to; that *this God* hath created all things that we see; and that the *God* who had given Being to herself and all other People, and had given her Child to her, was able to preserve and continue his Life.

On this she resolved that she would seek to God for that Mercy, and did accordingly; the Issue[199] was that her Child lived, and her Faith (such as it was) in him who had thus answered her Prayer, was wonderfully strengthened; and the Consideration of *God's Goodness* herein manifested to her, caused her to dedicate this Son of hers to the Service of that God who had thus preserved his Life: Of her doing of which she early informed him, and did, as far as as[200] she could, educate him accordingly. But this she did yet more vigorously, and to better Purpose prosecute, when a few Years after she was by the preaching of the Gospel, instructed in the way of Salvation by a Redeemer, and by the Grace of God enabled truly to believe in *Jesus Christ* our only Saviour.

Japheth's Father being also about this time converted, and so becoming a serious and godly Man, this his Son had the Advantage of a Christian Education, while he was but a Child, not only living in a Family where *God* was daily worshipped, but was himself taught to call on the Name of that God to whose Service he had been devoted: and when there was a School set up for the *Indians* on the Island in the Year 1651, his Father sent him to it, and he then learned to read both in the *English* and *Indian* Tongue, and also to write a very legible Hand, and was then also well instructed in his Catechism.

How he behaved himself while he was a Youth, I have no particular Account; however I never understood that he was viciously inclined.

---

197 Wuttunnohkomkooh (?–ca. 1675), *IC*, 135–37*.

198 Wampanoags had not usually been monotheistic before the arrival of the Puritans but traditionally worshiped a variety of manitous (spirits, gods, impersonal forces that permeate the world). See Bragdon, *Native People of Southern New England,* 184–86.

199 A pun: "issue" can mean either result or offspring.

200 The double "as" is in the original.

After he was grown up, he marry'd a Daughter[201] of a very godly Man, named *Keestumin,*[202] whom I shall afterwards mention; and she prov'd a very pious Person, and did *him Good and not Evil all the Days of her Life.*[203]

[46] When the first *Indian* Church was here gathered in the Year 1670, our *Japheth* was, as he himself told me, in a most distressed Condition for not being of the number of them who first confederated to walk together as a Church of Christ, according to the Order of the Gospel: he on the *one hand* greatly lamented his not being of that happy number, as he esteemed them; and on the *other,* at the same time fear'd to offer himself to the Society of God's People, lest he should be unqualified for the Privileges to which they were admitted.

But tho *Japheth* could not at this time enter into a solemn Covenant to serve the Lord, in an Attendance on all the Duties incumbent on particular Churches; yet it was not long after this, before he made a publick Profession of Repentance towards God,[204] and Faith towards our Lord *Jesus Christ,* and join'd as a Member in full Communion to the Church which he before long'd to be one of: in which Relation he from time to time behaved himself as became a good Christian.

He was not after this presently called to the Work of the Ministry, but was for a considerable time imployed in Offices civil and military, being first made a *Captain* over a Company of his own *Nation,* and also a *Magistrate* among them; in both which Places of Trust he behaved himself well, and to the Acceptation of both the *English* and *Indians*: and in the time of that War betwixt them, which began in the Year 1675, and was commonly call'd *Philip's War,*[205] good *Japheth* was very serviceable to both those of his *own Nation* and *ours* on this Island: for being firmly set, if possible, to maintain and preserve Peace betwixt the *English* and *Indians* here; and, being an *Indian* Captain, as has been already said, he was imployed by the *English* to observe and report how things went among the *Indians*: and to his Faithfulness in the Discharge of this Trust, I

---

201 Sarah Hannit, neé Sarah Mensoo of Chapaquiddick, *IC,* 74, 166–70*, 232.

202 *IC,* 74*, 87, 166.

203 Proverbs 31:12. This passage outlines the qualities of a good wife.

204 An example of a profession given by an Algonquian man at Natick is Ponampam's confession; see Eliot, *Further account,* 54–57.

205 Mayhew's emphasis on Japheth's loyalty to the English during King Philip's War (1675–76) stands in opposition to negative portraits of Christian Indians by Puritans during the war: e.g., Mary Rowlandson harps on Indian converts unregenerate conduct and propensity for violence in "A True History of The Captivity and Restoration of Mrs. Mary Rowlandson," 37. Many Indian converts were bitterly mistreated during the war; some were imprisoned on Deer Island in Boston Harbor without proper food or shelter. See Lepore, "When Deer Island Was Turned into Devil's Island," 14–19.

conceive that the Preservation of the Peace of our Island was very much owing, when the People on the Main were all in *War* and *Blood.*

Japheth's Fidelity to the *English* in this Affair gained him a high Esteem, and kind Treatment among them, he being generally look'd on as a godly and discreet Man by them; and being well accounted of among the *Indians* also, they not long after this called him to the Work of the Ministry among them. His Office of a Captain he now laid down, but that of a Magistrate he still sustain'd [47] for some Years after he began to preach, none else being thought so fit for that Trust. The Place he preached at was that wherein he liv'd and dy'd, being join'd in that Work with his Uncle *Janawonit,* before mentioned in Example the fifth.

Being called to the Work of the Ministry, he was very faithful and diligent in it, and was esteemed the best qualified of any *Indian* on the Island not yet in the Pastoral Office. He was therefore by *John Tackanash*[206] Pastor of the *Indian* Church here, in the time of his last Sickness, nominated as a fit Person to succeed him in the Office which he then expected a Discharge from; and the said *Tackanash* dying in *January* 1683-4, and being interred on the 23*d* of the same Month, the pious *Japheth,* who much lamented his Death, made a grave Speech at his Funeral, some of the Heads whereof being by my Father, who heard part of it, preserved in Writing, and now before me, I shall here insert them, and they are as followeth.

> We ought, *said he,* to be very thankful to God for sending the Gospel to us, who were in utter Blindness and Ignorance, both we and our Fathers. Our Fathers Fathers, and their Fathers, and we, were at that time utterly without any means whereby we might attain the Knowledge of the only true *God.* That People also which knew the Ways of God, were some thousands of Miles distant from us; some of whom, by reason of Difference among themselves about their Way, removed into this Land; but it was God that sent them, that they might bring the Gospel to us. Therefore, I say, we have great reason to be thankful to God; and we have reason to be thankful to them also, for that they brought the Gospel to us: but most especially we ought to thank God for this, for tho they taught us, it was God that sent them, and made choice of them for this Work, of instructing us in the Ways of the Lord.
>
> Before we knew God, when any Man dy'd, we said the Man is *dead*; neither thought we any thing further, but said he is *dead,* and mourned for him, and buried him: but now it is far otherwise; for now this good Man being dead, we have Hope towards God concerning him, believing that God hath received him into everlasting Rest.

---

206 *IC,* 14–16*.

[48] Now therefore we ought to improve the Benefit which we have by the Gospel. And first, such of us as had like not to have received this Kindness, I mean such of us as were grown up when the Gospel came to us, so that it only found us in being, such are strongly obliged to improve the same, since they scarcely received it, or were in danger not to have enjoyed it.

Secondly, There are others of us that have been born under the Gospel; and we that were so, ought duly to improve the same, inasmuch as we have received so wonderful a Benefit.

And now tho this Man that went before us, leading us in the Way of God according to the Gospel, be deceased, and helps us no more, yet his Doctrine remaineth still for us to improve; nor ought we to forget him, but should remember him by his Wife and Children, whom he hath left among us.

Thus far *Japheth's* Speech, which savoureth of the Piety of the Man by whom it was uttered.

Good *John Takanash* being thus laid in his Grave, Mr. *Japheth* was the next *Spring* called to succeed him in the same Place and Office; and in the Fulfilment of the Ministry thus committed to him, he continued about 28 Years, *viz.* till the Year 1712. He was faithful and diligent in the Work of God, unto which he was called, preaching the Word in season and out of season, reproving, rebuking, and exhorting, with all Long-suffering and Doctrine, and used frequently to catechise the Children of his Flock in publick.

He maintained a good Discipline in the Church over which the Holy Ghost had made him Overseer, knew, how to *have Compassion* on those whose Case called for it, and how *to save others with Fear.*[207] In difficult Cases that occurred, he was careful to take the best Advice he could get. He was not at all inclined to *lord it over his Flock*,[208] but willing in Meekness to instruct them. And when there was danger of Discord among his Brethren, he would not side with any Party of them, but would in such Case make most winning and obliging Speeches to them all, tending to accommodate the Matters about which they were ready to fall out; and so wonderful an Ability had he this way, that he seldom failed of the End he aimed at.

[49] He frequently visited the Families under his Care and Charge, especially when they were under Affliction by Sickness, or otherwise; and in the Visits he made them, he usually entertained them with serious and profitable Discourses, and I have heard him tell how very advantageous that kind of Visits had proved to some of his People.

---

207 Jude 1:23.
208 1 Peter 5:3.

He very often performed the Work of an Evangelist, in carrying of the Gospel into other Places, and endeavouring to promote the Kingdom of Christ in those of his own Nation; and God gave considerable Success to his Endeavours to do Good in this Way.

Tho his sermons were not very accurate, yet were they very serious, and had a great deal of good Matter in them, and he seem'd to me to do best when he did not try to oblige himself to any strict Method in them.

In Prayer he was very fervent, frequently praying with much Enlargement and Affection. On Sacrament Days I have more especially observed that he has done so; and God did sometimes shew a gracious regard to the Petitions by this his Servant put up to him. One Instance whereof has been formerly published in Dr. *Mather's* History of *New-England, Book* VI. *pag.* 63. But in nothing was he this way more highly favoured than in God's helping of him against a Temptation, with which for some time conflicting, and crying earnestly to God for Deliverance from it, he obtained the Mercy he sought to him for.

He was fully resolved that he and his House should serve the Lord; with them therefore he constantly prayed, and frequently sang Praises to God: he also read the Holy Scriptures in his House, and often gave serious Exhortarions to all that were about him.

He was much given to Hospitality:[209] for being frequently visited, both by Neighbours and Strangers, they were always kindly and generously entertained in his House with the best he had, or could readily procure.

He well understood, and steadily adhered to the Truths of our holy Religion in which he had been instructed, and would not be *driven about by every Wind of Doctrine.*[210]

One Instance of his Stability in the Truth, I think it may not be amiss here to give my Reader: A godly *Englishman,*[211] who had formerly been a School-master to the *Indians* here, and had taught *Japheth* and many others [50] to read and write, and had also learned them their Catechisms, and instructed them in the Principles of Religion, having unhappily imbibed the Errors of the *Antipedobaptists,* thought himself obliged to endeavour to bring Mr. *Japheth* over to his Persuasion: To this End he therefore visited him at his House, took much Pains to convince him that

---

209 The meaning of hospitality was different in English and Algonquian societies. At its most basic level, hospitality was for Mayhew a Christian virtue. It was also related, though, to social hierarchies: for Algonquians, giving hospitality conferred status on both giver and receiver, but English colonists often understood Algonquian hospitality as conferring status on the receiver alone.

210 Ephesians 4:14.

211 Peter Folger (1617–1690), who according to Mayhew was a forerunner of the Baptist church on the island.

theirs was the right Way, and that ours of baptizing Infants, and sprinkling in Baptism, was very wrong: But none of the Arguments used by
the Man, could convince *Japheth* of what they were brought to prove; at
length being just about to go away, *Japheth* told him he would only say
one thing more to him before he went.

> You know, Sir, *said he*, that we *Indians* were all in Darkness
> and Ignorance before the *English* came among us, and
> instructed us, and that your self are one of those *English* Men
> by whom we have been taught and illuminated. You taught us
> to read, and instructed us in the Doctrines of the Christian
> Religion, which we now believe, and endeavour to conform
> our Practices to. And when, Sir, you thus instructed us, you
> told us, that it may be there would shortly false Teachers come
> among us, and endeavour to pervert us, or lead us off from
> our Belief of the things wherein we had been instructed; but
> you then advised us to take heed to our selves, and beware
> that we were not turned aside by such Teachers, so as to fall
> into the Errors into which they would lead us. And now, Sir,
> I find your Prediction true; for you your self are become one
> of these Teachers you cautioned us against: I am therefore
> fully resolved to take your good Counsel, and not believe you,
> but will continue stedfast in the Truths wherein you formerly
> instructed me.

This Speech of *Japheth's* put an End to the Disputation.

As for *Japheth's* Morals, he was generally and justly esteemed, as well
by the by the *English* as *Indians*, a Person of a good Conversation: nor did
he discover any such Infirmity in his Life, or Deportment in the World,
as was inconsistent with such an Esteem; or which thro' Prayer, and the
Supply of the Spirit of Jesus Christ, he did not obtain a compleat Victory
over, being only privately admonished of a Failure, which some began to
be offended at.

As he was generally by the *English* esteemed a truly godly Man, so
being a Person of a very genteel and obli[51]ging Conversation, and one
who went clean and neat in his Apparel, he was every where courteously
received and entertained by them, the best Gentleman on the Island not
scrupling to invite him to sit at their Tables with them;[212] and speaking
English considerably well, Strangers that came to the Place took Delight

---

212 The status conferred on Japheth and on Wampanoag ministers on the island should be
compared with a case mentioned in the diary of Samuel Sewall. When the Indian minister John
Neesnummin visited in Boston in 1708, Sewall could find no one willing to lodge him: in part,
colonists feared the "contagion" of housing an Indian, but they also feared the lowered status
that would accompany hosting such an apparently undistinguished guest. Even the boarding-
houses refused him, and Sewall was finally forced to lodge the minister in his own study. See
Kawashima, *Puritan Justice and the Indian*, 108; Sewall, *Diary*, MHS, 5th ser., 5–7 (1878–82):
2:212–13.

in conversing with him. And once a Master of a Vessel discoursing with him, on the Morrow after the *Sabbath*, facetiously asking him, whether he prayed for him yesterday or not? *Japeth* readily reply'd, *Sir, I prayed for all God's People, and if you be one of them, I consequently prayed for you.*

Persons have sometimes had Premonitions of their own Death, and something of this Nature our *Japheth* did experience, as he did in the time of his last Sickness declare, together with the Influence the same had on his Life; an Account of which, with some of his dying Speeches, &c. his honest Son in law, *Job Soomannah*,[213] who was frequently with him in his Sickness, having written in *Indian*, communicated to me soon after *Japheth's* Death: An Extract of which Account I shall here in *English* insert, and it is as followeth.

He said, that about a Year before he was taken sick, he went out of his House, and walked alone in the Woods,[214] and there it was by God revealed to him, that he had but a little time to live in this World; and that being thereupon much concerned in his Mind, he did immediately set himself on doing all that he could to prepare for his approaching End, as taking it for a Truth that his End was now very near, an looking Day and Night for it: but he said, he still misliked himself, or reckoned that he came short.

Thus it was with him till *April* the 2d, 1712, which being a Day of Thanksgiving,[215] he went and preached thereon; but as with his Wife he returned home in the Evening, before they had gotten to their House he felt a Pain in his Side, and was never able after this to go to God's House of Prayer, his Sickness gradually encreasing on him from that time forward.

And having been sick about ten Weeks, he sent for the Brethren of the Church, and said to them as followeth, *viz. That it did often distress him in his Heart, and cáuse him to weep, when he saw the miserable Estate of all the People by reason of their Sins; but* [52] *especially how unapt the generality of the Church were to the Duties incumbent on them, and how often they did fall by reason of one kind of Infirmity or another, to which they were subject, tho he had very often instructed them in their Duty.*

---

213 *IC*, 110–13*.

214 The woods were not an unusual place for Algonquians to receive visions or encounter the divine: William Simmons notes that Native New Englanders often encountered manitous "at night 'in the most hideous woods and swamps' in the shapes of Englishmen, Indians, animals, inanimate objects, and mythical creatures"; Simmons, *Spirit of New England Tribes*, 39. Visions were also part of the popular religious practice that the colonists brought with them to New England. See Hall, *World of Wonders*, 86–87.

215 Feasts and thanksgiving days were important rituals for both the Wampanoags and the English colonists. For a list of Wampanoag thanksgivings, see "Wampanoag Celebrations."

I have, said he, *often wished for your sakes, that you might still enjoy*[216] *me; but now I am willing to die: however, as to this, let the Will of God be done. But do you go on to pray to God, and worship him both stedfastly and fervently.*

To his own Family, and such others as attended on him, he afterwards, not long before his Death, said, *Be not feeble in your Minds, I'm hitherto stedfastly resolved that I will love the Lord my God.*[217] *I shall*, said he, *now quickly go my last Journey, as others have done before me. Now I shall quickly set out. Thus it has been wont to be, when a Thing has here no further Use to be made of it. But Oh, what sweet Melody is there now in Heaven!* To his Son in law, the Writer hereof, he then said, *My Son, be thou of good Courage, and fail not to lay hold of the heavenly Salvation, for the sake of the things of this World But as for me*, said he, *I need to have my Mind further strengthened, and encouraged; for I think I shall now quickly leave you.*

The 28*th* of *July* 1712, was the last Day he lived in the World; for the Night following it, a little after Midnight, having desired those that were with him to praise God, by singing the 13*th* Psalm, and then by Prayer to commit both him and themselves to God, his Breath failed, and he resigned up his Spirit to God who gave it.

Thus far *Job Soomannah's* Memoirs of his good Father in law.

As I was well acquainted with *Japheth* in his Life, so I frequently visited him in the time of his last Sickness; and on the whole of my Acquaintance with him, I cannot but think, that he was a very serious and godly Man, and a Man of great Moderation and Prudence. His Discourse in the time of his last Sickness, when I was with him, was very pious and savoury.[218] He then expressed a humble Sense of the Sin of his Nature and Life, and yet his Hopes of eternal Salvation thro' the infinite Mercy of God, and Merits of his Son Jesus Christ. He then also expressed a Readiness and Willingness to resign [53] himself and all that the had into the Hands of God, his faithful Creator, and merciful Redeemer. I remember also that he told me, that God had in the latter Part of his Life given him a more effectual Sense of the Evil of Sin, than formerly he had had; and that he had also enabled him with more Vigilance and Industry, to endeavour the Mortification of the Corruptions of his Heart.

Among other *Evidences* of the *real Piety* of this good Man, the Grief of his Heart for the Sins of his Countrymen, especially those who had been

---

216 To have the use or benefit of, have for one's lot (*OED*).

217 The commandment to "love the Lord thy God" is invoked repeatedly in Deuteronomy and appears in Joshua as well. Jesus quotes this commandment in Matthew 22:37 and Mark 12:30.

218 In now obsolete religious phraseology, this word means "full of spiritual 'savour'; spiritually delightful or edifying," or "having the savour of holiness; of saintly repute or memory" (*OED*).

under his own Care and Charge, together with his Care and Concern for their Reformation, may justly be reckoned as *one*; for besides what of this Nature was discovered by him, in what is above-said, he a few Days before his Death, with his feeble and dying Hand wrote an affectionate Address to the People of his own Charge, which he desired might be communicated to them: which Writing of his being now by me, I shall render into *English*, and here insert, and with that conclude my Account of the Person that penned it. It is then as followeth:

Is it not a most desirable thing for Persons in this Life certainly to know, that they shall go to Heaven when they leave this World?

Therefore now take heed, and consider well what you do, and do not cast away such Hopes as these for nothing, nor for a little of the Pleasure of this World: for it is certain, that your carnal and worldly Actions can't give you Rest. Moreover, by these you do bring all sorts of Misery on your selves; yea, and not only so, but you do thereby trouble others also, so long as you remain unconverted.

Thus you trouble such as are Magistrates to rule and govern you, and by their penal Laws to punish you.

Next, you trouble such as are *Pastors* or *Ministers*, while you hate to hear, believe, and practice their Doctrine. While your Sin and Misery is great, their Trouble and Sorrow is so too here in this World.

You do also trouble the common People by your Sins, by bringing on them various Sicknesses and pestilential Diseases, and all other divine Chastisements.

You do also hereby hinder and disturb the holy Peace of God's praying People among the Churches, and make those ashamed that are religious; and you who are still ungodly laugh at it.

[54] Alas! Oh Lord, how very heavy is my Grief on the account hereof? seeing we now hear the Gospel preached to us, and have the Light of God's Word shining on us, and he in Peace giveth his *Sabbaths* to us.

God is constantly calling of us to Repentance, and has often repeated his Chastisements on us, by grievous Sicknesses; but, this notwithstanding, how full of Wickedness has he seen all our Towns? for both Men and Women, young Men and Maids, do all delight in Sin, and do things therein greatly grievous.

People should all of them now forsake their Sins, and turn to God; and they should come to their Ministers, and make penitential Confessions of their Transgressions to them, and entreat them to pray to God for them: then would God forgive their Iniquities, and teach them to do that which is right all the Days of their Lives.

Then also would God teach them to know Jesus Christ, and believe in him: and then they should receive Remission of all their Sins, and should be caused to walk according to the Word of God to the End of their Lives. Whoso heareth this, Oh let it put him on Consideration! These are my last Words to you. Now fare you all well. *Amen.*

EXAMPLE XVIII.
STEPHEN SHOHKAU, *a Preacher of the Word*
of God, who died in the Year 1713.

THe *Stephen* of whom I speak, was Son of *Nashohkow*, an *Indian* of *Takame* [now called *Tisbury*] and a Brother of that *Assaqunhut* and *Micah*, before mentioned.[219]

He lived some Years while he was young in a pious *English* Family, wherein God was constantly worshipped: and when he became himself Master of a Family, he followed the good Example that had been set him, praying constantly in his House, and frequently reading the Scriptures in it. He also, as I am credibly informed, frequently instructed and exhorted his Children, and so endeavoured to *bring them up in the Nurture and Admonition of the Lord.*[220]

[55] In his natural Parts he did not excel; yet being looked on as a serious and godly Man, and as having a competent Measure of Prudence and Discretion, he was imployed as a Preacher of the Word of God, to a few Families that lived in a Place something remote from the rest of the *Indians,* in the said *Tisbury,* and used his faithful Endeavours to promote the Interest of Religion in that little Village for many Years together, according to the Measure of Grace that he had received. I was well acquainted with him for more than three times seven Years, and always looked on him as a Man that *feared God and eschewed Evil.*[221] I have sometimes heard him preach and pray very piously, and have often heard him discourse discreetly and sensibly of the things of God and his Kingdom: and tho he might sometimes discover something of *Weakness* in his Discourses, yet I cannot think that any will say, that they ever knew him shew any *Wickedness* in them.

His Conversation was, so far as I can learn, always such as did *become the Gospel.*[222] I never heard that he was addicted to any Vice whatsoever, in all the time that I was acquainted with him, and with the Affairs of the

---

219 *IC*, 28–30*, 30–31*.
220 Ephesians 6:4.
221 Job 1:1, 1:8, 2:3.
222 Philippians 1:27.

Church to which he belonged; nor do I remember that he ever gave any Offence to his Brethren, or any other.

Tho he had two pious Women, one after another, for his Wives, who encouraged him in the Ways of Religion, wherein he was engaged, and were great Comforts to him; yet, as he was not *without those Chastisements, which they who suffer not are Bastards and not Sons,*[223] God gave him Grace to behave himself well under his afflictive Providences. No less than three of his Children were taken away by sudden and violent Deaths, and he gave Honour to God under those sore Trials.

As some of his Children dy'd sudden and violent Deaths, so he himself did, being drowned, as shall presently be declared; however, it seems that he was not without some Apprehensions, that the time of his Departure was at hand for some time before his Death. His Widow, whom I judge worthy of Credit, does inform, that some time before he dy'd he told her, that he thought he should before it was long die and leave her; and that, if it did fall out as he thought it would, he [56] would not have her discouraged, but continue to pray earnestly to God, and put her Trust in him: and, by the way, I think she followed his Advice in it.

As he foretold, so it came to pass, for about the *5th* or *6th* of *October* 1713, he with his Wife and two of her near Relations, *viz.* A young Woman and a Boy, essaying in a windy time to pass over a Pond, a little way in a small Canoo,[224] which his Wife was unwilling to venture her self in, till he had showen some Dislike at her being so fearful as she appeared then to be, the Canoo overset by the way, and his Wife and the other Woman, who could neither of them swim, got hold of it, and so got alive to the Shore: but our poor *Stephen* endeavoured so long to save the Boy whom he saw drowning, that at length he was not able to save himself, but sunk down and *died with the Youth*, which he would have had to *live with him.*[225]

EXAMPLE XIX.
ELISHA PAAONUT, *an* Indian *Minister, who died in the* Year 1714.

THis *Elisha*[226] was Son to an *Indian* living on the West End of *Martha's Vineyard*, called by the *Indians Paaonut;*[227] concerning whom it is said,

---

223 Hebrews 12:8.

224 A *mishoòn*, or dugout canoe. A number of these canoes have been found preserved in the lakes in Massachusetts. Roger Williams provides a description of them and notes how often they are overturned in *A Key into the Language*, 106–9.

225 Romans 6:8; 2 Timothy 2:11.

226 The uncle of Eleazar Ohhumuh (*IC*, 224). *WGH*, 331–32.

227 He may also have been the father of Deborah Ohhumuh (*IC*, 224). *WGH*, 331–32, 355.

that lying sick and nigh to Death so long ago, as before he and the rest
of *Indians* where he lived, had been instructed in the Doctrines and Pre-
cepts of the Gospel, he called his Children and other Relations, and spake
thus to them before he dy'd,

> If any fight against you, do not strive or fight with them. If
> any speak Evil of you, do not speak Evil of them. If any do
> Evil to you, do not Evil to them again. If you observe these
> things, you shall arrive at the good Place or Country that we
> hear of, above in Heaven.

Note here, that these *Indians* had heard a Rumour of that Life and
Immortality which is brought to Light by the Gospel, tho they were not
yet instructed in the Doctrines of Life contained therein.

Thus of *Elisha's* Father, whom leaving, I shall now come to what is
more certain concerning *Elisha* himself, giving a brief Account of him.

He was in his younger Days a Lover of strong Drink, and would
sometimes drink to Excess of it; however, [57] when the Gospel was
preached at the *Gayhead* where he lived, by that good *Mittark* who has
been already mentioned, he hearkened to the good Tidings published in
that Place, and became a serious Professor of the true Religion so made
known to him; and some Years after became an Assistant to the said *Mittark*, in preaching the Gospel to his Countrymen there; but after *Mittark's*
Death in the Year 1683, he did more fully devote himself to the Work of
the Ministry in the said Place.

In this Work he was employed when I first became acquainted with
him, about as long ago as the Year 1695, and I then thought him to
be a serious and good Man: yet he still, and for some time after this,
discovered so much of an Inclination to strong Drink, as gave some
Scandal to such as had otherwise a good Esteem of him; but his Fault
herein not being for some time reformed, it pleased God at length to
leave him once to fall into gross Drunkenness; for which Offence he
was brought into publick Church-Dealings, and now appearing to be
much awakened, and very deeply affected with a Sense of his Sin in
that Miscarriage, humbling himself very greatly before God and his
People, and promising, by the Help of Grace, to keep himself from that
Iniquity for the future, so far as did appear, he was as good as his Word
herein; for he no more, that ever I could hear of, to his dying Day did
in any degree return again to that Folly, but lived for many Years after
a very blameless Life, in the good Esteem of all that were acquainted
with him.

I have often heard him discourse very seriously, and heard him preach
and pray very understandingly and affectionately.

He seemed to be the best acquainted with the Scriptures of any *Indian* that ever I met withal, could most readily turn to almost any Text that one could mention to him, if a Word or two of it were but named. He used no Notes in preaching, nor did he seem to need any. When he began his Sermons, he used to give a fair Account of the Coherence of the Place from whence his Text was taken: and tho he never aimed at making any accurate Distribution of the things he discoursed on, yet he used to illustrate the Observations which he raised [58] from his Text, by other Places of Scripture pertinently alledged.

I have been informed, that he spent much time in reading and study, and by what I have observed in him, I can easily believe that he did so. Another *Indian* Preacher, who was a great Lover of the World, and proved a vile Apostate, would sometimes reflect on him as a slothful Man, and attribute his Poverty thereto: but others thought that his Care to approve himself to God, in a Discharge of the Duties of his Ministry, was that which hindered his pursuing the things of this World as some others did; but besides this, he was so lame in one of his Legs, that he was in some degree disabled from bodily Labour thereby.

As his Piety appeared in a faithful Discharge of the Duties of his publick Ministry, so it did likewise in his serious and constant Attendance on the Duties of that Family Religion, wherein all Masters of Families should resolve that they and their *Houses will serve the Lord:*[228] from this therefore he would not suffer any Thing or Business to divert him; and the Prayers Morning and Evening made in his House, were ordinarily attended with the reading of the Scriptures, and frequently with serious Exhortations to such as he had under his Care and Charge. I am also informed, that he frequently visited other Families in the Place where he lived, and gave much good Counsel to them.

He was sick a considerable while before he died, during which time he prayed much to God, for his Mercy to be extended both to himself and others, and gave a great deal of good Counsel to his Children,[229] and such as came to visit him.

A little before his Death he complained sadly of Moleslation from evil Spirits, yea affirmed they appeared in human Shape to him,[230] to trouble

---

228 Joshua 24:15.

229 One of his children was Elisha Elisha (alias Pianet, mentioned in William Homes's diary), who drowned in a pond with his daughter on May 12, 1746, at around age forty. Caleb Elisha, who is listed in Mayhew's disbursements to the poor, was probably also his child. *WGH*, 144, 233, 331–32, 431.

230 The belief in evil spirits was common in both Wampanoag and Puritan popular religion. In Puritan circles, people often spoke of the Devil as sending "temptations" to people on their deathbeds, since "the Devil liked to disrupt souls at peace"; Hall, *Worlds of Wonder*, 197. Although spectral evidence came into question during the witchcraft trials, many people in

and disquiet him. He then, tho there were no Signs of a Delirium on him, thus expressed himself to those that were with him.

> Thus it seems it is wont to be when Persons are drawing nigh to Death, the Devils do then make an Assault on them; they now continually come in so, that the House is filled with them, and they bring things and offer to me, but I do refuse to receive them, and do drive them away, and they quickly go out of the House again. I know but one of them, and that is _____ he is a[59]mong the Devils.

The Person whom he named was a Professor of Religion, who in a little time after became such an Apostate, that one would be ready to fear, that what was said of him had too much of Truth in it; but I shall not mention his Name.

That there was something of the Malignity of *Satan* against the good Man of whom I speak, appearing in what I have thus related, I make no question; but further I shall not attempt to make any Judgment of the Matter, but shall leave it to others to think what they please of it.

After this, just before he dy'd, seeing his Children weeping by him, he said to them, *Weep not for me, I do not think I am going to the Place of Torment,*[231] *but do believe I am going to leave all my Pain and Trouble here, and to enter into everlasting Happiness.*

EXAMPLE XX.
ISAAC OMPANY, *a* Ruling-Elder, *of the* Indian *Church* on Martha's Vineyard, *and a Preacher of the Word of* God *to the* Indians *on that Island.*

THe Father of this *Isaac*, whose Name was *Noquitompany,*[232] was a Man professing Godliness, and esteem'd by those that knew him as a pious and good Man.

But how good soever he was, his Son *Isaac* was in his younger Days sometimes guilty of the Sin of Drunkenness: but, so far as I can learn, he was on other accounts a very honest and just Man, and so generally looked on by his Neighbours, both *Indians* and *English*.

New England believed that Satan could take the shape of humans. Similarly the Wampanoag deity Hobbamock, associated with death, often appeared to Indians in the shapes of "Englishmen, Indians, animals, inanimate objects, and mythical creatures." See Simmons, *The Spirit of the New England Tribes*, 39.

231 Luke 16:28.

232 *IC*, 84–86*.

But there are yet *better things* to be spoken of this our *Isaac, and things that do accompany Salvation*;[233] for God having chosen him to Life eternal, was pleased, when he was, as I think, about forty Years old, effectually to call him, convincing him of his Sin and Misery by Nature, and enabling him to betake himself to *Jesus Christ* for Deliverance and Salvation.

Being thus turned from *Sin* to *God*, he made a publick Profession of *Faith* and *Repentance*, and was admitted as a Member in full Communion into the Church, whereof the memorable *Japheth* was then *Pastor*. And being now called with an *holy Calling*,[234] he after this always walked like an *holy Man*, behaving himself in all [60] respects *worthy of the Vocation*[235] with which he was so favoured, and was never more, so far as I can learn, overtaken with any Fault that was matter of Scandal, or stumbling to God's People, or any others that knew him. Even the Sin of Drunkenness, to which he had before his Conversion been somewhat inclined, he did now wholly abandon, living soberly, and as became a good Christian.

Having thus for some Years, by a good Conversation, recommended himself to the good Esteem of all his Brethren and Neighbours; and being also observed to be a Man of Prayer, and very devout and constant in his Attendance on the publick Worship, and Ordinances of God; and also one of a good Understanding in the holy Scriptures, and apt to instruct and exhort those with whom he conversed; he was sometimes called to preach the Word of God publickly, and did, to the good Acceptation of the better sort of People, perform that Duty.

He was a *Magistrate* as well as a Minister among his own Countrymen, and faithfully discharged the Duties of that *Office*, according to the best of his Skill and Judgment, not being a Terror *to good Works, but to those that were Evil*.[236]

He was also some Years before he dy'd, chosen and set apart to the Office of a *Ruling-Elder* in the Church whereof he was a Member, to supply the Place from which another *by his Transgression fell*,[237] and did with great Fidelity discharge the Trust therein reposed in him.

In his Preaching he was not very popular, and with many he was the less so, because he was a sharp and serious Reprover of the Sins, to which he could not but see his Countrymen were much addicted; and he has sometimes complained to me of several Preachers of his own Nation,

---

233 Hebrews 6:9.
234 2 Timothy 1:9.
235 Ephesians 4:1.
236 Romans 13:3.
237 Acts 1:25.

that they too much contented themselves with only teaching and exhorting the People, without sharply reproving and rebuking of them for the Sins and Vices wherein they lived.

Being such a Reprover of the unfruitful Works of Darkness, he was the fitter Person for the Office of a *Ruling Elder*, which he did now sustain and exercise, and the Duties whereof he did very faithfully discharge.

[61] He was not at all for the conniving at the Sins of his Brethren, nor willing to suffer Sin on them; when therefore Offenders were to be dealt with, he searched out Matters very diligently, and examined strictly into the Nature and Degrees of the Faults and Offences whereof they were guilty, and would sharply reprove them for their Sins, endeavouring with all his Might to convince them of the Evil of what they appeared to be justly charged with, and would most affectionately press them to a thorow[238] and hearty Repentance of their Miscarriages: all which he performed in such a manner as did plainly discover, that he was himself grieved and distressed on the account of the Sins and Faults of his Brethren, as I have many times observed.

As he was an *Elder that ruled well in the Church of God*,[239] so he did much more know how to rule his own House, tho, to his great Grief, some of his Children[240] behaved not themselves as they ought to have done.

He was constant and devout in his Family Worship, frequently read the Scriptures in his House before Morning and Evening Prayer, especially on *Sabbath* Days he did constantly do so; he then used to sing Psalms also.

It was likewise his constant Custom before he prayed, to let drop some serious and savoury Sentences in his Family, by way of Instruction, Exhortation, or Admonition, as he judged necessary.

He missed not of a considerable Share of those Afflictions, as Chastisements, which such that are *without, are Bastards and not Sons*:[241] for, beside the Trouble he met with from the Miscarriages of some of his own Children,[242] and the Hatred and Persecution which he endured from such of his Countrymen, as could not endure so strict a Discipline as he was for maintaining; he was also much vexed by some Controversies which arose, betwixt the *Indians* of the Place where he lived, and some of their *English* Neighbours, respecting the Title of the Land which the *Indians* claimed,

---

238 Thorough.

239 1 Timothy 5:17.

240 His children included David Ompany, Samuel Ompany, Naomy Sosamon (*IC*, 218), and Rachel Wompanummoo (*IC*, 212–16*). *WGH*, 115, 118, 146, 348, 350.

241 Hebrews 12:8.

242 His son David was sued for trespass; Samuel was sued for debt at least five times and involved in a legal suit for stealing. *WGH*, 115, 118, 146, 348, 350.

the Trouble whereof fell much on him, he being a leading Man in the Place: But I believe he acted with a good Conscience in that Affair.[243]

While he was under these Troubles, he discoursed frequently of the Frailty of human Life, and of the Vanity and Uncertainty of all sublunary[244] Enjoyments; but did [62] so more frequently and feelingly in the last Year or two of his Life, than before he had done. And the Winter before he dy'd, he spake frequently of *this World* as *none of his Home*, or *resting Place*, and of *Heaven* as the *Place of his Desires*, whither he hoped and expected shortly to go. He now also frequently magnified the Mercy of God discovered in the Redemption and Salvation of Sinners, by Jesus Christ our Lord.

About this time he more than once intimated, both to his own Family and others, that he was apprehensive that the time of his Dissolution was at hand; and withal declared his Willingness to leave this World, whenever it should please God to call him out of it: and so lively was the Impression he now had of the Shortness of his time here, that he seldom went out in a Morning without letting drop some Words to his Family, intimating the Uncertainty of his ever coming home alive again to them.

Thus, as at other times, he did on the fifth or sixth Day of *March*, in the Year 1716-7; for having early in the Morning of that Day instructed his Family, and prayed with them, as he used to do, and having told his Wife[245] and Children that he felt a Pain in his Side, which was not yet very troublesome to him, he went on a necessary Business from his own House in *Christian-Town* to *Edgartown*, about seven or eight Miles, telling them, that he designed to return home in the Evening if he could: but immediately subjoining, that *many went out in the Morning, and never returned to their Houses any more*, he did himself go out and do so; for having gotten well to the said Place, and done the Business he went on, he returned homeward in the Evening of the same Day, but never arrived alive at his *own House*, and was the next Day found dead in the Path, a Mile or two short of *it*; what the Cause of his Death was, never being discovered.

[63] EXAMPLE XXI.
JOASH PANU, *a Pastor of an* Indian *Church in* Martha's Vineyard, *who died* August 1720.

JOash Panu was a Son of *Annampanu*, otherwise call'd *Maattie*,[246] who, if he were not a good Man when his Son *Joash* was born to him, yet thro'

---

243 Some of the land transactions that bear his name are DCRD 1.123, 154, 417–18, and 9.400. He is also a witness to Japheth Hannit's will: DCRP 1.25a. *WGH*, 118, 127.
244 Inferior, ephemeral, and worldly, as opposed to spiritual (*OED*).
245 Elizabeth Ompany (*IC*, 212). *WGH*, 119, 316.
246 *IC*, 109–10*.

Grace became such a one, many Years before he dy'd; but more of him afterwards. The Woman by whom he had this Son, and some other Children, was a pious Daughter of that *Mittark* before mentioned.

When the *Joash* I am speaking of was a little Boy, some body was so kind to him as to put a little *Rum* in his Mouth, that so he might have an early Taste of that *Liquor* which our *Indians* do much admire; but it seems that this sort of Drink was somewhat too hot for the young and tender Mouth of the Lad; he therefore suddenly spurted it out, manifesting some Dislike of it. His Mother being present, and observing how he acted, spake to this Purpose to him, *Is this too hot for you, and so very offensive, as by your acting it seems to be? how much more would the Flames of Hell be so? and yet for drinking too much of this sort of Drink, there be many that go to that Place of Torment.*[247] *take heed therefore that you abstain therefrom, be sure to avoid the excessive Use of it.* This seasonable Word of Caution and Advice which his Mother thus gave to him, made such an Impression on the young Heart of this her Son, that he never forgot it as long as he lived; nor did he, so far as I can understand, ever taste one Drop more of that sort of Drink to his dying Day; neither did he use to drink any other sort of Drink that was strong or spirituous.[248]

I doubt not but that the pious Mother of this Son did in his Youth give him many other good Lessons, besides that already mention'd; but he was not put to School to learn to read and write in the proper Season of it, his Parents then living in a Place where there was no School at hand for him to go to, and 'tis like his Father was then too unmindful of things of that Nature: However, for the supplying of what was thus wanting, he did himself, when he was grown up to some Years of [64] Discretion, set on learning to read and write, and did, without the Help of a School, (being only assisted therein by such as he could in a transient way get to instruct him) make such Proficiency in the Work which he so happily attempted, that he learned to read *Indian* well, and advanced so far in learning to read *English* also, that an *English Bible* and *Concordance* was of considerable Use to him. He learned to write so well also, that he penn'd the Heads of the Sermons he preached, as also of those which he heard preached by others; and kept in writing Memorandums of such things as he thought should not be forgotten.

He appeared serious while he was but a *young Man*, was not known to be given to any Vice, nor much addicted to follow after such Vanities as most young Persons are too prone to pursue: and there's the more reason to think he was truly pious, while he was but a young Man, for that as soon as he was married, he did without any Delay set up the Worship of

---

247 Luke 16:28.
248 Beer was another common form of alcohol on the island and in Massachusetts generally.

God in his Family; and also frequently prayed to God in secret; especially in the Morning when he first rose, it was his Custom thus to do, as the pious Woman that was his Wife, who is yet living, does assure me.[249]

He was likewise very diligent in reading the holy Scriptures, and such other good Books as, being in the *Indian* Tongue, he could read with Advantage: and such as were acquainted with him, looked on him as a very just and honest Man in his Dealings with his Neighbours, and one whose Word might be rely'd on in what he spake or promised to them. The *English* as well as the *Indians* gave him this Testimony.

He did not join himself to any particular Church of Christ, as soon as the People of God thought him qualified for their Communion; but being concerned that he might approve himself to God in what he did, defer'd his asking an Admission to the Privileges of a Church State, until he was himself in some good measure satisfied, that he was qualified to enjoy them: nor did he ever after his Admission to them, by any Sin or Miscarriage, dishonour the Name of God, or scandalize any of his People, but *walked worthy of the Vocation wherewith he was called.*[250]

When he was called to the Work of the Ministry, he did undoubtedly study to approve himself to God in that [65] Work. He diligently read the Scriptures, and studied them; and not being furnished with Commentaries, was the more frequent in asking the meaning of difficult Places in them, and used also to propound many other profitable Questions about the Things of God and his Kingdom. He was a most zealous Preacher against the Sins of his own Countrymen, *crying aloud, and not sparing* to shew the *People their Transgressions.*[251] And by the just Complaints he sometimes made of the Wickedness of many of his Neighbours, I cannot but think he was one that did *sigh and cry for all their Abominations.*[252]

Nor did he thus shew to the People their Sins, without letting them know how they might be saved from them: he therefore preached *Jesus Christ* to his Hearers, shewing them who he was, and how he came into the World to save his People from their Sins, and what he did and underwent to that End; as also how sinful Men might come to have an Interest in him, and in all the Benefits, which by his righteous Life, and bitter Death, he purchased for them; and what would become of all those that refused to comply with the Terms of the Gospel.

Being so good a Man, and so faithful a Preacher, when one *Sowamog*[253] died, who was Mr. *Japheth's* immediate Successor in the Pastoral Office,

---

249 His wife, Naomi Panu, was still alive in 1732. *IC*, 247; *WGH*, 234, 345.

250 Ephesians 4:1.

251 Isaiah 58:1.

252 Ezekiel 9:4.

253 In contrast to Joash Panu, Sowamog was chosen against the advice of the commissioners. He was ordained on September 29, 1712: *WGH*, 315. His wife Pamie is mentioned in *IC*, 217.

the Flock over which these had been Overseers could think of no fitter Person to fill up that Vacancy, than this *Joash* was; to him therefore they committed the Care of their Souls, and he was accordingly solemnly ordained to be their Pastor in the Year 1716, and did faithfully discharge the Trust so commited to him, as long as his Life and Strength lasted, which was but about four Years.

He was humbly sensible of his Insufficiency for the great Work to which he was called, complained much of his own Ignorance and want of Learning; and would sometimes say to a Person whom he thought to have more Knowledge than himself,

> I would desire you to instruct me in my Duty, and shew me how the Affairs of the Church ought to be managed: we *Indians* are ignorant, and know not what to do, without Counsel and Direction from the *English*.

Nor was this merely a Compliment in him; for he constantly asked and received Advice in his Management of his Church-Affairs.

[66] Being thus willing to learn, he seem'd daily to increase in Knowledge, and I believe grew in Grace also. The longer he continued in the Work of the Ministry, the more zealous and earnest his Discourses appeared to be; nor were his Sermons impertinent, unstudied Discourses, but had many very good things in them, and these delivered in something of Order and Method.

In his Discipline he did constantly bear Testimony against *all the unfruitful Works of Darkness*;[254] very zealously reproving Offenders for their Miscarriages, and endeavouring to reclaim and reform them: *Drunkenness* especially was a Sin which he did most earnestly testify against, he spake of it with the greatest Indignation, and could hardly believe that it was lawful for Christians (except in extraordinary Cases)[255] so much as to taste of those Liquors, by the drinking whereof God is so much dishonoured, and so many Souls destroy'd. In discoursing of strong Drink and Drunkenness, he made great Use of that Text, *Wine is a Mocker, and strong Drink is raging, he that is deceived thereby is not wise:*[256] and he used in his Prayer to lament that there were so many Drunkards amongst the People of his own Nation.

The Overseers are the members of the "Honourable Company for the Propagation of the Gospel," to which *Indian Converts* is dedicated (*IC*, iii). The commissioners funded the Mayhew missions and oversaw practical affairs including the distribution of funds. *HMV*, 1:220.

254 Ephesians 5:11.

255 Although they strongly disapproved of drunkenness, Puritans were remarkably more liberal with (and addicted to) alcohol than one might suspect. Conroy, "Puritans in Taverns," 29–60.

256 Proverbs 20:1.

He was long sick of a consumptive Distemper[257] before he dy'd, which I have often thought he brought on himself by his excessive Labours. Not long after the Beginning of his Illness, he told his Wife and Children,[258] that he would not have them expect his Recovery; for he thought the Illness which he was under would end in his Death, and that he was going to his heavenly Father.

I saw him frequently in the time of his Sickness, and heard him utter many pious and savoury Expressions, which I cannot now repeat. However I remember that he did not appear to be at all dismay'd at the Thoughts of his approaching Dissolution; but said he was willing to die whenever God pleased that he should do so, whether it was sooner or latter. He owned himself to be a sinful Creature, and acknowledged, that if God should mark his Iniquity against him, he could not stand before him; yet he professed Hopes of Eternal Life *thro' the Merits of Jesus Christ his only Saviour.* [259]

His Church visiting him a little before his Death, he earnestly exhorted them to persevere in the Fear and Service of the Lord their God; and at their Desire, gave them his dying Counsel, respecting a Successor in the [67] Pastoral Care and Charge of their Souls: but they did not see Cause to take his Advice in this last Particular.

He towards the close of his Life did most earnestly exhort, and solemnly charge those of his own House, to *fear God, and depart from Iniquity;*[260] and particularly, that they should take heed of the Sin of Drunkenness, to which so many were inclined. And he then told them, that if they took his Advice in those things, they might again see him with Joy in his Father's Kingdom.

EXAMPLE XXII

ABEL WAUWOMPUHQUE, *Deacon of the* Indian *Church on the West End of* Martha's Vineyard, *and a Preacher of the Word of God at* Nashouohkamuk.

THis *Abel Waumompuhque*[261] was a Son of a godly Man of the same Name[262], who was Brother to *Mittark* before mentioned, who were both

---

257 Probably tuberculosis, also known as pulmonary consumption.

258 His children included Joseph Paneu (*IC*, 250), Laban Panu (*IC*, 247–50*), and probably Joash Panu, who kept school. *WGH*, 140, 234, 345, 355.

259 This phrase was commonly invoked in wills.

260 Proverbs 3:7.

261 An Indian laborer and deacon who was involved in numerous court cases and deeds. *WGH*, 360.

262 Abel Wauwompuhque Senior, a magistrate, preacher, and ruling elder. *IC*, 98–99*; *WGH*, 125.

of them Sons of *Nohtooksact*,[263] a *Sachim* that came from the *Massachusets Bay* many Years since.[264]

Our *Abel* was in his younger Years, and while yet in a State of Nature,[265] inclined to the same youthful Vanities as unconverted young Men generally are, and would sometimes drink to Excess; but when it pleased God to work a saving Change in his Heart, there followed thereon an evident Change in his Life, he then departed from the Sins which before he loved and practiced, and never, as did appear, return'd to them any more.

After he was married, and had some Children, he made a publick Profession of Religion, and joined as Member in full Communion to the Church whereof *John Tackanash* was Pastor; and for ever afterwards, so far as I can learn, walked worthy of the Vocation wherewith he was called. I never heard that he was once overtaken with strong Drink, from that time to the Day of his Death; or guilty of any other scandalous Offence whatsoever. And tho some of his Children were Persons of no good Character,[266] yet I never understood that he countenanced them in their Wickedness, or at all endeavoured to conceal their Faults; but on the contrary, always bore a Testimony against them.

He was a Person of good natural Parts, a ready Wit, and a very cautious and obliging Conversation; and seem'd [68] to be a very cordial Friend to the *English*, by whom he was generally well respected, and esteemed a sober and good Man.

It was not many Years after he had made an open Profession of Religion, before he was called to preach the Gospel occasionally to his own Countrymen; and was quickly esteemed and spoken of as a Person apt to teach, and would probably have proved as knowing and able a Man as any the *Indians* have had among them, had not that happened to him of which I shall now give an Account.

In the Year 1690, the *Indians* of *Martha's Vineyard* had a sore Fever among them, which proved mortal to many of them; of which number several of those who were most esteemed for Piety were a part.[267]

---

263 Also a sachem of Gay Head, mentioned in *IC*, 109. *WGH*, 155.

264 The Massachusett and Wampanoag peoples were closely connected linguistically and politically, as exemplified by their alliance against the Narragansetts in the early seventeenth century.

265 A "state of nature" is a translation of a Latin phrase referring to the "unregenerate moral condition of mankind, as opposed to a state of grace" (*OED*).

266 His known children are Noah Abel, a deacon and justice from 1729 to 1752 but also a debtor; Abel Abel, a preacher and debtor; Caleb Abel, sued for stealing a saddle; Cornelius Abel, a debtor who drowned; and Elias Able. *WGH*, 195, 213, 237–38, 261; *IC*, 70. It is worth noting that being a debtor would not be enough to qualify someone as being of "no good character": many of the Indian converts were debtors, and an account sheet from September 1715 records Experience Mayhew himself as owing money. MVHS 974.42, Doc R10, Box 5S, Env. 4.

267 As David Silverman notes (*Faith and Boundaries*, 126–27), the epidemic killed more than one hundred adults, three-quarters of whom were pious Indians.

With this Fever was our good *Abel* seized, and very sorely visited, insomuch that his Life was in a manner despaired of: but it pleased God in his great Goodness to spare the Man, only taking his hearing from him; so that after this he never heard a Word more so long as he lived.

This was a great Affliction to a Man who was much delighted in Conversation, and also a great Hindrance to his profiting by those Discourses of others, wherewith he might have been instructed and edified: However I have heard him say, that it may be God aimed at his Good in bringing such an Affliction on him,[268] and that it might have been worse with him if he had had the Use of his Ears than now it was.

Our *Abel* was not discouraged by this Disadvantage from endeavouring to gain more Knowledge than before he had: for having no Use of his Ears, he made the more Use of his Eyes; he took a great Delight in Books, and made much Use of them, was not willing to be without any that, being in his own Language, he could well read and understand; he made use of some *English* Books also: he would also ask many necessary Questions, and not be satisfied till either by writing, or some other Means, he had obtained an Answer to them.

He could understand Signs very readily:[269] but that which was yet more observable in him was, that by observing the Motion of the Person's Mouth that spake to him, if they spake very deliberately, he could understand almost every Word that they said, if not at the first yet at the Re[69]petition of the same Words to him; by which Means there was scarce any News going, but he knew what it was.

Being so notable a Man, he was not allowed to leave off *preaching*, when he was obliged to leave off *hearing*; and though he could not now modulate his Voice as he formerly could have done, yet he did good Service.

After the Death of *Deacon Jonathan Amos* before mentioned in our 15th Example, this *Abel* was chosen into that Office in his stead, and served faithfully in it as long as he lived, still continuing to preach occasionally as he had done before. But after Mr. *Japheth* his Pastor dy'd in 1712, he became a constant Preacher in his Room, and remained so as long as he lived.

---

268 This comment reflects good Calvinist doctrine: everything God did was the best, even though humans' often limited comprehension could not see the good in the details. This idea flies in the face of later American critics of Calvinism, who felt that predestination was immoral because it made God the author of evil: see, e.g., Channing's *Moral Argument against Calvinism* (1820). Here even seemingly "bad" events are truly good—it is just that the individual's understanding of the big picture is limited.

269 There is a long history of sign language on Martha's Vineyard, primarily because of the history of genetic deafness in the white community. The first known deaf white man arrived on the island in 1694, but there was a substantial community from the same gene pool by 1669. Nora Groce argues that a preexisting sign language system probably came with this community. Groce, *Everyone Here Spoke Sign Language*, 23, 35, 71.

I have heard him several times, and could not but observe, that he always expressed himself with great Earnestness and Affection; and did plainly hold forth Jesus Christ and him crucified to his Hearers, inviting them to come to him and lay hold of him, for eternal Life, and Blessedness, and denouncing Wrath to the uttermost in devouring Fire, and Everlasting Burnings, on all such as despise and disobey him. I also observed, that he cried aloud and spared not, to *shew the People their Transgressions and their Sins,*[270] telling them plainly of their Drunkenness, Whoredom, Thieving, Lying, Sabbath-breaking, &c. and letting them know, that those who do such things *should not inherit the Kingdom of God.*[271]

I have also heard him insisting with great Earnestness on the Necessity of Holiness in such as minister about holy things, and proving the same from *Isaiah* lii. ii. *Be ye clean that bear the Vessels of the Lord.*

In Prayer he used also to be very earnest, appearing therein to wrestle with God with all his Might: and I have sometimes heard him express his Sense of the Goodness of God to him, in granting gracious Answers to his Petitions; particularly, once in raising a Grandchild of his from the very Mouth of the Grave, and restoring it to Health, tho it had sometimes seemed to be quite dead.

He prayed frequently and earnestly for the *English* Ministers and Churches, and blessed God for the great Benefits which from them the *Indians* had received, in their bringing the Gospel to them.

[70] Tho he could not hear, yet he diligently attended the publick Worship of God when others preached; and that his doing so might be of the more Advantage to him, he used when he could to get some body or other to sit by him, and write the Heads of the Sermon preached, and shew them to him; or otherwise at least to shew him the Texts of Scripture quoted in the Discourse. He also often borrowed the Notes of such as used any, when they preached to the *Indians.*

As he was a devout Man in the publick Duties of Religion, so he was also very constant and serious in his Family Worship.

His Custom was to read a while in the *Practice of Piety*[272] before Morning and Evening Prayer, in which good Book he very much delighted; and while he had his hearing, he used also to sing Psalms in his House.

---

270 Isaiah 58:1.

271 1 Corinthians 6:9.

272 First printed in 1602, Lewis Bayley's *Practise of pietie* became the most popular devotional manual in seventeenth-century New England. John Eliot's Algonquian translation of it, *Manitowompae Pomantamoonk,* first appeared in 1665. Like the Bible and sermons, New England devotional manuals were a form of social literature, often being read within prayer groups, including all female prayer groups. Bayley's work offered practical advice for worshipers, such as "prayers for many different occasions, . . . advice on reading the Bible, practicing closet devotions, singing psalms, and observing the Sabbath." See Hayes, *Colonial Woman's Bookshelf,* 30, 43.

He frequently exhorted his Children to the Performance of the great Duties of Religion, and also reproved and rebuked them for their Miscarriages; and would sometimes tell them they made their Father weep when they took bad Courses.

There were three of his Sons who came to untimely Ends, *viz.* that *Elias*[273] and *Caleb*, whose Confessions are set down in Chapter third, and one called *Cornelius*, who was drowned not long since: which sad Providence made a deep Impression on the Heart of the good Man; yet he behaved himself very Christian-like under these Dispensations.

After the *Psalter* was printed for the Use of the *Indians* in 1709,[274] this godly Man delighted much to read and meditate therein; he therefore carried it about with him wherever he went to work, and whenever he sat down to rest him, he would look into it.

Being a *good Man*, he was a *merciful one*, and in that respect well qualify'd for the Office he sustained; he therefore wisely and compassionately considered the Poor, and was willing to do all that lay in his Power for their Relief.

He foretold that his Death was approaching, not far off, about a Year or two before he dy'd, when he seemed to others likely to live many Years longer; both to my self and others he thus gave notice of his End: but I thought what he said was but a mere Conjecture, and therefore did very little regard it: however, as he said so it prov'd.

[71] When in his last Sickness I visited him, I heard him express himself in such Language as became a dying Christian. He appeared not to be at all terrified at the Thoughts of his Dissolution, which he daily expected, but manifested a Willingness to leave the World, whenever it should please God to call him out of it; and also expressed his Hopes of a better Life, whenever his present Life should end.

He exhorted his Neighbours before he dy'd to take care that the *House of God did not lie waste*,[275] when he was laid in his Grave, and could not promote the repairing of it, as he had been wont to do. He also pressed

---

273 Elias Able (alias Elias Wauwompuque) was married to Hannah Tobe, the daughter of Japhet Hannit. They had at least four children: Sarah Gershom (alias Sarah Accouch), who was probably murdered by her stepson Jonathan Gershom; Bethia Abell, a spinster who kept a school; Jedidah Whitten, who married Benjamin Whitten; and Elizabeth Abel, a debtor. *WGH*, 127, 194, 196–97, 226, 261.

274 The publication of Experience Mayhew's Algonquian translation of *The Massachuset psalter* (1709) was an important milestone for the religious community on Martha's Vineyard. Although John Eliot's *Mamusse wunneetupanatamwe* (1663) had contained a metrical version of the Psalms, Mayhew's knowledge of *Wôpanâak*, particularly the version spoken on the island, was unsurpassed. See Scott, *Early Colonial Houses of Martha's Vineyard*, 3:231. By printing the book in parallel "columns of Indian and English," Mayhew also took an important step in aiding bilingual education on the Vineyard.

275 Perhaps a reference to Haggai 1:4.

them diligently to uphold the Worship of God in the Place; and did more particularly inculcate this Charge on a Son of his own, of whom he entertained some Hopes that he would serve the Lord in the Work of the Ministry, as he himself had done.

He told his Wife and Children, that he *would not have them much concerned about him, but rather be concerned to be true Worshippers of the Lord their God; for as for me,* said he, *I have a firm Persuasion, that when I shall leave this World, I shall leave all my Troubles behind me. And tho now I cannot hear, and can hardly see, but am every way weak and feeble; yet I shall shortly both see and hear, and walk, and leap in the Presence of the Lord.*

He in his Sickness very frequently called on God, and when others pray'd with and for him, tho he could not hear what they said, yet he himself still appeared very intent, and was supposed to be very seriously engaged in that Duty. And after he was speechless, he lifted up his Hands and Eyes towards Heaven, the Place where doubtless his Heart and Treasure were.

He dy'd *October* 1*st,* 1722.

[72] A
SUPPLEMENT
TO
The First Chapter:

Giving a more general Account of some other Godly Ministers.

BEsides the Persons already named, as Examples of Piety, in this Chapter, there have been several other Preachers and Deacons, who have been justly esteemed godly Men; and therefore such as ought not to be forgotten: but partly because I can give no very particular Account of them, and partly because a larger Account would swell the Essay now under my hand, beyond its intended Bigness, I shall make but a very general Mention of the other Persons whom I here design to name; and they are these here following, *viz.*

I. *Panupuhquah.*[276] This Man was an elder Brother of that *William Lay* before mentioned, *Example* the ninth.[277] He was one of the first *Indian* Preachers on this Island, and used to preach the Word of God at the Place now called *Nashouohkamuk*, alias *Chilmark*, and was accounted a very sober and godly Man. I cannot learn how long ago he dy'd, but I suppose well nigh sixty Years before the writing hereof in 1724.

II. *John Amanhut.*[278] This *John* was a Son of *Wannamanhut*,[279] who had for his Father a Sachim of the *Massachusets Bay*, by whom being sent hither to take care of the Rights he here claimed, he settled on the Island, and became a *Christian*, or *praying Man*: and his Son *John* being also a serious Professor of Religion, and one who could read, and was well versed in the Principles of Christianity, he was imployed as a Preacher of [73] the Gospel among his own Countrymen, and did good Service therein. He maintained a good Character as long as he lived, and was thought to die well. He was the Father of *Hosea Manhut*,[280] now one of

---

276 Father of Dinah Ahhunnut (*IC*, 126, 138–40*), who married Henry Ahhunnut (*IC*, 126–28*, 138). Henry (also known as Ianoxso) was the son of Ompohhunnut and hence a nephew of Mittark, son of Panunnut. *WGH*, 188, 334, 346.

277 *IC*, 24–28*.

278 Husband of Mary (Wana)manhut, alias Chachaconnonashk (*IC*, 217). They were married by 1666, when she attended a sermon at Takemmy. *WGH*, 201, 250.

279 The sachem at Takemmy who was married to Ushanapetow, a woman of nobility, also the father of Nanawit. John Ananhut, the half brother of Nanawit, appears to have been the son by a nonroyal mother, as he was involved in a controversy over his age and nobility status. In contrast, Nanawit's son Obediah Nananit was called a ruler on a Christiantown petition from 1741. See *WGH*, 148, 200–201, 249–50. For discussion of Indian marriage in colonial New England and its relationship to sachemships, see Plane, "Customary Laws of Marriage," and Plane, *Colonial Intimacies*, 153–77.

280 *IC*, 207, 217, 219, 269–70.

the *Pastors* of the *Indian* Church on the West End of this Island,[281] and of a very pious young Woman *Abigail Manhut*,[282] here after mentioned. I think he dy'd in *March* 1672.

III. *Lazarus*, called by the *Indians Kokesap*.[283] He was a very serious and godly Man, and a Person of a very exemplary Life and Conversation. He was the first *Deacon* of the Church whereof *John Tackanash* was Pastor, and dy'd at *Nunpang* in *Edgertown*, some Years before his Pastor did. I suppose about the Year 1677, he was one of the *Poor of the World*, but generally accounted by good People that knew him, *rich in Faith, and an Heir of God's Kingdom*.[284] He lived to be an old Man, and never married.

IV. *Joel Sims*.[285] This *Joel* was the Son of an *Indian* called *Pockqsimme*, and was well instructed in his Youth, so that when he grew up, he seemed to be a Person of better Knowledge than most of his Neighbours; and then appearing also to be seriously religious, and of a blameless Life, he was called to preach the Gospel at *Christian-Town*, the Place in which he lived, and was much esteemed for the Gifts and Graces wherewith he was endued. He dy'd while he was but a young Man, I think about the Year 1680, and was much lamented by good People among the *Indians*.

V. *James Sepinnu*.[286] This *James* was a Brother to *John Tackanash*, already frequently mentioned. He was a serious Professor of Religion, and a Man of a blameless Life and Conversation; and being also a Person of good Knowledge, he was called to preach the Word of God to the People of his own Nation, chiefly at a Place now called *Okokame*, or *Christian Town*, where he dy'd, if I mistake not, in the Year 1683.

VI. *Wompamog*,[287] commonly by the *English* called *Mr. Sam*. He was a *Sachim* of the East End of *Martha's Vineyard*, who, when he heard the Gospel preached, professed that he believed it; and having first learned to read, and been well instructed in the Principles of Christianity, he not

281 He was also a teacher at Christiantown and an Indian Justice of Tisbury. The commissioners allowed him to build an English-style house in 1723. Although Hosea is mentioned numerous times in passing in *Indian Converts*, he does not receive his own biography, since he did not die until after the book was published. *WGH*, 119–20.

282 *IC*, 219–22*.

283 Born ca. 1590. *WGH*, 340.

284 James 2:5.

285 Also known as Joell Poxim (*IC*, 184, 255), he was the father of Hannah Sissetom (*IC*, 184–87*) and hence probably related by marriage to the family of Cheeschumuck, the sachem of Holmes Hole. See *IC*, 148, 164; *WGH*, 144, 214, 335, 349.

286 James was paid as Indian schoolmaster, 1659–63. In 1661–62, he and eight others received roughly £3.75 each for their work each year. *HMV*, 1:237–38; *WGH*, 331.

287 Also known as Wapamauk or the "Sachim of Sanchakantacket," a place near what became Edgartown. He is the author of or mentioned in various documents in *Native Writings*: 1:77, 127, 205; 2:776. *WGH*, 97.

only joined himself to that Church of Christ whereof that *John Tackanash* was Pastor, but became himself a zealous Preacher to the People whose [74] *Sachim* he was. I have seen him divers times when I was a Youth, and remember that he was a Man of a very grave Deportment, and very full of serious and godly Discourse. I know he was charged with some Faults; but pleading his Innocency, nothing scandalous could be prov'd against him.

Some of our *English* People who were best acquainted with him, have given me a good Character of him. And I am credibly informed, that he triumphed over the King of Terrors at his Death. I can't certainly tell in what Year he dy'd, but I think it was in *October* 1689.

VII. *Kestumin.*[288] This Man was the first *Deacon* of the Church whereof the famous *Hiacoomes*[289] was Pastor. How early he was converted, I have never been informed: however, he was esteemed by all that were acquainted with him, as a Person of a very blameless Conversation, undoubted Piety, and an excellent Spirit. He was a devout Worshipper of God in Christ, praying constantly, in his House, and sometimes in publick also. He was a diligent Instructor of his own Family, and used to give many good Exhortations to his Neighbours. He faithfully and prudently discharged the Duties of the Office to which he was called. He was the Husband of one Wife only, and she a very pious Woman, and had, if no more, one very faithful and pious Child, *viz.* the prudent and godly *Sarah Hannit, Japheth's* Wife, hereafter to be mentioned. I remember the Man, and have heard him pray very affectionately, but cannot give a particular Account of him, nor can I learn what his last Words were.

VIII. *Job Peosin.*[290] This *Job* was a Preacher of the Word of God at *Sanchekantacket*, in *Edgartown*. And tho it must be confessed, that he discovered some Infirmity, in craving of strong Drink more than he ought to have done; yet I must say, that I cannot but hope, that he had the Root of the Matter in him, and did sincerely endeavour to mortify that Lust which did too *easily beset him.*[291] He preached, prayed, and discoursed like a Man that had a Principle of Grace in him, and was on all other Accounts, as far as I know, blameless; nor was he ever *drunk* that I know of, tho he sometimes drank more than he should have done.

[75] He lived to a great Age, and carried himself like a good Christian when he drew near to his End; for he then gave much good Counsel

---

288 Brother of Matthew Nahnehsheschat (*IC*, 87–88*). *WGH*, 156, 266.

289 *IC*, 1–12*.

290 A landowner in Sanchakantacket also known as "old Job," father of Isaac Tuckommy and Deborah Peoson. Deborah was probably the wife of Abel Sesetom, the son of the Indian minister Thomas Sussetom. Job's son Isaac was convicted of selling rum. *WGH*, 109–10, 122, 158.

291 Hebrews 12:1.

to his Relations and Neighbours, confessed his Unworthiness of Eternal Life, and yet professed Hopes of Everlasting Blessedness thro' the Mercy of God, and Merits of his Son Jesus Christ, and his Wilingness to die and leave the World, on the account of that Hope which he had in him. He dy'd in the Year 1723.

There have been several other Preachers among our *Indians*, which, tho I have had some Hopes, that they were not utterly destitute of the saving Graces of God's Spirit, yet such were the Infirmities with which they conflicted, that I think not convenient to mention them as Examples of Piety: nor would I have any to think, that because I mention them not, I look'd on them as such as were utter Strangers to a Life of Grace and Holiness.

[76] CHAP. II

Containing an Account of several Indian MEN, *not in any*
Church Office, *who have appeared to be truly good Men.*

WHEREVER God raiseth up a godly Ministry, and setteth them to
Work among any People, it seemeth more than probable that he hath
some Elect Souls, that he designs to extend his special saving Grace to,
and will by such a Ministry effectually call, and bring savingly home to
himself: But now, that God has raised up such a Ministry among our
Indians, seems evident by what has been said in the foregoing Chapter,
wherein I have instanced in a very considerable number of *Indian* Ministers, who have appeared to be truly godly.

I shall therefore now proceed to mention some that have not been
Ministers of the Word of God, nor sustained any Ecclesiastical Office
in our *Indian* Churches, who have yet been looked on as pious Persons;
and shall in this Chapter only instance in several *Men* that I judge so to
have been; purposing also to give an Account of some godly *Women* and
Children in the two next.

EXAMPLE I.

MIOHQSOO,[292] *an* Indian *of* Nunpang, *within the Bounds
of* Edgartown, *who was converted in the Year* 1646.

AFter the memorable *Hiacoomes*[293] had embraced the Christian Religion
in the Year 1643, he joined with Mr. *Mayhew,*[294] by whom he had been
instructed in the *Mysteries of God's Kingdom,* in an *Essay* to make known
those *Mysteries* to the rest of the *Indians* living on the [77] same Island
with them; but for the present, these could only treat with the said *Indians* in a private Way, about the Things of God, a publick Audience not
being yet attainable: nor were there many of them who were privately
instructed, that seemed much to regard the *great Things of God's Law,*[295]
that were declared to them, but rather looked on them as *a strange
Thing:*[296] and especially the *Sachims,* and chief Men among the *Indians,*

---

292 Father of Rachel Amos (*IC,* 152–54*), wife of Jonathan Amos (*IC,* 37–42*); David Okeiso,
who attended sermons and is mentioned in *Native Writings,* 1:81, 93, 115; and John Meoxo, who
also attended church services. Another son was lost at sea when he sailed for England with
Thomas Mayhew Jr. in 1657. *WGH,* 197, 259, 273, 290, 408; *HMV,* 1:227.
293 *IC,* 1–12*.
294 Thomas Mayhew the younger (1621–1657), grandfather of Experience Mayhew.
295 Hosea 8:12.
296 Hosea 8:12.

would not give any Countenance to that Religion which was then proposed to them; but did on the contrary most of them, either openly or secretly oppose it.

Thus Things remained till the Year 1646. at which time the *Indians* being visited with a soreDistemper[297] which God sent among them, and made mortal to many of them, but apparently less so to those who had given any Countenance to the great Truths that had been proposed to them, and *Hiacoomes* and his Family, who openly professed the same, were scarcely at all hurt by it:[298] Being, I say, thus visited by God, and observing the Distinction which he was then pleased to make betwixt those that favoured Religion, and such as did despise and reject it, they were many of them thereby put on a serious Consideration of the things which before they slighted; and some began earnestly to desire to have the Mysteries of Religion opened to them, and to hearken with great Attention to the Things that were by Mr. *Mayhew* and *Hiacoomes* preached among them.

About this time that *Miohqsoo* of whom I am speaking, being the chief Man of the Place where he lived, sent a Messenger in the Night to *Hiaccomes*, about five or six Miles, intreating him to come away to him: and *Hiacoomes* receiving the Message about break of Day, readily went to the said *Miohqsoo's* House, where when he came, there were many *Indians* gathered together, amongst which was *Tauwuhquatuck*,[299] the chief *Sachim* of that End of the Island, whom I shall have occasion again to mention.

Hiacoomes being come, *Miohqsoo* gladly received him, and told him what he desired of him; the Sum whereof was, *That he would shewhis Heart to them, and let them know how it stood towards God, and what they ought to do.*

Hiacoomes very gladly embraced this Call and Opportunity to instruct them, declaring to them all Things [78] which he himself had learned, concerning *God* the *Father, Son,* and *Holy Ghost,* shewing them what this *God* did for Mankind, and what their Duty was towards *him.*

Having finished his Speech, *Miohqsoo* asked him, How many Gods the *English* worshipped? *Hiacoomes* answered ONE, and no more. Whereupon *Miohqsoo* reckoned up about 37 principal Gods which he had;[300] and

---

297 It is unclear what this illness was, though its effect was severe. See Silverman, *Faith and Boundaries,* 22, 74.

298 This might be contrasted with the epidemic that ravaged the island in 1690, in which more than one hundred adult Wampanoags died, three-quarters of whom were pious Indians. Silverman, *Faith and Boundaries,* 126–27.

299 *IC*, 5, 80–82*, 282–85; *Native Writings,* 1:93, 109, 241. He was the first sachem to convert.

300 The Narragansetts also informed Roger Williams that they knew the names of thirty-seven gods. Simmons, *Spirit of the New England Tribes,* 41.

shall I, said he, *throw away all these 37 for the sake of one only?* What do you your self think, said *Hiacoomes?* for my part I have thrown away all these, and many more, some Years ago, and yet I am preserved as you see this Day. *You speak true,* said *Miohqsoo; and therefore I will throw away all my Gods too, and serve that one God with you.*

Miohqsoo having thus spoken, *Hiacoomes* proceeded more fully to instruct him, and the rest of the Company with him, and did, as *Miohqsoo* desired, open his Heart to them; he told them, that he did fear the great God only, and did greatly reverence his Son, who had suffered Death to satisfy the Wrath of God his Father, for all those that trust in him, and forsake their sinful Ways; and that the Spirit of God did work these things in the Hearts of the Children of Men. He told them also, that he was very sorry for his own Sins, and desired to be redeemed thro' Jesus Christ from them, and to walk according to *God's Commandments.*

Hiacoomes also now told these his poor Countrymen of the Sin and Fall of *Adam,* and what a dreadful Estate Mankind were thereby brought into; and did also boldly reckon up their own Sins to them, and charged them home on them,[301] as that of having many *Gods,* and going after *Pawwaws,* &c. And having thus opened his Heart to his Hearers, he concluded his Discourse by telling them, that if they could obtain such Hearts as, thro' Grace, he had, they should receive such Mercies as he did.

This Sermon *of Hiacoomes* being ended, several of his Hearers were much affected; and some of them said that now they had seen their Sins.

But it is time to return to *Miohqsoo.*

Miohqsoo having promised, as is above declared, to worship the *true God,* and serve him only, was as good as his Word; for he carry'd himself as a true Servant of God all the Days of his Life after it. Upon diligent Inquiry of such as knew him, I cannot understand that he was [79] ever known to be guilty of any considerable Fault after he made a Profession of Religion, but carry'd himself in all respects like a good Christian.

One thing in particular, wherein the sincere Piety of this *Miohqsoo* was discovered, I shall here relate. An *Indian* of some Note coming hither from the Main, good *Miohqsoo* fell into a Discourse with him, and told him many of the great Things of God, and of his Son, wherein he had been instructed; declaring also to him what a foolish and sinful People the *Indians* were, and how they might obtain the Pardon of all their Sins thro' *Jesus Christ,* the only Saviour of sinful Men; shewing him likewise what a good Life those lived, that were indeed the saved of the

---

301 "To charge home" is largely a military term meaning to bear down upon or attack (*OED*). It reflects Mayhew's vision of the struggle waged by Hiacoomes as part of the cosmic battle between good and evil.

Lord. And so greatly were they both affected with these things, that they continued their Discourse about them for near 24 Hours together, till their Strength was so spent, that they could discourse no longer. Among the Things which *Miohqsoo* now said to the Person with whom he discoursed, this was one, That true Believers did live above the World, and did keep worldly things always under their Feet; and this he said did appear in that, when they were either increased or diminished, it was neither the Cause of their Joy nor of their Sorrow; neither did they stoop so low as to regard them, but stood upright, with their Hearts heavenward, their whole Desire being after God, and their Joy in him only. Such a Christian it was much to be hoped this *Miohqsoo* was.

Miohqsoo himself being so good a Man, was very desirous that his Children should be so likewise; to this end he committed two of them, *viz.* a Son and a Daughter,[302] to the special Care and Charge of Mr. *Mayhew*,[303] who was very highly esteemed by him, being desirous that they should be well instructed. The Daughter will be afterwards mentioned; the Son Mr. *Mayhew* took with him, when he undertook that Voyage for *England*, in which he was lost, and all that went with him in the Ship, in the Year 1657.

After this *Miohqsoo* lived many Years, until he arrived to a great Age, and was looked on as a wise and good Man, both by the *English* and *Indians* that knew him. He frequently served his Generation in the Place of a Magistrate, and was esteemed faithful in the Discharge of that [80]Trust. The Year of his Death I cannot now find, nor can I give a more particular Account concerning him.

EXAMPLE II
TAWANQUATUCK,[304] *the first* Indian Sachim *that became a Christian on* Martha's Vineyard.

THis Person was the chief *Sachim* on the East End of *Martha's Vineyard*, where the *English* first settled in the Year 1642.

He was kind to the *English* at their first coming, and was, as I have been informed, willing to let them have Land to settle on; but several

---

302 Rachel Amos, *IC*, 152–54*. The name of the son is unknown.

303 Thomas Mayhew Jr., Experience Mayhew's grandfather.

304 Tawanquatuck is of further significance to those interested in gender studies, as his granddaughter Elizabeth Washaman (Wunnatuhquanmow) was one of a number of prominent female sachems of her generation in New England. Tawanquatuck's 1663 will left his lands to his grandchildren Joell and Wunnatuhquanmow: if both heirs were living at the time of his death, Joel was to have all of Tawanquatuck's land and property, and Wunatuhquanumow was to have her father Sakkagteanmou's land, as well as the tribute previously paid to her father by the

of his Council, or chief Men, called in *Indian Ahtoskouaog*, being much against his selling any Land to these *new Comers*, he to quiet them, gave several Parts of his *Sachimship* to them, and then sold to the *English* a considerable Part of what he reserved to himself, to make that Settlement on, now called *Edgartown*.[305]

But tho this *Sachim* was thus kind to the *English*, he did not presently see reason to imbrace their *Religion*; nor was he one of them that appeared as an Enemy thereto, being willing, as it seems, to consider what he did in a Matter of so great Importance.

However, in the Year 1646, when *Miohqsoo* above mentioned invited Hiacoomes to come to his House, and instruct him in the Religion which he professed, this *Tawanquatuck* was then present as an Auditor, with several other *Indians*, and in a short time after invited Mr. *Mayhew*[306] to preach publickly to his People, and he himself became a constant Hearer of him.

On Mr. *Mayhew's* first going to preach to the *Indians* on this Invitation, the *Sachim* told him,

> That a long time ago the *Indians* had wise Men among them, that did in a grave manner teach the People Knowledge; but they, *said he*, are dead, and their Wisdom is buried with; them and now Men live a giddy Life in Ignorance till they are white-headed, and tho ripe in Years, yet they go without Wisdom to their Graves.

He also told Mr. *Mayhew*, that he wonder'd the *English* should be almost thirty Years in the Country, and yet the *Indians* Fools still; but said he hoped the time of Know[81]ledge was now come. He then also (others joining with him in it) desired Mr. *Mayhew* to preach in a stated Course to the *Indians*, to make known the Word of God to them: and soon after going to Mr. *Mayhew's*, to encourage him to comply with his Request, told him that he should be to them as one that stands by a running River, filling many Vessels; *even so*, said he, *shall you fill us with Everlasting Knowledge*.

He likewise told Mr. *Mayhew*, that the reason why he desired him to preach to the *Indians* was, because he was desirous that the *Indians* should

---

Indians living on his land. See NCRD 2:39; *Native Writings*, 1:241, 2:780–81. After her grandfather's death Wunatuhquanumow became the squaw-sachem at Edgartown. *WGH*, 124–25, 132, 296. To satisfy debts, she was forced to sell much of her land to Englishmen and even her rights to drift whales (carcasses of stranded whales or whales that died at sea and either floated ashore or were found drifting). The erosion of the power and privileges of the sachemship during her lifetime reflects a general trend on the island from the end of the seventeenth to the middle of the eighteenth century. See Silverman, *Faith and Boundaries*, 136–38.

305 He also sold the Mayhews some of the lands at Chappaquiddick. *WGH*, 132.

306 Presumably Thomas Mayhew Jr.

grow more in Goodness, and that their Posterity might inherit Blessings after he was dead; and that he himself was also desirous to put the Word of God to his Heart, and to repent of, and throw away his Sins, that so after he should cease to live here, he might enjoy eternal Life in Heaven.

Mr. *Mayhew* complying with the pious Request of this good *Sachim*, and preaching to him, and as many of his People as were willing to come to hear him, the *Sachim* was hated and persecuted by such as were yet Enemies to the Christian Religion among the *Indians*. I shall here give one Instance of his Sufferings, and I shall set it down in Mr. *Mayhew's* own Words,[307] written on that Occasion about three Years after the thing happened,

> We had not, s*aith he*, long continued our Meeting, but the *Saggamore Tawanquatuck* met with a sad Trial; for being at a Weare,[308] where some *Indians* were fishing, where also there was an *English* Man present, as he lay along on a Mat on the Ground asleep, by a little light Fire, the Night being very dark, an *Indian* came down, as being ready fitted for the Purpose, and being about six or eight Paces off, let fly a broad-headed Arrow, purposing by all probability to drench the deadly Arrow in his Heart's Blood; but the Lord prevented it: for, notwithstanding all the Advantages he had, instead of the Heart he hit the Eye-brow, which like a Brow of Steel, turned the Point of the [82] Arrow, which glancing away, slit his Nose from the Top to the Bottom. A great Stir there was presently, the *Sagamore* sat up and bled much, but was thro' the Mercy of God not much hurt. The Darkness of the Night hid the Murderer, and he is not discovered to this Day.
>
> The next Morning I went to see the *Sagamore*, and found him praising God for his great Deliverance, both himself and all the *Indians* wondering that he was alive. The Cause of his being shot, as the *Indians* said, was for walking with the *English*: and it is also conceived both by them and us, that his Forwardness for the Meeting was one thing; which, with the Experience I have had of him, gives me Matter of strong Persuasion, that *he bears in his Brow the Marks of the Lord Jesus.*[309]

About a Year and a half after Mr. *Mayhew's* writing this Account, a great number of the praying *Indians*, of whom this *Tawanquatuck* was one of the most eminent, entered into a solemn Covenant to serve the

---

307 *See a Letter of Mr.* Mayhew's *to Mr.* Whitfield, *in his Light appearing more, and more* Pages 6, 7, 8. [Mayhew's note.]

308 Archaic form of "weir" (*OED*), a dam or fence built across a stream to catch fish.

309 Visible stigmata: the marks of Christ's Passion on hands, feet, side, or brow. Also see Ezekiel 9:4; Galatians 6:17.

true God, and him only; which Covenant was at their Request by Mr. *Mayhew* written in their own Language for them, and a Copy of it was soon after published in a Letter of his to the Corporation.

The praying *Indians* did also about the same time earnestly desire that Christian Civil Government might be set up over them, and that Transgressions of the Law of God might be punished according to the Rules of his Word, as Mr. *Mayhew* has in his said Letter declared;[310] which being according to their Desire, some time after done, this *Tawanquatuck* became a Christian Magistrate among the People, over whom he had before ruled as an *Indian Sachim*, and did so far, as I can learn, faithfully discharge that Trust so long as God continued his Life.

All, both *Indians* and *English* that I can meet with, who knew any thing of the Man while he lived, do give him this Testimony, that he continued all his Days to be a Person of a blameless Conversation. I cannot now find out in what Year he dy'd; but I think it was near about the Year 1670.

[83] EXAMPLE III
JOSEPH POMPMAHCHOHOO,[311] *who died at* Watshat,[312]
on Martha's Vineyard, in *the Year* 1687.

THe Father of this *Joseph* was an *Indian*, called *Pamanominnit*, which is all that I know of him; nor have I been informed how the Son carry'd himself in his younger Days: however, he became a Member in full Communion, of the Church whereof *John Tackanash*[313] was Pastor, well nigh as soon as that Church was first gathered, and was an Ornament to it as long as he lived.

Living some Years within about a Mile of my Father's House, we were all well acquainted with him, and looked on him as a grave and serious

---

310 *See Tears of Repentance, published by the Corporation in* 1653. [Mayhew's note.]

311 Joseph Pompmahchohoo owned the eastern half of Woachet neck. See *Native Writings,* 1:241, 245; *WGH,* 156.

312 As Charles Banks notes, Watshat (Watchet) in south-central Martha's Vineyard was an important demarcation point for original sachemships: "The Vineyard was apparently divided into four governmental sections, of which two, Chappaquiddick and Gay Head, were separated by natural boundaries from the main island. This latter territory being divided into two chief sachemships, which had a definite line of demarcation, represented as accurate a partition as could be devised. By a straight line drawn from the Blackwater brook emptying into the sound, to Watchet, the sachemships of Nunnepog and Takemmy were divided by the 'old Sachems and Cheefe men of Nunpoag on the one side, and the old Sachchims and Cheefe men of Takymmy on the other side'": *HMV,* 1:39.

313 *IC,* 14–17*.

Man, of a very blameless Conversation; and indeed all that knew him on the Island gave him such a Character.

He was justly esteemed a Person of great Prudence, Moderation, and Industry; and he accordingly ordered his Affairs with Discretion, provided well for his Family, and carry'd himself very obligingly to his Neighbours, both *Indians* and *English.*

He was observable for the excellent Memory wherewith God favoured him, and the good Use which he made of it. He could remember a great number of excellent Texts of Scripture, and had an Heart to improve them for the Edification of his Neighbours, when there was Opportunity and Occasion for it.

He constantly worshipped God in his Family, and used ordinarily to give some necessary Instructions and Admonitions to his Household, before Morning and Evening Prayer: but his Endeavours in this way to do them good had not the desired Effect.[314]

As he endeavoured to do good in his own House, so he did no less so in the Church to which he belonged, on all Occasions instructing, exhorting, and reproving his *Brethren,* as one that was not in doubt of the Obligations lying on him *to be their Keeper.*[315] nor did he perform this great Duty in private only, but did the same in publick also, when there was occasion for it.

He was constant in his Attendance on the publick Ordinances of God's Worship, as one that took Delight [84] and Pleasure in them: and he was in such Esteem for Wisdom and Piety among his Brethren, that if it had happened that the Minister that should preach was hindered from coming to the Place where he went to hear, they used to call on him to give a Word of Exhortation to them; and he several times did so, to the good Satisfaction and Edification of the most intelligent of them that heard him.

Another Way in which he served his Generation, by the Will of God, was, by sustaining and executing the Office of a Magistrate among his own Countrymen; in the Discharge of which Trust, being just, and ruling in the Fear of God, he did Good to his People.

This good Man made a good End. He was in his last Sickness visited by several of the most noted *Indians* on the Island, as particularly by *William Lay,* mentioned in *Chap.* I. *Example 9th,* and *John Hiacoomes,*[316] who afterwards preached at *Assawamsit* on the Main. And I have a Paper

---

314 His children probably include Joshua Teohoo, who was sued for debt, and Joseph Popmicho, who was sued both for debt and for stealing a horse. *WGH,* 156, 287, 307–8.

315 Genesis 4:9.

316 The son of Hiacoomes, the first Indian convert on Martha's Vineyard. *IC,* 35; *WGH,* 330.

now before me, subscribed by the two Persons last mentioned, wherein they testify, that he had good Hope in his Death; they declared that he had said,

> That having chosen the Lord to be his God, and being firmly persuaded of his great Power and Mercy, and also of the certain Truth and Faithfulness of the Promises of his Covenant, he had a strong Hope that he would eternally save him.

Nor will such a Hope ever make those ashamed, in whose Hearts the Love of God is shed abroad by the Holy Ghost.

EXAMPLE IV.
NOQUITTOMPANY, *an* Indian *of* Christian-Town,
who died in or about the Year 1690.

I Cannot tell who was the Father of this Man, but a Son of his I was well acquainted with, *viz.* that good *Isaac Ompany* mentioned *Chapter* I. *Example* 20.[317]

The Father did not presently embrace the Christian Religion, on the first preaching of it; nor did he for some time appear forward to attend the preaching of the Word of God, when it was brought nigh to him, but would either lie at home, or go a fishing or hunting on the *Lord's-Day*, to the great Grief of such as were better disposed. O[85]therwise he was generally esteemed a very honest and discreet Man among his Countrymen.

But what will moral Honesty without serious Religion profit a Man, in the Day that his Soul shall be taken from him, and when God shall enter into Judgment with such as obey not the Gospel? And our *Noquittompany* was at length convinced that he must become a praying Man, if he would enjoy that Salvation which none but such as call on the Name of the Lord may expect to obtain: God effectually convinced him,[318] that without Holiness no Man can see the Lord; and the next News of him was, *Behold he prayeth.*[319]

---

317 He was also the father of Sianum, whose daughter Margaret Osooit is highlighted in *IC*, 197–201*. Sianum was married to Keteanumin (alias Josias), the sachem of Takemmy. They had a house that adjoined on the northwest the lands of colonist William Rogers. Keteanumin is mentioned in numerous Duke County deeds from the colonial era. *WGH*, 204, 225, 108.

318 Mayhew's notion that God and not Noquittompany himself was responsible for this change of heart corresponds to Calvinist doctrine, which insists upon both unconditional election (God chooses certain individuals for salvation) and irresistible grace (the Holy Spirit extends to the elect a special inward call to salvation; the external call, which is made to the saints, cannot be rejected).

319 Acts 9:11.

He set up the Worship of God in his House, praying daily with his Family, and diligently instructing of them; nor were there now any more Complaints of his prophaning God's holy Day, but instead of going a hunting, as he used to do, he became a constant and diligent Attender on the publick Worship of God.

And being thus become a new Creature, living a new Life, he could not long content himself without *giving Glory to God by a professed Subjection to the Gospel*:[320] he soon asked Admission to all the Privileges of a Church State, and publickly professing *Repentance towards God, and Faith towards the Lord Jesus Christ*,[321] was readily admitted to them: nor did he ever after this bring any Discredit on Religion, or the Ways of God, by any immoral Practices, but continued a lively and bright Example of Piety to the End of his Life.

After his Wife dy'd, and his Children were all marryed, and settled in Families, he being old, used to live with them in their Houses, and sometimes lodged for a while in other Families, who were willing to receive and entertain him: and the Families wherein he for any time kept, were no Losers by having such a Man in them; for, being generally had in great Veneration among the *Indians*, they used wherever he lodged to desire him to lead in their Family Worship, and be instead of a Priest, to offer up their spiritual Sacrifices to God for them: and such was the excellent Gift and Spirit of Prayer, wherewith his God was pleased to favour him, that several *Indian* Ministers who heard him calling on the Name of the Lord, have assured me that his Prayers were very instructive and affecting.

[86] But there was nothing more remarkable in the Character and Carriage of this good Man, than his Ability and Willingness to entertain with good Discourses, all those with whom he conversed. His God and Saviour, and those things which have a Relation to another Life after this is ended, were the Subjects about which he continually delighted to confer; and he used earnestly to invite and excite his Neighbours and Friends to the great Duties which ought to be attended by all such as fear God, and would be happy in the Enjoyment of him.

He did also earnestly testify against the Sins to which he saw that his Neighbours and Countrymen were addicted, as more especially that of Drunkenness, which he himself abhorred and avoided. Especially before Morning and Evening Prayer he used to discourse after such a manner as has been now declared, as there be several credible Witnesses yet living that can testify.

---

320 2 Corinthians 9:13.
321 Acts 20:21.

He was exceeding sensible of the woful Depravation of the human Nature, thro' the Sin and Fall of the first *Adam.*[322] An *Indian* Minister worthy of Credit has informed me, that he once heard this Man making a Speech before he prayed in the Family where he lodg'd, and that Death being the Subject he then discoursed on, he declared, that every unconverted Man was really a dead Man[323]; *and that Men then came to Life again, when they were turned from Sin to God, so as to live to him from whom they had departed.* He knew well, that Men were by Nature dead in Trespasses and Sins.

When the Epidemical Fever began to rage, which swept away many of our *Indians* in and about the Year 1690, the good Man observing it, said, *That he hoped the time was then drawing on, when he should leave this troublesome World, and go to the Lord his God:* and it was as he conjectured and desired; for it was not long before he was seized with the Distemper which then prevailed, nor was he at all surprized *when it came on him.*[324] He with great Chearfulness entertained that *King of Terrors,* when it approached to him. He professed his Hopes in the Mercy of God, thro' the Merits of his Son, and greatly encouraged his Children and others, to seek that Kingdom to which he was going; and so yielded up his Spirit to the Hands of his Redeemer,

O Death, where is then *thy Sting! O Grave, where is thy Victory!*[325]

[87] EXAMPLE V.
MATTHEW, *called by the* Indians NAHNEHSHEHCHAT,
who died at Chappaquiddick in or about the Year 1690.

THo I cannot give a very particular Account of that Matthew of whom I here speak, yet he was so universally esteemed a good Man, that I can't

---

322 The doctrine of original sin was fundamental to New England theology and Puritan missionary activities. As the New England Primer put it, "In Adam's fall, we sinned all": learning to overcome one's natural depravity was the first step for every child and convert, whose entire life was expected to be a preparation for salvation. See Cooke et al., "Theories of Education," in *Encyclopedia of the North American Colonies,* 420. For Mayhew's discussion of how man's spiritual death began with Adam, see his *Grace defended,* 5.

323 For Puritans, sin was a spiritual death. In contrast, physical death might actually be a birth into eternal life for one who was saved. Because the unconverted were doomed not to be saved, they were denied that possibility.

324 In the Bible, the supernatural force that most often "comes upon" people and overwhelms them is the "Spirit of the Lord." This experience uusually is a source of power and prophesy (Numbers, Judges, 1 Samuel) and only rarely is an "evil Spirit from God" (1 Samuel 16:23). Mayhew's use of this phrase implies that the distemper not only was sent by God but also was in a way empowering or good.

325 1 Corinthians 15:55.

forbear mentioning of him, as one of the Examples of Piety that have been found among our *Indians.*

Who his Parents were I think I have never heard; but a Brother he was of that good *Kestumin,*[326] a Deacon mentioned in *Chap.* I. and there was another Brother of them that was esteemed a godly Man.

Tho this *Matthew* must needs have been a Man grown, before there was any School at which the *Indians* here might learn to read; yet, being desirous of such an Advantage, he happily attained the Skill, so that he was able to read the holy Scriptures, and such other Books of Piety as were extant in *Indian,* before he dy'd.

He was not long after the first preaching of the Gospel on the little Island where be lived, before he did embrace it; and he was one of the first Members of that Church whereof good *Hiacoomes* was the faithful Pastor; and his *English* Neighbours, as well as the *Indians,* that were well acquainted with him, do bear him Witness, that he was a person of a very blameless Conversation. I never met any one Person, either *Indian* or *English,* that could object any one Word against his Morals.

When the Church on the said *Chappaquiddick* was under flourishing Circumstances, he was esteemed as one of the principal Members of it, and was looked upon as a discreet, grave, and serious Man, whose Conversation was ordered as did become the Gospel.

He constantly upheld the Worship of God in his Family, every Day praying with them, and reading the Scriptures to them: and he used always to give some good Instructions and Exhortations to his Household, before Morning and Evening Prayer.

But there was scarce any Thing wherein this good Man did more evidently appear to be such a one, than in the Zeal for God, and earnest Desire of the Good of [88] Souls, which he continually manifested in the good Instructions, Admonitions, and Exhortations which he daily gave to his Neighbours. Several of them yet living, do affirm to me, that he used to go about from one House to another, earnestly exhorting, and pressing the People which he visited, to the great Duties of Religion, and reproving them for their Miscarriages, and cautioning them against the Sins to which he knew them to be most subject; therein doing what Christians are obliged to, when they are commanded to *exhort one another daily,*[327] &c.

But tho the Man I speak of, was a Person of undoubted Piety, yet there was one Failure of which he was guilty, which I think proper to mention.

---

326 *IC,* 45, 74, 166.
327 Hebrews 3:13.

After *Hiacoomes* his good Pastor was so superannuated, as not to be able so well to guard his Flock as he had been, there being a great Decay of Religion on the little Island where this Man lived, few godly Persons then remaining there, compared with what there had before been, our *Matthew* was drawn over to the Error of the *Antipedoptists*,[328] was re-baptized, and became one of their Communion.

But as I have no reason to think, that any carnal Interest prevailed with this Man to embrace the Opinion mentioned; but that he did that which appeared to him to be right, and most agreeable to the Scriptures, thro' his misunderstanding of them: So I never heard but that he carry'd himself in all other respects, very Christian-like towards those from whose Opinion he dissented. And as to his Conversation, it remained blameless to the last, as it had formerly been.

He dy'd of a strong Fever, which carried him off in a few Days, at time when many others were sick and dy'd; nor can I find any Person now living that can give me a distinct Account of what he said and did, betwixt the time of his being taken sick and his Death: but, this notwithstanding, I hope he dy'd in the Lord.

[89] EXAMPLE VI.
YONOHHUMUH, *who died at the* Gayhead *in the Year* 1698.

THis *Yonohhumuh* was an *Ohtoskow, i. e.* one of the *Indian* Nobility, being a Counsellor[329] to that *Mittark* mentioned in *Chap.* I. But it is much more to his Honour, that he became a Christian and a godly Man, not long after his *Sachim* himself did so, than that he was such an *Ohtoskow*, or Counsellor, as he was before his Conversion.

He was accounted a very just and honest Man in his Dealings with his Neighbours, and a Man of great Prudence and Moderation, and very courteous and obliging to all that he had any thing to do withal.

---

328 For more on the Antipedobaptists, see *IC*, 41.

329 Matthew Mayhew provides the following insight into Wampanoag social hierarchies: "Their government was purely monarchical and as for such whose dominions extended further than would well admit the Princes personal guidance it was committeed into the hands of Lieutenants, who governed with no less absoluteness, than the Prince himself: notwithstanding in matters of difficulty, the Prince consulted with his nobles, and such as whome he esteemed for wisdom; nobles were either such who descended from the Blood Royal, or such on whom the Prince bestowed part of his dominions with the Royalties, or such whose descent was from Ancestors, who had some time out of mind been esteemed such. Their yeomen were such who having no stamp of Gentility, were yet esteemed as having a natural right of living within their Princes dominion, and a Common use of the Land, and were distinguished by two names or titles, the one signifying the subjection and the other Tiller of the Land." M. Mayhew, *Brief narrative*, 7–9.

He was a Man of great Industry, one who labour'd diligently with his Hands, and taught his Children to work also; and with their Help raised yearly a good Store of Corn, Beans, &c.

He was observed to be a Person of remarkable Charity, used to give very liberally to the Poor of such Things as he had, was far from bringing the Curse of the People on him, by withholding Corn from them; so far from not selling it, that he was willing, if there were Occasion, to give it away freely.

He was not, that I can hear of, given to any Vice whatsoever, but lived in all Things blameless.

He appeared to be a Hater of Sin, by continually reproving of it, and bearing his Testimony against it, and by using his Endeavours to have it punished; of the last I shall give one Instance.

His own Son, the eldest he had, being charged with the Sin of Fornication,[330] and brought before the *Indian* Court to be examined about it, this good Man came to Court, and earnestly desired the Magistrates to search the Matter diligently, and not to spare his Son if he was found guilty; and when, on Enquiry, he was found so indeed, and Sentence was passed against him, he thanked the Court for the Judgment given, that he should have corporal Punishment inflicted on him; and again when that Sentence was executed, thanked the Officer by whom the Punishment was inflicted.

[90] He was a praying Man, as appeared not only by his joining with the People of God in their publick and solemn Worship; but also in that he prayed constantly and devoutly in his own Family, as all that fear God and desire his Favour ought to do.

His Piety and Charity were moreover further discovered in what shall be here related.

He frequently at his own Charges made Feasts,[331] to which many poor People were invited, and satisfy'd with Bread; and that their Souls might be fed also at the same time, he used to take care that they might then

---

330 Being formally charged with fornication was relatively rare on Martha's Vineyard. Most of the fornication cases recorded in the first book of the Dukes County Court Records, however, involved one or more Wampanoags, or people of partial Wampanoag ancestry. The prevalence of these cases may be strategic: as Ann Plane points out, "The prominence of marriage, fornication, and adultery themes in the narratives of Ponampam and the other Christian Indians suggests that missionaries took a special interest in altering these particular native relations": Plane, *Colonial Intimacies*, 43.

331 Feasts played an important role in pre- and postcontact Algonquian ritual in New England. Most descriptions by colonists include a discussion of feasting, which was a way to enhance the sense of community. And since food "has clear associations with abundance, health, and life," the "shared and joyous consumption of food, as well as its avoidance, marked equally the prodigality of spiritual relations and their cyclical renewal." Bragdon, *Native People of Southern New England*, 220.

also have the Bread of Life[332] broken to them, and always desired some Minister to preach a Sermon on these Occasions.

When he lay on his Death-Bed, but a few Days before he dy'd, *Peter Ohquonhut*[333] a Christian *Indian*, now a Minister worthy of Credit, going to his House to visit him, put some Questions to him, which, with the Answers he gave to them, here follow.[334]

Peter. *Do you believe that there is a God?*

Yonohhumuh. Yes, I believe that there is indeed a great God whose Name is *Jehovah*, and that he created the World, and all things in it.

Peter. *Do you know that you have sinned against the God that made you?*

Yon. Yes, indeed I do so, I know I have committed many and great Sins against him.

Peter. *Are you sensible that for your Sins you deserve to be tormented?*

Yon. Yes, I know that my Sins have deserved that I should be cast into Hell, and be there tormented for ever.

Peter. *Have you then any Hopes of being saved? and if so, by whom, and how?*

Yon. I have been informed, that God sent his Son into the World, to redeem and save sinful Men, and that such as come to him by true Faith and Repentance, are saved from Wrath by him;[335] and on this I ground my Hope for Salvation.

Peter. *Do you then repent of your Sins, and by Faith come to Christ, since you hope for Salvation in this Way?*

Yon. Yes, I do, I come, and come again to Christ, [or keep coming to him] and I mourn for my Sins, and intreat him to pardon them, and cleanse me from them. [91] And now bursting into Tears, he was not able for some time to say any thing more; but after a while he spake as follows.

Yon. Had God but *one Son*, and no more?

Peter. *He had but* one. He gave his only begotten Son, that whosoever believeth in *him* should not perish, but have everlasting Life.

---

332 The "bread of life" refers literally to the communion bread but figuratively to the nourishment of the word of God delivered by the ministers.

333 *IC*, 100, 110, 224. A minister at Gay Head. He was kidnapped by the French in 1711 or 1714 when crossing the sound in a canoe but was returned soon thereafter. *WGH*, 228.

334 Dialogues were an important and popular form of devotional literature in colonial New England. Other examples of this genre include John Eliot's *Indian dialogues* (1671). The dialogue format was also found in the catechisms used daily by children and early converts: Catechism, which involves "sending out a question and listening for the echo, the answer that fixes the depth of knowledge and understanding," had been popularized in Late Antiquity by St. Augustine and Erasmus; Martin Luther, John Calvin, and others brought it back to the forefront during the Reformation as a means of educating and saving souls. See Van Dyken, *Rediscovering Catechism*, 11, 14.

335 This differs from the standard Calvinist doctrine of unconditional election, since Yonohhumuh makes it sound as if all those that have come to Christ with faith will be saved.

Yon. Oh, the wonderful Love of God! that having but *one* Son, he was willing to give him to suffer and die for us miserable Sinners, that so we might live thro' him.

Thus far *Peter Ohquonhut's* Discourse with this good Man; after which I can obtain no particular Account of what he said and did, but am in general assured, that he continued stedfast in the Faith to the last, praying earnestly to God, and waiting for his Salvation.

EXAMPLE VII.
SAMUEL COOMES, *an* Indian *Magistrate, who died at* Nashouohkamuk, *alias* Chilmark, *in the Year* 1703.

SAmuel Coomes was the youngest Son save one of the memorable *Hiacoomes*, the first *Indian* Christian on *Martha's Vineyard.* He was by his Father when he was a Youth put to live with the worshipful *Thomas Mayhew* Esq;[336] the Father of that Mr. *Mayhew* by whom the *Indians* of this Island were first instructed; and living with one who had the Good of the *Indians* so much at his Heart as Mr. *Mayhew* had, he was very well instructed. He could read well, both in *Indian* and *English*, and well understood the Principles of the Christian Religion. He had no doubt also many good Instructions, and Counsels from his own Father, who lived and preached about two Miles from his Master's House.

But, notwithstanding all these Advantages, he was in his youthful Days a carnal Man. He would then sometimes drink to Excess; nor did he stay here, but fell also into the Sin of Fornication, with a white Woman living in the Town where he dwelt.[337] But tho he never that I could hear of, returned any more to the Sin and Folly last mentioned, yet he still continued to drink too [92] hard at sometimes, not being yet able to overcome his Lust after strong Drink, when he came where it was, tho he did not make a Trade of going after it.

---

336 Experience Mayhew's great-grandfather.

337 Abigail Norton (1666–ca.1724), the daughter of Isaac Norton and Ruth Bayes. *HMV,* 3:341–82, Norton Family #31. On December 28, 1680, Samuel was fined for fornication, and Abigail was ordered to marry him, pay five pounds, or be whipped: *WGH,* 142. Abigail must have chosen a whipping, as she went on to marry a white settler, Richard Weeks (1653–1724). The sentence reads as follows: "Samuell Iacombs and Abigaill Norton, for committing fornication are sentenced, the said Samuell to pay a fine of five pounds to the . . . [countey?] and twenty shillings to said Abigaill, and Abigaill is sentenced to pay five pounds, or be whipped (ten stripes; or Marry the said Samuell, Samuell to stand committed, till the Judgment be satisfied": DCCR I.25. Although fornication cases between Algonquian men and white women were unusual in the colonies, it was not unusual for adolescent sexual offenses in Massachusetts to transcend either church or class lines. See Thompson, *Sex in Middlesex,* 104.

After some Years he marry'd a Wife, to whom (as she, being a pious Woman yet living, informs me) he freely and fully confessed his great Sin, in that Uncleanness of which he had been formerly guilty, and told her that he was often grieved on the account of it.

When he was first marry'd, his aged and good Father lived some Years in his House with him, and while he did so, carry'd on the Worship of God in that House; and also frequently gave good Instructions to these Children of his,[338] and now his Son seemed in general to behave himself well, was exceeding diligent in his Business, seldom went where strong Drink was; yet when he came in the way of it, was apt to drink more of it than he should have done.

When his Father dy'd, he appeared to be much awakened, and of his own Accord offered to renew his baptismal Covenant, and actually did so: nor did he appear to do this in a mere formal manner, but with much Seriousness and Affection, at the same time acknowledging and lamenting the past Sin of his Life, and professing his Resolution by the Help of God, to forsake every evil and false Way, and that he would worship the God of his Father the remaining part of his Life.

The Vows of God being thus on him, he, without any further Delay, set up the Worship of God in his House, praying Morning and Evening in his Family as long as he lived. He now also read the Scriptures, and frequently sung Psalms in his House, and was careful to instruct his Children in their Catechisms, and *bring them up in the Nurture and Admonition of the Lord.*[339] And tho this Man had naturally a Thirst after strong Drink, yet thro' the Grace of God he so far overcame that Lust, that he never, as I could learn, was more than once overtaken with it from the time he renewed his Covenant to his dying Day; and then he confessed and bewailed his Sin therein, and renewed his Promise to watch more carefully against that Temptation.

I think he was universally esteemed a very just and righteous Man in his Dealings with his Neighbours, not willing to wrong any in their Estates. I am told by a credible Person that lived very near to him, that once he had a [93] Cow that broke into a little Piece of Corn that belonged to a poor Neighbour of his and devoured the most part of it; the which when he was informed of, he immediately killed the said Beast, and gave the poor Man a far greater Part of it than the Corn was worth,

---

338 Samuel's children included Simon Coomes (*IC*, 187), who married Martha Coomes (*IC*, 187–88*). Simon and Martha's children were Sarah Coomes, Thomas Coomes, and possibly Joseph Coomes. *WGH*, 142, 215–16, 337–38.

339 Ephesians 6:4.

which had been eat by her, and gave a considerable Part of the Remainder to his poor Neighbours.[340]

He seemed always to make Conscience of giving some Part of his little Incomes to pious Uses: to such therefore as taught him in the Word he communicated in all good things, tho he was not by any Law of Man obliged so to do: and scarcely any Man more carefully considered the Poor than he did; for he commonly made considerable Presents to his poor Neighbours, out of his Corn and Meat, and whatever else by his Industry was produced.

If a Meeting-house[341] was to be repaired, or any thing else was to be done for the promoting of Religion, none would contribute more liberally to it than he. And when there was a Day of publick Thanksgiving, and Provision to be made for it, which among our *Indians* is brought into common Stock, (which the Poor as well as the Rich may come to and be filled) this our *Samuel* was one of the principal Providers for that Feast.

Being thus liberal, I think in him, as evidently as in almost any Person that I have known, were those Texts fulfilled, *The liberal Soul shall be made fat, and he that watereth, shall be watered also himself: The Liberal deviseth liberal Things, and by liberal Things, and by liberal Things shall he stand.*[342] For altho this Man did not grow very great and rich in the World, yet the Blessing of God seemed to be on all that he had and did. His Stock lived and prospered, even then when he was but poorly provided to keep it. He generally raised Corn enough for the Supply of his Family, and had greater Plenty of the other Necessaries of this Life than most other *Indians* had.

---

340 Marauding livestock continued to be a problem on the island for both whites and Wampanoags. As early as 1633, Massachusetts laws were enacted that required cornfields to be fenced. See Dow, *Everyday Life in the Massachusetts Bay Colony*, 100. Although Puritans often required converts to fence their property as part of the mission to anglicize them, on Martha's Vineyard cows owned by whites often ran loose and damaged Wampanoag fields. On May 21, 1677, the court in Edgartown noted that "continuall complaint hath been made by the Indians, of tresspass don them in their corn fields by cattle, abiding continually abroad in the woods, to their great disturbance and dammage; uppon neglect of the owners of said cattle, the court have thought good for the maintainance of the quiet and peace, between the English, and Indians, to take speciall order therein and doe therefore order and appoint Joseph Norton, Richard Avy [Ivy?], and John Freeman, and have agreed with them, to use their utmost indeavour, seaven dayes nor comeing to bring in the said cattle to the plain at Edgartown": DCCR I.15.

341 Although voluntary donations for repairing meetinghouses were desirable, sometimes communities resorted to fixed contributions. For example, when the residents of Chilmark decided to build a new meetinghouse in 1724, they raised money through a tax on the heads of households in order to "Defray the Charge of building and finishing s'd house." 4 September 1723, Edgartown Records, transcribed in DRMV: Chilmark, 56–57.

342 Proverbs 11:25. Here liberal means generous with money, time, and goods.

Being called to serve his Generation for some Years, in the Place of a Magistrate, he was in the Discharge of that Office very just, *ruling in the Fear of God.*[343] And to the end that Things might be well managed in his Courts, he used to open them by Prayer to God for his Help and Direction. He was observed to be very impartial in giving his Judgment in any Case brought [94] before him; and he endeavoured as much as he could to be a Terror to Evil Doers,[344] by discountenancing and punishing their Offences.

But as good a Man as this Son of *Hiacoomes* was, he was guilty of one Fault, which I must mention, and a Fault it is which I believe many other good Men are guilty of: he never asked an Admission to the Table of the Lord, tho none that knew him would have scrupled to admit him to it.

However, I will do him the justice to declare how he excused his not doing this; he said,

> It was not because he despised that Ordinance of Christ, but because he feared that he was not well qualified for the Enjoyment of so high a Privilege; and further declared, that the dreadful Miscarriages of many that were admitted to this holy Feast made him afraid to venture to come to it, lest he also should dishonour God and Religion by the like Irregularities.

But it being now too late to retrieve a past Error, I fear there was never so much said to him as ought to have been, for the satisfying of his Scruples.

About a Year before he dy'd, he began to appear more serious than he used to do. He now spake frequently of the Frailty of human Life, and of his own in particular, and endeavoured to quicken himself and others to the Performance of the great Duties, which, if ever, must be done before the Night of Death overtake us. He about this time told his Wife, that he did not know how suddenly God might take him from her; but that if he left her a Widow, she should firmly trust in God, and see to it, that she did not let go her Hold of him; and be sure to take care to bring up her Children in his Knowledge and Fear.

He was sick but a few Days before he dy'd; and having, during that time, the perfect Use of his Reason and Understanding, he (tho naturally a reserved Man) discoursed freely, and his Discourses were then such as did very well become a sincere Christian, *viz.* very heavenly and gracious. He spake much of the Power and Providence of God, and of his Mercy and Faithfulness towards all such as love, fear, and serve him, and

---

343 2 Samuel 23:3.
344 Proverbs 11:25, Isaiah 32:8.

mightily encouraged all that were about him, to live to him, and follow hard after him. He also declared his Willingness to resign himself, and all his Concernments into God's [95] Hand, submitting all to his sovereign Goodwill and Pleasure. And he said, tho he was a great Sinner, and unworthy of God's Favour, yet he was not thereby discouraged from seeking to God for his pardoning Grace and Mercy, but was persuaded that he should not fail of obtaining it, could he but sincerely repent of his Sins, and by Faith lay hold of Jesus Christ his only Saviour; the which tho he acknowledged himself unable to do, yet he rely'd on the Holy Spirit of God for those gracious Assistances which were necessary to his so doing, and professed his Resolution to persevere in his Endeavours to come up to the Terms of the Gospel: and while these and such like Expressions were uttered by him, he intermingled with the Sentences he thus spake to Men, serious Petitions to God for the great Benefits of which he discoursed: besides which Ejaculations, he was frequently heard, during the time of his Sickness, in a more set and solemn manner, calling on God for his Mercy.

Thus he spake, thus he pray'd, and then he dy'd.

EXAMPLE VIII.
WILLIAM TUPHAUS, *who died in* Chilmark *in the Year* 1705.

THe Person I now speak of was a Son of *Taphus*,[345] an *Indian* of *Chappaquiddick*, of whom I have heard nothing remarkable. When he became a Man, he marry'd a Daughter of Deacon *Jonathan Amos*, mentioned *Chap.* I *Examp.* 15. And the Woman he thus marry'd[346] was a great Blessing to him; for being a very pious and godly Person, she was probably very instrumental in bringing him to be such a one too.

He had for some Years after he was marry'd, too plain and evident Marks of an unregenerate State on him; his godly Wife could not by any means persuade him to set up the Worship of God in his Family; and tho he was given to labour with his Hands, and did, by working among the *English*, frequently get Money, and bring it home, giving the same to his Wife to lay up for him, yet he would in a short time demand it again of her, and spend it all in Drunkenness, so that his Wife and Children were sometimes greatly strained [96] for want of such Things as should have been procured with what he wasted by his Intemperance.

---

345 Possibly also the father of Jonnat Tupshass and Peter Tuphose. *WGH*, 154, 270, 355.
346 Bethia Tuphaus (née Amos). *IC*, 98, 228, 230, 242.

His Wife being much afflicted with his bad Carriage herein, tho otherwise very kind to her, laboured, but in vain, to convince him of the Error of his Way; for nothing that she could say to him, seemed to make any considerable Impression on him: at length, she went in the bitterness of her Heart to her godly Father, and made her moan to him, declaring how much she was distressed for her poor Husband, and asked his Counsel what she should do in the Case that did so distress her? And he, in answer to her Requests, told her, that she should not suffer her Heart to be discomposed with the Trial that she met withal, but carry it well to her Husband, and commit the Matter to God, for he was strong, and Mens Hearts were in his Hands, and he could, when his time came, convince her Husband, and reform him, and that she ought with Patience to wait for that time.

With this so wise and pious Counsel of her Father's the Woman was much refreshed, and resolved to follow the Advice given her, and did accordingly.

It was not after this before she was taken with a grievous Fit of Sickness, whereof she had very like to have dy'd; and now her Husband being much distressed with a Sense of the Evil of what he feared was coming on him, in the Death of so good and kind a Wife as she was, was brought to a Sense of the Sinfulness of his Ways, confessing the same, and lamenting that he had not sooner hearkened to her Intreaties and Counsels, and made Promises to endeavour to reform his Life, leave off his Drunkenness, and set up the Worship of God in his House: and he did in some good measure fulfil these Engagements; for from this time forward he prayed in his Family, and was very rarely known to drink to Excess, as he had formerly done.

But being thus prevailed withal, not to waste what he had in Drunkenness, he fell into another Extreme, rarely to be found among our *Indians*, *viz.* that of being too sparing. He was so saving of what he had, as hardly to allow his Family what was necessary; and was not at all forward to give good Entertainment to such as came to visit him.

His good Wife observing this, was uneasy at it, and let him know that she was so. She told him, that they [97] were but Stewards of what God gave them, and they must be accountable to him how they disposed of it; and that what was put into their Hands was partly to improve for their own Comfort, and partly to do good withal to others, as they had Opportunity.

He seemed to take in good Part what his Wife thus said to him, and told her that all he had was before her, and he would leave the Management of what he had in the House to her, and she might use it in their own Family, or entertain her Friends with it as she thought convenient.

After this they lived comfortably, and served God chearfully; nor did the *good Man of this House*[347] now think it sufficient to serve God therein only, but thought himself obliged to devote himself to the Service of God in his House too: he therefore offered himself to the Communion of the Church in the Place where he lived, and on making a publick Profession of Faith and Repentance, was admitted as a Member in full Communion in it, and in general carry'd himself as a good Christian ought to do, as long as he lived after it, which, I think, was about ten Years.

Indeed once in the time he was charged with speaking untruly in a Matter, wherein he and another had a Controversy; and being convicted and convinced of his Error therein, he gave good Satisfaction to those whom he had offended. And he was also once overtaken with strong Drink, after he had made a publick Profession of Religion, when being admonished, he made a humble Confession of his Sin, promising to be more watchful against that Lust for the future, and was as good as his Word therein, no more that I could ever hear of returning to that Folly.

He dy'd of a lingring Distemper, which held him near a Year, before it put an End to his Life. During that time he carry'd himself as a sincere Christian ought to do. He gave much good Counsel to his own Family, and others that came to see him. He pray'd very much to God to pardon all his Sins, and be reconciled to, and at Peace with him thro' Jesus Christ his only Saviour. He instructed his Children in the great Truths of Religion, and exhorted them earnestly to the great Duty of Prayer, which they daily saw performed in the Family; and did particularly sometimes take into his Arms, and thus instruct [98] and exhort his little Daughter *Bethia*,[348] afterwards to be mentioned with some other of his Children.[349]

As I doubt not but that God gave him a true saving Faith, so he was also pleased to give him Peace in believing. He declared some time before he dy'd, that he had quitted all the Interest and Concernments which he had had in the Things of this Life and World, and was freely willing to leave them all, and go to his heavenly Father, in whose Mercy he trusted, and by whom he hoped he should be graciously received; and in this Hope he continued as long as his Life lasted.

---

347 Possibly a reference to the Interpreter in John Bunyan's *Pilgrim's Progress* (1678), a popular Puritan allegory in which "Christian" embarks on a perilous journey to salvation from the City of Destruction to Mount Zion. Early in his adventure, Christian calls upon the "good man of the house" (the Interpreter) who, he has been told, will show him "excellent things" and be a help on his journey. See Bunyan, *Pilgrim's Progress*, 33–34. The book was widely read in Massachusetts, in part because it showed rather than told people how to be good Christians. Hayes, *Colonial Woman's Bookshelf*, 44–45.

348 *IC*, 230–32*.

349 William Tuphaus (*IC*, 228–30*) and Job Tuphaus (*IC*, 242–43*).

EXAMPLE IX.
ABEL WAUWOMPUHQUE Senior, *who died*
at Nashowohkamuk *in the Year* 1713.

THis *Abel* was a Brother of the *Sachim Mittark*, mentioned *Chap.* I. *Examp.* 7. and the glad Father of that good *Abel* mentioned also in the same *Chapter, Example* 22.[350]

He was amongst the first that embraced Christianity in the Place where he lived and dy'd; nor did he ever after, that I can hear of, give Grounds to any to suspect his being a sincere godly Man.

He was either one of the very first of our *Indians* that confederated to serve the Lord in a particular Church State,[351] in an Attendance on all his Ordinances; or else joined to that Society soon after it was gathered, in the Year 1670: and having thus professed Subjection to the Gospel, he walked as did become a Person professing Godliness.

He used to read the Holy Scriptures in his Family, and prayed daily to God with them; and was also very constant in his Attendance on the publick Worship and Ordinances of God, and did appear very devout and serious therein.

He was a zealous Reprover of the Sins of the times in which he lived, especially the Sin of Drunkeness he did abhor, and earnestly testify'd against it.

He could not endure Contention among Brethren, but earnestly endeavoured to promote Peace and Unity among them: when therefore at Church-Meetings he saw [99] there was Danger of Discord, he would rise up and say, *Be at Peace one with another; consider that Christ hath said to you*, Peace I leave with you, my Peace I give unto you.[352]

He was sometimes called to the Office of a Magistrate among the People of his own Nation, and used to be a Terror to Evil Doers[353] when he was in that Place of Trust, by inflicting deserved Punishments on them.

So excellent a Gift of Prayer had he, that tho he was never that I know of, called to preach, yet our *Indian* Ministers did sometimes invite him to pray in publick, as on Days of Fasting and Prayer,[354] and on the *Lord's-Day* also; and I have my self heard him with very good Satisfaction.

---

350 Abel Wauwompuhque Sr. was the son of Nohtoakset, the sachem of Gay Head (*IC*, 67, 109) and the brother of Ompohhunnut. *WGH*, 125, 154–55; DCRD 6.369–70, SJC 43637.

351 Unlike Roger Williams and later Americans, mainstream New England Puritans believed that the church and state should be intertwined. Although Massachusetts laws would eventually change, originally only male church members could hold public office.

352 John 14:27.

353 Proverbs 21:15.

354 As Charles Hambrick-Stowe notes, fasts in Puritan New England were "a standard weapon in the arsenal of public rituals available in a time of trouble." Public fasts were held "in response

He used to sing Psalms in his House, while he had a Family of his own to join with him in that godly Exercise; and, after he was blind with Age, and lived among his Children in their Houses,[355] he continued to praise the Name of God, by singing to himself such Psalms as he had learned by Heart, while he had his Sight; as particularly part of the 18, also the 118, and 122.

He used to talk very piously and prudently, while he had the perfect Use of his Understanding; and tho he lived to so great an Age, that his Reason and Memory did at last in some measure fail him, yet his Piety and Charity did even then very much appear in his Discourses; and he had by Faith such a Prospect of things invisible and eternal, as made him very willing to leave this World, that so he might enter into the Enjoyment of them.

I believe none that knew this Man question his sincere Piety; I'm sure I my self do not.

The hoary Head is a Crown of Glory when it is thus *found in the way of Righteousness.*[356]

[100] EXAMPLE X.
JAMES NASHCOMPAIT, *of the* Gayhead, *who died at* Pashkehtanesit, alias Tuckers-Island,[357] *in the Year* 1713.

WHo the Parents of this *Indian* were I know not,[358] he being an old Man when I was first acquainted with him.

He was I think among the first of the *Indians* that embraced Religion at the *Gayhead*; and, as far I can learn, walked according to the Rules of it for ever after.

He appeared to be a Man that feared God and eschewed Evil, and was a sharp Reprover of Sin in his Brethren and Neighbours, would tell them plainly that they sinned against God when they did so.

He was all the while that I was acquainted with him, which was many Years, a Member of the Church of Christ in full Communion, and never

---

to dire agricultural and meteorological conditions, ecclesiastical, military, political, and social crises . . . and in preparation for important events such as the ordination of a minister or the militia's embarkation on a campaign." Similarly, days of public prayer were called in response to "speciall mercies" from God and other "extraordinary occasions." Hambrick-Stowe, *Practice of Piety*, 100–101.

355 The names of his other children besides Abel Wauwompaque Jr. are unknown. *WGH*, 125, 360, 613.

356 Proverbs 16:31.

357 One of the Elizabeth Islands off Cape Cod.

358 Segel and Pierce hypothesize that James's father was Nashkapeit, an "old Gentleman" on Nantucket: *WGH*, 112, 308.

that I heard of, gave any Offence to his Brethren, unless it were once to some of them in speaking too hastily, but he readily owned his Fault in it. He was none of those that followed after strong Drink, but testify'd against their Practice that did so.

He was a Person very zealous and affectionate in his Prayers, humbly confessing his own Sins, and the Sins of others in them, and the Mercy of God in sending his Son to redeem Mankind from Sin and Damnation, and pleading earnestly for Pardon and Mercy for himself and others, thro' Christ's Merits and Intercession for them, and for Sanctification[359] to be wrought in the Souls of Men, by the mighty working of God's Holy Spirit in them.

He used before he went to Prayer to utter some pious Sentences about the Things our Prayers should have a relation to; and I am told by *Peter Ohquanhut*,[360] the present Minister of the *Gayhead*, who is very worthy of Credit, that he has heard him on such an occasion magnifying the Power and Work of the Holy Spirit, discovered in the Impressions which he makes on the Souls of good People.

This good Man going to the Island above mentioned to see a Friend or two of his that lived there, returned not hither again, but went from thence to Heaven, as there is good reason to believe. I cannot attain so parti[101]cular an Account as I would have had of his Deportment in his Sickness; and at his Death: however, I am credibly informed, that his Discourses were to the last such as did become a dying Christian, and that he called often on the Lord while he was sick, as well as when he was in Health.

Tho he was an old Man when he ended his Days, yet I'm told he was able to stand and go, even to the Day on which he dy'd; and that having just before his Death been out of Doors, he came in and laid himself on his Bed; and then turning his Face to the side of the House,[361] and calling on his God, immediately resigned up his Spirit to him.

---

359 Sanctification is the action of the Holy Spirit in sanctifying or making holy the believer, by the implanting within him of the Christian graces and the destruction of sinful affections. Also, the condition or process of being so sanctified (*OED*). As Perry Miller explains, sanctification and moral behavior were intrinsically tied: "'*Sanctification* flowes from *Justification*; Being justified we are sanctified,' which meant simply that virtue and morality were useless if there were no regeneration." Miller, *New England Mind*, 49. Mayhew aims to prove that the converts are both moral and sanctified.

360 *IC*, 90–91, 110, 244.

361 Direction was and is important in northeastern Algonquian communities, and different directions were associated with particular manitous. Upon death, bodies were placed in the grave with a southwestern orientation, the direction of Cautantowwit's house. Bragdon, *Native People of New England*, 235; Simmons, *Cautantowwit's House*; Hammell, "Mythical Realities," 68.

EXAMPLE XI.
AKOOCHUK, *who died at* Gayhead, *November* 14*th*, 1714.

THis *Akoochuk* was esteemed a Person of good Quality among the *Indians*. And when he was a Man grown, he marry'd a Daughter of the *Sachim Mittark*,[362] formerly mentioned, and was afterwards one of his *Antoskouaog*, i.e. *Counsellors*.

He was while a young Man, somewhat given to strong Drink, and did sometimes drink to Excess; but embracing the Christian Religion, he obtained a Victory over his Lusts, and lived many Years very temperately and blamelessly among his Neighbours.

He worshipped God constantly in his House, and tho he was not a very good Reader, yet used Books, endeavouring to get Good out of them, and took Care to learn[363] his Children to read better than he could, and was a diligent Instructor of his Household: nor were his Endeavours to train up his Children for God without some good Effect, for some of his Children have already dy'd hopefully, and there is one of them yet living, who is a Man of a good Conversation, and a Preacher of the Word of God to his Countrymen, and has sometimes been a Schoolmaster among them.[364]

He was reckoned very charitable to the Poor, not only feeding them when they came to his House, but also giving them what was convenient to carry home with them. And he was esteemed a Person of Moderation and Discretion, and of a very kind and obliging Conversation.

[102] He several of the last Years of his Life served his Generation in the Place of a Magistrate; and while he did so, endeavoured to be a Terror to Evil Doers among his Neighbours, and used also to give much good Counsel to them.

He diligently attended on the publick Worship of God, and treated Christ's Ministers as Persons worthy of Honour: but in this he failed, that he did not ask an Admission to special Ordinances, tho none but himself questioned his being qualified to enjoy them; which his doing, and not a Contempt of them, kept him back from.

He was sick about a Month before he dy'd; and having the perfect Use of his Reason the greatest part of that time, he commended Religion to those of his own Family, and others that came about him, and exhorted them to pray constantly and fervently to God, and carefully to abstain from sinning against him. He then also professed his Hopes of Eternal

---

362 The sachem of Gay Head. *IC*, 21–23*.

363 Today, using "learn" to mean teach is considered the sign of an uneducated speaker, but during Mayhew's day this usage was perfectly acceptable (*OED*).

364 Probably John Akoochik, a ruling elder and later a minister at Gay Head, 1729–53. *WGH*, 182.

Life, thro' the Sufferings and Obedience of the Son of God, in whom he trusted for Salvation; and thus trusting and hoping in his Saviour, he willingly dy'd. And his Wife, who was, as there is reason to hope, a godly Woman, dy'd a few Days after him.

EXAMPLE XII.
JAPHETH SKUHWHANNAN, *who dy'd in* Chilmark
in the Year 1715, *when he was about* 26 *Years old.*

THis *Japheth* of whom I now speak, was a Son of *Nicodemus Skuhwhannan*,[365] and his Wife *Bethia*, Daughter of the well known, and frequently before mentioned Mr. *Japheth Hannit.*

His Father and Mother being both religious Persons, gave him good Instructions while he was a Child; and he early discovered some Inclinations to the Things that are good, so that his Friends had great Hopes of him.

When he was about ten Years old, his Grandfather *Hannit* having no Son living of his own, (all his own hopeful Sons dying while they were young) took him to live with him, and kept him for the most part as long as he lived; and I suppose educated him as well as he could, not only as being one of his own Family, and so under his special Care and Charge, but as being also [103] instead of an own Son to him, and one called by his Name.

He learned to read *Indian* well, and made a considerable Progress in learning to read *English* also; and could likewise write a legible Hand. He was also well instructed in his Catechism, and did himself take Pains to understand the great Truths contained in it. His Friends seemed very desirous that he should be a good Man, and endeavoured what they could, by good Counsels and Instructions, to dispose his Mind to things good and vertuous; nor did their Labour herein appear to be in vain, for there were some good things found in him towards the God of his Fathers while he was young: for he was observed soberly to attend religious Duties in the Family, to read good Books, and was also found sometimes praying in secret to God. He was also very obedient to his Parents, and seemed not to make a mock of Sin as many did.

After the Death of his Father, who dy'd at *Annapolis-Royal*,[366] after the Place was taken in the Year 1710. his Mother being left a Widow,

---

365 A sachem or gentleman of Chilmark (?–1710). *WGH*, 200.

366 Annapolis Royal (Nova Scotia), founded as Port Royal, was the oldest French settlement in North America. The English took it in an important victory in 1710, mainly with the help of colonial militia from Massachusetts, New Hampshire, Connecticut, and Rhode Island: Parkman, *Half Century of Conflict*, 1:141–49. Charles Banks notes that it was common to enlist the help

went to live with her Father where he before was; and his Grandfather dying not long after, *viz.* in the Year 1712, his Mother, Grandmother, and himself, were left to keep House together. And tho now deprived of so good a Relation as Mr. *Japheth* was, yet not being willing to lose the Presence of God also, which is infinitely better than that of any Man's in the World, they still carefully upheld the Worship of God in the Family, the Mother for the most part, but sometimes the Daughter leading in that Duty: but the Youth I'm speaking of, being arrived to those Years of Discretion,[367] wherein it might be more decent and proper for him to perform that Duty, they devolved that Work on him; and his Relations were now much comforted in him, and both those and others had very considerable Expectations concerning him.

However, it must be confessed, with respect to this young Man, that when he was about eighteen or nineteen Years old, he shewed too much Inclination to go into bad Company, and follow after strong Drink; of which Fault, being seriously admonished, he was obliged to acknowledge, that he had twice or thrice drunken more than he should have done; but being reproved for his Sin herein, he reformed, and never more that I have heard of, returned to that Folly.

[104] Soon after he was grown up to the State of a Man, he appeared to be unhealthy; and the ill Habits of his Body increasing more and more on him, he at length fell into a Consumption, that put an End to his Life.

When Sickness came on him, he freely acknowledged, and exceedingly lamented, the Follies and Irregularities of the former Part of his Life, own'd the Justice of God, in bringing on him the Affliction with which he was exercised, expressing at the same time his earnest Desire, that the same might turn to his spiritual Advantage, and his Hopes that it would do so. At present he was not sensible that his Sickness was like to be unto Death; he therefore made use of Medicines[368] in order to the

---

of Wampanoags in the fighting against the French. Transports from Martha's Vineyard were involved in two earlier but unsuccessful campaigns against Port Royal (1707, 1709) before the final successful campaign in 1710. *HMV*, 1:300–303; Johnson, "Search for a Usable Indian," 625–51.

367 Sixteen was considered the "age of discretion" in Plymouth Colony and marked the point at which adolescents had to swear an oath of allegiance to the king and were held responsible for heretical religious beliefs and crimes such as arson. Axtell, *School upon a Hill*, 99.

368 Native medicines greatly influenced white healing practices in New England. Relatively few doctors in colonial American had attended medical school: in 1721 only one of Boston's ten "doctors" had a degree. As Dr. William Douglass put it in 1760, "more die of the practitioner than of the natural course of the disease." The drugs used were prescribed in excessively large and unmeasured quantities. Even if given properly the prescriptions were of questionable use: e.g., Cotton Mather, a famous scientist, advocated the use of urine as an unparalleled "Remedy for Humane Bodies." In contrast Native healers used both local herbs and spiritual practices to tend the ill: *pawwaws* functioned as sucking doctors and used spirit helpers to rid the body of sickness. (A sucking doctor is a shaman who cures the patient by sucking out an intruding object that has been identified as the source of the illness. Lyon, *Encyclopedia of Native American Healing*, 264–66). Puritans feared that the *pawwaws'* invocation of spirits was satanic but looked more favorably upon herbal treatment and often learned from Native

recovering of his Health: but after some time perceiving that he grew worse, notwithstanding any means that he used, he told his Friends,

> that they had taken much Pains to get things for him, in order to the restoring and recovery of his Health, but God had not bless'd them to that end, and he thought he should not recover; and therefore did not desire that they should seek any more Medicines for him, but was willing to submit to the Goodwill and Pleasure of God concerning him; only earnestly desired that he might obtain an Interest in that Favour of his which is better than Life it self, and that he might when he dy'd enter into Eternal Rest and Happiness in the World to come.

This therefore he said *he was resolved to seek in the first Place.*

He accordingly now seemed diligent in his Preparations for his approaching Death. His Strength was not yet so far gone; but that he could pray in the Family, which therefore he daily did; and the Prayers which he now made were most earnest and pathetical, such as did well become a Man that expected very shortly to leave this World: and besides those wherein the rest of the Family joined with him, he very frequently poured out his Heart before the Lord more secretly, as when he thought the Family were asleep, and knew nothing of it, tho some or other of them at some times did so.

He now also most seriously exhorted all that came about him, young People especially, to take care of their Souls, and apply themselves in earnest to the great Duties of Religion, and that speedily while their Opportunities lasted. He likewise now comforted his Mother, and other Relations, exhorting them to go on stedfastly [105] in that Course of Religion and Godliness wherein they were engaged.

He discoursed frequently of *Jesus Christ*, and the Way of Life and Salvation provided for the miserable Children of Men[369] in and thro' *him.* He asserted his own Persuasion of the Truth of the Gospel, wherein this Way to Life is revealed; and magnify'd the Mercy of *God*, in contriving, providing, and revealing it, and sending his Ministers to persuade Sinners to be, in this way, reconciled unto *him.*

Not having in the time of his Health asked an Admission to the Ordinance of the Lord's-Supper, he now desired to renew his baptismal Cov-

---

healing practices; these were deemed so successful that colonial doctors sometimes trained with Native healers to learn about which roots, berries, blossoms, and herbs should be used and how. Duffy, *Epidemics in Colonial America*, 4, 7–8; Douglass, *Summary, historical and political*; Kavasch, "Native Foods of New England," 170; Bragdon, *Native People of Southern New England*, 204–5. For an example of a Native healer who was also a convert, see Hannah Nohnosoo, *IC*, 165.

369 In Genesis 11:5, the "children of men" rebel against God and build the tower of Babel. Augustine also uses this term in *The City of God* (15.2) to refer to the people who live in the city ruled by human standards, rather than those who live in the City ruled by God's standards.

enant; and that if it might be, he might partake of that Seal of the Covenant before he died. And in this his Desire was granted; for to the end he might do so, the Church met in the capacious Wigwam wherein he lay sick; where, after a serious Profession of Faith and Repentance, he solemnly renewed his Covenant with *God*, and was admitted as a Member in full Communion in that Church: And soon after it, the Lord's-Supper being for his sake celebrated in the same Place, he, with the rest of the Church, partook of it.

At his desire, there were also sometimes Sermons preached in the same House, once by my self, and at other times by some of the *Indian Ministers*; upon the hearing of which, he seemed much refreshed, and express'd his Thankfulness.

I sometimes went to visit him in his Sickness, and did with Pleasure hear his serious and savoury Discourses about the things of *God*, and another Life and World. He professed his Willingness to submit himself, and all his Affairs, to the good Will and Pleasure of the Lord his *God*; and professed his Hopes in the Mercy of *God* thro' *Jesus Christ* his Son, for eternal Life.

When he was going to die, he desired *Job Soomannan*,[370] afterwards to be mentioned, to commit him to God by Prayer: to which the said *Job* willingly consented; but desired to sing part of a Psalm before he prayed, (which by the way is very usual among the *Indians)* the doing of which was so acceptable to the dying Man, that he joined with the rest so audibly, that he was plainly heard among them; and he also shewed his consent to the Prayer then made, by repeating, with a low Voice, every Word and Sentence after him that pray'd, and frequently [106] lifting up his Hands towards Heaven, while the Prayer was sent up thither; at the conclusion whereof, his Hand that was up before falling down, he immediately expired, without ever speaking one Word more.

EXAMPLE XIII.
SAMUEL JAMES, *who died at* Sanchekantacket *in* Edgartown, *in the fall of the Year* 1715.

THE Father of this *Samuel James*, was *James Cowkeeper*,[371] an *Indian* of *Edgartown*, who died many Years since. His Mother was that good *Old Sarah* mentioned *Chap*. III. *Example* IV.

---

370 *IC*, 51–52, 110–13*.

371 As Mayhew notes (*IC*, 115), many of the Wampanoags had begun to keep domesticated animals; the name "Cowkeeper" probably reflects this practice. See Silverman, "We Chuse to be Bounded" for more on Wampanoags and animal husbandry.

He was taught to read when he was a Child, and otherwise well instructed by his godly Mother; but was nevertheless, while a young Man, a great Lover of strong Drink, and would drink to excess; and in his drunken Fits, fight and be very unruly; and the more so, for that he was a very strong Man, whom few could grapple withal, when there was occasion by strength of Hand to govern him.

I do not remember that I have heard that there was any observable Change in him, till after he was married; but the kind Providence of God directing him to marry a Woman that loved him much better than she did that sort of Drink which he much delighted in, and he also having a great Affection for her, it has been thought that she prevailed with him to leave off his Drunkenness, and follow after things that were of greater Advantage to him than strong Drink could be. However, he was after his Marriage very much reformed, and lived far more temperately than before he had done, and was very diligent in his Business, and carefully attended on the publick Worship of God; but still neglected to worship God in his Family, till an awakening Providence quicken'd him unto it.

His good and kind Wife had very like to have died in Child-bed with the first Child she had; and he was so much affected with the Sense of the Loss which he then greatly feared, that he could no longer keep Silence, but began to call on that God who is a Hearer of Prayers, and a Rewarder of them that diligently seek him: and having experienced the Goodness of God, in sparing his [107] Wife, and still continuing her to be a Blessing to him, he ceased not to call upon him as long as he lived afterwards; which, I think, was about five or six Years.

In his Concern for his Wife thus manifested, his Love to her was indeed very observable; and that he had Cause to be well affected towards her, on the account of her good Affections to him, I could not but my self observe in one Instance: He being pressed to go as a Soldier into the War,[372] he was most grievously distressed on that account, and came weeping to me, praying me, if it were possible to get him released; telling me, that his leaving of her would be a greater Grief to her than she was able to endure. But this being a Parenthesis, I shall go on with my Story of him.

Being thus become a *praying Man*, which among our *Indians* signifies a *godly one*, he in other regards behaved himself as a Person professing Godliness ought to do. He read the Scriptures in his Family, and conformed his Life unto the Law of God expressed in them: He was, I think,

---

372 Possibly the expeditions against Port Royal (1707, 1709, 1710), in which other members of the community fought (such as Nicodemus Skuhwhannan, *IC*, 103).

by all that knew him, *English* as well as *Indians*, esteemed as a Man of Truth, and as one that was just and honest in his Dealings.

As he was himself a constant Attender on the publick Worship of God, so he very much excited his Neighbours to do so too; and was a great Promoter of all things that are holy, just, and good; and a faithful Reprover of Sin, both in his own Family, and among others with whom he conversed. And he had this Testimony, that he was very kind and charitable to his poor Neighbours, being willing to distribute to them when there was occasion for it.

He was taken ill on a Lord's Day at Meeting, and was not able to set the Tune of the Psalm in the Afternoon, as for some time he had been used to do; and as he went home in the Evening, he told his Wife, he thought he should go to the House of God no more; and, as he said, so it proved, for on the next Saturday he died.

As soon as the Sabbath was over, on which he was first taken sick, he began to set his House in order, as tho he knew he was to die very speedily.

He took great care that all his just Debts might be duly paid after he was dead, letting his Wife know how all his Affairs were circumstanced, and giving her Di⌈108⌉rections how she should manage them after his Departure from her.

He set himself diligently to prepare for his own Dissolution, endeavouring to obtain the Pardon of all his Sins, thro' the Blood of his only Saviour.

He sent for a Minister to assist him in his Preparations for his Change, to whom he confessed and lamented the Miscarriages of his Life, and owned his Unworthiness of Mercy by reason of them, but expressed most Grief at his having neglected solemnly to give up himself unto God, to serve him in an Attendance on all the Ordinances of his instituted Worship. He also desired him to shew him the Incouragements given in the Gospel to such Sinners as he was, and direct him how to improve them: As also to pray to God for him, that he might have Grace to do what was incumbent on him, in order to his Salvation. Nor was he unwilling to put in practice the Advice given to him.

He expressed earnest Desires of being reconciled to God thro' the Merits of his Son Jesus Christ; and he cry'd earnestly to God for the Mercies he desired to obtain.

He earnestly exhorted his Relations and Neighbours to pray without ceasing to God for the good things they needed, and which none but he could bestow upon them; and to abstain from every thing that would provoke him.

He pray'd every Day with his Family, from the beginning of his Sickness to that whereon he died; and, that he might the better shew the Reverence which he did bear to the Object of his Worship, he always arose and stood on his Feet, while he called upon his Name; and tho he was so weak that he could not rise and stand without help that day he died, yet he would still stand up and call upon the Lord, 'twice doing so but a very little before his Death; in which Prayers of his, he with much Faith and Fervency committed his Soul into the Hand of God his Saviour.

Being told that he was too weak any more to rise and stand in Prayer, as he had done, he after this sent up some Requests to God as he lay upon his Bed, and so died.

Tho he had not a Plerophory[373] of Assurance that he should enjoy Life eternal, yet he appeared not to be [109] without that Hope which is *the Anchor of the Soul both sure and stedfast.*[374]

EXAMPLE XIV.
ANNAMPANU, *otherwise called* MAATTI, *an* Indian *of* Gayhead, *who died in* Dartmouth[375] *in the Year* 1715.

THIS Man was a Grandson to *Nahtoohsact*,[376] formerly a *Sachim* of the *Gayhead*, his Mother being Sister to *Mittark* before-mentioned, *Chap.* I. *Example* VII. and he was the Father of that excellent *Joash* mentioned in the same Chapter, *Example* XXI.

He was, as I have been informed, while a young Man, one that *walked in the Way of his own Heart, and in the Sight of his own Eyes,*[377] loving and following after strong Drink; and would also sometimes be in Broils, among those *who have Sorrow, Contention, Babbling and Wounds without Cause, &c.*[378] But it was not very long before he reformed these Disorders, and began to worship God in his House, and appeared to be a religious Man, shewing a Respect to God's People and Ways.

However, he was well in Years before he publickly professed Repentance towards God, and Faith towards the Lord Jesus Christ, and joined

---

373 A theological term, common in the seventeenth century, meaning full assurance or certainty (*OED*).

374 Hebrews 6:19.

375 Immediately following King Philip's War, Vineyard Wampanoags played a critical role in assisting mainland Wampanoags, like those at Dartmouth, to reconstitute their communities and establish churches. Silverman, *Faith and Boundaries*, 60.

376 *IC*, 67.

377 Isaiah 57:17; Proverbs 21:2.

378 Proverbs 23:29.

himself as a Member in full Communion to the *Indian* Church on the Island; but having once avouched the Lord to be his God, and promised to walk in his Ways, he for ever after adorned the Doctrine of God his Saviour, by walking as did become the Gospel. He was, I think, by all that knew him, esteemed a Person of a very blameless Life. I was my self many Years acquainted with him, and do not remember that ever I heard that he was guilty of any considerable Fault in all that time. Tho it is not to be doubted, but that he had his Failings as well as others.

He was one that used to discourse very seriously on matters of Religion: I remember I have heard him talk very sensibly of the Power of indwelling Sin[379] in Mens Souls, declaring how hard a thing it was for Persons to mortify it, and get the Victory over it; instancing, in particular, the Lusts forbidden, in the seventh Commandment.

[110] He was a praying Man: And as he pray'd in his own House, while he had one; so when, after he was grown old, he had no House of his own, but lived in other Families, he was a Blessing to them by his many good Prayers in them, and good Counsels given to them. He then also used to go about doing good, as in visiting the Sick and Afflicted, and counselling and comforting of them; and, as occasion was, praying with and for them.

Of his Charity and Piety this way manifested, I shall here give one Instance.

Peter Ohquanhut,[380] now Minister at the *Gayhead*, being in the Year 1714 taken by the *French*, and carry'd away to Sea, no body then knew whither, his Wife and Children were in great Distress about him, not knowing whether ever he would return to them again: But this good Man knowing how disconsolate their Condition was, and what Cares and Fears they were under, used almost every Day to visit them, speaking good and comfortable Words to them, and praying with and for them, till, by the good Providence of God, the good Man was returned to his Family again.

After this, our good *Annampanu* lived not long; for the next Year, going to visit his Friends on the Main, where he sometimes formerly lived, he there died: and tho I have had no Account how he carried himself in his last Sickness, yet I hope it is well with him; because *I know it is in the end always so with them that fear God, which fear before him.*[381]

---

379 "Indwelling sin" was one of the forces that battled for the souls of men. Even after sanctification (grace), the indwelling sin seeks to corrupt the believer from within while worldly pressures work to corrupt the Christian from without. The use of the term "Victory" by Annampanu reflects the perception of this cosmic struggle as a battle between good and evil.

380 *IC*, 90–91, 100, 244.

381 Ecclesiastes 8:12.

EXAMPLE XV.
JOB SOMANNAN, *who died at* Christian-Town, *in the Year* 1718.

THIS *Job* was a Son of a *praying Indian of Takame*, alias *Tisbury*, called *Somannan:*[382] His Mother was by some thought to be a *Heathen*, yet she owned the true God, and did sometimes call upon him.

Their Son *Job* was taught to read[383] *Indian* while he was a Youth; and he afterwards, by his own Industry, learned to read *English* pretty well. He also learn'd to write a very legible Hand, and was well instructed in his Catechism.

[111] Yet after all these Advantages received, the *Job* of whom I am speaking, did not in his younger Days appear *to fear God and eschew Evil*, as he ought to have done. He appeared to have such an Inclination after strong Drink, as to need the Grace of God to restrain him from the excessive Use of it: He was also charged with the Sin of Fornication,[384] nor did he, I think, deny that he was guilty of it.

But appearing after some time to be much reformed, and to live a sober and orderly Life, he married a Daughter[385] of Master *Japheth Hannit*, with whom he lived chastly all the rest of his Days.

As he was, before he married, observed by some to pray in secret to God; so as soon as he had taken a Wife to be a Meet-help[386] to him, he pray'd with her, and such others as happened to be present with them when that Duty was to be performed.

When *Japheth*, his good Father-in-Law, lay sick of the Illness whereof he died, having no Son of his own, this Son-in-Law of his did, in a very dutiful manner, wait on him, and take care of his Affairs; and prayed in the Family, and with him, as there was occasion for it. He also wrote down those dying Speeches of his, which my Reader has already had in his Life.

We were now ready to think that this *Job* was a good Man. However, it is reported, that after this he was guilty of dealing very unfairly with a

---

382 Also the father of Jonathan Sumanah, a poor man who lived with Elisha Amos, the son of Amos Ianoxso, who was most likely Mayhew's informant referred to in *IC*, 29. *WGH*, 122, 149–50, 349.

383 In the original, the "e" is missing: "r ad."

384 Fornication cases were rare in the courts on Martha's Vineyard, and very little information is provided in the court records. This example of a fornication case, registered on July 13, 1703, in Edgartown, involved an unnamed Indian man and woman: " Ordered that whereas an indian woman accused _____ an indian for the committing of fornication with her she being with child: that the sd _____ shall be punished by whipping the numbr of _____ stripes and sd to stand commited untill the next court of Sessions: in March 1704." DCCR I. 136?; blanks appear in the original.

385 Jerusha Job(e)(?–<1752). *WGH*, 126.

386 A biblical and Puritan term for wife, also called a helpmeet (see Genesis 2:18) or goodwife.

Neighbour of his; and that he confessed the Offence, and took the Shame of it upon him, and made Satisfaction for it: Which, if sufficient to prove that he was then a wicked Man, it must be acknowledged that he was unconverted till about five or six Years before he died; but the Truth of this Hypothesis I call in question. However, from this time forward I have not heard that he was ever guilty of any scandalous Offence whatsoever. He was a Man very diligent in his Business; and being a Weaver by Trade, wrought much for the *English* as well as the *Indians*, and so provided comfortably for his Family, tho lame in one of his Legs: and I think those that imploy'd him, generally accounted him very faithful.

He was a great Lover of good Books, was not willing to be without any such as had been translated into his own Mother-Tongue; and he used sometimes to read in *English* Books also.

[112] He had by his Wife but one Child, a Daughter,[387] who is yet living; and her he carefully instructed in her Catechism, and otherwise frequently taught and exhorted her. He also frequently gave good Instructions and Exhortations to others, especially his own Relations; and I believe did good by them.

He very constantly and diligently attended on the publick Worship of God, therein discovering a Love to God's House and Ordinances; yet he never offered himself to join as a Member in full Communion to any of the Churches on the Island. I was well acquainted with the Man, and had frequently Discourses with him on this and some Matters of Religion, and must testify that he used to talk seriously. He always expressed a sense of the Truth and Excellencies of our Holy Religion, and a Desire to conform his Life to the Rules of it; but had such Apprehensions of the Holiness that was necessary to qualify Persons for the Enjoyment of Church-Privileges, that he thought it not safe for him to venture to lay claim unto them.

He complained much of the Sinfulness of the Lives of many Church-Members; and seemed very desirous that some Way might be contrived for the Reformation of the Manners of his Countrymen, and would some times say he thought they were out of the way, in not being willing to have *Englishmen* for their Pastors.

He seemed to be a Person of a tender Conscience, and would, if seriously dealt withal for a small Fault, confess the same with Tears, and

---

387 Mehitable Keape (Cape), who inherited part of her grandfather Japheth Hannit's lands. Mehitable kept school at Christiantown, and her house was used for worship. She may have been the wife of David Cape (Keape), who, along with Mehitable Keape and her mother, Jerusha Job(e), was deeded one-third of "Japheth's Field" in Chilmark. David Cape was a preacher at Christiantown and the grandfather of Hannah Capey (Capon) and Elizabeth Occucha. *WGH*, 126–27, 311.

promise to amend what had been amiss in his Carriage, and would be as good as his Word therein.

He died of a Fever, which so disordered his Head that he was for the most part delirious in it: But when he was first taken, he said he questioned whether he should recover or not; and added, that he was willing to submit to the good Will and Pleasure of God concerning him, whether it were that he should live or die; only he earnestly desired to be reconciled unto him thro' Jesus Christ his only Saviour, and did trust and hope, that thro' his Mercy he should so be.

Finding that his Understanding began to fail him, he said he earnestly desired to meditate on God, but his Head was so disordered, that he could think but little of him. After this he was but little sensible; but when [113] he had any lucid Intervals, he confessed his Sins, and professed Hopes of finding Mercy with God; particularly just before he died he spoke to this Purpose. And why may we not hope that he obtained Mercy?

EXAMPLE XVI.
DAVID PAUL, *who died at a Place called* Nunpaug *in* Edgartown, *in the Spring of the Year* 1718.

THE Parents of this *David* were esteemed morally honest, and did sometimes pray to God; yet were they very faulty in that they did not send their Children to School as they ought to have done: So that neither this nor their other Children[388] were taught to read; nor was this *David* otherwise well instructed in his Youth; and not being *trained up in the way in which he should go*, he began while young to drink hard, and keep bad Company.

When he was of Age to marry, he took to wife the Daughter[389] of a praying Man, *Jacob Sockaconnit*,[390] hereafter mentioned. However, he did not for some time follow the Example of his Father-in-Law, in worshipping of God with his Family; yet it seems he had so much sense of God and Religion in his Heart, that he would, when he was in trouble, call upon him for Mercy. And having no Child for several Years after he was first married, he was much troubled at it; and not being so ignorant as not to know that Children were God's Gift, he prayed to him to give him

---

388 He may have been the brother of Peter Paul, an Indian laborer, and/or Joseph Paul. *WGH*, 179–80, 333.

389 Possibly Anna Paul, though this woman could also have been his daughter or sister. *WGH*, 251.

390 *IC*, 116–20*.

a Child; and vowed that if he did so, he should then be *his God*, and that he would love and serve him.

God condescended to hear this Prayer of his,[391] and so to put him upon the trial, whether he would be as good as his Promise or not: nor did the poor Man forget the Engagement that he had laid himself under, to serve the Lord, who had granted him the Mercy he desired. He declared that he received his Child as a Gift of God, in answer to the Prayer which he had made to him, and therefore acknowledged himself as bound by Promise to serve him.

The Vows of God being thus upon him, he without further Delay set up God's Worship in his House, praying Morning and Evening to him; and very much reformed ⌈114⌉ what was amiss in his Life: yet would sometimes drink too hard; and when he had so done, would be much troubled at it, and under such Discouragements about his own State as not to be able for some time to call upon God in his House, as he had been used to do. But then he would renew his Resolutions, *to look again towards God's Holy Temple*,[392] and would call upon the Name of the Lord.

After some time, his Mother dying, he was much affected at it, and renewed his Resolutions to abstain from the Sin of Drunkenness, with which he had hitherto been sometimes overtaken; and now God helped him to fulfil his Engagements herein. He (so far as I can understand) in the following Years of his Life lived very temperately;[393] and tho he still sometimes used those spirituous Liquors which had formerly hurt him, yet he took care not at all to abuse himself with them.

And having thus overcome the Lust and Sin that did before so easily beset him, he did for the future run with Patience the Race that was set before him.

He called on God daily in his House, making humble Confessions of his Sins, and imploring the pardoning Mercy of God thro' the precious Blood of his dear Son. He also very constantly and seriously attended the Worship of *God* in *his House*: and under the Advantage of publick Ordinances, and private Conferences with God's People, in which he delighted, he seemed to grow in Grace, and in the Knowledge of his Lord and Saviour; so that his Profiting was plainly discerned by such as were acquainted with him. And he grew into such Esteem for Piety and Wisdom, among the Christian *Indians* of the little Village to which he belonged, that on Days of Fasting and Prayer in that Place, he was sometimes desired to be

391 He was possibly the father of David Paul, an Indian of Edgartown who bought 100 acres in Southeast Tisbury from Samuell Nahomon (*IC*, 133–34), and of Sarah Amos, who married Amos Ianoxso (Amos Amos) Jr. *WGH*, 149, 159, 215, 251, 333.

392 Jonah 2:4.

393 Abstained from drinking.

a Mouth to the rest in the Duty of Prayer, wherein they spent the After-noon; several of the best qualified taking their turn to lead in that Duty.

Being now justly looked upon as a godly Man, he did in some good measure comply with the Duty required of such, when it is said to them, *Deut.* vi. 6, 7 *The Words which I command thee shall be in shall be in thine Heart; and thou shalt teach them diligently to thy Children,* &c. He having asked one Child of God, God was pleased to give him several more; and it was his Desire to give again to [115] *God* these kind Gifts of his to him; and he would sometimes express to others this Desire of his.

But this did most evidently appear in his Care to educate his Children for God, that so they might be prepared to live to him.

He took very great Care that his Children might not fail of being taught to read, being himself sensible of the Inconveniency of being without such Learning; and tho he was under a great Disadvantage, as living far from any School, in which they might be instructed, yet he was so set on their Learning, as for some time to get them boarded at a House near the School, to which he desired to send them. And which is yet more, there being no School in the Place the Year before he dy'd, he was himself at the Charge of hiring for several Months a sober young Man, who was then a Candidate for the Ministry among the *Indians*, on purpose to teach his Children to read and instruct them in their Cat-echisms; by which means they received great Advantages.

Some might possibly enquire, how this Man was able to be at such Charges; but I shall prevent this by informing them, that being a Person of great Industry in his Business, he provided for things honest and com-mendable, *not only in the Sight of the Lord, but in the Sight of Men also.*[394] He had his Cows, Oxen, Horses, and Swine,[395] also his Cart and Plough,[396] and Cribs, and Stacks of Corn, and his Wigwam well furnished with things necessary for the Use of his Family, and also to give to the Poor, when the Case called for it.

---

394 2 Corinthians 8:21.

395 Mayhew uses this impressive array of possessions and livestock to help establish David Paul's status and credentials as a sincere convert and good patriarch. As David Silverman notes, keeping livestock had important ramifications for maintaining land and power in Native com-munities: like other Native groups in New England, the Wampanoags of Martha's Vineyard "used animal husbandry as a multipurpose tool to denote their acceptance of colonial ways and to further distinctly native values and priorities. Livestock-holding allowed Indians to supple-ment the dwindling productivity of their hunting without abandoning the chase altogether. Its link with Christianity won native communities greater protection from colonial power bro-kers": Silverman, "We Chuse to be Bounded," par. 4–5.

396 This item is of interest in part because, as David Silverman notes (ibid., 5), "although Indi-ans grazed livestock, they rarely plowed, and most native men remained conspicuously absent from the planting fields."

Yet there was one thing that this good Man thought himself to want, and that was a comfortable Assurance of the Love of God to his Soul; tho God perhaps saw it best for him, that he should be without such Comfort, and that he should *be in heaviness thro' manifold Temptations.*[397]

When he discoursed concerning his own State before God, he still appeared to be in the dark about it, and used to reflect on himself as a most vile and sinful Creature; yet would in the Conclusion of his Discourses encourage himself in the Mercy of God, and the plenteous Redemption that is in his Son Jesus Christ: nor did he give over seeking for Mercy in the Way proposed in the Gospel. About a Year before he dy'd, he had a Fit of Sickness, wherein he, more especially, frequently talked as has now been declared.

[116] He was apprehensive that he had not long to live, for some time before he dy'd, while he seemed to be pretty well in Health, and would then say, that he would have such as had any Love for him, discover the same by taking care that his Children might be well instructed when he was dead; and he himself did frequently give good Instructions to them: he also charged his Wife to see to it, that they were well educated. When he was taken with the Fever, whereof he dy'd in about five Days, his Distemper[398] was so violent, that he had enough to do to conflict with the Pains of it; and he was so choaked with Phlegm, that he was capable of saying very little, so as to be understood: yet those that attended him perceived, that he cry'd earnestly to God for Mercy, and he thanked the Minister that came and prayed with him: And being asked, whether he still trusted in God his Saviour; he by Signs shewed that he did, and so dy'd.

EXAMPLE XVII.
JACOB SOCKAKONNIT, *who died at* Nunpaug
in Edgartown, *in the Year* 1721.

THis *Jacob*[399] was the eldest Son of *Thomas Sockakonnit,*[400] mentioned *Chapter* I. And being the Son of so good a Man, was well instructed in his younger Days; and was so far affected and influenced by the Means he enjoyed, and those Operations of God's Holy Spirit which did accompany

---

397 1 Peter 1:6.

398 Disease; sometimes used on the island to refer specifically to smallpox. See "At the Meeting of the Select Men, Dec. 14, 1737" and "At the Meeting of the Select Men, Dec. 26, 1737," in *A Report of the Record Commissions of the City of Boston containing the Records of Boston Selectmen, 1736 to 1742* (Boston: Rockwell and Churchill, City Printers, 1886), 15:89, 91.

399 His daughter married David Paul (*IC*, 113–16*).

400 *IC*, 35–37*.

them, that he acknowledged the *Truth* and *Excellency* of the *Christian Religion*, and appeared to have a Love to the House and Ordinances of God, and a high Esteem of good Men, and seemed himself to desire to be such a one.

He prayed daily in his House, and very constantly attended the publick Worship of God; and if at any time it happened that there was no publick Preaching in the Place where he lived, he appeared to be very uneasy at it, and would scarce give any rest to those that had the Management of the *Indian* Affairs on the Island, till there was a Preacher provided to dispense God's Word in that little Place. And when the *Indians* of that Village had for many Years no Meeting-house,[401] after the burning of one which they formerly had there, this *Jacob* kindly [117] invited them to meet in his own large Wigwam, and there courteously received them as long as he lived, professing a great Satisfaction in it, that the Word of God was brought so nigh to him, even into his own Dwelling.

He appeared to be much concerned if any of the People of the Place did not duly attend the publick Worship of God, and would do all that he could to persuade them to attend constantly on the Means of their Salvation. He did also much encourage the upholding of a School in the Place, and endeavoured to persuade the People to send their Children to it.

Thus forward and active was this our *Jacob* for the upholding of Religion in the little Place to which he belonged; but, alas! there was one grievous Temptation with which he conflicted, he had an excessive Love to strong Drink, and would sometimes be overtaken and overcome by it: and tho he seemed to strive against it, yet the Temptations were so powerful, that it did too often prevail against him.

Such, as has been now declared, was for many Years the Weakness of this poor Man; yet I could not but observe, that, when I discoursed with him about his Sin and Fault therein, he never endeavoured to justify himself, or extenuate the Evil, of which he was guilty, but judged and

---

401 One of the great innovations of Puritan worship was the symbolic structure of the meetinghouse. Meetinghouses differed from churches in that they were used for both secular and religious purposes, whereas churches were primarily places of worship. Puritan meetinghouses emphasized the Puritan plain style and the distrust of church hierarchy: the buildings were typically square or rectangular, and instead of stained glass, windowpanes were clear glass, allowing for the intense sun of New England summers to beat down upon worshipers and inspire them with God's unadulterated magnificence. Until the nineteenth century, meetinghouses were usually unheated and so cold in winter that the baptismal water and the communion bread often froze. Pews were narrow, and most prayers were performed while standing. See Sinnott, *Meetinghouse and Church in Early New England*, 5, 9–11. Much of the architectural information about the earliest Wampanoag meetinghouses has been lost, though early church services on the island appear to have been held in the oldest section of the Hancock-Mitchell House, which some conjecture was built by Rev. Thomas Mayhew Jr. as a one-room meetinghouse for the Wampanoags living in Chilmark and Takemy. Scott, *Early Colonial Houses of Martha's Vineyard*, 3:186–87.

condemned himself for it, and bewailed his Misery on the account of the Power of that Corruption that he had in him, and renewed his Resolution to strive against it, and to wait on God for his gracious Assistance therein. I also observed that he (especially towards the latter Part of his Life) more carefully shunn'd the Occasions and Temptations by which he was apt to be overcome. He went not so frequently to drinking Houses[402] as he had been wont to do: nor did he drink so hard when at them, as he had formerly done. However, he remained still too much under the Power of this Lust.

Thus the Case stood with him till about two Years before he dy'd, when being more tender thorow[403] Convictions, he declared to an *Indian* Minister the deep Sense he had of the great Sin of Drunkenness, to which he acknowledged he had hitherto been too subject; and withal declared his Apprehensions of an absolute Necessity of a thorow Reformation, and Resolution, by the Help of God's Grace, to live a new Life.

[118] After this there was a sensible Reformation in the Man, and I cannot learn that he was from thence forward ever guilty of Drunkenness.

However, about half a Year after he had privately manifested his Repentance to this Minister, as has been now related, he did on a Day of Fasting and Prayer renew his Profession of Repentance, declaring his Sorrow for all his Sins, and his Resolutions to depart from them, and live to God: and during that Year and half which he lived after this, he seemed to be a new Man, and to live a new Life; and I could not now but think that he was truly turned from Sin to God, whether he was before converted or not.

About this time I observed Things in him that confirmed me in my Opinion, that he was become a good Man. I heard him pray with such Fervency and Affection, as made me think he had the Spirit as well as the Gift of Prayer bestowed on him.

I also divers times heard him magnifying the Grace and Goodness of God, in granting to the *Indians* such excellent Means, as they in the Ministry of the Word enjoyed, and telling them how much it concerned them to lay to Heart, and diligently improve the great and excellent Truths which they heard preached to them.

---

402 As Charles Banks comments, it is likely that early drinking houses and taverns on the island were in the dwellings of owners who used "an adjoining building or 'leanto' . . . as a store and tap room where the guests could sit on the 'bench' and smoke, drink, and play cards, and hear the village gossip." There were laws regulating the selling of "strong drink"; most specifically, after 1676 it was illegal to sell or even "any way directly or indirectly furnish" beer and strong drink to the Wampanoags and other Indians. This prohibition was widely violated, however, as Jacob's habit and many court cases make clear. *HMV,* 1:462–63; DCCR I.14, June 27, 1676.

403 Through.

Being satisfied that he was qualified for Communion with the Church of Christ, in all the Ordinances of the Gospel, I put him on his Duty of asking an Admission to them; but found that he laboured under such Discouragements, with respect thereto, as he could not yet overcome. He feared that he had not yet experienced a Work of Regeneration,[404] or saving Conversion to God, and so remained unqualified for Communion with him in his Ordinances. However, I now observed that in him, which confirmed me in my good Opinion of him, as that he appeared to discourse on this Subject with very great Awe and Reverence, and such a Seriousness as would become one that set the Lord always before him. There was nothing light or trifling in his Discourse; nor did he seem at all unwilling to open the State of his Soul to me. And tho I could not at that time satisfy him, that it was his present Duty to ask an Admission to the Table of the Lord, yet a Duty in general he acknowledged it to be; and also owned the Obligations lying on him to prepare himself for it.

[119] A few Months before he dy'd, he so far overcame the Discouragements under which he thus laboured, as to signify his Desires of an Admission to the Privileges of which he before thought himself unworthy: but the Church to which he would have joined, being at that time without a Pastor, this for the present hindred his Proceeding; and being in a short time after taken with the Illness whereof he dy'd, he never had an Opportunity to enjoy that which he now much desired.

He was sick several Weeks before he dy'd, and some part of the time he was very much in the dark about the State of his Soul; so I found him to be when I visited him, and talked with him about his spiritual State. He then doubted whether his *Heart was sound in God's Statutes,*[405] and did not appear to have any Assurance of the Love of God to his Soul; yet I hoped by what he said of himself, that he truly hunger'd and thirsted after Righteousness, and therefore was one of them who would in due time be filled. He expressed a very deep Sense of his own Sinfulness, and earnest Desires of being reconciled to God, thro' the Blood of Jesus Christ his only Saviour, and of being sanctify'd by the Spirit of God, and fitted for his Kingdom; as also his Resolutions to continue seeking to God for these Mercies.

I intended to have again visited him, but he dy'd sooner than I thought he would have done; so I missed the Opportunity.

---

404 Theologically, regeneration is "the process or fact of being born again in a spiritual sense" (OED). As Perry Miller rightfully asserts, for Puritans, "regeneration began with the premise of an omnipotent God and an impotent man." That is, regeneration was the result of divine acts "which man himself could take no part." Miller, *New England Mind*, 26–27.

405 Psalm 119:80.

However, I have been informed by credible Persons, that were with him in his Sickness, that he was after I saw him often heard calling earnestly on God for his Mercy, and seen looking in his Bible, and reading Places of Scripture in it; and indeed his Bible was what (while he was in Health) he made much use of.[406]

The Persons who thus informed me, did also tell me, that he grew much more chearful before he dy'd, than in the former Part of his Sickness he had been; and that he obtained a comfortable Hope of the Love of God to his Soul, insomuch that he divers times expressed his Joy, by singing some Verses in the Psalms that were suitable for such a Purpose; and that he at last lamented his having too long delayed to ask an Admission to the Communion of God's People, whose Communion is with himself, and his Son Christ Jesus. However, I hope, he is [120] now joyned *to the General Assembly, and Church of the First-born, which are written in Heaven.*[407]

EXAMPLE XVIII.
JAMES SPANIARD, *who died in* Chilmark *in the Year* 1721.

THis Man was sirnamed *Spaniard,* because he was a Spanish *Indian,*[408] being, as I have heard, brought from some part of the *Spanish Indies*[409] when he was a Boy, and sold[410] in *New-England.*

He was not long after he came into the Country bought by a Gentleman[411] in *Chilmark,* with whom he lived many Years, and was kindly used; having, I doubt not, in that Family many good Instructions given him.

---

406 A common way in which both Wampanoags and colonists "made use of" their Bibles was to annotate them.

407 Hebrews 12:23.

408 As Alan Gallay notes, New Englanders sometimes referred to Native Americans from Florida (a Spanish colony) as "Spanish Indians." Alan Gallay, *The Indian Slave Trade,* 304.

409 See also Bannon, *Indian Labor in the Spanish Indies.*

410 James Spaniard's slavery represents a trend in early eighteenth-century New England to import "Eastern," "Carolina," and "Spanish" Indians. Although the majority of slaves in New England were of African descent, the Native population was also vulnerable to enslavement. Most New England Indians who were captured and enslaved were sold elsewhere, however, in places such as the Caribbean. James Spaniard's dislocation and separation from his family was a deliberate, rather than accidental, part of the English slave trade. Many more New England Algonquians served long terms as indentured servants in the eighteenth century, but slavery was not abolished in Massachusetts until 1783. For a more complete discussion, see Newell, "Changing Nature of Indian Slavery," 106–36.

411 *Major* Benjamin Skiff *Esq.* [Mayhew's note.] Major Benjamin Skiff (1651–1717/18) was one of the most prominent men in Chilmark and a leading citizen of the island. When he died, he left a large estate: appraised at just over £2,748, the property made him most likely the richest man in Chilmark. HMV, 2 (Annals of Chilmark): 36–38.

His kind Master dying a few Years before him, he was much affected at the Breach which God had made in the Family, and made this pious Reflection on it, *It is the Will of God that it should be so and we must be contented.*

Not long after this he, on very easy Terms, purchased his Freedom from his Mistress,[412] his Master having never designed to keep him a Slave all his Days: but tho he had met with very kind Usage here, yet he laid much to Heart the unkind Treatment he had met withal, in being separated from all his Friends and Relations, and brought out of his Country into a strange Land, from whence he never expected to return again, and at this he sometimes appeared to be discontented; which being informed of, I took an Opportunity to discourse with him about the Matter, telling him, that tho what had in this Particular befallen him, might be what was hard to be borne, yet God might design the same in Mercy to his Soul, inasmuch as he was brought from a Place where he would probably have perished for lack of Vision, into a Land of Light, where he might, if it were not his own Fault, attain to the Knowledge of the only true God, and Jesus Christ whom he had sent, whom to know is Life Eternal. I advised him therefore not to give way to Discontent on this account, but endeavour to make a [121] good Improvement of the Price which God had put into his Hand; which if he did, the Benefit which he would receive thereby, would infinitely more than compensate all the Wrong that had been done him. He seemed kindly to accept what I thus said to him, and I hope made a good Use of it.

Thus becoming a free Man, he quickly marry'd a Wife,[413] who had been well instructed by her pious Parents, and so knew God's Will, and approved of Things excellent, tho her Conversations was, in some respects, faulty.

It is to be hoped, that he had before this learned to pray in secret: for being now joined with one, who was willing to join in the Worship of God with him, he used to pray both Morning and Evening with her, and continued to do so as long as he lived.

Falling soon after he was first marry'd, into an Acquaintance with some of our *Indians*, which he had better been a Stranger to, he began to

---

412 Hannah Skiff (1660–1758). Her tombstone, with that of her husband, is in Abel's Hill Cemetery, Martha's Vineyard. *HMV*, 3:331, 2 (Annals of Chilmark): 36–38.

413 Intercultural marriages between Algonquians and other people of color became increasingly frequent in eighteenth-century New England but were still relatively rare when James Spaniard married his wife, see Plane, *Colonial Intimacies*, 146. Such marriages challenged the definition of "Indian" for both insiders of Native communities and outsiders. On intermarriage in the eighteenth and nineteenth centuries on Martha's Vineyard, see Silverman, *Faith and Boundaries*, 223–73.

learn their Ways, and once or twice drank more than he ought to have done: but being by a Friend privately admonished of his Sin and Danger, he without Delay separated himself from the Company, and Society of such wicked Persons, and walked no more in the Way with them, but refrained his Feet from their Path; nor did he fall into any other scandalous Immoralities.

He was constant and diligent in his Attendance on the publick Worship of God, and used to discourse seriously on Matters of Religion, and the Concerns of his own Soul; tho not being a compleat Master of either the *English* or *Indian* Tongue, he could not express himself very aptly in either the one or the other of them: but the *English* he seemed to understand best, in which therefore he generally prayed, his Wife understanding that also.

He was long sick and weak before he dy'd, and sometimes in such great Pain, as he could not endure without very sad Complaints, tho I never heard that he was charged with Impatience. He was also in the time of his Sickness deeply concerned about the State of his Soul, and very sollicitous that he might not fall short of Eternal Life; and did in his Distress often cry to God for his Mercy. He also divers times desired others to pray with him, particularly the Reverend Mr. *William Homes,*[414] besides others, both *English* and *Indians,* who do all te[122]stify, that he appeared very desirous to be reconciled to God, and made a Partaker of his Everlasting Mercies.

When I visited and discoursed with him, (which I several times did) I still found him in a very humble frame. He owned himself to be a great Sinner, altogether unworthy of God's Mercy; but yet said that he had some Hopes, and that he earnestly desired an Interest in the Mercy of God, thro' his Son Jesus Christ, and was resolved still to look to him for it, (or Words much to this purpose). And tho he seemed to want that *Joy of Faith*[415] which is much to be desired, yet I could not but hope that he was a true Believer.

Within a few Days after I last visited him, he died; and I am assured by some worthy of Credit, who were with him, that he then had *Peace* and *Joy in believing.*[416] He in the Morning of that Day, which was the Evening of his Life, experienced such Consolations as he never before enjoyed, and had such Foretastes of the Blessedness of *another World,* as

---

414 William Homes (1668–1746) taught for three years on Martha's Vineyard and then, starting in 1714, became the minister to the white community in Chilmark. See Homes, "Diary."

415 Philippians 1:25.

416 Romans 15:13.

did exceedingly refresh and delight him; and make him willing, yea and desirous, to leave *this* and go to *that.*

He now exhorted those that were with him, to trust continually in God, and be constant and diligent Seekers of him. He earnestly exhorted his Wife to take care that his little Son,[417] the only Child he had, might be taught to read, and trained up in the Way in which he ought to walk. He told her also, that when Persons went Journeys abroad, and left *their Families,* they used sometimes to commit them to the Care of some Man or Men, whom they desired to leave in Charge with them; but that the Journey he was going being long, he would commit *his* to the Care and Charge of God only; who he knew could, and he hoped would take care of them. He told her, that if she trusted in God, he hoped she would not in vain seek for Bread to satisfy her and her Child's hunger.

Having spoken to this purpose, he went smiling out of the World; and it is to be hoped, then went *unto God his exceeding Joy.*[418]

[123] EXAMPLE XIX.
JANNOHQUISSOO, *an old Man, who died at* Nashaun,
otherwise called Slocum's-Island,[419] *in* February 1722-3.

THis *Jannohquissoo* was in his younger Days a Person of a vitious[420] Conversation. He was given to Drunkenness, and such other Excesses as that Sin commonly leadeth Men into: nor did he become a *new Man* before he began to become an *old one*; but better late than never.

He was convinced of the Irregularity of his Life, and began to reform it, some Years before he was able to get a compleat Victory over his Lust after strong Drink, that being at some times too strong for him, as well as the Drink it self, which it drew him to follow after.

But God having a Design to subdue and conquer this Lust of his, was pleased by a very awakening Providence, to bring him under a solemn Obligation, to live more soberly for the future, than he had before done; for undertaking to go in a small *Canoo* a little way over the Water, to a Place where he expected to find Company and Drink, his *Canoo* overset,

---

417 James Spaniard, who appears in John Allen's "Supplies" list. Probably the husband of Phebe Spaniard, listed in Mayhew's distributions to the poor, and father of Sarah Spaniard, an Indian of Gay Head. *WGH,* 327, 333, 417; Mayhew "Distribution to the Poor"; Allen, "Account Book."

418 Psalm 43:4.

419 One of the Elizabeth Islands.

420 Vicious (*OED*).

and he had very like *to have perished in the Way.*[421] He was alone in the Sea; nor did he know that any Person either saw him, or could help him: and, being now in great Distress, he cry'd earnestly to God for Mercy, and made Vows to him, that, if he would deliver him, he would endeavour to part with all his Sins, and live to his Glory; and God was pleased to hear his Prayer, and send Deliverance to him. *This poor Man cried, the Lord heard him, and saved him out of all his Trouble.*[422] Some that saw him in Distress came and took him up, when it had been too *late,* if it had been one Minute later.

Being thus delivered, he performed to the Lord the Vows which he had made; for, tho many do quickly forget the Promises which they make to God when they are in Distress, yet all do not so, and this Man was one Instance of a Person that did not. He from this time for[124]ward forsook his Drunkenness, and all his drinking Companions, and *lived soberly;* and not only so, but also *righteously and godly in the World.*[423] If he was not before a praying Man, he now became one, worshipping God daily in his House; and appeared to take care that he might not *have any Fellowship with the unfruitful Works of Darkness, but rather reprove them.*[424]

Being thus reformed in his Life and Manners, the few Families on the little Island where he lived, did, with the Consent of the *English* Authority, who managed the *Indian* Affairs here, chuse him to be a Ruler over them; and he accepting the Office, did with much Fidelity discharge it as long as he lived.

He endeavoured to be a *Terror to Evil Doers*[425] among his Neighbours, frequently inflicting corporal Punishments on them for their Crimes, and not sparing his own Children when they appeared to be guilty.[426]

He shewed a great Desire that Religion might be upheld, and promoted in the little Island on which he lived; he used his utmost Endeavours, that the few Families there might constantly have a Minister to preach to them; and he himself, tho no Minister by Profession, yet carried himself very much like one in the Visits which he frequently made to the Houses of those whom he lived among, entertaining the Families with good Discourses when he was with them, and giving many good Instructions and Admonitions to such as he thought needed them.

---

421   Psalm 2:12.

422   Psalm 34:6.

423   Titus 2:12.

424   Ephesians 5:11. Mayhew's original reads "Followship," a typo.

425   Proverbs 21:15.

426   Like William Lay (*IC*, 26), the patriarch of this family has incorporated into his belief system some Puritan views on child rearing and corporal punishment.

He was very much grieved at the evil Conversation of some in the Place where he lived, and of his own Children in particular, whom he, not beginning early enough withal, was not able to restrain from their Wickedness; and as tho this had not been Affliction enough, he had a Wife, who being her self *like one of the foolish Women,*[427] too much countenanced her Sons in their Ungodliness, contending with her Husband for punishing their Offences, insomuch that he would sometimes say to her, that she acted as tho she desired to call her Children into everlasting Burnings: nor did she appear to repent of these Miscarriages until the Death of her Husband, which was but a very little while before she her self dy'd.

[125] This good Man, like some others, deferred his joining to the Church of Christ longer than he should have done, *viz.* till within a Year of his Death; but when he offered himself, gave great Satisfaction to those that admitted him, not only by manifesting a hearty Repentance for all the Miscarriages of his Life; but by professing Faith in Jesus Christ, as the only Saviour of sinful Men, such as he confessed himself to be: and that it might appear that he knew in whom he had believed, and that he was able to keep what he had committed to him, he particularly declared his Persuasion of what is revealed in the Scriptures, concerning his Person, Offices, Death, Resurrection, and Ascension into Heaven, &c.

He languished some Months before he dy'd; and, as the former Part of his Life had been very vicious, so in the former Part of his Sickness he was in great Distress about his Soul. God *made him to possess the Iniquitys of his Youth, caused the Iniquity of his Heels to compass him about.*[428] He confessed with bitterness of Soul the Drunkenness of which he had been guilty, yea and other Sins too, as Uncleanness, &c. and declared that his Sins were a *Burden too heavy for him to bear,*[429] and that he feared that God would cast him away for ever for them.

But yet God left him not utterly to despair of his Mercy, but enabled him to cry to him for the Pardon of his Offences, and that he might be reconciled to him thro' the Blood of Christ, which cleanseth from all Sin; and the Issue was, that God had Compassion on him, spake Peace to his distressed Soul, enabling him so to hope in his Mercy, as to be willing to die, yea even to desire to die, that he might go to his heavenly Father: and with such a Hope of a better Life, he ended his Life here in this World.

---

427 Job 2:10.
428 Job 13:26–27; Psalm 49:5.
429 Psalm 38:4.

[126] EXAMPLE XX.
HENRY OHHUNNUT, *alias* JANNOHQUISSOO, *an old Man,*
who died at Christian-Town, December 17th, 1724.

WHile this *Henry*[430] was but a young Man, meeting with some Trouble on *Martha's Vineyard,* which made his Mind uneasy, he left the Island, and travelled about on the main Land from one Place to another. At length coming to *Natick,*[431] and there abiding one Winter at least, hearing the Word of God preached, and beholding the Order of the *Indian* Church, which had been some time before that settled there, by the renowned Mr. *John Eliot,* whom our *Henry* sometimes heard preaching to the *Indians*; the Effect of his enjoying these Advantages was, that he believed the things which he heard, was awakened, and became a *Peantamaenin,* i.e. a *praying Man*; and being such a one, he professed Subjection to the Gospel of Christ, and was admitted as a Member in full Communion in the said Church.

Being returned to *Martha's Vineyard,* he there marry'd a Woman called *Dinah,*[432] who proved a good Wife to him, and a very good Christian; the same who is afterwards mentioned *Chapter* III. *Example* 2. By this Woman he was much encouraged in the Ways of God and Religion; and his Conversation was, so far as I can learn, constantly ordered as it became the Gospel.

He was diligent and steddy in his Business, labouring constantly with his Hands, to provide for his Family. He prayed daily in his House, and brought up his Children[433] *in the Nurture and Admonition of the Lord*: and they, several of them, dy'd very hopefully; but he living on the Main when they dy'd, I could not obtain so particular an Account of them as I would have done. However, there are two of them briefly mentioned in their Mother's Life.[434] He was also very constant in his Attendance on the publick Worship and Ordinances of God, as is well known to those who were acquainted with him.

---

430 Son of Ompohhunnut, the brother of Mittark (IC, 21–23*) and the uncle of Job Ahhunnut, the husband of Hannah Ahhunnut (*IC,* 140–41) and Abigail Ahhunnut (*IC,* 162–64). Job also married Ruth Awhunnt and two other women. *WGH,* 102, 154, 188.

431 A praying town in Massachusetts established by John Eliot.

432 The daughter of Panupuhquah, one of the first Wampanoag preachers at Chilmark. *IC,* 72, 138–40; *WGH,* 334, 346.

433 His children were Elisha Ahhunnut (?–>1684; *IC,* 139); Nathan Ahhunnut (?–>1684; *IC,* 139), and possibly John Ianoxso. Henry also had a son Amos Ianoxso (?–ca. 1752) by his second wife, Esther (Asquannit) Ahunnet. Amos Ianoxso's wife Jerusha Ionockso [Amos] is named in Mayhew's list of disbursements to the poor. *WGH,* 145, 170, 188, 192, 334, 427.

434 Elisha Ahhunnut and Nathan Ahhunnut both died at about age sixteen or seventeen: *IC,* 139.

Having been my self long and well acquainted with the Person I am speaking of, I can frely testify, that [127] he always appeared to me to be a very serious Man. I have divers times heard him pray very affectionately and understandingly; and I have also frequently heard him discourse very piously. He often lamented the Sins of his own Countrymen, but especially that of Drunkenness; which Evil, as he carefully abstained from, so he earnestly testify'd against in others, who were sometimes found faulty. Indeed he had a commendable Courage and Boldness in reproving the Sins of his Neighbours, of which Courage he made even his Superiors sensible, when there was Occasion for it.

He had a Heart to glorify God under afflictive Dispensations[435] owning his Wisdom, Sovereignty and Goodness in them: I shall here give one Instance of his so doing. Two or three Years before his own Death, he had a Son drowned, if not murdered, (which latter the poor old Man and some others suspected) and it was much to be feared too that he dy'd drunk, and so perished in his Sins. This was a most afflictive Providence to the aged Father, and such a fiery Trial to him, as was very hard to be endured. But while he was under this sore Affliction, lamenting to me the Loss he had sustained, and relating the sorrowful Circumstances with which it was attended, he told me that he quieted himself with this Consideration, that what had befallen him was ordered by God, who might do what he pleas'd, and who *ever* did all things well; and that having vowed to love his God as long as he lived, he was still resolved that he would do so, notwithstanding what was now come on him.

Observing not long before his Death, his constant and diligent Attendance on the publick Worship and Ordinances of God, notwithstanding his great Age, and the many bodily Infirmities which he was under, I one Day asked him, whether he experienced any Pleasure and Delight in hearing the Word of God preached, and attending on the Ordinances of his Worship? *Yes, very great*, said he to me. I also then asked him concerning his Hope of future Blessedness; in answer whereto he told me, that he had a strong Hope that God would save him: And he mentioned the Merits and Sufferings of Jesus Christ, as the Ground and Foundation of that hope of his. I asked him, whether he [128] found that he obtained a Deliverance from under that Power and Dominion of Sin, to which Mankind are naturally subject? To which he reply'd, that formerly he found his Lusts and Corruptions very strong, but of latter Years God had given

---

435 The ordering or arrangement of events by divine providence (*OED*). Mayhew means that Henry Ohhunnut gave glory to God by asserting God's "Wisdom, Sovereignty and Goodness," even when God's arrangement of the world (providence) was not to Henry's advantage, such as when his son died.

him Strength against them. How long is it, said I to him, since God has so helped you? I think about twenty Years, reply'd he to me.

He was sick but a few Days before he dy'd, and I saw him not during that time, (being from home on a Journey) tho he desired to have spoken with me: however, I am well informed, that he called much on God while he lay sick; and that declaring his Expectations of Death, he received the same joyfully, professing, that he hoped to enjoy Life Eternal thro' Jesus Christ his only Saviour. He also gave much good Counsel to his Son, who took care of him in his Sickness, exhorting him to be a constant and diligent Seeker of the Lord his God.

This was that poor old Man mentioned in *Chapter* IV. *Example* 20. in young *Joseph Peag's* Life, and he whom that Child would have taken Care of; of which there was indeed great need, he being grown very helpless.

[129] A
SUPPLEMENT
TO
The Second Chapter

Giving a more general Account of several Good Men not yet nam'd.

There have been many godly Men among our *Indians*, who may be justly named as Examples of Piety, besides those already mentioned; but I shall content myself with giving a more general Account of a few of them, than I have done of the Examples already given. And they are these.

I. *Pamchannit*,[436] who was a petty *Sachim* of part of the Island now called *Chilmark*, and the happy Father of the well known Mr. *Japheth Hannit*, who has been frequently before mentioned. He embraced the Christian Religion soon after the first publishing of the Gospel on the said Island, and continued a zealous Professor of it as long as he lived. He was a devout Worshipper of God in his Family, and a diligent Instructor of those under his Charge: he was one of the first Members of that Church whereof *Hiacoomes*[437] was the first Pastor, and behaved himself from his first Conversion to the end of his Life as did become the Gospel. He dy'd at *Nashouohkamuk* in the Spring of the Year 1672, but what he then said I have not heard, and so I cannot declare; yet there are good Grounds to hope that he dy'd in the Lord.

II. *Pehtauattooh*, who was a younger Brother of that *Pamchannit* but now mentioned. He was a Man of a very blameless Life, and undoubted Piety. Several that [130] were acquainted with him, yet living, do affirm, that he was a constant and serious Worshipper of God in his House, *walking with a perfect Heart*[438] in it, and that he was a sharp Reprover of Sin, and a diligent Instructor of his own Family and others. He was a Member of the Church whereof *John Tackanash* was Pastor, and he adorned the Doctrine of God his Saviour by a well ordered Conversation. I cannot certainly tell in what Year he dy'd, but I think it was near about the Year 1680. The Place was the East End of *Winthrop's* Island.[439]

---

436 The older brother of Janawannit, a sachem, minister, and schoolmaster in Chilmark. *IC*, 20–22*; *WGH*, 134, 211.

437 *IC*, 1–12*.

438 Psalm 101:2.

439 Naushon, one of the Elizabeth Islands.

III. *Lazarus.* The Person I here intend was before his Conversion called *Cain*, and by some so called afterwards.

He is by all acknowledged to be a *Pawwaw*, or *Wizard*, before he was by the Grace of God in the Gospel *turned from Darkness unto Light, and from the Power of Satan unto God.*[440] When the *Sachim Mittark*, of whom he was a Friend and Favourite, became a Christian, and a Preacher of the Gospel to his Countrymen at the *Gayhead*, this *Cain* renounced the Devil,[441] and became a Proselyte of *Mittark's*, and Disciple of Jesus Christ.

And, being some Years after admitted as a Member of the Church whereof Mr. *Japheth* was Pastor, he was baptized by the Name *Lazarus*, by which he was afterwards frequently called.

Being thus become a Christian, he lived and acted like one all his Life after. He no more returned to the Sorceries of which he had been formerly guilty; but instead of worshipping the Devil, as he had done, was a constant Worshipper of God in and thro' Jesus Christ; calling daily on him in his House, and publickly attending the Ordinances of his Worship on the *Sabbath*, or *Lord's-Day*.

I'm credibly informed, that when he lay a dying, he experienced such Consolations as were not small; and that being then by one spoken to about some of the Affairs of this World, he said to him, *Say no more to me of these Things, they are dull and insipid Things to me; but if you will speak to me of the Things of the World to come, I will hear you gladly about them.* He dy'd about the Year 1690.

[131] IV. *Amos*, who was a godly *Indian* of *Chappaquiddick*, and dy'd there in or about the Year 1690. He was one of the principal Members of the Church on that little Island, and by all acknowledged to have been a very serious Man, and one who lived a very holy and blameless Life: and being so *good* a Man himself, he endeavoured that his Children might be *so* too; and one of them, if no more, proved such a one, *viz.* the good Deacon *Jonathan Amos*, of whom I have before spoken.

In the same Year 1690, or not long before or after it, there dy'd at the said *Chappaquiddick* several other godly Men, whom I shall but name,

---

440 Acts 26:18.

441 *Pawwaws* were powerful visionaries and healers. They provoked great fear in the Puritan colonists, who often explained their power by aligning *pawwaws* with the devil. For example, Edward Winslow reported, "The office and duty of the powah is to be exercised principally in calling upon the Devil, and curing diseases of the sick or wounded. . . . If the party be wounded, he will also seem to suck the wound, but if they be curable (as they say) he toucheth it not, but *askooke*, that is the snake, *or wobsacuck*, that is the eagle, sitteth on his shoulder and licks the same. This none see but the powah, who tells them he doth it himself. If the party be otherwise diseased, it is accounted sufficient if in any shape he but come into the house, taking it for an undoubted sign of recovery." Winslow, *Good newes from New England,* 343–44.

viz. V. *Thomas Oonqun.*[442] VI. *Washamon.*[443] VII. *Jehu.* VIII. *Adam.*[444] IX. *Samuel Kohtohkomut.*

X. *John Kossunnut,* who was a Son in law of Hiacoomes.[445] These were Persons in such Esteem for Piety, that if I had not mentioned them, I am apt to think that some *English* People that knew them, would have blamed me for it, tho I can give no particular Account of them.

XI. *Paul,* commonly called *Old Paul,* who dy'd at *Christian-Town* about the Year 1676, was generally esteemed a godly Man, being a serious Professor of Religion, constant in the Performance of the Duties of it, and, as far I can learn, without any Stain in his Life and Conversation.

XII. *John Howwannan*[446] was another Person of the same Character with him last mentioned, and dy'd in the same Place about the Year 1678.

XIII. *Pattompan,*[447] who dy'd in *Tisbury* in the Year 1688. He was a Brother of three Ministers mentioned in the forgoing Chapter, *viz. John, Micah,* and *Stephen Shohkau,*[448] and was esteemed like them for Piety. There is another Brother yet living, tho a very old Man, his Name *Daniel Shohkau;*[449] he still preacheth the Gospel to a few Families at *Winthrops* Island, and is justly accounted a good Christian.

XIV. *Wuttahhannompisin,* an *Indian* of the *Gayhead,* who, by the oversetting of a *Canoo,* was drowned there, about the Year 1688. He was one of the first that embraced the Christian Religion in the said Place, when it was by *Mittark* preached to his Countrymen there in the Year 1663, and continued a constant Worship[132]per of God in and thro' his Son Jesus Christ, all his Days after, and was a Person of a very blameless Life. As he used to pray at other times, so God gave him Opportunity and a Heart to call on him, and commit his Soul to him while he was able to

---

442 The brother of James Oonqun and the son of Woompanummut (alias Oonqun). *WGH,* 266–67.

443 He was probably the father of Jacob Washaman, who married Elizabeth Washaman (Nataquanam), the squaw-sachem of Edgartown. Elizabeth Washaman was also the granddaughter and heir of Tawanquatuck. *IC,* 80–82*, 282–85; *WGH,* 117, 124–25, 132, 264.

444 Possibly Wisquannowas, alias Adam. His father and the sachem Pakkehpumassoo (*IC,* 3–4) were cousins. *WGH,* 106–7, 221.

445 *IC,* 1–12*.

446 Possibly the father of Asuh (Esau) Howanin, a minister of Christiantown. *WGH,* 120, 339.

447 Probably the father of Joseph Patompan and Josiah Pattompan (*IC,* 175, 218, 238), a minister at Christiantown and the husband of Ruth Pattompan (*IC,* 238). If so, this would make Pattompan the grandfather of Elizabeth Pattompan (*IC,* 176, 238–42*) and Jerusha Ompan (*IC,* 175–79*). If Joseph and Josiah were his sons, he might also possibly be the grandfather of Solomon Omppan (Patompan), the author of surviving "Biblical Marginalia" (*Native Writings,* 1:467, B47); Isaac Pentumpon, a debtor; Thomas Pontompon; and Didemus Pontompon. *WGH,* 124, 156, 199, 290, 346, 360–61.

448 *IC,* 28–30*, 30–31*, 54–56*.

449 Husband of Winnanmahkee. *WGH,* 238, 282.

keep his Head above Water, before he dy'd, as was reported by those that were with him and escaped. He dy'd a very old Man.

XV. *Simon Netawash,*[450] who dy'd at *Nashouohkamuk,* about the Year 1693. This Man was while young, somewhat given to the Sin of Drunkeness; but it pleased God some Years before he dy'd, to convince him of his Error herein, and enable him to live a sober Life: and not only so, but also to become a praying Man, worshipping God constantly in his House, and diligently attending the publick Worship of God in *his.* Being thus prepared by Grace for a Scene of Trouble and Affliction, God was pleased to send the same on him. He was taken with a Malady in one of his Hips, by reason whereof the Joynt at length perished, and also the Flesh that covered it. While he was thus visited, he endured a great deal of very strong Pain, but was exceedingly patient under it. He owned the sovereign Goodwill and Pleasure of God, in bringing the same on him, and manifested his Willingness to submit thereto. He daily cryed to God to sanctify the same to him, pardoning all his Sins, and fitting of him for his Eternal Kingdom: nor did he find it in vain thus to seek the Lord; for as his *outward Man decayed, his inner Man*[451] appeared to be *renewed Day by Day. In the Day that he cryed God heard him, and strengthened him with Strength in his Soul:*[452] so that when his Pain was almost insupportable, he experienced the Truth of that Word of God, *As thy Day is, so shall thy Strength be;*[453] he found Comfort in God when his outward Circumstances were most deplorable, and enjoyed great *Peace in believing.*[454] His last and dying Words were, *O Lord, I beseech thee to save my Soul.* While he uttered these Words, seeming to stretch himself on his Bed, his decayed Hip-Joynt came out of its Place, and lay naked without any Flesh or Skin on it, except that of his Hand, with which he at the same time laid hold [133] on it. Mr. *Japheth,* who was frequently with this Man before he dy'd, looked on him as an eminent Instance of Faith and Patience. I have heard that there was a Paper written of his dying Speeches; but it not coming to my Hand, I cannot here insert it.

XVI. *Isaac Wanahtak,* an *Indian* of *Christian-Town,* and a Member of an *Indian* Church on *Martha's Vineyard,* who dy'd in *Falmouth* on the Main, in the Year 1715. This was a Man of a very exemplary Conversation, as I, and many others that were acquainted with him, can testify. And I am credibly informed, that he dy'd as became a good Christian, calling upon

---

450 Father of Simon Netawash of Chilmark. *WGH,* 237, 354.

451 2 Corinthians 4:16.

452 Psalm 138:3.

453 Deuteronomy 33:25.

454 Romans 15:13.

God his Saviour, and putting his Trust in him for Life Eternal; and so laying down his Head with Comfort.

XVII. *Samuel Pashqunnahhamun*,[455] an old Man, who dy'd in *Tisbury* in the Year 1721. This Man was not effectually called until the eleventh Hour. He appeared to be a carnal and vitious Man till about three or four Years before, at a very great Age, he dy'd. He seldom went to any Meeting where the Word of God was preached, and was not known to call upon the Name of the Lord; and he would frequently drink to Excess when he had Opportunity for it. About eight Years before his Death he became naturally blind, and still remained spiritually so, about three or four Years of that time: and tho he could not now run about to seek after strong Drink, as he had formerly done, yet, if he could get any brought to him, he would abuse himself with it. But at length, it pleased God to open the Eyes of his Understanding, and to work such a great and gracious Change in him, that he saw, confessed and lamented the Sins of his Nature and Life, and called earnestly on God for his pardoning Mercy, thro' his Son Jesus Christ. He worshipp'd God every Day in his Family, put away his strong Drink, discoursed much about the things of God, and a future Life and World; and was so earnest to hear the Word of God preached, that being unable to go to the Place of publick Worship, he frequently desired Ministers to preach at his own House, and used to desire such as came to visit him, to pray and sing Psalms with him; and did sometimes send for Mini[134]sters to come to him for the same Purpose; so he did on the Day whereon he dy'd, and having obtained his Desire therein, he declared his Hopes of finding Mercy with God, and his Willingness to die and go to him; and then, as it is to be hoped, did so.

More Examples of good Men might have been here given; but, lest my Book swell to too great a Bigness, I shall add no more.

---

455 His father, Paskananhomon, was the brother of Keteanomin (*IC*, 197) and the son of Maukutoukquet, a sachem of Takemy. This would make Samuel Pashquannahhamun the first cousin of Margaret Osooit (*IC*, 197–201*). *WGH*, 159, 248.

[135] CHAP. III.

Containing an Account of several Indian WOMEN
that have been justly esteemed Religious.

THE number of *Women* truly fearing God, has by some been thought to
exceed that of *Men* so doing: but whether the Observation will generally
hold true or not, I shall not now inquire; or if it will, stay to consider
the Reasons of it.[456] However, it seems to be a Truth with respect to our
Indians, so far as my Knowledge of them extends, that there have been,
and are a greater number of their *Women* appearing pious than of the
Men among them.

But tho this be not what I have here undertaken to make good, yet
having in the foregoing Chapters instanced in several *Men,* that were
thought to be godly Persons by such as were acquainted with them, I
shall in this give an Account of some *Women,* of whom it may be justly
hoped, that they had Eternal Life abiding in them, and dy'd in the Lord.

EXAMPLE I.

WUTTUNUNOHKOMKOOH, *who was the Wife of* PAMCHANNIT,[457]
and the Mother of the memorable JAPHETH, *and died about the Year* 1675.

COnsidering whose Mother I have already said this *Wuttununohkomkooh*
was, and also what may be further related concerning her, it will not,
I suppose, be thought strange that I have mentioned her as my first
Example of *Women fearing God;*[458] tho, thro' want of Care to preserve her
Memory, I can give but a very general Account of her.

[136] There is one thing, however, to be said of her, which can scarce
be said concerning any other of our *Indians,* who lived a considerable
Part of their time before the Word of God was ever preached to them,
viz. That, by a due Improvement of the Light of Nature, assisted by the
Spirit of God, she attained to so right a Conception of the only true and
living *God,* and her own Relation to, and Dependence on *him,* as that
she did worship and call on *him,* and, as it seemeth, obtained a gracious
Answer to her Prayers. A particular Account of this being already given
in the Life of her Son *Japheth, Chap.* II. *Examp.* 17. I shall not again repeat

---

456 Ann Douglas discusses the rise in female church membership in *Feminization of American
Culture,* 97–99.

457 *IC,* 129*.

458 See Exodus 1:21 and 1 Peter 2–3.

[Figure 10.] Frontispiece from Experience Mayhew's *Narratives of the Lives of Pious Indian Women* (1830). Courtesy, Library of Congress, Rare Book/Special Collections Reading Room.

the same here, but refer my Reader to what is there said about it: only I must here say, that such a Discovery of the true God to her, before she was favoured with the Light of the Gospel, did very wonderfully prepare her for a ready Reception of it, when the Providence of God brought it to her, as within a few Years it did.

From whence it was thought, that as soon as this Woman heard of the Devotions of the *English*, who settled on the East End of *Martha's Vineyard*, in the Year 1642, at a considerable Distance from where she lived, she presently alledged that they were Worshippers of the same God to whom she had prayed: and she soon after found that she was not mistaken, when Mr. *Mayhew* began to preach the Word of God to the *Indians* on the Island; and when she heard the Gospel preached, she accordingly readily believed it and embraced it.

This Woman thus becoming a Christian, lived like such a one all the remaining Part of her Life, which was well nigh thirty Years, never that I can, on the strictest Enquiry, hear of doing any thing which might be an Occasion of stumbling to such as were acquainted with her, but did in all respects *order her Conversation as did become the Gospel.*[459]

---

459 Psalm 50:23. As Jane Kamensky points out, "conversation" for Puritans referred to both verbal exchanges and human conduct more generally. Cotton Mather included speaking "*cautiously, moderately, and deliberately*" in his rules for right speech; such rules also governed how Puritans felt that people should live their lives. Kamensky, *Governing the Tongue*, 4–5.

Her Husband also being, on the preaching of the Gospel, soon converted to Christianity, they lived together as *joint Heirs of the Grace of
Life*,[460] constantly worshipping the true and eternal God, both publickly
and privately, devoting also their Children to him, and *bringing them up
in the Nurture and Admonition of the Lord.*

[137] The Piety of this Woman was further discovered in that, as
she seriously joined with others in the Worship of God, when it was her
Duty so to do, so she was not ashamed her self vocally to call on him,
when it was proper and convenient that she should do so, as when the
Hour of Prayer being come, there was none present for whom it might
be more proper and decent to perform that Duty.[461] There are yet several
living Witnesses of the serious and fervent Prayers that this Woman
offered up to the Lord.

As Piety towards God was one Part of her Character, so Charity
towards her Neighbours was another; and for this latter, she was so
eminent an Example, that she was thereby distinguished, not only from
those who were totally destitute of a true Love to their Neighbours, but
even from most of them who have had some Measure thereof bestowed
on them. I have been credibly informed, that she was so extraordinary
courteous and obliging to all those that were about her, or whom she
had any thing to do withal, that herein she could scarcely be parallel'd;
and that she was unwearied in going about, and doing Good among the
Poor, and in communicating to them such good things as she was able to
bestow on them.

She was a little Woman, low in Stature, and withal of a most lowly[462]
Mind; and so exactly answered the Notation of her Name, which signi-
fyeth *a humble, or lowly Woman.* She discovered nothing of Pride in her
Deportment,[463] unless it were in honouring her self by a very regular
Conversation.

---

460 1 Peter 3:7.

461 By calling attention to her preference for allowing those for whom it was "more proper and
decent" (i.e., men) to pray for her, Mayhew distinguishes Wuttununohkomkooh from Puritan
women such as Anne Hutchinson, who, as Salem minister Hugh Peter put it, "stept out of . . .
[her] place" and "*bine a Husband rather than a Wife and a preacher than a Hearer; and a Magistrate
than a Subject.*" Qtd. in Kamensky, *Governing the Tongue*, 72.

462 Humble in feeling or demeanour; not proud or ambitious (*OED*). With this comment,
Mather emphasizes that she is modest, not that she is of limited intelligence.

463 Wuttununohkomkooh's modesty is particularly interesting when contrasted with the
deportment of other powerful Wampanoag women who during this era were sometimes deni-
grated by colonists for their "pride." A key example is Mary Rowlandson's description of Weet-
amoo, a Wampanoag squaw-sachem, whom Rowlandson condemned as "insolent" and "proud."
Although Puritan settlers expected women to be subordinate, subservient, unworldly, and self-
denigrating, Wampanoags would most likely have afforded Wuttununohkomkooh, the wife of
a sachem, a higher status. Arnold, "Now . . . Didn't Our People Laugh," 12–15; Rowlandson,
"True History," 43, 45, 53, 57–58.

I cannot obtain any particular Account of the Carriage of this Woman in her last Sickness, and at her Death; but I doubt not but that as she *lived the Life of the Righteous, so her last End was like his.*[464]

[138] EXAMPLE II.
DINAH AHHUNNUT, *who died at* Nashowohkamuk[465]
in or about the Year 1684.

THE Father of this Woman was, as I am inform'd, a praying *Indian*, who liv'd at *Monument*,[466] on the main Land, and was called by the *Indians Panupuhquah*.

When she was a Woman grown, she married an *Indian* of *Martha's Vineyard*, called *Henry Ahhunnut*, alias *Jannohquissoo*, (mention'd *Chap*. III. *Examp*. XX.) with whom she liv'd many Years, and had several Children;[467] to whom she was a kind and tender Mother, till God took her from them.

She was a Person of a very blameless Life. Neither was she the Subject of a mere negative Goodness only; for the good Works she did praised her: She was particularly a very remarkable Example of Kindness and Charity to her Neighbours, ready on all Occasions to visit and help them. This Testimony some of her *English* Neighbours, as well as many *Indians*, can and do give her.

She was much given to Hospitality; being always ready to entertain in her House such as Providence called her to receive into it, and chearfully performed all the Labour that was needful in providing well for them.

She living some Years near my Father's House, while I was a Youth, the Family had Opportunity and Occasion to take notice of her Carriage; and could not but observe that she was a very courteous, discreet, and diligent Woman; seldom went abroad, but tarried at home and minded her own Business, except when Duty called her to go out.

These things were commendable in her; but the best part of her Character is yet to be given: She was *a Woman that feared the Lord, and such a one is to be praised.*[468]

She not only with her Husband constantly worshipped God in the Family whereof they were the Parents, but did also publickly and sol-

---

464 Numbers 23:10.

465 Chilmark.

466 Monument Beach is near Buzzards Bay on Cape Cod.

467 Their children are Elisha Ahhunnut (?–>1684; *IC*, 139); Nathan Ahhunnut (?–>1684; *IC*, 139), and possibly John Ianoxso. *WGH*, 145, 170, 188, 192, 334, 427.

468 Proverbs 31:30.

emnly avouch *him* to be her God, and gave up her self unto him to be his, to love, fear, and serve[469] him for ever, and to expect all from him that she stood in need of.

[139] Being join'd in full Communion with the Church, whereof *John Tackanash* was the faithful Pastor, she highly praised, and diligently improved, the Privilege which she therein enjoy'd, constantly and seriously attending the Worship and Ordinances of God in his House; and therein shewing her Love to God, and his Word and Ways.

Her Piety was also further manifested in the Care she took to bring up her Children in the Knowledge and Fear of the Lord, by her constant Endeavours to instruct them in the Mysteries of Religion, and pressing them to the Duties in the Word of God requir'd of them: and there was, thro' Grace, a good Effect of her Essays to do them good in this way, several of them afterwards appearing to be pious, especially two of her Sons that died some time after, while they were but about sixteen or seventeen Years old; concerning one of which *Master Japheth* said he had scarce ever known so great Faith in so young a Person. The Name of this Youth was *Elisha*, and that of the other *Nathan*: but these Youths dying on the Main, whither their Father carried them after their Mother's Death, I cannot give a particular Account of them.

The Husband of the good Woman, who was a Person very worthy of Credit, told me but a few Months before he died, that he had great Reason to *praise her*, as such *a Wife as whoso findeth, findeth a good thing, and obtaineth Favour of the Lord*;[470] and as one that greatly helped and encouraged him in the Ways of God and Religion; wherein, by his Profession, he was obliged to walk. He said she not only excited him to pray without ceasing to God, but prayed her self also in the Family, when he was not present to do it.

She died of a strong Fever, which in a few Days carried her out of the World; tho I hope not before she was prepared for Death. In the time of her Sickness she professed her Reliance on the only Son of God, and her only Saviour, for the everlasting Mercies which she needed; and did, with Hands and Eyes lifted up towards Heaven, earnestly call upon God, that for his sake she might see and enjoy his Kingdom: and then with great Seriousness and Affection exhorted all about her, to *seek the Lord while he might be found, and call upon him while he was yet near*.[471]

[140] Blessed is that Servant, who when his Lord cometh he shall find so doing.

---

469 Deuteronomy 10:12.
470 Proverbs 18:22.
471 Isaiah 55:6.

EXAMPLE III.
HANNAH AHHUNNUT, *who died at* Nashouohkamuk,
alias Chilmark, *in or about the Year* 1704.

HANNAH Ahhunnut, commonly called by the *Indians Pahkehtau,* was a Daughter of an *Indian* who formerly liv'd in *Jokame,*[472] now *Tisbury,* of whom I know nothing remarkable.

Her first Husband's Name was *John Momonequem,*[473] a Son of that *Momonequem* mention'd *Chap.* II. *Examp.* II. The said *John* being a very worthy Man, a Preacher of the Word of God, and a *Ruling Elder* of the Church whereof Master *Japheth Hannit* was the *Pastor,* he was sent to preach the Gospel to the *Indians* at *Dartmouth,* and there died many Years since.

The *Hannah* of whom I am speaking, being there left a Widow, return'd again to *Martha's Vineyard,* the Place of her Nativity: She was a Member of the Church whereof her Husband was a *Ruling Elder* while he lived; and so far as I can understand, lived very blamelesly from the time she first join'd to it, to the end of her Life.

She was a Person of good Knowledge in the things of God, was able and willing to read the *Scriptures,* and other good Books translated into the *Indian* Tongue. And I have heard her discourse very understandingly and seriously in matters of Religion, and about the State of her own Soul; tho I cannot not particularly remember what she said.

She constantly attended God's publick Worship and Ordinances, and appeared very serious therein; was often much affected while she was waiting on God in the Duties of his House, wherein she drew nigh to him.

She was observed, by such as were acquainted with her, to make conscience of retiring for secret Prayer: I have heard an *English* Woman, worthy of Credit, with whom she labour'd some time, give her this Testimony.

Her second Husband, *Job Ahhunnut,*[474] whom I look upon as a godly Man, affirms, that she gave her self much to Prayer while she was his Wife. He says she [141] encourag'd him in his Duty towards God, and used to pray constantly in the Family when he was abroad.

She very frequently instructed and exhorted those of her own Sex, who stood in need of such Admonitions as she was able to give them: And young People especially, she in this way spake often to.

---

472 Probably a printer's error for Tokame (Takemmy).

473 *Native Writings,* 1:107–9.

474 *IC,* 163. He was the grandson of Ompohhunnut, Mittark's oldest brother and also the heir of Joel Aquanuat (*IC,* 202). His four other wives included Abigail Ahhunnut (*IC,* 162–64*) and Ruth Awhunnt. *WGH,* 102, 146–47, 154, 188.

She was very merciful to the Poor, tho she was not her self rich; and would very often extend her Charity towards them, by bestowing on them such things as she had, and as she thought their Needs called for.

She was remarkable for her Willingness and Ability to be helpful to the Sick; such she very often visited, carrying such things to them as she thought they needed, and doing such things for them, while with them, as she saw needful to be done. And being looked upon as a Woman of Prayer, and one who had an Interest in Heaven, Persons of her own Sex used to desire her to pray with and for them, when in their Sickness she visited them, and there were no Men present for whom it might be more proper to perform that Office. She used to perform the same Duty at Womens Travails also, when in difficult Cases there were special Occasions for it; and it has been reported, that she had sometimes very remarkable Answers.

She seemed to have a great Veneration for the *Ministers* of God, shewing by her Practice, that she *accounted them worthy of double Honour, esteeming them highly for their Work's sake*; and communicating to them in all such temporal good things as God had bestowed on her. And when there were Days of Thanksgiving[475] among our *Indians*, she was a most diligent Provider and Dresser of the Food wherewith the Poor as well as the Rich were then to be entertain'd; and usually order'd the setting of it on the Tables, at which People were to sit and eat it.

She died very suddenly of, as I suppose, an Apoplexy; but I trust Death did not find her unprepared for it.

[142] EXAMPLE IV.
ASSANNOOSHQUE, *commonly by the* English *call'd* Old Sarah,
who died in Edgartown, *about the Year* 1703.

WHO the Parents of this Woman were I know not: She was once married, and her Husband was commonly by the *English* called *James Cowkeeper*;[476] but he died before I had an Opportunity to have any Acquaintance with him; nor have I heard any thing remarkable concerning him. But good old *Sarah*, his Widow, was so observable a Person, that

---

475 Feasts and thanksgiving days were important rituals for both the Wampanoags and the English colonists. According to the Wampanoags of Gay Head, "In addition to daily thanks there have always been set times for celebration that coincided with changes of season and harvest times. Our New Year comes at the Spring planting time. Summer is celebrated with Strawberry Thanksgiving, at the time when the first wild berry ripens. Green Bean Harvest and Green Corn Harvest come at mid-summer. Cranberry Harvest celebrates the ripening of the last wild berry. A ceremony is held around the time of Winter solstice as well. The harvest celebrations are held after the work has been completed." See "Wampanoag Celebrations."

476 Father of Samuel James. *IC*, 106–9*.

many, both *English* and *Indians*, had some Knowledge of her. And I think every body that was acquainted with her, esteemed her as a Person of undoubted Honesty and Piety.

She was a serious Professor of Religion, one that gave her self up to God, joining her self to the *Indian* Church here, whereof she was long a Member. Nor was she ever known, as I can hear of, to do any thing that was matter of Stumbling or Offence to the Church to which she join'd; or any other of God's People, whether *English* or *Indians*.

She never would marry after her said Husband died, but chose to live in a State of Widowhood, saying, that if she married again, she might thereby bring such Troubles upon her self, as living a single Life she might be free from.

She was a Person of great Industry, kept her *Wigwam*, or *Indian* House, in very good Repair, and was generally well provided with all things necessary for the Support of her Family; so that she brought up her Children comfortably, both as to Food and Raiment, tho there were a considerable number of them; and which is yet more, she kept a very hospitable House, entertaining with much Kindness and Bounty such as came to visit her, tho the number of these were not very small: And Persons of the best Quality among the *Indians*, used frequently to lodge at her House, when they happened to be near the Place where she lived.

She was very observable for her *Charity* and *Compassion* to the Poor, which she manifested by feeding them when they were hungry, visiting them when they were sick; [143] and in every other way wherein she was able to help and relieve them.

But there must be a particular Remark here made on the Care she took of poor fatherless and motherless Children: when she heard of any such under suffering Circumstances, she used to fetch them to her own House, and there keep them, till they could in some other way be provided for.

When any of her own Houshold complained, as sometimes they did, that she gave away too liberally to others what was provided for the Use of her own Family; she used to tell them, there was no Danger in giving Victuals to such as needed it; for to such as did so God would send more, when more was necessary: which she ever found to be a Truth. And thus the Character of this Woman exactly answereth the Signification of her *Indian* Name, which properly signifyeth a *Woman that is a Giver of Victuals*, tho the Name was, as I suppose, given her while she was an Infant, and not after she appeared to be such a one.[477]

---

477 It would not have been unusual for Assannooshque to receive her name as an adult: Edward Winslow noted that around Plymouth, Algonquian names were given after adolescents had performed "some notable act" and marked the transition into adult status for both men and women. Bragdon, *Native People of Southern New England*, 170.

But the Charity of this Woman to her Neighbours did not only appear in what she did for the supplying of their bodily Wants; she was observable also for the Care she took of their Souls, and this appeared in her faithfully doing that which God's People are called to, when they are required to *exhort one another daily, lest any of them should be hardened thro' the Deceitfulness of Sin.*[478] She made it appear, that she did not hate her Brethren and Neighbours in her Heart, in that she did faithfully reprove them, and would not suffer Sin on them. She had a Courage to do her Duty, and such a Hatred of every Evil and sinful Way, that she would not willingly let any Miscarriage go unreproved; and I have been well assured, that not only common People, but even her Superiors, such as Magistrates and Ministers, &c. were by her (not to say rebuked) intreated as Fathers, when they did amiss, all her Admonitions being still managed with such Prudence and Compassion, that none could be justly offended at her, and so effectually to the End by her aimed at, that she had scarcely ever Occasion to proceed any further than the first Step in the Rule given by our Saviour, in the 18*th* of *Matthew*, and 15 *Verse.*

[144] Nor was the Person I am speaking of one that neglected her Duty towards God, while she so faithfully performed that which she owed to Men.

She therefore constantly upheld the Worship of God in her Family, praying ferrvently every Morning and Evening in it her self, unless there were any other Person present for whom it might be more proper. And tho it were her Unhappiness that she never was learned to read, yet she frequently ordered others to read the Scriptures in her House; and was a very diligent Instructor of her Children, in those things wherein she was able to teach them: and there were some of them that proved pious Persons, particularly her Son *Samuel,* mentioned in the forgoing *Chapter, Example* 13. and two others, that were Daughters.

Tho she lived something remote from the Place of publick Worship, yet she went so often to it, as to make it evident, that she had a great Love to God's House and Ordinances.

She was sick a considerable time before she dy'd; and her Deportment[479] was all that while suitable to the Description already given of the last Part of her Life. I cannot now obtain a very particular Account of her last Words and Speeches, but am in general informed, that she prayed earnestly to God, hoped stedfastly in his Mercy, thro' her only Redeemer, was willing to leave this World and go to Christ; exhorted her Relations and Neighbours to fear the Lord and serve him, and to

---

478 Hebrews 3:13.
479 "Depottment" in the original, probably a typo.

depart from all Iniquity, especially the Sin of Drunkenness, which as she avoided her self, so she could not endure in others.

Thus as this Woman *lived the Life of the Righteous, so her last End was like his.*[480]

EXAMPLE V.
ABIGAIL KESOEHTAUT, *who died in* Chilmark *in the Year* 1709.

THis *Abigail* was the Daughter of a praying Father and Mother, *viz. Pahahahkuh* and his Wife *Munuhkishque,* who formerly lived in the said *Chilmark,* the same being look'd upon as very just and honest Persons, tho they did not join as Members to any particular Church.

[145] This Daughter of the religious Parents now nam'd was taught to read very well, and was, I suppose, otherwise well instructed, she afterwards appearing to be a Person of good Knowledge in the things of God, as was well known by all those who were acquainted with her.

She, as I am informed, appeared to be sober and well inclined when she was but young, and was not known to be addicted to any Vice whatsoever.

She loved to read in good Books, and after she was marry'd,[481] and had some Children,[482] (not being nigh any School) she did herself teach them to read, and did otherwise carefully instruct them. She did also frequently and earnestly exhort them to fear and serve the Lord, and did in particular urge and press them to the Duty of secret Prayer, as some of them yet living do declare and testify.

She did not ask an Admission into the Church of Christ in the Place where she lived, till she had such Experience of a Work of Grace on her Soul, as did furnish her with Matter for a very affecting Profession of Faith and Repentance and encourage the Church to which she offered her self very gladly to receive her; nor did she ever afterwards make them ashamed by any such Irregularities in her Conversation, as many Professors of Religion are guilty of, her Conversation being for ever after such as did *adorn the Doctrine of God her Saviour.*[483]

---

480 Numbers 23:10.

481 Her husband was probably Harry Keseatow (Etoal) who owned land in Chilmark. He was the chief magistrate at Nashowakemuck. *WGH,* 170, 259.

482 If Abigail Kesoehtaut was the wife of Harry Keseatow, her sons were Andrew Harry, a laborer of Chilmark, and Henry Harry, a debtor. Harry Keseatow also had at least two daughters, whose names are unknown. *WGH,* 176–77, 259.

483 Titus 2:10.

As her Piety was otherwise conspicuous, so it did in particular shine forth in many gracious Expressions, which on all Occasions she used to utter, in which *God* was *acknowledged*, and those *edify'd* that conversed with her; besides what others inform me as to this Particular, I being my self acquainted with her, do judge worthy of such a Testimony.

She was much given to Prayer, and observed to be very earnest and affectionate in it; for she not only pray'd constantly and fervently in her own Family, when her Husband was gone from home, but was sometimes found praying abroad, where she did not expect any would see her, but *her Father who seeth in secret, and rewardeth openly.*[484]

As she pray'd much, so she frequently gave Alms of such things as she had, doing good, and being ready to distribute, and willing to communicate.

[146] In the beginning of the long Sickness whereof she dy'd, she was very deeply sensible of the Sins of her *Nature* and *Life*, and wanted a comfortable Assurance of the Love of God to her Soul; but was not wanting in doing all she could, that *being justify'd by Faith, she might have Peace with God thro' her Lord Jesus Christ.*[485] She then most frequently and earnestly pour'd forth her Soul before the Lord, intreating of him, for Christ's sake, to bestow on her those everlasting Mercies which she stood in need of, and to lift up the Light of his Countenance upon her; nor did God despise the Prayer of this his Handmaid, for after she had struggled a while with the Temptations of *Satan*, and the Unbelief of her own Heart, she first declared her firm Persuasion of the great Truths of the Gospel, wherein the way of Salvation by *Jesus Christ* the Son of God, is set forth and declared. She said she believed that *Jesus Christ* did indeed come into the World to save Sinners; that he dy'd, and rose again from the dead, to that End; and that there was Mercy and Forgiveness with God thro' him; and that she her self was not excluded from the Benefits of that Redemption, which he came to work out for his People.

By these Considerations her Heart was much quieted, and her Soul relieved; but God had yet higher Degrees of Consolation in store for her, for soon after this he gave to her a firm and strong Persuasion of her own personal Interest in the everlasting Mercies of that Covenant *which is well ordered in all things, and sure.*[486]

The Spirit of God did now bear Witness with her Spirit, that She was a Child of God, and had a Right to the Inheritance laid up in store for his Children.

---

484 Matthew 6:6.

485 Romans 5:1.

486 2 Samuel 23:5.

Having thus obtained Peace in believing, she opened her Mouth in the Praises of God to others. She told those that were about her, that what she had formerly heard of the Power and Mercy of God, she did now find and experience to be true; for he then had granted her the Mercies which she had long fought to him for, had pardon'd her Sins, and was reconciled to her Soul.

She then earnestly called on her Relations and Friends, to chuse God for their Portion, and love, fear, and obey him all the Days of their Lives, and be sure to avoid those things that were provoking in his sight. On her Husband in particular she did with much Earnestness press [147] these her dying Counsels, with which he appeared to be very much affected.

Having thus expressed her Sense of God's Goodness to her, and called on others to trust in him, and live to him, she declared that now she thought her End was very near at hand, and told her Friends, that being now to take her leave of them, if they would see her any more, they must be true Seekers of that God whom she had sought and found; which if they did, she and they would meet again, and see one another, in their Father's House, with great joy and Comfort.

After this she spake but little, and took very little Sustenance, but lay still for the most part with her Eyes closed as if she had been asleep; and yet she would answer when spoken to, and shew that she was not so, but was thinking on the things prepared for her in her Father's Kingdom: and being desired to take something to refresh here, she said she needed nothing of that Nature, having more to refresh her than they were or could be sensible of.

The real and solid Piety of the Person of whom I here speak, has, I think, been sufficiently evidenced in what has been already said of her; that therefore which I'm now going to relate is not brought in as any Proof of her Sincerity, but proposed to the Learned for their Thoughts on it.

The pious Woman of whom I have been speaking, had a godly Sister with her in the time of her Sickness, who had a most earnest Desire to know if her Sister dy'd, that she went out of this World in a State of Grace, and Favour with God, and should go into everlasting Joy: and tho her Sister expressed her self so very comfortably as she did, such was her Infirmity, that this did not satisfy her, but she long'd for a more full Assurance of her Sister's Well-being. Thus she continued in Distress for her until about twenty four Hours before she dy'd, when, being asleep in the House where her Sister lay, she, as she thought, plainly heard a Voice in the Air over the Top of the House, saying in her own Language, *Wunnantinnea Kanaanut*, the same being divers times repeated; which Words may be thus rendered in *English*, tho they are much more emphatical in *Indian, There is Favour now extended in* Canaan;[487] *there is Favour,* &c. The Person that in her Sleep thought she heard [148] such a Voice, supposed it to be a Voice from Heaven by the Ministry of Angels,[488] sent to give her Satisfaction in the Case that did distress her: and she was exceeding refreshed with the good Tidings which she thought she had in this wonderful Way received; but while she was transported with the Thoughts of God's condescending Goodness thus manifested to her, and her Heart filled with unspeakable Delight, to her great Grief, some Person, as she thought, awaked her, and wake she did, but she could not find that any Person called her. However, she then went to her Sister, and said, *Now, Sister, you are going into everlasting Happiness;* to which, her Sister being now speechless, could make no Answer, save that by a Sign she consented to what was said to her, and with a smiling Countenance lifted up her Eyes and Hands towards Heaven; after which she said no more, but the next Morning dy'd.

Query. *Whether the Person that dreamed the Dream now related, ought to take any other notice of it, than she should of any common Dream; or what she should think concerning it?*[489]

A Solution of this Problem would gratify both the Person that had the Dream, and him that has related it.

EXAMPLE VI.
ABIGAIL, *called by the* Indians AMMAPOO, *who died at* Sanchecantacket *in* Edgartown, *in the Year* 1710.

THIS *Abigail* was the Daughter of a petty *Sachim* of *Homes's Hole,* called *Cheshchaamog,*[490] and a Sister of that *Caleb Cheshchaamog,*[491] who took

---

487 The land promised in the Bible to the Children of Israel. The Puritans, who saw themselves as the "new Israelites," often referred to New England as the "new Canaan." Canaan is also used figuratively in hymns and devotional literature to symbolize both heaven and the Promised Land (*OED*).

488 Mayhew's acceptance of angels, dreams, and visions reflects the transitional period in New England theology following the witchcraft trials, after which angels, like other signs of the supernatural, were more likely to be dismissed as "delusions." Minister Increase Mather went so far as to argue that "appearances of angels have 'in a great measure ceased,'" and he doubted "most reports of apparitions, dreams, and voices." Qtd. in Hall, *World of Wonders*, 107.

489 Dreams played a central role in Wampanoag divination; Puritans, however, as David Hall notes, viewed dreams as significant but requiring caution in interpretation. Hall, *Worlds of Wonder*, 87, 213, 215–26, 222–23.

490 Today Holmes Hole is known as Vineyard Haven. Cheshchaamog ruled Nobnocket (West Chop). Besides Caleb and Abigail, his children included Ponit Cheeshamuck (*Native Writings*, 1:113, 149), Thomas Cheeshamuck, and Hannah Nohnosoo (*IC*, 164–66*), wife of John Nahnosoo (*IC*, 17–18*). *WGH*, 106, 144, 222, 335.

491 Caleb died of a "deep Consumptional epidemicall disease" in 1665, shortly after becoming the first American Indian to graduate from Harvard College. *WGH*, 288; Morison, *Harvard College in the Seventeenth Century*, 352–56.

a Degree in *Harvard* College[492] in the Year 1665. When she became a Woman, she was married to *Wunnannauhkomun* a godly Minister, mentioned *Chapter* I. *Example 5*. And, tho she was esteemed worthy to be a Wife to such a Husband, yet she made not a publick Profession of Religion until after the gathering of the first *Indian* Church on *Martha's Vineyard*, in the Year 1670.

She was taught to read while young, and made a good Improvement of that Advantage, till by a Scald in her Face, she in a great measure lost her Sight, within a few Years after she was first marry'd.

[149] She used, while her Husband lived, to pray in the Family in his Absence, and frequently gave good Counsel to her Children.

After she had lived so long with her Husband that the eldest of the three Daughters which she had by him, was become a Mother, he dy'd and left her a Widow; but just as he was going out of the World, desiring his Wife and Daughters to tell him what Petitions he should put up to God for them, before he took his leave of them, the Mother, her Daughters joining with her in it, requested him to pray for spiritual Blessings for her and them, which he did accordingly, as is related in his Life.

Being thus left a Widow, she lived in that Estate the greatest part of her time after; for tho she after some Years marry'd again, yet her Husband soon dying, she chose not to marry after this, but lived with her Children, and used to pray with them, and frequently gave many good Instructions to them, as two of them yet living do testify.

As she prayed much at other times, so she made God her Refuge in an evil Day, calling on him without fainting until he had Mercy on her; and experiencing the Mercy of God her self, she was very merciful to the Poor, being, according to her Capacity, *ready to distribute, and willing to communicate to them.*[493]

She delighted much in going to the House of God, and would scarce ever stay from Meeting, unless there were some very necessary Occasion for it.

She was a diligent Instructor of her Grandchildren,[494] as well as of her own, earnestly exhorting them to love and fear God, and believe in

---

492 The Indian College at Harvard was in use from 1655 to 1695, though part of this time it housed white students. It was "a structure strong and substantial, though not very capacious. It cost between three and four hundred pounds. It is large enough to receive and accommodate about twenty scholars with convenient lodging and studies." In addition to educating Algonquians for future missionary activities, the Indian College housed a press, which published New England best sellers and many of the early Algonquian books used on Martha's Vineyard, including the Eliot Bible. Morison, *Harvard College in the Seventeenth Century*, 343–44, 349–50.

493 1 Timothy 6:18.

494 The names of her daughters have been lost, but one of her grandchildren was Oggin (alias Haukkings) Sissetom, the husband of Hannah Sissetom (*IC*, 184–87*) and the father of Bethia Sissetom (*IC*, 255–57*). *WGH*, 137, 335, 349.

Jesus Christ their only Saviour; and lived to see some good Effects of her pious Endeavours in this Way: nor did she neglect to instruct and exhort other ignorant Persons.

When she prayed, she was careful not to forget her Enemies, and would seldom fail of putting up some good Petitions for them: and as she prayed for them, so she sought Oportunities to do good to them, and would sometimes say, that that was the way in which People should *heap Coals of Fire on the Heads of them that hated them.*[495]

She often spake of this World as none of our resting Place, and of her self and others as Strangers and Pilgrims[496] in it. But of Heaven she used to talk as a Place of excellent Glory, where God the Father, Son, and Holy [150] Spirit dwell, and from whence the holy Angels come to minister to the Saints on the Earth, and to which they would at their Death convey them. And of Death she would sometimes speak as the Hand of God, by which his People were removed into a better Place than this World is: and would also call it a *Ferryman,* by which we have our Passage out of this Life into the next.

As she was her self careful to abstain from Sin, so she was also a serieus and sharp Reprover of it, and used to call it the Way to Hell and Damnation.

She was long sick before she dy'd, and tho she underwent much Pain in that time, yet she bare it with Patience and Resignation, being full of heavenly Discourses, and calling often on God her Saviour.

One of her Daughters, who, I hope, is a pious Woman, affirms, that being much broken of her Rest, by tending her Mother Night and Day in her Sickness, and being her self not well, her Mother desired her to lie down and try to get a little Sleep, before it was well light, on the Morning of the Day on which she dy'd, but that telling her she was afraid she would suffer for want of Help if she did so, her Mother told her, that *God would take Care of her:* but this Argument not prevailing with her to lie down, she, as she sat in the Room drowsy, with her Eyes well nigh shut, suddenly saw a Light which seemed to her brighter than that of Noonday; when looking up, she saw two bright shining Persons, standing in white Raiment at her Mother's Bed-side, who, on her Sight of them, with the Light attending them, immediately disappeared;[497] and that hereupon saying something to her Mother of what she had seen, she replied, *This*

495 Romans 12:20.

496 On the centrality of the "pilgrim" metaphor in early New England society, see Hambrick-Stowe, *Practice of Piety*, 54–90.

497 Although Lutheran writers in Europe had tried to "define the spectrum of 'wonder works,'" including visions and signs, visions of Light and people bathed in white would have reminded at least some New England readers of Quakers or descriptions of visions experienced by people

is what I said to you, God taketh Care of me. She also, as I am informed, told another Person before she dy'd, that her Guardians were already come for her.

She, just before she departed this Life, prayed earnestly to God for all her Children and Offspring, as her first Husband did before he dy'd; nor did she now forget to pray for others also, and even for her Enemies. And having thus called on the Lord, she presently after committed her Soul into the Hands of her Redeemer, and so expired.

[151] I was long acquainted with the Person of whom these things are related, and always esteemed her a very godly Woman.

The Account given by her Daughter of what she saw before her Mother dy'd, being alone with her, she related soon after her Death, and still maintains the Truth of it.

EXAMPLE VII.
REBECCAH SISSETOM, *who died at* Sanchekantacket *in the Winter of the Year* 1719, *when she was about* 21 *Years old.*

THIS *Rebeccah* was a Daughter of *Deborah Sissetom,*[498] a very pious Woman yet living, and a great Granddaughter by the Father's side, to that excellent *Wannannauhkomun* mentioned *Chapter* II. *Example 5.* who dy'd calling upon God for his Blessing on his Offspring, as is there related.

She appeared sober, and well disposed from her very Childhood, was obedient to her Parents, and not so much given to Vanity as most Children are.

Having been taught to read while she was young, she soon appeared to delight in her Book. She seemed also to delight in going to Meetings; and, being about ten Years old when her Mother was admitted to full Communion in the Church of Christ, she her self manifested a Desire of being baptized before the same was proposed to her, and was accordingly admitted to that Privilege, being first examined, and found to understand the Nature of the baptismal Covenant,[499] as well as willing to give her Consent to it.

---

suffering from the cruelties of witches. Hall, *Worlds of Wonder,* 74, 86. Jonathan Edwards "A Divine and Supernatural Light" (1733), is a good example of attempts by Puritan divines to place limitations on direct revelation during the First Great Awakening.

498 Not the same woman as the Deborah Sissetom mentioned in *IC,* 272–75*, who died in 1724 at fifteen years of age. It was common for family members to share the same name.

499 On page 50 of *Indian Converts,* Mayhew distinguishes between "our" practice "of baptizing Infants, and sprinkling in Baptism" and the "Errors of the *Antipedobaptists,*" at Gay Head lead by Peter Folger. By definition Antipedobaptists were against infant baptism. Thus ironically in some ways the Baptist Church at Gay Head originally practiced a *stricter* form of Calvinism

After this she frequently discoursed of the things of God and another Life, and this in such a manner as shewed a becoming Seriousness, and manifested a Desire of obtaining that Knowledge which is necessary to Salvation, and also a great Concern that she might not fall short of eternal Life.

In her last Sickness she was often heard calling upon God for his Mercy, and pleading with him the Merits of his only Son Jesus Christ. She also declared that she feared that she might yet want something that was necessary to be known and done by her before she dy'd; and [152] therefore desired the Minister of the Place might be sent for to her, to instruct her: and pray with her: but he not coming as she hoped he would have done, and she being grieved at it, there providentially came in two other Ministers unsent for, but by God sent to her. These discoursed with her about the State of her Soul, instructed her, and prayed with her, yea and sang Psalms also. On this the young Woman was greatly comforted, and declared her Hope in the Mercy of God, thro' Jesus Christ her only Saviour, and withal her Willingness to die and leave this World: and accordingly having given many good Exhortations to her Relatives, and spoken some Words of Comfort and Encouragement to them, she called on her Saviour to receive her Soul, and then *slept in Jesus*.[500]

I shall only add this further concerning her, that, so far as I can learn, she was looked upon as a Person of a very blameless Life by all, whether *English* or *Indians*, that were acquainted with her.

EXAMPLE VIII.
RACHEL AMOS, *who died at* Chilmark *in the Year* 1711.

THIS Woman was the Wife of Deacon *Jonathan Amos*, mentioned *Chapter* I. *Example* 15. and was a Daughter of that good *Miohqsoo* mentioned *Chap.* I.[501]

She was, while young, put to live with that Mr. *Mayhew*, by whose Ministry the *Indians* here were first illuminated, her Father, no doubt, aiming at her spiritual Good therein; and she her self did afterwards acknowledge, that she had been a Gainer by that Disposal of her, and would sometimes speak of the good Instructions which she had in that

---

than the Mayhew's Congregationalist church, since the Baptists required every individual to attest to their salvation before baptism, rather than baptizing the children of Saints.

500　1 Thessalonians 4:14.

501　*IC*, 76–80*. Rachel Amos's siblings include David Okeiso, John Meoxo, and the brother who was lost at sea when he sailed for England with Thomas Mayhew Jr. in 1657. *WGH*, 197, 259, 273, 290, 408; *HMV*, 1:227.

Family received, and good Example therein set before her. More particularly the strict Observation of God's holy Day in the Family in which she had lived, was what she never did forget, and would frequently mention to her Children. I wish the Generality of *Indian* Youth that are put to live with the *English*, could give so good an Account of the Instructions given them in the House of their Masters.[502]

It is to be hoped that the good Instructions thus given her, had a good Effect upon her; for I cannot understand [153] but that she behaved her self well while she was a young Woman: however, it is certain that she appeared to be very pious afterwards.

As she was well instructed her self, so she was very exemplary for the pious Care she took to bring up her own Children *in the Nurture and Admonition of the Lord.* I suppose there are scare any of the eight Daughters whom she brought up, but what have on this Account risen up and called her blessed. I have my self heard several of them declare with much Affection and Tears, what good Instructions and Exhortations she used to give them: nor was her Labour herein lost and in vain, several of her Children so instructed having been, so far as could appear, truly godly Persons, some of which are hereafter to be mentioned.

As with her Husband she came from the Main, on purpose that she might enjoy God in all his Ordinances here, where they both thought Church-Discipline was better managed than there, so when they were come hither, she at the same time with him made a publick and solemn Profession of her Religion, and joined as a Member in full Communion with him, to that Church of which Mr. *Japheth* was Overseer; and was very constant and serious in her Attendance on, and Improvement of the Privileges to which she was admitted.

She was a praying Woman, and appeared so to be, not only in that she was careful to uphold the Worship of God in the Family, praying constantly her self in it when her Husband was not at home to lead in that Duty, but also in her frequent Retirements to seek him who seeth in secret and rewardeth openly.

A Daughter of this good Woman, which she had most reason to suspect to be still in a State of Nature[503] at the time to which this present Relation referreth, has with many Tears declared to me, that a little before her Mother was seized with the Illness whereof she dy'd, she meeting her alone where she was walking, did most solemnly charge

---

502 Wampanoag children who were raised by whites were actually less likely to be able to read English. Moreover, indentured children often lost their ability to speak the *Wôpanâak* language and the opportunity to learn folkways. Silverman, *Faith and Boundaries*, 217–18.

503 A "State of Nature" is a translation of a Latin phrase referring to the "unregenerate moral condition of mankind, as opposed to a state of grace" (*OED*).

her to depart from her Iniquities, and become a true Servant of God, and believe in his Son Jesus Christ; telling her then also, that she thought the time of her own Departure was at hand, and that she therefore gave this her dying Charge and Counsel to her.

[154] She, while she was in Health, used to discourse with her Husband concerning Death, and with him conclude, that it was a most necessary thing to be in a prepared Estate for it; and it is exceeding likely that she was her self well prepared for that Day and Hour.

In the time of her last Sickness she told her Children, that it was likely that she should now die and leave them: and after she had given much good Counsel to them, told them she would have them chear up their Minds, and not be too much grieved for her, for she had Confidence in her God, that he would save her: but yet she did at the same time acknowledge and lament the Sins of her Life, particularly those of her Youth, and the Slights she had put upon so good a God as hers was; and did exceedingly magnify his Mercy towards her, in that, notwithstanding her sinful and unworthy Life, he had still gone on to use Means with her for her Good, and had enabled her to hope and trust in his Mercy.

I had like to have forgotten to tell my Reader, that tho the Woman of whom I speak was in the general of a very blameless Conversation, yet, that she might be the more humble, and so the more pious and godly, she was once suffered to drink to Excess; and having done so, made a most humble and affecting Confession of her Sin therein,[504] and never was known to do so any more: which Fault of hers, if I had not thought here to have mentioned, would perhaps with some have been so great a one in me, as to have weakened the Credit of my whole History.

EXAMPLE IX.
ABIGAIL AMOS, *who died in* Chilmark *in the Year* 1711.

THIS *Abigail* was a Daughter of godly Parents, *viz. Jonathan* and *Rachel Amos*,[505] both before-mention'd; and these endeavour'd to bring her up, as they did the rest of their Children, in the Nurture and Admonition of the Lord.

She was taught to read, and well catechiz'd while young; and it is to be hoped, the good Instructions in her Childhood given to her, made good

---

504 For an example of a confession of drunkenness, see McCallum, *The Letters of Eleazar Wheelock's Indians*, 60–62.

505 *IC*, 37–42*, 152–54*.

Impressions on her [155] Soul, before she had passed the Years of her Minority, or was a Woman grown.

She was not while young given to keep evil Company, nor addicted to such Vices as many young People among the *Indians* are given to; but used to keep at home and mind her Business, working diligently with her Hands, that she might not eat the Bread of Idleness: and she was always very obedient to her Parents.

She appear'd to mind that which was good, not only by her constant and serious Attendance on Family Worship in her Father's House, and other Places where she occasionally was, and on the publick Worship of God in his House on the Lord's Day, and at other times; but also in her Forwardness to entertain serious and religious Discourses with God's People, as occasion offer'd for it.

Tho she appear'd to be a religious Person before the last and long Sickness which she died of, and was very blameless in her Life; yet it was more especially during that time, that she discover'd a pious Disposition of Soul, making it evident that she had a Principle of Grace in her Heart.

Soon after she was first taken ill, she manifested a deep Sense of the Sinfulness of her Nature and Life, comparing her self to those Swine who love to be wallowing in the Mire, alluding to that in 2 *Pet.* ii. 22. and seem'd to loath her self on the account of her moral Uncleanness;[506] and also called frequently and earnestly upon God, to pardon her Sins, and sanctify her Heart for the sake of Jesus Christ, whose Blood cleanseth from all Sin.

After this she said, That when God began a good Work on any Soul, his way was to carry it on to Perfection, and not to leave it unfinished; and that she hoped he had began such a Work of Grace in her, and would accordingly go on with it.

She was, during the time of her long and lingring Sickness, very full of such serious and heavenly Discourse, as to a Person, considering that out of the Abundance that is in the Heart the Mouth speaketh,[507] would strongly argue that she was indued with saving Faith, and other Graces of God's Holy Spirit. She now magnified the Power, Wisdom, and Grace of God, and asserted his Sovereignty over her and all his Creatures, declaring her Willingness to submit to his good Will and Pleasure with respect to the Issue of that Sickness with which he was pleased to visit

---

506 Self-loathing was a Puritan virtue: the self was "the great snare" and a "false Christ." Self-loathing was a sign that the Christian had placed God, not the self, at the center of the world. Bercovitch, *Puritan Origins of the American Self,* 14–18.

507 Luke 6:45.

[156] her, whether in her Life or Death: she also praised God for his Son Jesus Christ, and that way of Salvation thro' him which is revealed to Sinners in the Gospel, and professed her Hopes of obtaining everlasting Life in that Way.

To this purpose she discoursed when I visited her, not long before she died; and I am assured by others who are worthy of Credit, that her Discourses were generally of this Nature.

She also, before her Death, gave much good Counsel to her Relations and Visitors, exhorting them to take notice of her Frailty, and improve their time well in preparing for their own Death.

She was never married, but died a Maid, in, I think, the six or seven and twentieth Year of her Age.

EXAMPLE X.
HANNAH CHARLES, *who died in* Tisbury *in the Year* 1711.

THIS *Hannah Charles* was another Daughter of good Deacon *Jonathan Amos,* and *Rachel* his Wife before-mentioned,

Her godly Parents taught her to read, and gave her a religious Education; and she, thro' Grace, made a good Improvement of these Advantages.

I cannot understand but that she liv'd blamelesly while she was a young Woman; but after she was grown up, marrying with *Amos Charles,*[508] who proved a Lover and Follower of strong Drink, she was sometimes drawn into bad Company by him; and, as was reported, drank more than she should have done: but it was not long before, being convinc'd of all her Sins, she reform'd what was amiss in her Conversation,[509] made a publick Profession of Religion, and join'd her self as a Member in full Communion to the Church whereof Master *Japheth Hannit* was the Pastor.

Being now *a believing Wife,*[510] she endeavour'd to save her Husband; she prevail'd with him to worship God in his Family, and do some other things that were good and commendable. And thus putting on something of a form of Godliness, People for a time began to entertain good Hopes[511] concerning him; but his Religion did not hold out [157] to the

---

508 On March 28, 1699, Amos Charles accused a colonist, Ruth Cleveland, of selling rum. It was not unusual, when a complaint was made against a Wampanoag for selling rum to other Indians, for the accused to finger his suppliers. See DCCR I.114; *WGH,* 241–42.

509 This is a good example of using "conversation" to refer to both verbal exchanges and human conduct more generally. Kamenksy, *Governing the Tongue,* 4–5.

510 1 Corinthians 7:14.

511 This word is blurred in the original, but given the context and the letters that are clear, "Hopes" is the likely reading.

end: His Lust after strong Drink prevail'd too much over him; especially after the Death of his good Wife he appeared worse than ever.

But the Woman having once the *true Fear of God put into her Heart, never would any more depart from him.*[512] Tho she wanted not for Opportunities and Temptations to have Fellowship with her Husband, and others like him, in the Sin of *Drunkenness,* yet I can't understand that she was ever again overtaken *with it.*

She went but little abroad, but tarried at home with her Children; labouring diligently with her Hands, to provide the Necessaries of Life for them. She also diligently instructed them; and when her Husband was not at home, prayed with them.

Being sick a considerable while before she died, she carried her self like a good Christian during that time.

She acknowledg'd her utter Unworthiness of God's Favour, and magnify'd his Mercy, in that he had not for her many Sins utterly cast her away; but had been long waiting that he might be gracious to her, and had done much for her in order to her Salvation: and she was very sollicitous that she might not receive all this Grace of God in vain.

She called often and earnestly upon him, intreating him to pardon all her Sins, and be reconciled to her Soul, thro' the Merits of his dear Son, and her only Saviour.

She earnestly exhorted her Husband, and other Relations, to seek the Lord while he might be found, and call upon him while he was yet near, and to depart from all their Iniquity.

She told them that she would not have them to be much concerned about her, but be willing to part with her, as she was now willing to die and leave them; and all the Enjoyments of the World as well as all the Evils and Sorrows in it; that so she might go to her God, and enter into everlasting Rest and Peace, as thro' his Mercy she hoped to do; adding, that she and they might again see one another with much Joy, if they would truly love and serve the Lord their God.

I shall only add, that our *English* People who were acquainted with this Woman, do give a very good Character of her.

[158] EXAMPLE. XI.
ABIAH PAAONIT, *who died in* Chilmark *in the Year* 1712.

THIS Woman was the eldest Daughter of good Deacon *Jonathan Amos,* and *Rachel* his Wife before-mentioned; who, tho they had no Son, yet had

---

512 Jeremiah 32:40.

a great Blessing in their Children, the most of them proving very pious Persons: No less than four of the Examples mentioned in this History, have been found among them; and there are yet two of them living, who are justly esteemed sober and religious Women.

These godly Parents of this *Abiah*, took care to teach her to read when she was a Child, and did otherwise well instruct her; so that she was a Person of good Knowledge in the things of God, and was, I think, from her very Childhood, a sober and religious Person.

Elisha Paaonit, a Minister before-mention'd,[513] was her second Husband, as she was his second Wife; and they were both very happy in the Marriage in which they were joined. She was a Meet-help unto him, did much reverence him, and took great Care of him, keeping his Apparel whole and in good order, his Linen clean and neat, and carried her self in all respects towards him as a Minister's Wife should do.

She joined her self as a Member in full Communion to the *Indian* Church here, while she was but a young Woman; and she ever afterwards behav'd her self as a Person in Church-Relation is oblig'd to do, adorning the Doctrine of God her Saviour in all things: Only one failing she was guilty of, she was too apt to be offended, and to resent any Injury which she received higher than she should have done; but then she would be easily satisfied, and reconciled to the Person that wrong'd her, or which she supposed to have done so.

She was remarkable for her Love to the House and Ordinances of God; for no light thing could hinder or detain her from an Attendance on them: and when she was at them, she appear'd to be most devout and serious, being often much affected at publick Prayers, Sermons, and Sacraments.

[159] She was well known to be a praying *Woman*, or else should not have been mention'd as a pious *one*. She pray'd constantly in her Family in her Husband's Absence; and often with sick Women and Children, when there were Occasions for it; yea, in such esteem was she for the Gift as well as the Spirit of Prayer, wherewith the Holy Ghost had favoured her, that when there was any special occasion for Prayer, where any number of Women were met together without any Men with them, as at Womens Travails, &c. she, if among them, was commonly the Person pitched upon to be their Mouth to God, to make known their Requests to him.

She was very observable for her Forwardness to entertain religious Discourses, and her Ability to manage them to the Edification of those with whom she conversed; and tho she was a Woman of a commendable Industry, yet if any of her Neighbours came in to visit her, she would

---

513 *IC*, 56–59*.

ordinarily lay her Work aside, that she might sit and discourse with them: And her Discourses on such Occasions were not vain and frothy, but such as were good for the Use of edifying, and might administer Grace to the Hearers.

She was kind to her Neighbours Bodies as well as to their Souls; for tho she was but a poor Woman, yet she often distributed part of the little she had, to such as she thought were in more want than she was.

She died of a Consumption, under which she languish'd several Months before it put an end to her Life; but as her outward Man decayed, so her inward Man was renewed day by day.

She was in the former part of her Illness rather *disconsolate* than *joyful*; did not seem to be assured of her own personal Interest in the great and good things, the Existence whereof she doubtless by Faith realiz'd: and now she was very diligent in her Endeavours to make her Calling and Election sure, calling often and earnestly upon God, that for Jesus Christ's sake he would pardon all her Sins, and be reconciled to her; discoursing very seriously about the things of God and another World; but what in particular the Expressions were which she used, those who were with her do not so well remember as to undertake to relate, tho they affirm the same to have been very edifying.

As she drew nearer to her end, she appear'd more joyful than she had formerly been; and there was one thing [160] which happened not very long before she died, that seemed somewhat to affect her.

She being still able to sit up, and go out when she was minded so to do, she once late in the Night went out, as she had hitherto sometimes done;[514] but during the little time of her staying abroad, she was very suddenly refreshed with a Light shining upon and about her, which she thought to be brighter than that of the Sun at Noon-day. Being filled with Admiration at this *marvellous Light*,[515] and looking upwards to see if she could discern from whence it came, she saw, as she thought, as it were a Window open in the Heavens, and a Stream of glorious Light issuing out from thence, and lighting upon her; which, while she admired at it, in the twinkling of an Eye disappeared.[516]

This Account she presently gave to her Husband, from whom I had it presently after the thing happened. She related the same also to some

---

514 *Our* Indians *go out much more in times of Sickness than* English *People do.* [Mayhew's note.]

515 1 Peter 2:9.

516 The apocalyptic tradition of "visions, dreams, apparitions, unseen voices" had a long history in European Christianity and had been rampant in New England; following the witchcraft trials, however, these phenomena were viewed with increasing skepticism. See Hall, *Worlds of Wonders*, 86–87. Visions also played a central role in Wampanoag religious practice, and having a vision was one way that religious leaders gained their credentials. Simmons, *Spirit of the New England Tribes*, 38–45.

other credible Persons yet living, who still remember the Story, as it is here set down.

What notice ought to have been taken of this Phænomenon I shall not undertake to declare, but shall leave to the Judgment of the Judicious; but the Woman her self who saw this Light, was somewhat affected at what she had seen, and divers times spake of it as some little Glimpse of the Glory of the Heavenly World which God had been pleased to favour her withal. She thought she had seen some Rays of that glorious Light which the Saints[517] in Light do enjoy.

But however it was as to this, she had in some of the last Days of her Life a more sure and certain Discovery of the loving Kindness of God to her Soul, than any which such a Light appearing to the Eyes of her Body[518] could afford her: She had such Foretastes of the Joys of the Heavenly World, as made her heartily willing and desirous to leave this; and having experienced such a Mercy, she comforted her Relations whom she was to leave behind her, and earnestly exhorted them to go on to seek the Lord their God, and to be sure never to depart from him.

[161] Her last Words were, O Lord, I beseech thee be gracious to my Soul.

EXAMPLE XII.
MOMCHQUANNUM, *who died at* Sanchekantacket
in Edgartown, *in the Year* 1715.

WHO the Parents of this Woman were I cannot tell; but the Wife she once was of a praying *Indian*, whose Name was *Sissetome*, and the Mother of *Thomas Sissetome*,[519] an *Indian* Minister, who went from *Martha's Vineyard* to preach the Gospel on the main Land, I think at a Place called *Nammasohket*,[520] and died there at least thirty Years before the writing hereof, in 1724.

She was one of the first who embraced the Christian Religion in the Place where she lived, I suppose more than fifty Years before she died; and by the best Information that I can get, liv'd a sober and godly Life

---

517 For Puritans, "saints" refers to members of the elect rather than people officially canonized by the church.

518 For an analysis of the apocalyptic trope of the spiritual and "bodilie eye" in Puritan literature and culture, see Watters, *"With Bodilie Eyes."*

519 Thomas Sissetome may be the father of Oggin (Haukkings) Sissetom (*IC*, 184, 255), or Oggin may be descended by another line from the elder Sissetome. *WGH*, 122–23, 137.

520 Possibly a variant spelling of Namasket, now part of Middleborough in Plymouth County. *WGH*, 594.

for ever after; but I think did not make a publick Profession of that Faith and Repentance whereof she was long before thought to be the Subject, till after *Japheth* was ordain'd, which was in the Year 1683.

Being admitted to full Communion with the Church of Christ, in all the Ordinances of the Gospel, she highly prised, and diligently improved, the Advantages she enjoy'd, constantly attending on the Ministry of the Word and Sacraments, as that spiritual Food whereby she was to be nourished to Life eternal.

She appeared to profit by the Privileges which she enjoyed and improved; for out of the Abundance that was in her Heart her Mouth did continually utter very gracious and savoury Expressions, such as were good for the Use of edifying, and might administer Grace to the Hearers: and the longer she lived, the more she did excel herein,

She was both able and willing to give good Instructions and Exhortations to such as needed them, especially to young Men and Women, whom she frequently admonished for their Faults, and excited to their Duty.

She testified against the Sins of the Times wherein she lived, particularly against that of Drunkenness, and would not have any Fellowship with such unfruitful Works of Darkness.

[162] She was always, from her first Conversion to the Day of her Death, a praying Woman; not only joining with others in Prayer, when Duty called her so to do, but also her self calling audibly upon God as occasion required, and in her Devotions appeared to be very fervent.

As she prayed, so she gave Alms of such things as she had; and tho being a poor Widow she could give no more than two Mites,[521] yet she seemed to make conscience of doing that; and the most Miserable and Helpless were those to whom her Charity was chiefly extended: *Blessed are the merciful, for they shall obtain Mercy.*[522]

She liv'd to a great Age, yet not so long as to be past Labour before the Sickness whereof she died, nor did her Sight much fail her; and which was yet a further Favour of God to her, she in a good measure retained the Use and Exercise of her intellectual Powers, as long as her Soul, the Subject of them, continued in her.

During the time of her last Sickness, which was, I think, a Month at least, she behaved her self as a Child of God, going to her Heavenly Father, ought to do. She bare with much Patience the Pains with which God was

---

521 Originally a Flemish copper coin of very small value, in English "mite" was used mainly as a proverbial expression for an extremely small monetary unit. In books of commercial arithmetic in the sixteenth and seventeenth centuries, the "mite" commonly appears as the lowest denomination of English money. It is also an allusion to Mark 12:42–44, the story of the "widow's mite."

522 Matthew 5:7.

pleased to visit her: She gave good Counsel to those that attended on her: She expressed earnest Desires of enjoying that Favour of God which she acknowledged to be infinitely better than a temporal Life here in this World; and she prayed often to God that he would bestow on her the everlasting Mercies which her Soul stood in need of. She professed Hopes, that thro' the Merits of Jesus Christ, her only Saviour, she should obtain those Mercies; and she declared her hearty Willingness to leave this World, and go to the Fruition of them.

EXAMPLE XIII.
ABIGAIL AHHUNNUT, *who died at* Sanchekantacket, *in* Edgartown, *in the Year* 1715.

THIS *Abigail Ahhunnut* was a Daughter of a good Man who formerly lived at the said *Sanchekantacket;* his Name I have now forgotten.

She was generally esteemed as a sober and pious Person while she was a young Woman, not being given to any Vice that I can hear of.

[163] She was taught to read very well, and made much use of her Bible and other good Books, and was a Person of good Knowledge in the things of God, and could discourse very understandingly about them; tho being a Person of much Prudence, and not of many Words, she did not use to speak when there was not a proper Season and Occasion for it.

She made a publick Profession of Religion, and join'd her self to the Church of Christ, whilst she was, if I mistake not, but a young Woman; while *John Tackanash* was Pastor of the *Indian* Church here: and her Conversation was from thence forth, to the Day of her Dearh, very blameless. I cannot learn that she ever did, either in Word or Deed, give Offence to any of God's People.

She was very constant in her Attendance on the publick Worship of God, and seemed very serious and devout in it. She used to bring her Bible to Meeting with her, and as the Minister quoted Places of Scripture, she turned to and read them.

She had three Husbands, whereof the second was a Person eminent for Piety, *viz.* That Deacon *David*, whose Character I have given in *Chap.* I. *Examp.* 12. and she was such a Wife to them all, as whoso findeth, findeth a good thing, and obtaineth Favour of the Lord. As she encouraged them in the Duties of that Religion which they professed, so she her self acted like a religious Woman, as in other things so in this, That she constantly prayed in her Family when her Husband was from home; and while she was a Widow, she also did so.

Tho she used for the most part to keep silence where Men were present, yet as she was able to instruct most Women, so she was willing to give good Counsel to them when she saw occasion for it; and especially to young Women, she in this way used to shew her Charity. She was one of those blessed Persons who consider the Poor, on these Waters she often cast her Bread,[523] as there are still many that can testify.

The last of her three Husbands was that *Job Ahhunnut,* whose third Wife she was; of which three, that *Hannah* mentioned in our third Example was the second, and one now living the fifth, tho he be yet not sixty Years old. This Husband of hers praiseth her, declaring with much Affection what a Blessing he had in her; and all his Neighbours say the same of her.

[164] Two of her Sons, and some others, being gone on a Whale Voyage[524] to *Cape Cod,* in the Winter of 1715, she dreamed a little before their return, that they were come home, and that *she* was at the Point of Death, A few Days after they came home indeed; and she being seiz'd with the Measles about the same time, soon died of them.

In the time of her Sickness, she gave many good Exhortations to her Relations and Neighbours, and professed Hopes of everlasting Mercies thro' Jesus Christ her only Saviour; and then willingly left the World, and went to *him.*

EXAMPLE [X]IV.
HANNAH NOHNOSOO, *called by the* Indians NATTOOTUMAU, *who died in* Tisbury *in the Year* 1716.

THIS woman was a Daughter of a petty *Indian* Sachim, called *Cheshchaamog,*[525] who formerly owned the Lands about Homes's-hole. Being grown up, she was married to an *Indian* called *John Nahnosoo,* who was afterward a Ruling Elder of the Church whereof *John Tackanash* was Pastor; the same *Nahnosoo* spoken of *Chap.* I. *Examp.* 4.

How she carried herself in her younger Days I can't remember that I have heard; but she was happy in having so good a Man for her Husband as the said *Nahnosoo* was; and by the best Information I can get, she was

---

523 Ecclesiastes 11:1.

524 The whaling industry was an important source of revenue for the Wampanoags. During the eighteenth century they increasingly indentured themselves and their children on whaling vessels.

525 One of Cheshchaamog's sons, Ponit Cheeschamuck, inherited his father's sachemship; another son, Caleb Cheesechaumuck, was an early graduate of Harvard. Hannah Nohnosoo also had a sister, Ammapoo (*IC,* 148–51*), who was married to Wunnannauhkomun (*IC,* 18–20), another Indian minister.

a good Wife to him, doing him good and not evil all the Days of his Life, which expired about the year 1676,[526] after he had sustain'd the Office mention'd about nine or ten Years.

She join'd early to the Church already mentioned, and was a Member of it in full Communion, I suppose, at least forty Years before she died; in all which times I cannot learn that she was ever guilty of any scandalous Evil whatsoever, but constantly behav'd her self as became a good Christian, so as to adorn the Doctrine of God her Saviour in all things.

She was really, and not by Profession only, a praying Woman, praying always when there were proper Occasions for it; as in her own Family when she was a Widow and her Children lived with her, and afterwards in [165] the Houses wherein she lived with others, when there were none present for whom it might be more proper. And she always manifested a Love and Zeal for the House and Ordinances[527] of God, not in her Discourses only, but in her constant and serious Attendance on them.

She was very observable for her delighting much in serious and religious Discourses; she would on all Occasions be speaking something concerning her God and Saviour, and would frequently speak of the great things done by them for the sinful Children of Men.[528] I have my self divers times heard her talk very religiously; and there are many other Witnesses of her frequently doing so.

Having very considerable Skill in some of the Distempers to which human Bodies are subject, and in the Nature of many of those Herbs and Plants which were proper Remedies against them,[529] she often did good by her Medicines among her Neighbours, especially the poorer sort of them, whom she readily served without asking them any thing for what she did for them. Nor did she only serve the *Indians* this way, but was, to my knowledge, sometimes imploy'd by the *English* also. And I have sometimes heard her, when she has been asked whether she could help this or the other Person under the Indispositions wherewith they were exercised, make this wise and religious Answer: *I do not know but I may, if it please God to bless Means for that end, otherwise I can do nothing.*[530]

---

526 Mayhew gives conflicting information about John Nahnosoo's death: on page 18 he gives the date as approximately 1678 but later adjusts it to "about 1680." *IC*, 29.

527 In the original there is a printer's error: "Otdinances."

528 Genesis 11:5.

529 For more information on healing in Native New England see Kavasch, "Native Foods of New England," 17–21. Gladys Tantaquideon (Mohegan) also provides important early research into Algonquians medicinal practices; see Fawcett, "The Role of Gladys Tantaquidgeon," 141, 144–45. For the role of Algonquian women in domestic forms of production and internal trade, see Grumet, "Sunksquaws, Shamans, and Tradeswomen," 57–59.

530 Here Hannah paraphrases the doctrine of total depravity (one of the five main tenets of Calvinism): that is, that all man's senses are flawed, his will is imperfect, and he cannot will himself to salvation.

Among the Cases wherein she, by her Medicines, did good to her Neighbours, I shall particularly mention one only: Several Women, some *English* and some *Indians*, being divers Years after Marriage without the Blessing of Children, having barren Wombs and dry Breasts, which Persons in a married State are scarce ever pleased with, some of these Women applying themselves to the good old *Hannah* of whom I am now speaking, for help in Case that thus afflicted them, have soon after become joyful Mothers of Children; for which Comfort, under God, they have been oblig'd to her.

As for the Poor, as she expected no Reward for her Medicines of them, so she was observed to be otherwise very kind to them, readily administring to them for their Relief, such things as she was able to give them.

Her Charity to her Neighbours was also herein discover'd, that she improv'd the good Understanding which [166] it pleased God to give her, in giving good Counsels and Exhortations to such as she thought needed them, especially young People; and did likewise frequently admonish such as were guilty of Faults, for which they were worthy to be reproved.

But tho this *Hannah* did, by such things as have been mentioned, make it evident that she was such a one as we may well call *a good Woman*, yet so humble was she, that she did not use to call her self so; but reckoned her self so sinful a one, as to stand in absolute need of a Saviour to deliver her from Sin and Death, and would often speak of her self in these or such-like Words:

> I am a very filthy Creature; yet Jesus Christ my only Redeemer can, if he pleaseth, save me from my Sins, and all the Evil I deserve by them.

She frequently talked of Christ, and professed to trust in him alone for Salvation, both in the time of her Health, and after she was taken sick; but for some time before she died, was delirious, and said nothing worthy of Observation. It was well that she delayed not her Repentance till that time.

EXAMPLE XV.
SARAH, *formerly the Wife of Master* JAPHETH HANNIT, *who died* March 1716-17.

THE *Sarah* of whom I here speak, was the Daughter of a godly Man, named *Kestumin*,[531] mentioned in *Chap*. I. the same being afterwards Dea-

---

531 *IC*, 45, 74, 87.

con of the Church whereof good *Hiacoomes* was Pastor. She was married to *Japheth* whilst she was but young, was a good Wife to him as long as he lived; and like another *Sarah,*[532] did reverence her Husband and obey him.

Tho she carried her self soberly and well when she was first married, yet she did not, until several Years after, make a publick and solemn Profession of Religion, and join as a Member in full Communion to the Church of Christ, whereof her own Husband became afterwards the Pastor.

Her Conversation was from first to last very blameless and exemplary: She never was, that I have heard of, guilty of any Fault that was just matter of Offence to *God's People,* from the time she first joined to the Church of Christ till she died.

[167] She was *chaste, a keeper at home, that minded her own Business,*[533] and meddled not with what belong'd to others; and so no Busy-body, or Tale-bearer.

She was one of those *wise Women that builded the House,* and not of *the foolish ones that plucked it down with their Hands;*[534] for the fair and large *Wigwam*[535] wherein she with her Husband lived, was a great part of it her own Work; the Matts, or platted Straw, Flags and Rushes with which it was covered, being wrought by her own Hands; and those of them that appeared within side the House, were neatly embroidered with the inner Barks of Walnut-Trees artificially softned, and dyed of several Colours for that end: so that the generality of *Indian* Houses were not so handsome as this was; neither was it inferior to those the chief Sachims lived in.

The House thus built was kept clean and neat, all things in it being in their proper Places; the Clothing of the Family being also clean and whole, as by many has been observed: And in particular, this virtuous Woman's Husband was constantly so well clothed, and his Linen kept so clean and white, that he was always fit to go into the best Company, *and was known in the Gates when he sat amongst the Elders of his People.*[536]

When these good People had much Company at their House, as being given to Hospitality they frequently had, they were entertained with the best, and that ordered after the best manner, which their Circumstances

---

532 The "other" Sarah is the biblical matriarch and wife of Abraham in Genesis.

533 Titus 2:5.

534 Proverbs 14:1.

535 Wigwams were an inexpensive and flexible form of shelter: built out of wooden poles and removable mats, these homes were easily transportable when the Wampanoags moved between seasonable hunting and planting grounds. Wigwams were also well adapted to the island's climate. They could be double-matted with eelgrass stuffed between the layers, a technique that made the houses warmer than many Puritan-style dwellings and may have inspired the use of eelgrass for insulation in Puritan homes on the island. Scott, *Early Colonial Houses of Martha's Vineyard,* 1:52.

536 Proverbs 31:23.

would allow of; the good Woman and her Daughters serving chearfully on such Occasions, and shewing no Discontent.

But the Prudence and Industry of this Woman, in ordering her out-ward Affairs, tho it were very commendable, yet was not the best part of her Character; for tho she served with *Martha*, yet was she not so careful and troubled about many things, as not with *Mary* to chuse the one thing needful, even that good Part not to be taken away from her.[537]

We are told in the Description of a virtuous Woman, which we have in *Proverbs chap.* 31. *A Woman that feareth the Lord she shall be praised*; and such a one, the *Sarah* of whom I here speak was justly thought to be, by him who from that Text preached her Funeral Sermon when she was interred.

Her sincere Piety has been in part discover'd, in what has been already said of her; but this will be yet more [168] conspicuous in what may be further related concerning her.

She then carefully remembered the Sabbath Day to keep it holy,[538] constantly and seriously attending the Worship and Ordinances of *God* in his House on that Day.

She was careful to uphold the Worship of God in her Family, pray-ing constantly her self when her Husband was absent, (as on necessary Occasions he often was) unless there was some other Person present for whom it might be more proper; she also frequently retired to pray in secret, as was supposed by those that observed her.

Tho she could not read very well, yet she was not discourag'd from making the best use of Books she was capable of, reading frequently in such Books as she could make the most Advantage by: and Mr. *Per-kins's Six Principles of Religion*,[539] having been translated into the *Indian* Tongue, was what she took great delight in reading of.

She was careful to bring up her Children in the Nurture and Admo-nition of the Lord, frequently gave them good Instructions, and would faithfully reprove them when they did amiss; and did also frequently exhort them to the great Duties of Religion, and particularly of that of secret Prayer to God.

She was taken sick of a Fever on the second Day of the Week, and died on the Saturday next following. She told her eldest Daughter[540] then with her, that she was apprehensive that the Sickness with which she was seiz'd would be her last; and withal, expressed such a Submission and

---

537 Luke 10:38–42. Cotton Mather references this allusion in the preface to his conduct book for women, *Ornaments for the daughters of Zion* (1692), which provides standards for female behavior to which the women in *Indian Converts* are held.

538 Exodus 20:8.

539 Perkins, *Foundation of Christian religion*.

540 Bethia Escohana, *IC*, 102–3; *WGH*, 126.

Resignation to the Will of God with respect to her own Life, and all her temporal Concernments, as did become a true Saint.

She then also expressed her Desire to see and speak with her other two Daughters before she died; who being come, she expressed to them all a very deep Sense of the many Sins and Failures of her Life; but told them, that what she now most especially blamed her self for, was her not having taken so much Care for her eternal Good as she ought to have done: *for tho,* said she, *I have sometimes instructed and exhorted you, yet I should have done this more earnestly and pressingly than I have, and should even have commanded you to love and serve the Lord your God: But having fallen far short of my* [169] *Duty herein in times past, I must now be the more earnest with you, being now about to leave the World and you.*

And she did accordingly now, in the most affecting and pressing Language of a dying Mother, urge and command these her Children to love the Lord their God with all their Hearts and Souls, Mind and Strength;[541] and did even intreat them to avoid and abstain from those Sins which she thought them most inclined to, and all other Sins whatsoever.

She had, in times past, frequently discoursed of the woful Condition, into which, by the Sin of our first Parents, Mankind were fallen; but now she seemed with more than ordinary Earnestness, to endeavour to affect her own Heart, and the Hearts of all about her, with the deepest Sense of the Guilt and Corruption whereinto all the Posterity of the first *Adam* had, by his Apostacy, been plunged; and among other things, she then said, that we who were created in the Image of God, or made like to him, did, by *Adam's* Sin and Fall, lose that *Image* with which we were indued, and became like Devils for Wickedness.

This being said, she proceeded to magnify the Riches of God's Grace, in finding out and providing that Way for the Salvation of Sinners which is revealed in the Gospel, declaring in general Terms what that Way was, *viz.* that of Redemption by the Blood of *Christ,* the only Son of *God.*

She then declared, that as to her self she had hopes thro' the Mercy of God in *Jesus Christ,* the only Saviour of sinful Man, she should, notwithstanding all her Sin and Guilt, obtain everlasting Life and Happiness in the World to come; and having thus professed her own Hopes of everlasting Mercies, she exhorted all about her to have continual recourse to the Blood of *Christ* for cleansing from all Sin. She told them they could never wholly cease from committing Sin as long as they lived in this World, and therefore had need constantly to apply to the Blood of Christ for Pardon and Cleansing; and this she declared her own Intentions to do as long as her Life continued.

---

541 Deuteronomy 6:5.

After she had thus discoursed, she said but little to any but God, to whom she was frequently heard pouring out her Soul; and she also desired some that came in to [170] pray for her. The last Words that ever she was heard to say were, *O Lord I beseech thee to save my Soul.*

EXAMPLE XVI.

KATHERINE, *called by the* Indians Wuttontaehtunnooh, *who died at* Sanchecantacket *in* Edgartown, *in the Year* 1718.

THIS Woman was the Daughter of an *Indian* called *Mechim*,[542] and this is all the Account I can give of him. Her Mother was a Woman very much noted among the *Indians* for her Piety. Her Name was *Suioknumau.*

The Daughter's Husband dying long since, I have not heard any thing remarkable concerning him; of her therefore I am now only to give some Account.

How she carry'd her self in the first Part of her Life, I do not remember to have heard; but have been told, that she joined as a Member in full Communion to the Church whereof *John Tackanash* was Pastor, no Body now knows how long ago; it is thought at least forty Years before she dy'd; and was, so far as I can learn, without Spot and blameless all that while. I was my self acquainted with her about thirty Years, and do not remember that in that Time I ever heard that she was guilty of any considerable Fault, tho doubtless she had her Infirmities as well as other People.

She was well known to be a Person of great Industry, labouring diligently with her Hands to provide her self an honest Livelihood.

She was one of those blessed Persons who prudently and compassionately considered the Poor; for tho she had no outward Means but her own Labour, to depend upon for her Support, yet she frequently gave Alms to poor and needy People; and that even after she was so old, that she was scarce able to provide the Necessaries of Life for her self.

If she knew of any Person sick that wanted Relief, she used to make Baskets,[543] or something else that she could dispose of to the *English*, or some of the best Livers[544] among the *Indians*; and having sold the same for something the Sick most needed, she would then visit them, and carry those good things to them.

---

542 Mechimes's Field in Edgartown Plain may be named after him. *WGH*, 356.

543 Baskets have long been an important financial resource and art form in Native New England, particularly for women. See Wolverton, "Precarious Living," 341–68; and Lester, "Art for Sale," 151–67.

544 Living (*OED*): i.e., the wealthiest of the Indians.

[171] She was very pious towards God, as well as charitable towards Men; there be many that can bear Witness that she was a praying Woman; while she had a Family of her own, after she became a Widow she used to pray with them, and afterwards when she dwelt in other Families, she frequently, when there was Occasion for it, prayed in them: yea, so much was she esteemed for the Gift and Spirit of Prayer, wherewith God had favoured her, that when she was occasionally with other Women, where no Men were present, she was frequently the Person singled out among them, as their Mouth, to make known their Requests unto God. Just now a good Woman told me she had on such Occasions several times heard her call upon the Lord very affectionately and understandingly.

Yea such was the Gravity of this Woman, and the high Esteem which she had for her Piety among all that knew her, that I have been credibly informed, that when she happened to lodge in Houses where the Man of the House did not himself pray in his Family, she was by such invited to pray with and for them.

As she was grave and serious in her Deportment, so she used to discourse very religiously, frequently instructing and exhorting her Neighbours, especially the young People of the Place in which she lived.

Her Love to the House and Ordinances of God appeared to be such, as was very rarely equalled; for on them she attended with very great Constancy and Seriousness, and that even when she was grown so old that she could hardly go, and was but meanly clothed, travelling many times a considerable Way to Meeting, tho the Weather was so cold and stormy, that one could scarce have thought it possible that she should have endured it.

She seemed to have such a Veneration for the Ministers of God's Word, that she has often brought that Text to my Mind, *How beautiful are the Feet of them that preach the Gospel, and publish glad Tidings of good Things.*[545] She would, on the Sight of a Minister coming to preach in the Place where she lived, discover all the Signs of Joy and Reverence, proper to be manifested towards a Person coming in the Name of the Lord to a People.

[172] She living to be so very old, as to be almost past all Labour, needed to have some of her Wants charitably supplyed and as she had, while she was able, shewed Mercy to others, so she sometimes received the like Favours, tho she never appeared to crave them: for, as she never asked for them, so when she at any time received them, she used first to express her Thankfulness to God, from whose bountiful Hand she affirmed that all her Supplies came; and then in the second Place, gave

---

545 Romans 10:15.

Thanks to those Men whose Bounty and Kindness she experienced in the Favours she received.

One would have hoped, that so good a Woman as this was, would have had a most comfortable *Exit*, had we not known, that the Godly do often experience the Reverse of what is in Scripture said of the Wicked, when we are told, *That there are no Bands in their Death, their Strength is firm: They are not in Trouble like other Men,*[546] &c. The contrary to which, this godly Person had by a sovereign God ordered out to her.

She was in the last Year of her Life very frequently miserably distracted, and was, when out of those Fits, very much troubled with melancholy Vapours,[547] which did much annoy her. She was ready to fear that God had suffered the Devil to take some kind of Possession of her,[548] and this Fear did somewhat disquiet her Soul; yet she was not hereby discouraged from her Duty when she was able to attend it. She still attended the publick Worship of God as often as she could, and prayed earnestly to God in private, as I have been well assured. I discoursed with her while she was under the Cloud which I have mentioned, and plainly perceived that her Desires were still after God, and the Remembrance of his Name; yet she dy'd a while after terribly distracted, and under such violent Agitations of Body as were very uncomfortable to those that tended her.

However, I hope, she was one of those whom nothing could *separate from the Love of God which is in Christ Jesus.*[549]

[173] EXAMPLE XVII.
ALANCHCHANNUM, *who died at* Nunpaug *in* Edgartown, *in the Year* 1720.

THIS Woman was the Wife of that *John Tackanash* of whom I have given some Account, *Chapter* I. *Example* 3.[550]

She was, as I have been informed, a Person of no very good Character for some time after the said *John Tackanash* first marry'd her; but at

---

546 Psalm 73:4–5.

547 An archaic medical term common ca. 1665–1750: a morbid condition caused by exhalations originating from within the organs of the body (especially the stomach); also a depression of spirits, hypochondria, hysteria, or other nervous disorder (*OED*).

548 Sickness, Satan, and sin were often connected in the New England mind: as Lewis Bayley put it in the *Practice of pietie*, "sickness comes not by hap or chance . . . but from mans wickedness" (quoted in Hall, *Worlds of Wonder*, 197). Bayley's work was translated into Algonquian by John Eliot.

549 Romans 8:39.

550 Their eldest son was Joshua Tackanish. *Native Writings*, 1:205; *WGH*, 105, 272.

length it pleased God by his Word and Spirit, in some measure, to convince her of the Sinfulness of her Heart and Life, and put her on a serious
Consideration of her State and Ways, and to strive with her, in order to a
forsaking of her Sins, turning unto him, and becoming his Servant.

Hereupon she began to entertain Thoughts of giving up her self to
God, by laying hold of his Covenant, and so joining her self to that Church
whereof her Husband was then the faithful Pastor: but then *Satan*, the
great Enemy of Souls, and the Lust and Corruption of her own so evil
Heart, did make a violent Resistance against her doing so.[551]

The Case standing thus with her, she now experienced a very sore
Combat betwixt the Flesh and the Spirit in her. Sin and the World on the
one hand, being presented with all their Charms to her; and on the other
hand, Life and Death, Blessing and Cursing, Heaven and Hell being set
before her, with the absolute Necessity of her chusing the one, and fly-
ing from the other. In this Combat, which Side would prevail seemed to
her for some time doubtful; but at length Grace so far overcame Sin and
Corruption, that she was enabled publickly to avouch the Lord to be her
God, and promise to deny all Ungodliness and worldly Lusts, and to live
to him all her Days.

Of this her Conflict with Sin and *Satan*, she her self did some Years
since give me a good Account, the Sum whereof I have now given to my
Reader.

But this *Alanchchannum* having, thro' Grace, been of so *good Courage*,
(which, by the way, is the Signification of her Name) as to have overcome,
and become Conqueror in this her first and great Combat with her spiritual Enemies, we may henceforward consider her as [174] a new Creature, interested in the new Covenant, and so united to Jesus Christ, and
living a new Life, not unto herself, but to him that dy'd for her.

We accordingly from this time forward hear no more of her falling
into those Miscarriages, which she had been before guilty of, but are on
the contrary informed, that she lived soberly, righteously, and godly in
the World. She in near fifty Years time was not once that I can hear of,
left to dishonour God, wound her own Soul, and offend her Brethren, by
any scandalous Miscarriage, but did all that while walk as did become
the Gospel. She lived a Widow from the Death of her Husband *Tackanash*
until her self dy'd, which was about thirty seven Years; in all which time,
as I am credibly informed, she prayed constantly in her House, and used
to entertain with good Discourse such as went to visit her.

---

551 As Andrew Delbanco and others have noted, the Puritans had a much more concrete and
personal relationship with Satan than did later Americans. Although Satan was gradually "dismissed" in the eighteenth century, he still held sway in popular religion. See Delbanco, *Death
of Satan*, 64.

I observed my self, that she was very constant in her Attendance on the publick Worship and Ordinances of God, and she always appeared to me to be a very serious Woman.

She was a Person of very much Sorrow: Several of her Children lived somewhat viciously, and tho, as I am informed, she endeavoured to reclaim and reform them, yet she saw little or no good Effects of her Essays to do them Good.

Two of her Sons that were Men grown, and had Families, came to untimely Ends, and so did a Grandson of hers, all three drowned at several times; which Bereavements made a deep Impression on her, and would perhaps quite have overcome her, had she not cast her Burden on the Lord, in whom she believed and trusted: when her Spirits were ready to faint within her, she us'd to comfort her self in God, owning his absolute Dominion over all his Creatures, and Right to dispose of them as he pleas'd, acknowledging him to *be righteous in all his Ways, and holy in all his Works*,[552] owning also his Wisdom and Goodness in them.

There are yet living Witnesses of her quieting her self by such Considerations, when she was under the most grievous Pressures of outward Grief and Trouble.

She was an old Woman when she dy'd, yet retained the Use of her Understanding, and improved the same well to the last. In her Sickness she prayed earnestly to God, and gave good Counsel to her Friends, and took [175] her leave of this World with good Hopes, that she was going to a better Place, thro' the Merits of her Redeemer.

EXAMPLE XVIII.
JERUSHA OMPAN, *who died in* Tisbury September 18, 1721.

THIS *Jerusha Ompan* was a Daughter of religious Parents, *viz. Josiah Patumpan*, and *Ruth*[553] his Wife, of the said Place, he the said *Josiah* being sometimes imployed in dispensing the Word of God to his Countrymen on *Martha's Vineyard*.

The Parents of this young Woman taught her to read while she was young: she was also instructed in her Catechism, and as I have been informed, had much good Counsel by her Parents given to her.

And as she had a competent Measure of Knowledge in the things of God, so she soon appeared to have a serious regard to them. She seemed to have the Fear of God in her Heart, while she was but a young Girl,

---

552 Psalm 145:17.
553 *IC*, 218, 238. Josiah was probably the son of Pattompan. *IC*, 131; *WGH*, 156, 290.

was very dutiful to her Parents, and was not known to be given to any Vice. She never much affected going to Huskings[554] and Weddings, and if at any time she went to them, she would be sure to come home seasonably, not tarrying too long, as the Generality of Persons did.

She was a Person of very remarkable Industry, labouring daily with her Hands for her Livelihood. She us'd, when she could be spared from her Father's House, to work with her *English* Neighbours, with her Labour purchasing such things as she her self needed, and also Necessaries for the Family to which she belonged.

She did not appear to affect gay and costly Clothing, as many of the *Indian* Maids do, yet always went clean and neat in her Apparel, still wearing such things as were suitable to her own Condition and Circumstances.[555]

She delighted much in going to the Assemblies of God's People, and used to attend the Exercises in them with a very becoming Sobriety, as both my self and others have frequently observed; and at the Conclusion of them she used to hasten home to the Place of her own Abode, and not go a visiting to other Places. And when she was not her self to go to Meeting, she used to quicken others in the Family to do so, telling them, that there was no need for them to stay at home when she did.

[176] She much delighted in reading her Books, and if she could not get time in the Day, she would not ordinarily fail of reading in the Night; and for that End always used to be provided with something to make a Light withal.

She constantly attended Prayers in her Father's House; and that she was her self a praying Woman, I shall here manifest by one Instance.

When her Sister *Elizabeth*,[556] after mentioned *Chap*. IV. lay sick and like to die, about eleven Years before her own Death, being then scarce nineteen Years old, she observing her to be in great Pain and Distress, and there being none else present but her Mother, unless it were some Children, she fell to comforting her Sister, and at the same time offered to pray to God for her, and with much Affection did so, as the sick Maid and the Mother told the Father at his coming home.

---

554 Huskings, or husking bees, were parties or gatherings at which neighbors and friends assisted in the husking of corn (*OED*).

555 The sumptuary laws of Massachusetts Bay did not prevent all extravagance in clothing but rather limited it to people with estates greater than £200. In this way clothing communicated one's position, economic achievement, and social standing. Earle, *Two Centuries of Costume in America*, 17; Welters, "From Moccasins to Frock Coat," 13. Although Puritans generally felt that plain, dark clothing made from wool or cotton best reflected their plain style ideals, Puritan clothing could be brightly colored in yellow, green, red, and even purple, and for wealthy Puritans ornamentation was not unusual. See Rubinstein, *Dress Codes*, 286.

556 *IC*, 238–42*.

It may be wondered by some how this Maid came to offer to pray with her Sister when her Mother was present; which, that People may think the less strange, I shall here inform them, that it has been a Custom amongst our *Indians* to teach their Children Forms of Prayers, and sometimes to call them to make use of them in their Presence; and hence, as I suppose, it hath come to pass, that young People among the *Indians* have thought it no Presumption to call upon God for his Mercy, when their Parents have been by, and heard them: and I think it is better it should be so, than that for want of such Instructions they should not know so much, as how to desire a Blessing on their Food, and be so afraid of being put upon it, as rather to lose their Meals, than sit down at a Table where they fear they shall be called to this Duty.

But to go on with my Account of the Maid of whom I am now speaking, I am informed by a Person very worthy of Credit, that she was deeply concerned how she might approve her self to God under a sore Trial wherewith she was for some time exercised, and did more than once with much Affection and many Tears, ask to be advised how she should govern her self in the Case that did distress her; and having received the best Counsel she could get, she carefully followed it, committing her Cause to God, and relying on him in a way of well-doing; and so doing, found his Grace suffici[177]ent for her. What her Trial in particular was, I think not convenient to relate, only will say it was what was no Fault in her.

She used to ask serious Questions in Matters of Religion, as particularly of one she enquired, Whether *Adam* had Free-will before his Fall, and how his Sin came to be imputed and propagated to his Posterity, and how we might be delivered from it? And, lastly, how she ought to order her Prayers with respect to it?

She was, I think, by all that knew her, both *English* and *Indians*, esteemed a Person of a very blameless Conversation: some of her *English* Neighbours that us'd to employ her do bear Witness, that she was a Person of great Integrity, true to her Word, just and honest in her Dealings, and of a most obliging Carriage and Temper.

Some of her Relations that survive her, do testify concerning her, that she was a serious and faithful Reprover of their sinful Miscarriages, and that she did often give them good Counsel: particularly one of her Brothers,[557] that was younger than she, gives this Testimony concerning her; and says also that she used to instruct him in his Catechism.

---

557 Josiah's second wife was a widow when he married her; hence, he became a stepfather to at least one son. In addition, Josiah was probably the father of Solomon Omppan (*Native Writings*, 1:467), Isaac Pentumpon, Thomas Pontompon, and perhaps Didemus Pontompon, an Indian whaleman. *WGH*, 124, 199, 232, 290, 299, 360.

She was about 29 Years old before she dy'd; and tho she had had some
Offers of Marriage made to her, yet she would accept of none of them,
alledging to her Friends as the reason of her Refusal, that of the Apostle
in the first Epistle to the *Corinthians, Chap.* vii. *The unmarried Woman
careth for the Things of the Lord,* &c.[558]

She dy'd of a lingring Distemper; and as her outward Man gradually
decay'd, so it appeared that her inner Man was renewed Day by Day.[559]

Her Discourses were during that time very pious and edifying; particularly she declared, that she saw no Beauty in the most desirable
things and Enjoyments of this World, and wished that all her Relations
and Friends had the same Sentiments concerning them as she had. She
talked of Heaven as a Place of transcendent Excellency and Glory, and
manifested earnest Desires of going to that Place. She declared, that if
she were clothed with the Righteousness of Christ, that would entitle
her to the Blessedness which was to be enjoyed in the Kingdom of God;
and that *his Ressurrection* would preserve her from a State of Sin and
Death, to an eternal Life of [178] Glory. She exhorted her Relations and
Visitors to be diligent Seekers of God, and to depart from all Iniquity.
She expressed her Willingness to die, whenever it should please God
that she should so do; only she most earnestly desired, that she might be
first reconciled to him, and made meet for the Enjoyment of him.

After this manner she discoursed when I went to visit her; and tho I
cannot affirm, that she said to me all that is above related, yet to others
worthy of Credit she said the rest, and more than I have here set down.

She took care that all the little Debts which she owed might be
exactly paid;[560] and one of her *English* Neighbours enquiring of her a
little before she dy'd, how he should come by the small Matter which she
owed him, she first gave him a satisfactory Answer to his Demands, and
then exhorted him to take heed, that he did not lose his Soul for a little
of the rotten Dirt of the World.

As she discoursed piously, so she prayed earnestly to God for the
Mercies she needed: some of the Expressions which she used, her Father
having penn'd in *Indian,* and put into my Hand, I shall here insert in
English, and they are these which here follow,

---

558 1 Corinthians 7:34.

559 The perception that illness, particularly consumption (tuberculosis), wasted away the
body, leaving the true self or spirit behind, was common through the nineteenth century. Sontag, *Illness as Metaphor,* 20–26.

560 Debt was a rampant problem on Martha's Vineyard, and Wampanoags were often sued for
debt. David Silverman notes that during the eighteenth century "the intersection of changes in
native economy and Indian tastes in food and clothing, with the debilitating effects of disease,
meant that natives generally became dependent upon store credit for clothing and sustenance":
Silverman, *Faith and Boundaries,* 186.

I beseech thee, O my God, to pardon all my Sins before I die; for I now know that I shall not recover, and live any longer in this World; nor are my Desires after any of the things here below; but I do most earnestly crave thy pardoning Mercy, thro' the Death of thy Son Jesus Christ.

For verily thy Death, O Christ, is sufficient for the Salvation of my Soul from Death, when the time of my Death cometh. And when I die, I beseech thee, O my Redeemer, to receive my Soul, and raise it up to thy heavenly Rest. Thus have Mercy on me, O my God; and then I know when my time ends in this World, I shall be exceedingly happy in thine House for ever.

About a Week before she dy'd, she thought her Understanding began to fail her; at which she seemed to be troubled, and prayed to God that he would not deprive her of her Reason, while he continued her Life: and the Lord granted her Request.

[179] Several Persons that were with her in the two or three last Days of her Life, do, with one Consent, assure me, that she enjoyed much Consolation in her Soul, and declared her Willingness to leave her *earthly House of this Tabernacle,* and go to that *not made with Hands, eternal in the Heavens.*[561]

EXAMPLE XIX.
MARY COSHOMON, *who died in* Chilmark, March 1721-2.

THIS *Mary* was a Daughter of pious Parents, (*viz.* Deacon *Jonathan Amos* and his Wife, before mentioned) who taught her to read, and instructed her well in the Principles of the true Religion: and she, so far as I can learn, was of a sober and regular Conversation from her Youth up.

When she came to Years of Discretion, she used to ask her Parents serious Questions in Matters of Religion, desiring to be instructed by them in the things of God and his Kingdom.

When she was a Maid grown, she was married to *Eliab Coshomon,*[562] since a Preacher of the Word of God to the *Indians* in the said *Chilmark:* and as soon as she was become a Wife, she encouraged her Husband to set up, and constantly uphold the Worship of God in his House and used her self to pray in the Family when he was not at home.

When she had been marry'd about two Years, she began to express a deep Sense of the Obligations lying on her, publickly and solemnly to

---

561 2 Corinthians 5:1.

562 An inhabitant of the northeast end of Gay Head, son of Samuel Coshomon, a minister at Sanchakantacket (*IC*, 218). *WGH*, 128–29, 138.

devote her self to the Fear and Service of God, in an Attendance on all the Ordinances of his instituted Worship. She then said, that when she saw the People of God sitting at his Table, and enjoying Communion with him, she thought with her self, that if she did not draw nigh to him here, in the great Duties in which his People were bound to wait on him, she should be excluded from his Presence in the World to come, and not be admitted into the Company of such as would be then happy in the Enjoyment of him, but only *see them afar off, she her self being shut out from among them.*

[180] She also declared that she look'd on the Officers of the Church of Christ, as Dressers of the Trees planted in God's Vineyard;[563] and that she greatly needed to be under such Cultivations, by Instructions, Admonitions, and Reproofs, as Members of Churches might expect to enjoy. Such Thoughts as these drew many Tears from her Eyes, when she saw the Lord's Supper administered, and put her upon seeking earnestly to God to prepare her for the Privileges which she earnestly desired to enjoy.

Having opened her Case to some *Indian* Ministers that lodged at the House, one Night after the *Sacrament,* and having received Counsel and Advice from them, she was, on her desiring of it, readily admitted to a Participation of all the Ordinances of the Gospel, having, in order thereto, made a Profession of that Faith and Repentance, which God by his good Spirit had wrought in her Soul.

Some time after her Admission to those Privileges, she declared to her Husband, that she had found Rest and Comfort in the Enjoyment of them; but said, that she must notwithstanding expect to meet with Troubles and Temptations, while she remained here in the World; and that therefore she desired him to be helpful to her under them; and that in order to his being the more so, he would give up himself unto God also, and submit to those Rules which Christ had commanded his Disciples to follow: and this Duty she continued to press on him, until he not long after joined as a Member in full Communion to the Church whereof she was before one.

But tho a Desire of being under Discipline in the Church was one thing that made this good Woman seek to become a Member of it, yet being so, she never did by any Miscarriages offend her Brethren, and put them to the Trouble of dealing with her, but walked very blamelessly from the time of her first Admission to the Day of her Death.

She was a great Lover of the House and Ordinances of God, and would never unnecessarily stay from them, and did appear very serious and devout while she attended them.

---

563 Luke 13:6–7.

She was a diligent Instructor of her Children;[564] and one little Girl in particular, which she could not send to School because there was none near, she did her self teach to read, and say her Catechism competently well [181] by that time she was six Years old, and did otherwise well instruct her.

She was remarkable for her dutiful Carriage towards her Husband, ever shewing him great Reverence and Respect; and when he was guilty of any Miscarriage, she would bring no railing Accusations against him, but would in a very submissive manner advise and intreat him.

She carried her self very obligingly to all her Neighbours, yet seldom went to visit them unless there were some special Occasion for it; but generally kept at home, and minded her own Business, working very diligently with her Hands.

Tho she was not her self rich, yet she charitably and wisely considered the Poor, and was forward when they needed to give them part of that little which she enjoyed.

As this good Woman *glorified God*[565] while she was well and in Prosperity, so she did no less *so* in those *Fires*, which in a Furnace of Affliction[566] he was pleased in his wise and holy Providence to cause her to endure.

She was, after she had lived to be about forty Years old, in the manner already declared, helping her Husband in *Indian* Harvest time, to put up his Corn into a Crib prepared for that use; and the same falling suddenly upon her, with a considerable Quantity of Corn in it, did most grievously crush and bruise her, insomuch that, besides several other Hurts, some of the Joints of her Back were somewhat displaced.

She was for the present speechless, and appeared to be in a manner dead; but after a while coming a little to her self, she justified God in respect of what had befallen her, declared her Expectation of a speedy Death, and prayed that her Soul might not perish, but enjoy everlasting Mercies, altho her Body was thus sorely broken.

Nor her self only, but all others about her did now continually expect her Dissolution, nor was there here any Chirurgeon[567] to be had that could help her; but after she had lain some Days in this Condition, perceiving that she was yet alive, and not knowing how long God might still preserve her *so*, she said, that she had but a little while to live when she came first into the World, and much less now; yet God had lengthened her Life much longer than she thought he would have done, when that Evil befel her under which she now [182] suffered: and she then

---

564 Her husband's known children included Esop Coshomon and Samuel Coshomon. *WGH*, 138, 184, 308, 338.
565 A phrase used in the Gospels and in Acts (and in the catechism).
566 Isaiah 48:10.
567 Surgeon (*OED*).

magnify'd the Mercy of God in preserving her so long, and declared that she looked upon the Evil wherewith God had visited her, as design'd by him for her spiritual Advantage, and prayed that her suffering of it might not be in vain to her; 'For so,' *said she,*

> the Pain which I must afterwards endure will be infinitely greater than that which I here undergo: I therefore intreat the Lord to help me so to improve this, and all other Providences of his towards me, that I may have all my Pain and Sorrow here in this World, and be for ever happy in that which is to come.

This poor Woman lived after this about three Years and a half, but was never able to sit up again: and a great Part of the time she was exercised with such grievous Pains as were hard to be endured, but was exceeding patient under them; and so excellent and exemplary was her Carriage from first to last, as cannot easily be expressed.

I divers times visited and discoursed with her, while she was in this low Estate, and cannot but testify that her Discourses were always very heavenly and gracious: and there be many others that can give the like Testimony.

She owned the Wisdom, Goodness and Sovereignity of God, in visiting her with the Affliction under which he was pleased to exercise her. She confessed, that what she suffered was far less than her Sins deserved; and affirmed, that she was obliged to bear with Patience what her heavenly Father was pleased to lay on her. She asserted, that what she suffered was but little and light, compared with what her Saviour had suffered for her, and with the Happiness and Glory to be enjoyed by God's People in another Life and World. She constantly declared her Willingness to die, whenever it should please God that she should so do: and on the other hand, that if God pleased to lengthen out her Life a while longer, she was content that he should so do.

She also declared how very apt God's own People were in their Prosperity to forget him, and how much they often needed Affliction on that Account; and did confess to his Praise, that he had done her Good by that wherewith she had been visited.

[183] She prayed without ceasing to God for the Mercies she needed, and did not neglect to pray for others also; and sometimes in her Prayers said to God, that she had no Righteousness of her own to recommend her to his Favour, but must with the poor Publican smite upon her Breast, and say, *Lord be merciful to me a Sinner.*[568]

About three or four Weeks before she dy'd, she was in the Night heard calling upon God, and, among other things, then spake to this Purpose:

---

568 Luke 18:13. Publicans were much-hated tax collectors for the Roman Empire in the time of Christ.

O Lord, I beseech thee, consider the Case of my poor Husband and Children, consider the great Trouble and Difficulty which they have undergone in looking after me, so long as they have done; is it not time to give them rest? However, I may not prescribe unto thee, do as thou thinkest best.

A little after this she was again heard pleading with God after the fame manner.

Not long before she dy'd, she gave much good Counsel unto her Husband and Children. Something of what she said to him, I think worthy to be here inserted.

She intreated him to be sure to endeavour to keep a Fear and Awe of God alive in his Heart; *for if,* said she, *that be wanting, you will soon fall into Sin, and that will bring Evil upon you: but if God should at any time suffer you to be overcome by Temptations, so as to sin against him, see that you be not discouraged so as to despair of his Mercy, for so your Condition will be exceeding miserable.* Other good Advice she gave to him, which he had need to remember and improve.

Having finished the Counsel which she gave to her Friends, she spent much of her few remaining Hours in speaking and praying to *her God*; but was now so weak and low, that not much of what she said could be heard and understood by those that were with her.

Thus she lived, and then dy'd, and we hope does now thro' Faith and Patience inherit the Promises.

[184] EXAMPLE XX.
HANNAH SISSETOM, *who died at* Sanchekantacket
about the latter end of September 1722.

THIS *Hannah* was a Daughter of *Joel Sims*[569] mentioned in *Chapter* I. who dy'd while she was young. She was put to live in a religious *English* Family on the Island, where she was taught to read, tho not very well, and instructed in the first Principles of Religion;[570] and she carry'd her self well in that Family.

After she was grown up, she marry'd an *Indian* called *Oggin* [alias *Haukkings*] *Sissetom,* who was a Grandson of that very pious *Wunnannauhkomun* mentioned *Chapter* I. *Example 5.*[571] and one for whom his said

---

569 *IC*, 73*, 255.

570 Usually the "first principles" were taught through the catechism. For a fuller version of them, see Fitch, *First pinciples [sic] of the doctrine of Christ.*

571 *IC*, 18–20. Husband of Ammapoo (*IC*, 148–51*) and hence the brother-in-law of John and Hannah Nahnosoo. Oggin Sissetom's brothers included Abel Sesetom and Caleb Seaton (*IC*, 272).

Grandfather was very solicitous, that he might *be* and *do* Good, as is there declared: but his Character was not at all answerable to the Desires of that godly Man, or of his godly Mother yet living; for tho he frequently worshipped God in his Family, and was also pretty constant in his Attendance on God's publick Worship, yet he had such an excessive Lust after strong Drink, that he was frequently overcome by it, so as that he might be justly looked upon as one of those Drunkards who, without a true Repentance, *shall not inherit the Kingdom of God;*[572] and tho he sometimes appeared to be under great Convictions, yet still the Temptation prevailed too much against him, and sometimes overcame him; and it is uncertain whether God ever gave him a true Repentance or not: however he appeared so remarkably penitent in the eight or nine Days of his last Sickness, that there may be some Room to hope, that he may be found among the number of those who are called at the eleventh Hour.

But I did not intend this Man as one of my Examples of Piety, tho I have said thus much concerning him; it was his Wife that I intended to give some Account of.

And the first thing which I shall take notice of in her Character, was her remarkable Dutifulness to her Husband; for tho by his frequent Drunkenness he very much unman'd himself, and forfeited the Honour which had been otherwise due to him, yet, this notwithstanding, his good Wife carried her self towards him, his own Relations being Judges, as she ought to have done if he [185] had not been so faulty, constantly yielding Obedience to his just Commands, and not vexing and provoking of him by any hard Words, but used in a very dutiful manner to advise and intreat him.

But as on the one hand she would not unnecessarily provoke him; so on the other, she would have no Fellowship with him in the Sin in which he lived; but on the contrary, endeavoured to persuade him to refrain from it. Her Life was also on all other accounts very blameless.

The ill Courses which her Husband took, kept his Family very poor and needy, so that she was forced to labour extremely hard for a Livelihood for her self and Children:[573] for, tho he was a labouring Man, yet he, as some *English* Men do, spent almost all he got in strong Drink, bringing very little home for his Wife and Children to live upon.

Yet these Inconveniencies the poor Woman bore very patiently, still following her Business, and endeavouring to keep her Children to work also: nor was this the best Part of her Character, for unto Patience and

---

572 1 Corinthians 6:9–10; Galatians 5:21; Ephesians 5:5.

573 Her children include Bethia Sissetom (IC, 186, 255–57*) and Thomas Organ, a debtor. Bock (Rebecca) Organ, a debtor, was also probably her child. *WGH*, 138, 238, 348–49.

Diligence she added Prayer to God for his Blessing on all that belonged to her: she prayed with her Children when her Husband was not at home with her, seeking the Presence of God, which she knew would more than supply the want of any other Comfort which she needed.

A good *English* Neighbour observing how her Husband spent what he got in strong Drink, which did but hurt him, one said to her, that she thought she ought to talk to him for wasting what he got, and bringing so little home to her and his Children: unto which she answered, that she was loth to do so; for if she should, she should thereby only vex him without doing any Good. No doubt she had before this made the Trial.

One Comfort she had under this Affliction; her Husband's pious Mother before-mentioned living much in the House with her, was very kind and obliging to her, endeavouring to comfort her under all her Trials; and used to exhort her to devote her self to the Service and Glory of the God of her good Father, who had devoted her to him in Baptism while she was a Child. This her Mother-in-law used also, sometimes to pray with [186] her and her Children, her Daughter in her Husband's Absence desiring her to do it.

But tho she kindly accepted of her Mother's Goodwill towards her, yet she had not the Courage to ask an Admission to full Communion in the Church of Christ, but alleged, that she feared she was not qualif'd for so high a Privilege.

Near a Year before she dy'd, she buried a very pious Daughter, *Bethia Sissetom,* afterwards to be mentioned in the fourth Chapter of these Examples;[574] whom having seen laid in the Grave, she was herself immediately taken ill, the same Sickness increasing on her, till it put an End to her Life: and during the time of this her long Sickness, she labour'd abundantly to prepare for her great Change, calling very often and earnestly upon God to pardon her Sins, sanctify her Heart, and fit her for his Kingdom; and used, as long as she was able, to read and meditate as well as pray, and was very full of such serious Discourse as does become a Person leaving this World, and entring on an eternal Estate of Weal or Woe in another.

Her *English* Neighbours before-mentioned visiting of her in her Sickness, were entertain'd by her with serious and good Discourses.

She then blamed her self for having let her Heart and Time be too much taken up about the things of this Life and World, of which she said her Poverty and Want had been one Occasion; but added, that she had

---

574 *IC*, 255–57*.

now seen her Error, and that the Concerns of our Souls should be more taken care of.

She also declared, that the Sickness and Death of her Daughter before-mentioned, had been a Means to affect her and do her good, taking notice at the same time of the Grace of God manifested in her and towards her.

It pleased God very much to enlighten and comfort her before she died. She expressed her Hopes of everlasting Mercies thro' the Merits of her only Saviour Jesus Christ, and her Willingness to die and leave this World, and all the Enjoyments of it, as well as all the Sorrows and Troubles she met withal in it. She mightily comforted and encouraged her pious, but poor Mother-in-Law, who had been so very good and kind to her: and she gave much good Counsel to her Husband and Chil[187]dren and others, exhorting them earnestly to forsake every evil Way, and follow hard after God: and so left this Vale of Tears.

EXAMPLE XXI.
MARTHA COOMES, *who died at* Nashouohkamuk
in the Summer of the Year 1722.

THIS Woman was a Daughter of religious Parents, *viz. Gershom Wompanummoo,*[575] and *Sarah* his Wife, of the Place already mentioned; her Mother being a Daughter of that good Deacon *Jonathan Amos,* of whom I have spoken in *Chap.* I. *Examp.* 15.

She was solemnly devoted to God in her Infancy, and had a religious Education; but notwithstanding the Advantages she enjoyed, she was by some said to be vicious while she was a Maid, and for some time after: The Sins which she was chiefly charged withal, were such as against the eighth and ninth Commandments. But having been some few Years married to *Simon Coomes,*[576] a hopeful young Man, whose Grandfather *Hiacoomes,* and Father *Samuel Coomes,*[577] have been already mention'd, as remarkable Examples of Piety, she began to appear more serious than

---

575 Called "Great Gershom," he was probably also the father of Daniel Wompanumoo (*IC,* 213); Matthew Gershom, jailed for assault on James Mason of Boston; Aron Gershom, sued for stealing wool and given a Bible by Society for the Propagation of the Gospel in 1732; and Simon Garsham, assistant to Pastor Hosea Manhut (IC, 73, 207, 217, 219, 269–70) at Nashouakomack 1735–39). *WGH,* 119, 226, 236, 241, 278, 350.

576 After Martha died, Simon married Jean Coomes, the granddaughter of Kisquish, the sachem of Chilmark. Simon's children probably included Thomas and Joseph Coomes. *WGH,* 136, 215–16, 246–47.

577 *IC,* 91–95*.

before she had been, and carried her self much better than formerly she had done. And now it might be said of her, *behold she prayeth;*[578] for she not only join'd with others in the Worship of God, which she before appear'd to do, but was also observed to pray by her self alone, where she did not design that any but God should see and hear her.

She also, before that long and lingring Sickness whereof she died, expressed Desires of giving up her self publickly to God, that so she might enjoy him in all his Ordinances; but was under such a Sense of her sinful Unworthiness, that she durst not ask an Admission to the *Table of the Lord,*[579] tho she said she desired to serve *him.*

After she had been sick a while, she expressed her Apprehensions of the Approaches of Death towards her; and withal, a deep Concern that she might not fall short of the everlasting Mercies offered to Sinners in the Gospel, and her Resolutions to seek earnestly to God for an Interest in them.

[188] She was accordingly, in the time of her sickness, often heard pouring out her Soul before the Lord; but with so low a Voice, that very little of what she said could be understood: and she now professed her Faith and Hope in Christ her only Saviour.

The Evening before she died, she mightily comforted and encouraged her Relations: She told them she would not have them much grieved at her Death; for she believed, that when she left this World she should enter into Rest in the Kingdom of God;[580] and then exhorted them to be constant and earnest Seekers to that God in whom she trusted; telling them, that if they were so, they might again see her with Comfort in the other World.

The next Morning she desired that her Father, then abroad, might be called to come to her; and being come, she gave some serious and good Counsel to him, and then presently died, calling on her Saviour to receive her Soul.

She left one little Daughter behind her when she died, *viz. Sarah Coomes,* afterwards mentioned in *Chap.* IV.[581]

Let none object against this Woman the Faults of which she was guilty before her Conversion; *for such were some of you, but ye are washed, but ye are sanctified, but ye are justified in the Name of the Lord Jesus, and by the Spirit of one God.*[582]

---

578 Acts 9:11.

579 A phrase used by the prophets Ezekiel and Malachi, and by St. Paul.

580 A phrase used extensively in the Gospels and by St. Paul.

581 *IC,* 263–64*.

582 1 Corinthians 6:11.

EXAMPLE XXII.
ABIGAIL SEKITCHAHKOMUN, *an old Maid, who died at* Nashaun,
alias Slocums Island, *in the Year* 1722.

THIS *Abigail* had a very good Report, even from her Childhood, and made a public Profession of Religion while she was but a young Maid, joining her self while a very young Woman to that Church of *Antipedobaptists* whereof good *Stephen Tackmasson*[583] before-mentioned was the Pastor.

She had the Happiness of being taught to read while she was young; and she made a good use of the Advantage, reading abundantly in the Bible, and such other good Books as our *Indians* have among them; and she ordered her Conversation[584] as did become the Gospel.

She sometimes said, that having long had a Desire to love and serve the Lord, she used to think that her loving and keeping bad Company would not agree there[189]withal, and that she had therefore resolved to be separate from them, and not to walk in their way: And herein she kept her Resolution to the last; when many of her Neighbours had their drunken Meetings, she would not go to them, but tarried home and minded her Business, labouring diligently with her Hands for a Livelihood.

She living with her Mother, and Mother's Sister, used to take her turn to pray in that little Family, and was probably the best qualified to perform the Duty of any Person in it.

She was constant and serious in her Attendance on the publick Worship of God, and heard indifferently those of her own Persuasion, and those who were for Pedo-Baptism; nor could she endure to hear those of her own Profession revile those from whom they dissented.

Being sick almost a Year before her Death, she was in that time very full of good and heavenly discourses; she talked much of the Vanity and Uncertainty of all things in this lower World, and the Excellency and Glory of that which is above: she expressed a deep Sense of the Evil of Sin, and of the Excellency of a Life of Faith and Holiness; and earnestly exhorted her Relations and Visitors to fear God and keep his Commandments.

She professed Faith in the Son of God, and said that her believing in him, was that which had encourag'd her to join the Church whereof she was a Member.

She said she had rather leave this World and go to God, than remain any longer here below; and she desired those about her, in the time of her Sickness, to let their Discourses be about the things of God and his

---

583 *IC*, 42–44*.
584 Psalm 50:23.

Kingdom: and when some began to talk of other things in her hearing, she let them know that she took no delight therein.

Thus setting her Affections on things that are above, and not on things below, she willingly left this World and went to the other.

[190] EXAMPLE XXIII.
HANNAH TILER, *who died at* Sanchecantacket *in* Edgartown, *in the Summer of the Year* 1723.

THIS Woman's Father was a praying *Indian*, named *Maquane*,[585] who died many Years since. Her Mother's Name was *Susannah*, and she was a pious Person, and of a blameless Conversation; she lived to a great Age, and died at the little Island of *Chappaquiddick*, but a few Days before the writing hereof.

As this Daughter of hers was as bad by Nature as any others, so the former part of her Life was no better ordered than the Lives of Persons in a State of Nature generally be. Nor was the Husband[586] she married after she was grown up, a Person of so good Qualifications, as that it might be justly hoped concerning him, that he would *save his Wife*.[587] He lived but viciously before he married her, and continued so to do for some Years afterward. He would frequently have his drunken Fits, and was often very contentious in them; and his Wife, who had too much Fellowship with him in these unfruitful Works of Darkness,[588] being the weaker Vessel,[589] often went by the wall when there were Contentions between them.

But the Woman being at length convinced of the great Evil there is in the Sin of Drunkenness, resolved that she would forsake it, and God helped her so to do; so that she overcame her Temptations to that Vice, and lived in that regard very temperately: but being her self in that Particular reformed, and Drunkenness now becoming exceeding offensive to her, she could not bear with it in others, and therefore could not forbear talking too angrily to her Husband when she saw him guilty of that Crime;[590] and this was an Occasion of sore Contentions betwixt them.

---

585 Owner of land at Chikkemmo which was given to him by Tawanquatuck, the first sachem to become a Christian (*IC*, 80–82*). *WGH*, 132, 197.

586 Probably Thomas Tyler Jr., who was accused of stealing rum on May 28, 1685. His mother was the sister of Wompamog, alias Mr. Sam (*IC*, 73–74*). *WGH*, 97, 154, 171, 217.

587 1 Corinthians 7:16.

588 Ephesians 5:11.

589 1 Peter 3:7. Puritans felt that women were spiritually weaker than men and more susceptible to the devil and sin. For the impact of New Testament misogyny on Puritan beliefs about women, see Thickston, *Fictions of the Feminine*.

590 The original reads "Crimel," probably a printer's error.

But the *Wrath of Man worketh not the Righteousness of God;*[591] and this poor Woman quickly saw, that her contending so sharply with her Husband about his Drunkenness, was not the way to cure him of it: She therefore resolved to try another Method with him, and see if by mild Intreaties, and a good Carriage towards him, she could not gain him; and she accordingly put this Method in practice with him, patiently bearing both [191] with his excessive Drinking, and other things hard to be indured, which, when he was in drink, she suffered from him. And tho this Method had not presently the desired Effect, yet she found Peace in it; and God helped her, in this way of well-doing, to cast all her Care on him.

Being thus reform'd in her Life, she made a publick Profession of Religion, and joined her self to the Church of Christ about nine or ten Years before that wherein she died; during all which time, she walked, as far as I can understand, very blamelessly, ordering her Conversation as did become the Gospel. However, some of her Neighbours yet observed, that she still suffered such things from an unreasonable Man, as they thought to be intolerable; and advised her to apply her self to the Civil Authority for the Redress of her Grievances: But she peremptorily refus'd to take this Course, as prudently forseeing and considering the evil Consequences that would be apt to attend it, and as being in some hopes, that by continuing in the Method which she had begun, she might possibly at length *save her Husband.*[592]

Accordingly she, after some time, did so far overcome his Evil by her Goodness, that he carried himself more kindly to her than formerly he had done; and appeared to become religious, put on a Form of Godliness, prayed in his House, took some care about the Instruction of his Children, and made a publick Profession of Faith and Repentance, joining himself to the Church of Christ; so that People were in hopes that he was become a good Man. Yet he still appear'd to be somewhat faulty; and one thing objected against him was, that he was not yet so kind to his Wife as he should have been, especially considering how well she constantly carried her self towards him; but still she bore, with the greatest Patience, all his Unkindness towards her, being glad that she had gained so far on him as she had done. Her Neighbours bear her witness, and her Husband also confesseth, that such as has been now declared was her Carriage towards him.

Nor did this good Woman neglect to do all she could for the good of the rest of her Household, either by providing Necessaries for their Bodies, or giving them those good Instructions which tended to the

---

591 James 1:20.

592 1 Corinthians 7:16.

Salvation of their Souls, A Son which her Husband had by a former Wife[593] has declared to me, that she carried it towards him as [192] tho she had been his own Mother, and did frequently give good Instructions and Exhortations to him.

She saw, and rejoic'd in, one good Effect of her Endeavours to bring up her Children in the Fear of God: A little Daughter of hers, who died a few Months before her, appeared so pious in her Life, and had such Hopes in her Death, that she declared to some of her Friends, that the Comfort she had in respect of the happy Change which she hoped her Child had experienced, had in a great measure swallowed up that Grief which otherwise her Death would have brought on her.

She was good to her Neighbours, as well as to those of her own House, as all that lived near her can testify. Her Charity, or Kindness, was more especially discovered to such of her Neighbours, as, being sick and weak, were unable to take care of themselves; to such she frequently made Visits and carried Presents: and tho she had nothing to carry them that was of any considerable Value, yet she would pray them to accept of what she brought them, telling them that others had need take care of them, when they were unable to go abroad to provide for themselves such things as they wanted.

Nor was the Charity of this Woman confin'd to those of her own Nation only: Some of her *English* Neighbours do testify concerning her, that she did good to them when they had need of it. Thus an *English*[594] Gentleman who lived near her, lately told me, that when by reason of Sickness he much needed Help in his Family, this Neighbour of his did of her own accord come frequently to his House, and perform such Services in it as were most necessary to be done, without the least Intimation of her expecting any Reward for what she did.

One Instance more of her Charity I shall here insert: She had a poor *English* Neighbour that had a Daughter to whom God had not given that use of her Reason as People ordinarily enjoy, by reason whereof she was very helpless, and not able to do such things for her self as otherwise she might. This being observed by the charitable Woman of whom I write, she every Year, just before Winter, began to knit the poor Girl a Pair of Stockings, her Mother finding Yarn for it; the doing of which [193] she

---

593   If her husband was Thomas Tyler Jr., his only known son was James Tiler. Both Thomas and James were still living when *Indian Converts* was written. *WGH*, 99, 154.

594   Joseph Norton *Esq;* [Mayhew's note.] Joseph Norton (1652–1741/42) of Edgartown was "one of the leading citizens of the Vineyard and its first representative to the General Court of Mass. in 1692." He was briefly sheriff of the county and served as justice of the Court of Common Pleas. He lived at Major's Cove near Miober's Bridge and is buried at Tower Hill Cemetery. *HMV*, 3:357. He was the uncle of Abigail Norton, who was convicted of fornication with Samuel Coomes (*IC*, 91–95*).

freely gave her, and would not by any means be hindred from doing so as long as she lived.

Nor can the Character of this Woman be fully given, without an Account of the *Piety* as well as *Charity* wherewith she was indued. Besides what has of this nature been already related concerning her, I must here further add, that those who were well acquainted with her, do affirm concerning her, that she was much in Prayer to God, and was sometimes observed (according to the good Example by another *Hannah* set her) to be *pouring out her Soul before the Lord.*[595]

She did also, with great Constancy and Seriousness, attend the publick Worship and Ordinances of God; scarce any Weather being bad enough to hinder her from going to God's House of Prayer, when she was not by Sickness disenabled for it.

She also used on all Occasions to discourse very piously; frequently using such Expressions as tended to the Honour of God, and the Edification of those with whom she conversed: for this she was so observable, that some of her *English*, as well as *Indian* Neighbours, took notice of it; especially when she visited the Sick she was wont to talk seriously with them about the things of God, and another Life and World; and she would sometimes, when she saw Persons, as she thought, too impatient under the Pains which they endured, speak to this Effect to them: *Consider how light and short the Pains are which you so much complain of, compared with those which the Damned undergo in the Place of eternal Torments.*

As she thus excited others to Patience, so she was exceeding patient her self under those Afflictions wherewith it pleased her heavenly Father to visit her.

In her last Sickness she discovered a temper[596] of Soul well becoming a Person, whose Conversation in the foregoing Years of her Life, had been such as has been now described. She trusted in the Mercy of God, thro' Jesus Christ her only Saviour, and called frequently on him for the Favours and Benefits which she needed, expressing her Hopes of receiving the Mercies which she called on the Lord her God for. She declared her Willingness to die whenever it pleased God that she should so do: And she earnestly exhorted all that were about her to be diligent Seekers of that God in whom she believed and [194] trusted, and to take heed that they did not by their Sins provoke him.

---

595 The biblical Hannah was barren but poured out her soul to God and vowed that if God gave her a child, she would give the child to the Lord. God listened to her, and she bore Samuel, a great judge and prophet and the last ruler before Saul, the first king of Israel. 1 Samuel 1–9.

596 Temperament (*OED*).

Thus she lived, and thus she died; and is, I hope, gone to that Place where the Wicked cease from troubling, and where the Weary be at rest.

EXAMPLE XXIV.
ELIZABETH UHQUAT, *who died at* Christian-Town *in the Year* 1723.

AS by Faith *Rahab* the Harlot perished not,[597] so there is good Reason to believe that the same may be truly said of the poor Woman of whom I here speak.

She was, while young, put to an *English* Master on the main Land, who neither taught her to read, nor took care to instruct her in the Principles of the true Religion, the Knowledge whereof is necessary to Life eternal; which is the unhappy Case of many of our *Indian* Youth that go to live among the *English*, tho there be others of them who are well instructed.[598]

Being very ignorant, she was also exceeding wicked while she was a young Woman; and a Violation of the seventh Commandment was the Sin of which she appeared to be most deeply guilty, having by her Whoredoms been the Mother of two Children, before ever she had a Husband to be the Father of them.

After this she married, but her Husband did, in a short time, treacherously depart from her, and took another Wife;[599] she not being, as I could understand, any blameable Cause of his so doing, but was much troubled at his so forsaking her. However, being irrecoverably gone from her, she afterwards married another Man, *viz. Joseph Uhquat*[600] of the Place above-named; with whom she lived and was, as far as did appear, a faithful Wife to him to the Day of her Death.

While she lived with this Husband, she was observed to keep much at home, and to mind her own Business labouring diligently with her Hands to provide for her self and him such things as were necessary:

---

597 Joshua 2 and 6.

598 In spite of her own negative experiences, Elizabeth Uhquat still chose to send her son Tobit to an English family. Tobit's family seems to have treated him better, however, and educated him. See *IC*, 257–61*. On the factors that led to Tobit's being bound out, see Silverman, *Faith and Boundaries*, 185–87.

599 As Ann Marie Plane notes, Native American marriages in New England did not always look like white marriages and did not follow the same rules. Plane discusses Uhquat's marriage and sexuality at length in *Colonial Intimacies*, 113–17, 129–33.

600 Joseph Uhquat was the son of Sarah Unquit and Elias (Ely) Unquet. He was also married to Dorcas Onquet, the mother of his son Joseph Unquet Jr., who was bound out to colonist Thomas Arey. *WGH*, 116, 147–48, 239, 318–19, 395–95.

but he being for some time given to Idleness, and to follow after strong Drink, she was grieved and disturbed at it; and this sometimes caused Difference and Contention betwixt them. However, it seems that her Uneasiness at his [195] Conduct, and her Endeavours to reform him, had a good Effect on him; it being very apparent to their Neighbours, that he after some time became a better Husband: And he and his Wife lived more comfortably together than formerly they had done.

But the Woman I am speaking of being thus settled in a Family, and that in a Place where the Word of God was constantly preached, became a diligent Hearer of the same, and seemed to take heed how she heard; giving, so far as could be observed, a very great Attention to the things which she heard preached from the Scriptures of Truth: and the longer she continued in this Course of hearing the Word of God, the more serious she seemed to grow; and her Neighbours began to observe and say, that she was much altered in her Countenance and Behaviour from what she had formerly been. I could not my self but observe a very remarkable Change in her, she appearing to me as a Woman of a sorrowful Countenance; and I sometimes saw her much affected at Sermons which she heard preached.

She was about this time very much affected at the Death of one of her fore-mentioned Children, who will be afterwards spoken of.[601] The Piety which she beheld in her dying Child, was a means to stir up in her earnest Desires to be made a Partaker of the like gracious Endowments, and put her upon endeavouring to obtain the like Qualifications,

Her Husband being gone from home on a Whaling-Voyage when this happened, when he returned in the Spring (as he himself declares to me) she told him, That God had since he had been gone given her a more deep and affecting Sight and Sense of her Sins, than she had ever before had, and that he had made her to see a Necessity of true Repentance and of a new Life; and did withal, earnestly desire him to assist her therein, and that he would to that end set up the Worship of God in his House, which he had hitherto neglected, &c. These things he says she pressed upon him with such Importunity, that he could not withstand the Motion made by her, but did, as far as he was able, comply with her Desires therein. This was early in the Spring in the Year 1722-3.

After this, the Woman continued to be of a sorrowful Countenance; and I not fully understanding what was the [196] matter with her, waited for a convenient Opportunity to discourse with her about the State of her

---

601 Tobit Potter: *IC*, 257–61*.

Soul: but not speaking with her before I went to *Boston* in *June*,[602] she died before my Return; which, when I understood, I repented the Delay. However, there was a godly understanding Woman, who observing how melancholy she appeared to be, discoursed several times seriously with her about her spiritual State, and much encouraged her to follow hard after God, and to apply her self to some Minister for further Advice and Direction; for which Counsel, tho she was very thankful, yet she was under such Discouragements as never to speak with any Minister about her Case, till after she was seized with the Sickness whereof in a few Days she died.

But being sick and like to die, she sent for a Pastor of an *Indian* Church who lived not far from her, and fully and freely opened the State of her Soul to him, and desired his Counsel and Prayers respecting the Difficulties which she was under; yea, earnestly begged the Prayers of all God's People for her.

She now owned her self to be a most vile and sinful Creature, and said God had made her deeply sensible that she was so; having set all her Sins in order before her Eyes, and made them exceeding bitter to her Soul: she further said, That such was the Load of Guilt which lay on her, that were it not that she believed that the Son of God came into the World to save such miserable Sinners as she was, and had laid down his Life and shed his most precious Blood to that end; and that the Mercy of God was exceeding great, and ready to be extended to all such as truly lay hold of the same, she should despair of obtaining Pardon of Sin and Life eternal; but being persuaded of these things, she was resolved that she would seek to him, and do all that she could that if it were possible she might make her Peace with him, and intreated that the People of God would help her by their Prayers in this great Work.

She also now lamented that she had so long neglected publickly and solemnly to give up her self to God, to be his Servant all the Days of her Life; and said that she feared she had missed an Opportunity of doing this; but if God would please to spare her Life, and enable her to do it, she was resolved to delay this Work no longer. [197] She was very thankful to the Minister that came to visit, counsel and pray with her, and so he left her.

After this she called frequently and earnestly upon God for his Mercy; and before she died, obtained a comfortable Hope of eternal Blessedness.

---

602   On July 3, 1723, Mayhew received an honorary degree of Master of Arts at the commencement ceremonies at Harvard College. He had originally excused himself from the honor but was overruled by the college. Prince, "Some Account of those English Ministers," 307.

EXAMPLE XXV.

MARGARET OSOOIT, *commonly called by the* Indians Meeksishqune,
who died at the Gayhead December *the Fifth* 1723.

THIS Woman was a Daughter of a petty Sachim of *Tisbury,* called by
the *English Josiah,* and by the *Indians Keteanomin;*[603] but of him I can give
no very good Character. Her Mother's Name was *Sianum,* a Daughter of
Noquittompane,[604] formerly mentioned; the same being esteemed a good
Woman, in some of the last Years of her Life.

But whatever the Father or Mother of this Person was, it is much to
be hoped she her self was *a Woman that feared the Lord,*[605] and served him
with Integrity and Uprightness of Heart.

She was happy in this, that she was, while young, taught to read very
well; and God gave her a Heart afterwards to make a good Use of this
Advantage, wherewith in his good Providence he favoured her, as we
shall have further occasion to observe.

She was, so far as I can learn, while a Maid, of a sober Conversation,
and free from any moral Scandal whatsoever; but I do not know that she
was religious while a young Woman, tho 'tis probable that she was so.

She was, after she had been some time a Woman grown, married to
Zachariah Osooit,[606] an *Indian* of the *Gayhead;* and lived with him about
thirty three Years, and did bear many Children to him.

As soon as she became a Wife, she began to discover such things as
gave some grounds to hope that she had the Fear of God in her; for it then
appeared that she often read the Word of God, and such other Books of
Piety as were so long ago published in the *Indian* Tongue: She also then
excited her Husband to pray to God in his House, and prevailed with
him so to do; and whereas he was very apt to follow after strong Drink,

---

603 Keteanomin frequently appears in the early deeds from Martha's Vineyard. He was the son
of Maututoukquet, the sachem of Takemy in the 1640s. His other children included Alexander,
the next sachem of Takemy, and Zachariah Papmick, a jack of trades who worked as a cooper,
town clerk, and preacher at Christiantown. The sons also had a "wild" side: Alexander was an
accessory to murder (DCCR I.61), and Zachariah was presented to the court for breaking the
Sabbath. *WGH,* 108–9, 114, 248.

604 *IC,* 84–86*.

605 Proverbs 31:30.

606 This Zachariah was an Indian magistrate. He died sometime before December 1732.
Their children include Zachariah Hossueit (?–1774), a pastor at Gay Head, and possibly Moses
Osooit, who was sued for debt by Experience Mayhew in 1734. *WGH,* 130–31, 140, 357. Zachariah Hossueit was one of the most significant ministers on the island; as David Silverman puts
it, "For almost a half a century Hossueit was the Indians' unrivaled master of the written word,
translating the passages of God's book into plain speech for the people and interpreting the
natives' language for colonial authorities." Numerous examples of Hossueit's writing survive
in archives and in print; see *Native Writings,* 1:5, 69, 175, 415. On the Hossueit family and their
legacy, see Silverman, *Faith and Boundaries,* 157–84.

[198] she used her utmost Endeavour to restrain him from that way of Wickedness, and would have no Fellowship with him in it.

Only she was once guilty of great Folly this way; for being vexed with the Intemperance of her Husband, and having some Rum ready at hand which she might drink of if she pleased, Satan tempted her to taste the Liquor, and to take so plentifully of it, that she might see how good a thing it was to be drunk as many others were: and drunk she was to some purpose, so that falling down on the Earthen Floor of her House, and sleeping some time there, she at length awaked so sick and out of frame, that she thought it no good thing to be drunk; and was yet more sick at the thoughts of her Sin and Folly, in trying the wicked Experiment by which she had made such a Beast of her self as she had done: And it pleased God, that instead of now becoming in love with the Liquor by which she had so basely fallen, her Aversion to it was so abundantly increased, and she never more returned to that Folly of which she had been guilty: Nay, she could hardly be persuaded to taste of that Liquor again as long as she lived; and she grew more earnest with others to refrain from the excessive Use of it.

As she appeared to fear God and eschew Evil, so she made conscience of worshipping God, and calling upon his Name. When her Husband was gone from home, as he too often was, she constantly pray'd with her Children; nor did she pray in her Family only, but frequently went into secret Places to call upon the Name of the Lord: at which Devotion she was sometimes accidentally surprized, by her Relations and Neighbours.

As her Children became capable of receiving Instructions, she endeavoured to train them up in the way in which they should go: several of them have with Tears told me what Pains she used to take with them, as by teaching them their Catechisms, and also reading the Scriptures to them, and pressing them to the Duties mentioned in them, and warning them against the Sins therein forbidden. Her Husband and Neighbours do likewise give the same Testimony concerning her.

She was often grieved at her Husband's erring thro' strong Drink, and was unwearied in her Endeavours to persuade him to refrain from that Sin: but alas! she [199] had not the Success in it which she desired; and such were the Hardships which she was by this means brought under, that it must be confessed, it made her sometimes speak unadvisedly, which she would readily confess and lament: but considering how much Poverty and Grief she underwent, it is more to be admired that her Patience held out as it did, than that she sometimes shewed some Infirmity.

She was looked upon as a Person so well qualified for the Communion with the Church of Christ, that many wondered that she did not ask an

Admission thereunto; and some discoursed with her about the matter, but she had such Apprehensions concerning the Holiness required of those who are admitted to Fellowship with God in his Ordinances, that she could not be persuaded that she was her self qualified for so high Privileges, and would declare how grievously God was dishonour'd by such as had given themselves to him, and yet did not walk worthy of the Vocation wherewith they were called.

When she discoursed on these things, she used to take her Bible, to which she was no Stranger, and turn to and read such Places in it as she apprehended to intimate what Holiness was required to be in such as so drew nigh to God, as particularly *Psalm* xv. and xxiv. 3, 4. and many other Places.

She seldom went abroad, unless there were some special Occasion that called for it; and indeed while her Children were young, it was thought by some she did not go to Meeting so often as she should have done: but others have alleged in her favour, that the miserable Condition which she and her Children were in, rendered it almost impossible that she should frequently leave her own House and go to God's, which they judge she would have otherwise gladly done. She was her self most miserably clothed, and her Children were no better of it; nor had she ordinarily, while they were small, any body to leave with them: and the Diligence with which she afterwards attended God's publick Worship, when her Children were grown more able to help themselves, gave grounds to think that she did not stay from publick Ordinances for want of an Heart to attend them.

She mightily delighted in *The Practice of Piety*,[607] a Book which our *Indians* have in their own Language, [200] and would scarce pass a Day without reading something in it.

As she grew in Years, she seemed to grow in Grace, and in the Knowledge of her Lord and Saviour Jesus Christ; which many ways appeared to those that observed her.

She often confessed and lamented the Sins of her Heart and Life, and talked much of that way of Redemption by the Son of God which is revealed in the Gospel, magnifying the Grace of God therein manifested to Sinners.

She complained often of the Sins of the Times, and mourn'd for them, particularly the Sin of Drunkenness, of which she knew many of her Neighbours were frequently guilty; and that any in publick Stations were in this way faulty, seemed to her intolerable.

---

607 First printed in 1602, Lewis Bayley's *Practise of pietie* became the most popular devotional manual in seventeenth-century New England. See Hayes, *Colonial Woman's Bookshelf*, 43. John Eliot's Algonquian translation of it, *Manitowompae Pomantamoonk*, was printed in 1665 and 1685.

She frequently dealt with Persons privately for their Sins, especially with those of her own Sex; and if they were Persons who had made a publick Profession of Religion, she would declare to them the solemn Obligations they lay under to live to God, and to depart from all Iniquity: And when she had begun to deal with any for their Miscarriages,[608] she would not willingly leave them till she had brought them to a Confession of their Faults, sometimes with Tears, and to engage to endeavour to reform what was amiss in them.

After she had been supposed to have been several Years past Childbearing, and was, I suppose, upwards of fifty Years old, she brought forth a Son, who is still living; but not long after this she grew unhealthy, and was grievously exercised with a sore Breast, which in the Issue put an end to her Life.

She was for some time towards the beginning of her Illness in *much Heaviness thro' manifold Temptations*,[609] complaining of her Sins as a Burden too heavy for her to bear, and mourning under the Weight of them; yet God did not suffer her to despair of his Mercy, but enabled her to believe the Gospel of his Son, and endeavour to obtain Reconciliation to God thro' him, and a Sense of his loving Kindness to her Soul. She her self cry'd earnestly to God for his Mercy, and she called others to help her by their Prayers in that time of her Trouble, and she now declared, that she utterly disregarded every thing in this World, and was only concer[201]ned that she might not fall short of the Favour of God, without which nothing else could give Rest and Comfort to her Soul: nor did God deny the humble Requests of this his poor Handmaid, but did graciously lift up the Light of his Countenance upon her, giving her Peace in believing, and that Joy of Faith which passeth all Understanding.

She was now not only willing to die, whenever it should please God that she should so do, but even longed for that happy Hour; and yet said, that she was content still to bear more Affliction, if her heavenly Father saw it needful that she should.

She was wonderfully carry'd out in her Endeavours to affect the Hearts of her Relations and Neighbours, with a Sense of the Necessity and Excellency of Religion, and did with all possible Earnestness press them to engage thorowly in the great Duties of it, and to avoid every thing that might bring the Displeasure of God on them.

To this End she was not only spake to them all jointly, but having first spoken to her Husband giving him the best Counsel she could, and committing the Care of her Children to him, earnestly desiring him to *bring*

---

608 Misconduct, misbehaviour (*OED*).
609 1 Peter 1:6.

them up in the Nurture and Admonition of the Lord; she called her Children, all one by one, giving such Advice to them as she thought respectively most needed, and telling them she had often instructed and exhorted them, but that being now to leave them, that was the last time that she should ever speak to them.

She also declared before she dy'd, that she saw the Error she had been in, in not joining to the Church of Christ, as she ought to have done; and she lamented this Fault.

Some Christians that were with her when she was dying, having at her Desire commended her to God by Prayer, and sung a Psalm of Praises to him, she manifested a Desire to be gone, and intimated, that the Messengers of Heaven were already come to receive her: and two Persons that were then abroad, near the House where she lay a dying, do affirm, that they then plainly heard a melodious singing in the Air,[610] over the House where this Woman lay; but whether that be a Mistake or not, there is reason to believe that she dy'd well, and that she is gone to the *innumerable Company of Angels, and to the Spirits of just Men made perfect.*[611]

[202] EXAMPLE XXVI.
HEPZIBAH ASSAQUANHUT, *who died at*
Christian-Town, October 20, 1723.

THE Parents of this *Hepzibah* were *John Whitten*[612] (as he is commonly called) and *Jerusha* his Wife, *Indians* of the Place already mentioned.

They put this their Daughter while young, to live in a good *English* Family in *Tisbury*, where she continu'd I think seven Years, and until she was a Woman grown. And the pious People with whom she lived do bear her Witness, that she appeared all the while she was with them to be a sober, orderly, and well disposed Person, not given as they could perceive to any Vice whatsoever; but was faithful to her Trust, and diligent in her Business, and very willing and forward to go to Meeting, but not at all inclined to go into any bad Company. She also appeared willing to learn to read, but did not take her reading so easily as many do, and so did not learn to read so well as was to be desired.

---

610 Wampanoag oral tradition recounts that when the Gay Head Community Baptist Church was rebuilt, the old rafters were reused in a nearby house and that members of that household could sometimes hear Wampanoags singing hymns of praise. See "Aquinnah."

611 Hebrews 12:22–23.

612 John Whitten was accused repeatedly of supplying rum, and he later fingered others for the same crime. His wife Jerusha was also informed against for selling rum. *WGH*, 351–52.

Not long after she went from her said Master, she was marry'd to *Joel Assaquanhut*[613] of the Place aforesaid, and was a good Wife to him, being a discreet and chaste Keeper at home, and one that loved her Husband and Children, being also very obedient to him; and was one that laboured diligently with her Hands, to provide Necessaries for the Family.

Tho she lived very much in the Day of Temptation to the Sin of Drunkenness, yet I can't, upon strict Enquiry, understand, that she was in the least degree stained with that Vice, but on the contrary she used to bear a Testimony against the immoderate Use of strong Drink, and pleaded with her Relations to abstain from it.

She encouraged her Husband to worship God in his Family, and frequently read in such Books of Piety as she was able to read in.

I visited her more than once in the time of that Sickness whereof she dy'd, and then heard her express her self well, with respect to the Concerns of her own Soul, and a future Life and World. She acknowledged her self to be an unworthy Sinner, yet said she had prayed often to God for his Mercy, and that not only now since [203] she was sick, but also long before; and she hoped he would not utterly cast her off, but pardon her Sins and save her Soul.

She also professed Faith in the Son of God, and a Trust in the Merits of his Sufferings and Obedience, for all the Mercies she needed, and her Resolutions to continue seeking to God for them, and then desired me to pray with and for her.

As the time of her Dissolution approached, her Hopes and Consolations increased: she declared that she had no Pleasure in any of the Things and Enjoyments of this Life, but was willing to leave Parents, Husband, and Children, and all she had here, for the sake of those things which were above, which she hoped she was going to the Enjoyment of.[614]

She lamented the Sinfulness of the Lives of some of her Relations, and particularly of her own Father and Mother; and gave them her dying Charges to depart from those Iniquities, which she had formerly without any good Effect, cautioned them against; and declared that having done so, she was willing to die and leave them.

She also declared her hearty Willingness to forgive all such as had done her any Wrong, mentioning in particular one Instance wherein she had been greatly injured.

---

613 The son of Constable John Shohkow, alias Assquanhut (*IC*, 28–30*), and Esther Ahunnet, whose first husband was Henry Ohhunnut (*IC*, 126–28*). Joel was presented to the court in 1730 for stealing and killing sheep. *WGH*, 146, 188, 202, 427.

614 This is a good example of someone who possessed the virtue of "weaned affections."

As she appeared willing to forgive Men their Trespasses, so it is much to be hoped, that her heavenly Father was also willing to forgive hers.

EXAMPLE XXVII.
SARAH PEAG, *who died at* Christian-Town October *the* 30, 1723.

THE Father of this *Sarah* was one *Samson Cahkuhquit*, of whom I can give no good Report. Her Mother was a Person yet living whose Name is *Elizabeth*, the same being a Woman of good Knowledge, and one who, as I hope, truly feareth God.

The Daughter was, while she was young, put to live in a good *English* Family in *Chilmark*, where she was taught to read, and had, I doubt not, many good Instructions and Admonitions given to her, but did not behave her self answerably to the Advantages she enjoyed. She [204] was sometimes guilty of stealing, lying, and running away from her Master; and yet she did not appear to be ashamed when she had committed these Abominations, but was proud and haughty, and much set upon making her self fine with her Ornaments.[615]

After her time was out with her said Master, there appeared for some time no remarkable Change in her. But what I then heard her most blamed for, was her giving way too much to her irregular Passions, so as often to transgress that Rule, *Be angry and sin not.*[616] It is certain that she was a Person of a very unhappy Temper, and naturally so much inclined to Contention, as to need a great Measure of Grace for the rectifying and regulating of that perverse Spirit, which she had in her.

She had not been long grown up before she marry'd to one *Jacob Peag*,[617] to whom the Hastiness of her Spirit proved a great Exercise and Trial, and perhaps much greater than it would have been, if he himself had not been of too hasty a Spirit also. Two such Persons meeting together lived somewhat uncomfortably, especially the first Part of the time which they lived together.

Having such an unruly Spirit, she very much needed to have it broken and humbled; and God suited his Providences unto her Necessities, causing her to experience such Changes, as some because they have not, do not fear God.

---

615 Wordly adornments contrast with the spiritual "ornaments" with which true "daughters of Zion" should adorn themselves, as explained by Cotton Mather in *Ornaments for the daughters of Zion.*

616 In other words when you are angry, keep silent so that you do not sin. Psalm 4:4.

617 Jacob Peag was sued for debt at least three times between 1723 and 1734. *WGH*, 337.

Among those Afflictions and Trials which he brought upon her, the Sorrows with which she brought forth some of her Children were none of the least, nor was she unaffected with the afflictive Hand of God upon her herein.

After she had her first Child, who was that *Joseph Peag* hereafter mentioned in *Chapter* IV. *Example* 20. she appeared more serious than she had formerly done, and attended the publick Worship of God as one that sought spiritual Advantage thereby: and so plain a Change was there in her Countenance and Behaviour, that I could not my self but take much notice of it.

She was also about this Time sometimes observed to withdraw her self from Company into a Wood near her Dwelling; and her Mother informs me, that once she found her praying and weeping in a Place where she was after this manner retired, and that her Daughter perceiving that she had discovered what she was doing, called [205] her, and opened the sorrowful Condition of her Soul to her, letting her know, that her spiritual Wants were the Cause of her being there, in the Employment which she found her at.

She did not on her becoming thus serious presently overcome the irregular Passions to which she had been subject; yet there was this observable Change in her, with regard thereto, that when she had been unreasonably angry, she would when her Passion was over, confess her Fault, and appear to be much troubled at her Miscarriages.

After her second Child was born, she appeared yet more concerned about her spiritual State, and discoursed frequently with her Husband about the Obligations which those who fear the Lord lay under to give up themselves to him, to be his Servants, and to attend all his Ordinances: and the Issue of their Conferences on this Subject quickly was, that first the Wife, and soon after the Husband gave up themselves unto God, and were admitted to full Communion in all his Ordinances.

The poor Woman having at her Admission into the Church, made a humble Confession of her Sins, and professed Faith in Christ, and her Resolutions to live to him, seemed to endeavour to fulfil the Engagements she had brought her self under: and she was I think on all accounts blameless, saving that she was still apt to be overcome with Passion, and be so angry as to sin therein.

From hence on her part were those sad Jars betwixt her and her Husband, mentioned in her Son's Life: but when God took this dear and precious Child from her, he by this Affliction brought her to a more full Sight and Sense of her Sin in those Contentions, by which she had dishonoured God, grieved his holy Spirit, and wounded the Heart of her said Child, than she ever before had. From this time forward there was a great Change in her, and she governed her Passions much better than ever she had done before, insomuch that those that observed her, looked upon her as in that regard a new Creature.

But soon after this, falling her self into a weak and languishing Condition, she lived not many Months, but after the Birth of a third Child, in a few Weeks dy'd.[618] I twice visited her in the time of her last Sickness, and when at the first of those times I came to the House [206] where she lay ill, I found her in a grievous Agony, confessing and bewailing the Sins of her Heart and Life. She with many Tears cry'd out against her self as a most vile and wicked Creature, unworthy of the least of God's Mercies, but worthy to be eternally rejected of him, and to be cast into Hell for ever. Then she proceeded to magnify the infinite Grace and Mercy of God in sending his own only dear and precious Son into this World, to save such sinful and wretched Creatures as she was, expressing withal her Hopes in the Mercy Of God thro' him, and her Resolutions to continue to seek for the Pardon of her Sins and the eternal Salvation of her Soul, thro' the Merits of his Suffering and Obedience.[619]

I now asked her, whether she could charge her self with dealing hypocritically in that Transaction with God, wherein she publickly gave up her self to him? To this she answered, that she could not; but said, that such was the Power of her Corruptions, that they had sometimes been too hard for her, yet God had not left her to commit any of those more heinous Offences into which the Children of Men do sometimes fall.

Having heard those things from her, I thought it my Duty to encourage her to rely on the Mercy of God in Christ for Salvation, and spake some Words of Comfort to her; which having done, and at her Desire pray'd with her, I left her.

Some Days after this I went again to see her, and found her in a more quiet and composed Frame than before. She still own'd her self to be a sinful and unworthy Creature; and in particular confessed her Sin in giving way to her Passions as she had done, and being so contentious as she had often been; but added, that her Husband's sometimes using strong Drink too freely, had been one thing which had much disturbed her. She at the same time professed her Hopes in God thro' Christ for the Forgiveness

---

618 Sarah Peag's experiences should be contrasted with Roger Williams's optimistic statement that "it hath pleased God in wonderfull manner to moderate that curse of the sorrowes of Child-bearing to these poore Indian Women: So that ordinarily they have a wonderfull more speedy and easie Travell [labor], and delivery then the Women of *Europe*": Williams, *A Key into the Language*, 149.

619 There is a certain pleasing circularity in that Sarah Peag's own sufferings mirror Christ's. As Laurel Ulrich points out, Christ himself "had likened his own death and resurrection to the sorrow and deliverance of a pregnant women whose 'time had come'" (John 16:21–22). Ulrich, *Good Wives*, 131.

of all her Iniquities. She also professed her Willingness to die, if it were the Will of God that she should so do. After I had again said to her what I thought proper, and had at her Request prayed with her, I took my leave of her, she with much Affection then thanking me for all the Instructions and Exhortations that I had ever given her.

[207] After this she lived but a few Days, and was, during that time, as she had been before, very diligent in preparing for her approaching End, which she daily expected. She called often upon God for Mercy, and gave much good Counsel to her Relations and Visitors. She expressed her earnest Desires, that, if she had offended any by any Miscarriages of which she had been guilty, they would bring her Faults to remembrance, that she might confess them, and ask for the Pardon of them.

In the Morning of the Day on which she dy'd, in the Afternoon she was under some Discouragements, and in Heaviness by reason of Temptations; but having sent for an *Indian* Minister to give her Counsel, and pray with her, the Clouds wherewith her Soul was overshadowed, were all dispersed, and she enjoyed Peace in believing, and declared that she was willing to die, and go to her heavenly Father; which said, she expired, calling on her Redeemer to receive her Spirit.

EXAMPLE XXVIII.
MARY MANHUT, *a Maid, who died at* Christian-town April 8, 1724.

MARY Manhut was a Daughter of Christian Parents, who devoted her to God in Baptism while she was a Child, *viz. Hosia Manhut*,[620] now a Pastor of an *Indian* Church on *Martha's Vineyard*, and *Quakshomoh*[621] his Wife, who is esteemed a sober and godly Woman.

She was by these her religious Parents well instructed while she was young, being taught to read, and well catechised, and had, I doubt not, very frequently good Counsel given her. She was likewise kept under good Family Government,[622] not suffered to run abroad at Pleasure, but

---

620 *IC*, 73, 217, 219, 269–70. The son of John Amanhut and grandson of Wannamanhut (*IC*, 72); his mother was Mary Manhut. He served as a teacher at Christiantown, as pastor of the Indian church at the west end of the island, and as an Indian justice at Tisbury (*IC*, 217). *WGH*, 119–20, 200–202, 250.

621 Also known as Abigail Manhut. She is listed among those receiving disbursements to the poor. Her other child with Hosia Manhut was Hannah Adams, who lived in Tisbury. *WGH*, 116, 248–49.

622 "Family Government," or the disciplining and ordering of family life, was an important subject for New England Puritans, who believed that *"Well-ordered Families* naturally produce a *Good Order* in other *Societies"*: Axtell, *School upon a Hill*, 146.

obliged to attend Family Religion in her Father's House, and also to attend the publick Worship of God on the Lord's Days, and at other times as might be convenient.

Enjoying these Advantages, she seemed to make some good Improvement of them. Her Conversation was generally blameless. Her Parents affirm, that she was very obedient to them, and that she used frequently to read in good Books, especially *the Practice of Piety* [208] she much delighted in; and she would be affected and weep when discoursed withal about the Affairs of another Life, owning the Truth and Importance of what was said to her, as I have my self upon Trial experienced.

After she had been some Years a Woman grown, there being a Motion made, that the Children of the Church arrived to Years of Discretion, would renew their baptismal Covenant,[623] and explicitely chuse the Lord to be their God, devoting themselves to his Service, and putting themselves by their own Act and Deed under the Watch and Government of the Church of which they were before Members, there was none more forward than she was to comply with what was proposed; and it happening, that about this time she and some others of the said young People were together discoursing concerning what was proposed to them, some of them shewed a Backwardness to consent unto that whereunto they were invited, but this young Woman freely declared her Approbation of the thing proposed, and pleaded the Reasonableness of it, and the Advantage that might attend it, with such Cogency as to silence her Gainsayers,[624] and to bring over some of them to be of her Mind. And what she thus pleaded for, she soon put in Practice, some of those that had before shewn an Aversion to it, now also doing as she did.

Not long after this solemn Transaction with God, in which she appeared very serious, she was taken with the Sickness whereof she dy'd.

Quickly after she was first taken ill, she expressed a deep Sense of the solemn Obligations which she had brought her self under, to live to God, and her continued Resolutions to perform the Vows she had made, saying, that if it pleased God that she might recover again, she desired to be more considerate than she had been, and more fully to obey his Word than she had hitherto done.

---

623 The extension of baptism to the unsaved was one of the controversies inherent in the dispute known as the "Half-Way Covenant." Although New England churches began to offer infant baptism to children such as Mary Manhut, who were born to church members, and although infant baptism provided some comfort to parents, it was often not considered the same as a baptism performed on a saved adult. Hence, "renewals" of the covenant once the baptized infants reached an age of consent, were popular. Hall, *Worlds of Wonder*, 150–55.

624 Those who speak against or oppose (*OED*).

And then she said, *I have destroyed my self by my Sins, but O Lord Jesus Christ, I believe thou canst wash and cleanse my Soul from them all, by thy Blood that was shed for the Remission of our Offences. I believe that how many soever the Sins of a Sinner are, yet, if he truly repents, and turns from them, he shall be saved.*

[209] She some Days after this declared, that if it would please God to save her, she had rather he should do it now, than lengthen out her Life any longer in this World, so that she should live to sin any more against him.

A few Days after this she spake to this Purpose: *I am grieved that I have so often broken my Covenant with God as I have done. Sometimes when I have been sick I have thought, that I would, if I recovered, go and join my self to the Church; but when I have been well again, I have not done it. This has been a great Sin in me. But now I desire Help from God in this Affair. O Lord God, I now long to be in my Place [or enjoy my Privileges] in the Church before I die; for there, O Lord, it is that I may expect to receive Help from thee. I believe in the Father, and in his Son Jesus Christ, and in the Holy Ghost, who is the Instructor and Illuminator of Souls.*

Our *Indians* can hardly believe that they are fully in the Church, till they are admitted to full Communion in all the Ordinances there to be enjoyed: they suppose that till this be done, they are as it were but in the Porch of the House into which they would enter, in hopes of finding and enjoying God there; and this was what this poor Woman now earnestly thirsted after, and lamented that she had so long neglected to ask and seek for: Nor could her Mind be quiet, till the Church-Meeting at her Father's House admitted her into their Communion in the Ordinance of the Lord's-Supper, which she was not before admitted to; and this seemed to be some Satisfaction to her, tho God never gave her an Opportunity to partake of it. But I am not yet in my Story arrived to the time when this was done.

Having manifested her Desire hereof, she thus pray'd: *I beseech thee, O God, to forgive my Sins, and save my Soul; I'm sorry for my Sins, and now see what the Desert*[625] *of them is. And then she said to those about her: I am grieved that I did not diligently obey the Commandments of God. When I was in Health my Sins were many, and I often did Evil against God; but these my Sins I do now plainly see. There is especially one thing that does trouble me, I went to Meeting on the Lord's Day from my Father's House; and when Meeting*

---

625 Deserved reward or punishment.

was done, my Mother called me to go home with her, but I did it not, but went away with another Person: not [210] *going to my father's House as I should have done: this was a great Sin, I now see it. O Lord, I beseech thee to forgive this Sin of mine.*

My Mother, if it please God that I should live any longer, I will no more disobey you as I have formerly done; it would be an Evil in me thus again to fall.

Three Days after she had thus discoursed, the Weakness of her Body growing on her, she earnestly desired that God would lengthen out her Life, till she had publickly renewed the Dedication of her self to him, and been admitted into a State of nearer Communion with him than she had hitherto been in. And she then said, *My Desire is, and I now intreat God, that I may live a little longer, and do a little more of what he has commanded me to do. Nothing indeed that I do can merit that I should be saved, Jesus Christ only does this. Let his Merits be upon me, who has wrought many good Works for poor Sinners: and I believe that he that does his Commandments shall be saved. But if it please God that I may live a little longer, I would fain*[626] *do that which is well-pleasing to him; for while I was in Health, I too much slighted his Word: yet now am I unwilling to go to Hell, but if God would please now to save me, to that I willingly consent.*[627] She meant by this, as I suppose, that she was willing then to die, if the Will of God were so, if so be he would please to save her.

When the time came that she should be admitted into full Communion with the Church, her Father read a Paper which he had written from her Mouth, expressing her Repentance towards God, and Faith towards the Lord Jesus Christ, (the Sum whereof is drawn into this Account of her) and she further answered to such Questions as any for their Satisfaction desired to propound to her: And then also confessed a Fault of which she had been formerly guilty, and which she could not be easy till she had declared, and manifested her Repentance of it. It was this, she once eat some Fish, which she knew the Persons had no Right to who invited her to partake of it with them. This she declared to have been a great Trouble to her.

After this she expressed a great Concern for the young People that had renewed their baptismal Covenant, and the Engagements which they were under to serve the Lord, *I should,* said she, *be very sorry if they*

---

626 Gladly, eagerly, willingly (*OED*).

627 Silverman notes that Wampanoags required conversion narratives for church membership long after many English congregations had eased that standard: message to author, May 5, 2006.

should [211] *again fall into Sin. We have,* said she, *engaged to be subject to the Discipline of the Church, and to obey the Lord.*

About this time some of the Children of the Church coming to visit her, she spake thus to them: *O take heed to your selves, for you have been baptized; depart from all Iniquity, for that brings the greatest Miseries. The Doors of Hell are opened, and the Wicked do go in at them; Oh let us turn now, that we may not go in thither. When I was in Health, I was too unconcerned about this; but now Affliction is come upon me, I see my Sin therein, and that the same carried me towards Hell. Let us pray to God to pardon our Sins, and let us do what in his Word he requires of us.*

On the last *Sabbath* save one which she lived, she said; *I now desire a little Rest,* [meaning here, if it would please God to give it] *or otherwise if the Will of God were so, that he would now save me. O God, I beseech thee have Compassion on me, and now wash and cleanse my Soul, that so I may be saved. O now open the Gates of Heaven to me, and receive my Soul there; but shut, I beseech thee, the Gates of Hell for me, that I may not go into that Place.*

Then speaking to her Relations, she said, *Do not be too sorry for me, nor weep excessively when I die; for this Body of mine is a weak and frail Thing, that must quickly pass away: but let him that weepeth, weep for his own sins and Miseries; and O pray earnestly!*

On the last *Sabbath* which she lived, she earnestly desired to hear the Word of God preached; and her Father at her Request preached a Sermon in his House from *John* iv. 42. at the hearing whereof she was refreshed.

After this she was able to say very little, but what she did say was comfortable, as importing the good Hopes she had, that she should enter into Rest, when she should leave this World. Among other things of this Nature, she, before she dy'd, spake of the ministring Spirits as coming to receive her.

Her Father just before she dy'd singing the fourth Psalm, and praying with her, she seemed observably to attend to what was done; and particularly shewed her Pleasure in that Psalmody, not only by looking most earnestly and pleasantly towards her Father, while he read [212] and sang, but also by stretching out her Hand, and laying it on his Book while he did so, he then sitting nigh to her.

When I visited her during the time of her Sickness, her Discourse was such as gave me great Hopes, that she was a truly penitent and believing Sinner. She then gave much good Counsel to her Relations and Neighbours, and particularly to her own Father, from whose Papers the Substance of this Account is taken; nor have I the least Suspicion of the Veracity of what he has therein written concerning her.

EXAMPLE XXX.
RACHEL WOMPANUMMOO, *who died in* Christian-town,
June 15. 1724, *in the 25th Year of her Age.*

THIS Woman was a Daughter of godly Parents, *viz. Isaac Ompany*[628] formerly mentioned, and his Wife *Elizabeth* yet living. These devoted her to God in her Infancy, and took care to teach her to read while she was a Child; also taught her her Catechism, and did otherwise piously educate her.

Of these Advantages she appeared to make a good Improvement. She was very obedient to her Parents, loved to read her Book,[629] and go to Meeting, while she was young, and carry'd her self as she ought to do.

When she was grown up, she appeared to be much inclined to Diligence, and used, when she could be spared from the Family to which she belonged, to work by the Week or Month among the *English* in the Vicinity, by her Labour purchasing such things as she needed: and I think all that employed her, counted her faithful in her Work, and true to her Word; and she having frequently lived and laboured in the Family of the Writer hereof, he cannot but give her such a Testimony.

Having been much among the *English*, and so got the Knowledge of their Language; she, after she was a Woman grown, learned to read *English*, and also to write a legible Hand, (having only learned to read *Indian* before) which having done, she used to read *English* Books when she had any Opportunity for it.

[213] Tho, as she afterwards declared, she used sometimes to pray to God before her Father's sudden Death, when she was about 17 Years old, of which I have given an Account *Chapter* I. *Example* 20. yet being much awakened and affected with that awful Providence, she became more serious than she had before been, and with greater Constancy called on the Name of the Lord, being deeply concerned about the State of her Soul; and her godly Mother has assured me, that she about this time and afterwards frequently found her in secret, calling on God; and that she used to give good Counsel to her Sisters, and seriously reprove them when they did amiss.

Being something more than twenty Years old, she marry'd to *Daniel Wompanummoo*, commonly called *Daniel Gershom*; unto whom, his

---

628 *IC*, 59–62*. His other children included David Ompany, Samuel Ompany, and Naomy Sosamon (*IC*, 218). Elizabeth was the mother of at least Naomy and Rachel and possibly the others. *WGH*, 115, 118, 316, 348.

629 Her Bible.

own Relations being Judges, she carried her self very dutifully, and as a Wife ought to do, who wisely considers that of the Apostle, *How knowest thou, O Woman, but thou may'st save thine Husband?*[630] The Man, tho a Child of praying Parents,[631] and one that had been well instructed, yet did not, when she first married him, walk answerably to the Benefits he had received, but would frequently drink to Excess, nor could he be persuaded to pray in his Family; at which Miscarriages, tho his Wife was much grieved, yet she would *bring no railing Accusations against him,*[632] but used to advise and intreat him to reform what was amiss in him: and she did after some time so far overcome his Evil by her Goodness, that there appeared to be a sensible Reformation in him; for he more carefully abstained from strong Drink than he had formerly done, and called upon God in his House, and carried himself kindly to his Wife, which was a great Comfort to her.

This godly Young Woman having thus prevailed with her Husband to pray in his House, was so much concerned that the Worship of God might be constantly upheld therein, that when he was gone from home, she desired her good Mother that lived with her, to perform the Duty; and sometimes at her Mother's Request, did her self perform it.

Having made so good Progress in Religion, as has been now declared, she began to be very desirous to approach yet nearer to God, in an Attendance on all the Ordinances of his instituted Worship: but such humble Thoughts had she of her self, that she durst not ask an [214] Admission to the Table of the Lord, as fearing lest she was not well qualify'd for it. However, she desired publickly and solemnly to renew her baptismal Covenant, and did so; and did not make a mere formal Business of it, but at the same time made a very humble, and affecting Confession of the Sins of her Life, and a Profession of her Resolutions to endeavour to walk more closely with God than she had hitherto done: and I doubt not but she did as she promised.

It was not long after she had thus owned the Covenant, before she was taken ill of the Sickness whereof she dy'd, within a few Weeks after.

Some of the Circumstances attending her Illness made her *Indian* Neighbours suspect, that it was by Witchcraft brought on her; and if what is credibly asserted be true, it is to be feared that it was so, and she her self suspected it: however, she told me, that she received what she

---

630 1 Corinthians 7:16.

631 He was the son of Gersom Wampanumoo (*IC*, 187) and probably Sarah Wompanummoo (*IC*, 187), who was herself the daughter of Jonathan and Rachel Amos (*IC*, 37–42*, 152–54*). *WGH*, 236, 259, 290, 350, 352.

632 2 Peter 2:11; Jude 1:9.

suffered as from the Hand of a righteous, holy, and sovereign God, without whose Goodwill and Pleasure no Evil could befall the Children of Men. And during the whole time of her Sickness, she behaved her self as a true Christian ought to do. I divers times visited her, and received from her own Mouth an Account of what God had done for her Soul, and what her Carriage had from time to time been towards him. She very humbly confessed the Sinfulness of her Heart and Life, and her utter Unworthiness of God's Mercy, but withal declared her Belief of the Gospel, and that Jesus Christ was an all-sufficient Saviour: she professed she hoped in the Mercy of God thro' him, and called earnestly on him Day and Night for the Pardon of her Sins, and Salvation of her Soul.

This was the Sum of what she said to me some of the first times I visited her in her Sickness and what she said to others was agreeable hereunto.

But there is one thing which I think I may not omit in the Account I am giving of this pious Person: being sick and like to die, she was grieved that she had not before asked an Admission to full Communion in the Church of Christ, and could not be satisfy'd till she had done it, and obtain'd what she desired, the *Indian* Church meeting at her House for that End: but then being not able to say much, she was only desired briefly to answer to some Questions, both doctrinal and practical, which she [215] had then propounded to her; and the Answers she then gave to them, contained in them so good a Profession of Repentance towards God, and Faith towards the Lord Jesus Christ, that they were very satisfactory.

Having been a Witness to this her Profession, I asked her, Whether the Reason why she desired to be admitted by the Church into full Communion with them, was, because she thought that without being so she could not be saved? *No,* said she, *I do not think so.* Why then, said I, do you desire this, seeing probably you may not live to have any Opportunity to partake of the Lord's Supper? Unto which she answered, *That she desired this, because she thought it her Duty, to approach as nigh to God while she lived as she could do*: which being said, the Church very gladly received her into their Communion.

About a Fortnight before she dy'd, her Pastor *Hosea Manhut* being sent for to pray with her, she spake thus to him, as in a Paper of his now before me, he informs me: *If it be the Will of God that I should now die, I am satisfied that it should be so. But, Oh! that God my Redeemer would now pardon all my Sins. I have often broken the Commandments of God, and cannot escape Damnation, if dealt withal according to my Sins: I therefore intreat Christ to wash and cleanse my Soul. And I do believe that he is able to save me; and if he please so to do, I desire he would now save me.*

I'm credibly informed, that both before and after this, she was very frequently heard, both by Night and Day, crying earnestly to God for Mercy, and pleading with him the Merits of his Son, her only Saviour. And the last time save one that I went to visit her, she declared, that this was the Course she took, in order to her finding Favour with God, and obtaining his Salvation; and that she had great Hopes that God would not cast her off, but give eternal Life to her.

She underwent a great deal of strong Pain in the time of her Sickness, but shewed much Patience under it, giving Glory unto God all the while, by owning his Sovereignity, Justice, and Mercy, and that she had no Reason to complain.

About three or four Days before her Death, she declared to those about her, that she was now ready to die, and desired Death rather than Life. She said, she had [216] been long and earnestly seeking unto God for his Mercy, and that she firmly hoped that he had heard her, and would receive her into his heavenly Kingdom. She said she had wholly quitted any Interest she had in any of the Things and Enjoyments of this World, being willing to leave them all and go to God: even her little Son and only Child, she said she was willing to depart from, and leave him with God, who could, and she hoped would provide for him, and be a Guide to him. She also now charged her Relations not to be overmuch troubled at her Death, but that they should love God, and seek to him continually.

After this she said very little to any body that was about her, except it were to answer a Question propounded to her: nor did she much complain of any Pain, but appeared to have such a chearful Countenance, as bespake inward Peace and Comfort in her Soul. I once saw her in that time; and tho I was ready to think she had been just dying when I came in, yet when I spake to her, she looked chearfully on me, and said she knew me. I asked her if she were now willing to die? To which she answered, that she was. I further asked her, whether she had Hopes in the Mercy of God, thro' his Son Jesus Christ? To which she answered, she had; which said, having committed her to God, I left her.

Being divers times after this asked concerning her Hope, she either by Words or Signs gave very comfortable Answers; and then dy'd, much lamented by her Relations and other good People.

[217] A
SUPPLEMENT.
TO
The Third Chapter:

Wherein some other Religious Women are nam'd.

THERE have been several other very pious Women among our *Indians*, of whom I intended to have given a brief Account: but this Work being already grown on my Hands beyond what I expected, I shall only briefly name some of them, and such were these here following, *viz.*

I. *Mary Manhut*,[633] the Wife of *John Ammanhut*,[634] and Mother of *Hosea Manhut*,[635] now Pastor of an *Indian* Church at *Martha's Vineyard.* This *Mary* dy'd at *Nashouohkamuk*, in or about the Year 1689.

II. *Mary Coshomon*, who was the first Wife of *Samuel Coshomon*,[636] an *Indian* Minister yet living, and dy'd in *Chilmark* in the Year 1691.

III. *Siokunumau*, who was the Wife of an *Indian* called *Mechim*, and the Mother of that *Katherine*, of whom I have given an Account in the foregoing *Chapter, Example* 16. She dy'd about the Year 1690.

IV. *Nahpunnehtau*,[637] who dy'd at *Christian-Town* about the Year 1703. She was first the Wife of an *Indian* Magistrate called *John Papamek*,[638] and after that was the Wife of a praying *Indian* called *Paattoohk*.[639]

V. *Pamie*, formerly the Wife of *Sowamog*[640] an *Indian* Minister. She was esteemed a Person of very remarkable Piety by all that were acquainted

---

633 Also known as Mary Wanamanhut or Chachaconnonashk. *WGH*, 250.

634 *IC*, 72, 219. He was the son of Wannamanhut, the sachem at Takemy (*IC*, I.72). *WGH*, 200–201.

635 Their other child was Abigail Manhut (*IC*, 219–22*). Hosea was an important minister on the west end of the island and an Indian justice, but since he was still alive when *Indian Converts* was written, Mayhew did not include a biography of him. *WGH*, 119–20, 201, 250, 347.

636 Also known as Samuel Mukkuhkonitt. His father was probably Mokokinnet, a sachem of the land near Chilmark/Tisbury, who was the great-grandson of Pakkehpumassoo (*IC*, 3–4). *WGH*, 106, 128–29, 135.

637 Probably the mother of Zachariah Papamick, a preacher at Christiantown who was at one point presented to the court for Sabbath-breaking. *WGH*, 114, 340.

638 Probably a first cousin on his father's side of Keteanomin, alias Josias, the sachem of Takemmy (*IC*, 197). *WGH*, 103–4, 108, 200.

639 Referred to in other colonial records as a justice, Indian magistrate, and the late sachem of Chechemmo. *WGH*, 222. The fact that Nahpunnehtau married two members of royal families suggests that she, too, may have been of royal descent.

640 *IC*, 65. A minister at Gay Head who was ordained on September 29, 1712. He later replaced Japheth Hannit. He was the father of Jeremiah Sowamog and possibly Pilot Sowamog. *WGH*, 235–36, 314–15.

with her. I am not [218] certain in what Year she dy'd, but there are many yet living that knew her.

VI. *Rebeccah Lay*, the last Wife of good *William Lay*, of whom I have given an Account *Chap.* I. *Examp.* 9. This Woman died about the Year 1708.

VII. *Johanna Coshomon,*[641] the last Wife of *Samuel Coshomon* above mentioned. She dy'd at *Sanchekantacket* in the Year 1711.

VIII. *Ruth Pattompan,*[642] the Wife of *Josiah Pattompan,*[643] who dy'd in *Tisbury* in the Year 1722.

IX. *Naomy Sosamon,*[644] the Wife of *Thomas Sosamon,*[645] and a Sister of that *Rachel* mentioned in the last *Chap. Examp.* 30. who dy'd at *Christian-town May* 21, 1726. This Woman was a Daughter of that *Isaac Ompany* mentioned *Chap.* I. *Examp.* 20. She was, so far as I can learn, a Person of a good Conversation; and she professed when she was dying, that she had been a Seeker of God ever since she was ten Years old; and that God had since her Sickness enabled her to cry earnestly to him for his Mercy. She said also, that she was willing to die, having Hopes that, thro' the Merits of Jesus Christ her only Saviour, she should obtain Life eternal.

I do not think that any that were acquainted with the *nine Women last named*, have any doubt of their real Piety. And I at this time think of divers others, who might have been very justly numbred with them; but tho their Names be not written in this Book, yet, I hope, it will one Day appear that they are written in Heaven.

---

641 The daughter and heir of Wompameg "Mr. Sam" (*IC*, 73–74*), the sachem. *WGH*, 97, 144. Again notice that members of royal families on the island tended to marry other people of royal descent.

642 Mother of Elizabeth Pattompan (*IC*, 238–42*) and Jerusha Ompan (*IC*, 175–79*). *WGH*, 346.

643 *IC*, 175, 218, 238. Probably the son of Pattompan and the grandson of Nashohkow (*IC*, 28, 54; *WGH*, 156, 290, 331); which would make him the nephew of Micah Shohkan (*IC*, 30–31*), Stephen Shohkau (*IC*, 54–56*), Pattompan (*IC*, 131), and Daniel Shohkau (*IC*, 131).

644 Daughter of Isaac and Elizabeth Ompany (*IC*, 59–62*).

645 They were probably the parents of Micah Sosaman, a whaleman from Tisbury who was accused of stealing a horse. *WGH*, 348, 350, 400.

[219] CHAP. IV.

Early Piety exemplified, in an Account of several *Young Men, Maids,* and *Children,* that have appeared to be truly pious.

I Doubt not but that where there is any thing considerable of true Piety and Religion among a People, God does extend his special and saving Grace to some of every Age, whether elder or younger among them.[646]

As therefore it appears by what has been already said, that there have been many grown Persons who have been converted and saved among our poor *Indians,* so I believe it will be evident by that which here followeth, that there have been also many young People savingly brought home to God among them. I shall here instance in several such, as I cannot but hope have been effectually called.

EXAMPLE I.
ABIGAIL MANHUT, *who died at* Nashouohkamuk,
in or about the Year 1685, *when she was about twenty Years old.*

ABigail Manhut was a Daughter of *John Ammanhut,*[647] an *Indian* Minister formerly mentioned, and a Sister of *Hosea Manhut,* now one of the Pastors of the *Indian* Church on the West End of *Martha's Vineyard*: She was piously educated by her Father and Mother,[648] who were both esteemed godly Persons; and she her self appeared pious from her very Childhood.

She was taught to read well while she was young, and delighted much in reading the Scriptures and other good Books.

[220] She also loved to go to Meeting and hear the Word of God preached, and was a strict Observer of God's Holy Day.

She was not given to run about with rude and wicked Company, as many young People are, but constantly and seriously attended the

---

646 This assertion would not have been so obvious to the first- or second-generation ministers in New England; for Thomas Hooker, e.g., even children of ten or twelve years "lived the life of a beast" and were not yet rational enough to understand "the mysteries of life and salvation." See Brekus, "Children of Wrath," 302, 313. Mayhew's confidence in children is a sign of the influence of Enlightenment thought in New England and the movement toward the First Great Awakening.

647 *IC,* 72, 217. John was the son of Wannamanhut, the sachem at Takemy (*IC,* I.72). *WGH,* 200–201.

648 Her mother was Mary Manhut (*IC,* 217).

Worship of God in the Family to which she belonged; and was always very dutiful and obedient to her Parents.

She had not, so far as did appear, any Fellowship with the unfruitful Works of Darkness; but was on the contrary, a zealous Reprover of them.

Her Relations yet living, do affirm that she used Boldness and Courage in reproving their Miscarriages, when she knew them to be guilty of any Fault.

Such as were acquainted with her do also affirm that she used to pray by her self, and that very frequently; and that when she had none with her but Children, she was sometimes found praying with them.

She used, in the time of her Health, to discourse very seriously about the things of God and another Life; and having learned of her Mother, with whom she lived after her Father's Death, to sing *Psalm* Tunes, she used not only to sing with the rest of the Family before Morning and Evening Prayer, but was also frequently heard singing Psalms by her self alone.

It is so long since this Maid died, that I cannot distinctly remember any thing concerning her: but while I was writing this Account of her, my aged Mother[649] came in and told me, that she lived and laboured some time in my Father's House, carrying her self very well while she was there; and that my Father esteemed her a very pious Person.

She died of a lingring, consumptive Distemper,[650] and so was sensible of the gradual Approaches of Death towards her; and in the time of her Sickness, behaved her self as one that had lived well ought to do: She prayed often to God, and desired others to pray with and for her, and gave many good Exhortations to her Relations, and others that came to visit her; and her Mind appeared to be calm and serene, as being possessed with Peace in believing.

When she was going to die she was sensible of it, and told those about her, that she should now presently leave them; but seemed not at all surprized at the Approach [221] of the King of Terrors. She comforted her Relations by telling them, that she was heartily willing to die, as being persuaded that she was now going to God, in whose Presence there was Fullness of Joy; yea, she rejoiced that that happy time was now come. She now also exhorted and encouraged those about her to love God, and live to him; telling them how good and profitable it was so to do.

---

649 Elizabeth (Hillard) Mayhew (1654–1746). When John Mayhew died in 1688, he left his house to Experience Mayhew, his eldest son, who lived there with his mother and younger siblings until 1695, when the Mayhew-Whiting House was built nearby. Scott, *Early Colonial Houses of Martha's Vineyard*, 3:189–91.

650 Probably tuberculosis.

Having spoken to this purpose, she seeming to be nigh to Death, her Friends that were with her committed her to God by Prayer; and she appeared evidently to join with them therein, by lifting up her Hands and Eyes to Heaven, from whence she well knew that all her Help came. After this she spake no more; but being asked whether her Desires were still after God, she by a Sign answered that they were so; and so went to him after whom her Soul longed.

I cannot forbear here relating a very observable thing that happened at the time of this young Woman's Death, of which there are three or four credible Witnesses yet living: It being a dark Night when she died, the Moon not then shining, and many of the Stars being covered with Clouds, the People who were with her and tended her, were on a sudden put to a great Strait for something to make a Light withal, whereby they might see to do what was needful to be done for her, their Dry-Pine or Light-wood, which they had hitherto used for this purpose, being all spent. But while they were in some surprize on this account, they were on a sudden more surprized by perceiving that there was a Light in the House, which was sufficient for them to see to do any thing by, that the dying Maid could need them to do for her. All present wondered from whence it was that this marvellous Light came to them;[651] and several of them went out to see if they could discover the Cause of it, but could see nothing that could afford[652] such a Light as that wherewith they were favoured; and therefore concluded it was something extraordinary, and such of them as are still living think so. They say it was not a sudden Flash of Light only, but lasted several Hours, even from the time they first needed it, till the young Woman was dead, and they had no more Occasion for it: Nor was this Light so dim, but that it was as sufficient to all the ends for which a Light was necessary, as tho it had been [222] as bright as that of the Sun at Noon-Day, so clear that they did plainly see the Signs which the Maid, being speechless, made in answer to such Questions as they thought proper to put to her.

I shall leave others to think of this matter as they please; but the Story is so well attested, that I cannot but give credit to it; and I believe there was something extraordinary in it. Herein, it seems, that that Word was in the most literal Sense fulfilled: *Unto the Upright there ariseth Light in Darkness.*[653]

---

651 William Simmons notes that John Josselyn (1673) records the belief of Native New Englanders that sometimes a light would appear over a wigwam when someone died. Simmons, *Spirit of New England Tribes*, 120.

652 Furnish (*OED*).

653 Psalm 112:4.

EXAMPLE II.

JOSEPH NAHNOSOO, *who died at* Nashouohkamuk, *now* Chilmark, *if I mistake not, in the Year* 1685, *when he was about twenty Years old.*

THIS *Joseph* was a Son of that good *John Nahnosoo*, of whom I have spoken in *Chap.* I. *Examp.* 4. Some time after the Death of his Father, he was committed to the Care of Master *Japheth Hannit*, with whom he dwelt several of the last Years of his Life.

He was taught to read both in *English* and *Indian*, and was well instructed in his Catechism; and I doubt not but that he was taught to write also.

He spent much of his time in Reading and Meditation,[654] and seemed to delight very much therein: nor did he appear to be any ways viciously inclined, or to delight in such Company as were known so to be.

When good *Japheth* was at any time gone from home, as about that time on necessary Occasions he often was, this sober and pious young Man read the Scriptures, prayed, and sung Psalms in the Family, as he himself did when at home with them.

By wrestling at a Husking, he brake one of his Legs, and lay lame a great while with it; lamenting the Vanity of which he had been guilty, and saying that he should not from thenceforth delight in such Exercises.

When he was taken with the Fever whereof he died, he quickly declared his Apprehensions, that that Sickness would put an end to his Life; and withal, expressed his Willingness to submit to the Will of God therein: He then also confessed his Sins, and lamented them, and [223] prayed earnestly to God for the Pardon of them, and for cleansing from them.

He declared his firm Belief of the great Truths revealed in the Word of God, particularly those which relate to the Person of Jesus Christ, and his Meditation betwixt God and Sinners; and professed that he did rely on the Mercy of God thro' him.

He earnestly exhorted all that were about him, to pray constantly and earnestly to God, and to lay hold of him, and cleave continually to him; and so died, hoping in the Lord.

Good *Japheth*, from whom I received a considerable Part of what I have written concerning this young Man, was exceedingly troubled at his Death, as having had great Hopes of his proving very serviceable among his own Countrymen. But God had otherwise determined.

---

654 See, e.g., Edward Taylor's *Preparatory Meditations Poems of Edward Taylor*, 3–259.

EXAMPLE III.
JEREMIAH HANNIT, *a Son of Master* JAPHETH HANNIT,
who died at Chilmark, *in or about the Year* 1686,
when he was about fifteen Years old.

THIS *Jeremiah* was *Japheth's* eldest Son, and was looked upon as a very hopeful Youth by all that knew him, whether *English* or *Indians.*

He was much kept at School, and plyed his Time well at it. He was also taught his Catechism, and well instructed in the Principles of Religion, and had the Advantage of a very strong Memory to facilitate his Learning.

He was very sober from a Child, and not given to such idle Talk as most young People are addicted to; and was very obedient to his Parents, and very faithful and diligent in any Business which they set him about. Nor was he known to be given to any of those Vices, which Persons of his Age are apt to run into: and what more strongly argued his real Piety than any thing yet said of him was, that he used to pray in secret Places, as some yet living can of their own Knowledge testify.

He was long sick and weak before he died, and in that time expressed a deep Sense of the Sins of his Nature and [224] Life, and earnest Desire, that God would pardon all his Transgressions, and renew and sanctify his Soul.

He said he believed that Jesus Christ was an all-sufficient Saviour, and would be a Saviour to him, if he could by Faith lay hold of him. He declared his Resolution to seek to him as long as he lived, and did accordingly call often upon him. And he exhorted his Relations and others to pray always to the Lord.

Falling more violently sick a few Days before his Death, he declared his Expectations of dying speedily; and withal, his Hopes of obtaining eternal Life, thro' Jesus Christ his only Saviour; and continued to the last calling on him for his Mercy.

When he perceived himself dying, he looked about on his Friends, and said, *Fare ye well.*

My Father,[655] who was acquainted with this Youth, looked on him as truly pious, and very much lamented his Death. *Japheth* had another Son, whose Name was *Joshua*, and he was also said to die hopefully; but of him I cannot give any particular Account.

---

655 John Mayhew (1652–1688).

EXAMPLE IV.
ELEAZAR OHHUMUH, *who died at the* Gayhead *in or about the Year* 1698, *when he was sixteen Years old.*

THE Parents of this *Eleazar, viz. Caleb Ohhumuh,*[656] and *Deborah*[657] his Wife, sent him to School to learn to read and write while he was a young Boy; and he made such Proficiency therein, that he soon read competently well, and could write a legible Hand. He also learned his Catechism by Heart, and was not ignorant of the first Principles of the Oracles of God.

He was also taught to call upon the Name of the Lord while he was but a Child, as many of our *Indian* Children have been, which has proved of great Advantage to some of them.

Not only his own Parents, but *Elisha*[658] also, an *Indian* Minister of the *Gayhead* formerly mentioned, who was his Uncle, used to instruct and exhort him.

All that knew him bear him witness, that he appeared sober and serious from his very Childhood; and his Mother, who is a Professor of Godliness, yet living, and I hope a good Woman, informs me, that he used frequently [225] of his own accord to pray to God while he was very young, and used also to tell others that they ought to do so.

I'm likewise informed, that when he came to Years of such Discretion, as to be sensible that it would not be decent for him to pray vocally where others were present, and yet not joining with him in the Duty, he used frequently to withdraw himself into obscure Places, whither it was supposed he went to pray in secret to God, being there sometimes found kneeling down, or lying prostrate on the Ground, or otherwise leaning against some Trees, as tho he was praying.

He was diligent in reading his Book, willing to go to Meeting, and used often to repeat his Catechism, and that without being called to it, and was very obedient to his Parents.

He divers times confessed the Sinfulness of that Estate which by Nature he was in, and expressed earnest Desires of being delivered therefrom; and used to manifest a Dislike of the Sins of others, and would sometimes reprove them for their Faults.

The Father of this *Lad* being somewhat addicted to follow *strong Drink* while the Son lived, so that he was by bad Neighbours too often

---

656 Possibly the son of Yonohhumuh (*IC*, 89–91*), an Indian noble. *WGH*, 157, 291, 331.

657 Probably the daughter of Paaonut. *WGH*, 331, 355.

658 Probably Elisha Paaonut (*IC*, 56–59*); most likely Deborah Ohhumuh was his sister. *WGH*, 331.

drawn into the Company of such as inflame themselves *therewithal,* the pious Youth laid grievously to heart his Sin and Error therein, and did divers times go to the Places where his Father was drinking, and with such Earnestness, and so many Tears, intreat him to leave his drinking Company and go home to his own House, that he was not able to withstand the Importunity of his afflicted Child, but at his Desire left the drinking Tribe; and when he came home, owned the Victory which his Son had obtained over him.

Such was the Gravity of his Deportment, that all who knew him took notice of it; especially his Behaviour while he attended the Worship of God, either in publick or in the Family to which he belonged, was remarkably serious.

It seems this Youth thought it his Duty sometimes vocally to call upon God in the Presence and Hearing of others; for he divers times requested his Father, when the Hour for Family-Prayer came, to permit him to call on the Name of the Lord; which Desire his Father willingly granting, he discharged the Duty with that Un[226][der]standing,[659] Gravity, and Affection, which argued that he had the Spirit of God helping his Infirmities, and that he was no Stranger to the Duty of Prayer: tho what his particular Expressions were at such times, cannot now be remembred.

He was sick something more than half a Year before he died; and soon after he was taken ill, he told his Relatives, that he thought the time of his Dissolution was now drawing on, and prayed them not to be much troubled at his Death; for that he hoped that God would, thro' his Son Jesus Christ, have Mercy on him, pardon his Sins, and save his Soul for ever. He told them, that he had from his childhood chosen God for his Portion, and that beholding with Grief the Miscarriages of that wicked Generation among whom he had lived, he had earnestly intreated the Lord, by any means to keep him from the Company and Society of such as they were, and not suffer him to go astray in their Paths; and that he therefore hoped that God would, when he died, take him to himself. He earnestly requested them to be earnest Seekers of that God in whom he trusted, and to depart from all Iniquity, that so they might also go to Heaven, where they might again see him with Comfort.

The good Hopes which this Youth had that it would be well with him after Death, did not make him grow remiss in his Preparations for his End: He, as long as he was able, made use of his Books by reading in them, and meditating on what he read. He also called frequently and

---

659 A printer's error here omitted "der": p. *225* ends with "Un-" p. *226* completes only "standing."

earnestly on God for the Mercies he needed, especially for the Pardon of all his Sins, thro' the Mediation of Jesus Christ his only Saviour.

He also sent for the Elders of the Church, Master *Japheth*, and many others, to come and pray with him, not to request that he might be recovered and live any longer in the World, (for he thought that God had determined the contrary, and declared his Willingness to submit to his Sovereign Pleasure therein) but that which he desired was, that he might be prepared for his great Change, and that the same might be made safe and comfortable to him.

The Ministers meeting on this occasion, discoursed with him about the State of his Soul, and received great Satisfaction respecting the Reasons of that Hope which he [227] had in him; some of them declaring that they had scarcely ever seen so bright an Example of Piety in so young a Person.

Not long after this, the Youth perceiving himself nigh to Death, sent for some of the Neighbours to come and commit him to God, and as he expressed it, to give him a Lift towards Heaven; which, according to his Desire, they did, then also singing a Psalm of Praise to God his Saviour; which he being well pleased at, and not able to shew it by joining with his Voice, shewed his Consent to what was done, by laying hold with his Hand on the Book out of which they read and sung, and keeping hold of it till the Psalm was finished, and looking all the while with a most chearful Countenance.

Soon after this Exercise was over, the pious young Man looking up towards Heaven, and smiling as tho he had seen something that did greatly delight and comfort him, surrendred his Soul into the Hands of his Redeemer.

Some who were with him when he died have told me, that they thought themselves as sure that he was gone into the Kingdom of God, when he left this World, as tho they had seen the Angels of God come down and convey him to that Place of Glory.

I have now finished what I had to say of this godly Youth; but considering what has been above said of his Father, it may perhaps be grateful to my Readers, if I here give some further Account of him.

He was exceedingly affected at the Sickness and Death of this Son of his, who had performed the Part of a Father towards him: He totally quitted his immoderate Use of strong Drink; he lived very inoffensively among his Neighbours; he join'd himself to the Church of Antipedo-baptists[660] in the Place where he lived, and behaved himself like a good Man among them, reproving their sinful Miscarriages, and trying to

---

660 The Gay Head Community Baptist Church.

reform them; but at length being extremely vexed and grieved at the evil Conversation of many of his Brethren, he was so discouraged, that he would not hold Communion with them any longer, but totally left them. After this he seldom went to Meeting; but when he did so, it was to another Assembly than that to which he had belonged. Nor was he now so constant in praying in his Family as he had formerly been; but he still continued in other Respects a [228] Person of good Morals: He dissuaded his Family and Neighbours from sinning against God, and mightily commended and pressed the internal Duties of Religion, and urged those of his House to be much in secret Prayer to God; and in this Course he continued some Years, and then died very suddenly. I do not understand that he gave any Account how he expected it would fare with him in the other World.

EXAMPLE V.

WILLIAM TUPHAUS, *who died in the Year* 1703,
when he was about twelve Years old.

THIS *William Tuphaus* was a Son of *William Tuphaus,* an *Indian* of *Chilmark,* mentioned *Chap.* II. and his Wife *Bethiah,* a Daughter of good *Jonathan Amos* also formerly mentioned.

His godly Parents, especially his Mother (being a very knowing and pious Woman) instructed both him and their other Children while young, endeavouring to teach them to know *God,* and call upon him. And this Boy had been for a considerable time before his Death, a very orderly and obedient Child; and his Friends observed, that he frequently retired into some Place by himself, which was, as they supposed, for secret Prayer to God.

Once when a Brother of his who was younger than himself, was suddenly taken very sick, and his Mother had no body else but *him* with her, who then stood by observing the Sickness and Pain of his said Brother, and the Affliction and Distress of his Mother on the Account thereof, he on a sudden said to her, *Let us pray;* and immediately putting him self into a proper Posture for it, began audibly to call upon the *Lord:* and he did then in the first Place humbly confess his own Sins, and utter Unworthiness of the least of *God's* Favours, and beg the Pardon of them; praying also that *God* would renew and sanctify him, and teach and enable him to do his Duty. Then he prayed for his sick Brother,[661] that God would spare his Life, and recover him to Health; and that he might be taught to know and serve the *Lord;* but that if otherwise, his Brother were then

---

661 Possibly Job Tuphaus (*IC*, 242–43), who would have been about two years old at the time.

to die, yet God would have Mercy on him, and save him with an eternal Salvation. He also then prayed for his poor af[229]flicted Mother, that she might be comforted and enabled to indure the Trial which she was then under. He pray'd also for his absent Father, that God would preserve him, indue him with his Grace, and make him meet for his eternal Kingdom: then he prayed for all his other Relations, that they might be Partakers of special and saving Mercies. He also prayed for all Mankind; particularly for little Children, that they might find Mercy with *God*: and in this Prayer of his, he pleaded the Merits and Intercession of Jesus Christ the Son of *God*, and only *Saviour* of Sinners. This was when he was about *ten Years old.*

After this Youth had thus prayed, he appeared yet more grave and serious than he had formerly done. He did not any longer carry himself like a young Boy; but rather like some Man of Years, who had his Heart seasoned[662] with the Grace of *God*: he kept at home and took care of the Affairs of the House when his Father was gone abroad to work, and was as dutiful to his Parents as any Child could be.

The Mother of this Lad took notice, that when his Father began to eat without asking a Blessing on the Food prepared, (which tho a good Man he sometimes did) he used to go out, and not begin to eat when the rest of the Family did: But the Reason of this she did not at first understand; but at length observing whither he went, and what he did, she perceived that he went by himself to pray to God, and she concluded it was to perform the Duty which her Husband neglected; because as soon as he had done, he would come in and eat.

He was sick but three Days before he died, in which time he called frequently and fervently upon God for Mercy; but generally spake so low, that but little of what he said could be understood by those who were with him.

On the Day on which he died, a little before it was light, his Mother perceived he was awake, and heard him praying to *God*, tho but with a low Voice, as he had done before during the time of his Sickness. At length, when his Prayer was ended, she spake to him, and asked him if he were awake; to which replying that he was, and was not sleepy, she told him it was good to wake early in the Morning, and to think upon God, and upon the things of another World, &c. continuing her Discourse till Day-light; which having finished, he thanked her [230] for what she had said to him. But then appearing very ill and full of Pain, much worse than he had hitherto been, he again began to call upon God, and that with a louder Voice than before he had done, so that he might be plainly heard

---

662 Matured, brought to a state of perfection (*OED*).

and understood. He prayed God to pardon all his Sins, and to renew and sanctify him by his Holy Spirit, and so to fit him for his eternal and heavenly Kingdom. He earnestly intreated that God would not cast him off and reject him; and in the whole, pleaded the Merits and Intercession of *Jesus Christ*, on whom he affirmed that he did put his trust, as the only Saviour of Sinners, and Refuge of his Soul.

When he had thus prayed, his Mother perceiving that he looked very earnestly upon her, asked him, if he desired any thing of her; *Yes*, said he, *I have a great Desire you should once more pray for me.* She very readily complied with his Desire therein, there being none but Children in the House with her; and she says, that God then enabled her not only to ask for him the Mercies which she then thought he needed, but did also help her to resign him up to that God who had lent him to her, and to give her Consent that he should take him away from her, if so it seemed good in his sight.

Having thus resigned him to *God*, she perceiving that he was nigh to Death, presently sent for his Grandfather *Jonathan Amos*, to come and pray with and for him; which he having with much Affection done, the pious Youth presently expired.

EXAMPLE VI.
BETHIA TUPHAUS, *who died in the Year* 1704, *when she was not quite four Years old.*

THIS *Bethia* was a Daughter of that *William* and *Bethia Tuphaus* above-mentioned, and a Sister of the Youth last spoken of. Her godly Father and Mother began to instruct her in the things of God, as soon as she was in any measure capable of understanding them; and it seems that these Essays of her godly Parents, to make good Impressions on the young Heart of their little Daughter, had, by God's Blessing, the desired Effect: She seemed to take much notice of what they said to her, [231] as tho she desired to receive Instruction, and know her Duty.

When she was but a little above three Years old, her good Father being very sick, and nigh to Death, her Mother saw her kneeling down in the Room where he lay, and soon perceived that she was speaking and praying to God; when observing what she said in that Address to *him*, she first plainly heard her confessing her Sins, and utter Unworthiness to speak to the Lord; and then intreating of *him* to have Mercy on, and pardon and save her. She then prayed God to have Mercy on her sick Father; and she requested, that if it were not the Will of *God* that he should recover and live longer in the World, yet he would please to give him Life eternal in Heaven with himself: then she prayed for her little

Brothers,[663] that God would bless and save them. And lastly, she prayed for all other little Children, that *God* would extend his Favour to them.

This was the first time that this Child was observed to call upon the *Lord;* but after this, her Mother frequently heard her praying to *God*, and that with more Enlargements than at first.

She was not at home, but kept with her godly Grandmother[664] at the time of her Father's Death; which was not very long after her praying for him, as has been related. This Tidings, when heard by her, seemed to make a great Impression upon her; insomuch, that she thereupon grew melancholy, and would be much grieved at every little thing that happened, which was not agreeable to her; and in a short time appearing not to be well, her Illness grew so fast upon her, that in a few Days she died.

Her Mother observing what Heaviness she was in about the time she was first taken ill, discoursed with her about the Vanity and Uncertainty of all the Things and Enjoyments of this *lower World*, and the Excellency of those which are above in the *other*, where *Christ sits* at *God's Right-Hand:*[665] upon the hearing of which Discourse, the Child seemed to be much comforted, and expressed a Willingness to die; yea, and a Desire to go to Heaven and be with *God*.

Her good Grandfather[666] was from home when she drew nigh to Death, and did not return till after she was become speechless; but on his coming, he presently recommended her to *God* by Prayer; and she, soon after he [232] had so done, left this World, and I hope went into the Kingdom of *God*.

EXAMPLE VII.

JEDIDAH HANNIT, *who died in* Chilmark October *the* 14*th* 1725,[667] *being about seventeen Years old.*

JEdidah Hannit, of whom I here speak, was a Daughter of Master *Japheth Hannit*, and *Sarah* his Wife. She was religiously educated while she was a Child; and it is very probable that the Spirit of God did make good

---

663 Including presumably Job Tuphaus, *IC*, 242–43*.

664 Presumably Rachel Amos (*IC*, 152–54*), though it could also be her paternal grandmother, whose name is unknown.

665 Mark 16:19; Luke 22:69; Colossians 3:1; Hebrews 12:2.

666 Presumably Jonathan Amos (*IC*, 37–42*), since this man is identified as "good," and Mayhew comments about her paternal grandfather, Taphus, that he "has heard nothing remarkable" about him. *IC*, 95; *WGH*, 232–33, 355.

667 The death date of 1725 is clearly an error, since Japheth lived only until July 29, 1712, and Sarah until March 1716–17, yet Jedidah spoke to "her Father and Mother" when her death approached, and her father made a speech as Jedidah's end neared. I am grateful to my student Mackenzie Cole (Reed College, 2006) for pointing out this discrepancy.

Impression on her Soul some Years before that in which she died. She was very obedient to her Parents, was very apt and willing to learn her Catechism, and delighted much in reading her Book. Nor was she much inclined to go into such vain Company as many young People delight in: And her Friends sometimes found her praying in secret Places, where she intended that none but God should see or hear her.

In the Night on which she was taken with the Sickness whereof she died, she dreamed, as she in the time of her Sickness declared, that there was a very dark and dismal time shortly coming on the *Indian* Nation; with which Dream being much distressed, she waked out of her Sleep, and had such an Impression made on her Mind, that what she had so dreamed would come to pass, and of the Dreadfulness of the thing so apprehended, that she immediately prayed earnestly to God, that she might not live to see the thing feared, but that she might be removed out of the World before it came to pass. After this, having again fallen asleep, she after some time awaked very sick: and the Sickness whereof she was so seized, did in a few Days put an end to her Life.

The Distemper with which she was thus taken being a Fever, with a Pain in her Side, was so very violent from the beginning of it, that she was neither able to say much to her Friends, or do much for the Safety or Welfare of her Soul, if that Work had not been done already by her. Her Illness still increasing, she in a little time appeared to be dying, and her Friends were grieved and surprized at what was coming so suddenly on them. But having lain for some little time wholly speechless, and to appearance senseless, and almost breathless, she began to [233] revive, breathed better, and was in a short time able to speak, and that sensibly, and remained so for several Hours together; nor was her Pain so violent as it had before been: Being thus revived, she said she seemed to her self to have been in a Dream; but whether she were so or not, she could not determine. However, she said she was going to a Place which she much desired to be at, and was exceedingly delighted with the thoughts of her going to it; but she then thought that her Brother-in-Law, naming him, came after her, and called her to come back again, telling her that her Father and Mother and other Friends would be exceedingly troubled, if she went away so suddenly and left them.

While she seemed to be dying, as is above related, her Brother-in-Law,[668] by whom she thought she had been called back from her

---

668 Probably Job Soomannah. The reference to her brother-in-law again points to the error in Mayhew's death date for Jedidah, since all of Jedidah's known brothers-in law died before 1723, yet Jedidah's illness came upon her suddenly in 1725. Her known brothers-in-law were Job Soomannah (?–1718), the husband of Jerusha Job(e); Elias Able(?–<1723), the husband of Hannah Tobe; and Nicodemos Skuhunnan (?–1710), the husband of Bethia Escohana. *WGH*, 126–27, 261.

Journey, as is above-said, went out of the House; and not long after him, her Father also; and the last mentioned of these Persons walking by the side of an Hedge-Fence, not far from the House, overheard the other, on the other side of the Hedge, pleading most earnestly with God, that his Sister might not be so suddenly taken away from her Friends, as to appearance she seemed likely to be: Soon after this, the Father of the Maid returning to the House, found her revived, as has been declared, and was told what she had said before he came in; and soon after her said Brother came in also, and to his great Comfort saw her, as one in a manner raised from the Dead.

But lest the Relations of this young Woman, and particularly her Brother-in-Law mentioned, should be too much transported at the sudden Alteration which they saw in her, Mr. *Japheth* made a very grave and seasonable Speech to them, telling them that they should by no means conclude from his Daughter's being thus revived, that God designed to recover her from this present Sickness; but think it sufficient, that God had so far heard Prayers for her, as not to take her so suddenly away as they feared he would have done, and had given her and them a further Opportunity to speak one to another before she died and left them: and to this purpose he more particularly addressed himself to his Son-in-Law, who had prayed for his Daughter, as has been declared.

However, the Maid thus far revived, had now a further Opportunity to look up to God for his Mercy, and [234] let her Friends understand that she did not leave the World without committing the Care of her Soul to Jesus Christ, her only Saviour. Having such Opportunity, she now declared, that she did no longer set her Mind upon any of her worldly Enjoyments, but was willing to die and leave them. *There is*, said she, *but one thing that I am now concerned about. I am now troubled for my Sins against my God, and my not keeping his Commandments as I ought to have done. I have made Promises to him, and have not duly performed them. I desire that God's People would pray to him for me.*

After this she said, *I believe in Jesus Christ, that he is my only Saviour;* and then praying, called thus upon him, *O my God, thou who takest away the Sins of the World, forgive my Sins, I beseech thee, and save my Soul for ever.*

She also took her leave of her Relations and others in Words to this Effect: *Farewel all ye my beloved Friends! Farewel all ye young People, fear ye God greatly, pray earnestly to him, sanctify his Sabbath, and be sober on that Day in his Fear.*

As for me, said she, *my Days are cut off, and I groan by reason of the Pain which I endure; but I am willing to die, because I believe in Christ that he is my Salvation.*

EXAMPLE VIII.

JEREMIAH WESACHIPPAU, *a Youth of the* Gayhead, *who died in* Chilmark *towards the latter End of the Year* 1705, *when he was about 18 Years old.*

THE Parents of this young Man, *viz. Elisha Wesachippau* and his Wife, were both of them esteemed[669] Persons of a vicious Conversation, and were some Years before this their Son dy'd, both at once drowned in the Sea, being supposed to be drowned in Rum at the same time: They had a Son that was esteemed a pious Youth, drowned with them.

But it is their Son *Jeremiah* that I am here to give a short Account of; and as bad as his Parents on other Accounts were, yet they sent him to School when he was a Child, where he was taught to read, and also learned his Catechism, and heard many Prayers put up to God; for it is the Custom of our *Indian* Schoolmasters to pray [235] with their Scholars. He was also taught to write a legible Hand. Living also with an Uncle of his, [his Mother's Brother] especially after the Death of his Parents, that House then becoming his Home; he there enjoyed considerable Advantages, Reading and Prayer being attended in that Family, and something of good Order upheld.

The Lad enjoying those Advantages, was enabled thro' Grace, to make a good Improvement of them. He was sober and orderly from a Child, loved his Book well, studied his Catechism diligently, delighted in going to Meeting, and behaved himself soberly there; was very obedient to his Uncle, and faithful in any Business which he set him about; would not go into bad Company, but saved himself from that untoward Generation among whom he lived.

These things were observed in him by many of his Neighbours: but his Piety did yet more evidently appear in that he was a praying Youth. He was observed to pray in secret to God, being several times found at his secret Devotions, in obscure Places unto which he used to retire: nor did he pray in secret only, but gave Honour to God, by praying in the Family to which he belong'd when his Uncle was gone from home, and there was no Person present for whom it was more proper to lead in the Duty.

He dy'd of a violent Fever, which carry'd him off in a few Days; but it is to be hoped that Death did not find him unprepared. He in the time of his Sickness, as well as before, sought earnestly to God for Mercy, calling often upon him, and desiring others to pray with and for him; and owning his Unworthiness of the great Salvation which he thus sought for, he professed his Hopes of obtaining it thro' the Merits of Jesus Christ

---

669 Judged (*OED*).

his only Saviour. Tho a more particular Account cannot be now given of him, yet he was so generally esteemed a godly young Man by such as were acquainted with him, that I could not forbear[670] instancing in him as an Example of early Piety.

[236] EXAMPLE IX.

ABIGAIL KENUMP, *who died in* Chilmark, *in or about the Year* 1710, *being 16 Years old, or thereabouts.*

THIS *Abigail Kenump* was the Daughter of *Amos Kenump*[671] and *Abigail* his Wife, who lived in the said *Chilmark.* She seemed to be very sober and considerate while she was but a Child, was remarkably observant and dutiful to her Parents; and after she had learned to read, was observed to be often looking in her Book, and seemed to meditate much on the things which she read in it. She loved to go to Meeting while she was but young, and seemed to take heed that she sinned not, as if she had an Awe of God in her Heart.

One Morning, when some young People who lodged in the House with her, were, when they first waked, entred into a Discourse which was vain and unsavoury,[672] she very seriously reproved them, telling them, *That the God of their Lives and of all their Mercies, ought to have the first of their Thoughts when they awaked in a Morning: And declared to them, how unfit a thing it was for Persons to begin the Day with such vain and unprofitable Discourses.*

Some time after this she grew unhealthy, and was long sick of a languishing Distemper before she dy'd; yet she was not so bad for a considerable time, but that she could go to Meeting: And being willing to omit no Opportunity to wait on God in the publick Ordinances of his Worship, while she had Ability to attend them, she frequently desired some Body or other to carry her on a Horse, when she had not Strength to go up to the House of God on Foot.

When her Strength so failed that she could not go to Meeting any longer, she appeared careful to spend her time well at home; and Reading and Meditation was now a great part of her Employment.

This pious Maid was also much in Prayer, or else she had not deserved such a Character: but tho she seemed to aim at Secrecy herein, yet those that dwelt in the same House with her could not but observe, that she was often alone pouring out her Heart before the Lord.

---

670 To dispense with, do without, spare (a person or thing); obsolete (*OED*).

671 Owner of forty acres east of Joseph Kehannit's property in Gay Head. *WGH*, 187.

672 Objectionable on moral grounds; unpleasant, disagreeable (*OED*).

[237] When young People came to visit her in her Sickness, as sometimes they did, she used to desire such of them as she knew could read,
to read some Portion of God's Word to her, and would take that Opportunity to let fall some Words of Caution and Counsel to them. She would
then speak to them of the Frailty and Uncertainty of this present Life,
and declare to them the exceeding Evil of Sin, and let them know how
needful a thing it was for young People *to remember their Creator in the
days of their Youth, &c.*[673]

She in the former part of her Sickness made use of Medicines, in order
to the recovering of her Health; but some time before she dy'd, she said,
she had no need to make use of such Medicines any longer; *for,* said she,
the Lord Jesus Christ is the only Medicine that I now stand in need of.

Some time after this, a little before her Death, she spake to this Effect
to her sorrowful Mother: *Be not, my Mother, overmuch grieved at my Death;
for, tho I have been guilty of many Sins, yet I have Hopes in the Mercy of God,
thro' Jesus Christ my only Saviour, that I shall when I die leave all my Pain
and Affliction behind me, and enter into everlasting Rest and Happiness. And
if you do by a thorow Repentance turn unto God, and truly seek and serve him,
you may yet again see me with great Joy and Comfort.*

She was very sensible of the Approaches of Death towards her, as the
time of her Dissolution drew near; but was able, thro' Grace, to look *that
King of Terrors* in the Face.

Just as she was dying, she called her Mother to her, and spake such
good and comfortable Words to her, as she had formerly done, and then
lifting up her Hands towards Heaven, said, *Oh! my gracious Saviour, have
Mercy on me a miserable Sinner, who am but Dust and Ashes;*[674] which having
said, her Hand dropped down, and she immediately expired.

[238] EXAMPLE X.
ELIZABETH PATTOMPAN, *who died in* Tisbury, July *the* 6th, 1710,
in the 17th *Year of her Age.*

THIS *Elizabeth* was a Daughter of *Josiah Pattompan*[675] and *Ruth*[676]
his Wife, both Professors of Religion, and, as I have been informed,

---

673 Ecclesiastes 12:1.

674 Genesis 18:27; Job 30:19, 42:6.

675 Probably the son of Pattompan and the grandson of Nashohkow (*IC,* 28, 54; *WGH,* 156,
290, 331). This would make her father the nephew of Micah Shohkan (*IC,* 30–31*), Stephen
Shohkau (*IC,* 54–56*), Pattompan (*IC,* 131), and Daniel Shohkau (*IC,* 131). Josiah and Ruth
Pattompan were also the parents of Jerusha Ompan (*IC,* 175–79*).

676 *IC,* 218.

diligent Instructors of their Children in the Mysteries and Duties of Christianity.

When this Daughter of theirs was about eleven Years of Age, they put her to live in an *English* Family in the Town in which they themselves lived; and she carry'd her self very orderly and well while she tarried there, being willing to learn to read, and receive such other Instructions as those she lived with thought themselves obliged to give her: but the Death of her pious Mistress, about a Year, as I think, after her first coming to that House, occasioned her returning to her Father's House again, tho her Master would not otherwise have parted with her, not having observed any thing in her Carriage which he misliked.

After her Return to her Father and Mother, she continued to behave her self well, being very obedient to them. She was exceeding diligent in her Business, minded her Book, and was willing to go to Meeting as oft as she could.

She appeared also careful to abstain from Sin, and her Parents observed that she prayed in secret Places; and once when they had been abroad, and did not return till after she had done looking for them, they, when they came to the Door, heard her praying with the Children which they had left under her Care and Charge.

As she took heed that she sinned not, but lived very blamelessly, so she was a very serious Reprover of Sin in others, especially those of the Family in which she lived; insomuch that her Father assures me, that all that belonged to the House stood in Aw of her, even her Parents as well as others, she having the Courage to let them know, that she was grieved at such Miscarriages as she saw in them, or otherwise knew that they were guilty of; and yet had the Prudence to manage her Re[239]proofs so inoffensively, as not to give them any Occasion to be angry with her.

Growing unhealthy some Years before she dy'd, as her bodily Weakness grew upon her, her spiritual Strength seemed to increase more and more: she therefore now discoursed more freely about the Concerns of her Soul and another World, than she had formerly been wont to do; and she told her Relations, that great Seriousness which she observed in her Mistress with whom she lived, and her Earnestness in prosecuting the Work of Religion wherein she was engaged, was that which first put her upon a deep and serious Consideration of her own State and Ways: she said, that she then thought, that if she would obtain eternal Life, she must work out her own Salvation with Fear and Trembling,[677] as she saw her Mistress did, and indeed which all about her could not but observe.

---

677 Philippians 2:12.

One Instance of this Maid's following the Example herein set her, I shall here make a particular mention of.

One Morning her Father going out of his House before it was well light, and walking towards a Spring not far off, which the Family used to fetch Water from, he thought he heard near that Place the Voice of his said Daughter, who went out some time before him; and going a little further that way, he found that he was not mistaken, for he then plainly heard his Daughter speaking, and calling on God for his Mercy to be extended to her. She then humbly confessed to him the Sins of her Nature and Life, and earnestly entreated him for the Merits sake of his Son Jesus Christ, to pardon and blot out all her Transgression,[678] and to renew and sanctify her Heart,[679] saying to him, that if he would graciously please so to do, she should be then willing to leave this World, and all her Enjoyments in it, that she might go to him, and be happy in the Enjoyment of him for ever, &c.

On the same Day wherein her Father heard her thus praying to God, she fell more violently ill, and remained so till she dy'd. Being now much worse than she had hitherto been, she expressed her Apprehensions that she should not recover of the Sickness with which she was visited, and her Willingness to submit to the Will of God therein, also her earnest Desires of being recon[240]ciled to him, and her Hopes of eternal Salvation thro' Jesus Christ her only Saviour. She also now called earnestly on God for the Manifestation of his Favour to her Soul, gave many good Exhortations to all her Relations, and forewarned her Father of something that befel him, according to her Words, soon after her Death.

Some Days before she dy'd, she earnestly desired her Father to commit to writing, for the Benefit of her Relations, some things which she then uttered: which her Father doing not long after, he since presented me with a Copy of the said Writing; which having now before me, I shall here insert the Substance of it, and it is as followeth.

I know assuredly, said she, *that such is the Condition of Mankind, that there is no Rest for them any where in this World: I chuse therefore to go to my Father, rather than tarry any longer in it.*

Then praying, she said, *Therefore now, O my heavenly Father, if thou pleasest so to do, prepare my Soul to be saved by thee in the Place of heavenly Rest, which thou hast prepared for thy People; and then I know I shall certainly have everlasting Joy in thy Salvation. If therefore, O God, thou takest me away, take away likewise my Sinfulness from me. And O that thou, O God, wouldst deal thus mercifully with all my Friends and Brethren.*

---

678 Psalm 51:1; Isaiah 43:25.
679 1 Peter 3:15.

Having thus prayed, she further spake thus to her Relations: *And you my Brethren and Friends, I desire you would not be over much grieved at my Death, but instead thereof turn to, and call on God, and then we shall see one another again in Heaven.*

Lastly, said she, *I speak to you my Father. I find in my Heart, my Father, something that is a Matter of very great Consequence, or Importance to you; it greatly concerns you, that turning to God, you call constantly upon him as long as you live, which if you do, your God will shew a great Favour to you, [or will greatly bless you,] and you shall have great Joy, [or Comfort] but if you do not, you will be wretched and miserable for ever.*

You ought to consider how exceeding dreadful their Pain and Torment will be, who go to Hell, [or to the Place of Devils.]

[241] I would have you, my Father, remember one thing more: after I am dead you will quickly lose all your Estate, but if you worship and serve God as you ought to do, you will receive it again.

[See that you abstain from Drunkenness.*] I intreat you, my Father, in the Name of our merciful King in Heaven, that you would write these Words for the Use of my Brethren and Friends, that so they may duly consider their own Souls.*

Tho the Father of this young Woman was so earnestly desired by her to commit to Writing the Words above recited, yet having for some time neglected so to do, he does with great Assurance and Confidence affirm, that the Spectre[680] of his said Daughter did after her Death one Day plainly appear to him, being so near to him, that he plainly saw that she appeared with the same Clothes which she commonly wore before her Death. He also saw some Warts on one of her Feet, which were, in appearance, such as his Daughter had on hers.

He says he had not the Power to speak to the *Apparition,* nor did *that* say any thing to him, but soon vanished out of his Sight. He also says, that on the Sight of the Spectre his Breath and Strength did in a great measure fail him, and that he remained weak, and uncapable of any Business; till advising with some on the Case, he was told that he had best fulfil the Will of his Daughter, by committing her Words to Writing as she had desired him to do, but that on his doing it, he was, after he had slept a little, as well as he used to be. This Account he gave to several Persons soon after the thing happened, as some of them do still testify.

And whereas his Daughter told him before she dy'd, that soon after her Death he would lose all his Estate, &c. he affirms that this came to

---

680 Specters or ghosts of the living, as well as the dead, appeared to people in New England and were a great source of controversy, particularly in the years surrounding the witchcraft trials. It was generally believed that the devil used apparitions of the living to do his bidding, though theologians debated whether the devil did so with or without the person's consent. See Reis, *Damned Women,* 57 n, 72–75. Spectral evidence became more suspect after the witchcraft trials, which may be why Mayhew says (*IC,* 242) that he will "leave these strange Occurrences to the Thoughts of others, without spending my own Judgment on them."

pass according to that Prediction of hers; for his Horses, Swine, and his other Cattle, all dy'd in a short time, [if I mistake not] within a Year; and whatever else he had, went unaccountably to Ruin, so that he became poor and miserable; but that in a few Years he again got things about him, so as to live comfortably, as he does to this Day: Nor has his Account of what thus befel him his own Word only, to support the Credit of it, there being several others that took notice of the sad Decay of his Estate, &c.

[242] I shall leave these strange Occurrences to the Thoughts of others, without spending my own Judgment on them; only I shall take the Liberty to say, that I hope the Maid to whom these Passages relate, was a truly pious Person.

EXAMPLE XI.

JOB TUPHAUS, *who died in or about the Year* 1714, *in the* 15th *Year of his Age.*

THIS Youth was another son of that *William* and *Bethia Tuphaus* above mentioned. His Mother has informed me, that the first Child she had being a Daughter, and dying while very young, she had none but Sons for many Years after;[681] and that being very desirous of having another Daughter, she prayed earnestly to God, that he would, if it pleased him so to to do, bestow one upon her; but if he saw good to deny her Request herein, he would then please to give her such a Son, as would be as great a Comfort to her as a Daughter would be if she had one.

The next Child which this good Woman had after she had thus prayed, was this *Job*, and such a Son he proved to be as she had prayed he might, if it did not please God to bestow a Daughter upon her; and for her further Comfort, the next after this was one of the same Sex as she had desired, even that *Bethia* who is above mentioned.[682]

But it is the said *Job* that I am now giving some Account of, and he appeared to have in him such good Things as God does indue those withal, whom he has a Favour for, and intends to make Heirs of his eternal Kingdom.

This *Job* was then *one* that *feared God and eschewed Evil.* He seemed, when he was but a Child, *to stand in awe that he sinned not;*[683] was not, as did appear, given to any of those Vices that the Generality of Boys are addicted to. He was very obedient to his Parents, and diligent and faithful in any Business that he was set about. He was very willing and

---

681 Including William Tuphaus Jr.: *IC*, 228–30*.

682 *IC*, 230–32*.

683 Psalm 4:4.

desirous to go to Meeting, and seemed loth to omit any Opportunity of attending the publick Duties of Religion. He was also very careful to attend Family Worship, and seemed to be very serious in it.

[243] He was sick near a Year before he dy'd, in which time he shewed a great Delight in hearing the Word of God read; and sometimes desired his Mother to read in the Book of the *Psalms* to him; and Psalms of Prayer he was most desirous to have read in his hearing, and would seem to be delighted and refreshed when they were so, and would lift up his Hands and give Thanks. When Psalms were sung in the Family, he used to join with his Voice in the singing of them, tho the State of his Body was very weak and low.

Once after Family Prayer, his Mother asked him what his Thoughts of his own Condition were? Unto which he answered, that he thought he should now quickly die. And are you, said she, willing so to die? *I am*, said he, *if God will please to bestow his Grace upon me; for then he will deliver me from all my Pain and Sorrow for ever. I love my Relations*, said he, *but I am willing to leave them all and go to God; and I desire that God would help me more and more to put my Trust in him. I would not have you troubled at my Death, for we must all of us die, one as well as another. And tho I go a little before my Friends and Relations, they must quickly follow after me.* But do you, said his Mother, hope you shall be saved? *I earnestly desire*, said he, *that God would have Mercy on me, and I do put my Trust in my God.*

The Day before his Death his Mother again asked him, Whether he was willing to die? Unto which he answered, *that he was.* But do you, said she, love God? *Yes*, said he, *I do.*

After he was speechless, he held out his Hand to his Mother, Grandmother,[684] and Brother severally, and took them by theirs: and so, taking his leave of them, went, as 'tis to be hoped, to that God in whom he trusted.

[244] EXAMPLE XII.
JERUSHA OHQUANHUT, *who died* November 14th 1714,
in the 18th *Year of her Age.*

THIS *Jerusha Ohquanhut* was a Daughter of *Peter Ohquanhut*,[685] and *Dorcas* his Wife; the said *Peter* being one of the present Pastors of the *Indian* Church on the West End[686] of *Martha's Vineyard.*

---

684 Probably Rachel Amos (*IC*, 152–54*).

685 *IC*, 90–91, 100, 110. Their other children were Lydia Ohquonhut (*IC*, 246–47*) and Dorcus Amos (*Native Writings*, 1:165, 175), who was probably the wife of Israel Amos. Israel Amos was the grandson of Henry Ohhunnut (*IC*, 126–28*) and his second wife, Esther Ahunnut. *WGH*, 147, 149, 228, 341, 427.

686 Gay Head.

Her religious Parents taught her to read, and say her Catechism, while she was but young; they also taught her to call upon God while she was but a little Girl, and she seemed to be very sober while she was but a Child, and used to pray according to the Instruction given her: nor was she, as did appear, addicted unto any Vice, but carried her self well, and was very obedient to her Parents.

When she was scarcely 15 Years old, her Father endeavouring to pass the Sound in a *Canoo*, was there taken by a *French* Privateer,[687] and carried away; but whither, neither his own Family, nor any other here, could tell.

At this Mishap this Daughter of his (as well as the rest of his Family and others) was exceeding troubled, but did at the same time encourage her self and the rest of her Relations, in the Power, Goodness, and Providence of God, and expressed her Dependence on him for the Preservation and safe Return of her Father, in his good time. She now put her Friends in mind how God delivered *Daniel* out of the Lions Den,[688] and the three Children out of the fiery Furnace,[689] into which they were cast; and from thence inferred how easy a thing it was with God to set her Father at Liberty, and bring him home to his Family again.

Having such a Faith, she exercised the same in fervent Prayer for her Father's Return: and her Mother perceiving that she was now very constant and earnest in her secret Devotions, and knowing that she had been long used to call on the Lord, did sometimes invite and persuade her to pray in the Family, there being none but themselves and little Children in it; nor was she at a loss how to express her self pertinently in the Duty, but [245] prayed like one that was used to it, as indeed she was, and had for a long time been.

In these Addresses to Heaven she prayed with much Affection, and ordinarily with Tears, inforcing her Petitions with proper Arguments taken out of the Word of God, which she was no Stranger to; nor did she fail of mentioning her Father's Case in any of the Prayers thus sent to God by her.

And while she was thus earnest with God for the Return of her Father, he put it in the Hearts of the *French* to release him, and set him on Shore at   ;[690] who, being at Liberty, got home to his Family at *Gayhead* in about a Month after he was taken.

This young Woman on the News of her Father's Return, and being already come as far as the next Town, was so exceedingly affected, as for

---

687 For examples of captivity narratives by Wampanoags who were captured by the French, see the narratives of Phillip Metack and Joseph Matark, two descendants (probably grandsons) of Mittark: MA Arc. 33.73–74, 33.161, 97.283, 98.481, 133.98; *WGH*, 425–26.

688 Daniel 6:22–23.

689 See Daniel 3. The three men were Shadrach, Meshach, and Abednego.

690 The blank space is in the original.

the present to fall into a Swoon; but being in a short time recovered out of it, she expressed her great Joy and Thankfulness to God for his great Goodness therein manifested.

Not long after this she signified her Intentions to her Parents of renewing her Covenant with God, and asking an Admission to the Table of the Lord: and being encouraged by them so to do, did it accordingly; and giving good Evidences of a Work of Grace on her Soul, was by the Church readily admitted when she was but very little above 15 Years of Age: nor did this young Woman ever, by any Miscarriage, bring Reproach on Religion, or the Church whereof she was a Member.

As she appeared to be a very pious Person in the time of her Health, so she did in the time of that Sickness also whereof she died, she then behaving her self as became an Heir of God's eternal Kingdom. I shall conclude my Account of her with the last Words she spake before she died; which being penned by her Father, to whom, with the rest of her Friends, she spake them, were in Writing delivered to me, and they are these:

> My Father, these are my last Words to you, now in my End: Worship God fervently, and be not much troubled for me; for as for me, I'm going to my heavenly Father: serve God therefore with greater Diligence and Fervency than you used while I was well in Health. And all you my other Friends, whom I know to have lov'd me, and who are also beloved of me, if you are sorry for my leaving of you, seek for me with Jesus Christ, and there [246] you shall find me, and with him we shall see one another for ever.

EXAMPLE XIII.
LYDIA OHQUANHUT,[691] *who died in the Year* 1715, *when she was five Years old.*

SHE was a Sister of *Jerusha Ohquanhut,* last mentioned.

She was, like her Sister, instructed in the first Principles of Religion as soon as she was capable of such Instructions: and it seems that it pleased the Holy Spirit of God, by his sanctifying Influences, to make very early Impressions on her Soul. She carried her self on all accounts very inoffensively, before she was seized with the Sickness whereof she died; being very obedient to her Parents, and not, as did appear, addicted to any Vice: but it was not till after she was taken with that Sickness that put an End to her Life, that such things did appear in her, as did more fully discover

---

691 The daughter of Peter and Dorcas Ohquanhut, *IC,* 90–91, 100, 110. Besides Lydia and Jerusha (*IC,* 246–47*), they were the parents of Dorcus Amos (*Native Writings,* 1:165, 175), who was probably the wife of Israel Amos. *WGH,* 147, 149, 228, 341, 427.

her to be *a new Creature*,⁶⁹² and an Heir of that Salvation of which those
who call on the Name of the Lord, have a Promise made to them.

Her Father being affected with some of the Expressions she then
used, committed them to Writing, and thereby furnished me with what I
shall here further relate concerning her.

When her Mother perceived that she was dangerously ill, she wept
over her; which the sick Child observing, said to her, "My Mother, do
not weep, for it is to Heaven that I'm going. *Jerusha* is already gone to
Heaven, and now I am going to Heaven also." She further said at the
same time, "We must all of us die, we must all of us die, we must all of
us die."⁶⁹³

Two Days after this she called on the Lord, and said; "Oh God! have
Mercy on me; Oh God! have Mercy on me, Oh God! have Mercy on me."

A while after she spake thus to her Father, "My Father, I desire you
would teach me how I ought to pray." Her Father, in answer to her
Requests, taught her several Petitions as he thought proper, and suitable
for her to make use of; and she did still as fast as she could, learn them,
with great Affection improve them, calling on the Lord in the Words in
which she was so directed to [247] pray to him, and frequently repeating the Petitions so put up by her. At length her Friends perceiving that
she was just a dying, her Father taught her to call upon her Saviour
in these Words, *Lord Jesus Christ receive my Soul*; and she most readily
accepting her Father's Direction, thus to commit her Spirit to the Hands
of her Redeemer, did frequently, while she lay dying, in these Words
call upon him: and after she was so far spent, as not to be able to speak
audibly, she was supposed to continue so praying, her Lips continuing to
move as long as she had any Life left in her.

Thus this Child breathed out her Soul into the Hands of God her
Saviour.

EXAMPLE XIV.
LABAN PANU, *who died at* Gayhead, November 6th, 1715,
when he was ten Years and about nine Months old.

THIS Child had for his Father a godly *Indian* Minister, *viz. Joash Panu*,⁶⁹⁴
formerly mentioned. His Mother was a pious Woman who is yet living,
Naomi Panu, the Widow of the said *Joash*.

---

692 2 Corinthians 5:17; Galatians 6:15.

693 The bleak statement "we must die" is softened by the assurance of the thriple repetition:
three was considered a perfect or heavenly number in Christianity, since it reflects the Trinity.

694 *IC*, 63–67*. Joash was the son of *Annampanu*, otherwise called *Maattie* (*IC*, 109–110).

He did not appear to have any Fear of God before his Eyes till about two Tears before he dy'd, but seemed rather to be an evident Instance of the Verity of that Word of God, *the wicked are estranged from the Womb, they go astray as soon as they are born.*[695] He was till he was near nine Years old, rude and disorderly, was apt to profane the *Sabbath* Day, and could scarcely be restrained from playing at Meeting: nor did the many good Instructions and Exhortations given him by his Parents appear to have any good Effect upon him.

His Parents, grieved with his Miscarriage, at length began to deal more sharply with him, taking therein that Advice of the wise Man, *Corect thy Son, and he shall give thee rest:*[696] and as they found the *Counsel* good, so they found the *Promise true*; for due Corrections thus added to good Instructions, did, by God's Blessing, soon produce a remarkable Change in the Carriage and Behaviour of their Child. He very suddenly appeared to be much more sober and orderly than he use to be; and thus [248] becoming sober, he soon discovered a religious Seriousness also.

He about this time told his Mother, that formerly he had not believed there was a God, but now he was persuaded that there was one, who had placed him here in the World. And for what End, said his Mother, do you think that God has placed you here as he has done? *That I might seek and serve him,* said the Child; *and as God has placed us here upon Earth, so he will shortly remove us again from it.* His knowing and pious Mother then proposing the Doctrine of the final Judgment to him, he readily asserted his firm Persuasion of the Truth and Certainty of that Doctrine: and he then carried himself as one, that must be brought into Judgment for all he said and did, ought to do.

Being thus become serious, he applied himself with Diligence to the reading of his Books, which he had before too much neglected; and he now also studied his Catechism, and would often of his own accord repeat by Heart the Questions and Answers, which he had before learned: and he and some of the other Children of the Family,[697] and some also of another Christian Family that lived near by, used by turns to catechise one another; by which Means the Knowledge of this Child, as well as some of the rest, was considerably increased.

His Mother sometimes hearing of him at these Exercises, would ask him, whether he really believed the Truth of the Answers in his Catechism

---

695 Psalm 58:3.

696 Proverbs 29:17.

697 His siblings include sisters whose names are known, as well as Joseph Paneu (*IC*, 250), who was active in the "Nahuakamuk" Church from 1746 to 1767, and Joash Panue, a laborer who kept the school from 1726 to 1744. *WGH*, 140, 234, 345, 355.

which he repeated; making this Demand more especially when he came to Answers of the greatest Importance: and he would still, in Answer to her, declare his firm Belief of the Truths which he so learned.

Thus believing, it might soon be said of him, *Behold he prayeth:*[698] he was sometimes heard and seen calling upon God his Saviour.

His Mother several times observing that he was alone, saying something which she could not so hear as to understand, she once asked him what, and to whom he used to speak in his Retirements? To which he answered, that he used to speak to God, and pray to him, to pardon all his Sins, and make him good [or godly.] His Father also sometimes found him alone in the Woods, calling on the Name of the Lord; and sometimes heard him in the Depth of the Night, when he was upon his Bed, cry[249]ing to God for his Mercy and Salvation; as in a Paper wherein he hath set down the time of his Birth and Death, he has declared.

The Father of this Child observing such good things as these in him, would sometimes tell his Wife and others, that he thought he should not long enjoy him: by which he was supposed to intend, that his little Son had his Conversation so much in Heaven, that he thought he would be soon ripe for that Place, and removed to it.

He divers times confessed the Sinfulness of his Heart and Life, especially to his Father, when he was instructing and exhorting of him; and he particularly lamented his Miscarriages before-mentioned, and he sometimes cautioned his younger Brothers and Sisters against such Evils.

He talked often of his own Frailty and Mortality, and that even while he appeared to be in Health; and sometimes let fall such Expressions as seemed to intimate, that he thought he should very shortly die. And he did as he conjectured, living a natural Life scarcely two Years after he began to live a spiritual one.

He was sick but about a Month before he died; in which time he behaved himself as became a Youth that remembered his Creator.[699]

Soon after he was taken ill, his Mother asking him whether he was willing to die and leave this World, and all his Enjoyments in it, he after a little Pause said, that *he found in himself an Unwillingness at present so to do.* But why so? said his Mother to him, this is a very troublesome World, here are many Afflictions to be undergone; whereas Heaven is a most excellent Place, wherein there is no Trouble or Sorrow to be indured. *I am concerned,* said the Child weeping, *for my little Brother,* (one younger than himself) *I now keep with him and look after him; but if I die, I can take*

---

698 Acts 9:11.
699 Ecclesiastes 12:1.

no more care of him.[700] Don't, said his Mother, let that trouble you; if you die before your Brother, it will not be long before he will follow after you; and if you go to Heaven, he will, if he loves and serves God, come thither to you, and there live with you for ever; the which that he may do, I will endeavour to teach him to know and serve the Lord. Do you therefore seek to God to prepare you for your End; and be willing to die, and go to your God, when he sees meet to call you. *Yea*, said the Lad [250] smiling, *I will be so; I will not set my Heart no longer upon my Brother, nor be unwilling to leave him: Come hither* Joseph,[701] said he to him; who then coming to him, he took him by the Hand and said, *Farewel my Brother, you shall not offend (or hinder) me any longer, be thou diligent in seeking after God!*

After this, he never discovered the least Unwillingness to die, but set himself to seek the Lord with his whole Heart, and called daily upon him for his Mercy, to be extended to him for the sake of Jesus Christ his only Saviour; and also frequently desired his Father to pray for him, and sometimes his Mother also in his Father's Absence.

He also now discoursed much of the things of God and another World, frequently calling God his Heavenly Father, and speaking of Jesus Christ as his only Redeemer and Saviour: but what the Sentences were he then uttered, cannot now be distinctly remembered, not having been committed to Writing.

He underwent much Pain in the time of his Sickness, and sometimes said that he could not forbear groaning under his Affliction; yet he said it was God that laid the same upon him, and he did bear with much Patience the mighty Hand of God[702] which he was then under, constantly trusting in and crying to him only for Deliverance.

When he perceived that he was nigh to Death, he said but little to any that were about him, but kept almost continually praying to God, often saying, *Oh! my Heavenly Father, have Mercy on me.*

When his Friends asked him whether he was willing to die, and whether he had Hopes that God would save him, he still answered affirmatively to these Questions.

After his Voice so failed him that he could not pronounce perfect Sentences, he still kept praying to God, and saying, *Woi—Woi—Woi*; which may be rendred in *English, I pray—I pray—I pray—*, which were the last Words he ever was heard to speak.

---

700 This concern for one's siblings and their physical and spiritual health should be compared with Jonathan Edwards's transcription of the conversion of Phebe Bartlet in "A Faithful Narrative," 199–205.

701 Joseph appears to have followed his brother's lead: he was active in the Wampanoag church at Nashuakamuk (Chilmark), 1746–67. *WGH*, 140.

702 An echo of Job 19:21.

[251] EXAMPLE XV.

JANE POMIT, *who died in* Nashouohkamuk, *alias* Chilmark,
in March 1716-17, *in the eighteenth Year of her Age.*

THIS *Jane* was a Daughter of *Jesse Pomit,* an *Indian* of the *Gayhead,* (who died
while she was a Child) and his Wife *Jane,* who is yet living in *Chilmark.*

She was taught to read while young, and was also instructed in her
Catechism, and had by her Mother and Grandmother many good Counsels given her. Nor were the Means used for her Good lost; for she was
obedient to her Mother, willing to receive Instructions, and loved to read
her Book and go to Meeting.

When she was ten or eleven Years old, the good Instructions given
her began to make a very observable Impression upon her: she would
then weep and be much affected, when spoken to about the things of God
and another World, seeming to lay to heart what was said to her.

Some time after this, her Mother being poor, and living with her and
one or two more of her Children in a little sorry Cottage, and having a
little Son some Years younger than this Daughter, then in a sick and low
Condition, was put to great Straits for a Livelihood for her self and little
ones, undergoing such Difficulties as People were not generally so sensible of as they should have been; and particularly her little Son *David,*
for that was his Name, did somewhat suffer for want of such things as, in
regard of his present low and weak Condition, he needed: which being
observed and considered by his Sister, of whom I am here speaking, she
with great Compassion and Sympathy applied her self to him, condoling
the Misery of the present State which he was in, and declaring to him
how much better it would be for him, if he were fit to die, to leave this
World, and go unto that better Country which is above in Heaven; and
earnestly pressed him to prepare to go to that good Place, telling him, as
well as she could, what we must do to be saved, as that he must love God,
and call upon his Name, &c.

[252] Nor did she once only thus address herself to him, but did several times with much Affection so do; telling him what an excellent and
glorious Place Heaven was, and how dreadful the Torments of Hell were,
and how much it concerned him to endeavour to escape the one and obtain
the other; declaring withal, her own Resolutions so to do: and so earnest
was she sometimes with him, that she would not leave him till he owned
the Truth and Importance of what she said to him. I'm informed, that the
Girl her self was wont to be thus treated while she was a Child; and if so, it
is the less wonder she should deal so pungently[703] with her little Brother.

---

703 Sharply, pointedly (*OED*).

I desire my Reader to pardon the Digression, if I here, as in a Parenthesis, give some further Account of the little Boy so instructed by his Sister: He did not at first seem to be very much affected with what she said to him; but before he died, which he did not long after, when he was about nine Years old, he was concerned about his eternal Estate, and called upon God for Mercy; so that there was some ground of hope that he died well: and this is all that I have to say about him.

The young Maid being sick her self, after the Death of her Brother, called earnestly upon God to extend his Favour to her; she intreated him to spare and lengthen out her Life a little longer, and made Promises that she would endeavour to live to him. God heard her Requests, spared her Life; and she performed her Vows to him, owning her Obligations so to do.

Being arrived to sixteen Years of Age, or something upwards, she expressed a great Desire of enjoying God in all his Ordinances; and gave so good an Account of her Knowledge of the only true God, and Jesus Christ whom he hath sent, and Experience of a Work of Grace on her Soul, that she was with good Satisfaction admitted to full Communion in the Church whereof Master *Joash Panu* was the Pastor. Nor did she ever, while she lived, give the Church any Cause to repent of their having admitted her.

About the time of her being thus admitted to the Privileges of a Church State, or rather before it, her Mother's Wigwam being gone to ruin, they had no House of their own to dwell in, but were fain to get Entertainment as they could in the House of others. But this way of living did not please the Daughter, who there[253]fore told her Mother, that she earnestly desired that she would again endeavour to get her a little Wigwam to live in; for, said she to her, we cannot worship and serve God so constantly and comfortably in the way we are in, as we might if we had a House of our own, in which we might daily call upon him. She further told her Mother, that being fallen into an unhealthy State of Body, she should on that account chuse rather to have a House of their own, in which she might live and die, than to be in other Peoples Houses.

Her Mother hearkning to her, and getting a little Wigwam according to her Desire, they there lived together, and called daily on God, as the Daughter had proposed; and there she also died about a Year after.

Being settled in their much desired Wigwam, the Daughter prayed her Mother to grant her the Privilege of sometimes expressing orally, or with her Voice, the Prayers to be jointly put up to God by them; which Requests her Mother readily and with much Pleasure granted, desiring her Daughter to pray every Evening, she taking her turn in the Morning: Nor was the Mother any ways disadvantag'd, in her own Apprehen-

sions, by thus imploying her Daughter, but much edified with the Gift of
Prayer wherewith God favoured her. She has told me, that as her Daughter was able, in a very suitable manner, to express the Wants and Desires
of her own Soul, and those of others whom she was bound to pray for, so
she generally called upon God with much Fervency and Affection, and
often with many Tears poured our her Soul before him.

Bodily Weakness increasing apace on this pious young Woman, she
never was more than twice able to attend the Administration of the
Lord's Supper, after she was admitted to a Participation in it, tho she
very much desired to have partaken of it oftner; and yet the Comfort she
received at the Table of the Lord, when she was enabled to come to it,
was such as that she was no Loser by seeking an Admission thereunto.

When she came home in the Evening, the first time she was at this
Feast, she opened her Mouth in the Praises of God, for that he had
granted her the Favour which she had desired of him; and professed that
she had met with Comfort and Refreshment in the Duty she had been
attending. She likewise experienced divine [254] Consolation the last
time she was at the Sacrament, declared the same to her Relations at her
Return from it; adding at the same time, that she thought she should
no more in this World partake of the Feast at which she had then been
entertained; but that she hoped she should be again admitted to it in the
Church that is above.

This being in *August*, she died the next Spring after, being in the mean
time very diligent in her Preparations for that great Change which she
expected and waited for. She often called upon God for the Mercies she
needed, not forgetting to pray for others also; she utter'd also many pious
and savory Sentences, which cannot now be distinctly remembred. She
mightily encouraged her poor afflicted Mother, desiring her to put her
trust in God, and pray without ceasing to him. Master *Joash*, her Pastor,[704] often visited and discoursed with her, and was well satisfied with
what she said to him: others who were well acquainted her, have given
her a good Character.

One Day, a little before she died, she bemoaning her Brother whom
she was like to leave alone, (the rest of her Brothers and Sisters being
dead) her Mother told her she should not distress her self about him,
God would provide for him after her Death as well as while she lived:
upon the hearing of which, after a little Pause, she called to her Mother
and said, *My Mother, I will no more love my Brother, or any thing else here, I
will henceforth love none but Jesus Christ.*[705]

---

704 Joash Panu (*IC*, 63–67*).
705 Jane's statement reflects the doctrine of weaned affections.

She accordingly, after this, spake of this World and the Enjoyments of it, as things which she did not set her Heart upon; but professing Hopes of enjoying everlasting Mercies thro' the Merits of the Son of God her only Saviour, she declared her Willingness to die, and go to the Enjoyment of them; and so took her leave of this Vale of Tears.[706]

[255] EXAMPLE XVI.

BETHIA SISSETOM, *who died at* Sanchekantacket, *in* October 1721, *when she was about eighteen or nineteen Years old.*

THIS young Woman was a Daughter of an *Indian* commonly called *Oggin*, alias *Haukim*, and his Wife *Hannah*, a pious Woman beforementioned, in *Chap.* III. *Examp.* 20.[707]

She had also a very pious Grandfather, *viz. Joel Sims*[708] formerly mentioned, and a godly Grandmother yet living; the last of whom had Opportunity and a Heart, by her good Example and Instructions, to promote her Salvation: And if I may go a little further back, she was a great Grandchild of that excellent *Wunnannauhkomun*, who prayed so very earnestly for his Offspring when he was dying, mentioned *Chap.* I. *Examp.* 5.

These were great Advantages; but it seems God still deigned *some better thing for her*,[709] which those mentioned were but means and steps towards her Attainment of. She behaved her self from a Child in some good measure as a Person so privileged ought to do; was very obedient to her Parents, diligent and faithful in what she was set about, and not known to be any ways vicious; and yet not free from some of those Vanities to which young People are very commonly subject.

There being seldom, while she was young, any School near to which she could be sent, and she being so exceedingly desirous to learn to read, that no Difficulties lying in the way could discourage her from it, she used to catch at every Opportunity she could get to read a Lesson to any one that would hear her: and her Mother being but a poor Reader, and her Father seldom at home, some of her Neighbours seeing how much she was set upon learning her Book, and kindly offering to hear her read

---

706 Psalm 84 ("valley of Baca," or weeping). The phrase "vale of tears" is also used in the rosary—"Hail, Holy Queen, Mother of Mercy"—though it is unlikely that Mayhew intended this allusion.

707 Hannah Sissetom (*IC*, 184–87*). As mentioned on *IC*, 184, *Oggin* [alias *Haukkings*] *Sissetom* was a grandson of *Wunnannauhkomun* (*IC*, 18–20*). Oggin was also the grandson of Ammapoo (*IC*, 148–51*), and hence through him Bethia is related to John and Hannah Nahnosoo. Oggin Sissetom's brothers include Abel Sesetom and Caleb Seaton (*IC*, 272).

708 *IC*, 73*, 184: Hannah Sissetom's father.

709 Hebrews 6:9, 11:40, 12:24; Ecclesiastes 7:8.

if she would come to them when they could attend it, she thankfully accepted the Offer, going very often to them; and tho the Circumstances of the Family to which she belonged, were such that she could scarcely be spared long enough from it to go and read a Lesson or two in a Day, yet she would by her great Industry redeem time, for that wherein she so much delighted; and in this way [256] she learned to read better than many do who have a School to go to, and time to attend it.

Having with such Difficulty attained this Skill, she with a proportionable Diligence improved it, delighting much in reading such Books as might be advantageous to her; and in this way especially, arrived to some good measure of Knowledge in the things of God and his Kingdom, insomuch that her Mother, after she died, acknowledged that she had got the start of her, and knew so much more than she did, that she either did or might have learned of her.

Tho she made a good use of her Books while she was in Health, yet they became more especially serviceable to her after she fell into a Consumption,[710] under which she lingred, I think, a Year and half before she died, being unable for the greatest part of that time to go to Meeting.

When she first began to languish, she thought she saw Death approaching towards her, but was then far from being able to bid the same welcome to her: she still saw Terror in the Face of that King of Terrors; and she could not yet say with pleasure, "I shall go to the Gates of the Grave, I'm deprived of the Residue of my Years, I shall not see the Lord, even the Lord in the Land of the Living; I shall behold Man no more, with the Inhabitants of the World."[711]

It seems she was still in the dark, as to her Estate[712] before God; and she could not be willing to die without a comfortable Hope of his Love to her Soul: she was therefore now, more than ever before, observed to work out her own Salvation with Fear and Trembling, and to use all Diligence to make her Calling and Election sure. She now confessed the Sins and Failures of her Life, and cried daily to God her Saviour, that his Grace and Mercy might be extended to her, and that her Sins might be all pardoned, and her Soul saved.

Her pious Grandmother before-mentioned, being now with her, frequently comforted her in her Affliction, and greatly encouraged her in

---

710 Although later the term referred specifically to pulmonary consumption (tuberculosis), in the colonial era it could also apply more generally to a "wasting of the body by disease" (*OED*).

711 Isaiah 38:10–11.

712 The state of her salvation or "election." No Puritan knew for certain that she or he was saved, as this decision was God's alone; however, individuals were still obliged to hope and call upon God.

the Work wherein she was engaged; but which was infinitely better, God wrought in her both to will and to do of his own good Pleasure.

God thus speeding the Work, it was not long before it was with her, as the Light of the Morning when the Sun riseth, even as a Morning without Clouds.[713] All her [257] Fears of Death were now vanished away; and not this World, but Heaven, was now the Place of her Desires. She declared that she could leave Father and Mother, and Brethren and Sisters, and all that had been dear unto her here, that she might go to God who was her exceeding Joy.

About this time, a godly *English* Neighbour going to visit her, was edified by hearing many good and comfortable Expressions which she uttered: among other things, she said that the thoughts of Death had been, in the first of her Sickness, very bitter to her; but that having got over that Difficulty, she was now willing to die and leave this World, and all the Enjoyments in it.

Her Discourses, after she thus attained to Peace in believing, were continually such as became a Child of God, living within the Views of that Glory which she expected in a short time to arrive to: but those who were then frequently with her, will not trust their Memories so far as to undertake to give a particular Account of what she said; only they affirm, she expressed her self very piously and comfortably, and that she did mightily exhort and encourage her Relations to depart from all Iniquity, and be diligent Seekers of that God to whom she hoped she was going; and did, I trust, do so to her unspeakable Joy.

EXAMPLE XVII.
TOBIT, *commonly called* TOBIT POTTER, *who died at* Okahame, *alias* Christian-Town, *in the Winter of the Year* 1722, *when he was in the thirteenth Year of his Age.*

THE Lad of whom I here write, was a Son of *Elizabeth Uhquat,* spoken of in the foregoing Chapter, *Example 24.*[714]

He was in the ninth Year of his Age put to live in a religious *English*[715] Family in *Tisbury,* where continuing about four Years, he was carefully instructed in the great Truths of Religion; and it is from the

713 2 Samuel 23:4.

714 *IC,* 194–97*. Plane discusses Elizabeth Uhquat and her son at length in *Colonial Intimacies,* 113–17.

715 *Mr.* Edward Milton, *and* Mary *his Wife.* [Mayhew's note.] Edward Milton (?–1733) arrived in Tisbury around 1700 after having served as a soldier in King Philip's War. He was an upstanding member of the town, though not particularly prominent: he served as "Surveyor of Highways Constable, tithing-man, and Grand Juror." Banks indicates that his wife's name

pious Mistress whom he lived with, that I have received the Substance of what I have to relate *concerning him*. He was very [258] ready and apt to learn his Catechism, and to receive such other Instructions as were given to him, increasing daily in Knowledge by the Means for that End used with him.

As he increased in Knowledge, he appeared to be under Convictions, and said he was in trouble and needed more Instructions; and would, if he were not ashamed, speak with some Minister about his Case; for he said he thought that Ministers knew more than others, and should be honoured more, as coming to us in Christ's stead.

He also enquired whether Ministers prayed for all, saying he thought they did, but did not know whether their Prayers would reach him who was of another Nation. In answer to which, he was told that none were excluded, and was put in mind of that Place of Scripture, *God is no Respecter of Persons; but in every Nation, he that feareth him and worketh Righteousness, is accepted with him.*[716]

He was very willing to go to Meeting as often as might be; and he told his Mistress, that tho he could remember but little of what he heard, yet he made as good use as he could of what he did remember, and studied the same daily.

He was very careful to attend Reading and Prayer in the Family wherein he lived, and hearkned diligently to what he heard read, endeavouring to remember as much as he could of it.

Questions being put to him on the Answers in the Assembly's Catechism, he would give pertinent Answers to them; so that it appeared that he was not only able to say his Catechism, but that in some good measure he understood it.

He learned several pious Poems by heart; and among others, those Verses for Children wherein are these Words:

> *I may not sin as others do,*
> *Lest I lie down in Sorrow too.*[717]

Which Verse having once repeated, he said, To lie down was to die, and in Sorrow was in Hell; and he would often make such pertinent Observations on other things which he read.

[259] He was careful to pray in secret towards the latter part of his time; and also manifested a Desire to see the Lord's Supper administred, and more than once did so.

---

was "Mercy" not Mary; however, Mercy was a common nickname for Mary. Mercy Hamlin was Edward's third wife. His previous wife died before Tobit came to live with the family. Mercy survived Edward. *HMV* 3:335.

716 Acts 10:34–35.

717 *New-England primer.*

He once said, that when he looked on the Moon and Stars, &c. he considered that these things could not have been, if there had not been a God that made them.

He said he loved good People better than others, because he thought they belonged to God; and being desired by a Minister to do a Chore or two for him, he said he had rather do things for him than not, and that because he was a Minister; and that he did not desire any Reward for what he did.

Having a sore fit of Sickness about a Year before he died, he then said he prayed daily for himself as well as he could, but he desired that his Master would also pray for him: Being asked what he desired, he answer'd, That God would forgive all his Sins, and give him an Interest in his Son Jesus Christ.

After his Recovery, he told his Mistress, that he had been sometimes formerly guilty of Lying; but that he was resolved to do so no more, tho he should suffer for what Faults he committed, being known.

Once speaking of a Servant who had been unfaithful, he said he would not do as he did; for he had heard that read, *Servants obey your Masters*, &c.[718]

He would sometimes say, that he thought he should be willing to die if he were fit for it; and being once asked why so? he answered, because he should then enjoy God, which he thought was Man's greatest Happiness.

He said once when he came from Meeting, that hearing the Minister mention those Words, *If my Father and Mother forsake me, the Lord will take me up*;[719] he was glad to hear this, for that he thought he had no body to take care of him. And he would frequently mention Passages in Sermons which he heard, and make pertinent Remarks upon them.

He was often affected, and would weep when he was catechiz'd, and when any good Instructions were given to him,

He appear'd to have a great Love to his Books, and once said, that he would not take twenty Shillings for one of them.

[260] If there were, on any occasion, Prayers in the Family, and he not there, he would be troubled that he was not at them.

He was always thankful for such good Instructions as were given to him; and when he went from his Master, a few Months before he died, he told his Mistress he thanked her for all the Good she had ever done him.

Being unhealthy when he left his said Master, and went to another with whom he had formerly for some time lived, it was so order'd, that he returned to his Mother, and not long after died.

---

718 Colossians 3:22.
719 Psalm 27:10.

His Behaviour and Discourses, from the time he went to his Mother till his Death, were still such as they formerly had been, *viz.* very serious and pious: but he not being able to speak *Indian* any thing well, and none of the *Indians* with him in the time of his Sickness, excepting his Mother, being able fully to understand what he said in *English,* I cannot obtain a particular Account of what he said in that time; especially considering that his Mother died a little after him, before I had a good Opportunity to inquire of her about him.

However, I am in general well informed, that he was sensible that he was like to die, and very diligent in preparing for his Change. He prayed much himself, and desired others to pray with and for him: and he attained to comfortable Hopes of his eternal Happiness in another World, before he left this; and comforted his distressed Mother, by acquainting her therewithal.

Particularly on the Morning of the Day wherein he died, he did so; for being then observed to look more lively than he had for some time done, and his Mother observing him to clap his Hands and smile, she asked him why he did so? to which he answered, because I am to die this Day. How know you that, said his Mother to him? I do know, said he, that it will be so. Are you then willing to die, said she to her Son? I am so, said he unto her. And why so, said his Mother to him? Because, said he, I shall then go to Jesus Christ, and be with him for ever.

This his Mother related to the Mistress with whom he had lived, on the Day in which he was interred.

His pious Mother sent for me to come and pray with him a little before he died; but he was become speechless before I could get to him ; and so I could then have [261] no Discourse with him, which I was troubled at. However, I doubt not but that he died in the Lord.

EXAMPLE XVIII.
HANNAH SOOPASUN, *a Daughter of* JOEL[720] *and* SARAH SOOPASUN *of* Christian-Town, *who died there* May *the* 12th 1723, *when she was about eleven Years and two Months old.*

THE Parents of this Child being both of them Professors of Religion, devoted her to God in her Infancy, and took care that she might be educated accordingly. They sent her to School while young, that so she might

---

720 Joel Soopasun was a deacon at Christiantown, but he also appears commonly as both a victim and a defendant in the Dukes County Court Records and Deeds, including DCRD 4.217, 6.292, 7.183, 9.166; DCCR (Vols. 1–2), MVHS, Box 17A, Env. 27; DCRP 1.107, MA Arc. 31.315. He was charged with trespass, shooting and wounding a mare, and being a debtor. He was listed in Mayhew's disbursements to the poor (1755). *WGH,* 205.

learn to read; and she made good Proficiency therein for the time she was kept at it. She was also pretty well instructed in her Catechism, so that she understood in some good measure the great Truths of Religion.

The School failing which she was sent to, her Parents put her to an *English* Master and Mistress, intending that she should have lived some Years with them, and there have received such farther Instructions as were necessary for her. But the Girl proving sickly at that House, after she had been some time there, both Parties agreed that she should again go and live with her Parents; and she accordingly did so, her said Master and Mistress speaking well of her after her removing from them.[721]

She delighted much in going to Meeting, so that she would not willingly miss any Opportunity for doing so; she was also still very apt and willing to learn to read, and to receive such other Instructions as were needful for her.

She seemed grieved, when by her long Sickness she was detained from the House of God; and told one of her Sisters, that she would not stay at home as she did, if she was well enough to go to Meeting.

When she grew so ill that her Friends suspected she would not recover, and understood what their Apprehensions were concerning her, she seemed to be much concerned about it, and Death for some time appeared very terrible to her: And now she seemed to be very sensible of her Sins, and confessed some of which she had been guilty. She also frequently desired her Father to pray [262] for her, which he at her Request readily did, and made it one of his Requests to God for her, that her Life might be spared, and her Health again restored to her; but she at length told him, that she desired he would no longer pray for her Life, telling him that she thought that God intended her Sickness should be unto Death; and she now earnestly desired him to pray for the Pardon of her Sins, and the eternal Salvation of her Soul. She also now told him that she wholly disregarded all her worldly Enjoyments, and was only concerned about the things of another Life and World.

She understood the Doctrine of Redemption by Jesus Christ;[722] and sometimes discoursed about it, improving of it for her Relief and Comfort, when she was under a deep Sense of her own Sinfulness.

As the time of her Death drew near, she was very sensible of it, and was not at all terrified at it; but told her Relations, that she desired they

---

721 For more about indenturement of Wampanoag and Algonquian children see Silverman, *Faith and Boundaries*, 185–222; and Herndon and Sekatau, "Colonizing the Children," 137–73.

722 The Puritan version of the doctrine of redemption is outlined in the Westminster Confession of Faith (1644), chaps. 10–13. Redemption was carefully framed as a balance between God's acts and human responsibility.

would not lay the same much to heart, since she had Hopes of changing this Life for a better whenever she should leave this World.

A little before her Death, she desired that one of the *Indian* Ministers might be sent for to come and pray with her; but by her Mother desired him not to pray for her Recovery, but only that God would fit her for and bring her to his everlasting Kingdom.

After this, she encouraged her Relations to be diligent Seekers of God; and told her Father, that she was troubled that he went so often, and stayed so long at drinking Houses, and that he sometimes seemed to her to have drank too hard when he came from them: and then earnestly intreated him to reform what was amiss in that respect.

When she perceived that she was dying, she desired her Father to commit her to God by Prayer; the which having done, she did her self call upon him, concluding with that Form of Prayer which our Lord taught his Disciples to use.

She then told her Friends, that she saw a shining Person clothed in White, standing by the Foot of her Bed; nor did she seem at all delirious when she thus spake; yet none else in the Room saw any thing of that Nature.[723] Her Father then told her, that she should rather think upon God, and call upon him, than mind any such thing; [263] which said, she again, in a few Words, prayed to *God* for his Mercy, and then, as it is to be hoped, went to *him.*

EXAMPLE XIX.
SARAH COOMES, *who died in* Chilmark, March 10. 1723,
when she was six Years and nine Months old.

THIS Child had for her Great-Grandfather, on the Father's side, the memorable *Hiacoomes,* frequently before-mentioned; and for her Grandfather, that good *Samuel Coomes* mention'd in *Chap.* II. *Example* 7. On the Mother's side she was a Grandaughter to that good Deacon, *Jonathan Amos,* mentioned *Chap.* I. *Example* 15.[724]

Her Mother being very sickly, and dying some time before her, she lived much with her good Grandmother, her Mother's Mother, who carefully instructed her in the things of God, and taught her to call upon him, as soon as she began to be capable of receiving such Instructions;

---

723 On Wampanoag dreams and visions, see Plane, "Falling 'Into a Dreame,'" 84–105.

724 Her mother was Martha Coomes (*IC*, 187–88*), who, according to Mayhew's earlier statements, was actually Jonathan Amos's granddaughter, so Sarah would be his great-grand-daughter. Sarah's maternal grandmother was Sarah Wompanummoo (*IC*, 187), the daughter of Jonathan Amos.

who, to her great Satisfaction, quickly found that she had a Relish for them, by her frequently desiring of her further to open and explain the Mysteries of Religion to her.

When she asked her Grandmother to instruct her, she usually did it in these Words, *Kukkootammah Mannit*; that is, *Teach me God*, or instruct me concerning him: And her Grandmother finding her so willing to hear and receive Instructions, was as willing to go on in the good Work which she had so happily begun, and had such Incouragements to go on withal.

And as the Child increased in Knowledge, so she appeared to be more and more affected with a Sense of the Reality and Importance of the Truths wherein she was instructed; and would, when the same were at her Desire proposed to her, frequently affirm her Belief of the Truth and Certainty of them, saying, that tho she could not her self express them, yet she firmly believed them.

Nor did this Child rest in the bare and naked Knowledge of the things she learned, but endeavour'd also to put the same in practice; and did evidently appear to be influenced thereby in her Life.

Her Grandmother having frequently observed that she was unwilling to go to bed early in the Evening, tho she appeared to be very drousy, and not knowing the Reason [264] of it, the Girl after some time told her, that she desired to stay up till her Grandfather[725] had been at Prayers in the Family; and from thence forward used to do so. Nor did she content her self with being at Family Worship, without making her Address to God by her self alone, as her Grandmother, and others in the Family, soon observed.

She lay sick a considerable while before she died; and in that time continued to crave Instructions in the things of God and the eternal World, and to express her Assent to, and acquiesce in them. She in particular expressed her stedfast Belief of the Doctrines of Christ's Person, Suffering, and Intercession for Sinners; and when she prayed, she called upon God to have Mercy upon her for his sake.

She seemed to have a lively Apprehension of a future Life and World, wherein Rewards and Punishments should be distributed unto all, according to their Works in this.

When she drew near her End, she desired her Grandmother not to be too much grieved for her; for, said she, I am now going to the House of God, and when you go to God's House also, we shall again see one another with Joy; and we shall there see others also, who are gone before us, leaving us sorrowful here behind them; and then we shall be where there is everlasting joy.

---

725 Gershom Wompanummoo (*IC*, 187).

She also, before she died, desired her Grandmother to be of good Courage, and go on stedfastly to serve God, notwithstanding any Opposition which she might meet withal in the way wherein she ought to walk.

EXAMPLE XX.
JOSEPH PEAG, *who died at* Christian-Town, July 20. 1723.
being four Years and twenty one Days old.

THIS Child was a Son of *Jacob Peag*, and *Sarah* his Wife,[726] both of them Persons professing Godliness; and who, as they did devote him to God in *Baptism*, while he was an Infant, so they took care to instruct him in the things of God. As soon as he was capable of receiving the most familiar Instructions that could be given to him, his pious *Grandmother*[727] also laboured to make him understand the first Principles of Religion.

[265] The little Child thus instructed was scarce three Years old, before the Instructions thus early given to him, began to make some observable Impressions on his Soul. He would of his own accord mention God, and call him good and gracious, and speak of the Benefits which he received as bestowed by him.

He used in the fourth Year of his Age to ask very notable Questions in Matters of Religion; to instance some of them, he one Day asked his Grandmother, how it was said that good People went to Heaven when they dy'd, when yet there was a Hole dug in the Ground, and they were put into it, and buried in it? His Grandmother, in answer to him, instructed him in the Doctrine of the *Immortality of the Soul*, its Separation from the Body at Death, and its *Return to God who gave it*,[728] &c. All which the Child seemed to understand, and appeared to be well satisfy'd with the Answer.

At another time the Child asked his Grandmother, *Why People, when they prayed, used to say* God *and* Christ; *are there*, said he, *two of them?* Yes, said his Grandmother, there are; yea, indeed there are *Three. What*, said the Child, *is the Name of the other which ye speak of?* The *Holy Ghost*, said the Grandmother to him.—*Are there then three Gods*, said the Child to her? No, said the Grandmother, there is but *one* God, yet that *one* God is some ways distinguished into *three*,—which is a Mystery too deep for us to understand.—Upon the hearing of which Answer, the Child fell to admiring of God as a most wonderful Being, saying, *O tamosnuksoo Mannit!* i.e.

---

726 *IC*, 203–7*.

727 Probably his maternal grandmother, Elizabeth Cahkuhquit, who was referenced earlier (*IC* 203).

728 Ecclesiastes 12:7.

Yea God is very wonderful! And he appeared to be well satisfy'd with what was said, without making any further Enquiries.

At another time this Child asked his Grandmother, *Whether Jesus Christ was really God, or not?* To which his Grandmother answered, that he was, telling him that he was God's only Son, and that he was equally God with his Father; and further familiarly instructing him in the Doctrine of Christ's Incarnation, and of his suffering in our Stead to reconcile us to God. The Child seemed to understand, and receive what she said, and did appear to be much affected therewithal, *Expressing his Admiration at the Goodness of God and Christ, appearing in this wonderful Way contrived far the Sal[266]vation of such wicked Creatures, as the Children of Men.*

He one Day asked his Father, *For what End People sung when they went to Meeting?* His Father told him, that it would be the great Work and Business of good People to praise God when they came to Heaven; and that singing being one Way in which they would then praise him, they were *now before-hand learning* to praise and glorify God's Name.—*I desire then,* said the Child, *to learn to sing too, may I not,* said he, *so do?* To which his Father answering him, that he might, he seemed to be mightily pleased with that Answer. And after this, whenever he heard Persons singing of Psalms, which was frequently practiced at the House of an *Indian* Minister[729] just by, the Child would slip away thither, and with great Sobriety attend that Exercise to the Conclusion of it; and did also frequently attempt to sing by himself, tho being but a Child, he therein acted as a Child.

There being frequently unhappy Jars[730] betwixt the Parents of this poor Child, he appeared to be much distressed at them, and would sometimes *run out of Doors,* as if he were not able to endure the House, where his Parents were contending; yea, so much affected was he at their Quarrels, that he could not forbear telling his Parents, *That they were very evil, and God was offended at them, desiring them to leave them off, lest by them they should provoke God to bring Evil upon them,* And one Day he told his Grandmother, (being abroad with her) *That he was weary of living in the World, by reason of the Sin and Disorder he saw in it, instancing in particular in the Differences of his Parents, telling her that he had rather die, and go to the House of God, than live any longer in so bad a Place as this was.*—And such a Desire of dying, and going to the House of God, he at another time expressed to a pious Aunt of his, who meeting him abroad, spake something of God and Heaven to him.

When this Child saw his Parents under any Straits and Difficulties, he would frequently express his Grief at them, but would say withal to

---

729 *Hosea Manhut.* [Mayhew's note.] An Indian minister at the West End of the Island, he was still alive when *Indian Converts* was written. *IC,* 73, 207, 217, 219, 269–70.

730 Discord, quarreling (*OED*).

them, *That, if they* [267] *would love and serve God, they should shortly go to his House, where they should be happy for ever.*

When he saw some *Indians* drunk, he asked, *What was the Matter with them?* and being informed, he manifested a great Abhorrence of their Wickedness. And one Day hearing that there were some *Indians* drinking at House near by, he asked, *where his Grandfather was?* and being answered, that he was at home, he expressed his Joy at it, and said, *That his Grandfather should not drink, as other* Indians *do, for he was a* Mannittoomp, i.e. A Man of God, *and God would be greatly offended at it if he drank to Excess.* He also desired his own Parents to abstain from the Sin of Drunkenness, to which he saw many addicted.

He told his Father and Mother, *That they ought to be always very kind to old Men and Women; for* (said he) *they belong to God, and God has a great respect for them, and will be angry with you if you slight them, and do not carry well towards them.* And he now mentioned in particular one old and good Man that used to come to the House, as one that he would have kindly treated.

When this Child received any Benefit, he used to acknowledge that it was God that bestowed the same upon him, and would bless and praise him for it; thus he used to bless God for his Food when he received it, and to call him a *good God* on the account of it.

The Relations of this Child frequently heard him *calling upon the Lord* for his Mercy; and do affirm, that in his Prayers he used to mention all the Persons in the adorable *Trinity,* asking the Favours for which he prayed in the *Name of Christ,* to be communicated by the *Holy Spirit.* And that he distinctly prayed, *that he might be fitted to dwell in the House of God, and then go to it.* He had once asked his Grandmother, *Whether any sinful or unclean thing could be in God's House?* meaning Heaven: and being informed by her, that there could not, he probably from thence saw it needful so to pray.

At the very first of his being taken ill, about a Fortnight before he dy'd, he earnestly desired his Grandmother to lay him into a Chest that stood in the House, without any Lid to it, that he might go to sleep in it. To please the Child she did as he desired; but as soon as he was laid down, he looked on her with a smiling Coun[268]tenance, and said, *As you now see me laid in the Chest, into which you have put me, so you will very soon see me laid in another,* (meaning a Coffin) *whereinto I shall be put and buried.*

In the former Part of his Sickness he talked much of God and Heaven, and expressed earnest Desires of leaving the World, and going to the House of God, for so Heaven was constantly called by him: yet he seemed to have something lying on his Mind, that did still much afflict him; nor did he long conceal it, that the foresaid Contentions of his Parents was the thing that did so trouble him. But now the *Indian* Minsiter before mentioned, being sent for to pray with him, and knowing what Burden the Child was under, on the Account mentioned, would not go to Prayer in the afflicted Family, till he had first laboured to convince the Parents of the distressed Child, of the Sinfulness of those Jars of theirs, whereby God was greatly dishonoured, and on the Account whereof their poor sick Child was sorely afflicted. And the Effect of this Essay was, that they both confessed their Sins and Error therein, and made Promises, that they would endeavour to live more peaceably for the future.

The Minister having succeeded so well in his Essay to make Peace in the Family, prayed with the sick Child, who was now very low and weak: he also recommended to God the Affair in which he had just then been labouring with some Appearance of Success. But while he thus prayed, the Parents of the Child sitting by him, one of them on the one side, the other of them on the other side, the Child stretched out his Hands, with one of them laying hold on the Hand of his Father, and with the other on the Hand of his Mother, and then pulled their Hands together, and put them one into the other; which having done, he let them go again, as if he had accomplished what he desired.

After this the Child appeared very much refreshed and comforted, but still expressed earnest Desires to die, and go to the House of the Lord. He very frequently thanked and blessed God for sending that Sickness upon him: and when his Pain grew stronger, he would renew his Thanksgiving, and would still speak of his Sickness as the Messenger of God, sent to call him out of this World to the House of God, unto which he desired to be gone. Once he held up his Hand, and beckoned with it, as tho [269] he desired that some Person would come to him; and being asked why he did so? he said, *he desired that God would come and take him home to his own House.* Soon after this he dy'd: and 'tis to be hoped, that, according to his Desire, he went to the House of the Lord, there to dwell for evermore.

EXAMPLE XXI.
JESSE QUANNOOHUH, *who died* June 5th, 1724, *when he was seven Years and about two Months old.*

THE Boy of whom I here speak was a Child of religious Parents, who gave him up to God in Baptism while he was an Infant, *viz. Jeremiah Quanoohuh,* and his Wife *Hannah*[731] of *Okokame,* alias *Christian-Town.*

---

731 Hannah was sued for stealing by Zachriah Papamick in 1727 but was acquitted. *WGH*, 347, 114. Zachriah was the son of John Papamek and probably Nahpunnetau, both of whom are mentioned on in *IC,* 217. *WGH,* 103, 340.

He was put to School to learn to read while young, and made good Progress therein, as long as the School continued; but that failing for a while, before there was another for him to go to, he fell into that languishing Distemper whereof he dy'd.

Observing while he lay sick, that his Parents were apt to contend one with another, without any just Cause, he told them that he was greatly troubled, and feared that he should not be saved. His Mother asking what the reason of his Fear was? he told her, he feared he should suffer for the Sin of which his Father and she were guilty in their Contentions, *You often,* said he, *contend about nothing, so that the House is defiled thereby.* Upon the hearing of this his Parents were so affected, as to promise to endeavour to reform, and prayed their little Son to forgive them; at which he appeared to be greatly comforted.

Being apprehensive, after be had been sick a while, that he was like to die, he of his own accord sent for *Hosea Manhut,*[732] an *Indian* Minister of the said Place, to come and pray with him, and, as he himself expressed it, *to receive him, and give him up to Jesus Christ.* Hosea being come, asked him, if he believed the Being of God? *Yes, I do,* said the Child to him. Where is he? said *Hosea* to him. *In Heaven,* said the Child, holding up his Hand. *Hosea,* Do you believe that Jesus Christ is the Son of God? *Jesse, Yes, I do. Hosea,* Where is Christ? *Jesse, In Heaven. Hosea,* Do you believe that he is able to save you? *Jesse, I do so believe.* And do you, said [270] *Hosea,* desire that he should so do? Yes, said the Child, *I do desire it.*

After this Confession of Faith, *Hosea* received him as a believing Child, and prayed, that Christ would also receive him, as the Child desired he should.

Hosea being some time after this, on a *Lord's-Day,* betwixt the fore and afternoon's Exercises,[733] sent for to pray with him, I being then at that Place went with him; and before he prayed put several Questions to the Child then very sick and weak, in order to my knowing what Knowledge of God, and Sense of Religion he had in him. And by his Answers, which much exceeded my Expectations, I found that he was not ignorant of those great Truths, the Knowledge whereof are ordinarily necessary to Salvation. He satisfied me, that he believed the Being of the only true God, by whom all things are created that do exist: also the Doctrine of the Immortality of the Soul, and of eternal Rewards and Punishments either in Heaven or Hell, after this Life, he appeared to have a lively Apprehension of. He conceived of Heaven as the Place where the blessed and glorious God was himself graciously present; but

---

732 *IC,* 72, 207, 217, 219, 266.
733 I.e., between ministerial duties at Sabbath services (*OED*).

Hell he conceived of, as the Place of Devils and wicked Men, where they must be tormented for ever.

He was not ignorant of that Estate of Sin and Guilt, into which all Mankind have fallen. And he acknowledged himself a sinful Creature, that needed Pardon and Cleansing.

The Doctrine of Redemption by Christ he appeared not to be ignorant of, but acknowledged him to be the only Saviour of Sinners. He owned[734] his Divinity, as being the Son of God; also his Incarnation, Obedience, and Sufferings for Sinners, &c.

He understood that the Benefits purchased by Christ were not promiscuously applied to Mankind; but that they are only repenting and believing Sinners that are made Partakers of them.[735]

He professed his Desire to be interested in the Redemption purchased by Christ, and that he might be qualified to receive them.

This Child was not indeed able in a suitable Language to express these things; and indeed his bodily Weakness was such that he could not have done it, had he been otherwise capable of it, but being tried by [271] Questions, the most whereof either yea or nay was a sufficient Answer to, he gave very proper Answers to the most of them, and such as made it evident that he had been well taught; and I before knew that he had been instructed in his Catechism.

After the *Indian* Pastor mentioned had prayed with him, I could not but observe, that he seemed to be sensibly revived, and was much better able to speak than he was before.

I then asked him whether he did not expect to die within a little while? To which he answered, that he did. I again asked him, whether he was willing to die, and leave this World, and all the Enjoyments in it? Unto which he replied, that he was. I asked him, whether he hoped that God would save him, and that he should go to Heaven when he dy'd? To which his Answer was affirmative. I asked him, whether he was sensible of his Sins, and grieved that he had sinned so much against God as he had? To which he said, that he was. I further inquired of him, whether he himself ever called upon God for his Salvation? Unto which he answering, that he did, his Parents bare Witness to the Truth of what he said, declaring, that they had sometimes heard him calling on the Name of the Lord, and that before he was sick, and not since only. And a very credible Person that sometimes was in the House, did also give that Testimony.

A few Days before this Child dy'd, I went again to visit him, but he was then so weak that he could say little to me, only he answered some

---

734 Acknowledged (*OED*).

735 The doctrine of limited atonement.

Questions that I put to him, thereby giving me to understand, that being sensible of his Sins, he trusted in Christ as his only Saviour, and prayed to God for Pardon and eternal Life thro' him, and had such a Hope of receiving the same on his Account, that he was very willing to die, and leave the World, and all things in it; yea, that he chose to die rather than live, and should not be unwilling to die tho it were then immediately, but yet was content to live longer if God pleased that he should so do.

His Father and Mother have both declared to me, that he used frequently to call upon them to teach him to pray to God; and that they, according to his Desire, furnishing of him with the best of Expressions they could, to address himself to the Lord in, he still as soon as he [272] had learned them, improved them to the end for which he desired to be taught them, using them in Prayer to the Lord his God.

Thus calling on the Name of the Lord, it is to be hoped that he is saved.

EXAMPLE XXII.
DEBORAH SISSETOM, *who died at* Sanchekantacket
February 12, 1724, *in the* 15th *Year of her Age.*

THIS *Deborah* was a Daughter of *Caleb Sissetom*[736] and his Wife, of the Place already mentioned. Her Mother, who dy'd within less than two Years before her, made, as many hoped, a good End, being very penitent, and seeking earnestly to God for Mercy in the time of her Sickness.

The Grandmother of this young Maid was a very pious Woman, who is yet living; and this good Woman had for her Father a godly *Indian* Minister formerly mention'd, (*Chap.* 1. *Examp.* 5.)[737] as one that prayed very earnestly to God for his Offspring when he was dying.

A little above a Year before this young Woman dy'd, I went to her Father's House, on purpose to visit the Family, and inform my self what Knowledge of God and Sense of Religion there was in it; but when I came thither, I found none but Children in the House; and of these this Maid, of whom I then knew nothing that was remarkable, was the eldest.

Providence ordering it thus, I resolved to say something to them; and directing my Speech to the said *Deborah*, and putting some such

736 Caleb Sissetom was the brother of Abel Sissetom and Oggin [Haukkings] Sissetom (*IC*, 184, 255), hence also the brother-in-law of Hannah Sissetom (*IC*, 184). Caleb was probably the son of Thomas Sussetom, an Indian minister, and he was the father of Joseph Seatom (who owned land in Farm Neck, and was probably the father of Robert and John Seatom) and the grandfather of Caleb Setom. Caleb Sr. was a justice at Sanchakantacket, 1752–55, and also a debtor. *WGH*, 101, 122, 137, 220, 254–55, 279.

737 Wunnanauhkomun (*IC*, 18–20*).

Questions to her as I thought proper, she answered me very discreetly to them all, and appeared to be exceeding serious in what she said. I found she understood the first Principles of the Christian Religion, and she professed that she believed them; and she seemed to have an affecting Sense of the Excellency and Importance of what she said she did believe. She affirmed she had Desires after God, and was a Seeker of him. When I instructed and counselled her, she was much affected with what I said; and when I went away, gave me very hearty Thanks for the Instructions I had given her.

[273] I observed at this time, that she appeared to be unhealthy, and I heard a while after that her Friends feared she was falling into a Consumption: however, I did not see and speak with her again, till at least a Year after I had my first Discourse with her; but hearing that she was grown worse, and was like to die, I again visited her, and I shall here set down the Substance of what she said to me, chiefly in answer to such Questions as I then put to her.

She said she remembred the Discourse which I formerly had with her, and said she had been thereby encouraged to seek after God, and she manifested a Desire that I would further instruct her.

I then put many Questions to her for the Trial of her Understanding, and found she well understood the Principles of the Christian Faith; as the Doctrine of Original Sin, the Guilt which it brought on all Mankind, and the Depravation of the humane Nature by it, by which Man is now naturally inclined to that which is evil only, and that continually. She owned, that from this corrupt Fountain all those actual Sins do flow, which Mankind commit, and said, her own Sins had been very many and great.

I found also that she had a distinct Understanding of the Doctrine of Redemption by Jesus Christ. I put several Questions to her concerning his Person, Offices, and the Righteousness he fulfilled in his Obedience and Sufferings for Sinners; all which she answered well, and declared her Belief of his Resurrection from the dead, and Ascension into Heaven, &c.

I likewise found that she understood the Doctrine of Regeneration, and the absolute Necessity of it, in order to the eternal Salvation of Sinners. She owned, that without Holiness of Heart and Life, none could have any saving Benefit by Jesus Christ, or ever enter into the Kingdom of God.

She declared, that the Mercy of God in giving his Son to die for Sinners, and his, in undertaking the Work of our Redemption, was exceeding great, and that Mankind are thereby brought under the strongest Obligations to love God, and not to live to themselves, but to him that dy'd for them.

She declared to me that she repented of all her Sins, and endeavoured to forsake them; and that she [274] Prayed earnestly to God for Christ's sake to pardon them all, and to give her a new Heart; and that God would please to continue to her the use of her Reason as long as he continued her Life, that so she might be able to think of him.

She said she used to pray in secret to God before she was sick, but that she had especially since her Sickness prayed earnestly to him.

She said also, she had taken delight in going to Meeting, and hearing the Word of God preached; and had sometimes been much affected with what she heard, so as to be afraid of Sin and Hell.

She said, she hoped she had a sincere Love to Jesus Christ, that she was grieved at the Miscarriages[738] of those who sinned against him, and had a Desire that all People would obey and serve him.

She said, she hoped she had experienced the sanctifying Influences of God's Spirit on her Soul, working good Affections and Desires in her; and that she was willing to die whenever it should please God to remove her out of this World, as firmly hoping she should obtain Life eternal; and that when lately she thought she was dying, she was not surprized with the Thoughts of her Change, but had Peace and Comfort in her Soul.

She desired me to pray with her before I left her, and to ask of God the Pardon of all her Sins, and that he would please to continue to her the use of her Understanding as long as she lived.

Having done as she desired, she expressed much Thankfulness to me for the Pains I had taken for her Good, and so I took my leave of her.

After this, I saw and discoursed with her divers times before she died, and always found her in such a frame as has been expressed. She said that her Desire of being freed from Sin, unto which she was subject while she was here, and to enjoy the Blessedness of the Heavenly World, caused her to desire Death rather than Life; and tho her outward Circumstances were very mean, yet she seemed to me to be rich in Faith, and to enjoy great Peace in believing.

Her Relations affirm, that she used to pray in secret Places, having several times found her alone, pouring out her Heart before the Lord with many Tears.

[275] Not having been baptized in her Infancy,[739] she desired to have received that Seal[740] before she died; but Providence denying her an Opportunity for it, she expressed her Submission to the Will of God with respect thereto.

---

738 Instances of misconduct or misbehavior (*OED*).

739 The significance of baptism was debated in New England: some argued that it conveyed "saving grace," whereas others saw it as "an element of nurture." Either way, it was a comfort to parents: Cotton Mather, for example, assured his readers in *Baptismal piety* (1727) that "if children who were baptized died as infants, 'They shall none of them be lost, as minute as they are.'" Quoted in Hall, *Worlds of Wonder*, 155.

740 Baptism was also considered a token or symbol of the covenant with God (*OED*).

She was very sensible of the Approaches of Death, as the time of her Departure drew near. She called often upon God for his Mercy; and as she had Opportunity, desired others to pray with her.

She gave much good Counsel to her Relatives, and told them that she was willing, yea desirous to die, as being weary of this World, and as longing to be with her Saviour: And it is to be hoped that she went to him.

Conclusion of Chap. IV.

THERE have been many other young Persons among our *Indians,* who have been thought to die well: But not being able to give a particular Account of them, I shall add no more to the Instances already given, in some of whom that Word has been very observably fulfilled: *Out of the Mouth of Babes and Sucklings hast thou ordained Strength, because of the Enemies, that thou mightest still the Enemy and the Avenger.*[741]

---

741 Psalm 8:2.

[277] SOME
ACCOUNT
OF THOSE
ENGLISH MINISTERS
WHO

Have successively presided over the Work of Gospelizing
the *Indians* on *Martha's Vineyard*, and the adjacent Islands.

By another Hand.[742]
Exemplo monstrante Viam. Manil.

LONDON,
Printed in the Year M.DCC.XXVII.
[279] SOME
ACCOUNT
OF THOSE
ENGLISH MINISTERS

Who have successively presided over the Work of Gospelizing the Indians *on
the* Vineyard, *and adjacent Islands: By whose special Care and Labour it was
at first begun, and has been carried on and continued down to this Day.*

THE worthy *Collector* of the foregoing Instances having very well
expressed his Concern that GOD may have the Glory of his Works of
Grace upon that People, it must needs be very fitting there should now
be some Account of those more principal *English* Instruments, which
Heaven has been pleased to qualify, and inspire with Zeal for this difficult Employment, and then to crown and honour with such remarkable
Successes. And as the Author happens to be restrained from publishing a
just Account of these, by his near Relation to them, and his commendable
Modesty, it is but Gratitude and Justice that *some other* Hand should now
take the Pen, and draw something of those worthy Gentlemen, who have
chiefly laboured in this Evangelick Service, and by whose Care and Pains
such happy Fruits have sprung and grown.

---

742 Thomas Prince (1687–1758), the minister of Old South Church (Boston). He was one of
the greatest of New England book collectors. After his death, his library went to Old South
Church and later to the Boston Public Library. See Hill, *History of the Old South Church*, 1:386–
95, 2:42–44.

This I shall therefore, with all Faithfulness and convenient Brevity, endeavour, partly from several Books and Pamphlets published both in *Old England* and *New*, [280] partly from two or three Manuscripts of Credit I have now in my Hands, and partly from my own Enquiries and Informations of the living.

Mr. *Thomas Mayhew senior*, coming over as a Merchant to the *Massachusets*, in the early times of that Plantation, and meeting with Disappointments in his Business, he first purchases a Farm at *Watertown*, and applies himself to Husbandry: and then in 1641 he procures a Grant or Patent of Sir *Ferdinando Gorges*, the Earl of *Sterling's* Agent, for *Martha's Vineyard, Nantucket*, and *Elizabeth* Isles, to make an *English* Settlement, &c.

In 1642, he sends Mr. *Thomas Mayhew junior*, his only Son, being then a young Scholar about 21 Years of Age, with some other Persons, to the *Vineyard*, where they settled at the East End; and quickly after the *Father* followed, and became their Governor. But because the Son appears to be the first that laboured in the *Indian* Service, on those Islands, I shall therefore here begin with *him*.

EXAMPLE I.
The Reverend Mr. THOMAS MAYHEW junior, *the only Son of the worshipful* Thomas Mayhew *Esq*.

HE was a young Gentleman of liberal Education, and of such Repute for Piety as well as natural and acquired Gifts, having no small Degree of Knowledge in the *Latin* and *Greek* Languages, and being not wholly a Stranger to the *Hebrew*, that soon after their Settlement on the Island, the new Plantation called him to the Ministry among them.

But his *English* Flock being then but small, the Sphere was not large enough for so bright a Star to move in. With great Compassion he beheld the wretched *Natives*, who then were *several thousands* on those Islands, perishing in utter Ignorance of the *true GOD*, and eternal Life, labouring under strange Delusions, Inchantments, and panick Fears of *Devils*, whom they most passionately worshipped, and in such a miserable Case as those *Eph*. ii. 12. *Without CHRIST, being Aliens from the Commonwealth of* Israel, *and Strangers from the Covenants of Promise, having no Hope, and without God in* [281] *the World*. But GOD, who had ordained him an Evangelist for the Conversion of these *Indian Gentiles*,[743] stirred

---

743 The Puritans saw themselves as "New Israelites." The author's emphasis on the Wampanoags as Gentiles and *"Aliens from the Commonwealth of* Israel, *and Strangers from the Covenants of Promise"* distinguishes him from missionaries who thought that Indians were one of the lost tribes of Israel.

him up with an holy Zeal and Resolution, to labour their Illumination and Deliverance.

He first endeavours to get acquainted with them, and then earnestly applies himself to learn their *Language*. He treats them in a condescending and friendly manner. He denys himself, and does his utmost to oblige and help them. He takes all Occasions to insinuate and show the sincere and tender Love and Goodwill he bare them; and as he grows in their Acquaintance and Affection, he proceeds to express his great Concern and Pity for their *immortal Souls*. He tells them of their deplorable Condition under the Power of malicious *Devils*, who not only kept them in Ignorance of those earthly good things, which might render their Lives in this World much more comfortable, but of those also which might bring them to eternal Happiness in the World to come; what a kind and mighty GOD the *English* served, and how the *Indians* might happily come into his Favour and Protection.

The first *Indian* that embraced the Motion of forsaking their false Gods, and adoring the true one, was *Hiacoomes*, which was in the Year 1643; an Account of whom we therefore have in the first of the foregoing *Examples*.[744] This *Indian* living near the *English* Settlement,[745] quickly grew into an Acquaintance with them. And being a Man of a sober, thoughtful, and ingenuous Spirit, he not only visited their Houses, but also their publick and religious Meetings; at which time Mr. *Mayhew* took particular Notice of him, discoursed often with him, invited him to his House every *Lord's-day* at Evening, gave him a clear Account of the Nature, Reasonableness, and Importance of the *Christian* Faith, and quickly brought him to a firm and resolute Adherence to it.

Mr. *Mayhew* having gained *Hiacoomes*, he first imploys him as a faithful Instrument to prepare his Way to the rest of the *Natives*, instructing him more and more in this new Religion, showing him how to recommend it to them, and to answer all their Arguments and Objections against it. And then in 1644, he proceeds to visit and discourse them *himself*, carrying a greater and more irresistible Light and Evidence with him. And whereas at first he could not hope to be heard in *pub[282]lick*, he therefore begins to instruct them in a more *private* way, sometimes going to the Houses of those he esteemed most rational and well qualified, and at other times treating with particular Persons.

And as Mr. *Mayhew* endeavoured the Good of these Heathens, by discoursing with as many as were willing to have any Conference with him, so with *Hiacoomes* in particular, whom he from time to time directed to

---

744 *IC*, 1–12*.
745 Edgartown.

communicate the Knowledge received to those that Mr. *Mayhew* could not so easily meet with. And thus they united their Counsels, and wrought together, and by the Blessing of GOD soon gained some others.

But that which especially favoured the Progress of Religion among them, was a *universal Sickness,*[746] wherewith they were visited in the *following Year;* wherein it was observed by the Heathen *Indians* themselves, that those who hearkened to Mr. *Mayhew's* pious Instructions did not taste so deeply of it, and *Hiacoomes* and his Family in a manner nothing at all. This put the *Natives* who lived within six Miles of the *English,*[747] upon serious Consideration about this Matter, being much affected, that he who had professed the *Christian* Religion, and had thereby exposed himself to much Reproach and Trouble, should receive more Blessings than they: whereupon *Myoxeo*[748] the chief Man of that Place, and *Towanquatick*[749] the *Sagamore,*[750] with many others, sent for *Hiacoomes* to tell them what he knew of *the God* which the *English* worshipped.

At this very Meeting, which was in 1646, *Myoxeo* was happily enlightened, and turned to chuse and acknowledge *this God* for his own; and *Towanquatick* soon after, encouraged by some others, desired Mr. *Mayhew* to give them a publick Meeting, to make known to them the Word of GOD in their own Tongue: and, among other Incitements, addressed him thus,—*You shall be to us as one that stands by a running River, filling many Vessels; even so shall you fill us with everlasting Knowledge.* So Mr. *Mayhew* undertook to give them a Meeting once a *Month;* but as soon as the first Exercise was over, they desired it oftener than he could well attend: however, once a *Fortnight* was the settled Course; and as this was [283] the *first* publick Audience among them, so from hence, both Mr. *Mayhew* on the Week-days Lecture, and *Hiacoomes* on the *Sabbaths,* were constantly heard in *publick* as long as they lived.

However, Mr. *Mayhew* here met with three very great *Obstacles:* for, (1.) Many strongly stood for their own Meetings, Ways and Customs, as being in their account much more advantageous and agreeable than ours, wherein they have nothing but talking and praying, and this in a manner too still and sober for them. (2.) Others alledged, that the *Sagamores* were generally against this new Way. But the (3.) and greatest of all was, how they should come off from the *Pawaws.*[751] This was the strongest Cord

---

746 A smallpox epidemic ravaged the New England tribes in 1643 (Bragdon, *Native People of Southern New England,* 26), which, together with that of 1645, may have reduced the Wampanoag population on Martha's Vineyard by half: Silverman, *Faith and Boundaries,* 22.

747 In Nunpang (*IC,* 76).

748 Spelled "Miohqsoo" by Mayhew (*IC,* 5, 38, 76–80*, 152).

749 Spelled "Tawanquatuck" by Mayhew (*IC,* 5, 77, 80–82*).

750 *A sovereign Prince.* [Prince's note.]

751 *Such as cure, or hurt and kill by diabolick* Sorcery, *and to whom sometimes the* Devil *appears.* [Prince's note.]

that bound them;[752] for the *Pawaws*, by their diabolical Sorceries, kept them in the most slavish Fear and Subjection to them. There were about twelve at the Meeting who were halting between two Opinions, and others only came to see and hear what was done: for tho they had heard something of the ONE GOD of Heaven, yet such was their unspeakable Darkness and Bondage to Sin and the *Pawaws*, that they durst not for Fear desert them: and tho a few were better enlightned, yet the *Natives* round about stuck fast in their Brutishness.

The *Sagamore Towanquatick* was exceeding malign'd by them, and in 1647 his Life was villanously attempted for his favouring the *Christian* Religion:[753] but his great Deliverance, with a due Reflection on the Villany, the rather confirmed him in it, and inflamed him with the more active Zeal to espouse and assert it; and the Meeting went on to the Joy of some *Indians*, and the Envy of the rest, who derided and scoffed at those who attended the Lecture, and blasphemed *the God* whom they worshipped, which very much damped the Spirits of some for a time in his Ways, and hindered others from looking towards them. But *Towanquatick* and *Hiacoomes* were inspired with a wonderful Courage and Constancy: And [284] in the *following Year* had a *general Meeting* of all that were inclined for *Christianity*, to confirm and assist one another in their abiding by it.

This Assembly was held in Mr. *Mayhew's* Presence, and therein he tells us, that twelve of the young Men went and took *Sacochanimo*,[754] *Towanquatick's* eldest Son, by the Hand, telling him, *They loved him, and would go with him in GOD's Way*; and the elder Men encouraged them, and desired them never to forget these Promises. And so after they had eaten, and sang part of a *Psalm* in their own Language, and Mr. *Mayhew* had prayed, they returned home with Expressions of great Joy and Thankfulness.

The next Year there was a greater *Convention*, wherein was a mixt Multitude, both of *Infidel* and *Christian Indians*, and those who were in doubt of Christianity; but Mr. *Mayhew* it seems was not now present. In this Assembly the dreadful Power of the *Pawaws* was publickly debated, many asserting their Power to hurt and kill, and alledging numerous Instances that were evident and undoubted among them: and then some asking aloud, *Who is there that does not fear them?* others reply'd, *There is not a Man that does not.* Upon which *Hiacoomes* breaks forth, and boldly

---

752 A figure of speech derived from the Bible: see Job 36:8; Judges 15:13; Psalm 118:27.

753 *See the* Story *in Mr.* T. Mayhew's *Letter of* September 7, 1650. *Printed at* London 1651. *and in Mr.* E. Mayhew's Indian Converts, Chap. II. [Prince's note.]

754 Sacochanimo also appears in *Native Writings*, 1:245; and *HMV* 1:216. He was the father of the squaw-sachem Elizabeth Washaman and the brother of Wunnappushkkattoosq. *WGH*, 124–25, 296, 284.

declares, that *tho the* Pawaws *might hurt those who feared them, yet he believed and trusted in the GREAT GOD of Heaven and Earth, and therefore all the* Pawaws *together could do him no Harm, and he feared them not.* At which they all exceedingly wondred, and expected some dreadful thing to befal him; but observing he remained unhurt, they began to esteem him happy in being delivered from their terrible Power. Several of the Assembly declared they now believed in the *same God* too, and would be afraid of the *Pawaws* no more: and desired *Hiacoomes* to tell them what this GREAT GOD would have them to do, and what were the things that offended him; he immediately fell to Prayer and Preaching, and by a rare and happy Invention, he readily discovered and mentioned forty five or fifty sorts of *Sins* committed among them, and as many contrary *Duties* neglected; which so amazed and touched their Consciences, that at the End of the Meeting there were twenty two *Indians* who resolved against those Evils, and to walk with GOD, and attend his Word, among whom was *Momonequem*, a Son of one of the principal [285] *Indians*, who some time after became a Preacher, and of whom we may read in the *second Example.*[755]

And now in 1650, comes on the critical Point of the Credit and Power of the *Pawaws* among them: for *Hiacoomes* thus openly renouncing and protesting against the false Gods he had worshipped, with all the *Pawaws* their familiar Ministers; and with an amazing Courage, despising and defying their Power, the *Pawaws* were greatly enrag'd, and threatened his utter Destruction; but to their own and their Peoples Surprize and Confusion, were unable to hurt him.

Mr. *Mayhew* improves the Advantage, and redoubles his Diligence, is incessant in his pious Endeavour: And now, while many are in doubt of their way, he offers to show them the right one; he spares not his Body either by Day or by Night: He readily travels and lodges in their smoky *Wigwams*,[756] when he usually spends a great part of the Night in relating the ancient Stories of GOD in the *Scriptures*, which were very surprizing and entertaining to them, and in other Discourse which he conceives most proper. He proposes such things to their Consideration which he thinks firstly requisite: he fairly solves their subtle Objections, and tells them they might plainly see, it was purely in good will to them, from whom he could expect no Reward, that he spent so much Time and Pains, and endured so much Cold and Wet, Fatigue and Trouble.

---

755 *IC*, 12–14*.

756 Indian Dwellings, *like* Tents, *framed with small Poles set in a Ring, bowed inwards, tied above, and covered with* Bark *or* Matts; *with a Hole at the top to let out the Smoke from the Fire in the midst of the Ground at the bottom.* [Prince's note.] For superb colonial illustrations of New England wigwams, see Ezra Stiles's diagrams reprinted in Plane, *Colonial Intimacies*, 108–9.

But as GOD was pleased to animate,[757] uphold and preserve him, so also quickly to give a growing *Success* to his painful Labours.

For soon after, an *Indian* standing up at the *Lecture,* confessed his Sins, declared his Repentance and Desire to forsake them, and to go in GOD's Way; and then going to *Towanquatick,* took him by the Hand, and in his native Simplicity said, *I love you, and do greatly desire to go along with you for GOD's sake:* the same he said to some others; and then coming to Mr. *Mayhew* he said, *I pray you to love me, and I do love you, and desire to go with you for GOD's sake;* upon which they ⌈286⌉ received him with Gladness of Heart. After this, there came five Men more; and by the *End of the Summer,* there were thirty nine *Indian Men* of this Meeting, who had not only the Knowledge of the main Points of Religion, and professed their Belief of them, but had also solemnly entered into a *Covenant* to live agreeably to them: Besides the well-instructed and believing *Women,* who were supposed to exceed the number of the *Men,* tho they had not yet entered the *Covenant.*

Mr. *Mayhew's* way in Publick now is, by a *Lecture* every *Fortnight,* whereto both Men, Women and Children come; and first he prays, then preaches, then catechizes, then sings a *Psalm,* and all in their own Language. After Sermon, he generally spends more time than in the Sermon it self, in a more familiar Reasoning with them. And every *Saturday* Morning, he confers with *Hiacoomes* more privately about his subject matter of preaching to the *Natives* on both the Parts of the following Day; Mr. *Mayhew* directing him in the choice of his Text, and in the Management of it.

About this time, *viz.* the *End of the Summer,* the Rev. Mr. *Henry Whitfeld,*[758] Pastor of the Church at *Guildford New England,* in his Voyage to *Boston,* in order to his Return to *England,* happened to put in at the *Vineyard,* and to stay there ten Days.

There he tells us, he found a small Plantation, and an *English* Church gathered, whereof this Mr. *Mayhew* was Pastor; that he had attained a good Understanding in the *Indian* Tongue, could speak it well, and had laid the first Foundation of the Knowledge of CHRIST among the *Natives* there, by preaching, &c.

Mr. *Whitfeld* attends Mr. *Mayhew* to a more private *Indian* Meeting, and the next Day to the *Indian* Lecture, where Mr. *Mayhew* preached; and then catechiz'd the *Indian* Children, who answered readily and modestly

---

757 To give spirit, inspire (*OED*).

758 Author of *The light appearing more and more towards the perfect day* (1651); *Some helpes to stir up to Christian duties Wherein is explained the nature of the duty of stirring up our selves* (1634); and *Strength out of weaknesse* (1652).

in the Principles of Religion; some of them answering in *English*, and others in the *Indian* Tongue: And then Mr. *Whitfeld* adds the following Lines.—

Thus having seen a short Model of his Way, and of the Pains he took, I made some Inquiry about Mr. Mayhew *himself, and about his* Subsistence; *because I saw but a small and slender Appearance of outward Conveniences of Life in any comfortable way: The Man himself was modest, and I could get little from him; but after, I un[287]derstood from others how short things were with him, and how he was many times forced to labour with his own Hands, having a* Wife and three small Children, *who depended upon him to provide Necessaries for them; having* not half *so much yearly coming in, in a settled way, as an ordinary Labourer gets there among them; yet he is chearful amidst these Straits, and none hear him complain.* The Truth is, *he will not leave the Work in which his Heart is engaged; for on my Knowledge, if he would have left the Work, and employed himself other where, he might have had a more competent and comfortable* Maintenance. *I mention this the rather, because I have some hope, that some pious Mind who reads this, might be inwardly mov'd to consider his Condition and come to his Succour, for his Encouragement in this great Work.*

Thus—Mr. *Whitfeld*—But quickly after he left Mr. *Mayhew*, there happened a thing which amaz'd the whole Island, and turned to the great and speedy Advancement of the *Christian* Religion.

For it pleased GOD, who had drawn the *Indians* from the *Pawaws* to worship himself, whereat the *Pawaws* were greatly offended; yet now to persuade even *two* of themselves to run after those who sought him, and desire they might also go with them in the ways of *that God* whose name is JEHOVAH. They came very deeply convinced of the Sins they had liv'd in, and especially *Pawawing*; revealing the diabolical Mysteries, and expressing the utmost Repentance and Detestation of them; intreating that GOD would have Mercy upon them, pardon their Sins, and teach them his Ways, for CHRIST JESUS his sake. And very affecting it was to Mr. *Mayhew* and all who were present,

To see these poor naked Sons of Adam, *and Slaves to the Devil from the Birth, to come towards the Lord as they did,[759] with their Joints shaking and their Bowels trembling; their Spirits troubled, and their Voices with much Fervency uttering Words of sore Displeasure against Sin and Satan, which they had embraced from their Childhood with* [288] *great Delight.* And now accounting it also their Sin that they had not the Knowledge of GOD, that they had served the *Devil*, the great Enemy both of GOD and Man, and had been so hurtful in their Lives; but yet

---

759 *Mr.* T. Mayhew's *Words in his* Letter *of* Octob. 16. 1651, *published at* London *in* 1652. [Prince's note.]

being very thankful that thro' the Mercy of GOD they they had an Opportunity to be delivered out of their dangerous Condition.

The *Christian Indians* exceedingly rejoic'd to see the *Pawaws* begin to turn from their wicked Ways to the Lord; and in a little time after, on a *Lecture-Day*, at the close of the Exercise, there were several more of the *Natives* who expressed their Desire to become the Servants of the MOST HIGH GOD; among whom was *Tequanonim*,[760] another *Pawaw* of great Esteem and very notorious. And now indeed both the common *Indians*, and the *Pawaws* themselves, began to observe and confess, that since the *Gospel* had been preached to them, the *Pawaws* had been very much foil'd in their diabolical Essays;[761] and instead of curing as formerly, they now had rather killed many.

At the *same time* there came pressing in about *fifty Indians* more in *one Day*, desiring to join with the Worshippers of GOD in his Service, confessing their *Sins*; some—those actual ones they had liv'd in, and others—the Naughtiness of their Hearts: Desiring to be made better; and for this end, to attend on the *Word of God*, and looking only to CHRIST for Salvation. And upon this occasion, Mr. *Mayhew* observes that they generally came in by *Families*; the *Parents* also bringing their *Children* with them, saying, *I have brought my Children too, I would have my Children serve God with us, I desire that this Son and this Daughter may worship JEHOVAH*. And if they could but speak, their Parents would have them say something to shew their Willingness to serve the LORD: and when the *Commandments* were repeated, they all acknowledged them to be good, and made choice of JEHOVAH to be *their God*, promising by his Help to walk according to his Counsels. And when they were received by those that were before in this *General Covenant*, it was by loud Voices, giving Thanks to GOD that they were met together in the ways of JEHOVAH.

This was all before the End of the Year 1650.

[289] And by the midst of *October* 1651, there were *one hundred ninety nine* Men, Women and Children, who had professed themselves to be Worshippers of the great and ever-living GOD. And now there were *two* Meetings kept every *Lord's Day*, the one three Miles, the other about eight from Mr. *Mayhew*'s House. *Hiacoomes* taught twice a day at the nearest, and *Mononequem* as often at the farthest: On every *Saturday* they both came to Mr. *Mayhew* to be informed and instructed in the Subject they were to treat of, and GOD greatly assisted them. And Mr. *Mayhew*

---

760 *IC*, 13, 297.

761 Trials or experiments; hostile attempts (*OED*).

had then undertaken, by divine Assistance, to keep *two* several *Lectures* among them, which would be at each Assembly once a Fortnight.

On *January* 11. 1651-2. Mr. *Mayhew* set up a *School*, to teach the *Natives* to read, *viz.* the Children, and any young Men who were willing to learn, whereof they were very glad: And as there quickly came in about *thirty* Indian *Children*, he found them apt to learn; and more and more were coming in every Day.

In the *Spring* of the Year 1652, the *Indians*, of their own accord made a Motion to Mr. *Mayhew*, that they might have some Method settled among them for the Exercise of *Order and Discipline*, that so they might be obliged to live in a due Subjection to the *Laws* of GOD; whereto they desired to enter into a *Covenant*: they desired him also to inform them what were the *Punishments* which GOD had appointed for those who brake his Laws, to which they were also willing to subject themselves; and that they might have some Men chosen among them, with his *Father* and *himself*, to see that the *Indians* walked in an orderly manner; encouraging those who did so, and dealing with those who did not, according to the Word of GOD.

In order to this, a Day of *Fasting and Prayer* was appointed to repent of their Sins, and seek the divine Presence and Help; and another shortly after, to finish the Work. Being then assembled together, some *Indians* spake for their Excitation, and about ten or twelve of them prayed, as Mr. *Mayhew* describes it,[762] *not with a* [290] *set Form like Children, but like Men indued with a good Measure of the Knowledge of GOD, their own Wants, and the Wants of others, with much Affection, and many spiritual Petitions, favouring of an heavenly Mind.*

The same Morning Mr. *Mayhew* drew up an excellent *Covenant* in their native Language, which he often read and made plain to them: and they all with free Consent and Thankfulness united in it, and desired the Grace and Help of GOD to keep it faithfully; which, were it not for making this Account too large, I should have here inserted. And Mr. *Mayhew* observed, that when they chose their *Rulers*, they made choice of such as were best approved for *Piety*, and most like to suppress all Wickedness, and encourage Goodness; and that afterwards they were upon all Occasions forward to show their earnest Desire of the same.

In short, by the end of *October* 1652, there were *two hundred eighty two* Indians, not counting young Children in the number, who were brought to renounce their *false Gods, Devils and Pawaws*, and publickly, in set Meetings, before many Witnesses, had freely disclaimed and defied their tyrannical Power; yea, *eight* of their *Pawaws* had now forsaken their dia-

---

762 *In his* Letter *of* Octob. 22. 1652, *and published at* London *in* 1653 [Prince's note.]

bolical Craft, and profitable Trade, as they held it, to turn into the ways of GOD. And as not any of these were compelled thereto by Power, so neither were they allured by *Gifts*, having received none from the very Beginning.

Indeed the *Natives* in general observed to their wonder, that the *Christians* were all along exempted from being hurt by the *Pawaws*; even some of the Heathen *Pawaws* themselves at length came to own, that they could not make their Power to seize on a *Christian*: and those who yet were Enemies to the *Christian Indians*, could not but acknowledge that the Blessing of Heaven was in an eminent manner among them. But this was intirely the distinguishing Favour of *Providence*, to recommend this Religion to those who were not otherwise yet induced to see the Excellence of it.

The *praying Indians*, as the *Christianiz'd Indians* were commonly called, being distinguish'd by this pious Exercise, were constant Attenders on the publick Worship; and even the *barbarous Indians*, both Men and Women, came often to Mr. *Mayhew's* Lectures, bewail[291]ing their Ignorance, disliking their sinful Liberty, and seeking Subjection to GOD, to be taught, governed and saved by him, for CHRIST JESUS's sake.

Thus this worthy Gentleman continued his almost inexpressible Labour, and vigilant Care for the Good of the *Indians*, whom he justly esteemed his Joy and Crown. And GOD was pleased to give such a victorious Success to his painful and unwearied Labours, that by the Year 1657, there were *many hundred* Men and Women added to the *Christian Society*, of such as might truly be said to be holy in their Conversation; and for Knowledge, such as needed not to be taught the first Principles of the Oracles of GOD: besides the *many hundreds* of looser and more superficial Professors.

While he was labouring in this blessed Work with indefatigable Pains and Difficulties, expecting no Reward but from him who said, *Go teach all Nations, lo I am with you,*[763] GOD was pleased to move the Hearts of many good People in *England*, who had heard of the same, to advance a considerable Sum, to encourage the Propagation of the Gospel among the *New-England Indians*. And having seen so great a Blessing on his painful Labours, and seeing the Spirit given to sundry *Indians*, with the Gift of Prophesying, according to the Promise made by *him* who *ascended on High, and gave Gifts to Men*; having also an able godly *Englishman*, named *Peter Foulger*,[764] employed in teaching the Youth in Reading, Writing,

763 Matthew 28:19–20.

764 Historian Isaac Backus credits Peter Folger (1617–1690) with instigating the founding of the Wampanoag Baptist church: Backus, *A history of New-England*. When Folger began to preach Anapaptist heresies, he was run off the island in 1662. Silverman, *Faith and Boundaries*, 55, 110–11.

and the Principles of Religion by Catechizing; being well learned likewise in the Scripture, and capable of helping them in religious matters:
And Mr. *Mayhew*, the *Father*, being pretty competently skilled in the
Indian Language, and highly honouring the Labour for their Conversion, whereby, if any Difficulties should arise, they might have suitable
Assistance, in the Year 1657, which was the 37th of his Age, he intended
a short Voyage to *England*, to give a more particular Account of the State
of the *Indians* than he could well do by Letters, and to pursue the most
proper Measures for the further Advancement of Religion among them.

He accordingly took Passage in a Ship, with his *Wife's own Brother*,[765]
and with an *Indian* who was a Preacher among the *Natives*.[766] But alas!
the mysterious Ways of [292] Providence! neither the Ship, nor any of
the Passengers were ever heard of more!—

Thus came to an immature Death Mr. *Mayhew* junior; who was so
affectionately beloved and esteemed of the *Indians*, that they could
not easily bear his Absence so far as *Boston*, before they longed for his
Return; and for many Years after his Departure, he was seldom named
without Tears.

I have my self seen the *Rock* on a descending Ground, upon which he
sometimes used to stand and preach to great numbers crouding to hear
him: And the *Place* on the Way-side, where he solemnly and affectionately took his leave of that poor and beloved People of his, was for all that
Generation remembred with Sorrow.

In a Letter of the famous Mr. *Eliot*, of *Dec.* 28. of the *following Year*,
and published at *London* in 1659, he thus expresses himself: *The LORD
has given us this amazing Blow, to take away my Brother* Mayhew. *His aged*
Father *does his endeavour to uphold the Work among the poor* Indians, *whom
by Letters I have encouraged what I can*, &c.

This brings me therefore to give some Account of,

EXAMPLE II.
The worshipful THOMAS MAYHEW Esq; *the Father of the other.*

THIS Gentleman was both *Patentee*[767] and *Governor* of this and the neighbouring Islands, as has been stated[768] before.

---

765 His wife was Jane Paine, neé Gallion. *HMV* 1:118, 3:301.

766 A son of Miohqsoo (*IC*, 76–80*), who had been raised in Mayhew's own house. *HMV*
1:227.

767 I.e., he held the "patent" (title) for the island that allowed him to settle there.

768 There are three missing letters at the beginning of this word ("___ted") in the original. I
have filled in "stated," based on context.

And while his *Son* was with such Success endeavouring to gospel-
ize the *Natives,* the *Father* greatly favoured and encouraged the Work,
and forwarded his Son therein not only by affording his best Advice,
but also by labouring in a most prudent manner with the *Indian Sachims*[769]
to govern their People according to the *English* Laws, and at length
submit to the Authority of the Crown of *England,* and admit of such
as were best qualified to as[293]sist them in Government. By affording them his own Help also, and so wisely managing Affairs among
them, that in a little time he was most highly esteemed and reverenced
by them, and even generally looked upon as both their principal *Ruler*
and *Patron.*

It is an Honour due to his Memory, and may be of great Use to others,
especially in our *Eastern* and *Northern* Borders, to trace and describe the
Steps of his *excellent Conduct.*

This Gentleman observing that the *Indian Governments* were very
absolute *Monarchies,* one main Obstruction to the Progress of the Gospel
in the Island, seemed to be the Jealousy the *Princes* conceived of the Invasion of their Government thro' the Pretence of Religion, and the eclipsing
their Monarchical Dignity: and finding that the *Princes* on these *Islands,*
tho they maintain'd their absolute Power as *Kings,* were yet bound to do
certain Homage to a more potent *Prince* on the bordering *Continent;* and
tho they were no great People, had yet been wasted by intestine[770] Wars,
wherein the greater *Princes* on the *Main,* not unlike *European Princes,* for
like Reasons of State, were not unassisting;[771] whereby the *Islanders* were
necessitated to make those *Princes* the Ballance[772] or Umpires to decide
their Controversies, by *Presents* annually sent to oblige them to give
their Assistance as occasion required.[773] And seeing his *Son,* as aforesaid,
in a zealous Endeavour for their Conversion, he judges it meet, that as
Moses and *Aaron* they should unite in their several Places to promote the
great Design;[774] and therefore he most wisely takes the Advantage of
this Situation of the *Indian* Affairs, to attach them to him by the *following
Method.*

---

769 *A general Name for* Princes, *both supreme and subordinate.* [Prince's note.]

770 Internal, with regard to a country or people; usually said of war or feuds (*OED*).

771 I.e., the sachems on the mainland did assist in the wars.

772 Judges.

773 This section suggests a common English misunderstanding of the significance of gift giving in Algonquian cultures.

774 In Exodus 4:14, God commands Moses to seek his brother Aaron's help in convincing
the Israelites that God has appeared to Moses and has both renewed his covenant with the
Israelites and commanded them to leave Egypt. Moses needed Aaron's help because he was a
poor speaker (a man of "uncircumcised lips": Exodus 6:12), whereas Aaron could "speak well."
See Exodus 3–4.

He tells the *Island-Indians,*

> That by Order from the Crown of *England,* he was to govern
> the *English* who should inhabit these *Islands;* that his *Royal*
> *Master* was in Power far above any of the *Indian Monarchs.*
> But that as he was great and powerful, so he was a Lover
> of Justice; that therefore he would in no measure invade
> their Jurisdictions, but on the contrary, assist them if need
> required; that *Religion* and *Government* were distinct things,
> and their *Sachims* might retain their just Authority, tho their
> Subjects were *Chris*[294]*tians.*

And thus, in no long time, he brought them to conceive no ill Opinion of
the *Christian* Religion.

When afterwards the number of the *Christian Indians* increased, he
advised and persuaded them to admit the *Counsels* of judicious *Christians*
among themselves; and in Cases of more than ordinary Consequence, to
erect a *Jury* for Tryal; promising his own Assistance to the *Indian Princes,*
whose Assent was always to be obtained, tho they were not Christians.
And thus in a few Years time, he settled an happy Administration among
them, to their great Content: and *Records* were kept of all Actions and
Acts passed in their several *Courts,* by such who having learned to write,
were appointed thereto.

By his prudent Measures and Reasonings, he brought even the *Princes*
themselves, with their *Sachims* or Nobles, to see the distinguishing
Excellence of the *English* Government. And in his Administration, he
gave them so fair an Example of the Happiness of it, as not only charmed
them into an earnest Desire of copying after it, and coming into the
same Form themselves, but even induced them to make a publick and free
Acknowledgment of their Subjection to the Crown of *England:* Tho still
they were always mindful to be understood as *subordinate Princes,* to govern according to the Laws of GOD and the *King,* which they very much
aspired to know.

In his *Administration* towards them, he was always ready to hear and
redress their Grievances upon the first Complaint, without the least
Delay; whereby he wisely prevented any ill Impressions from so much
as ever getting into their Minds against the *English,* thro' a neglect of
Justice. Whenever he decided any Causes between them, he not only
went by the Rules of the most impartial Equity, and gave them equal
Justice with the *English,* as being Fellow-Subjects of the same *Sover-*
eign; but he also took care to convince and *satisfy* them, that what was
determined was right and equal. He would not suffer any to injure them
either in their Goods, Lands, or Persons. They always found a *Father* and
Protector in him: and he was so far from introducing any *Form of Gov-*

ernment among them against their Wills, that he first convinced them
of the Advantage of it, and even brought them to *desire* him to intro-
duce and settle it. [295] He took care to keep up the State and Authority of a Royal *Governor*, not with ostentatious Pomp or Show, but with
such superior constant Gravity, and wise and exact Behaviour, as always
raised and preserved their Reverence; and so to govern, as that his Acts
of Favour appeared to proceed, not from Fear, Constraint, or political
Causes, but from a gracious and condescending Temper of Mind; and to
make it evident, that he was not ruled by Self-Interest, Will or Humour,
but by Wisdom, Goodness, Justice, Reason, and the Laws of GOD.

By such *wise* and *Christian Conduct*, there was no Difference between
the *English* and *Indians* on these *Islands*,[775] as long as he lived among
them, which was for near *forty* Years. The *Indians* admired and loved
him as the most superior Person they had ever seen before: and they
esteemed themselves so safe and happy in him, that he could command
them any thing without giving them any Uneasiness; they being satisfied he did it because it was most fit and proper, and in due time it would
appear to be so.

And by such means as these, he not only gained their perfect Confidence in him, but also most firmly attach'd them to him, and to the
English Interest. A remarkable *Instance* whereof they gave in a time of the
greatest Danger; and it is *as follows.*

During the late *distressing War* between the *English* and *Indians* in
New-England, in the Years 1675 and 1676,[776] wherein almost all the
Indian Nations on the *Main* were united against us, a censorious Spirit
possessed too many of the *English*, whereby they suffered themselves
to be unreasonably exasperated against all the *Indians*, without distinction. Of such there were some on these *Islands*, who could hardly be so
moderated by Mr. *Mayhew* and others in Government with him, as to be
restrained from rising to assay the disarming even these *Island-Indians*;
they being then *twenty* to *one* of the English, and having Arms.

For the Satisfaction of these jealous *English*, Capt. *Richard Sarson*
Esq;[777] being ordered with a small Party to treat with the *Natives* on
the *West-End* of the *Vineyard*,[778] who were most to be doubted, as
being nearest the *Continent*, about *three Leagues* off, having the greatest
Ac[296]quaintance and Correspondence there, and being the latest

---

775 Court records suggest that this is an exaggeration.

776 King Philip's War.

777 Richard Sarson (1637–1703) married Mrs. Jane (Paine) Mayhew, the widow of Rev.
Thomas Mayhew Jr., ca. 1667. When he died, he left an estate of £163 and a homestead. *HMV*
2 (Edgartown): 104–8, 3:430.

778 Gay Head.

that had embraced *Christianity*, he returns with this wise and amicable *Answer*,

> That the delivering their Arms[779] would expose them to the Will of the *Indians* engaged in the present War, who were not less their own than Enemies to the *English*; that they had never given occasion for the Distrust intimated; that if in any thing not hazarding their Safety they could give any Satisfaction or Proof of their Friendship and Fidelity, they would readily do what should reasonably be demanded of them: But in this Particular, they were unwilling to deliver their Arms, unless the *English* would propose some likely Means for their necessary Safety and Preservation.

With *this Reply*, they drew a *Writing* in their own Language, wherein they declared, *That as they had submitted freely to the Crown of* England, *so they resolved to assist the* English *on these* Islands *against their Enemies*,[780] *which they accounted equally their own, as Subjects to the same King.* And this was subscribed by Persons of the greatest Note and Power among them.

Having *this Return*, the *Governor* resolved, and accordingly imployed them as a *Guard* in this time of eminent Danger; furnishing them with suitable Ammunition, and giving them Instructions how to manage for the common Safety. And so faithful were they, that they not only resolutely rejected the strong and repeated Sollicitations of the *Natives* on the neighbouring *Main*, but in observance of the general Orders given them, when any landed from thence to sollicit them, tho some were nearly related by Marriage, and others by Blood, yet the *Island-Indians* would immediately bring them before the *Governor* to attend his Pleasure: yea, so entire and firm did their Friendship appear, that tho the War, on account of the Multitudes of *Indians* then on the *Main*, had a very dismal Aspect; yet the *English* on these *Islands* took no care of their own Defence, but left it wholly to these *Christian Indians* to watch for and guard them; not doubting to be advertised by them of any approaching Danger from the Enemy. And thus while the *War* was raging in a most dreadful manner thro'out the *Neighbouring Countries*, these *Islands* enjoyed a perfect *Calm* [297] *of Peace*; and the People wrought, and dwelt secure and quiet.

---

779 I.e., surrendering their guns and weapons to the English colonists.

780 As Prince notes here in "Some Account," a number of these "enemies" would have been their kin by blood or marriage. For more on the English use of Wampanoags to fight other Native Americans, see Johnson, "Search for a Usable Indian," 625–51. Mayhew's willingness to arm a Wampanoag militia should be contrasted with the incarceration and mistreatment of Indian converts on Deer Island during King Philip's War. See Lepore, "When Deer Island Was Turned into Devil's Island," 14–19.

This was the genuine and happy Effect of Mr. *Mayhew* the Governor's excellent *Conduct*, and of the Introduction of the *Christian Religion* among them.

But having thus considered him in the Exercise of his *Civil Authority*, we proceed now to view him in his *Ministerial Service*. And here we must needs return to his *first Access* to the *Island*.

Being then about fifty five Years of Age, yet his Place both as *Patentee* and chief *Ruler*, obliged him not only to a frequent Converse with the *Natives*, but also to learn so much of their Language as was needful to understand and discourse with them. And as he grew in this Acquirement, his pious Disposition and great Pity for that miserable People, led him to improve it in taking all proper Occasions to tell them of their deplorable State, and to set them in the Way of Deliverance.

His grave and majestick *Presence*, accompany'd with his superior *Station*, struck an Aw[781] into their Minds, and always raised their great Attention to what he spake; and his *Words* were so wise and weighty, and expressed with so much Concern and Seriousness, as, by *God's* Blessing, made such deep Impressions on many, that they could never lose. Among the rest, the forementioned famous *Pawaw Tequanonim*,[782] who was taken off from his diabolick Trade, and became a *Christian* in 1650, declared that his Conversion was chiefly owing to some things he had heard from the Governor, who took Occasion to discourse him about true Happiness, and the Way thereto, which the poor *Indian* said he could never forget.

Thus this pious *Gentleman* concurred with his lovely *Son* aforesaid in his Endeavours, to open the Eyes of these wretched *Heathens*, and to *turn them from Darkness to Light, and from the Power of Satan to GOD*.[783] And the surprizing and sore *Loss* of this his excellent and only Son in 1657, was perhaps as grievous to him for the dismal Aspect it had upon the *Indian Work*, as for his own want of him, tho he was now in the *seventieth* Year of his Age.

In this dark and melancholy Hour the bereaved *Father* looks on the more disconsolate and bereaved Na[298]tives; and pitying and mourning for them, he considers what he should do.

He sees no Probability of obtaining so sufficient a *Salary* as might invite a *regular Minister* to engage in the *Indian* Service; he has little or no Hopes of finding any of the Spirit of his deceased *Son*, to bear the Burden attending, and at this time of Necessity to be undergone,

---

781 Awe, dread mingled with veneration (*OED*).

782 *IC*, 13, 288.

783 Acts 26:18.

with a Prospect of more than could well be expected, to encourage to so toilsome a Work; he considered, that his excellent *Son* had spent his Strength, and yet rejoiced in the midst of those many Aches, Pains and Distempers, contracted by his often lodging on their hard Matts, in their exposed Wigwams,[784] and enduring wet and cold, in Faith of *God's* accepting and prospering him in that painful Work, whereto he could see no earthly Advantage that might rationally move or encourage him. The pious *Father* concludes that this was all of GOD, and not merely of Man: and when he looked on the *Indians*, he could not bear to think that the Work so hopefully begun, and so far advanced by his Son, should now expire with him also.

In the Consideration of these things, an holy Zeal for the Glory of GOD, and a most compassionate Charity for the Souls of this bereaved and perishing *People*, kindle up in his Breast. They raise him above all those Ceremonies, and petty Forms and Distinctions that lay in the Way, and which he accounted as nothing in competition with their *eternal Salvation*: and he therefore resolves to do his utmost, both to preserve this most important Work, and to carry it on under all external Difficulties and Discouragements.

He determines frequently to visit and encourage this poor People. He goes once every Week to some of their Plantations.[785] At so advanced an Age he sets himself with unwearied Diligence to perfect himself in their difficult Language; and tho a *Governour*, yet is not ashamed to become a *Preacher* among them.

He ordinarily preached to some of their Assemblies one Day every *Week*, as long as he lived. And his Heart was so exceedingly engaged in the Service, that he spared no Pains nor Fatigues, at so great an Age therein; sometimes travelling on Foot nigh *twenty Miles* thro' the Woods, to preach and visit, when there was [299] no *English* House near to lodge at, in his Absence from home.

Nor does he content himself with the Progress which his *Son* had happily made before him, but indefatigably labours for a further Advancement. And in a *few Years* time, with the Assistance of those religious *Indians* who taught on the *Lord's-day*, he persuaded the *Natives* on the *West End*[786] of the *Island* to receive the Gospel, who had been many Years obstinately resolved against it, being animated by the neighbouring *Sachims* on the

---

784 In spite of what Prince believes, wigwams were well adapted to the island's climate; see note 535.

785 Settlements or farms (*OED*).

786 *Known by the Name of the* Gayhead, *from the various coloured* Oker, *which makes the high* Cliffs *appear very beautiful at a great distance, both on the Lands and Seas, when the Sun shines on them.* [Prince's note.]

Shores of the *Continent*: so that now the *Indians* on the Isles of *Martha's Vineyard* and *Nantucket*, might justly bear the Name of *Christian*; the number of their *Adult* on both these Islands being then about *three thousand*.

About the Year 1664, he was greatly relieved and assisted by the reverend Mr. *John Cotton*,[787] who came to the *Vineyard*, and preached to the *English* at the *East End* of the Island;[788] and having attained a considerable Knowledge in the *Indian Tongue*, he also preached to the *Natives* for about two Years. But in *November* 1667, upon a repeated Invitation, he removed to *Plimouth*, near fifty Miles to the northward.

However, Mr. *Mayhew*, far from being discouraged, goes on alone again in the laborious Work. He aspires most earnestly to bring it on to Perfection. And now the *Natives* being generally brought over to the *Christian* Faith, and many of them desiring to be formed into a Church by themselves, that they might walk together in all the Ordinances and Commands of CHRIST; this honoured Gentleman, with the reverend Mr. *Cotton* aforesaid, who made a journey from *Plimouth* on purpose, being fully satisfy'd they were suitably qualify'd, after mature Advice and Consideration, concluded to give their Assistance thereto.

And Mr. *Mayhew* being a Person of such eminent Prudence and Piety, and full of devout and heavenly [300] Discourses, the *Indians* were so edify'd and pleased with his Labours, that they desired him, tho now above *fourscore* Years of Age, to accept the *Pastoral Charge* over them: but he thought this would not so well consist with the *prime Place* he held in the Civil Government, wherein they also very greatly wanted him; and therefore advised them to chuse such *Indian Pastors* as he thought would do good Service among them; which they accordingly did, making choice of *Hiacoomes* and *Tackanash* for their Pastors.[789]

The Day appointed being come, which was *August* 22, 1670. an *Indian Church* was compleatly formed and organized, to the Satisfaction of the *English* Church, and other religious People on the Island, who by Advantage of many Years Acquaintance, had sufficient Experience of their Qualifications.

At this *Solemnity* it seems the famous Mr. *Eliot* was also present; for in a Letter of *September* 20, 1670, published the Year after at *London*, in a

---

787 John Cotton Jr. (1640–1699) was the son of renowned Boston minister John Cotton and the uncle of Cotton Mather. See his "Missionary Journal," 52–101. For an analysis of Cotton's journal, see Silverman, "Indians, Missionaries, and Religious Translation," 141–74. Also see McIntyre, "John Cotton, Jr.," 119–39.

788 Edgartown. With "regular educated clergymen . . . now settled amongst them," the town decided to built a second and larger meetinghouse: *HMV*, 2 (Edgartown): 146–47.

789 The ordination of Wampanoag pastors increased Wampanoag independence in church matters.

tract entituled, *A brief Narative of the Progress of the Gospel among the* Indians *in* New-England, *in the Year* 1670, he gives an Account of the State of the Natives under the Hands of this Mr. *Mayhew*, and tells us,

> That passing over to the *Vineyard*,[790] many were added to the Church of that Place, both Men and Women, and were all of them baptized, and their Children also with them; and that the *Church* was desirous to have chosen Mr. *Mayhew* for their *Pastor*, but he waved it, conceiving that in his present Capacity, he has greater Advantages to stand their *Friend*, and do them Good, to save them from the Hands of such as would bereave them of their Lands, &c. But they should always have his Counsel, Instruction, and Management in all their Ecclesiastical Affairs, as they hitherto had; that he would die in this Service of CHRIST; and that the *praying Indians*, both of the *Vineyard* and *Nantucket*, de[301]pend on him as the great Instrument of GOD for their Good.

Nor did the Settlement of a *Church* with Pastors among them, abate of his ministerial Care or Pains for these aboriginal *Natives*: but this honourable and ancient *Gentleman* still proceeds in the laborious Work, even to the *ninty third* Year of his Age, and the *twenty third* of his Ministry, which was in 1681, when he dies, to the great Lamentation both of the *English* and *Indians*.

Not long before his Death he had a very *ill Turn*, which his Relatives thought would have carried him off; but he told them, *The time was not yet come, and that he should not die with that Fit of Sickness*: and as he said, it accordingly proved, he recovering and preaching again several times. After this he told a Grandson of his, yet living, *That the time of his Departure was near at hand*; but he earnestly desired that GOD *would give him one Opportunity more in publick to exhort the* English *of the Town where he lived*,[791] which he had for some time been also obliged to teach, thro' the want of a regular Minister. GOD granting his Desire, he taught them the *following Sabbath*, and then took his affectionate *Farewel* of them: and falling ill that Evening, he assured his Friends, *That his Sickness would now be to Death, and he was well contented therewith, being full of Days, and satisfied with Life*, &c. He gave many excellent Counsels and Exhortations to all about him; his Reason and Memory not being at all impaired, as could be perceived. And he continued full of Faith, and Comfort, and holy Joy to the last.

---

790 *Dr.* Increase Mather *says, that both Mr.* Eliot *and Mr.* Cotton *went over, and assisted in the Ordination, in his* Latin Letter *to the famous Mr.* Leusden *of* Utrecht, *wrote in* 1687, *and published at* London *in* 1688. [Prince's note.]

791 Viz. Edgartown, *on the* East *End of the Island.* [Prince's note.]

His *great Grandson,* now the Reverend Mr. *Experience Mayhew,* tells me, that when his *Father*[792] went to visit the *Governour* in his last Sickness, he took this his young *Son*[793] with him, being then about *eight* Years old; and he well remembers his *great Grandfather's* calling him to his Bedside, and laying his Hands on his Head, and blessing him in the Name of the LORD.

[302]Tho the Loss of his *only Son* in his old Age, was a great and lasting Sorrow; yet by GOD's lengthning out his Life to so uncommon a Term, he had the reviving Consolation, to see a very valuable *Son* of *that Son* associated with him in the *Indian Service,* to their great Acceptance, a few Years before he dy'd: and which doubtless made his Departure much more easy and joyful to him.

We therefore now come to

EXAMPLE III.
The Reverend Mr. JOHN MAYHEW, *the youngest* Son of Mr. THOMAS MAYHEW junior.

BUT by the way we may observe, that the Governour's only Son, Mr. *Thomas Mayhew junior,* left three Sons, *viz. Matthew, Thomas,* and *John. Matthew* the eldest, upon his Grandfather the Governour's Death, became the chief Person, both of the Civil and Military Order on the Island, and died in 1710. *Thomas,* born in 1648, became one of the Justices of the inferiour Court of Common Pleas, and Quarter Sessions there, and died in 1715. And this *John* the youngest, born in the beginning of 1652, applied himself intirely to the Work of the *Ministry,* wherein he was for some small time contemporary with his aforesaid Grandfather, and succeeding him, continued therein to his Death.

This Gentleman being but about *five* Years of Age at the Loss of his Father, thereby unhappily missed the Advantage of a learned Education; for want of which, together with his full Employment at home, and his not being inclined to appear abroad, he very much confined himself to the Island, and was not so extensively known: and hence it is, there has been too little hitherto publickly said of this Gentleman, considering his great Worth and Usefulness. But I can assure my Reader that he fell not short either of the eminent *Genius* or *Piety* of his excellent *Progenitors.*

---

792 John Mayhew (1652–1688).

793 I.e., Experience Mayhew, who was born in 1673 and would have been eight at the time of his great-grandfather's death.

He was early inclined to the *Ministerial* Work: and having the Benefit of his Grandfather's wise Instructi[303]ons, and of his Father's Library; and being a Person of more than ordinary natural Parts, great Industry and sincere Piety, he made such a large Proficiency in the Study and Knowledge of divine Things, that about 1673, when he was but twenty one Years of Age, he was first called to the Ministry among the *English* in a new and small Settlement, at a Place named *Tisbury*, near the midst of the Island; where he preached to great Acceptance, not only of the People under his Care, but of very able Judges that occasionally heard him.

But he also naturally cared for the Good of the *Indians*,[794] and, understanding their Language well while he was a very young Man, he used frequently to give them good Instructions, and even the chief *Indians* on the Island often resorted to him for Counsel. And being arrived at the Age above-said, they would not be contented till he became a publick Preacher to them likewise: so ardent and urgent were their Desires, that he could not deny them, even tho his thrice honoured *Grandfather* was then a laborious and acceptable Preacher among them.

He taught alternately in all their Assemblies a *Lecture* every *Week*, and assisted them in the Management of all their Ecclesiastical Affairs. And tho what was allowed him was very inconsiderable indeed, yet he went steadily on in this pious Work, and would not suffer any Affairs of his own to divert him from it, nor was there scarce any Weather so bad as to hinder him.

And having both the *English* and *Indians* under his Care, his Diligence was now to be doubled, especially after his *Grandfather's* Death in 1681; and this much the more, by reason of certain erroneous Opinions in danger of taking Root in the Island.[795] Mr. *Mayhew* was rightly for repelling them with spiritual Weapons: and being a Person of very superior Abilities, and Acquaintance with the Scriptures, he used to desire such as began to imbibe those Principles, to produce their Reasons; and those who wanted to be resolved in their Difficulties, to give him the Advantage to resolve them in publick, that others might also receive Light and Satisfaction; whereby they came to be more clearly instructed, and more fully convinced and satisfy'd, than in the ordinary Way of [304] *Preaching*, which yet always preceded the other. In short, he had such an excellent Talent for the *Defence* of the *Truth* against Gainsayers, that those who

---

794 In West Tisbury there was the Christiantown Indian Church and the Takeme Praying Town. Rhonda, "Generations of Faith," 376.

795 The spread of the Antipedobaptist doctrines that eventually led to the establishment of the Wampanoag Baptist church, which was officially organized in 1693. As Banks rightly points out, the Baptists did eventually succeed in replacing Puritanism as the dominant form of Wampanoag Christianity on the island. *HMV* 1:248.

would have spread their Errors, found themselves so effectually opposed by the Brightness of his Knowledge and Piety, and the Strength of his argumentative *Genius*, that they could make no Progress in their Designs on the Island: and the Churches and People, and in them their Posterity were happily saved from the spreading of those *erroneous Opinions*, and the Disturbance and Troubles they would have produced among them.

And as for the *Indians*, his Custom was to tarry some time with them after the publick Exercise was over, allowing them to put *Questions* to him for their own Instruction, and also trying their Knowledge, by putting *Questions* to them. And he was so very well skilled in their *Language*, as to be able to discourse freely with them upon any kind of Subject, and to preach and pray in their Tongue with the greatest Readiness.

He was a Person of clear Judgment, great Prudence, and of an excellent Spirit; and the *Indians* very much repaired to his House for Advice and Instruction, and also for Relief in their Wants. And as he was fully persuaded, that many of them were truly *religious*, he would sometimes say, *that tho he had but little Reward from Men*, (having but about *five Pounds* a Year for his Labours among them) *yet if he might be instrumental in saving any, he should be fully satisfy'd and think himself to be sufficiently recompensed*. But after the honourable *Commissioners*[796] came to be acquainted with him, and the eminent Service he did, they raised his Salary to *thirty Pounds*, which was but about two Years before his Death.

He walked in his House with a perfect Heart; having his Children and Servants in all Subjection, they both loving and fearing him, and being frequently and seriously instructed and counselled by him.

He lived and dy'd within the Bounds of *Chilmark*;[797] but constantly preached to the *English* at *Tisbury*, for the [305] space of *fifteen Years* to his Death, and about as long *once* every *Week* to one or other of the *Indian* Assemblies on the Island; besides abundance of Pains he took more privately with them. He rather made it his aim to serve his Generation by the Will of GOD, than to be known or observed in the World; and therefore went but little abroad. The whole of what was allowed him for his incessant Labours both among the *English* and *Indians*, put together, would scarce amount to *ten Pounds per Annum*, except the *two last* Years of his Life, as aforesaid; and yet he went on chearfully, in Hopes of a rich and joyful Harvest in *Heaven*.

And having finished what GOD in his all-wise and perfect Providence saw meet to imploy him in, he deceased on *February 3*, 1688-9, about two in the Morning, in the *37th* Year of his Age, and the 16*th* of his Ministry;

---

796 Commissioners of the Society for the Propagation of the Gospel.

797 *The Name of the* English *Town towards the* West End *of the* Vineyard. [Prince's note.]

leaving the *Indians* in a very orderly Way of assembling on the *Lord's Day* for publick Worship in four or five several Places, and of hearing their several well instructed Teachers, who usually began with Prayer, and then after singing part of a *Psalm*, from some Portion of Scripture spake to the Auditors: as also an *Indian Church*, of *one hundred Communicants*,[798] walking according to the Rule of the *Scriptures*.

In his last Sickness he expressed a Desire, "if it were the divine Will, that he might live a while longer, to have seen his Children a little grown up before he died, and to have done more Service for CHRIST on the Earth." But with respect to his own State before GOD, he enjoyed a great Serenity and Calmness of Mind, having a lively Apprehension of the Mercy of GOD, thro' the Merits of CHRIST: Far from being afraid to die, having Hopes, thro' Grace, of obtaining eternal Life by JESUS CHRIST *our Lord.* He counselled, exhorted and encouraged his Relatives and others who came to visit him: And with respect to himself, among other things, said, *He was persuaded that GOD would not place him with those after his Death, in whose Company he could take no Delight in his Life-time.*

His Distemper was an heavy Pain in his Stomach, Shortness of Breath, Faintness, &c. and continued from the End of *September* to the time of his Death. And [306] thus expired the *third* successive *Indian Preacher* of this worthy Family; after he had set another bright Example of disinterested Zeal for the Glory of GOD, a lively Faith of the invisible and eternal World, and a generous and great Concern for the Salvation of all about him.

And now I need not say, that his Loss in the Flower of his Age, and especially so soon after his *Grandfather*, was much lamented by both *English* an[d] *Indians*; and many good People yet living express a very grateful Remembrance of him.

He left *eight Children*;[799] the eldest of which was but *sixteen* Years of Age, and soon after succeeded him in the *Indian Service*. And this is now

EXAMPLE IV.
The Rev. Mr. EXPERIENCE MAYHEW,
the eldest Son of Mr. JOHN MAYHEW.

THIS Gentleman was born *January* 27. 1672-3; he began to preach to the *Indians* on the *Vineyard* in *March* 1693-4, when he was a little above

---

798 Those who partake of or receive Holy Communion (*OED*).

799 Experience Mayhew (1673–1758), John Mayhew (1675–1763), Elizabeth Mayhew (1677–1729), Benjamin Mayhew (1679–1717), Deborah Mayhew (1681–1772), S. Ruthamah Mayhew (1685–1781), and Simon Mayhew (1687–1753); another daughter, Ruth (1683–1683) died in infancy. Jonathan was married to Elizabeth Hillard (1654/55–1746). *HMV* 3:302–3.

twenty one Years of his Age, and about *five* Years after his Father's Decease: and has continued on in the same laborious Employment, having the prudential Care and Oversight of five or six *Indian Assemblies;*[800] to whose Service he has been wholly devoted, and to one or other of which he has constantly preached for above these *thirty two* Years.

Tho *this* Gentleman also unhappily missed of a learned Education in his younger days; yet by the signal Blessing of GOD on his diligent Studies and Labours, he grew so conspicuous by that time he was about *twenty five* Years of Age, that the Rev. Dr. *Cotton Mather,* first in a Sermon printed at *Boston* 1698, and then reprinted in his *Magnalia* in *London* 1702, speaking of more than *thirty Indian Assemblies,* and of more than *thirty hundred* Christian *Indians* then in this Province, he adds in the *Margin* the following Words,

> That an hopeful and worthy young Man, Mr. *Experience Mayhew,* must now have the Justice done him of this Character, That in [307] the *Evangelical Service among the* Indians, *there is* [no] Man that exceeds this Mr. Mayhew, *if there be any that equals him.*

The *Indian Language* has been from his Infancy natural to him, and he has been all along accounted one of the greatest Masters of it that has been known among us. The honourable *Commissioners* therefore employed him to make a *new Version* of the whole Book of *Psalms,* and the Gospel of *John;* which he did in collateral Columns of *English* and *Indian,* with a great deal of Accuracy, in 1709.

And such an extraordinary Progress has he made in Knowledge, that for many Years since, he was offered the Degree of a *Master of Arts* at *Cambridge,* tho he was pleased to excuse himself from the Honour. However, the *College* saw Cause at length to over-rule his Modesty, and to confer it upon him at the *publick Commencement* on *July* 3. 1723. to the Approbation of all that know him.

He for his first Wife married a Daughter of the late Honourable *Thomas Hinckley* Esq; of *Barnstable;*[801] for his second, a Daughter of the late honoured *Shearjashub Bourn* Esq; of *Sandwich;*[802] by both of whom he

---

800 The Wampanoag congregations covered in the 1698 report by the Society for the Propagation of the Gospel, along with their number of congregants, were (1) Nashauekemmuk (Chilmark), 231; (2) Onkonkemme (Tisbury), 72; (3) Seconkgut (Chilmark), 35; (4) Gay Head, 265; (5) Sahnchecontuckquet (Edgartown), 166; (6) Nunnepoag, 84; and (7) Chaubaqueduck (Chappoquiddick), 138. *HMV* 1:250–51.

801 Thankful Hinckley (1671–1706). *HMV* 3:305. She is buried in West Tisbury Cemetery.

802 Remember Bourne (1683–1721/22). *HMV* 3:305. She is buried in the Abel's Hill Cemetery in Chilmark with Experience Mayhew. Shearjashub is a biblical name from Isaiah 7:3.

has several Children living,[803] and is now endeavouring to bring up *one* of them for the *College*, in order to the *Indian Service.*[804]

But this worthy Gentleman, the Compiler of the foregoing *Indian Examples*, being now alive and flourishing among us, I may not venture to trespass so much on his Modesty, as to enter into any further Description of his Life or Character. And if I had said nothing of him, as *this Composure* is without his Desire or Knowledge, and he'll be surprized to see it when it appears in Publick; so I have Reason to know, it would be Satisfaction enough, to have only mention'd his *Name* as *Successor* in the same *Indian Ministry* to his pious and dear *Progenitors.*

[308] And thus of my own mere Motion have I given a plain and unadorned Account of these excellent *Gentlemen*; whose *Names* I could not but think, and doubt not but my Readers will readily judg, to be worthy of everlasting Remembrance and Honour. I have endeavoured to search out and collect their precious and dispersed *Remains,* and to set them in order, that here they may lodge and appear as in one *Shrine* together. I might have possibly made the Account somewhat more agreeable to some sort of Readers, if I had given my self the liberty of running out into a florid Style and Expression, or of setting every Particular in the most beautiful Light; but as I was inclined to croud as many *Historical Passages* into as *small a Compass* as I conveniently could, so where I found them pretty well expressed in the *Memoirs* before me, I chose to depart as little as possible from the *Terms* themselves, that I might be sure of keeping the nearer to the naked *Truth,* and the less disguise or embellish it by artful Glosses or Words of my own.

I might also have given an entertaining Description of the *original State* of the *Natives* in these *Islands,* when the *English,* with Mr. *Mayhew,* first went among them; their *Genius, Language, Government, Customs, Notions of things, Religion, Pawaws,* &c. But as these would have too much swelled the Composure, I was obliged to wave them, and confine

---

803 Experience had three children by his first wife: Reliance (1696–1729/30), Samuel (1700–1746), and Mary (?–?). Although Mary's dates are unknown, she lived long enough to marry John McGee and have a child named Reliance, who died in 1754 at twelve years of age and whose gravestone is in the West Tisbury Cemetery. Experience Mayhew also had five children by his second wife: Nathan (1712–1733), Abigail (1714–?), Eunice (1716–?), Zachariah (1718–?), and Jonathan (1720–1766). Of his children, Jonathan is the most famous. *HMV* 3:305.

804 ——*Nec desine Tales, / Nate, sequi.*——Claud. [Prince's note.] A quotation meaning "Fail not to make such as he thine example, my son" (the original is actually "*ne desine tales,*" not "*nec*"): Claudius Claudiani, "Panegyricus," 310–11. Just as the Roman writer Claudian suggests that Trajan's kindness to his people makes him a worthy examplum for the emperor Honorius, so too Thomas Prince suggests Experience Mayhew's dedication to continuing his family's mission serves as an exemplum for both Mayhew's own son and Prince's readers.

my self more strictly to those things only that had a more immediate Relation to the *Gentlemen* wrote of; whose *Lives* I chose to give as intire by themselves as might be, and refer the Reader for *those other matters* to the four *Letters* of Mr. *Thomas Mayhew* junior above-said, printed at so many several times in *London*; which are full of Entertainment, and breathe a most excellent Spirit, and from whence I collected a main Part of the History under *his Name*; as also to a *Tract* composed by his eldest Son *Matthew Mayhew* Esq; and published both in *New-England* and *Old*, under the Title of *The*[805] *Conquests* [309] *and Triumphs of Grace*, &c. From which I have also taken a great many Passages, and even all I could there find relating to my *three first Examples*.

If I had Leisure enough, and could think it a grateful thing to the Publick, I should be inclined to draw up a complete and regular *History* of the *New-England Indians*, as far as has come to our Knowledge, from the very Beginning; having already collected a considerable Stock of printed *Materials* for it in *England*, where I found them much more plentiful than on this side the Water. By which it would yet further appear, that contrary to the ungenerous and unworthy Aspersions cast on this Country by Mr. *Oldmixon*, *Moll*, and some others, there have been such *zealous Endeavours* to christianize the *aboriginal Natives*, as have deserved a better Regard, and instead of slighting Expressions, a very grateful and respectful Mention: And with so much *Success*, as has rather required their more becoming Ascriptions of Praise to GOD, than Contempt of the Works of his Grace, in producing as evident Instances of pure, sincere, and unaffected Piety among that poor and unpolished People, as are to be seen in the politest Nations.

But doubtless, what has been done above and before will suffice.

However, whether the World be informed and convinced or not, let those who labour even in the obscurest Corners, still go on in their Work, like their Companions, the *Angels*, invisible to the Eyes of Mortals, and receiving no personal Praises or Acknowledgements from them; or like that great and affecting Example of Mr. *Mayhew* the *third*. And the less Honour they receive from Men in this Life, they will doubtless have the more from GOD in the other: they'll now have such solid Satisfaction within, as the World cannot give them; and the Day will certainly come, when all their secret Services to the Kingdom of CHRIST will be produced with themselves into the most publick Sight; they'll be applauded by *him* the omniscient and most righteous Judge in the face of the

---

805 *Reprinted in* Dr. Cotton Mather's Magnalia, *Book* VI. [Prince's note.]

Universe; and he'll most openly honour and reward them with this, *Well done good and faithful Servant, enter into the Joy of our Lord.* Their Honours [310] will subsist and flourish universal for ever; while the high but hollow Applauses of many others on Earth will intirely sink and vanish in eternal Oblivion.

Boston, New-England,   T. P.
    Novemb. I. 1726.

FINIS.

Appendix

A Brief Account of the State of the Indians *on* Martha's Vineyard, *and the small Islands Adjacent in* Duke's-Country, *from the Year* 1694 *to* 1720. By the Reverend Mr. Experience Mayhew Preacher of the Gospel to the Indians in *Martha's Vineyard.*

Ezek. 34.last. *And ye the Flock of my Pasture are MEN, and I am your GOD.* Hos. 11.4. *I Drew you with cords of A MAN, and with Bands of Love.*

[1] *Martha's Vineyard* is an Island lying in about the Latitude of 41. and about 22 Miles in length, from East to West, *Chapaquidick* and *Capoag*, near adjoyning at the East end, being included; the said Island being about 8 Miles in breadth towards the East end of it, and about 3 towards the West end, but the Soil of much of it, is very barren and uncultivated. The Sound of the North-side is about 3 Leagues over, *viz.* To *Falmouth* on the Main, and to *Elsabeth's*-Islands, which lye South-Westward of *Falmouth.*

From the *Gayhead* at the West end of the Island, to *Rhode-Island*; it is about 12 Leagues. and from *Edgartown* Harbour at the East end of it, to *Nantucket*; is as Vessels sail, about 10.

The Island called *No-mans-land* lies Southward from the West end of *Martha's Vineyard*, about 4 Miles from the *Gayhead.*

[2] Concerning the Conversion of the *Indians* on these Islands, and places adjacent on the Main, there was a brief Narrative written by *Matthew Mayhew*, Esq; Eldest Son of the Rev. Mr. *Thomas Mayhew*, who first Preached the Gospel unto them; which Narrative was Printed at *Boston* in the Year 1694. and Reprinted at *London* the next Year, under the Title of, *The Conquests and Triumphs of Grace*, &c. The same, for Substance, being again Printed some Years after, in Dr. *C. Mather's* History of *New-England.*[1]

I shall begin my Account of the State of the *Indians* from the time the said Book was first Published, that being about the time that I first began to Preach to them.

The Number of *Indians* on these Islands is very much diminished, since the *English* first settled on *Martha's-Vineyard*, which was in the Year 1642 there being then as was supposed on that Island about 1500 Souls. At present

---

1 Mather, *Magnalia Christi Americana*, 2:422–40.

there are in the *Vineyard* six small Villages, containing in all of them, about 155 Families, and the Number of Souls may be about eight hundred.[2]

Each of these Villages is provided with an *Indian* Preacher to dispense the Word to them on the Lord's Days, when I am not with them. They meet for the Worship of GOD twice a Day on the Sabbath, and after Prayer, sing a Psalm; then there is a Sermon Preached on [3] some Portion of Scripture, which being ended, they sing again; while the Days be of a sufficient length; and then conclude with Prayer.

Besides the *Indians* on the *Vineyard*, there is a small Assembly on *Winthrop's* Island, the Eastermost of *Elsabeth's* Islands before mentioned; and these also have ordinarily an Indian Minister to Preach the Word of GOD to them, and Mr. *John Weeks* an *Englishman* formerly Preached to them; but has lately, as I am informed, desisted from that Work.[3]

At *Tucker's*-Island, & at *Nashaun* or *Slocum's* Island, which lie near together, Westward of *Winthrop's* Island, are about 12 or 14 Families, and these, tho' their Number be small, are provided with an Indian Preacher.

At the before mentioned *No mans land*, there are now so few Indians left, that they have none to Preach constantly to them.

Besides the *Indian Assemblies* already mentioned, there is one Assembly of *Anabaptists* at the *Gayhead*; but the number of People belonging unto this, is very inconsiderable.[4]

Tho' there are many *Indians* on these Islands, who are negligent as to their Attendance on the Publick Worship of GOD; yet I know of none, but what do make some Profession of Religion, and will talk soberly, when treated withal about it; having made a trial on some that have been most suspected.

---

2 This estimate should be compared with censuses later in the century which give the following headcounts:

Area and Year	"Indians"	"Negroes"	Total Population
Dukes County, 1764	313	46	2,300
All of Massachusetts, 1763	1,493	5,214	23,5800

Felt, *Census of Massachusetts, 1763–1793*; Benton, *Early Census Making in Massachusetts*. Racial categorization became more complicated as the eighteenth century progressed, and Wampanoags on the island intermarried with African Americans: Silverman, *Faith and Boundaries*, 223–41.

3 Banks notes that "John Weeks was preaching to the Indians in 1700 at a salary of £10 per annum, and later a native preacher, Jannohquosso, held services here." *HMV*, 2 (Annals of Gosnold): 8.

4 This is somewhat optimistic on Mayhew's part. Although the Baptists did not dominate Aquinnah (Gay Head) until the nineteenth century, the popularity of the Baptist church "spiked soon after the New England Company pressured the Aquinnah and Nashemuck Congregationalists to replace their deceased pastor, Japheth Hannit, with Experience Mayhew" (Silverman, *Faith and Boundaries*, 238–39, 163).

−5⌝

[4] And tho' there are among these *Indians*, a great many who are very defective in their Morals; yet there are a considerable number, even of those not yet joyned in Church Communion, who live soberly, and Worship GOD in their Families.

There has, from time to time, been much care taken that the several Villages might be provided with School Masters to teach the Children to Read and Write; yet some of them have not been so constantly supplied, as is to be desired; and generally when the Spring of the Year comes on, the Indians take their Children from School, alleging they want them for Tillage of the Land; and so the Schools fail till the Fall; and this has much hindred their Progress in Learning: Nevertheless, I think the greatest number can Read, either in the *English* or in the *Indian* Tongue; and some in both.

There is also care taken to *Catechise* the Youth, For besides what is done in this kind, by the *Indian* School-Masters & Preachers, I frequently examine the Young People my self, and have determined to attend this Service once a Fortnight, in some or other of the forementioned Villages; and this Method will I hope, prove very advantageous, many grown People as well as Children, attending these Exercises.

[5] The *Indian* Church at *Martha's-Vineyard*, whereof Mr. *Japheth Hannit*[5] an excellent *Indian Minister* was formerly the Pastor, but died in the Year 1712. had after his Death another Pastor, called *Sowomog*:[6] but he being an Old Man when he was first called unto that Office, lived but a very few Years.

The Name of the present Pastor of that Church is *Joash Panu*,[7] who is a very serious prudent & pious Man, of a good Conversation, and one who drinks no strong drink, but is much grieved at those of his Country-men who do err by means of it. If it please GOD to continue his Life, he is like to prove a good Instrument; but being lately fallen into a Languishing Distemper, I fear what the issue of it may be.[8]

The number of Communicants, both Men and Women, in this Church, is about 110. the most of these are Inhabitants of *Martha's-Vineyard*, but not all; there being a few that have joyned themselves there-unto, not only from *Elsabeth's* Islands, but from the Main Land also, lying next unto the *Vineyard*.

The Lord's Supper is ordinarily Administred in that Church about 7 or 8 times in a Year, and Discipline is in some measure kept up in it. Unto this

---

5 *IC*, 44–54*.

6 *IC*, 65, 217.

7 *IC*, 63–67*.

8 Joash Panu died of "consumptive Distemper" in August 1720, the year this account was published. *IC*, 63–67*.

End, besides other Church Meetings, there is constantly on the *Thursday* or *Friday* before that Sacrament is Admini[6]stred, a Meeting of the Church, wherein such are suspended from the Lords Table as having been overtaken in any fault, have not given due satisfaction. At this Meeting also there is ordinarily a Sermon Preached suitable to the occasion.

It must be acknowledged that as the *Indians* are many of them addicted unto strong drink; so some of the Members of the Indian Church have been sometimes found very faulty, on this account; yet it is also true, that such as these have generally appeared very Penitent. And tho' some have fallen quite away, and so have been cut off by the Sword of Discipline; yet others thro' the Grace of GOD, have been so far recovered out of the Sins into which they have fallen, as that it may be hoped they will not again return to them; and there have all along been, and still are, a considerable number, whose Conversation is, so far as I can understand, very blameless, and who may be justly looked upon as Exemplary Christians; what ever such *English Men* as are filled with Prejudices against the *Indians*, may say to the contrary.

Some Years after I first began to Preach to the *Indians*, the *Church* on *Martha's-Vineyard*, did on a day of *Fasting* and *Prayer* appointed for that End, solemnly renew their Covenant [7] with GOD, engaging to endeavour to forsake those Sins with which they confessed they were to easily beset; and there was after this, for a Time, some Reformation: but I observed that two or three of the Brethren that could not be perswaded to joyn in the Action, soon after fell into Scandalous Misdemeanours.

I also observed, That after the Church had thus renewed their Covenant, the Means of Grace offered unto the *Indians*, seemed for a time to be attended with more of the Presence of GOD, and the Influences of His Spirit, than they were before, or have been since.

It was then frequent to see Persons at the Hearing of Sermons, very much affected, and some times as soon as Sermon was ended, there would stand up several, one after another, and make very Penitential Confessions of their Sins, with Promises to endeavour to Live new Lives, desiring also the Prayers of the People of GOD for them.

About this time there joyned in full Communion unto that small Church on the *Vineyard*, in one Year, at least 30 Persons, the behaviour of many of whom did very much resemble that of the Jailor, at his Conversion, *Acts* 16. GOD shewing us herein that He can make the *Indians* as well as Others a *willing People in the Day of His Power.*

[8] There is an Increase of Knowledge among these *Indians*, tho' it must be confessed that their progress herein is but slow, by reason of the want of

a Learned Ministry constantly to Instruct them. Their ordinary Preachers having but little Learning, are not so able to feed them with Knowledge and Understanding as is to be desired; yet some of these have Gifts not to be despised in *a day of small things.*

These *Indian* Ministers as they are Members in full Communion of the Church on the *Vineyard,* so they do not engage in the work of the Ministry without the Consent & Approbation of that Church, as well as of the *English* Ministers that Preach unto the Indians, and have an Inspection over them.

Having now Preached to the *Indians* upward of Twenty-five Years, I have never yet had any special charge of any one single Congregation committed to me; but have visited the several fore-mentioned Assemblies alternately, as I have thought most necessary; Preaching ordinarily, unto some or other of them every Lord's Day, and on working days once a Fortnight; constantly also attending their Church-Meetings, to assist & direct them.

The *Indians* when they are Sick, generally send for their Ministers, and some times other Christians with them, to visit them, and Pray with, and for them. I have some times [9] been with them on such occasions, and heard them profess a great concern about their Souls; declaring that they did not regard any thing in this World, so they might obtain and Interest in GOD's Favour; and I have known many of them who have professed a good hope thro' CHRIST in their Death, and who have behaved themselves on all accounts as does become dying Saints; nor have I any doubt, but that many of them have died in the Lord.

The Reverend Mr. *Josiah Torrey,* Pastor of the *English* Church in *Tisbury* on the *Vineyard,* has also for many Years past Preached as a Lecturer unto the *Indians* on that Island, having for that End learned their Languge. He Preacheth in some or other of their Assemblies once a Fortnight, and goes frequently to their Church-Meetings, to advise and assist them; so that the *Indians* have a Sermon every *Thursday* Preached to them, either by Mr. *Torrey,* or my self: And we strengthen the hands of one another, by going together to these Weekly Exercises.[9]

The Reverend Mr. *Samuel Wiswall*[10] Pastor of the Church in *Edgartown,* has also almost learned the *Indian* Tongue, with a design to do what Service he can among that People.

---

9 As I noted in the introduction, this is a highly generous account of Torrey's work on the island: Rev. William Homes comments in his diary that Torrey "drunk too freely and too frequently of spirits." Qtd. in *HMV,* 2 (Annals of West Tisbury): 81.

10 Wiswall (?–1746) received his B.A. from Harvard in 1701. *HMV,* 2 (Annals of Edgartown): 152.

The *Indians* on *Martha's Vineyard* and the adjacent Islands, do hitherto understand the [10] *Indian* Tongue much better than that of the *English*; and therefore complain much for want of *Indian* BIBLES, having now but very few among them. Nor are there any to be had; the last Edition being now gone. These *Indians* are therefore very desirous of another Impression of the Bible, if it might be obtained; and divers of them have told me as well of some of those on *Nantucket*, (whom I have divers times visited) that they should be willing according to their capacity, to contribute to it.[11]

But the disadvantage which the *Indians* are under thro' the Scarcity of the BIBLES is some-what helped by the Care of the Honourable Commissioners to supply them with other useful Books in their own Language, *viz.* The *New-England* Confession of Faith; Several Catechisms; The Practice of Piety; Mr. *Shepard's* Sincere Convert; Mr. *Baxter's* Call to the Unconverted. And several Sermon Books of Dr. *Mather's*, &c. besides the Psalter, and the Gospel of JOHN, Printed in the Year 1709. And the *Indian* Primer Printed this Year, in *Indian* & *English.* All which Books are now very useful unto them.

As to their Civil Government, the *Indians* in *Dukes* County, (as well as in other Places) are wholly under the *English*; [11] But because their State does yet somewhat differ from that of their *English* Neighbours, there are several Laws made by the General Court of this *Province*, with a particular regard to the *Indian* Inhabitants of the same: And there are some *English* Justices especially Commissionated to take care of the *Indians* Inhabiting the several Counties of it; and *these* are directed to Nominate and Appoint several Officers among the *Indians* themselves, to assist under their regulation in the Government of that People.

In *Dukes* County, *Thomas Mayhew* Esq;[12] Second Son of the fore-mentioned Mr. *Thomas Mayhew*, who first Preached to the *Indians* on the *Vineyard*, was long improved in the Government of the *Indians* there, and was both singularly Spirited & Accomplished for that Service; as he was on divers other accounts, a very excellent Person: But he finished his course *July* 21.

---

11 In spite of this plea, no more editions of the Eliot Bible were printed.

12 Thomas Mayhew Esq. (1650–1715), Experience Mayhew's uncle, was an "associate justice of the King's Bench from 1692 to 1699 and chief justice from 1699 to 1713." Interestingly enough, Rev. William Homes notes in his diary that Thomas Mayhew Esq. was treated for "distemper" by an "Indian doctor" and "recovered so far that he was able to rid[e] about and look after his affairs, but in the latter end of the spring or beginning of summer this year," he had new symptoms that eventually led to his death. Homes further notes that Mayhew "was a man of good sense considering his education and seemed to be piously inclined tho he did entertain some singular opinions in religion" qtd. in *HMV*, 2 (Annals of Chilmark): 35; 3:302.

1715. And his Son *Zacheus Mayhew*[13] succeeding him in that necessary but troublesome Office and Imployment, does good Service in it.

There are yet but few *Indians* on *Martha's-Vineyard* that have Houses of the *English* fashion, tho' the number of these is of late increased; but in respect of their Apparel, they are generally Cloathed as the English are, and they by degrees learn the English [12] way of Husbandry:[14] Several of them have good Teams of Oxen, with which they Plough and Cart, for themselves and Neighbours, as the English do. Many of them have also Horses, Cows, Sheep and Swine. They have also among them some that have learned Trades; as at *Martha's-Vineyard* there are several Weavers, One or two House-Carpenters, One Wheel-wright, who is so good a Work-man, as to be frequently employed by his English Neighbours. There are several Tailors, and one if not more Shoemakers, and one Black-smith, who not only took his Trade himself, but also made his Bellows, and other Tools; and one Cooper, *Viz. William Charles*, who is a good Work-man. And tho' some of these may not be so accurate as our English Trades-men, yet this shews that as the *Indians* are capable of Learning such Callings as *English* Men follow; so they begin to come to it.

Experience Mayhew
June, 2d.
1720.

---

13 Zaccheus Mayhew (1684–1760), a lawyer and farmer, was appointed "justice of the Court of Common Pleas . . . in 1718 and sat on the bench with his cousin Paine [Mayhew] . . . for over thirty years. . . . He also acted as agent for the Indians of the Island for many years." *HMV,* 3:304.
14 For more on Wampanoag animal husbandry, see Silverman, "We Chuse to Be Bounded," 511–48.

Bibliography

Adams, James Truslow. "Disfranchisement of Negroes in New England." *American Historical Review* 30, no. 3 (1925): 543–47.

Akers, Charles W. *Called unto Liberty: A Life of Jonathan Mayhew, 1720–1766.* Cambridge: Harvard University Press, 1964.

Albanese, Catherine L. *Nature Religion in America: From the Algonkian Indians to the New Age.* Chicago: University of Chicago Press, 1990.

Allen, John. "Account Book of John Allen." 1730–59. MVHS.

Amatya, Alok, and Taylor Smith. *Map of Colonial New England with Algonquian Confederacies.* Portland, Ore.: Computer User Services of Reed College, 2007.

———. *Map of Martha's Vineyard with Towns and Sachemships.* Portland, Ore.: Computer User Services of Reed College, 2007.

Amussen, Susan Dwyer. *An Ordered Society: Gender and Class in Early Modern England.* Oxford: B. Blackwell, 1988.

Anderson, Benedict. *Imagined Communities: Reflections on the Origin and Spread of Nationalism.* New York: Verso, 1991.

Antoun, Richard T. *Understanding Fundamentalism: Christian, Islamic, and Jewish Movements.* Walnut Creek, Calif.: AltaMira Press, 2001.

Apess, William. *On Our Own Ground: The Complete Writings of William Apess, a Pequot.* Ed. Barry O'Connell. Amherst: University of Massachusetts Press, 1992.

"Aquinnah." *Wampanoag Tribe of Gay Head (Aquinnah).* 1999–2003. Online at http://www.wampanoagtribe.net/education/text/aquinnah.htm (accessed August 18, 2004).

Archer, Richard. *Fissures in the Rock: New England in the Seventeenth Century.* Hanover, N.H.: University Press of New England, 2001.

Armstrong, Karen. *The Battle for God.* New York: Random House, 2000.

Arnold, Laura. "'Now . . . Didn't Our People Laugh?' Female Misbehavior and Algonquian Culture in Mary Rowlandson's *Captivity and Restauration.*" *American Indian Culture and Research Journal* 21, no. 4 (1997): 1–28.

Attaquin, Helen, et al. *Wampanoag Cookery.* Boston: American Science and Engineering, 1974.

Athearn, Simon. *Map of Martha's Vineyard.* 1968. MVHS.

Augustine. *City of God.* 413–27. Ed. David Knowles. New York: Penguin Books, 1972.

Axtell, James. *The School upon a Hill: Education and Society in Colonial New England.* New Haven: Yale University Press, 1974.

Backus, Isaac. *A history of New-England, with particular reference to the denomination of Christians called Baptists.* Boston: Edward Draper, 1777.

Banks, Charles Edward. "Documents Relating to Martha's Vineyard." Manuscript. MHS.

——. *The History of Martha's Vineyard: Dukes County, Massachusetts.* 3 vols. Boston: G. H. Dean, 1911–25.

Bannon, John. *Indian Labor in the Spanish Indies.* Boston: Heath, 1966.

"Barnstable, Mass., Vital Records vol. 1." *Early Vital Records of Barnstable, Dukes & Nantucket Counties, Massachusetts to about 1850.* CD-ROM. Wheat Ridge, Colo.: Search & ReSearch, 1999.

Bayley, Lewis. *The practice of pietie directing a Christian how to walke that he may please God.* 2nd ed. London: Felix Kingston, 1619. EEBO.

——. Trans. John Eliot as *Manitowompae Pomantamoonk: Sampwshanau Christianoh Uttoh woh an Pomantog Wussikkitteahonat* [sic] *God.* Cambridge: Samuel Green and Marmaduke Johnson, 1665; and *Manitowompae Pomantamoonk Sampwshanau Christianoh: Uttoh woh an Pomantog Wssikkitteahonat God.* Cambridge: Corporation in London for Gospelizing the Indians in New-England, 1685.

Beeman, Richard R. *The Varieties of Political Experience in Eighteenth-Century America.* Philadelphia: University of Pennsylvania Press, 2004.

Benton, Josiah H. *Early Census Making in Massachusetts, 1643–1765.* Boston: Charles E. Goodspeed, 1905.

Bercovitch, Sacvan. *The Puritan Origins of the American Self.* New Haven: Yale University Press, 1975.

Blodget, Harold. *Samson Occom.* Hanover, N.H.: Dartmouth College, 1935.

Bradstreet, Anne. *The Works of Anne Bradstreet.* Ed. Jeannine Hensley. Cambridge: Harvard University Press, 1967.

Bragdon, Kathleen J. "'Emphaticall Speech and the Great Action': An Analysis of Seventeenth-Century Native Speech Events Described in Early Sources." *Man in the Northeast,* no. 33 (1987): 101–11.

——. *Native People of Southern New England, 1500–1650.* Norman: University of Oklahoma Press, 1996.

Breen, Timothy H. "Who Governs: The Town Franchise in Seventeenth-Century Massachusetts." *William and Mary Quarterly* 27, no. 3 (1970): 460–74.

Brekus, Catherine. "Children of Wrath, Children of Grace: Jonathan Edwards and the Puritan Culture of Child Rearing." In *The Child in Christian Thought,* ed. Marcia J. Bunge, 300–328. Grand Rapids, Mich.: Eerdmans, 2001.

Brooks, Joanna. *American Lazarus: Religion and the Rise of African-American and Native American Literatures.* New York: Oxford University Press, 2003.

Bross, Kristina. *Dry Bones and Indian Sermons: Praying Indians in Colonial America.* Ithaca: Cornell University Press, 2004.

Brown, B. Katherine. "Freemanship in Puritan Massachusetts." *American Historical Review* 59, no. 4 (1954): 865–83.

Brown, Michael F. "On Resisting Resistance." *American Anthropologist,* n.s., 98, no. 4 (1996): 729–35.

Brown, Richard D. *Modernization: The Transformation of American Life, 1600–1865.* New York: Hill and Wang, 1976.

Bunyan, John. *The Pilgrim's Progress.* 1678, 1684. New York: Penguin Books, 1964.

Chalcraft, David J., and Austin Harrington, eds. *Protestant Ethic Debate: Max Weber's Replies to His Critics.* Liverpool: Liverpool University Press, 2001.

Channing, William Ellery. "The Moral Argument against Calvinism." 1820. In *The Works of William E. Channing,* 8th ed., 2:217–41. Boston: J. Munroe, 1848.

Christie, Francis Albert. "The Beginnings of Arminianism in New England." *Papers of the American Society of Church History,* ser. 2, 3 (1912): 151–72.

Clark, Michael P., ed. *The Eliot Tracts: With Letters from John Eliot to Thomas Thorowgood and Richard Baxter.* Westport, Conn.: Praeger, 2003.

Claudiani, Claudius. "Panegyricus de Quarto Consulatu Honorii Augusti" [Panegyric on the fourth consulship of the Emperor Honorius (CE 398)]. In *Claudian, with an English Translation by Maurice Platnauer,* vol. 1. New York: Putnam, 1922.

Collins, James, and Richard Blot, *Literacy and Literacies: Texts, Power, and Identity.* New York: Cambridge University Press, 2003.

Conroy, David W. "Puritans in Taverns: Law and Popular Culture in Colonial Massachusetts, 1630–1720." In *Drinking: Behavior and Belief in Modern History,* ed. Susanna Barrows and Robin Room, 29–60. Berkeley: University of California Press, 1991.

Cooke, Alexander. *Saint Austins religion Wherein is manifestly proued out of the works of that learned father, that he dissented from popery, and agreed with the religion of the Protestants in all the maine points of faith and doctrine. Contrary to that impudent, erronious, and slanderous position of the bragging papists of our times, who falsely affirme, we had no religion before the times of Luther and Caluine.* London: Augustine Mathewes, 1624.

Cooke, George Willis. *Unitarianism in America: A History of Its Origin and Development.* Boston: American Unitarian Association, 1902.

Cooke, Jacob Ernest, et al., eds. *Encyclopedia of the North American Colonies.* New York: Scribner, 1993.

Cooper, James F. *Tenacious of Their Liberties: The Congregationalists in Colonial Massachusetts.* New York: Oxford University Press, 1999.

Coote, Edmund. *The English skoole-master.* London: Widow Orwin, 1596.

Corrigan, John. *The Hidden Balance: Religion and the Social Theories of Charles Chauncy and Jonathan Mayhew.* Cambridge: Cambridge University Press, 1987.

Cotton, John, Jr. "The Missionary Journal of John Cotton Jr., 1666–1678." Ed. Len Travers. *Proceedings of the Massachusetts Historical Society* 109 (1998): 52–101.

Crayon, Porte, illus. "Summer in New England." *Harper's New Monthly Magazine* 21, no. 124 (1860): 442–61.

Cremin, Lawrence Arthur. *American Education: The Colonial Experience, 1607–1783.* New York: Harper and Row, 1970.

Crosby, Thomas. *The history of the English Baptists, from the Reformation to the beginning of the reign of King George I.* London: The editor, 1738–40.

Deetz, James, and Edwin S. Dethlefsen. "Death's Head, Cherub, Urn and Willow." *Natural History* 76, no. 3 (1967): 29–37.

de las Casas, Bartolomé. *The devastation of the Indies: A brief account.* 1542. Trans. Herma Briffault. Baltimore: Johns Hopkins University Press, 1992.

Delbanco, Andrew. *The Death of Satan: How Americans Have Lost the Sense of Evil.* New York: Farrar, Straus and Giroux, 1995.

Demos, John Putnam. *Entertaining Satan: Witchcraft and the Culture of Early New England.* New York: Oxford University Press, 1982.

Des Barres, Joseph F. W. *Chart of Buzzards Bay and Vineyard Sound.* London, 1776. Library of Congress Geography and Map Division. Online at *American Memory Map Collections:* http://hdl.loc.gov/loc.gmd/g3762b.ar098100.

Dierks, Konstantin. "The Familiar Letter and Social Refinement in America, 1750–1800." In *Letter Writing as a Social Practice*, ed. David Barton and Nigel Hall, 31–41. Philadelphia: John Benjamins, 2000.

"Divine examples of God's Severe Judgements upon Sabbath-Breakers, in their unlawful sports, collected out of several divine subjects . . ." [Broadside]. London: T.C., 1671.

Dollimore, Jonathan. *Sexual Dissidence: Augustine to Wilde, Freud to Foucault.* Oxford: Clarendon Press, 1991.

Douglas, Ann. *The Feminization of American Culture.* New York: Anchor Press, 1988.

Douglass, William. *A Summary, Historical and Political, of the first planting, progressive improvements, and present state of the British settlements in North-America.* London: R. and J. Dodsley, 1760.

Dow, George Francis. *Everyday Life in the Massachusetts Bay Colony.* 1935. Dover: New York, 1988.

Duffy, John. *Epidemics in Colonial America.* Baton Rouge: Louisiana State University Press, 1953.

Dukes County Court Records. Office of the Clerk of Courts, Dukes County Courthouse, Edgartown, Mass.

Dukes County Deeds. Dukes County Registry of Deeds, Dukes County Courthouse, Edgartown, Mass.

Dukes County Registry of Probate, Dukes County Courthouse, Edgartown, Mass.

Earle, Alice Morse. *Two Centuries of Costume in America, MDCXX–MDCCCXX.* New York: Macmillan, 1903.

Early American Imprints. Series I, Evans (1639–1800). Worcester, Mass.: American Antiquarian Society, 2002–6. Online at http://infoweb.newsbank.com.

Early English Books Online. Ann Arbor: Bell & Howell Information and Learning, 1999. Online at http://eebo.chadwyck.com.

Edwards, Jonathan. "A Faithful Narrative." *The Works of Jonathan Edwards*, vol. 4. Ed. John E. Smith, 199–205. New Haven: Yale University Press, 1972.

———. *Images or Shadows of Divine Things.* Ed. Perry Miller. Westport, Conn.: Greenwood Press, 1977.

———. "The Importance and Advantage of a Thorough Knowledge of Divine Truth." In *Works*, 4:1–15. New York: Leavitt and Allen, 1843.

————. *A Narrative of Surprising Conversions: The Distinguishing marks of a Work of the Spirit of God; An Account of the Revival of Religion in Northampton, 1740–2; Sermons.* London: Banner of Truth Trust, 1965.

Edwards, Morgan. *Materials towards a History of the American Baptists.* Philadelphia: Historical Society of Pennsylvania, 1770.

Eisenstadt, Shmuel N., and Wolfgang Schluchter. "Introduction: Paths to Early Modernities—A Comparative View." *Daedalus* 127 (1998): 1–18.

Eliot, John. *A brief narrative of the progress of the Gospel amongst the Indians in New England.* London, 1671.

————. *A further account of the progress of the Gospel amongst the Indians in New England.* London: John Mancock, 1660.

————. *Indian dialogues, for their instruction in that great service of Christ, in calling home their country-men to the knowledge of God, and of themselves and of Iesus Christ.* Cambridge, Mass.: Marmaduke Johnson, 1671.

————. *The Indian primer; or, The way of training up of our Indian youth in the good knowledge of God, in the knowledge of the Scriptures and in an ability to read.* Cambridge, Mass.: Marmaduke Johnson, 1669.

————. *The Logic Primer.* 1672. Intro. Wilberforce Eames. Cleveland: Burrows Brothers, 1904.

————, trans. *Mamusse wunneetupanatamwe Up-Biblium God naneeswe Nukkone Testament kah wonk Wusku Testament.* Cambridge, Mass.: Samuel Green and Marmaduke Johnson, 1663.

Eliot, John, and Thomas Mayhew. *Tears of repentance, or, A further narrative of the progress of the Gospel amongst the Indians in New-England.* London: Peter Cole, 1653.

Fawcett, Melissa. "The Role of Gladys Tantaquidgeon." In *Papers of the Fifteenth Algonquian Conference,* ed. William Cowan, 135–45. Ottawa: Carleton University, 1984.

Felt, Joseph B. *Census of Massachusetts, 1763–1793.* MHS.

Fitch, James. *The first pinciples [sic] of the doctrine of Christ; together with stronger meat for them that are skil'd in the word of righteousness. Or, The doctrine of living unto God, wherein the body of divinity is briefly and methodically handled by way of question and answer.* Boston: John Foster, 1679.

Forbes, Allan. *Other Indian Events of New England.* Boston: State Street Trust Company, 1941.

Ford, Paul Leicester, ed. *The New-England primer; a reprint of the earliest known edition.* New York: Dodd, Mead, 1899.

Gallay, Alan. *The Indian Slave Trade: The Rise of the English Empire in the American South, 1670–1717.* New Haven: Yale University Press, 2002.

The Geneva Bible, a Facsimile of the 1560 Edition. Madison: University of Wisconsin Press, 1969.

Godbear, Richard. *The Devil's Dominion: Magic and Religion in Early New England.* New York: Cambridge University Press, 1992.

Goddard, Ives, and Kathleen J. Bragdon, eds. *Native Writings in Massachusett.* 2 vols. Philadelphia: American Philosophical Society, 1988.

Goodwin, Thomas. "The Government and Discipline of the Churches of Christ." In *Works*, vol. 4. London: J.D. and S.R. for Thomas Goodwin, 1697. Appendix 1:3–35.

Gookin, Daniel. *Historical collections of the Indians in New England: Of their several nations, numbers, customs, manners, religion, and government, before the English planted there.* 1792. New York: Arno Press, 1972.

Groce, Nora Ellen. *Everyone Here Spoke Sign Language: Hereditary Deafness on Martha's Vineyard.* Cambridge: Harvard University Press, 1985.

Grumet, Robert Steven, "Sunksquaws, Shamans, and Tradeswomen: Middle Atlantic Coastal Algonkian Women during the 17th and 18th Centuries." In *Women and Colonization: Anthropological Perspectives*, ed. Mona Etienne and Eleanor Leacock, 43–61. New York: Praeger, 1980.

Hall, David D. *Worlds of Wonder, Days of Judgment: Popular Religious Belief in Early New England.* New York: Knopf, 1989.

Hambrick-Stowe, Charles E. *The Practice of Piety: Puritan Devotional Disciplines in Seventeenth-Century New England.* Chapel Hill: University of North Carolina Press, 1982.

Hamell, George R. "Mythical Realities and European Contact in the Northeast during the Sixteenth and Seventeenth Centuries." *Man in the Northeast* 33 (1987): 63–87.

Hannah, John D. *Charts of Reformation and Enlightenment Church History.* Grand Rapids, Mich.: Zondervan, 2004.

Harlan, David. *The Clergy and the Great Awakening in New England.* Ann Arbor, Mich.: UMI Research Press, 1980.

Hariot, Thomas. *A briefe and true report of the new found land of Virginia.* 1590. New York: Dover Publications, 1972.

Harris, Benjamin. *The Protestant Tutor.* London: Ben. Harris, 1679.

Havelock, Eric. *The Muse Learns to Write: Reflections on Orality and Literacy from Antiquity to the Present.* New Haven: Yale University Press, 1986.

Hayes, Kevin J. *A Colonial Woman's Bookshelf.* Knoxville: University of Tennessee Press, 1996.

Hermes, Katherine. "'Justice Will Be Done Us': Algonquian Demands for Reciprocity in the Courts of European Settlers." In *The Many Legalities of Early America*, ed. Christopher L. Tomlins and Bruce H. Mann, 123–49. Chapel Hill: University of North Carolina Press, 2001.

Herndon, Ruth Wallis, and Ella Wilcox Sekatau. "Colonizing the Children: Indian Youngsters in Servitude in Early Rhode Island." In *Reinterpreting New England Indians and the Colonial Experience*, ed. Collin G. Calloway and Neal Salisbury, 137–73. Boston: Colonial Society of Massachusetts, 2003.

Hill, Hamilton Andrews. *History of the Old South Church (Third Church) Boston, 1669–1884.* 2 vols. Boston: Houghton, Mifflin, 1890.

Homes, William. "Diary of Rev. William Homes of Chilmark, Martha's Vineyard, 1689–1746." In *The New-England Historical and Genealogical Register*, vol. L, 155–66. Boston: Published by the Society, 1896.

Iacocci, Joseph. "Martha's Vineyard Gravestones from 1688 to 1804: An Historical Study." *Dukes County Intelligencer* 20, no. 3 (1979):125–59.

Ivimey, Joseph. *A History of the English Baptists*. London: Printed for the Author, 1811. Online at http://www.vor.org/rbdisk/ivimey/html/index.htm.

Johnson, Richard R. "The Search for a Usable Indian: An Aspect of the Defense of Colonial New England." *Journal of American History* 6, no. 3 (1977): 623–51.

Kamensky, Jane. *Governing the Tongue: The Politics of Speech in Early New England*. New York: Oxford University Press, 1997.

Kavasch, Bonnie. "Native Foods of New England." In *Enduring Traditions: The Native Peoples of New England*, ed. Laurie Weinstein, 5–30. Westport, Conn.: Bergin and Garvey, 1994.

Kawashima, Yasuhide. *Puritan Justice and the Indian: White Man's Law in Massachusetts, 1630–1763*. Middletown, Conn.: Wesleyan University Press, 1986.

Kidd, Thomas S. *Protestant Interest: New England after Puritanism*. New Haven: Yale University Press, 2004.

Lamert, Charles. "Foreword—1905: Weber in the Year of Miracles." In *The Protestant Ethic Turns 100: Essays on the Century of the Weber Thesis*, ix–xii. Boulder, Colo.: Paradigm, 2005.

Lee, Charles R. "Public Poor Relief and the Massachusetts Community, 1620–1715." *New England Quarterly* 55, no. 4 (1982): 564–85.

Lepore, Jill. *The Name of War*. New York: Vintage, 1999.

———. "When Deer Island Was Turned into Devil's Island." *Bostonia* (1998): 14–19.

Lester, Joan. "Art for Sale: Cultural and Economic Survival." In *Enduring Traditions: The Native Peoples of New England*, ed. Laurie Weinstein, 151–67. Westport, Conn.: Bergin and Garvey, 1994.

Lockeridge, Kenneth A. *Literacy in Colonial New England*. New York: W.W. Norton, 1974.

Lyon, William S. *Encyclopedia of Native American Healing*. New York: W.W. Norton, 1996.

MacKinnon, Malcolm. "The Longevity of the Thesis: A Critique of the Critics." In *Weber's Protestant Ethic: Origins, Evidence, Contexts*, ed. Hartmut Lehmann and Guenther Roth, 211–44. New York: Cambridge University Press, 1993.

Mancall, Peter C. *Deadly Medicine: Indians and Alcohol in Early America*. Ithaca: Cornell University Press, 1995.

March, Kathleen Davidson. *Uncommon Civility: The Narragansett Indians and Roger Williams*. Ann Arbor: University Microfilms International, 1985.

Marten, Catherine. "Wampanoags in the Seventeenth Century: An Ethnohistorical Survey." Plimoth Plantation Inc. Occasional Papers in Old Colony Studies, No. 2. December 1970.

Martin E. Marty and R. Scott Appleby, eds. *Fundamentalisms Observed*. Chicago: University of Chicago Press, 1991.

Mather, Cotton. *Baptismal piety*. Boston: 1727.

————. *Family-religion urged.* Boston: Benjamin Harris, 1709. *Early American Imprints*, Series I, no. 1403.

————. *Magnalia Christi Americana; or, the ecclesiastical history of New-England, from its first planting in the year 1620, unto the year of our Lord, 1698.* London: T. Parkhurst, 1702.

————. *Ornaments for the daughters of Zion; Or, The character and happiness of a vertuous woman: In a discourse which directs the female-sex how to express the fear of God, in every age and state of their life; and obtain both temporal and eternal blessedness.* Cambridge: Samuel and Bartholomew Green, 1692.

————. *Teashshinninneongane Peantamooonk* [Family religion excited, and assisted. Algonquian]. Boston: B. Green, 1714.

Mayhew, Ezperience. *All mankind, by nature, equally under sin. A sermon preach'd at the public lecture in Boston. On Thursday, Dec. 3. 1724.* Boston: B. Green, 1725. *Early American Imprints*, series I, no. 2677.

————. *A Brief Account of the State of the* Indians *on* Martha's Vineyard, *and the small Islands Adjacent in* Duke's-Country, *from the Year 1694 to 1720.* Boston: B. Green, for Samuel Gerrish, 1720.

————. "Disbursements Given to the Indian Poor" (1755). In *Papers of Experience Mayhew, Missionary to the Indians at Martha's Vineyard, Mass.* MHS.

————. "*A Discourse shewing that God Dealeth with Men As with Reasonable Creatures … With a brief account of the State of the Indians on Martha's Vineyard, & the Small Islands adjacent in Dukes County, from the Year 1694. to 1720.* Boston: B. Green, for Samuel Gerrish, 1720.

————. "Distribution to the Poor." 1733. MVHS.

————. *Grace defended.* Boston: B. Green, 1744.

————. *Indian converts; Or, Some account of the lives and dying speeches of a Considerable number of the Christianized Indians of Martha's Vineyard in New England.* London: S. Gerrish, 1727.

————. *The Massachuset psalter; or, Psalms of David with the Gospel according to John, in columns of Indian and English: Being an introduction for training up the aboriginal natives, in reading and understanding the Holy Scriptures.* Boston: B. Green and J. Printer, 1709.

————. *Papers of Experience Mayhew, Missionary to the Indians at Martha's Vineyard, Mass.* MVHS.

————. *A right to the Lord's Supper considered in a letter to a serious enquirer after truth.* Boston: J. Draper, 1741.

Mayhew, Matthew. *A brief narrative of the success which the Gospel hath had, among the Indians, of Martha's Vineyard,* including "Description of Sachems." 1694. *Massachusetts Historical Society,* 2nd ser., no. 119 (1940): 7–9.

McCallum, James Dow, ed. *The Letters of Eleazar Wheelock's Indians.* Hanover, N.H.: Dartmouth College Publications, 1932.

McGiffert, Michael, ed. *God's Plot: Puritan Spirituality in Thomas Shepard's Cambridge.* Amherst: University of Massachusetts Press, 1994.

McIntyre, Sheila. "John Cotton, Jr.: Wayward Puritan Minister?" In *The Human Tradition in Colonial America*, ed. Ian K. Steele and Nancy L. Rhoden, 119–39. Wilmington, Del.: SR Books/Scholarly Resources, 1999.

McLaughlin, William G. *New England Dissent 1630–1833: The Baptists and the Separation of Church and State*. Cambridge: Harvard University Press, 1971.

———. *Revivals, Awakenings, and Reform: An Essay on Religion and Social Change in America, 1607–1977*. Chicago: University of Chicago Press, 1978.

———. *Soul Liberty: The Baptists' Struggle in New England, 1630–1833*. Hanover: University Press of New England, 1991.

McMillan, Jill. "Institutional Plausibility Alignment as Rhetorical Exercise: A Mainline Denomination's Struggle with the Exigence of Sexism." *Journal for the Scientific Study of Religion* 27, no. 3 (1988): 326–44.

Millar, Robert. *History of the propagation of Christianity, and overthrow of Paganism. Wherein the Christian religion is confirmed*, 2 vols. Edinburgh, 1723.

Miller, Perry. *The New England Mind: The Seventeenth Century*. Cambridge: Harvard University Press, 1982.

———. *Transcendentalists*. Cambridge: Harvard University Press, 1950.

Mills, Earl, Sr., and Betty Breen. *Cape Cod Wampanoag Cookbook*. Santa Fe, N.M.: Clear Light, 2001.

Monaghan, E. Jennifer. "Literacy Instruction and Gender in Colonial New England." *American Quarterly* 40, no. 1 (1988): 18–41.

———. "'She Loved to Read Good Books': Literacy and the Indians of Martha's Vineyard, 1643–1725." *History of Education Quarterly* 30, no. 4 (1990): 492–521.

Morgan, Edmund S. *The Puritan Family*. New York: Harper and Row, 1966.

Morison, Samuel Eliot. *Harvard College in the Seventeenth Century*. Cambridge: Harvard University Press, 1936.

Muldoon, James, ed. *The Spiritual Conversion of the Americas*. Gainesville: University Press of Florida, 2004.

Murdock, Kenneth B. "Clio in the Wilderness: History and Biography in Puritan New England." *Church History* 24, no. 3 (1955): 221–38.

Murray, Laura J., ed. *To Do Good to My Indian Brethren: The Writings of Joseph Johnson, 1751–1776*. Amherst: University of Massachusetts Press, 1998.

Nantucket Registry of Deeds. Nantucket Town and County Building, Nantucket, Mass.

The New-England Historical and Genealogical Register. Vol. L. Boston: Published by the Society, 1896.

The New-England primer improved. Boston: S. Adams, 1762.

Newell, Margaret, "The Changing Nature of Indian Slavery in New England, 1670–1720." In *Reinterpreting New England Indians and the Colonial Experience*, ed. Colin G. Calloway and Neal Salisbury, 106–36. Boston: Colonial Society of Massachusetts, 2003.

Nicholas, Mark A. "Mashpee Wampanoags of Cape Cod, the Whalefishery, and Seafaring's Impact on Community Development." *American Indian Quarterly* 26, no. 2 (2002): 165–97.

Nielsen, Donald A. *"The Protestant Ethic and the 'Spirit' of Capitalism* as Grand Narrative: Max Weber's Philosophy of History." In *The Protestant Ethic Turns 100: Essays on the Centenary of the Weber Thesis,* ed. William H. Swatos Jr. and Lutz Kaelber, 53–76. Boulder. Colo.: Paradigm, 2005.

O'Brien, Jean. *Dispossession by Degrees: Indian Land and Identity in Natick, Massachusetts, 1650–1790.* New York: Cambridge University Press, 1997.

Occom, Samson. *A sermon preached at the execution of Moses Paul.* New Haven: T. and S. Green, 1772.

Ong, Walter. *Orality and Literacy: The Technologizing of the Word.* London: Methuen, 1982.

Parkman, Francis. *A Half Century of Conflict.* Boston: Little, Brown, 1902.

"Pelagianism." *The Concise Oxford Dictionary of the Christian Church.* Ed. E. A. Livingstone. Oxford: Oxford University Press, 2000. Online at http://www.oxfordreference.com/views/ENTRY.html?subview=Main &entry=t95.e4376.

Perkins, William. *The foundation of Christian religion gathered into six principles and it is to be learned of ignorant people that they may be fit to hear sermons with profit, and to receive the Lords Supper with comfort.* Boston: Samuel Green, 1682.

Piff, David, and Margit Warburg, "Seeking for Truth: Plausibility Alignment on a Baha'i Email List." In *Religion and Cyberspace,* ed. Morten Hojsgaard and Margit Warburg, 86–101. London: Routledge, 2005.

Plane, Ann Marie. *Colonial Intimacies: Indian Marriage in Early New England.* Ithaca: Cornell University Press, 2000.

———. "Customary Laws of Marriage: Legal Pluralism, Colonialism, and Narragansett Indian Identity in Eighteenth-Century Rhode Island." In *The Many Legalities of Early America,* ed. Christopher L. Tomlins and Bruce H. Mann, 180–213. Chapel Hill: University of North Carolina Press, 2001.

———. "Falling 'Into a Dreame': Native Americans, Colonization, and Consciousness in Early New England." In *Reinterpreting New England Indians and the Colonial Experience,* ed. Colin G. Calloway and Neal Salisbury, 84–105. Boston: Colonial Society of Massachusetts, 2003.

Plane, Ann Marie, and Gregory Button, "The Massachusetts Indian Enfranchisement Act: Ethnic Contest in Historical Context, 1849–1869." *Ethnohistory* 40, no. 4 (1993): 587–618.

Porterfield, Amanda. "Women's Attraction to Puritanism." *Church History* 60, no. 2 (1991): 196–209.

Prince, Thomas. *A Chronological History of New-England in the Form of Annals.* Boston: Kneeland and Green for S. Gerrish, 1736. Early American Imprints, Series I, no. 4068.

———. "Some Account of Those English Ministers who have successively presided over the Work of Gospelizing the Indians on Martha's Vineyard, and the adjacent Islands." In *Indian Converts,* ed. Experience Mayhew, 279–310. London, 1727.

Queen, Edward L., et al. *The Encyclopedia of American Religious History.* New York: Facts on File, 2001.

Rabasa, José. "Writing and Evangelization in Sixteenth-Century Mexico." In *Early Images of the Americas: Transfer and Innovation*, ed. Jerry Williams and Robert Lewis, 65–92. Tuscon: University of Arizona Press, 1993.

Reis, Elizabeth. *Damned Women: Sinners and Witches in Puritan New England.* Ithaca: Cornell University Press, 1997.

Report of the Record Commissions of the City of Boston containing the Records of Boston Selectmen, 1736 to 1742. Boston: Rockwell and Churchill, City Printers, 1886.

Revere, Paul. "Philip. King of Mount Hope," *The Entertaining History of King Philip's War* by Benjamin Church. Newport, R.I.: Solomon Southwick, 1772.

Rhonda, James P. "Generations of Faith: The Christian Indians of Martha's Vineyard." *William and Mary Quarterly*, 3rd ser., 38, no. 3 (1981): 369–94.

Richardson, James B., III. "Death's Heads, Cherubs, Urn and Willow: A Stylistic Analysis of Martha's Vineyard Tombstones." *Dukes County Intelligencer* 10, no. 3 (1969): 179–200.

Rowlandson, Mary. "A True History of the Captivity and Restoration of Mrs. Mary Rowlandson." 1682. Ed. Amy Schranger Lang. In *Journeys in New Worlds: Early American Women's Narratives*, ed. William Andrews, 11–66. Madison: University of Wisconsin Press, 1990.

Rubinstein, Ruth P. *Dress Codes: Meanings and Messages in American Culture.* Boulder, Colo.: Westview Press, 2001.

Salisbury, Neal. *Manitou and Providence: Indians, Europeans, and the Making of New England, 1500–1643.* New York: Oxford University Press, 1982.

Salwen, Bert. "Indians of Southern New England and Long Island: Early Period." In *Handbook of North American Indians*, ed. Bruce Trigger, vol. 15. Washington, D.C.: Smithsonian Institution, 1978.

Schaff, Philip. *America: A Sketch of Its Political, Social, and Religious Character.* Cambridge: Belknap Press of Harvard University Press, 1961.

Schreiner, Susan. *The Theater of His Glory: Nature and the Natural Order in the Thought of John Calvin.* Durham: Labyrinth Press, 1991.

Schutte, Anne. "'Such Monstrous Births': A Neglected Aspect of the Antinomian Controversy." *Renaissance Quarterly* 38, no.1 (1985): 85–106.

Scott, Jonathan Fletcher. "The Early Colonial Houses of Martha's Vineyard." Ph.D. dissertation, University of Minnesota, 1985.

Segel, Jerome D., and R. Andrew Pierce. *The Wampanoag Genealogical History of Martha's Vineyard, Massachusetts.* Vol. 1. Baltimore: Genealogical Publishing, 2003.

Sekatau, Thomas. *Narragansett Indian Recipes.* Haffenretter Museum Library, 1970.

Sewall, Samuel. *Diary of Samuel Sewall, 1674–1729.* In *Collections of the Massachusetts Historical Society*, 5th ser., 5–7 (1878–82).

Shea, Daniel B. *Spiritual Autobiography in Early America.* Madison: University of Wisconsin Press, 1988.

Silverman, David J. "The Church in New England Indian Community Life." In *Reinterpreting New England Indians and the Colonial Experience*, ed. Colin G. Calloway and Neal Salisbury, 264–98. Boston: Colonial Society of Massachusetts, 2003.

————. "Conditions for Coexistence, Climates for Collapse: The Challenges of Indian Life on Martha's Vineyard, 1524–1871." Ph.D. dissertation, Princeton University, 2000.

————. *Faith and Boundaries: Colonists, Christianity, and Community among the Wampanoag Indians of Martha's Vineyard, 1600–1871.* New York: Cambridge University Press, 2005.

————. "Indians, Missionaries, and Religious Translation: Creating Wampanoag Christianity in Seventeenth-Century Martha's Vineyard." *William and Mary Quarterly* 62, no. 2 (2005): 141–74.

————. "'We Chuse to be Bounded': Native American Animal Husbandry in Colonial New England." *William and Mary Quarterly* 60, no. 3 (2003): 511–48.

Simmons, William. *Cautantowwit's House; An Indian Burial Ground on the Island of Conanicut in Narragansett Bay.* Providence: Brown University Press, 1970.

————. "The Great Awakening and Indian Conversion in Southern New England." In *Papers of the Tenth Algonquian Conference*, ed. William Cowan, 25–36. Ottawa: Carleton University, 1979.

————. *Spirit of the New England Tribes: Indian History and Folklore, 1620–1984.* Hanover, N.H.: University Press of New England, 1986.

Sinnott, Edmund Ware. *Meetinghouse and Church in Early New England.* New York: McGraw-Hill, 1963.

Solberg, Winton U. *Redeem the Time: The Puritan Sabbath in Early America.* Cambridge: Harvard University Press, 1977.

Sontag, Susan. *Illness as Metaphor* and *AIDS and Its Metaphors.* New York: Anchor Books, 1990.

Sperry, Kip. *Abbreviations and Acronyms.* 2nd ed. Provo, Utah: Ancestry, 2003.

Stannard, David E. *The Puritan Way of Death: A Study in Religion, Culture, and Social Change.* New York: Oxford University Press, 1977.

Stevens, Laura M. *The Poor Indians: British Missionaries, Native Americans, and Colonial Sensibility.* Philadelphia: University of Pennsylvania Press, 2004.

Strother, D. H. "Summer in New England." *Harper's New Monthly Magazine* 21, no. 124 (1860): 442–61.

Stout, Harry S. "Word and Order in Colonial New England." In *The Bible in America*, ed. Nathan Hatch and Mark Noll. New York: Oxford University Press, 1982.

Taylor, Edward. *The Poems of Edward Taylor.* Ed. Donald E. Stanford. Chapel Hill: University of North Carolina Press, 1989.

Theophano, Janet. *Eat My Words: Reading Women's Lives through the Cookbooks They Wrote.* New York: Palgrave Macmillan, 2002.

Thickston, Margaret Olofson. *Fictions of the Feminine: Puritan Doctrine and the Representation of Women.* Ithaca: Cornell University Press, 1988.

Thomas à Kempis. *The Imitation of Christ.* Ca. 1420. Trans. W. P. Oxford: Leonard Lichfield, 1639.

————. *The Imitation of Christ: A Modern Version Based on the English Translation made by Richard Whitford around the Year 1530.* Ed. Harold C. Gardiner. Garden City, N.Y.: Hanover House, 1955.

Thompson, Roger. *Sex in Middlesex: Popular Mores in a Massachusetts County, 1649–1699.* Amherst: University of Massachusetts Press, 1986.

Tichi, Cecilia. "Spiritual Biography and the 'Lords Remembrancers.'" *William and Mary Quarterly* 28, no. 1 (1971): 64–85.

Tolles, Frederick B. "'Of the Best Sort but Plain': The Quaker Esthetic." *American Quarterly* 11, no. 4 (1959): 484–502.

Twisse, William. *The riches of Gods love unto the vessells of mercy.* Oxford: L. L. and H. H. for Thomas Robinson, 1653.

Ulrich, Laurel. *Good Wives: Image and Reality in the Lives of Women in Northern New England, 1650–1750.* New York: Vintage Books, 1991.

———. "John Winthrop's City of Women." *Massachusetts Historical Review,* NA 2001. Online at http://www.historycooperative.org/journals/mhr/3/ulrich. html (accessed August 1, 2006).

van der Wall, Ernestine. "Arminianism." In *Encyclopedia of the Enlightenment,* ed. Alan Charles Kors. Oxford: Oxford University Press, 2003. Online at http://www.oxfordreference.com/views/ENTRY.html?subview=Main &entry=t173.e031.

Van Dyken, Donald. *Rediscovering Catechism: The Art of Equipping Covenant Children.* Phillipsburg, N.J.: P and R, 2000.

Van Lonkhuyzen, Harold W. "A Reappraisal of the Praying Indians: Acculturation, Conversion, and Identity at Natick, Massachusetts, 1646–1730." *New England Quarterly* 63, no. 3 (1990): 396–428.

Vernant, Jean-Pierre. *The Origins of Greek Thought.* Ithaca: Cornell University Press, 1962.

"Wampanpoag Celebrations." In *Wampanoag Tribe of Gay Head.* 1999–2003. Online at http://www.wampanoagtribe.net/education/celebrat.htm (accessed August 10, 2004).

Watters, David H. *"With Bodilie Eyes": Eschatological Themes in Puritan Literature and Gravestone Art.* Ann Arbor: University of Michigan Research Press, 1981.

Weber, Max. *The Protestant Ethic and the "Spirit" of Capitalism and Other Writings.* Ed. and trans. Peter Baehr and Gordon C. Wells. New York: Penguin Books, 2002.

Welters, Linda. "From Moccasins to Frock Coat and Back Again: Ethnic Identity and Native American Dress in Southern New England." In *Dress in American Culture,* ed. Patricia A. Cunningham and Susan Voso Lab, 6–41. Bowling Green, Ohio: Bowling Green State University Popular Press, 1993.

"The Wetu or Native House." Plimoth-on-Web, http://www.plimoth.org/ Museum/Hobbamock/wetu.htm (accessed 2000–2001).

Wheelock, Eleazar. *A plain and faithful narrative.* Boston: Richard and Samuel Draper, 1763.

White, Richard. *The Middle Ground: Indians, Empires, and Republics in the Great Lakes Region, 1650–1815.* Cambridge: Cambridge University Press, 1991.

Wigglesworth, Michael. *The day of doom; or, A poetical description of the Great and Last Judgment.* Cambridge: Samuel Green, 1666. Early American Imprints, Series I, no. 112.

Williams, Roger. *A Key into the Language of America.* 1643. Ed. John J. Teunissen and Evelyn J. Hinz. Detroit: Wayne State University Press, 1973.

Wilson, John, Thomas Shepard, and John Eliot. *The Day-breaking, if not the sun-rising of the Gospell with the Indians in New-England.* London: Richard Cotes, 1647.

Winslow, Edward. *Good newes from New England.* London: W. Bladen and J. Bellamie, 1624. In *Chronicles of the Pilgrim Fathers,* ed. John Masefield, 267–357. New York: Dutton, 1910.

Winthrop, John. "Reasons to Be Considered for . . . the Intended Plantation in New England." 1629. *Proceedings of the Massachusetts Historical Society* 8 (1864–65): 420–25.

Wolverton, Nan. "'A Precarious Living': Basket Making and Related Crafts among New England Indians." In *Reinterpreting New England Indians and the Colonial Experience,* ed. Colin G. Calloway and Neal Salisbury, 341–68. Boston: Colonial Society of Massachusetts, 2003.

Wyss, Hilary E. "'Things That Do Accompany Salvation': Colonialism, Conversion, and Cultural Exchange in Experience Mayhew's *Indian Converts.*" *Early American Literature* 33, no. 1 (1998): 39–61.

———. *Writing Indians: Literacy, Christianity, and Native Community in Early America.* Amherst: University of Massachusetts Press, 2000.

Index

Numbers in this index refer to pages in this volume; page numbers for *Indian Converts* in footnotes refer to the original edition. An asterisk preceding the page number indicates the primary biography for the individual in *Indian Converts*.

LAURA ARNOLD LEIBMAN was born in Ann Arbor, Michigan, and received her PhD from University of California, Los Angeles. An associate professor of English and humanities at Reed College, she is the author of several articles and the academic director of *American Passages* (Annenberg/CPB). Leibman is the recipient of a Fulbright grant and two grants from the National Endowment for the Humanities. She currently lives in Portland, Oregon, with her husband, Eric Leibman.